THE
NAVY LIST
2014

Compiled on the 26 January 2015

Available from:
Dandy Booksellers Limited
Units 3 & 4, Opal Mews
31-33 Priory Park Road,
London NW6 7UP
Telephone: 020 7624 2993
Fax: 020 7624 5049
orders@dandybooksellers.com
www.dandybooksellers.com
www.publicinformationonline.com

Printed in the UK by Dandy Booksellers under
the Open Government Licence V3.0.

ISBN 9780117731257

PREFACE

This edition of the Navy List has been produced largely from the information held within the Ministry of Defence's "Joint Personnel and Administration" system (JPA) as at 26 January 2015.

Officers who succeed to peerages, baronetcies or courtesy titles should notify their Career Manager.

Serving officers who notice errors relating to their data in the Navy List should ensure that the data held within JPA is accurate & up to date. If you are unable to make these corrections within your JPA account, you should seek assistance either from your JPA administrator or Career Manager. All other errors or omissions should be brought to the attention of the Editor of the Navy List. Readers who should wish to comment on this edition of the Navy List are invited to write to:

Mrs Jacqui Farmer
The Editor of the Navy List
Mail Point 2.2
West Battery
Whale Island
PORTSMOUTH
PO2 8DX

Due to the wide-availability of the Navy List on the Defence Intranet and the RN Website, free distribution of the Navy List in hard copy format has ceased.

CONTENTS

Section 8

Section 9

MEMBERS OF THE ROYAL FAMILY

HIS ROYAL HIGHNESS THE PRINCE PHILIP, DUKE OF EDINBURGH, KG, KT, OM, GBE, ONZ, AC, QSO, , GCL, CC, CMM

Lord High Admiral of The United Kingdom...10 Jun 11
Admiral of the Fleet ....15 Jan 53
Captain General, Royal Marines ....Jun 53
Admiral of the Fleet Royal Australian Navy .... 1 Apr 54
Admiral of the Fleet Royal New Zealand Navy...15 Jan 53
Admiral of the Royal Canadian Sea Cadets..15 Jan 53
Admiral of the Royal Canadian Navy ....Jun 11

HIS ROYAL HIGHNESS THE PRINCE OF WALES, KG, KT, GCB, OM, AK, QSO, PC, ADC

Admiral of the Fleet ....16 Jun 12
Commodore-in-Chief, Her Majesty's Naval Base, Plymouth.................................... 8 Aug 06

HIS ROYAL HIGHNESS THE DUKE OF CAMBRIDGE. KG, KT ADC

Commodore-in-Chief Scotland... Aug 06
Commodore-in-Chief Submarines .... Aug 06

HIS ROYAL HIGHNESS PRINCE HENRY OF WALES,

Commodore-in-Chief Small Ships and Diving .... Aug 06

HIS ROYAL HIGHNESS THE DUKE OF YORK, KG, GCVO, ADC

Rear Admiral .... 19 Feb 10
Admiral of the Sea Cadet Corps... 11 May 92
Commodore-in-Chief Fleet Air Arm... Aug 06

HIS ROYAL HIGHNESS THE EARL OF WESSEX KG, GCVO, ADC

Commodore ....1 Jan 11
Commodore-in-Chief Royal Fleet Auxiliary .... Aug 06

HER ROYAL HIGHNESS THE PRINCESS ROYAL, KG, KT, GCVO, QSO

Admiral Chief Commandant for Women in the Royal Navy .... 15 Aug 12
Commodore-in-Chief, Her Majesty's Naval Base Portsmouth .... Aug 06

HER ROYAL HIGHNESS THE DUCHESS OF CORNWALL, GCVO

Commodore-in-Chief Naval Medical Services .... Aug 06
Commodore-in-Chief Naval Chaplaincy Services .... 2 Oct 08

HIS ROYAL HIGHNESS PRINCE MICHAEL OF KENT, GCVO

Honorary Rear Admiral Royal Naval Reserve ....1 Jun 04
Commodore-in-Chief Maritime Reserves .... Aug 06

HER ROYAL HIGHNESS PRINCESS ALEXANDRA THE HON. LADY OGILVY, KG, GCVO

Patron, Queen Alexandra's Royal Naval Nursing Service ....12 Nov 55

VICE ADMIRAL OF THE UNITED KINGDOM

Honorary Rear Admiral Sir Donald Gosling KCVO RNR .... 2 Apr 12

PERSONAL AIDES-DE-CAMP TO THE QUEEN

Admiral His Royal Highness The Prince of Wales, KG, KT, GCB, OM, AK, QSO, PC, ADC
Vice Admiral His Royal Highness The Duke of York, KG, GCVO, ADC
Commodore His Royal Highness The Earl of Wessex, KG, GCVO, ADC
Vice Admiral Sir Tim Laurence, KCVO, CB, ADC

PRINCIPAL NAVAL AIDE-DE-CAMP TO THE QUEEN

Admiral Sir George Zambellas KCB, DSC, ADC, DL...9 April 13

NAVAL AND MARINE AIDES-DE-CAMP TO THE QUEEN

Commodore P A McAlpine CBE, ADC .... Appointed 19 Dec 11 Seniority 08 Feb 11
Brigadier R A W Spencer OBE ADC .... Appointed 17 Nov 14 Seniority 22 Jul 11
Commodore I Shipperley ADC ....Appointed 12 Jan 15 Seniority 28 Aug 12
Commodore J C Rigby ADC... Appointed 16 Jun 14 Seniority 01 Jul 13
Commodore A M Adams ADC..Appointed 20 Oct 14 Seniority 20 Oct 14
Captain T J Gulley ADC... Appointed 16 Jun 14 Seniority 25 Jan 11
Captain R J A Bellfield ADC.. Appointed 03 Sep 14 Seniority 27 Sep 11

EXTRA NAVAL AND MARINE EQUERRIES TO THE QUEEN

Vice Admiral Sir James Weatherall KCVO, KBE
Vice Admiral Sir Tom Blackburn KCVO, CB
Vice Admiral Tony Johnstone-Burt CB OBE
Rear Admiral Sir John Garnier KCVO, CBE
Rear Admiral Sir Robert Woodard KCVO
Commodore A J C Morrow CVO

NAVAL AND MARINE RESERVE AIDES-DE-CAMP TO THE QUEEN

Commodore A C Jameson ADC ....Appointed 23 Apr 13 Seniority 01 Jul 11
Captain N R V Dorman ADC .... Appointed 01 Sep 14 Seniority 01 Sep 09
Colonel J Marok ADC .... Appointed 06 Jan 15 Seniority 08 Oct 13

HONORARY APPOINTMENTS

HONORARY CHAPLAINS TO THE QUEEN

The Venerable Ian Wheatley QHC Bth
The Reverend Monsignor Andrew McFadden QHC PhB STL VG
The Reverend Tim Wilkinson QHC BA
The Reverend Roland Wort QHC BA BSc FRSA

HONORARY PHYSICIANS TO THE QUEEN

Surgeon Rear Admiral C McArthur, QHP, BM, BCh, BAO, MRCGP, LRCP, DObst, RCOG Dip FFP
Surgeon Commodore A.S. Hughes, QHP, MBChB, MRCGP
Surgeon Commodore P J Buxton OBE, QHP, FRCR

HONORARY SURGEON TO THE QUEEN

Surgeon Commodore A Walker OBE, QHS, FRCS
Surgeon Captain M J Midwinter CBE QHS RN

HONORARY DENTAL SURGEON TO THE QUEEN

Surgeon Captain (D) R.E. Norris, QHDS, MA, FFGDP, MDGS, RCS(Eng), BDS(Lond)

HONORARY NURSE TO THE QUEEN

Commodore I.J. Kennedy, QHNS, QARNNS
Captain S J Spencer QHNS, QARNNS

HONORARY OFFICERS IN HER MAJESTY'S FLEET

ADMIRAL

His Majesty King Carl XVI Gustaf of Sweden, KG ....25 Jun 75

His Majesty Sultan Haji Hussanal Bolkiah Mu'izzaddin Waddaulah Sultan and Yang Di-pertuan of Brunei Darussalam, GCB, GCMG .... 4 Aug 01

HONORARY OFFICERS IN HER MAJESTY'S ROYAL MARINES

COLONEL

His Majesty King Harald V of Norway, KG, GCVO ....18 Mar 81

Defence Council 2014

The Rt Hon
Michael Fallon MP
Secretary of State for Defence

Lord Astor of Hever DL
Parliamentary Under Secretary of State and the Lords Spokesman on Defence
Unpaid

Philip Dunne MP
Parliamentary Under Secretary of State and Minister for Defence Equipment, Support and
Technology (including Defence Exports)

The Rt Hon
Mark Francois MP
Minister of State for the Armed Forces

Anna Soubry MP
Minister of State for Defence Personnel, Welfare and Veterans

Julian Brazier MP
Parliamentary Under Secretary of State and Minister for Reserves

Jon Thompson
Permanent Under Secretary; Non-Executive Director, Crown Commercial Services (CCS)

Admiral Sir George Zambellas KCB DSC ADC
First Sea Lord and Chief of Naval Staff

General Sir Nicholas Patrick Carter KCB CBE DSO ADC Gen
Chief of the General Staff

Air Chief Marshal Sir Andrew Pulford KCB CBE ADC RAF
Chief of the Air Staff

General Sir Nicholas Houghton GCB CBE ADC Gen
Chief of the Defence Staff

Air Chief Marshal Sir Stuart Peach KCB CBE ADC DL BA MPhil DTech DLitt RAF
Vice Chief of the Defence Staff

General Sir Richard Barrons KCB CBE ADC Gen
Commander of Joint Forces Command

Professor Vernon Gibson
MOD Chief Scientific Adviser

Bernard Gray
Chief of Defence Materiel

David Williams
Director General Finance

THE ADMIRALTY BOARD

Chairman

THE RIGHT HONOURABLE PHILIP HAMMOND MP
(Secretary of State for Defence)
(Chairman of the Defence Council and Chairman of the
Admiralty Board of the Defence Council)

THE RIGHT HONOURABLE MARK FRANCOIS MP
(Minister of State for the Armed Forces)

MR PHILIP DUNNE MP
(Minister for Defence Equipment, Support and Technology)

MR ANDREW MURRISON MP
(Minister for International Security Strategy)

MISS ANNA SOUBRY MP
(Minister for Defence Personnel, Welfare and Veterans)

LORD ASTOR of HEVER, DL
(Under-Secretary of State and the Lords Spokesman on Defence)

ADMIRAL SIR GEORGE ZAMBELLAS KCB, OBE, ADC, DL
(First Sea Lord and Chief of Naval Staff)

VICE ADMIRAL PHILIP JONES KCB
(Fleet Commander)

VICE ADMIRAL DAVID STEEL CBE
(Second Sea Lord)

VICE ADMIRAL SIMON LISTER CB, OBE
(Chief of Fleet Support)

REAR ADMIRAL JAMES MORSE
(Controller of the Navy)

REAR ADMIRAL CLIVE JOHNSTONE CBE
(Assistant Chief of Naval Staff)

MISS LOUISE TULETT CBE
(Finance Director (Navy))

KEY PERSONNEL

4* NAVY COMMAND

Chief of Naval Staff/First Sea Lord
Admiral Sir George Zambellas KCB DSC ADC DL

3* NAVY COMMAND

Fleet Commander & Deputy Chief of Naval Staff
Vice Admiral Sir Philip Jones KCB

Chief of Naval Personnel & Training and Second Sea Lord and Chief Naval Logistics Officer
Vice Admiral Sir David Steel KBE DL

Chief of Materiel (Fleet)
Vice Admiral S R Lister CB OBE

CHIEF OF STAFF (INTEGRATED CHANGE PROGRAMME)

2* Chief of Staff (Integrated Change Programme) (COS(ICP))
Rear Admiral M C Cree

1* Assistant Chief of Staff (Integrated Change Programme) (ACOS(ICP))
Brigadier R A Spencer OBE

ASSISTANT CHIEF OF NAVAL STAFF (POLICY)

2* Assistant Chief of Naval Staff (Policy)
Rear Admiral C C C Johnstone CBE

1* Head of Naval Staff
Commodore J M Lines RN

COMMANDER UK MARITIME FORCES

2* Commander UK Maritime Forces (COMUKMARFOR)
Rear Admiral A D Radakin

1* Deputy COMUKMARFOR (DCMF)
Commodore J J F Blunden LVO

1* Commander UK Task Group (COMUKTG)
Commodore J P Kyd

COMMANDER UK AMPHIBIOUS FORCES & COMMANDANT GENERAL ROYAL MARINES

2* Commander UK Amphibious Forces & CGRM (COMUKAMPHIBFOR & CGRM)
Major General M L Smith MBE

COMMANDER OPERATIONS

2* Commander Maritime Operations (COMOPS)
Rear Admiral M J Parr CB

KEY PERSONNEL

1* Commander 3 Commando Brigade RM (Comd 3CDO BDE RM)
Brigadier C R Stickland OBE

ASSISTANT CHIEF NAVAL STAFF (AVIATION & CARRIERS)

2* Rear Admiral Fleet Air Arm and Assistant Chief of Naval Staff (Aviation & Carriers)
Rear Admiral R G Harding CBE

1* Assistant Chief of Staff Carrier Strike & Aviation (ACOS CSAV)
Commodore M P Briers

1* Commanding Officer RNAS Yeovilton (CO VL)
Commodore R S Alexander OBE

ASSISTANT CHIEF OF NAVAL STAFF (CAPABILITY)

2* Assistant Chief of Naval Staff Capability (ACNS Cap)
Rear Admiral J A Morse

1* Assistant Chief of Staff Maritime Warfare (ACOS MW)
Commodore G A Robinson OBE

1* Assistant Chief of Staff Information Superiority (ACOS IS)
Brigadier D M M Evans

1* Assistant Chief of Staff Surface Ships & Submarines (ACOS SSM)
Commodore C R S Gardner

1* Assistant Chief of Staff Land & Littoral Manoeuvre (ACOS LLM)
Brigadier M W Dunham OBE

1* Assistant Chief of Staff Maritime Capability (ACOS Mar Cap)
Commodore J Morley

ASSISTANT CHIEF OF NAVAL STAFF (SUPPORT)

2* Assistant Chief of Naval Staff (Support) (ACNS Spt)
Rear Admiral I M Jess CBE

1* Commodore Portsmouth Flotilla (COMPORFLOT)
Commodore P A McAlpine OBE ADC

1* Commodore Devonport Flotilla (COMDEVFLOT)
Commodore R Farrington CBE

1* Commodore Faslane Flotilla (COMFASFLOT)
Commodore M J D Walliker OBE

1* Assistant Chief of Staff Afloat Support (ACOS AFSUP)
Commodore R W Dorey RFA

1* Assistant Chief of Staff Logistics & Infrastructure (ACOS Logs & Infra)
Commodore A T Aplin MBE

KEY PERSONNEL

Commanding Officer HMNB Clyde
Commodore A M Adams

Commanding Officer HMNB Devonport
Commodore I Shipperley

Commanding Officer HMNB Portsmouth
Commodore J C Rigby ADC

Naval Base Transfer
Mr David Diamond

ASSISTANT CHIEF OF NAVAL STAFF (PERSONNEL) AND NAVAL SECRETARY

2* Assistant Chief of Naval Staff (Personnel) and Naval Secretary
Rear Admiral S J Woodcock OBE

1* Commander Maritime Reserves (COMMARRES)
Commodore A C Jameson

1* Commodore Naval Personnel Strategy (CNPS)
Commodore M A W Bath

1* Commodore Naval Personnel (CNPers)
Commodore M E Farrage CBE

1* Naval Assistant (NA)
Commodore R Albon OBE

1* Assistant Chief of Staff Medical (ACOS MED)
Surgeon Commodore P Buxton OBE

1* Commodore Naval Legal Services (CNLS)
Commodore A B Spence

FLAG OFFICER SEA TRAINING & ASSISTANT CHIEF OF NAVAL STAFF (TRAINING)

2* Flag Officer Sea Training (FOST/ACNST)
Rear Admiral B J Key

1* Deputy Flag Officer Sea Training (DFOST)
Commodore J S Weale OBE

1* Commander Operational Training (COM OT)
Commodore T J L Williamson MVO

1* Commander Core Training (COMCORE)
Brigadier G M Salzano MBE

KEY PERSONNEL

FINANCE DIRECTOR NAVY

2* Finance Director (Navy)
Louise Tulett CBE

1* Assistant Chief of Staff Resources & Plans (ACOS RP)
Commodore D Dutton OBE

1* Command Secretary & Deputy Civilian Workforce Advisor
Giles Ahern

1* Head of RN Communications
Commodore G B Sutton

CHAPLAIN OF THE FLEET

2* Chaplain of the Fleet
The Venerable I J Wheatley QHC

Deputy Chaplain of the Fleet
The Reverend M Gough

COMMANDER REGIONAL FORCES

1* Commander Regional Forces (CRF)
Commodore M J Atherton OBE

1* Naval Regional Commander Eastern England (NRC EE)
Commodore M J Atherton OBE

1* Naval Regional Commander Northern England (NRC NE)
Commodore G Doyle

1* Naval Regional Commander Scotland & Northern Ireland (NRC SNI)
Captain C J Smith

1* Naval Regional Commander Wales & Western England (NRC WWE)
Commodore A J G Miller CBE

OFFICERS ON THE ACTIVE LIST
OF THE ROYAL NAVY, THE ROYAL MARINES,
THE QUEEN ALEXANDRA'S
ROYAL NAVAL NURSING SERVICE
AND RETIRED AND EMERGENCY OFFICERS SERVING

Name	Substantive Rank	Seniority	Branch	Specialisation	Organisation Name	Location Name

A

Name	Substantive Rank	Seniority	Branch	Specialisation	Organisation Name	Location Name
Abbey, Rachel F.	Lt RN	07-Sep-10	ENG	ME	FOST DPORT	PLYMOUTH
Abbiss, Jack E C	Mid	08-Sep-14	ENG	ME	BRNC	BRNC DARTMOUTH
Abbott, Duncan A J	Lt RN	01-Nov-07	WAR	GSX	HMS DIAMOND	
Abbott, Grant P	Maj	01-Oct-09	RM	GS	NATO-ACO-JFC	BRUNSSUM
Abbott, Katherine Y L	Lt RN	01-Dec-03	WAR	PWO	HMS DAUNTLESS	
Abbott, Sir Peter (Charles) GBE KCB	Adm	03-Oct-95				
Abbotts, Michael C	Lt Cdr	01-Oct-11	ENG	AE	CHFHQ	RAF BENSON
Abel, James A	Lt RN	01-Nov-05	ENG	WESM(SWS)	DES COMFLEET	USA
Abel, Nigel P	Lt Cdr	01-Oct-07	WAR	P MER CDO	CHF(MERLIN)	RAF BENSON
Abernethy, James R G	Capt RN	24-Mar-14	WAR	PWO(N)	COMDEVFLOT	PLYMOUTH
Ablett, Daniel J	Surg Lt Cdr	01-Nov-09	MED	GS	MTM INM ALVERSTOKE	GOSPORT
Ablett, Eleanor L MBE	Cdr	30-Jun-11	LOGS	L	MOD CNS/ACNS	LONDON
Abouzeid, Adam A	Capt	01-Sep-09	RM	GS	CTCRM	EXMOUTH
Abraham, Paul CBE	Capt RN	30-Jun-08	WAR	SM(CQ)	DI - ICSP	LONDON
Ackerman, Richard J	Lt RN	09-May-99	WAR	MTO N (RES)	FLEET CMR	PORTSMOUTH
Ackers, Simon S	Mid	01-Feb-14	LOGS	L	BRNC	BRNC DARTMOUTH
Ackland, Heber K MVO	Capt RN	10-Dec-13	LOGS	L	DES COMLAND	ABBEY WOOD
Adam, Ian K	Cdr	30-Jun-09	WAR	PWO(A)	FLEET MARITIME WARFARE	HMS COLLINGWOOD
Adam, Murray W	Lt Cdr	01-Oct-14	WAR	PWO(SM)	HMS ARTFUL	
Adams, Alistair J	Cdre	05-Nov-12	WAR	PWO(C)	HDPROG	CORSHAM
Adams, Andrew M	Cdre	20-Oct-14	ENG	MESM	NBC CLYDE	HMNB CLYDE
Adams, Benjamin L	Mid	01-May-14	WAR	HM	BRNC	BRNC DARTMOUTH
Adams, Edwin S	Lt Cdr	01-Oct-09	WAR	P SK4	HMS OCEAN	
Adams, George	Lt Cdr	01-May-09	ENG	ME	FLEET CAP SSM	PORTSMOUTH
Adams, Henry D	Lt RN	01-Sep-12	WAR	GSX	MCM1	FASLANE
Adams, Joanne F	Lt RN	01-Apr-08	WAR	O SKW	MASF	RNAS CULDROSE
Adams, Jonathan T	Capt	03-Sep-14	RM	GS	42 CDO RM	PLYMOUTH
Adams, Joseph M	Mid	01-Feb-14	WAR	GSX	BRNC	BRNC DARTMOUTH
Adams, Keith J	Lt RN	01-Sep-11	ENG	AE	FLEET CSAV	PORTSMOUTH
Adams, Lee M	Capt	01-Apr-11	RM	GS	NCHQ	PORTSMOUTH
Adams, Matthew	Maj	01-Oct-14	RM	SCC	HQ ARTD OPS	WARMINSTER
Adams, Megan A	Surg SLt	25-Jul-14	MED	Medical	BLAKE	BRNC DARTMOUTH
Adams, Peter	Cdr	01-Sep-09	ENG	TM	FOSNI - YOUTH MSCC	ROSYTH
Adams, Victoria R A	Lt RN	01-Sep-12	WAR	GSX	HMS DAUNTLESS	
Adams, William J MBE	Lt Cdr	01-Oct-08	WAR	GSX	OCLC ROSYTH	HMS CALEDONIA
Adcock, Markus	Lt RN	01-Nov-12	ENG	WE	HMS SUTHERLAND	
Addison, Timothy M B	Capt	01-Sep-10	RM	GS	40 CDO RM	TAUNTON
Adekoluejo, Gbadebowale A	Lt RN	05-Nov-14	ENG	TM	CTCRM	EXMOUTH
Adey, Joanna L	Lt Cdr	01-Oct-10	ENG	TM	NCHQ CNPERS	PORTSMOUTH
Adkins, Paul S	Lt RN	16-Dec-11	WAR	C	FOST DPORT	PLYMOUTH
Adkins, Rhys T	2Lt	25-Aug-14	RM	N/A	CTCRM	EXMOUTH
Adlam, Charlotte	Lt RN	01-Jan-09	ENG	WE	DI - SA	LONDON

Name	Substantive Rank	Seniority	Branch	Specialisation	Organisation Name	Location Name
Adshead, Stephen P	Surg Lt RN	01-Mar-12	MED	GDMO	HMS VIGILANT	
A'Hern, Paul V	Lt RN	01-Sep-09	WAR	GSX	RN EXCHANGE NORWAY	OSLO
Ahlgren, Edward G OBE	Cdr	30-Jun-07	WAR	SM(CQ)	UKMARBATSTAFF	PORTSMOUTH
Aindow, Alice L	SLt	01-Nov-14	WAR	GSX	MWS COLLINGWOOD	HMS COLLINGWOOD
Ainscow, Anthony J	Lt Cdr	01-Oct-09	ENG	ME	NCHQ CNPS	PORTSMOUTH
Ainscow, Peter D	Lt RN	17-Nov-14	ENG	ME	HMS ARGYLL	
Ainsley, Alex S	Capt	03-Sep-14	RM	GS	45 CDO RM	DUNDEE
Ainsley, Andrew M J	Lt Cdr	01-Oct-08	WAR	PWO	HMS MONMOUTH	
Ainsworth, Alan	Lt RN	01-Jul-04	ENG	WE	DEFENCE ACADEMY	SHRIVENHAM
Aird, Pauline	Lt Cdr	01-Apr-05	ENG	ME	HQ RS	AFGHANISTAN KABUL
Aitken, Andrew J	Cdr	30-Jun-11	WAR	SM(CQ)	DEFENCE ACADEMY	SHRIVENHAM
Aitken, Neil D	Lt RN	01-May-07	WAR	ATC	ARCC KINLOSS	RAF KINLOSS
Aitken, Steven R	Lt RN	01-Jan-01	WAR	P LYNX	RN EXCHANGE FRANCE	PARIS
Akerman, Andrew E	Lt RN	01-Aug-08	LOGS	L	HMS OCEAN	
Alberts, Ian	Surg Lt RN	07-Aug-13	MED	Medical	BLAKE	BRNC DARTMOUTH
Albon, Joshua G	Lt RN	01-Apr-14	WAR	P MER CDO	CHF(MERLIN)	RAF BENSON
Albon, Mark	Cdr	30-Jun-06	WAR	HM	DEFENCE ATTACHE	SANAA
Albon, Ross OBE	Cdre	07-Jul-08	LOGS	L BAR	NAVSEC	HMS EXCELLENT
Alcindor, David J	Lt Cdr	22-Apr-10	WAR	SM(AWC)	FLEET MARITIME WARFARE	HMS COLLINGWOOD
Alcock, Christopher	Capt RN	30-Jun-07	WAR	O SK6	FLEET CSAV	PORTSMOUTH
Alder, Mark C	Lt Cdr	01-Oct-10	ENG	MESM	DES COMFLEET	HMS DRAKE
Alderson, Richard J	Lt Col	30-Jun-14	RM	GS	MTM RN GLOBAL	AUSTRALIA
Alderson, Stuart J	Lt RN	01-Sep-13	ENG	MESM	HMS VANGUARD	
Alderton, Paul A	Lt Cdr	01-Oct-09	ENG	WE	NCHQ CNPS	PORTSMOUTH
Aldous, Benjamin	Lt Cdr	01-Nov-07	WAR	PWO(A)	MTM NELSON	HMS NELSON
Aldridge, Rachel	SLt	01-Jan-14	MED	Medical	BLAKE	BRNC DARTMOUTH
Alessandro, Santino S P	Lt	02-Sep-14	RM	GS	45 CDO RM	DUNDEE
Alexander, Amy L	Lt Cdr	01-Oct-08	ENG	WE	DES COMLAND	ABBEY WOOD
Alexander, Daniel D P	2Lt	25-Aug-14	RM	N/A	CTCRM	EXMOUTH
Alexander, Oliver D D	Lt Cdr	01-Oct-06	WAR	MCD	MTM DRAKE	HMS DRAKE
Alexander, Phillip M D	Lt Cdr	01-Jan-09	ENG	MESM	NBC CLYDE	HMNB CLYDE
Alexander, Robert S OBE	Cdre	04-Dec-12	WAR	P SK6	RNAS YEOVILTON	YEOVILTON
Alexander, William A D	Lt RN	01-Jan-06	WAR	HM	RN EXCHANGE N ZLAND	NEW ZEALAND
Allan, Chris R	Lt Cdr	01-Dec-05	WAR	PWO(C)	FLEET COMOPS NWD	NORTHWOOD
Allan, Fraser S	Maj	01-Oct-09	RM	GS	NCHQ	NCHQ
Allan, John M	Lt RN	08-Dec-09	WAR	O SKW	750 SQN	RNAS CULDROSE
Allan, Robert C	SLt	01-Sep-14	ENG	AE	DCEME SULTAN	HMS SULTAN
Allcock, Andrew J	RN Chpln	05-Jan-09	Ch S	Chaplain	DEFENCE ACADEMY	SHRIVENHAM
Allcock, Edward C	Surg Cdr	01-Jul-14	MED	Anaes	MDHU PORTSMOUTH	PORTSMOUTH
Alldridge, George M	Lt RN	01-Feb-14	WAR	HM	MTM MWS HMTG (D)	HMS DRAKE
Allen, Alexander P	Lt Cdr	01-Oct-14	ENG	ME	DES COMFLEET	ABBEY WOOD
Allen, Benjamin J	SLt	01-Sep-14	WAR	GSX	MCM2	PORTSMOUTH
Allen, Elinor J	Cdr	30-Sep-05	WAR	OP INT	FOSNI - CNR	PORTSMOUTH
Allen, Jason L	Lt Cdr	01-Oct-13	WAR	PWO	MWS COLLINGWOOD	HMS COLLINGWOOD
Allen, Lloyd N	Lt RN	11-Dec-09	LOGS	L	HMS OCEAN	
Allen, Nicholas C	Lt RN	08-Jul-12	WAR	P UT	MTM SHAWBURY	RAF SHAWBURY
Allen, Patrick L	Cdr	30-Jun-08	WAR	O SKW	FOST DPORT	PLYMOUTH
Allen, Paul M	Lt Cdr	01-Oct-04	WAR	O LYNX	NC REQUIREMENTS MANAGERS	YEOVIL
Allen, Richard	Cdr	30-Jun-06	WAR	SM(CQ)	MTM NELSON	HMS NELSON
Allen, Richard M	Cdre	01-Jul-13	WAR	SM(CQ)	BDS	WASHINGTON
Allen, Stephen M	Capt RN	08-Jan-13	WAR	O SK6	MTM FLEET HQ	PORTSMOUTH
Allen-Scholey, Spencer G	Lt RN	09-Apr-10	ENG	MESM	NCHQ CNPS	PORTSMOUTH
Allen-West, Bart J	Lt RN	05-Aug-11	LOGS	L	HMS NORTHUMBERLAND	
Allfree, Joseph	Lt Cdr	01-Jan-03	WAR	AAWO	HMS DRAGON	
Allibon, Mark C	Cdr	30-Jun-00	WAR	PWO(A)	FLEET FOST ACOS(Trg)	PORTSMOUTH
Allison, Glenn	Lt Cdr	01-Oct-08	WAR	P SK4	5 REGT AAC	RAF ALDERGROVE
Allsopp, Mark D	RN Chpln	02-Jun-08	Ch S	Chaplain	30 CDO IX GP RM	PLYMOUTH
Almond, Nicholas	Lt Cdr	01-Oct-12	ENG	AE	DES COMJE	YEOVIL
Alston, Richard	Maj	01-Oct-08	RM	C	MTM DEFAC JSCSC	SHRIVENHAM
Althorpe, Damian S	Capt	01-Apr-11	RM	SCC	NCHQ CNPERS	PORTSMOUTH
Alvey, Joshua T D	SLt	01-Nov-14	WAR	GSX	MWS COLLINGWOOD	HMS COLLINGWOOD
Amery, Miles I	SLt	01-Mar-14	WAR	GSX	HMS MONMOUTH	

Name	Substantive Rank	Seniority	Branch	Specialisation	Organisation Name	Location Name
Amor, Matthew	Lt RN	01-Sep-10	ENG	WESM(TWS)	NBC CLYDE	HMNB CLYDE
Amorosi, Riccardo G F L	Lt Cdr	01-Oct-11	ENG	WE	HMS DUNCAN	
Amphlett, Nigel G	Capt RN	07-Jun-10	WAR	O LYNX	SERV ATTACHE/ADVISER	LONDON
Ancona, Simon J	R Adm	14-Oct-13	WAR	O SK6	ACDS	LONDON
Anderson, Andrew E	Lt Cdr	01-Oct-10	WAR	ATC	FLEET AV VL	RNAS YEOVILTON
Anderson, Bruce W D	Maj	01-Oct-11	RM	GS	NCHQ	PORTSMOUTH
Anderson, Bryan A	Lt RN	12-Jul-13	WAR	INT	FLEET COMOPS NWD	HUNTINGDON
Anderson, David E A	Lt RN	06-Apr-07	WAR	O SK6	MTM DRAKE	HMS DRAKE
Anderson, Garry S	Lt Cdr	01-Oct-07	WAR	INT	EU OHQ	NORTHWOOD
Anderson, Joseph	SLt	01-Jul-14	LOGS	L	COMPORFLOT	PORTSMOUTH
Anderson, Kevin	Lt RN	01-Jun-03	ENG	TM	DEFENCE ACADEMY	SHRIVENHAM
Anderson, Mark E J	Cdr	30-Jun-14	WAR	PWO	HMS RICHMOND	
Anderson, Martin	Lt RN	31-Jul-09	WAR	SM(X)	MTM RALEIGH	HMS RALEIGH
Anderson, Michael I C	Lt RN	01-May-07	WAR	O MER	750 SQN	RNAS CULDROSE
Anderson, Neil	Lt Cdr	01-Oct-11	ENG	WE	DES COMLAND	ABBEY WOOD
Anderson, Peter D	SLt	01-Sep-14	WAR	GSX	MWS COLLINGWOOD	HMS COLLINGWOOD
Anderson, Richard	Mid	08-Sep-14	FNG	AE	BRNC	BRNC DARTMOUTH
Anderson, Robert G	Capt RN	01-Jul-08	ENG	WE	FLEET CMR	PORTSMOUTH
Anderson, Stephen R	Cdr	30-Jun-14	WAR	O LYNX	HMS SUTHERLAND	
Anderson, Timothy J R	Surg Lt RN	04-Aug-10	MED	EM	MTM INM ALVERSTOKE	GOSPORT
Andrew, Paul R	RN Chpln	04-Jan-10	Ch S	Chaplain	CTCRM	EXMOUTH
Andrews, Alistair J	Lt RN	01-Apr-09	WAR	P SKW	OCLC PETERBRGH	PETERBOROUGH
Andrews, Christopher	Lt Cdr	01-Oct-09	WAR	IS	FLEET CAP IS	PORTSMOUTH
Andrews, David	SLt	19-Sep-14	WAR	O UT	MTM RAF CRANWELL	RAFC CRANWELL
Andrews, Dominic M	Lt Cdr	01-Oct-13	ENG	WE	MTM FLEET HQ	PORTSMOUTH
Andrews, Iain S	Lt RN	01-Sep-01	WAR	MW	HMS SUTHERLAND	
Andrews, Justin P	Lt Cdr	01-Oct-11	WAR	WE	MTM NELSON	HMS NELSON
Andrews, Liam J R	Lt RN	01-Nov-13	WAR	GSX	MCM2	PORTSMOUTH
Andrews, Louisa J	Lt Cdr	01-Oct-10	WAR	HM(AM)	LOAN DSTL	FAREHAM
Andrews, Nicholas G	Lt RN	01-Mar-11	WAR	GSX	HMS MONMOUTH	
Andrews, Paul	Lt Cdr	01-Jun-94	LOGS	L CMA	SMC MARCHWOOD	SOUTHAMPTON
Andrews, Rick	Lt RN	01-Sep-07	ENG	MESM	DES COMFLEET	ABBEY WOOD
Andrews, Robert C	Lt RN	01-Sep-14	WAR	P	MTM 820 SQN CULDROSE	RNAS CULDROSE
Andrews, Steven J	Lt RN	13-Oct-12	MED	MS(CDO)	MED SQN CDO LOG REGT RM	RMB CHIVENOR
Angliss, Roger J	Lt RN	08-Apr-05	WAR	O MER	820 SQN	RNAS CULDROSE
Angus, Donald J C	Surg Lt Cdr	19-Aug-13	MED	GMP	MTM INM ALVERSTOKE	GOSPORT
Aniyi, Christopher B J	Cdr	30-Jun-09	ENG	ME	DES COMFLEET	ABBEY WOOD
Ankah, Gregory K E	Lt Cdr	01-Dec-04	ENG	ME	DES COMFLEET	ABBEY WOOD
Annett, Ian C	Capt RN	11-Mar-13	ENG	WE	FLEET CAP IS	PORTSMOUTH
Anrude, Jack F	Capt	01-Sep-10	RM	GS	43 CDO FPGRM	HELENSBURGH
Ansell, Christopher	Lt Cdr	01-Oct-06	WAR	PWO(C)	HMS ARGYLL	
Anstey, Robert J	Capt RN	25-Mar-14	WAR	SM(CQ)	FOST SM SEA	HMNB CLYDE
Aplin, Adrian T MBE	Cdre	01-Jul-14	LOGS	L	FLEET SPT LOGS INFRA	PORTSMOUTH
Apps, Julian C	Maj	01-Oct-14	RM	GS	UKMARBATSTAFF	PORTSMOUTH
Arend, Faye M	Lt Cdr	01-Oct-06	LOGS	L	NCHQ CNPERS	PORTSMOUTH
Arkell, Thomas C	Capt	01-Sep-13	RM	GS	42 CDO RM	PLYMOUTH
Armand-Smith, Penelope H	Lt Cdr	01-Oct-14	WAR	HM	FLEET COMMANDER DCNS	PORTSMOUTH
Armitage, David G	Lt RN	01-Feb-14	WAR	P UT	MTM RAF CRANWELL	RAFC CRANWELL
Armitage, John J	Mid	01-Feb-14	WAR	SM(X)	BRNC	BRNC DARTMOUTH
Armour, Angela B	Lt RN	01-Sep-05	ENG	TM	HMS QUEEN ELIZABETH	
Armour, Graeme A	Col	02-Sep-14	RM	GS	1 ASSLT GP RM	PLYMOUTH
Armstrong, Alison C	Lt RN	01-Nov-14	WAR	HM	HMS ENTERPRISE	
Armstrong, Christopher T	Capt	01-Sep-09	RM	GS	HQ 3 CDO BDE RM	PLYMOUTH
Armstrong, Colin D	Lt Cdr	01-Oct-14	WAR	PWO	MTM NELSON	HMS NELSON
Armstrong, David M	Lt Cdr	01-Oct-12	WAR	MCD	PJHQ (UK)	NORTHWOOD
Armstrong, Katharine L M	Lt Cdr	01-Mar-05	WAR	INT	PJHQ (UK)	NORTHWOOD
Armstrong, Nicholas P B	Lt Cdr	01-Oct-96	WAR	O MER	RNAS CULDROSE	HELSTON
Armstrong, Paul	Lt RN	01-Apr-12	WAR	P UT	MTM WMO YEOVILTON	GRANTHAM
Armstrong, Paul C	Lt RN	13-Jul-12	ENG	WE	HMS SOMERSET	
Armstrong, Rory J	Lt Cdr	01-Oct-12	WAR	MCD	HMS KENT	
Armstrong, Scott T	Lt Cdr	01-Oct-04	WAR	P SK4	771 SQN	RNAS CULDROSE
Armstrong, Stuart M	Lt Cdr	01-Oct-07	WAR	SM(CQ)	NCHQ CNPS	PORTSMOUTH

Name	Substantive Rank	Seniority	Branch	Specialisation	Organisation Name	Location Name
Arnold, Lee J	Lt RN	01-Sep-11	ENG	MESM	HMS VANGUARD	
Arr Woodward, Robert W	Surg Lt RN	01-Aug-12	MED	GDMO	HMS RICHMOND	
Arscott, James S	Lt	02-Sep-14	RM	GS	42 CDO RM	PLYMOUTH
Arthur, Calum H C	Surg Lt Cdr	01-Aug-06	MED	T&O	MTM INM ALVERSTOKE	GOSPORT
Asbridge, Jonathan I	Cdr	30-Jun-08	LOGS	L SM	UK MCC	BAHRAIN
Ashby, Maxine	Lt RN	01-Dec-00	LOGS	L	RNAS CULDROSE	HELSTON
Ashcroft, Adam C	Capt RN	30-Jun-08	WAR	P LYNX	SERV ATTACHE/ADVISER	TOKYO
Ashcroft, Benjamin J	Capt	01-Sep-09	RM	GS	42 CDO RM	PLYMOUTH
Ashley, Elizabeth A	Surg Lt RN	01-Aug-12	MED	GDMO	HMS VIGILANT	
Ashley, Scott M MBE	Maj	01-Oct-14	RM	SCC	FOSNI - CNR	PORTSMOUTH
Ashley, Stephen J	Lt RN	01-Sep-08	ENG	WE	UKMARBATSTAFF	PORTSMOUTH
Ashley-Smith, R	Lt RN	01-Mar-09	ENG	ME	DES COMFLEET	ABBEY WOOD
Ashlin, James M	Lt Cdr	01-Oct-12	WAR	P FW	750 SQN	RNAS CULDROSE
Ashman, Rodney G	Cdr	30-Jun-07	LOGS	L CMA	FLEET SPT LOGS INFRA	PORTSMOUTH
Ashmore, Sir Edward (Beckwith) GCB DSC	Adm of Fleet	09-Feb-77				
Ashton, James	Lt Cdr	01-Mar-10	ENG	MESM	HMS VICTORIOUS	
Ashton, Karl	Lt RN	01-Jan-12	LOGS	L	COMPORFLOT	PORTSMOUTH
Ashton, Megan E	Lt RN	01-Mar-09	ENG	AE	DCDS PERS TRG	LONDON
Asker, Tristan	Lt RN	01-Sep-14	ENG	WE	HMS OCEAN	
Askham, Mathew T	Lt RN	01-Jun-06	WAR	P MER	MTM RAF CRANWELL	RAFC CRANWELL
Aspden, Andrew M	Capt RN	21-Oct-08	WAR	O SK6	MTM DCLC RN STUDENTS	SHRIVENHAM
Asplin, Jacob N	2Lt	25-Aug-14	RM	N/A	CTCRM	EXMOUTH
Asquith, Simon P OBE	Capt RN	28-Apr-14	WAR	SM(CQ)	HMS PORTLAND	
Astley, Daniel	Lt RN	01-Sep-13	ENG	WE	HMS LANCASTER	
Astley, William E	Lt RN	23-Jul-13	ENG	ME	HMS MONMOUTH	
Aston, James A	Lt RN	01-Aug-10	ENG	TM	FOST FAS SHORE	HMNB CLYDE
Aston, Mark W	Surg Cdr (D)	30-Jun-97	DENTAL	GDP	RNAS YEOVILTON	YEOVILTON
Atherton, Bruce W	Maj	01-Oct-04	RM	P LYN7	MTM APACHE	IPSWICH
Atherton, Martin J OBE	Capt RN	30-Jun-03	LOGS	N/A	COMMANDER REG FORCES	LONDON
Atkins, Ian	Cdr	30-Jun-09	ENG	ME	DES COMFLEET	ABBEY WOOD
Atkinson, Andrew W	Capt	21-Mar-13	RM	SCC	HMS BULWARK	
Atkinson, David	Capt	21-Mar-13	RM	GS	NCHQ	PORTSMOUTH
Atkinson, James D	Lt RN	26-Feb-06	WAR	OP INT	NATO ACO	NORTHWOOD
Atkinson, Kevin A	SLt	01-Nov-14	ENG	WESM	MWS COLLINGWOOD	HMS COLLINGWOOD
Atkinson, Mark	Cdr	30-Jun-08	WAR	MCD	DSEA MARITIME	PORTSMOUTH
Atkinson, Neil C	Maj	01-May-06	RM	GS	MTM NELSON	HMS NELSON
Atkinson, Richard J	Cdr	30-Jun-13	WAR	AAWO	HMS DUNCAN	
Attrill, Jonathan D N	Capt	01-Sep-13	RM	GS	40 CDO RM	TAUNTON
Attwater, Richard P	Lt Cdr	01-Oct-14	WAR	PWO	HMS DUNCAN	
Attwood, Keith A	Lt RN	01-Sep-04	WAR	P LYNX	LHF 815 SQN	RNAS YEOVILTON
Atwal, Kamaldip	Lt RN	01-Jan-02	ENG	TM	DMSTG	BIRMINGHAM
Atwill, John W O	Cdr	30-Jun-11	LOGS	L BAR	MOD CNS/ACNS	LONDON
Aujla, Pavandip S	SLt	08-Dec-12	WAR	GSX	HMS ARGYLL	
Auld, Douglas	Lt Cdr	01-Oct-06	ENG	MESM	FLEET CAP SSM	PORTSMOUTH
Austin, Peter N	Lt Cdr	01-Oct-07	ENG	WESM(SWS)	DES COMFLEET	PLYMOUTH
Avison, Christopher J	SLt	01-Apr-12	WAR	P UT	MTM RAF LINTON-ON-OUSE	RAF LINTON ON OUSE
Ayers, Oliver R B	Lt RN	01-Nov-06	WAR	PWO	HMS DARING	
Aylmer, Matthew A	Lt RN	01-Apr-14	WAR	ATC	RNAS CULDROSE	HELSTON
Ayrton, Robert E	Lt RN	01-Dec-02	WAR	HM(AS)	FLEET HM UNIT	PLYMOUTH
Ayto, Lydia Jane	SLt	08-Oct-12	WAR	GSX	HMS PORTLAND	

B

Name	Substantive Rank	Seniority	Branch	Specialisation	Organisation Name	Location Name
Babington, James H	Mid	05-May-14	LOGS	L	BRNC	BRNC DARTMOUTH
Back, Charles P D	Capt	01-Sep-13	RM	GS	45 CDO RM	DUNDEE
Bacon, David R	Lt RN	09-Apr-12	LOGS	L	DES HR	ABBEY WOOD
Bacon, Thomas G	Maj	01-Oct-14	RM	GS	HQ 3 CDO BDE RM	PLYMOUTH
Baddeley, James	Lt RN	01-Sep-13	ENG	ME	HMS DUNCAN	
Baggaley, Jason A L	Cdr	30-Jun-11	ENG	WE	FLEET ACOS(RP)	PORTSMOUTH
Bagnall, Sally-Anne E	Cdr	06-Aug-12	QARNNS	Nurse Officer	DMS WHITTINGTON	LICHFIELD
Bagshaw, James R W	Lt Cdr	01-Oct-08	WAR	PWO(A)	FLEET COMOPS NWD	NORTHWOOD
Bailes, Kenneth	Lt Cdr	01-Oct-10	WAR	PWO	FLEET SPT FGEN	PORTSMOUTH

Name	Substantive Rank	Seniority	Branch	Specialisation	Organisation Name	Location Name
Bailey, Andrew P	Lt RN	01-Apr-11	WAR	O SKW	857 NAS	RNAS CULDROSE
Bailey, Angus W C	2Lt	25-Aug-14	RM	N/A	CTCRM	EXMOUTH
Bailey, David J	Lt RN	01-Oct-09	WAR	MW	MCM2	PORTSMOUTH
Bailey, Ian J	Lt Cdr	01-Oct-10	ENG	WE	HMS ARGYLL	
Bailey, Jeremy J	Capt RN	16-Dec-14	ENG	ME	FLEET CAP SSM	PORTSMOUTH
Bailey, Michael	Lt Cdr	01-Oct-10	WAR		NCHQ	PORTSMOUTH
Bailey, Oliver J	Mid	01-Feb-14	ENG	ME	BRNC	BRNC DARTMOUTH
Bailey, Sian	Lt RN	01-Aug-99	ENG	TM	MTM RMR MERSEYSIDE	LIVERPOOL
Bailey, Simon	Lt Cdr	01-Oct-11	WAR	PWO	FLEET COMOPS NWD	NORTHWOOD
Baillie, Robbie W	Lt Cdr	01-Oct-11	ENG	TM	CTCRM	EXMOUTH
Bainbridge, John R	Lt Cdr	01-Oct-07	WAR	MCD	FOST MPV SEA	HMNB CLYDE
Bainbridge, Paul A	Lt Cdr	01-Oct-11	LOGS	L	OCLC PETERBRGH	PETERBOROUGH
Bainbridge, Stuart D	Lt Cdr	01-Oct-08	WAR	P MER	FLEET AV CU	RNAS CULDROSE
Baines, David M L	Cdr	30-Jun-10	ENG	IS	MCSU	FLEET HQ
Baines, Gary A	Maj	01-Oct-06	RM	SCC	MTM HASLER COY	HMS DRAKE
Baines, Liam P	Lt RN	01-Sep-12	ENG	WESM(TWS)	HMS TORBAY	
Bains, Baldeep S	Surg Lt Cdr	01-Aug-06	MED	GMP	DPHC SW	RNAS YEOVILTON
Baish, Christopher D	Mid	08-Sep-14	WAR	GSX	BRNC	BRNC DARTMOUTH
Baker, Adrian P	Cdr	30-Jun-13	WAR	O LYNX	DIRECTOR (JW)	NORTHWOOD
Baker, James E G	Lt Cdr	01-Oct-10	WAR	PWO	HMS DEFENDER	
Baker, James K	Lt RN	01-May-06	WAR	P SK4	AACEN	STOCKBRIDGE
Baker, James O	Surg Lt Cdr	01-Mar-13	MED	GDMO	HQ SQN CDO LOG REGT RM	RMB CHIVENOR
Baker, Kyle L	Lt RN	01-Sep-13	ENG	MESM	HMS AUDACIOUS	
Baker, Luke D	Surg Lt RN	03-Aug-11	MED	GDMO	HMS VANGUARD	
Baker, Mark A	Lt RN	08-Dec-09	LOGS	L SM	COMDEVFLOT	PLYMOUTH
Baker, Michael	Maj	01-Oct-05	RM	P LYN7	HQ JHC DCOMD	ANDOVER
Baker, Nicholas	Lt Cdr	01-Oct-05	LOGS	L	DMLS	HMS RALEIGH
Bakewell, Emma C	Lt RN	01-Jan-07	ENG	ME	FLEET FOST TBTU	HMS COLLINGWOOD
Bakewell, Timothy D	Lt Col	30-Jun-12	RM	HW	SERV ATTACHE/ADVISER	BUCHAREST
Bakker-Dyos, Joshua J	Surg Lt RN	01-Aug-12	MED	GDMO	NCHQ	PORTSMOUTH
Balcam, Jonathan E W	SLt	01-May-12	LOGS	L	824 SQN	RNAS CULDROSE
Baldie, Steven A H	Lt Cdr	01-Oct-11	WAR	P MER CDO	CHF - 846	RAF BENSON
Balfour, Andrew J	2Lt	25-Aug-14	RM	N/A	CTCRM	EXMOUTH
Balfour, Daniel M	2Lt	25-Aug-14	RM	N/A	CTCRM	EXMOUTH
Balfour, Ross D	Lt Cdr	01-Oct-12	WAR	MCD	RN EXCHANGE USA	WASHINGTON
Balhetchet, Adrian S	Cdr	30-Jun-09	ENG	AE	MOD NSD	LONDON
Ball, Ian N	SLt	01-Sep-13	WAR	SM(X)	MTM RALEIGH	HMS RALEIGH
Ball, Jacob	Lt RN	01-Sep-12	WAR	SM(X)	HMS VIGILANT	
Ball, Liam	SLt	01-Sep-12	ENG	AE	DCEME SULTAN	HMS SULTAN
Ball, Samuel P	Mid	01-May-13	WAR	O UT	BRNC	BRNC DARTMOUTH
Ball, William J E	Lt Cdr	01-Oct-09	ENG	ME	HMS QUEEN ELIZABETH	
Ballantyne, Craig	Cdr	30-Jun-14	WAR	SM(CQ)	HMS TALENT	
Ballard, Adam P V	Lt Cdr	01-Oct-12	WAR	PWO(N)	HMS PROTECTOR	
Ballard, Danelle R	Lt Cdr	01-Oct-12	WAR	PWO(N)	RN ACQUAINT CENTRE	HMS COLLINGWOOD
Ballard, Mark L	Cdr	30-Jun-11	ENG	WESM(SWS)	COMFASFLOT	HELENSBURGH
Balletta, Rene J	Lt Cdr	01-Nov-04	WAR	PWO(C)	RN EXCHANGE FRANCE	PARIS
Balls, Christopher F	Lt RN	01-Sep-11	ENG	WESM(TWS)	RNSMS	HMS RALEIGH
Balmer, Guy A	Lt Col	30-Jun-14	RM	GS	NAVY CORE TRG HQ	PLYMOUTH
Balmond, Samuel J	Lt RN	01-Feb-11	ENG	TM	JFC - DCTS (H)	AYLESBURY
Bamber, Michael S	Surg Lt Cdr (D)	05-Jul-12	DENTAL	GDP	MTM DEFAC JSCSC	SHRIVENHAM
Bambro, Calum A	SLt	01-Feb-12	WAR	GSX	HMS CLYDE	
Bamford, Alexander	Surg Lt RN	07-Aug-13	MED	Medical	BLAKE	BRNC DARTMOUTH
Bamforth, Christian J M	Cdr	30-Jun-13	ENG	WESM(TWS)	FOST SM SEA	HMNB CLYDE
Bance, Nicholas D	Lt Cdr	01-Oct-04	WAR	P LYNX	WMF 825 SQN HQ	RNAS YEOVILTON
Band, James W	Cdr	30-Jun-04	ENG	AE	MTM FLEET HQ	PORTSMOUTH
Band, Sir Jonathon GCB DL	Adm	02-Aug-02				
Bane, Nicholas S	Lt Cdr	01-Oct-13	WAR	P SK4	RAF SHAWBURY	SHREWSBURY
Banfield, Steven D	Lt Cdr	01-Oct-10	WAR	PWO	HMS SEVERN	
Bannister, Jonathan	Lt Cdr	01-Oct-12	WAR	PWO	RN EXCHANGE AUSTRALIA	CANBERRA
Banyard, Adelaide C	SLt	01-Nov-14	WAR	HM	MWS COLLINGWOOD	HMS COLLINGWOOD
Barber, Alexander S L	Lt RN	01-Jan-05	WAR	INT	NATO ACO	NORTHWOOD
Barber, Christopher J	Lt RN	01-Apr-11	WAR	MCD	MCM1	FASLANE

Name	Substantive Rank	Seniority	Branch	Specialisation	Organisation Name	Location Name
Barber, Christopher J H	Lt Cdr	01-Oct-07	WAR	O SKW	RNAS CULDROSE	HELSTON
Barber, Gregory A	SLt	01-Jan-14	LOGS	L	HMS ALBION	
Barber, Mark	Lt RN	01-Sep-03	WAR	P SK6	DEF HELI FLYING SCH	SHREWSBURY
Barber, Max A J	SLt	01-Sep-13	WAR	GSX	HMS DARING	
Barber, Ralph W	RN Chpln	31-Mar-08	Ch S	Chaplain	FOST DPORT	PLYMOUTH
Barber, Thomas E	Capt	01-Sep-10	RM	GS	RMR MERSEYSIDE	LIVERPOOL
Barclay, Alastair J	Lt RN	21-Jun-96	WAR	ATC	RNAS CULDROSE	HELSTON
Barden, Paul E	Maj	01-Oct-10	RM	SCC	NC REQUIREMENTS MANAGERS	ABBEY WOOD
Barfoot, Peter M	Lt Cdr	01-Oct-10	WAR	PWO	HMS DAUNTLESS	
Barham, Edward	Lt RN	01-Sep-06	WAR	O LYNX	FLEET CAP IS	PORTSMOUTH
Bark, James S	Lt Cdr	01-Sep-96	WAR	SM(CQ)	CAPTAIN HMS NEPTUNE	HMNB CLYDE
Barker, Helen A	Lt RN	01-Sep-07	LOGS	L	DES COMLAND	ABBEY WOOD
Barker, Paul D	Lt Cdr	01-Apr-08	ENG	AE	HMS SULTAN	GOSPORT
Barker, Peter R	Lt Cdr	01-Oct-14	LOGS	L BAR	NCHQ - CNLS	PORTSMOUTH
Barker, William G	Lt RN	16-Mar-13	ENG	MESM	HMS VANGUARD	
Barkey, Barry J	Lt RN	01 Sep-11	WAR	P MER	820 SQN	RNAS CULDROSE
Barks, Nicholas	Capt	30-Mar-12	RM	GS	NCHQ	PORTSMOUTH
Barley, Andrew G W	SLt	01-Feb-12	LOGS	L	MTM FLEET HQ	PORTSMOUTH
Barlow, James A	2Lt	25-Aug-14	RM	N/A	CTCRM	EXMOUTH
Barlow, Jay P	Lt RN	05-Aug-11	ENG	WE	MCM2	PORTSMOUTH
Barlow, Leonard J	Lt RN	30-Jul-10	ENG	WESM(TWS)	MTM NEPTUNE	HMNB CLYDE
Barlow, Martin J	Cdr	30-Jun-12	WAR	O SKW	HQ AIR - COS(OPS) - JALO	HIGH WYCOMBE
Barlow, Matthew J	Capt	01-Aug-07	RM	GS	MTM HASLER COY	HMS DRAKE
Barlow, Paul R	Lt RN	01-Sep-12	ENG	WESM	DES COMFLEET	ABBEY WOOD
Barnard, Edward B G	Surg Lt Cdr	04-Aug-09	MED	EM	MTM INM ALVERSTOKE	GOSPORT
Barnes, David C	Lt RN	01-Sep-09	ENG	WE	DES COMLAND	ABBEY WOOD
Barnes, Paul F	Lt RN	14-Aug-07	ENG	TM	HQ DISC	CHICKSANDS
Barnes, Thomas M	Lt RN	01-May-13	WAR	GSX	HMS NORTHUMBERLAND	
Barnes-Yallowley, Jonathan	Lt Cdr	16-Jul-92	WAR	P SK6	HMS QUEEN ELIZABETH	
Barnett, Caila	Lt RN	01-Sep-06	ENG	TM	URNU SOUTHAMPTON	SOUTHAMPTON
Barnett, Christopher J	Lt RN	01-Apr-12	LOGS	L	HMS VICTORIOUS	
Barnick, Sebastian G D	SLt	08-Mar-13	WAR	GSX	HMS SOMERSET	
Barnicoat, Karen	Lt RN	01-Jan-06	WAR	O MER	MTM MWS COLLINGWOOD	HMS COLLINGWOOD
Barnwell, Alan F	Capt	21-Jul-01	RM	P SK4	CHFHQ	RNAS YEOVILTON
Barr, Andrew R	Lt RN	01-Feb-14	WAR	SM(X)	HMS ARTFUL	
Barr, Derek D	Lt RN	01-Apr-02	ENG	AE	MTM CULDROSE	RNAS CULDROSE
Barr, Simon J C	Lt RN	09-Apr-10	ENG	MESM	SFM CLYDE	HMNB CLYDE
Barrand, Stuart M	Cdr	30-Jun-02	WAR	AAWO	MTM NELSON	HMS NELSON
Barratt, Stephen	Lt Cdr	01-Oct-02	LOGS	L	LSP OMAN	MUSCAT
Barrett, Benjamin T	Lt Cdr	01-Oct-14	WAR	HM	DI - ICSP	LONDON
Barrett, Scott	Lt RN	01-Jan-04	WAR	INT	FLEET COMOPS NWD	HUNTINGDON
Barrie, Stuart	Lt Cdr	01-Oct-10	ENG	WESM(TWS)	FOST SM SEA	HMNB CLYDE
Barritt, Oliver D	Lt Cdr	01-Oct-07	WAR	HM (H CH)	HMS ECHO	
Barron, Jeremy M	Lt Cdr	01-Oct-13	ENG	WESM(TWS)	DES COMFLEET	ABBEY WOOD
Barron, Philip R	Lt Cdr	01-Oct-13	WAR	O LYNX	HMS OCEAN	
Barrow, Charles M	Lt Cdr	01-Oct-09	WAR	PWO(U)	MTM MWS COLLINGWOOD	HMS COLLINGWOOD
Barrowclough, William G	Lt RN	01-Nov-12	WAR	GSX	HMS PROTECTOR	
Barrows, David M	Lt Cdr	01-Oct-03	ENG	WE	NATO - BRUSSELS	BRUSSELS
Barry, Emma L	Lt RN	31-Jan-12	ENG	TM	NCHQ	PORTSMOUTH
Barry, John P	Lt Cdr	01-Oct-02	WAR	PWO(U)	FOST DPORT	PLYMOUTH
Bartlett, David L	Lt Cdr	01-Oct-14	ENG	AE	MTM DEFAC JSCSC	SHRIVENHAM
Bartlett, David S G	Capt RN	01-Jul-12	ENG	AE	MTM FLEET HQ	PORTSMOUTH
Bartlett, Ian D	Cdr	30-Jun-08	ENG	MESM	DES COMFLEET	PLYMOUTH
Bartlett, Kathleen	Mid	08-Sep-14	WAR	GSX	BRNC	BRNC DARTMOUTH
Bartlett, Marie-Claire	Lt RN	01-Sep-07	ENG	AE	MTM NELSON	HMS NELSON
Bartlett, Simon	Lt RN	01-Apr-11	ENG	ME	DES COMFLEET	ABBEY WOOD
Barton, Jenny	Surg SLt	29-Jul-14	MED	Medical	BLAKE	BRNC DARTMOUTH
Barton, Keith J A	Lt Cdr	01-Oct-08	ENG	AE	MAA	ABBEY WOOD
Barton, Mark A	Cdr	30-Jun-13	ENG	ME	NCHQ CNPS	PORTSMOUTH
Barton, Peter G	Cdr	30-Jun-99	ENG	WE	UKTI - DSO	LONDON
Barton, Sarah J	Surg Lt Cdr	04 Aug-04	MED	GMP	FWO DEVPT SEA	PLYMOUTH
Bartram, Gregory J	Lt Cdr	01-Oct-12	ENG	WE	DCD - MODSAP KSA	RIYADH

Name	Substantive Rank	Seniority	Branch	Specialisation	Organisation Name	Location Name
Bartram, Richard	Lt Cdr	01-Oct-12	WAR	P LYN7	CHF - 846	RAF BENSON
Basketfield, Wayne	Lt RN	17-Dec-09	WAR	INT	FLEET CAP IS	PORTSMOUTH
Bass, Andrew G G	Lt RN	01-May-13	LOGS	L	HMS BULWARK	
Bass, Emma	Lt Cdr	01-Oct-09	ENG	WE	OCLC MANCH	MANCHESTER
Bass, Paul W	Lt Cdr	01-Oct-09	ENG	WESM(TWS)	NBC CLYDE	HMNB CLYDE
Bassett, Daniel S	Lt RN	01-Sep-13	WAR	O SKW	857 NAS	RNAS CULDROSE
Bassett, Dean A	Capt RN	09-Sep-13	WAR	PWO(A)	HMS BULWARK	
Bassett, Karen	SLt	14-Sep-13	LOGS	L (RES)	FLEET CAP IS	PORTSMOUTH
Bassett, Nicole	Lt Cdr	01-Oct-13	LOGS	L	LOAN DSTL	FAREHAM
Bastiaens, Paul A	Lt Cdr	01-Oct-13	ENG	AE	FLEET AV VL	RNAS YEOVILTON
Bate, Christopher	Lt RN	20-May-10	WAR	SM(X)	HMS TALENT	
Bates, Nicholas	Lt Cdr	01-Oct-12	WAR	O MER	829 SQN	RNAS CULDROSE
Bates, Oliver J	Capt	01-Sep-09	RM	P UT	MTM 847 SQN MIDDLE WALLOP	STOCKBRIDGE
Bateson, Timothy N	Lt RN	01-Sep-11	ENG	WESM(TWS)	MTM DEFAC JSCSC	SHRIVENHAM
Bath, Edward G	Lt Cdr	27-Dec-95	WAR	AAWO	MWS COLLINGWOOD	HMS COLLINGWOOD
Bath, Michael A W	Cdre	01-Jul-12	LOGS	L SM	DCDS PERS TRG	LONDON
Bathurst, Benjamin G H.	Capt	03-Sep-14	RM	GS	40 CDO RM	TAUNTON
Bathurst, Sir (David) Benjamin GCB DL	Adm of Fleet	09-Jul-95				
Batsford, Gareth E	Lt RN	13-Jun-08	ENG	MESM	FLEET CAP SSM	PORTSMOUTH
Batten, Nicholas J	Capt	01-Sep-12	RM	GS	NCHQ	PORTSMOUTH
Baum, Stuart R	Capt RN	30-Jun-06	WAR	SM(CQ)	FOSNI - NRC NE	LIVERPOOL
Baverstock, Andrew P	Lt Cdr	01-Oct-09	WAR	INT	MTM DEFAC JSCSC	SHRIVENHAM
Baxendale, Robert F	Lt Col	30-Jun-08	RM	GS	CDO LOG REGT RM	RMB CHIVENOR
Baxter, Arran C	Lt RN	01-May-02	ENG	MESM	HMS TIRELESS	
Baxter, Iain M	Cdr	30-Jun-10	ENG	AE	FU OHQ	NORTHWOOD
Baybutt, Thomas J	Capt	01-Sep-11	RM	GS	42 CDO RM	PLYMOUTH
Baylis, Matthew F P	Capt	01-Sep-08	RM	GS	FLEET DRM	PORTSMOUTH
Dayliss, Annabel M	Lt Cdr	16-Mar-12	WAR	ATC	FLEET AV VL	RNAS YEOVILTON
Bayliss, James E L	Lt RN	01-Jan-08	WAR	P LYNX	RNAS YEOVILTON	YEOVILTON
Bayliss, James P	Lt RN	01-Apr-09	WAR	P SK4	CHF(MERLIN)	RAF BENSON
Beacham, Philip R	Lt Cdr	01-Jul-03	WAR	P MER	829 SQN	RNAS CULDROSE
Beacham, Sophie R	Lt RN	01-Jun-08	LOGS	L	RNAS CULDROSE	HELSTON
Beadnell, Robert M	Lt Cdr	01-Jan-04	ENG	TM	FLEET FOST ACOS(Trg)	PORTSMOUTH
Beale, David J	Capt	01-Sep-12	RM	GS	40 CDO RM	TAUNTON
Beale, Joshua L	SLt	01-Feb-12	WAR	GSX	HMS MERSEY	
Beale, Michael D	Lt Cdr	01-Oct-07	WAR	MCD	MWS DDS	PORTSMOUTH
Bean, Edward C	Lt RN	09-Apr-10	LOGS	L	NAVY ICP	PORTSMOUTH
Beaney, Jonathan M	Lt	02-Sep-14	RM	GS	CTCRM	EXMOUTH
Beanland, Peter L	Lt Cdr	01-Oct-10	WAR	PWO(C)	COMUKTG	PLYMOUTH
Beard, David J	Surg Lt Cdr	01-Aug-06	MED	Anaes	RCDM	BIRMINGHAM
Beard, Hugh D	Capt RN	03-Jan-12	WAR	SM(CQ)	NEP	LONDON
Beardall, Michael J D	Capt RN	27-Jun-11	WAR	PWO(A)	DDC	LONDON
Beardall-Jacklin, Paul A	Lt RN	03-Nov-14	ENG	TM	MTM FLEET HQ	PORTSMOUTH
Beardmore A S	Mid	08-Sep-14	WAR	SM(X)	BRNC	BRNC DARTMOUTH
Beardsley, Nigel A	RN Chpln	03-May-05	Ch S	Chaplain	HMS RALEIGH	TORPOINT
Beasley, Adam C	Mid	05-May-14	WAR	GSX	BRNC	BRNC DARTMOUTH
Beaton, Iain	Lt Cdr	01-Oct-14	WAR	INFO OPS	UKMARBATSTAFF	PORTSMOUTH
Beattie, Paul	Capt RN	10-Nov-14	WAR	AAWO	UKMARBATSTAFF	PORTSMOUTH
Beaumont, Alan J	Lt RN	09-Apr-09	ENG	ME	DES COMFLEET	ABBEY WOOD
Beaumont, Richard	Lt RN	01-Sep-08	ENG	AE P	820 SQN	RNAS CULDROSE
Beaver, Robert M S	Lt Cdr	01-Oct-06	ENG	ME	FLEET COMOPS NWD	NORTHWOOD
Bebbington, David M	Lt RN	17-Feb-06	WAR	C	HDNET	CORSHAM
Beck, Andrew J	Lt RN	01-May-07	WAR	SM(N)	HMS TRIUMPH	
Becker, Robert K	Lt Cdr	01-Oct-13	WAR	INT	PJHQ (UK)	NORTHWOOD
Becker, Thomas O	Lt RN	01-Sep-06	WAR	HM	HMS SEVERN	
Beckett, Keith A CBE	R Adm	04-Nov-14	ENG	MESM	DES COMFLEET	ABBEY WOOD
Bedford, Daniel J	Capt	01-Sep-11	RM	GS	CTCRM	EXMOUTH
Bedford, Jonathan	Surg Lt Cdr	01-Jul-00	MED	GMP	DPHC LONDON & SE REGION	NORTHWOOD
Beech, Christopher M	Cdr	30-Jun-11	WAR	PWO(C)	NATO - BRUSSELS	BRUSSELS
Beeching, Lee G	Lt RN	20-Oct-06	WAR	MCD	MCM1	FASLANE
Bees, Thomas D	Mid	01-May-14	WAR	GSX	BRNC	BRNC DARTMOUTH
Beete, Jon E	Capt	01-Aug-07	RM	GS	OCLC BIRMINGHAM	BIRMINGHAM

Name	Substantive Rank	Seniority	Branch	Specialisation	Organisation Name	Location Name
Behan, Oliver M	Lt RN	01-Jul-11	WAR	GSX	HMS IRON DUKE	
Bekier, Oliver	Lt RN	01-Sep-12	WAR	GSX	HMS LANCASTER	
Bell Williamson, T.	Lt RN	01-Nov-14	WAR	GSX	MWS COLLINGWOOD	HMS COLLINGWOOD
Bell, Catriona M	Lt Cdr	01-Oct-08	WAR	PWO(N)	BRNC	BRNC DARTMOUTH
Bell, David	Lt RN	01-Feb-10	LOGS	L	HMS SULTAN	GOSPORT
Bell, Jeffrey M	Cdr	24-Jun-13	ENG	AE	NATO - BRUSSELS	BRUSSELS
Bell, Lewis G	Lt RN	01-Feb-06	WAR	HM	MTM DRAKE	HMS DRAKE
Bell, Michael H	Capt	16-Apr-10	RM	SCC	30 CDO IX GP RM	PLYMOUTH
Bell, Nicholas A G	Lt RN	01-May-04	WAR	P MER	829 SQN	RNAS CULDROSE
Bell, Richard J	Lt RN	01-May-06	WAR	O LYNX	LHF 815 SQN	RNAS YEOVILTON
Bell, Robert D	Lt Cdr	01-Mar-97	WAR	MCD	MCM1	HMNB CLYDE
Bell, Scott W	Lt Cdr	01-Oct-07	LOGS	L SM	NCHQ CNPS	LONDON
Bell, Tristan A	SLt	01-Jul-12	WAR	GSX	HMS LANCASTER	
Bellfield, Robert J A	Capt RN	27-Sep-11	WAR	PWO(U)	HMS RALEIGH	TORPOINT
Benbow, James A K	Lt RN	01-May-04	WAR	P LYNX	DCDS PERS TRG	LONDON
Benbow, Melanie	Lt RN	01-Feb-09	WAR	GSX	FOST DPORT	PLYMOUTH
Benbow, William	Lt RN	01-Feb-09	WAR	GSX	EU OHQ	NORTHWOOD
Bence, David E	Cdr	30-Jun-08	WAR	MCD	UK MCC	BAHRAIN
Bending, Shaun P	Lt RN	01-Mar-13	WAR	P UT	MTM RAF CRANWELL	RAFC CRANWELL
Benfell, Niall A	Cdr	30-Jun-13	LOGS	L	COMUKTG	PLYMOUTH
Bennet, Matthew J	Capt	01-Sep-12	RM	GS	40 CDO RM	TAUNTON
Bennett, Ashley S	SLt	01-Nov-14	WAR	GSX	MWS COLLINGWOOD	HMS COLLINGWOOD
Bennett, Brian	Lt RN	01-Nov-01	ENG	TM	HQ DISC	CHICKSANDS
Bennett, Christopher	Lt Cdr	01-Oct-09	WAR	P LYN7	FLEET SPT FGEN	PORTSMOUTH
Bennett, Elizabeth C	Lt RN	01-Jan-08	LOGS	L	MCM1	HMNB CLYDE
Bennett, Graham	Lt Cdr	01-Jul-93	WAR	PWO(U)	HMS VIVID	PLYMOUTH
Bennett, Ian J	Lt RN	01-Sep-07	WAR	O MER	820 SQN	RNAS CULDROSE
Bennett, Joseph P G	Capt	01-Sep-12	RM	GS	BRNC	BRNC DARTMOUTH
Bennett, Mark A	Lt Cdr	01-Oct-10	ENG	WESM(SWS)	HMS VICTORIOUS	
Bennett, Oliver F	Lt RN	01-Jan-12	LOGS	L	NCHQ - CNLS	PORTSMOUTH
Bennett, Paul OBE	R Adm	04-Feb-13	WAR	PWO(A)	JFC HQ	NORTHWOOD
Bennett, Philippa	Surg Lt RN	03-Aug-11	MED	GDMO	DPHC SOUTH	PORTSMOUTH
Bennett, William E	Cdr	30-Jun-14	ENG	ME	DES COMFLEET	ABBEY WOOD
Bennett-Smith, Paula	Lt RN	31-Jul-09	WAR	C	FLEET CAP IS	PORTSMOUTH
Benney, Jordon R	SLt	01-Sep-14	WAR	SM(X)	MWS COLLINGWOOD	HMS COLLINGWOOD
Benson, Adam D M	Lt RN	01-Feb-14	ENG	WESM	HMS VENGEANCE	
Benstead, Neil	Lt Cdr	01-Oct-04	ENG	ME	UKMARBATSTAFF	PORTSMOUTH
Bentley, Grant	Lt RN	01-Aug-06	WAR	GSX	PJHQ (UK)	NORTHWOOD
Benton, Angus M	Lt Cdr	01-Sep-96	WAR	MCD	AIB	HMS SULTAN
Benton, Peter J	Surg Capt RN	31-Dec-08	MED	Occ Med	DPHC SW	HMS DRAKE
Benton, Simon A	Lt RN	01-Apr-08	ENG	TM	HMS SULTAN	GOSPORT
Benton, William A J	Lt RN	06-Apr-07	WAR	AV	FLEET CAP SSM	PORTSMOUTH
Benzie, Andrew	Lt RN	23-Oct-08	WAR	SM(N)	HMS AMBUSH	
Berger, Angus E	Capt	01-Sep-13	RM	GS	TGHQ	AFGHANISTAN
Bernacchi, Jonathan P	Lt RN	15-Apr-11	ENG	WESM(TWS)	HMS VIGILANT	
Bernau, Jeremy C	Lt Cdr	01-Nov-91	WAR	SM(CQ)	COMFASFLOT	HELENSBURGH
Bernstein, Khan H	2Lt	25-Aug-14	RM	N/A	CTCRM	EXMOUTH
Berridge, Matthew J	Lt RN	01-May-14	WAR	SM(X)	MTM RALEIGH	HMS RALEIGH
Berrill, Simon P	SLt	19-May-14	WAR	GSX	MTM FLEET HQ	PORTSMOUTH
Berry, David H	Lt RN	01-Jun-07	WAR	FC	MTM MWS COLLINGWOOD	HMS COLLINGWOOD
Berry, Ian MBE RD	Cdr	30-Jun-13	WAR	MW (RES)	FLEET CMR	PORTSMOUTH
Berry, Thomas P	Lt	02-Sep-14	RM	GS	40 CDO RM	TAUNTON
Berry, Timothy J	Lt Cdr	01-Oct-06	WAR	PWO(N)	HMS CLYDE	
Bessant, Matthew	Lt RN	01-Apr-05	WAR	GSX	FLEET COMOPS NWD	HUNTINGDON
Best, Alexander	Lt RN	01-Jan-11	WAR	O MER	820 SQN	RNAS CULDROSE
Best, Hannah J	Lt RN	01-Sep-12	WAR	O MER	814 SQN	RNAS CULDROSE
Best, Paul N	Maj	01-Oct-13	RM	SCC	FLEET SPT LOGS INFRA	PORTSMOUTH
Best, Robert M	Lt Cdr	01-Oct-13	ENG	MESM	HMS TALENT	
Beswick, Mark D	Lt RN	03-May-13	MED	MS(CDO)	MED SQN CDO LOG REGT RM	RMB CHIVENOR
Betchley, Hannah M	Lt RN	01-Sep-08	ENG	AE	DES COMJE	ABBEY WOOD
Betchley, James W	Lt Cdr	01-Oct-14	WAR	PWO(SM)	HMS TORBAY	
Bethwaite, Jonathan	SLt	18 Oct-12	WAR	GSX	HMS TYNE	

Name	Substantive Rank	Seniority	Branch	Specialisation	Organisation Name	Location Name
Betteridge, Carol A OBE	Capt RN	26-Feb-13	QARNNS	Nurse Officer	DMS WHITTINGTON	LONDON
Bettles, John	Lt Cdr	25-Nov-11	WAR	PWO	UKMARBATSTAFF	PORTSMOUTH
Betton, Andrew OBE	Cdre	01-Dec-14	WAR	O LYNX	PJHQ (UK)	NORTHWOOD
Betts, Andrew T J	Lt Cdr	01-Oct-14	ENG	AE	FLEET CSAV	PORTSMOUTH
Betts, Peter R	Lt Cdr	01-Oct-14	ENG	WESM(TWS)	FLEET COMOPS NWD	NORTHWOOD
Bevan, Hector H	2Lt	25-Aug-14	RM	N/A	CTCRM	EXMOUTH
Bevan, Jeffrey R MBE	Lt Cdr	01-Oct-10	WAR	P MER	4 REGT AAC	IPSWICH
Beveridge, Simon A R	RN Chpln	28-Apr-93	Ch S	Chaplain	NEPTUNE 2SL/CNH - CHAP	HMNB CLYDE
Beverstock, Mark A	R Adm	23-Jul-12	ENG	WESM(SWS)	ACDS	LONDON
Bevis, Timothy J	Brig	21-Feb-11	RM	GS	OPS DIR	LONDON
Bewley, Geoffrey RD	Cdr	28-Oct-08	WAR	MW (RES)	NCHQ CNPS	PORTSMOUTH
Bhaduri, Thomas	Mid	17-Nov-14	WAR	GSX	BRNC	BRNC DARTMOUTH
Bhagwan, Gavin S	Mid	01-May-14	ENG	WE	BRNC	BRNC DARTMOUTH
Bicker, Richard E	Lt RN	09-Apr-09	ENG	WESM(SWS)	DES COMFLEET	ABBEY WOOD
Bickley, Gary N	Lt RN	01-Jan-03	WAR	PWO(N)	MWS COLLINGWOOD	HMS COLLINGWOOD
Bicknell, Neil D	Lt RN	12-Jul-13	ENG	WE	HMS DRAGON	
Bicknell, Richard	Lt Cdr	31-Mar-01	WAR	MW (RES)	MCM2	PORTSMOUTH
Biddlecombe, Hugh R	Lt RN	01-Apr-11	LOGS	L	DCD - MODSAP KSA	RIYADH
Biddulph, Andrew R	Lt RN	15-Apr-11	WAR		UKMARBATSTAFF	PORTSMOUTH
Biggs, David M	Lt Cdr	01-Oct-96	WAR	O SKW	849 SQN	RNAS CULDROSE
Bignell, Stephen	Cdr	30-Jun-14	ENG	WE	DES COMLAND	ABBEY WOOD
Billam, David A	Lt RN	01-Apr-13	WAR	FC	HMS DUNCAN	
Billings, Andrew J	Lt Cdr	01-Oct-13	WAR	REG	NPM WESTERN	HMS DRAKE
Bilson, Gavin	Lt RN	01-May-06	ENG	IS(SM)	NATO-ACO-SHAPE	CASTEAU
Bing, Neil A	Lt Cdr	01-Oct-05	WAR	P FW	FLEET AV CRANWELL	RAFC CRANWELL
Bingham, Alexander A J	Lt Cdr	01-Oct-11	ENG	ME	FLEET CAP SSM	PORTSMOUTH
Bingham, David S	Lt Cdr	01-Mar-99	WAR	AAWO	FLEET CSAV	PORTSMOUTH
Bingham, Edward	Lt RN	15-Jul-12	WAR	INFO OPS	MTM NPT RES MOBILISATION	PORTSMOUTH
Binns, James B	Lt RN	01-Sep-06	ENG	MESM	DES COMFLEET	ABBEY WOOD
Binns, John R	Lt Cdr	01-Oct-09	ENG	WE	COMDEVFLOT	PLYMOUTH
Binns, Jon F	Lt Cdr	01-Oct-08	WAR	INT	FLEET COMOPS NWD	NORTHWOOD
Birbeck, Keith	Lt Cdr	01-Oct-98	ENG	WESM(TWS)	D STRAT PROG	ABBEY WOOD
Birch, Peter L	Lt Cdr	01-Oct-13	WAR	P LYNX	FLEET CSAV	PORTSMOUTH
Bird, Andrew W	Lt RN	01-Sep-04	WAR	P MER	824 SQN	RNAS CULDROSE
Bird, Gary M	Lt Col	30-Jun-13	RM	GS	MTM RN GLOBAL	SPAIN
Bird, Jonathan M	Cdr	30-Jun-14	WAR	O MER	MASF	RNAS CULDROSE
Bird, Matthew G J	Cdr	30-Jun-14	ENG	AE	MAA	ABBEY WOOD
Bird, Michael P	Lt Cdr	01-Oct-14	WAR	PWO	HMS PORTLAND	
Bird, Richard A J	Cdr	30-Jun-11	WAR	HM (H CH)	HMS PROTECTOR	
Bird, Timothy M	Lt RN	01-Jun-06	LOGS	L	HMS QUEEN ELIZABETH	
Birkby, Christina	Lt Cdr	01-Oct-13	WAR	PWO	JFHQ	NORTHWOOD
Birley, Daniel T	Surg Lt RN	01-Mar-14	MED	Medical	BRNC	BRNC DARTMOUTH
Birley, Jonathan H	Lt Cdr	01-May-95	WAR	PWO(U)	FLEET COMOPS NWD	NORTHWOOD
Birrell, Stuart DSO	Brig	14-Jun-13	RM	GS	MTM DEFAC RCDS	LONDON
Birse, Gregor J	Cdr	30-Jun-13	WAR	HM (M CH)	DI - ICSP	LONDON
Birt, David J	Surg Cdr	30-Jun-01	MED	Anaes	MDHU DERRIFORD	PLYMOUTH
Bishop, Alexander N S J	Mid	01-May-14	WAR	P UT	BRNC	BRNC DARTMOUTH
Bisson, Ian J P	Cdre	13-Jan-14	ENG	WE	DBS MIL PERS	GOSPORT
Black, Charlotte J	Lt RN	01-Mar-04	ENG	IS	JFCIS(I)	QATAR
Black, Dominic J	Lt RN	01-Sep-12	LOGS	L	HMS IRON DUKE	
Black, Edward J	Lt Cdr	01-Oct-12	WAR	MCD	LSP OMAN	MUSCAT
Black, Joanna M	Lt Cdr	01-Oct-12	WAR	PWO	MWS COLLINGWOOD	HMS COLLINGWOOD
Black, Kenneth J	Lt RN	01-Mar-08	LOGS	L	MWS COLLINGWOOD	HMS COLLINGWOOD
Black, Malcolm DL	Lt RN	09-Apr-12	ENG	MESM	HMS VANGUARD	
Blackbourn, Stephen A	Lt RN	27-Jul-07	ENG	WE	COMDEVFLOT	PLYMOUTH
Blackburn, Andrew R J	Cdr	30-Jun-14	ENG	AE	HMS QUEEN ELIZABETH	
Blackburn, Craig J	Lt RN	01-Sep-04	WAR	GSX	MTM MWS COLLINGWOOD	HMS COLLINGWOOD
Blackburn, Emma C	Lt Cdr	01-Oct-09	ENG	AE	HMS OCEAN	
Blackburn, Ewan J S	SLt	01-Sep-14	ENG	WE	MTM FLEET HQ	PORTSMOUTH
Blackburn, Lee R	Lt Cdr	01-Sep-08	ENG	ME	HMS SULTAN	GOSPORT
Blackburn, Stephen A	Lt Cdr	01-Mar-98	ENG	ME	FLEET CAP SSM	PORTSMOUTH
Blackburn, Stuart J	Cdr	30-Jun-14	WAR	SM(CQ)	D STRAT PROG	ABBEY WOOD

Name	Substantive Rank	Seniority	Branch	Specialisation	Organisation Name	Location Name
Blackburn, Thomas E.	Lt RN	01-Sep-11	ENG	AE	HMS SULTAN	GOSPORT
Blackett, William P H	Lt Cdr	01-Oct-12	WAR	PWO	HMS DARING	
Blackford, Alexander G	2Lt	25-Aug-14	RM	N/A	CTCRM	EXMOUTH
Blackledge, Benjamin P	Lt RN	01-Jan-12	ENG	TM	RMB STONEHOUSE	PLYMOUTH
Blackman, Nicholas T OBE	Capt RN	25-Jan-11	ENG	AE	DES COMJE	YEOVIL
Blackmore, Andrew M	Lt Cdr	01-Oct-13	ENG	WESM(TWS)	NC REQUIREMENTS MANAGERS	ABBEY WOOD
Blackmore, James	Cdr	30-Jun-14	WAR	P FW	FLEET CSAV	WASHINGTON
Blackmore, Mark S	Cdr	30-Jun-02	WAR	O SK6	FLEET CSAV	NORFOLK
Blackwell, Mark E	Lt RN	01-Sep-08	LOGS	L BAR	DCDS PERS - SPA	RAF NORTHOLT
Blackwell, Richard E	Cdr	30-Jun-09	LOGS	L SM	IPP	LONDON
Blagden, Laura J	Lt RN	01-Mar-14	ENG	AE	MTM 814 SQN CULDROSE	RNAS CULDROSE
Blair, Duncan G S	Surg Cdr	30-Jun-03	MED	GMP (C&S)	MED OP CAP	NORTHWOOD
Blake, Jeremy G	2Lt	02-Sep-12	RM	GS	40 CDO RM	TAUNTON
Blake, Matthew G	Lt RN	01-May-05	WAR	O MER	HMS PORTLAND	
Blakeman, Philip M	Lt RN	01-Aug-08	ENG	WE	DHU	CHICKSANDS
Blanchford, Daniel	Lt Col	30-Jun-10	RM	GS	NCHQ	PORTSMOUTH
Bland, Christopher D	Lt Cdr	01-Oct-08	ENG	WESM(SWS)	NUCLEAR CAPABILITY	LONDON
Bland, Steven A	Surg Cdr	07-Aug-07	MED	EM	PCRF	RFA ARGUS
Blatcher, David J	Lt RN	01-Sep-08	ENG	ME	COMPORFLOT	PORTSMOUTH
Blatchford, Timothy P	Lt RN	08-Apr-05	ENG	AE	RNAS CULDROSE	HELSTON
Bleasdale, Daniel R	Lt Cdr	01-Oct-12	ENG	TM	NETS (OPS)	PORTSMOUTH
Blenkinsop, Graham J	Lt RN	02-May-07	WAR	HM	HMS GLEANER	
Blethyn, Catherine	Lt Cdr	01-Oct-12	ENG	TM	NCHQ CNPERS (HRTSG)	PORTSMOUTH
Blethyn, Hugh P	Lt Cdr	01-Oct-11	ENG	IS	MCSU	FLEET HQ
Blick, Graham M J	Lt RN	30-Jul-10	WAR	AV	RNAS YEOVILTON	YEOVILTON
Blick, Sarah L	Lt RN	01-Jan-02	LOGS	L	AIB	HMS SULTAN
Bligh, Sarah L	Lt RN	01-May-04	WAR	FC	MTM NELSON	HMS NELSON
Blight, Phillip R R	Lt RN	03-May-13	ENG	WESM	HMS TRENCHANT	
Block, Andrew W G	Cdr	30-Jun-10	WAR	PWO(A)	HMS KENT	
Blois, Simon D	Lt Cdr	01-Oct-09	ENG	WE	NAVY MCTA	PORTSMOUTH
Bloor, Thomas W	Capt	03-Sep-14	RM	GS	40 CDO RM	TAUNTON
Blount, Keith E OBE	Cdre	27-Aug-13	WAR	P SK6	UK MCC	BAHRAIN
Blower, Amy	Lt RN	01-Sep-12	WAR	GSX	OCLC MANCH	MANCHESTER
Blunden, Jeremy J F LVO	Cdre	22-Oct-12	WAR	PWO(N)	UKMARBATSTAFF	PORTSMOUTH
Blunden, Katie L	SLt	07-Aug-13	LOGS	L	HMS SOMERSET	
Blythe, James	Lt Cdr	01-Oct-09	WAR	PWO	MCM1	FASLANE
Blythe, Paul C	Cdr	30-Jun-09	WAR	SM(CQ)	CBRN POL	LONDON
Blythe, Tom S	Lt Col	30-Jun-09	RM	LC	MTM DEFENCE ACADEMY	SHRIVENHAM
Boaden, Christopher S	Lt RN	19-Feb-09	WAR	O LYNX	LHF 815 SQN	RNAS YEOVILTON
Boak, Charlotte L	SLt	01-Jul-14	WAR	GSX	MWS COLLINGWOOD	HMS COLLINGWOOD
Boak, Philip R	Lt RN	01-Apr-11	WAR	HM	HMS ECHO	
Boakes, Philip J	Lt Cdr	01-Oct-09	ENG	ME	FLEET CAP SSM	PORTSMOUTH
Boarder, Richard J	Lt RN	01-Sep-10	ENG	MESM	NBC CLYDE	HMNB CLYDE
Boardman, Andrew	Lt RN	01-Sep-08	ENG	MESM	DES COMFLEET	THURSO
Boardman, Daniel	SLt	01-Sep-12	ENG	AE	DCEME SULTAN	HMS SULTAN
Boast, Rachel	Lt RN	22-Oct-12	WAR	O SKW	OCLC ROSYTH	HMS CALEDONIA
Boddington, Hannah	Lt RN	01-Jan-12	WAR	GSX	UK MCC	BAHRAIN
Boddington, Jeremy D L	Cdr	30-Jun-07	WAR	P MER	FLEET CSAV	RNAS YEOVILTON
Bodkin, Lee	Lt RN	01-Jul-09	ENG	ME	RNLA	HMS COLLINGWOOD
Bodman, Simon A	Lt Cdr	01-Oct-09	WAR	PWO(C)	HMS NORTHUMBERLAND	
Boeckx, Thomas J F	Lt Cdr	01-Oct-07	WAR	PWO(N)	HMS SOMERSET	
Bolam, Samual P P	Capt	01-Sep-13	RM	GS	43 CDO FPGRM	HELENSBURGH
Bolland, Amy	Lt RN	01-Mar-13	ENG	ME	HMS DIAMOND	
Bollen, Johanna M	Cdr	30-Jun-14	LOGS	L	DES HR	ABBEY WOOD
Bolton, James D	Lt RN	01-Aug-10	WAR	SM(X)	MTM NEPTUNE	HMNB CLYDE
Bolton, Jonathan P	Cdr	30-Jun-10	ENG	ME	FLEET ACOS(RP)	PORTSMOUTH
Bolton, Matthew T W	Cdr	30-Jun-08	ENG	ME	COMPORFLOT	PORTSMOUTH
Bolton, Stephen J	Cdr	30-Jun-13	WAR	P LYNX	HQ AIR - COS(TRG) - DFT	ABBEY WOOD
Bomby, Ross A	Lt	02-Sep-14	RM	GS	43 CDO FPGRM	HELENSBURGH
Bond, Frances	Lt RN	01-Nov-10	WAR	HM	FLEET COMOPS NWD	NORTHWOOD
Bond, Ian	Lt RN	19-Dec-08	ENG	WESM(SWS)	HMS SULTAN	GOSPORT
Bond, Nigel D MBE	Cdr	31-Dec-00	LOGS	L	NCHQ CNPERS	PORTSMOUTH

Name	Substantive Rank	Seniority	Branch	Specialisation	Organisation Name	Location Name
Bond, Robert D A	Lt Cdr	01-Oct-11	WAR	P SK4	845 SQN	RNAS YEOVILTON
Bond, Robert J	Lt RN	01-Apr-06	WAR	P MER	814 SQN	RNAS CULDROSE
Bond, Stuart J	SLt	01-Apr-12	WAR	HM	MTM MWS HMTG (D)	HMS DRAKE
Bone, Darren N	Capt RN	01-Jul-09	WAR	PWO(A)	UKMARBATSTAFF	PORTSMOUTH
Bone, Jonathan D	Surg Lt RN	07-Aug-13	MED	Medical	BLAKE	BRNC DARTMOUTH
Bone, Louise	Lt RN	01-Sep-13	WAR	HM	HMS ENTERPRISE	
Bone, Matthew	Lt RN	01-Sep-10	ENG	AE	HMS SULTAN	GOSPORT
Bone, Richard C	Cdr	30-Jun-08	ENG	TM(SM)	NC REQUIREMENTS MANAGERS	ABBEY WOOD
Bonin-Casey, Patrick J	Lt	01-Jul-13	RM	SCC	42 CDO RM	PLYMOUTH
Bonnar, John A	Cdr	30-Jun-12	ENG	WE	COMPORFLOT	PORTSMOUTH
Bonner, Daniel	Cdr	27-Jul-07	ENG	AE	DES COMJE	YEOVIL
Bonner, Timothy J	Surg Lt Cdr	09-Aug-06	MED	T&O	MTM INM ALVERSTOKE	GOSPORT
Boon, Gareth	Lt Cdr	01-Oct-07	WAR	HM (M CH)	FLEET COMOPS NWD	NORTHWOOD
Boon, Simon E	Lt Cdr	01-Oct-10	LOGS	L SM	JFLogC	NORTHWOOD
Boorn, Andrew E	2Lt	25-Aug-14	RM	N/A	CTCRM	EXMOUTH
Boot, Stephen	Lt Cdr	01-Oct-09	LOGS	L	NBD COB LO HMS DRAKE	HMS DRAKE
Booth, Alan K	Lt RN	01-Sep-07	WAR	P MER	MTM SHAWBURY	RAF SHAWBURY
Booth, Anthony R	Lt RN	01-Mar-12	WAR	O UT	MTM 750 SQN CULDROSE	RNAS CULDROSE
Booth, Ben	Surg Lt RN	01-Aug-12	MED	GDMO	30 CDO IX GP RM	PLYMOUTH
Booth, Diccon P P	Lt RN	01-Sep-01	ENG	TM	DEFENCE ACADEMY	SHRIVENHAM
Booth, Rachael M	Surg Lt Cdr	02-Aug-11	MED	GMP	DPHC SW	BRNC DARTMOUTH
Booth, William N	Lt Cdr	01-Oct-06	ENG	ME	FOST DPORT	PLYMOUTH
Boothroyd-Gibbs, Adam P	Lt RN	01-Jan-08	WAR	O MER	MTM MWS COLLINGWOOD	HMS COLLINGWOOD
Borbone, Nicholas	Cdr	30-Jun-11	WAR	AAWO	DDC	LONDON
Boreham, Daniel J R	Lt RN	01-Sep-13	ENG	MESM	HMS TRENCHANT	
Borland, Kate E	Lt RN	01-May-13	WAR	GSX	MCM1	FASLANE
Borland, Stuart A	Capt RN	10-Jan-11	ENG	WE	SERV ATTACHE/ADVISER	NEW DELHI
Borrett, John E	Lt RN	01-Jul-05	WAR		RN REAPER - 39 SQN	RAF WADDINGTON
Borthwick, Christopher D	SLt	01-Feb-14	WAR	ATC UT	RNAS CULDROSE	HELSTON
Boston, Justin	Lt Cdr	01-Jan-05	ENG	TM	FLEET FOST ACOS(Trg)	ABBEY WOOD
Bosustow, Antony M	Cdr	30-Jun-07	ENG	WE	NCHQ CNPS	PORTSMOUTH
Boswell, Emma J	Lt RN	30-Jul-10	MED	MS(SM)	FLEET CAP SSM	PORTSMOUTH
Boswell, Laura J	Lt RN	29-Jan-07	QARNNS	ITU	MTM RALEIGH	HMS RALEIGH
Botham, Adrian M	Lt RN	16-Dec-05	ENG	WE	NAVY MCTA	PORTSMOUTH
Botterill, Hugh W S	Lt Cdr	01-Oct-10	WAR	AWO(U)	FOST DPORT	PLYMOUTH
Botting, Neil A	Lt Cdr	01-Oct-10	WAR	SM(CQ)	HMS TALENT	
Botwood, Tudor J MBE BD	RN Chpln	09-Sep-02	Ch S	Chaplain	RNAS CULDROSE	HELSTON
Boucher, Jonathan R	Capt	01-Sep-10	RM	GS	CTCRM	EXMOUTH
Boucher, Peter J	Lt	02-Sep-14	RM	GS	42 CDO RM	PLYMOUTH
Boughton, Jonathan A L	Lt Cdr	01-Oct-10	ENG	WE	HMS SUTHERLAND	
Boulding, Andrew D	Lt RN	13-Jun-08	ENG	MESM	NBD NB SAFETY DEVONPORT	HMS DRAKE
Boulind, Matthew A	Lt Cdr	01-Oct-11	WAR	O LYNX	FLEET CSAV	PORTSMOUTH
Boulton, David S	Lt RN	01-Sep-05	ENG	IS(SM)	CBRN POL	LONDON
Boulton, Graham R	Lt Cdr	01-Oct-14	WAR	MW	HMS COLLINGWOOD	FAREHAM
Bourn, Sebastian J N	Surg Lt Cdr	31-Jul-12	MED	Anaes	MTM INM ALVERSTOKE	GOSPORT
Bouyac, David R L	Lt Cdr	01-Oct-13	WAR	P FW	736 NAS	RNAS CULDROSE
Bovill, Christopher	Lt Cdr	31-Jul-03	ENG	AE	MTM WMO CULDROSE	RNAS CULDROSE
Bowbrick, Richard C	Capt RN	26-Aug-14	WAR	AAWO	NCHQ CNPERS	PORTSMOUTH
Bowden, Matthew J	Lt RN	01-May-14	WAR	GSX	MTM NORTHWOOD HQ	NORTHWOOD
Bowden, Matthew T E	Cdr	30-Jun-12	WAR	PWO(C)	FLEET CAP IS	PORTSMOUTH
Bowe, Alexander B	Mid	17-Nov-14	WAR	P UT	BRNC	BRNC DARTMOUTH
Bowen, Nigel T	Cdr	30-Jun-05	WAR	O LYNX	MTM NELSON	HMS NELSON
Bowen, Richard J	Lt Cdr	01-Oct-12	ENG	WE	PJHQ (UK)	NORTHWOOD
Bower, Andrew J OBE	Cdr	30-Jun-08	WAR	SM(CQ)	MOD NSD	LONDON
Bower, Dean A MSC	Lt RN	09-Apr-09	ENG	ME	MWS EXCELLENT	HMS EXCELLENT
Bower, Nigel S	Cdr	30-Jun-05	WAR	SM(CQ)	HMS ARTFUL	
Bowerman, James W	Capt	01-Sep-09	RM	P SK4	845 SQN	RNAS YEOVILTON
Bowers, John P	Capt RN	08-Dec-14	WAR	O LYNX	DOC	LONDON
Bowers, Keith J	Lt Cdr	01-Oct-12	ENG	WE	HMS PORTLAND	
Bowers, Mark R	Lt RN	01-Aug-03	ENG	IS	NC PSYA	PORTSMOUTH
Bowers, Thomas M E	Lt RN	01-Nov-14	ENG	WE	HMS ST ALBANS	
Bowgen, John	Capt	16-Apr-10	RM	MLDR (SCC)	CTCRM	EXMOUTH

Name	Substantive Rank	Seniority	Branch	Specialisation	Organisation Name	Location Name
Bowhay, Simon	Lt Cdr	01-May-99	ENG	WESM(TWS)	HDNET	CORSHAM
Bowie, Alan N	Surg Cdr	28-Oct-05	MED	GMP	DPHC SW	RNAS CULDROSE
Bowie, Richard	Lt Cdr	01-Oct-10	ENG	WESM(TWS)	COMFASFLOT	HELENSBURGH
Bowler, James R	Lt RN	01-Apr-11	ENG	MESM	HMS AMBUSH	
Bowler, Thomas	Lt RN	01-Sep-10	ENG	ME	HMS BULWARK	
Bowles, Daniel J	Lt RN	01-Nov-10	WAR	SM(X)	MTM RALEIGH	HMS RALEIGH
Bowman, Dean E	Lt RN	01-Sep-07	ENG	MESM	HMS ARTFUL	
Bowman, James A	2Lt	25-Aug-14	RM	N/A	CTCRM	EXMOUTH
Bowman, Robert	Cdr	30-Jun-13	ENG	AE	NATO-ACT-HQ	NORFOLK
Bowman, Simon K J	Lt RN	01-Jun-05	WAR	ATC	RNAS YEOVILTON	YEOVILTON
Bowmer, Christopher J	Lt RN	01-Sep-08	ENG	MESM	MOD CNS/ACNS	LONDON
Bowness, Zoe J	Lt RN	01-Jan-15	WAR	ATC	RNAS YEOVILTON	YEOVILTON
Bowra, Mark A MBE	Lt Col	30-Jun-11	RM	GS	MTM HASLER COY	HMS DRAKE
Bowyer, Richard	Maj	10-Oct-06	RM	GS (RES)	RN EXCHANGE AUSTRALIA	CANBERRA
Boyall, Duane R	Lt RN	01-Jun-09	ENG	TM(SM)	NCHQ CNPERS (HRTSG)	PORTSMOUTH
Boyce, the Lord KG GCB OBE DL	Adm of Fleet	13-Jun-14				
Boyd, Elaine M	Lt Cdr	01-Oct-11	LOGS	L	PJHQ (UK)	NORTHWOOD
Boyd, Nicholas	Cdr	30-Jun-05	ENG	ME	FLEET CAP SSM	PORTSMOUTH
Boyes, Georgina K L	Surg Lt Cdr	05-Aug-14	MED	Med	MTM INM ALVERSTOKF	GOSPORT
Boyes, Martyn R	Cdr	30-Jun-13	ENG	MESM	DES COMFLEET	ABBEY WOOD
Boyes, Richard A	Lt Cdr	01-Oct-06	WAR	P MER	771 SQN	RNAS CULDROSE
Bradbury, Simon	RN Chpln	18-Sep-96	Ch S	Chaplain	DEFENCE ACADEMY	ANDOVER
Bradford, Malcolm H	Capt	01-Sep-04	RM	P SK4	4 REGT AAC	IPSWICH
Brading, Roland D	Maj	01-Oct-10	RM	GS	43 CDO FPGRM	HELENSBURGH
Bradley, Matthew	Lt Cdr	01-May-02	WAR	PWO(U)	COMUKTG	PLYMOUTH
Bradley, Rupert	Lt Cdr	01-Oct-10	WAR	P SKW	771 SQN	RNAS CULDROSE
Bradley, Trevor A	Lt Cdr	01-Oct-09	ENG	WE	HMS SOMERSET	
Bradshaw, Emma R	Lt RN	01-Feb-13	LOGS	L	MWS COLLINGWOOD	HMS COLLINGWOOD
Bradshaw, James P	Lt RN	01-Oct-09	WAR	SM(N)	MTM RALEIGH	HMS RALEIGH
Bradshaw, Kieran J	Lt RN	01-Sep-14	ENG	AE	RNAS YEOVILTON	YEOVILTON
Bradshaw, Matthew P	Mid	17-Nov-14	WAR	HM	BRNC	BRNC DARTMOUTH
Brady, Matthew V	Lt RN	01-Nov-06	WAR	ATC	RNAS CULDROSE	HELSTON
Brady, Sean E	Cdr	30-Jun-08	WAR	PWO(U)	HMS RALEIGH	TORPOINT
Brady, Sean P	Lt Col	30-Jun-12	RM	GS	CTCRM	EXMOUTH
Brain, Brandon J	SLt	01-Nov-14	WAR	P UT	BRNC	BRNC DARTMOUTH
Brain, Terri	Lt RN	01-Mar-12	ENG	WE	FOST DPORT	PLYMOUTH
Brain, William J	Maj	01-Oct-06	RM	GS	OPS DIR	LONDON
Braithwaite, Geoffrey C	Lt Cdr	01-Oct-12	ENG	ME	NATO-ACO-JFC HQ	NAPLES
Brand, James A	Mid	08-Sep-14	ENG	ME	BRNC	BRNC DARTMOUTH
Brand, Simon	Capt RN	08-Sep-08	WAR	P LYNX	SERV ATTACHE/ADVISER	CAIRO
Brann, Robert W	Lt Cdr	01-Oct-10	WAR	PWO(A)	NCHQ CNPERS	PORTSMOUTH
Brannighan, David M	Lt Cdr	01-Oct-14	WAR	SM(N)	HMS VIGILANT	
Brannighan, Ian D	Lt RN	01-Sep-04	WAR	P LYNX	LHF 815 SQN	RNAS YEOVILTON
Bratt, James J	Lt RN	01-Nov-08	WAR	SM(N)	MWS COLLINGWOOD	HMS COLLINGWOOD
Bravery, Martin A E	Cdr	30-Jun-10	WAR	P MER	TIO	LONDON
Bray, Andrew	Lt Cdr	01-Oct-13	LOGS	L	HMS DRAGON	
Bray, Matthew	Lt RN	24-Feb-11	WAR	FC	FOST DPORT	PLYMOUTH
Bray, Michael A	Lt RN	09-Apr-10	ENG	WE	HMS COLLINGWOOD	FAREHAM
Bray, Michael P	Lt RN	01-Sep-14	ENG	WESM	HMS VIGILANT	
Brayson, Mark	Lt Cdr	01-Oct-05	WAR	P LYNX	MTM WMO CULDROSE	RNAS CULDROSE
Brazenall, Benjamin C	Lt RN	01-Jan-04	WAR	P SK4	MTM CHF (MERLIN)	RAF BENSON
Breach, Charles E M	Maj	01-Oct-10	RM	MLDR (SCC)	45 CDO RM	DUNDEE
Breach, Pamela	Lt Cdr	01-Oct-09	WAR	ATC	MTM WMO YEOVILTON	RNAS YEOVILTON
Breaks, James	Lt RN	01-May-14	WAR	GSX	MWS COLLINGWOOD	HMS COLLINGWOOD
Brearley, Nathaniel L	Mid	08-Sep-14	WAR	GSX	BRNC	BRNC DARTMOUTH
Breckenridge, Iain G OBE	Capt RN	07-Jan-14	WAR	SM(CQ)	NATO ACO	NORTHWOOD
Breckenridge, Robert J	Lt RN	01-Jun-07	WAR	P SK6	MTM 771 SQN CULDROSE	RNAS CULDROSE
Bree, Stephen E P	Surg Capt RN	01-Jul-11	MED	Anaes	DMS WHITTINGTON	WASHINGTON
Breen, John E	Lt Cdr	01-Oct-10	ENG	AE	AWC	PATUXENT RIVER
Breen, Paul R	Lt RN	15-Apr-11	ENG	AE	RNAS CULDROSE	HELSTON
Breet, Max W D	Capt	01-Sep-12	RM	GS	43 CDO FPGRM	HELENSBURGH
Brehaut, John R	Lt RN	01-Apr-13	LOGS	L	CHFHQ	RNAS YEOVILTON

Name	Substantive Rank	Seniority	Branch	Specialisation	Organisation Name	Location Name
Brenchley, Nigel G	Cdr	30-Jun-08	LOGS	L	DIO SAPT	HMS COLLINGWOOD
Brennan, John P	Lt Cdr	01-Oct-12	ENG	WE	FOST DPORT	PLYMOUTH
Brennan, Paul A	Lt Cdr	01-Oct-06	ENG	MESM	DES COMFLEET	HMS DRAKE
Brennan, Richard D	SLt	01-Sep-14	ENG	ME	DCEME SULTAN	HMS SULTAN
Brereton, Charles	Lt RN	01-Feb-15	WAR	GSX	HMS TYNE	
Brettell, Jeremy D	Lt Cdr	01-Oct-13	WAR	PWO(N)	HMS RICHMOND	
Bretten, Nicholas J	Lt RN	01-Jul-06	WAR	INT	JFIG - JT IP	RAF WYTON
Breward, Daniel P	Lt RN	01-Jan-10	WAR	O SKW	857 NAS	RNAS CULDROSE
Brewer, Christopher E	Lt Cdr	01-Oct-06	WAR	SM(AWC)	MTM DEFAC JSCSC	SHRIVENHAM
Brian, Neil	Lt Cdr	01-Oct-02	WAR	O MER	824 SQN	RNAS CULDROSE
Brian, Stephen	Lt Cdr	01-Oct-14	WAR	PWO(SM)	HMS TALENT	
Bridge, James G	Lt RN	15-Apr-11	WAR	HM	1 GP MARHAM	KINGS LYNN
Bridger, Callum J	2Lt	25-Aug-14	RM	N/A	CTCRM	EXMOUTH
Bridges, John M	RN Chpln	02-Jul-05	Ch S	Chaplain	CHAPLAIN OF THE FLEET	PORTSMOUTH
Bridson, Andrew	Capt	28-Jul-06	RM	LC (SCC)	6 OPS SQN	PLYMOUTH
Brierley, Natalie L	SLt	01-Sep-14	WAR	ATC UT	RAF SHAWBURY	SHREWSBURY
Brierley, Simon P J	Lt Cdr	01-Oct-09	ENG	AE	CHF - 846	RAF BENSON
Briers, Matthew P	Cdre	22-Apr-14	WAR	P SK4	FLEET CSAV	PORTSMOUTH
Briggs, Cathryn S	Lt Cdr	01-Oct-04	QARNNS	OT (C&S)	PCRF	RFA ARGUS
Briggs, Christopher J	Lt RN	16-Dec-11	ENG	WESM(SWS)	MTM FOST FAS	HMNB CLYDE
Briggs-Mould, Timothy P	Lt Cdr	16-Mar-99	ENG	WE	SVCOPS/DHDREG5/EPI	EPISKOPI
Brighouse, Neil G	Maj	24-Apr-02	RM	P SK4	RNAS YEOVILTON	YEOVILTON
Bright, Amanda C	Lt Cdr	01-Oct-12	WAR	REG	RNP - HQ PMN	HMS EXCELLENT
Bright, Jack MBE	Lt RN	01-Sep-09	LOGS	L	USSC JERUSALEM	ISRAEL
Brindley, Alice E	Lt RN	10-Nov-13	ENG	WE	HMS DUNCAN	
Brindley, Mark W	Lt Cdr	01-Oct-10	ENG	WE	MWS EXCELLENT	HMS EXCELLENT
Briscoe, Daniel A	Lt RN	01-Jan-09	WAR	GSX	MTM MWS COLLINGWOOD	HMS COLLINGWOOD
Briscoe, James W A	Lt Cdr	01-Oct-12	ENG	WE	HMS OCEAN	
Bristow, Paul C	Lt Cdr	01-Oct-12	ENG	TM	NCHQ CI TEAM	PORTSMOUTH
Britten, Benjamin T	Lt RN	01-Sep-08	WAR	P FW	HQ AIR HQ 1GP LTNG	MCAS CHERRY POINT
Britton, Gemma L	Lt RN	01-Apr-08	WAR	PWO(N)	HMS EXPRESS	
Broad, Annabel E	SLt	01-May-13	WAR	GSX	HMS OCEAN	
Broad, James W	SLt	01-Mar-14	WAR	GSX	MTM NELSON	HMS NELSON
Broadbent, Nicholas J	Maj	01-Oct-14	RM	SCC	FLEET SPT LOGS INFRA	PORTSMOUTH
Broadley, Kevin J	Cdr	30-Jun-00	WAR	P SK6	NATO - BRUSSELS	BRUSSELS
Brock, Danny R	Lt RN	20-Jul-12	LOGS	L SM	HMS ASTUTE	
Brock, Mathew J	Lt RN	01-Jan-02	WAR	MCD	MTM NELSON	HMS NELSON
Brockie, Alan F	Lt Cdr	01-Oct-13	QARNNS	OT (C&S)	DMRC HEADLEY COURT	EPSOM
Brocklehurst, Judith E	Lt Cdr	01-Oct-09	QARNNS	ITU	RCDM	BIRMINGHAM
Brodie, Duncan J	Lt Cdr	01-Oct-10	ENG	AE	814 SQN	RNAS CULDROSE
Brodie, Stephen D	Lt Cdr	01-Oct-09	QARNNS	EN (C&S)	JFC HQ	NORTHWOOD
Brogden, Thomas G	Surg Lt Cdr	02-Aug-11	MED	GS	MTM INM ALVERSTOKE	GOSPORT
Brokenshire, Matthew W	Capt	01-Mar-09	RM	GS	MTM NELSON	HMS NELSON
Bromage, Kenneth	RN Chpln	02-Aug-92	Ch S	Chaplain (RES)	HMS DRAKE	PLYMOUTH
Brook, Sophie A	SLt	01-Sep-13	WAR	SM(X)	HMS VIGILANT	
Brooking, Gary N	Lt RN	12-Jul-11	QARNNS	ITU	MASF	RNAS CULDROSE
Brooks, Alexandra L	Lt Cdr	01-Oct-11	WAR	MEDIA OPS	MTM NELSON	HMS NELSON
Brooks, Daniel	Mid	01-May-14	WAR	GSX	BRNC	BRNC DARTMOUTH
Brooks, Gary	Cdr	30-Jun-08	WAR	HM (H CH)	DEFENCE ACADEMY	SHRIVENHAM
Brooks, Nicholas R	Lt Cdr	01-Oct-09	ENG	MESM	DES COMFLEET	ABBEY WOOD
Brooks, Paul N	Lt Cdr	01-Oct-09	ENG	WE	FLEET COMOPS NWD	NORTHWOOD
Brooksbank, Oliver	Lt RN	01-Nov-10	WAR	P LYNX	LHF 815 SQN	RNAS YEOVILTON
Broster, Lee J	Lt RN	01-Jul-04	ENG	WE	NATO - BRUSSELS	BRUSSELS (MONS)
Brotherton, James M	Mid	01-Feb-14	LOGS	L	HMS BULWARK	
Brotherton, John D	Lt Cdr	16-Apr-02	WAR	P MER	849 SQN	RNAS CULDROSE
Brotton, Peter J	Lt Cdr	01-Apr-06	WAR	PWO(C)	HMS SUTHERLAND	
Broughton, Arron M	Capt	01-Sep-13	RM	GS	CTCRM	EXMOUTH
Broughton, Jack E	Capt	03-Apr-09	RM	SCC	FLEET SPT LOGS INFRA	PORTSMOUTH
Browett, Jon J	Lt Cdr	01-Oct-12	WAR	PWO	HMS ARGYLL	
Brown, Alastair D	Lt Cdr	01-Oct-12	ENG	ME	FOST DPORT	PLYMOUTH
Brown, Andrew	Lt Cdr	01-Dec-04	ENG	WE	JSSU (CYP) - 2 SQN	AYIOS NIKOLAOS
Brown, Andrew MBE	Surg Cdr	20-Jul-10	MED	GMP	DPHC SW	EXMOUTH

Name	Substantive Rank	Seniority	Branch	Specialisation	Organisation Name	Location Name
Brown, Andrew S	Lt Cdr	01-Oct-08	WAR	PWO	MCM2	PORTSMOUTH
Brown, Benjamin E	Lt RN	01-Feb-12	WAR	MCD	MCM2	PORTSMOUTH
Brown, Callum J	SLt	01-Oct-13	ENG	WE	MWS COLLINGWOOD	HMS COLLINGWOOD
Brown, Elliot L	SLt	01-Aug-13	ENG	AE	RNAS YEOVILTON	YEOVILTON
Brown, Harry G	SLt	01-Sep-14	WAR	SM(X)	MCM2	PORTSMOUTH
Brown, James A	Lt Cdr	01-Oct-10	WAR	HM	HMS ENTERPRISE	
Brown, James A	Lt Cdr	01-Oct-11	ENG	WESM(TWS)	SFM CLYDE	HMNB CLYDE
Brown, Joe H	Lt	02-Sep-14	RM	GS	CTCRM	EXMOUTH
Brown, Joshua	SLt	01-Sep-12	MED	Medical	BLAKE	BRNC DARTMOUTH
Brown, Leonard A MBE	Lt Col	30-Jun-09	RM	P LYN7	CHFHQ	RNAS YEOVILTON
Brown, Lynda E M	Lt Cdr	01-Oct-13	LOGS	L	HMS PROTECTOR	
Brown, Marc A	Lt RN	11-Apr-08	WAR	O SKW	849 SQN	RNAS CULDROSE
Brown, Matthew O	Lt RN	01-Sep-13	WAR	GSX	MCM1	FASLANE
Brown, Michael A	Lt Cdr	01-Oct-14	WAR	P SK4	845 SQN	RNAS YEOVILTON
Brown, Nathan D	Lt	01-Mar-14	RM	GS	42 CDO RM	PLYMOUTH
Brown, Neil L	Cdre	01-Jul-10	LOGS	L BAR	MTM NELSON	HMS NELSON
Brown, Nigel	Col	30-Jun-06	RM	C	NATO - BRUSSELS	BRUSSELS (MONS)
Brown, Oliver G	SLt	01-May-13	WAR	GSX	MWS COLLINGWOOD	HMS COLLINGWOOD
Brown, Peter S J	Lt Cdr	01-Jun-95	ENG	MESM	NATO-ACO JFC HQ	NAPLES
Brown, Rebecca J	Lt RN	01-Mar-09	LOGS	L	BRNC	BRNC DARTMOUTH
Brown, Rebecca K	Lt RN	01-Apr-12	WAR	GSX	HMS CLYDE	
Brown, Simon J	Lt RN	28-Jul-06	ENG	AE	DES COMJE	YEOVIL
Brown, Simon J J	Cdr	16-Jun-87	WAR	PWO(U)	DMS WHITTINGTON	LICHFIELD
Brown, Stephen H	Lt Cdr	15-Jan-01	WAR	MCD	NDG	HELENSBURGH
Brown, Steven	Lt RN	01-Mar-11	ENG	MESM	HMS VIGILANT	
Browne, James B	Mid	08-Sep-14	ENG	ME	BRNC	BRNC DARTMOUTH
Browne, James M O	Mid	17-Nov-14	WAR	GSX	BRNC	BRNC DARTMOUTH
Browne, Kevin M	Lt Cdr	01-Oct-13	WAR	INT	JFC HOC C4ISR	ABBEY WOOD
Bruce, Robin P M	Capt	01-Sep-12	RM	GS	CLR ASG	WAREHAM
Bruford, Robert M C	Cdr	30-Jun-10	WAR	AAWO	SERV ATTACHE/ADVISER	RIYADH
Brunsden-Brown, Sebastian E	Lt Cdr	01-Oct-01	WAR	P MER	824 SQN	RNAS CULDROSE
Brunton, Steven B CBE	R Adm	24-Feb-12	ENG	WESM(TWS)	DES COMFLEET	ABBEY WOOD
Bruzon, Charles	RN Chpln	01-Sep-04	Ch S	Chaplain	COMPORFLOT	PORTSMOUTH
Bryan, Rory J L OBE	Capt RN	08-Sep-14	WAR	PWO(U)	HMS PROTECTOR	
Bryant, Nathan C	SLt	01-May-12	ENG	WE	MWS COLLINGWOOD	HMS COLLINGWOOD
Bryce, Andrew A	Capt	01-Sep-13	RM	GS	45 CDO RM	DUNDEE
Bryce, Graeme E	Surg Lt Cdr (D)	29-Jun-05	DENTAL	GDP	MTM INM ALVERSTOKE	GOSPORT
Bryce, Jenny E	Lt RN	01-Feb-14	LOGS	L	HMS NORTHUMBERLAND	
Bryce-Johnston, Fiona L S	Lt RN	16-Jul-01	QARNNS	PHC	DPHC LONDON & SE REGION	NORTHWOOD
Bryden, David G	Lt Cdr	01-Oct-14	WAR	GSX	MTM MWS COLLINGWOOD	HMS COLLINGWOOD
Bryers, Matthew P	Lt RN	01-Jun-13	WAR	MCD	MCM1	FASLANE
Bryson, Susan	Lt Cdr	01-Oct-05	WAR	PWO(N)	BRNC	BRNC DARTMOUTH
Bubb, Jonathan D	Lt Col	30-Jun-12	RM	C	1 ASSLT GP RM	PLYMOUTH
Buchan, James	Lt RN	01-Apr-11	WAR	GSX	MTM STONEHOUSE	PLYMOUTH
Buchan, Sarah R	Lt RN	01-May-98	ENG	TM	NCHQ CNPERS (HRTSG)	PORTSMOUTH
Buchanan, Nathan G	2Lt	25-Aug-14	RM	N/A	CTCRM	EXMOUTH
Buchan-Steele, Mark A	Cdr	31-Dec-00	LOGS	L SM	FOSNI - NRC	HMS CALEDONIA
Buck, James E	Cdr	30-Jun-13	WAR	PWO(N)	FLEET CAP SSM	PORTSMOUTH
Buck, Thomas A J	Capt	03-Sep-14	RM	GS	45 CDO RM	DUNDEE
Buckenham, Peter J	Lt Cdr	01-Oct-08	ENG	ME	FOST DPORT	PLYMOUTH
Buckland, Richard J F	Cdr	31-Dec-99	WAR	O SKW	NCHQ - NAVY CMD SEC	PORTSMOUTH
Buckle, Iain L	Cdr	30-Jun-05	ENG	WE	FMC NAVY	LONDON
Buckley, James D	Maj	01-Oct-14	RM	GS	NCHQ	PORTSMOUTH
Buckley, Martin	Lt Cdr	16-May-85	WAR	N/A	NCHQ CNPS	PORTSMOUTH
Bucknall, Robin J W	Lt Col	30-Jun-09	RM	HW	IPP	LONDON
Bugg, Christopher G	Lt RN	01-May-13	WAR	O UT	MTM SHAWBURY	RAF SHAWBURY
Bukhory, Hamesh	Lt Cdr	01-Oct-12	ENG	AE	DES COMLAND	ABBEY WOOD
Bulgin, Martin R	Lt RN	01-Jan-05	WAR	ATC	3FTS - CMD	RAFC CRANWELL
Bull, Christopher M S	Cdr	30-Jun-04	ENG	WESM(TWS)	DIST/COR	CORSHAM
Bull, Louis P	Lt Cdr	01-Oct-09	WAR	SM(AWC)	HMS AMBUSH	
Bullock, James	Lt RN	01-Aug-02	WAR	P SK4	202 SQN - E FLT	HULL
Bullock, John B	Lt Cdr	01-Oct-10	ENG	ME	HMS DUNCAN	

Name	Substantive Rank	Seniority	Branch	Specialisation	Organisation Name	Location Name
Bullock, Robert A	Lt Cdr	01-Oct-11	WAR	PWO(C)	FOST NWD (JTEPS)	NORTHWOOD
Bulmer, Renny J MBE	Maj	01-Oct-00	RM	SCC	FLEET CMR	PORTSMOUTH
Bundock, Oliver J	Lt RN	01-Apr-14	WAR	P	MTM 815 SQN YEOVILTON	RNAS YEOVILTON
Burbeck, Leslie R L	Lt RN	01-Nov-14	WAR	O UT	RNAS CULDROSE	HELSTON
Burbidge, Kay	Lt Cdr	01-Oct-10	WAR	O MER	MWS COLLINGWOOD	HMS COLLINGWOOD
Burbidge, Richard L	Lt RN	01-May-14	WAR	GSX	MTM YEOVILTON FCC	RNAS YEOVILTON
Burcham, Jason R	Maj	01-Oct-09	RM	BS	RM BAND PLYMOUTH	HMS RALEIGH
Burge, Roger	Cdr	30-Jun-11	ENG	WESM(SWS)	DES COMFLEET	ABBEY WOOD
Burgess, Andrew J	Surg Capt RN	17-Apr-07	MED	Anaes	MDHU DERRIFORD	PLYMOUTH
Burgess, Mark J	Capt	01-Apr-03	RM	P LYN7	MTM WMO CULDROSE	RNAS CULDROSE
Burgess, Maxine J	Lt RN	11-Dec-09	WAR	AV	HMS OCEAN	
Burgess, Philip G	Lt Cdr	01-Oct-13	ENG	ME	HMS PORTLAND	
Burgess, Thomas A	SLt	01-Sep-14	ENG	AE	DCEME SULTAN	HMS SULTAN
Burghall, Rebecca C	Lt Cdr	01-Oct-13	WAR	HM(AS)	HMS PROTECTOR	
Burgoyne, William	Lt RN	01-May-06	WAR	PWO(SM)	HMS VICTORIOUS	
Burke, Helen E	Lt RN	01-Sep-12	ENG	ME	MTM DCEME SULTAN	HMS SULTAN
Burke, Michael C	Lt Cdr	01-Sep-95	WAR	SM(X)	FLEET FOST ACOS(Trg)	PORTSMOUTH
Burke, Paul D OBE	Capt RN	28-May-10	WAR	SM(CQ)	MOD NSD	LONDON
Burkin, Craig R	Capt	01-Sep-11	RM	GS	NCHQ	PORTSMOUTH
Burlingham, Alexander C R	Lt RN	01-Aug-03	ENG	TM	FOST DPORT	PLYMOUTH
Burlingham, Brett L	Cdr	30-Jun-03	ENG	ME	NAVY ICP	PORTSMOUTH
Burlton, Patrick	Lt	01-Sep-13	RM	GS	CLR ASG	WAREHAM
Burnell, Jeremy	Col	14-Dec-14	RM	GS	MTM 43 CDO FPGRM	HELENSBURGH
Burness-Smith, Oliver N	Lt RN	01-Mar-12	WAR	GSX	LOAN NEW ZEALAND DGHR(N)	WELLINGTON
Burnett, Daniel D	Lt RN	09-Apr-12	WAR	P UT	MTM SHAWBURY	RAF SHAWBURY
Burnett, Paul H	Cdr	24-Feb-14	MED	MS	NCHQ MEDDIV	PORTSMOUTH
Burningham, Michael R	Capt RN	12-Mar-12	LOGS	L SM	FLEET SPT LOGS INFRA	PORTSMOUTH
Burns, Adrian C OBE	Cdr	30-Jun-10	LOGS	L SM	RNAS YEOVILTON	YEOVILTON
Burns, Amy	SLt	01-Sep-12	ENG	MESM	DCEME SULTAN	HMS SULTAN
Burns, Andrew P	Capt RN	03-Jan-12	WAR	PWO(A)	JFC HQ	NORTHWOOD
Burns, David I	Capt RN	02-Jul-13	WAR	PWO(C)	FLEET COMOPS NWD	NORTHWOOD
Burns, David M	Capt	01-Sep-09	RM	GS	CLR ASG	WAREHAM
Burns, Natalie J	Lt RN	01-Jan-12	WAR	GSX	MTM YEOVILTON FCC	RNAS YEOVILTON
Burns, Richard	SLt	01-Sep-12	ENG	WE	MWS COLLINGWOOD	HMS COLLINGWOOD
Burns, Richard J	Lt RN	01-Sep-13	WAR	GSX	MCM2	PORTSMOUTH
Burr, Amapola E	Mid	01-Feb-14	WAR	SM(X)	BRNC	BRNC DARTMOUTH
Burr, Christopher J	Maj	01-Oct-13	RM	GS	CTCRM	EXMOUTH
Burrell, David J	Lt Cdr	01-Oct-11	WAR	SM(CQ)	HMS TALENT	
Burrows, James R	Lt RN	01-Apr-12	WAR	P UT	MTM RAF CRANWELL	RAFC CRANWELL
Burrows, Oliver R	SLt	01-Sep-14	ENG	AE	DCEME SULTAN	HMS SULTAN
Burrows, Thomas G	Lt RN	01-Sep-08	WAR	P SK4	RMAS SANDHURST GP	CAMBERLEY
Burton, Alex	Lt Cdr	01-Nov-08	WAR	PWO(U)	FOST NWD (JTEPS)	NORTHWOOD
Burton, Alexander J	R Adm	28-Oct-14	WAR	PWO(U)	FLEET CAP MARCAP	PORTSMOUTH
Burton, James H	Lt RN	01-Jan-06	WAR	PWO(SM)	MTM MWS COLLINGWOOD	HMS COLLINGWOOD
Burton, Joe S	Mid	01-Feb-14	WAR	GSX	BRNC	BRNC DARTMOUTH
Burvill, Justin P	Cdr	30-Jun-12	ENG	MESM	DES COMFLEET	USA
Buscombe, Leo N P	Mid	01-May-14	WAR	O	BRNC	BRNC DARTMOUTH
Bush, Alexander J T	Cdr	30-Jun-14	WAR	MCD	DEODS	ANDOVER
Butcher, Mark W	Lt RN	01-Sep-08	WAR	HM	MCM1	FASLANE
Butler, Adam	Lt RN	01-Oct-10	WAR	HM	HMS PROTECTOR	
Butler, James M	Lt RN	17-Dec-10	LOGS	L	MTM DEFAC JSCSC	SHRIVENHAM
Butler, Jason N	Mid	17-Nov-14	WAR	O UT	BRNC	BRNC DARTMOUTH
Butler, Jonathon E	Lt Cdr	01-Oct-11	ENG	WESM(TWS)	HMS VANGUARD	
Butler, Philip M	Lt Cdr	01-Oct-13	WAR	P SK4	HQ JHC DCOMD	ANDOVER
Buttar, Daniel M I	SLt	01-May-12	WAR	GSX	HMS DRAGON	
Butterworth, Chester O	SLt	01-Sep-13	WAR	GSX	MCM2	PORTSMOUTH
Butterworth, Leslie MBE	Lt RN	16-Jan-99	LOGS	L FS	NATO ACO	NORTHWOOD
Butterworth, Sophie	Surg Lt RN	04-Aug-10	MED	EM	MTM INM ALVERSTOKE	GOSPORT
Buttery, Stephanie A	Lt RN	01-Sep-14	WAR	GSX	RN EXCHANGE GERMANY	BERLIN
Buxton, Joshua L	2Lt	02-Sep-12	RM	GS	CTCRM	EXMOUTH
Buxton, Peter OBE	Surg Cdre	15-Aug-11	MED	Radiologist	NCHQ MEDDIV	PORTSMOUTH
Bye, Ashley	Lt RN	01-Oct-08	WAR	P SK4	COMUKTG	PLYMOUTH

Name	Substantive Rank	Seniority	Branch	Specialisation	Organisation Name	Location Name
Bye, Kyo	Surg SLt	28-Jul-14	MED	Medical	BLAKE	BRNC DARTMOUTH
Byrd, Liam	Lt Cdr	01-Oct-13	LOGS	L	HQ JHC DCOMD	ANDOVER
Byrne, Christopher J	2Lt	25-Aug-14	RM	N/A	CTCRM	EXMOUTH
Byron, Douglas C	Lt Cdr	01-Oct-12	LOGS	L	LO HMS NEPTUNE	HMNB CLYDE
Byron, James D DSC	Cdr	30-Jun-13	WAR	PWO(U)	MTM DEFAC JSCSC	SHRIVENHAM

C

Name	Substantive Rank	Seniority	Branch	Specialisation	Organisation Name	Location Name
Cabot, Thomas L J	Capt	01-Mar-14	RM	GS	43 CDO FPGRM	HELENSBURGH
Cabra Netherton, K.	Mid	01-Feb-14	WAR	GSX	BRNC	BRNC DARTMOUTH
Cackett, Thomas E R	Lt RN	01-May-06	WAR	P SK4	845 SQN	RNAS YEOVILTON
Caddick, Andrew	Lt RN	01-Sep-03	ENG	MESM	HMS TRENCHANT	
Caddick, David	2Lt	25-Aug-14	RM	N/A	CTCRM	EXMOUTH
Caddy, Paul D	Lt RN	01-Sep-08	WAR	GSX	MTM MWS COLLINGWOOD	HMS COLLINGWOOD
Cahill, Karen A	Lt Cdr	01-Aug-03	WAR	GSX	COMPORFLOT	PORTSMOUTH
Cain, John D	Capt	03-Sep-14	RM	GS	45 CDO RM	DUNDEE
Cairns-Holder, Declan P	Lt RN	20-Aug-10	ENG	WE	NAVY MCTA	PORTSMOUTH
Caithness, Julian C	Mid	08-Sep-14	WAR	GSX	BRNC	BRNC DARTMOUTH
Calder, Thomas A	Lt RN	01-Mar-12	ENG	AE	820 SQN	RNAS CULDROSE
Caldwell, Daniel J	Maj	01-Oct-09	RM	GS	PJHQ (UK)	NORTHWOOD
Calhaem, Richard T	Lt Cdr	01-Oct-08	WAR	P SK4	771 SQN	RNAS CULDROSE
Callaghan, John J	Surg Lt RN	01-Aug-12	MED	GDMO	HMS DAUNTLESS	
Callear, Ben	SLt	01-May-12	ENG	WESM	HMS AMBUSH	
Callender, James T	Lt RN	01-Apr-12	WAR	GSX	HMS KENT	
Callis, Gregory J	Lt RN	01-Sep-02	ENG	ME	COMPORFLOT	PORTSMOUTH
Calvert, Charles W A	Mid	08-Sep-14	ENG	WE	BRNC	BRNC DARTMOUTH
Calvert, Lauren J	Lt RN	01-Apr-10	WAR	HM	FLEET COMOPS NWD	NORTHWOOD
Cambrook, Laura	Lt RN	01-Sep-09	WAR	O LYNX	LHF 815 SQN HQ	RNAS YEOVILTON
Cameron, Alastair J	Capt	01-Sep-13	RM	GS	MTM CTCRM	EXMOUTH
Cameron, Fiona	Lt Cdr	01-Oct-08	ENG	TM	COMPORFLOT	PORTSMOUTH
Cameron, Fraser I	SLt	01-Sep-14	WAR	GSX	MCM1	FASLANE
Cameron, Mark J	Capt RN	06-Nov-12	ENG	WE	FOSNI - CNR	PORTSMOUTH
Cameron, Peter S OBE	Brig	13-May-14	RM	GS	DIRECTOR (JW)	NORTHWOOD
Cameron, Sam	Lt RN	01-Mar-10	ENG	MESM	HMS ASTUTE	
Campbell, Alastair	Lt RN	01-May-04	WAR	P MER CDO	CHF - 846	RAF BENSON
Campbell, Colin	Lt RN	01-Jan-09	WAR	SM(X)	HMS VIGILANT	
Campbell, David C	Lt RN	01-Nov-14	WAR	GSX	MCM2	PORTSMOUTH
Campbell, Edward J	Lt RN	01-Jul-11	WAR	P UT	MTM SHAWBURY	RAF SHAWBURY
Campbell, Felicity	Cdr	01-Jul-12	QARNNS	Nurse Officer	RCDM	BIRMINGHAM
Campbell, Jonathan G	Lt RN	01-Sep-07	WAR	MCD	FDU	PORTSMOUTH
Campbell, Michael M	Maj	01-Nov-04	RM	GS (RES)	FLEET CAP IS	PORTSMOUTH
Campbell, Robin D H	Cdr	30-Jun-07	ENG	WESM(TWS)	DES COMJE	ABBEY WOOD
Campbell, Scott L	SLt	01-Nov-14	WAR	P UT	MWS COLLINGWOOD	HMS COLLINGWOOD
Campbell, Thomas C	Lt	01-Sep-12	RM	GS	RN EXCHANGE NETHERLANDS	DEN HELDER
Campbell-Baldwin, James W	Lt Cdr	01-Oct-14	WAR	PWO	MWS COLLINGWOOD	HMS COLLINGWOOD
Camplisson, Owen G	Lt RN	01-Jul-06	WAR	P SK4	DEF HELI FLYING SCH	SHREWSBURY
Canale, Andrew J	Cdr	01-Jun-13	WAR	PWO(U)	DCDS PERS TRG	LONDON
Cane, Jonathan	Lt RN	01-Aug-08	LOGS	L	BRNC	BRNC DARTMOUTH
Canning, Christopher P MBE	Cdr	30-Jun-13	WAR	O SK6	MAA EXEC GP LONDON	LONDON
Canosa, Luis J	Lt RN	01-Jan-12	LOGS	L	HMS MONMOUTH	
Cantellow, Stuart J	Lt Cdr	01-Jun-09	ENG	AE	RNAS CULDROSE	HELSTON
Cantillon, Lloyd M	Lt RN	16-Jun-08	QARNNS	ITU	PCRF	RFA ARGUS
Cantrill, Richard J OBE MC	Lt Col	30-Jun-11	RM	MLDR	42 CDO RM	PLYMOUTH
Canty, Thomas A	Lt Cdr	01-Feb-10	ENG	ME	NAVY MCTA	PORTSMOUTH
Capes, Stuart G	Cdr	30-Jun-08	WAR	SM(CQ)	OPS DIR	LONDON
Capewell, David A KCB OBE	Lt Gen	01-Dec-11	RM	GS	MTM NELSON	HMS NELSON
Caple, Jonathan N	Cdr	30-Jun-14	LOGS	L	NATO-ACO-SHAPE	CASTEAU
Capps, James A	Lt RN	01-Jan-05	WAR	P SK4	MWS COLLINGWOOD	HMS COLLINGWOOD
Carbery, Stephen J	Lt Cdr	01-Oct-09	ENG	WE	JFC HOC C4ISR	ABBEY WOOD
Carden, Peter D	Cdr	30-Jun-99	WAR	O SK6	AIB	HMS SULTAN
Cardy, Lloyd E	Lt RN	01-Apr-12	WAR	GSX	MTM MWS COLLINGWOOD	HMS COLLINGWOOD
Carey, Trevor	Lt Cdr	01-Oct-14	ENG	ME	HMS IRON DUKE	
Carlisle, Jack C	SLt	01-Nov-14	WAR	P UT	MWS COLLINGWOOD	HMS COLLINGWOOD

Name	Substantive Rank	Seniority	Branch	Specialisation	Organisation Name	Location Name
Carlton, Paul D	Lt RN	01-May-06	ENG	MESM	DES COMFLEET	ABBEY WOOD
Carman, Felix	Lt RN	01-Dec-04	WAR	HM	HMS ENTERPRISE	
Carne, Richard J P	Lt Cdr	01-Oct-08	WAR	O MER	829 SQN	RNAS CULDROSE
Carnell, Richard P	Lt Cdr	01-Oct-09	QARNNS	EN (C&S)	JFHQ	NORTHWOOD
Carnew, Sean F	Lt RN	01-Sep-03	WAR	O MER	RNAS CULDROSE	HELSTON
Carney, Joseph	SLt	01-May-12	WAR	O UT	MTM RAF CRANWELL	RAFC CRANWELL
Carnie, Christopher	Lt RN	01-May-13	LOGS	L	HMS TALENT	
Carnie, Manson J	Cdr	30-Jun-13	WAR	P LYNX	MTM DEFAC JSCSC	SHRIVENHAM
Carns, Alistair S MC	Maj	01-Oct-10	RM	GS	NCHQ	PORTSMOUTH
Carpenter, Bryony H	Lt Cdr	01-Oct-04	ENG	TM	DCTT HQ	HMS SULTAN
Carpenter, Gary J	Lt Cdr	01-Oct-12	ENG	WESM(SWS)	HMS VIGILANT	
Carpenter, James E	Lt RN	01-Jun-11	WAR	GSX	MCM2	PORTSMOUTH
Carpenter, Neil P	Lt RN	01-Apr-11	LOGS	L	COMUKTG	PLYMOUTH
Carr, David J	Lt Cdr	01-Oct-13	WAR	PWO	MTM MWS COLLINGWOOD	HMS COLLINGWOOD
Carr, Stephen A J	SLt	01-Nov-14	WAR	GSX	MWS COLLINGWOOD	HMS COLLINGWOOD
Carrick, James P	Lt RN	01-Sep-98	WAR	SM(N)	NATO-ACT-JWC	STAVANGER
Carrick, Richard J	Capt RN	06-Sep-11	ENG	MESM	MTM DRAKE	HMS DRAKE
Carrigan, Jonathan A	Cdr	30-Jun-12	LOGS	L	FLEET SPT LOGS INFRA	PORTSMOUTH
Carrioni-Burnett, Ivana M	Lt RN	20-Oct-12	WAR	H	HMS ECHO	
Carroll, Paul C	Capt RN	06-Oct-14	ENG	ME	FLEET CAP MARCAP	PORTSMOUTH
Carroll, Stephen	Lt Cdr	01-Oct-08	ENG	AE	ACDS	LONDON
Carson, Daniel	2Lt	25-Aug-14	RM	N/A	CTCRM	EXMOUTH
Carter Quinn, M G	Lt Cdr	01-Oct-09	WAR	AAWO	MCM1	FASLANE
Carter, Andrew J M	Lt RN	01-May-07	WAR	O MER	824 SQN	RNAS CULDROSE
Carter, Christopher	Lt RN	18-Feb-05	WAR	GSX	RNLA	BRNC DARTMOUTH
Carter, David	Lt RN	22-Mar-99	WAR	AW (RES)	MWS COLLINGWOOD	HMS COLLINGWOOD
Carter, Holly	Lt RN	01-Apr-09	WAR	ATC	RNAS CULDROSE	HELSTON
Carter, Jonathon M	Lt Cdr	01-Jun-96	ENG	WESM(SWS)	SUPERINTENDENT WEAPONS	HMNB CLYDE
Carter, Kevin	Lt Cdr	27-Aug-02	WAR	GSX	NATO-ACO-SHAPE	CASTEAU
Carter, Kevin C GM	Maj	01-Oct-13	RM	GS	NCHQ	PORTSMOUTH
Carter, Laura J	Lt RN	08-Jul-10	LOGS	L	COMDEVFLOT	PLYMOUTH
Carter, Paul	Lt Cdr	01-Oct-06	ENG	WESM(TWS)	FLEET ACOS(RP)	PORTSMOUTH
Carter, Robert I	Lt Cdr	01-Oct-95	WAR	ATC	DIO INTL & DTE DTE HQ	WARMINSTER
Carter, Simon N	Capt RN	07-Sep-11	LOGS	L SM	PJHQ (UK)	NORTHWOOD
Carthew, Richard J	Lt Cdr	01-Oct-09	LOGS	L SM	RNAS CULDROSE	HELSTON
Carthey, Ben	Lt RN	01-Jan-09	WAR	P SK6	854 NAS	RNAS CULDROSE
Cartwright, Darren OBE	Cdr	30-Jun-05	WAR	O SK6	FLEET COMOPS NWD	NORTHWOOD
Carty, Michael G	Maj	01-Oct-14	RM	P FW	HQ AIR - HQ1GP - OPS&FD	YUMA, USA
Carver, Charles A	Lt Cdr	01-Oct-14	LOGS	L	NCHQ - CNLS	HELENSBURGH
Carver, James D	Lt RN	01-Nov-10	WAR	P SK6	771 SQN	RNAS CULDROSE
Carvill, Joe J	Capt	01-Sep-13	RM	GS	FLEET COMOPS NWD	NORTHWOOD
Cary, Matthew R	Lt RN	01-Sep-13	WAR	GSX	MCM1	FASLANE
Cash, Rupert	Lt RN	19-Nov-10	WAR	HM	FLEET HM UNIT	PLYMOUTH
Cassells, Benjamin T C	Capt	01-Sep-08	RM	GS	NCHQ	PORTSMOUTH
Cassidy, Stuart M	Lt RN	01-Sep-03	WAR	P SK4	GANNET SAR FLT	HMS GANNET
Casson, Paul R OBE	Capt RN	10-May-10	ENG	ME	MTM DEFAC RCDS	LONDON
Castle, Alastair S	Lt Cdr	01-Dec-01	WAR	P MER	824 SQN	RNAS CULDROSE
Castle, Colin	Lt Cdr	01-Oct-06	WAR	AAWO	RN EXCHANGE FRANCE	PARIS
Castledine, Benjamin C	Surg Lt Cdr	03-Feb-14	MED	GMP	MTM INM ALVERSTOKE	GOSPORT
Castroyannakis, Timothy	Lt RN	01-Oct-08	WAR	MCD	MCM1	FASLANE
Caswell, Neil C	Lt Cdr	01-Oct-13	LOGS	L	RNLA	HMS COLLINGWOOD
Cataffo, Paul J	SLt	01-Apr-12	WAR	O SKW	854 NAS	RNAS CULDROSE
Catchpole, Andrew D	Capt	21-Mar-13	RM	SCC	ES SQN CDO LOG REGT RM	RMB CHIVENOR
Cator, Benjamin H	Lt RN	03-Sep-13	ENG	WE	HMS RICHMOND	
Cattanach, James I	Lt RN	01-May-08	WAR	SM(X)	MTM RALEIGH	HMS RALEIGH
Catton, Innes C	Maj	01-Oct-10	RM	GS	40 CDO RM	TAUNTON
Cave, George	Lt RN	01-Sep-14	ENG	ME	HMS DEFENDER	
Cave, Simon J	Lt RN	09-Apr-10	ENG	ME	COMPORFLOT	PORTSMOUTH
Cavendish, Gavin W	Lt RN	11-Oct-13	WAR	INT	854 NAS	RNAS CULDROSE
Cavill, Niki R D MBE	Lt Col	30-Jun-13	RM	GS	DCDS MIL STRAT OPS	LONDON
Chadfield, Laurence J	Lt Cdr	01-Oct-04	WAR	PWO(C)	PJHQ (UK)	NORTHWOOD
Chadwick, Kara	Lt Cdr	01-Oct-08	LOGS	L BAR	DCDC	SHRIVENHAM

Name	Substantive Rank	Seniority	Branch	Specialisation	Organisation Name	Location Name
Chaffe, Sebastian S R G	2Lt	07-Sep-14	RM	N/A	CTCRM	EXMOUTH
Chalk, Martin J	2Lt	25-Aug-14	RM	N/A	CTCRM	EXMOUTH
Challans, Benjamin	Lt RN	01-Mar-12	ENG	ME	HMS DRAGON	
Chalmers, Donald P	Cdr	31-Dec-99	WAR	PWO(U)	NATO - BRUSSELS	BRUSSELS (MONS)
Chambers, Christopher M	Mid	01-May-14	WAR	GSX	BRNC	BRNC DARTMOUTH
Chambers, Gary J	SLt	01-Aug-13	ENG	WE	MWS COLLINGWOOD	HMS COLLINGWOOD
Chambers, Harry	Capt	01-Sep-09	RM	GS	MTM 30 CDO IX GP	PLYMOUTH
Chambers, Joanne M	Lt RN	01-Jan-09	ENG	WE	DES COMFLEET	ABBEY WOOD
Chambers, Lee	SLt	01-Jan-14	WAR	SM(X)	MTM NELSON	HMS NELSON
Chambers, Mark W	Lt RN	13-Apr-12	MED	MS(SM)	NBC CLYDE	HMNB CLYDE
Chambers, Richard	Lt Cdr	01-Oct-10	WAR	PWO(C)	HMS IRON DUKE	
Chambers, William J	Lt RN	30-Apr-94	WAR	MCD	DCDS PERS TRG	LONDON
Chan, Deona Mei Lam	Surg Lt RN	06-Aug-14	MED	Medical	BLAKE	BRNC DARTMOUTH
Chandler, Philip	Lt RN	01-Sep-00	ENG	TM	HQ JHC	ANDOVER
Chandler, Rory G	Lt RN	01-Sep-13	ENG	MESM	HMS AMBUSH	
Chandler, Russell S	Lt RN	01-Apr-09	WAR	O LYNX	LHF 815 SQN	RNAS YEOVILTON
Chang, Christopher J	Lt Cdr	01-Oct-09	LOGS	L	DES COMFLEET	ABBEY WOOD
Chang, Hon W	Lt RN	01-Aug-02	ENG	TM	CHAPLAIN OF THE FLEET	PORTSMOUTH
Chapman, Anthony	Cdr	30-Jun-11	WAR	MEDIA OPS	UK MCC	BAHRAIN
Chapman, Charles L	Cdr	30-Jun-10	ENG	WESM(TWS)	NCHQ CNPERS	PORTSMOUTH
Chapman, Christopher	Lt RN	01-Sep-12	WAR	GSX	HMS WESTMINSTER	
Chapman, James L J	Lt Cdr	01-Oct-09	WAR	HM(AS)	HMS SCOTT	
Chapman, Martin S	Lt Cdr	01-Oct-08	LOGS	L CMA	ACDS	ABBEY WOOD
Chapman, Nicholas J	Lt Cdr	01-May-90	WAR	SM(CQ)	LOAN DSTL	FAREHAM
Chapman, Peter	Cdr	30-Jun-12	ENG	WE	NATO-ACT-HQ	MONS (CASTEAU)
Chapman, Simon OBE	Lt Col	30-Jun-07	RM	GS	HQ 3 CDO BDE RM	PLYMOUTH
Chapman, Simon J	Lt Cdr	01-Apr-98	WAR	AAWO	FLEET ACOS(RP)	PORTSMOUTH
Chappell, Benjamin J	Capt	01-Sep-10	RM	GS	CTCRM	EXMOUTH
Charles, Steven R	Lt RN	19-Dec-08	LOGS	L	NCHQ CNPS	PORTSMOUTH
Charlesworth, Graham	Capt RN	19-Apr-10	ENG	WESM(TWS)	DES COMFLEET	WASHINGTON
Charlesworth, Nicholas J	Lt RN	01-Jan-09	WAR	P SK4	MTM CHF (MERLIN)	RAF BENSON
Charlton, Andrew R	Lt RN	01-Jan-12	WAR	P UT	MTM SHAWBURY	RAF SHAWBURY
Charlton, Kevin W	Cdr	11-Aug-13	QARNNS	Nurse Officer	NCHQ MEDDIV	PORTSMOUTH
Charnley, David J	Capt	01-Sep-12	RM	GS	INFANTRY BATTLE SCHOOL	BRECON
Charnock, Simon J	Lt Cdr	01-Apr-13	LOGS	L	NCHQ CNPS	LONDON
Charters, Emma	Lt RN	01-Sep-13	LOGS	L	HMS DUNCAN	
Chaston, Stephen P	Lt Cdr	01-Mar-01	WAR	SM(AWC)	HMS TRENCHANT	
Chatterjee, Shatadeep MBE	Lt Cdr	01-Oct-10	ENG	ME	FOST DPORT	PLYMOUTH
Chatterley-Evans, Dawn A	Lt RN	01-Jan-07	LOGS	L	JFC HQ	NORTHWOOD
Chatwin, Nicholas J OBE	Cdr	30-Jun-05	WAR	P LYNX	FOSNI	LONDON
Chawira, Denis	Lt Cdr	01-Oct-10	WAR	MCD	DEODS	ANDOVER
Cheal, Andrew J	Lt Cdr	01-Oct-14	ENG	TM	CTCRM	EXMOUTH
Cheema, Sukhdev S	Lt RN	01-Jul-04	ENG	WESM(TWS)	HDNET	CORSHAM
Cheesman, Daniel MBE	Lt Col	30-Jun-10	RM	C	45 CDO RM	DUNDEE
Chenery, Alexander C	Lt RN	01-Sep-14	ENG	ME	NAVY MCTA	PORTSMOUTH
Cheshire, Thomas E	Cdr	30-Jun-12	ENG	MESM	COMFASFLOT	HELENSBURGH
Cheshire, Thomas S	Lt RN	01-Jan-07	WAR	GSX	BRNC	BRNC DARTMOUTH
Chestnutt, James	Cdr	30-Jun-13	ENG	AE P	DCTT HQ	HMS SULTAN
Chew, Christopher	Lt RN	20-May-13	WAR	GSX	HMS PURSUER	
Cheyne, Rory P	SLt	01-Feb-12	WAR	P UT	MTM RAF CRANWELL	RAFC CRANWELL
Chidley, Timothy J	Capt RN	08-Jan-09	ENG	ME	DES COMFLEET	ABBEY WOOD
Child, William M	SLt	01-Sep-12	ENG	WESM	HMS RALEIGH	TORPOINT
Childs, David G	Capt RN	26-Apr-10	ENG	AE P	MOD CNS/ACNS	PORTSMOUTH
Childs, John R	Lt Cdr	01-Apr-02	WAR	AAWO	NCHQ CNPS	PORTSMOUTH
Chin, Henry R	Lt RN	01-Mar-12	ENG	WESM(TWS)	HMS ASTUTE	
Chirnside, Gabriella F	Surg Cdr	30-Jun-06	MED	GMP (C&S)	MTM NELSON	HMS NELSON
Chisholm, David C	Lt RN	07-Apr-06	ENG	WE	COMDEVFLOT	PLYMOUTH
Chisholm, David T	Lt RN	01-May-06	ENG	MESM	HMS VIGILANT	
Chisholm, Philip J H	Lt Cdr	01-Oct-14	WAR	PWO(C)	UKMARBATSTAFF	PORTSMOUTH
Chittick, William	Surg Lt Cdr (D)	10-Jul-02	DENTAL	GDP	ROYAL BRUNEI ARMED FORCES	SERIA
Chitty, Jack E	Lt	02-Sep-14	RM	GS	CTCRM	EXMOUTH
Chivers, Paul A OBE	Cdre	10-May-11	WAR	O LYNX	MAA	ABBEY WOOD

Name	Substantive Rank	Seniority	Branch	Specialisation	Organisation Name	Location Name
Choules, Barrie	Lt Cdr	01-Sep-02	ENG	TM(SM)	FLEET FOST ACOS(Trg)	ABBEY WOOD
Chowdhury, Devarun	Mid	01-Feb-14	WAR	P UT	BRNC	BRNC DARTMOUTH
Christie, Andrew J	Lt RN	14-Aug-11	ENG	TM	NETS (OPS)	HMS DRAKE
Christie, Laura	Lt RN	01-Jul-11	LOGS	L	COMPORFLOT	PORTSMOUTH
Christie, Rhys L	SLt	18-May-14	WAR	SM(X)	MWS COLLINGWOOD	HMS COLLINGWOOD
Christie, Tom C	Capt	01-Mar-14	RM	GS	42 CDO RM	PLYMOUTH
Chudley, Ian V	Lt RN	01-May-03	WAR	P SKW	849 SQN	RNAS CULDROSE
Church, Simon J	Lt Cdr	01-Oct-14	ENG	MESM	HMS TORBAY	
Churcher, Jeremy E	Cdr	30-Jun-06	WAR	HM (H CH)	COMMANDER OP TRAINING	HMS COLLINGWOOD
Churchward, Matthew J	Maj	01-Oct-04	RM	LC	FLEET CMR	PORTSMOUTH
Ciaravella, Timothy J	Lt Cdr	01-Oct-13	ENG	ME	HMS WESTMINSTER	
Clague, John J	Lt Cdr	01-Oct-06	WAR	PWO(U)	FOST DPORT	PLYMOUTH
Clapham, Grantley T	Lt Cdr	01-Oct-14	ENG	IS	NATO-NCSA-NCSA SECTOR MONS	STAVANGER
Clapham, Philip A	SLt	03-Jul-13	DENTAL	GDP(VDP)	BLAKE	BRNC DARTMOUTH
Clare, Jonathan F	Maj	01-Oct-04	RM	MLDR (SCC)	43 CDO FPGRM	HELENSBURGH
Clare, Katharine	Lt Cdr	01-Oct-05	ENG	IS	SVCOPS/DHDOPSPLANS/COR	CORSHAM
Claridge, Alexander M	Lt Cdr	01-Oct-13	QARNNS	OT (C&S)	DHFT - DMS WHITTINGTON	LICHFIELD
Claringbold, Neill R	Lt RN	01-Nov-14	WAR	ATC UT	RNAS YEOVILTON	YEOVILTON
Clark, Benjamin	SLt	01-Sep-14	ENG	AE	DCEME SULTAN	HMS SULTAN
Clark, Craig S	Lt RN	01-Sep-13	WAR	GSX	HMS ARGYLL	
Clark, David J	Lt RN	11-Apr-08	ENG	WE	DES COMLAND	ABBEY WOOD
Clark, Gary R G	Lt RN	01-Jan-15	WAR	P UT	MTM RAF VALLEY	HOLYHEAD
Clark, Gordon D	Lt RN	08-Jul-10	LOGS	L SM	FOST SM SEA	HMNB CLYDE
Clark, Ian D	Cdr	30-Jun-03	ENG	MESM	MTM NELSON	HMS NELSON
Clark, James C	SLt	01-Jan-13	WAR	O UT	MTM 849 SQN CULDROSE	RNAS CULDROSE
Clark, Matthew H R	Lt RN	01-Sep-11	WAR	P UT	MTM 845 SQN YEOVILTON	RNAS YEOVILTON
Clark, Matthew T	Capt RN	02-Oct-12	LOGS	L	MTM NELSON	HMS NELSON
Clark, Michael H	Lt Cdr	01-Mar-04	WAR	AAWO	FLEET FOST ACOS(Trg)	HMS COLLINGWOOD
Clark, Oliver R	Lt RN	01-Jan-08	LOGS	L	MTM NELSON	HMS NELSON
Clark, Paul A	Lt Col	30-Jun-10	RM	SCC	DIU	ANDOVER
Clark, Paul A	Lt RN	01-Jan-04	ENG	TM(SM)	FOST FAS SHORE	HMNB CLYDE
Clark, Philip J	Lt RN	01-Sep-05	WAR	O SKW	MTM 824 SQN CULDROSE	RNAS CULDROSE
Clark, Rachael H	SLt	01-May-12	WAR	GSX	MCM1	FASLANE
Clark, Russell A	Lt Cdr	01-Aug-08	WAR	O LYNX	MTM DEFAC JSCSC	SHRIVENHAM
Clark, Simon	Cdr	30-Jun-05	LOGS	L CMA	DCDC	SHRIVENHAM
Clark, Stephen M	Lt Cdr	01-Oct-10	LOGS	L CMA	FLEET ACOS(RP)	PORTSMOUTH
Clark, Stephen R	Lt Cdr	01-Oct-06	ENG	TM	MTM FLEET HQ	PORTSMOUTH
Clark, Steven R	Mid	01-Feb-14	WAR	GSX	BRNC	BRNC DARTMOUTH
Clark, William P G	2Lt	25-Aug-14	RM	N/A	CTCRM	EXMOUTH
Clarke, Adam G	Lt Cdr	01-Oct-07	ENG	IS	FLEET CAP IS	PORTSMOUTH
Clarke, Andrew P MBE	Lt Cdr	01-Oct-00	WAR	P SK4	845 SQN	RNAS YEOVILTON
Clarke, Benjamin J	SLt	01-Sep-14	ENG	WESM	HMS RALEIGH	TORPOINT
Clarke, Bernard R MBE	RN Chpln	30-Jun-81	Ch S	Chaplain (RES)	HMS COLLINGWOOD	FAREHAM
Clarke, Charles M L OBE	Capt RN	01-Jul-09	WAR	PWO(U)	NCHQ CNPS	LONDON
Clarke, Christopher	Mid	01-May-14	LOGS	L	BRNC	BRNC DARTMOUTH
Clarke, Daniel	Cdr	30-Jun-12	WAR	SM(CQ)	MTM NEPTUNE	HMNB CLYDE
Clarke, Danny T	Mid	01-May-14	LOGS	L	BRNC	BRNC DARTMOUTH
Clarke, David W D	Maj	01-Oct-12	RM	GS	COMUKAMPHIBFOR	PORTSMOUTH
Clarke, Ian	Cdr	30-Jun-10	WAR	PWO(A)	NATO-ACO-SHAPE	CASTEAU
Clarke, James P	Lt RN	01-Sep-07	ENG	WE	LOAN DSTL	FAREHAM
Clarke, John	Surg Cdr	30-Jun-02	MED	Occ Med	RN EXCHANGE USA	WASHINGTON
Clarke, Marcus	SLt	01-Sep-12	MED	Medical	BLAKE	BRNC DARTMOUTH
Clarke, Matthew	Lt Cdr	01-Oct-14	WAR	PWO	MWS COLLINGWOOD	HMS COLLINGWOOD
Clarke, Matthew D	Lt Cdr	01-Oct-07	ENG	TM	MTM NELSON	HMS NELSON
Clarke, Paul A	Lt RN	21-Feb-09	WAR	SM(X)	NATO ACO	NORTHWOOD
Clarke, Peter M	Maj	01-Oct-09	RM	P SK4	847 SQN	RNAS YEOVILTON
Clarke, Richard	Cdr	30-Jun-07	ENG	TM	NCHQ CNPS	PORTSMOUTH
Clarke, Richard	Cdr	30-Jun-11	ENG	AE	DES COMAIR	WASHINGTON
Clarke, Richard A	Lt RN	20-Oct-06	ENG	MESM	FLEET CAP SSM	PORTSMOUTH
Clarke, Richard W	Lt RN	01-Mar-10	ENG	MESM	DES COMFLEET	ABBEY WOOD
Clarke, Robert W J	Lt RN	01-Nov-12	ENG	MESM	DCEME SULTAN	HMS SULTAN
Clarke, Samuel A S	Surg Lt RN	01-Mar-14	MED	Medical	BRNC	BRNC DARTMOUTH

Name	Substantive Rank	Seniority	Branch	Specialisation	Organisation Name	Location Name
Clarke, Steven P	Lt RN	01-Nov-08	WAR	SM(X)	HMS VICTORY	HMNB PORTSMOUTH
Clarke, William	Lt Cdr	31-Mar-00	WAR	MW (RES)	JFC HQ	NORTHWOOD
Clarkson, Andrew	Lt Cdr	01-Oct-09	QARNNS	EN (C&S)	PCRF	RFA ARGUS
Clarkson, Antony M	Lt Cdr	01-Oct-10	ENG	WE	MTM MWS COLLINGWOOD	HMS COLLINGWOOD
Clarkson, Paul J I	Lt RN	01-Aug-08	WAR	INT	DSI	CHICKSANDS
Clasby, Lorraine	Lt RN	21-Aug-09	WAR	GSX	HMS DIAMOND	
Claxton, Alistair	Capt	03-Sep-14	RM	GS	40 CDO RM	TAUNTON
Claxton, Andrew G D	Lt Cdr	01-Oct-14	WAR	HM	FLEET COMOPS NWD	NORTHWOOD
Clay, Toby	Lt Cdr	01-Oct-08	WAR	P LYNX	PJHQ (UK)	NORTHWOOD
Clayton, Andrew M	Slt	01-Sep-14	ENG	MESM	DCEME SULTAN	HMS SULTAN
Clayton, David H	Lt RN	01-May-14	ENG	WE	HMS DAUNTLESS	
Clayton, John D	Lt RN	01-Mar-11	WAR	O SKW	857 NAS	RNAS CULDROSE
Clear, Nichola J	Lt Cdr	01-Oct-09	ENG	ME	COMPORFLOT	PORTSMOUTH
Cleary, Christopher M	Lt Cdr	01-Oct-08	LOGS	L	COMDEVFLOT	PLYMOUTH
Cleaves, Richard A	Lt RN	19-Oct-07	WAR	C	PJHQ (UK)	NORTHWOOD
Clee, James S	Lt Cdr	01-Oct-12	WAR	HM(AM)	FLEET COMOPS NWD	NORTHWOOD
Clegg, Ross E	Lt RN	03-May-13	ENG	AE	829 SQN	RNAS CULDROSE
Clements, Elizabeth J	Lt Cdr	01-Oct-07	LOGS	L	DES COMLAND	ABBEY WOOD
Cleminson, Mark D	Lt Cdr	01-Feb-05	ENG	MESM	COMFASFLOT	HELENSBURGH
Clifford, Stephen D		13-Jul-12	WAR		NCHQ	PORTSMOUTH
Clingo, Thomas W	Surg Lt RN	01-Mar-13	MED	GDMO	MASF	RNAS CULDROSE
Clink, Adam D	Cdr	30-Jun-11	WAR	P FW	FLEET CSAV	RNAS YEOVILTON
Clink, John R H	R Adm	26-Aug-14	WAR	PWO(N)	FOSNI	HELENSBURGH
Clough, Christopher R	Capt RN	12-Apr-10	ENG	WE	SERV ATTACHE/ADVISER	PARIS
Clough, Warren S	Lt RN	19-Dec-08	WAR	INT	NATO-ACO-JFC HQ	BRUNSSUM
Clouter, Timothy C	Mid	17-Nov-14	WAR	GSX	BRNC	BRNC DARTMOUTH
Clow, Jennifer	SLt	24-Jul-13	DENTAL	GDP(VDP)	BLAKE	BRNC DARTMOUTH
Clow, Thomas W	Capt	03-Apr-09	RM	LC (SCC)	CTCRM	EXMOUTH
Coackley, Jane	Lt Cdr	01-Oct-10	ENG	TM	MTM DEFAC JSCSC	SHRIVENHAM
Coard, Thomas J	Maj	08-May-14	RM	GS (RES)	RMR SCOTLAND	HMS CALEDONIA
Coatalen-Hodgson, Ryan	Lt RN	01-Sep-06	WAR	INT	NEP TEMP SERV ATTACHE ADV	LONDON
Coates, Aaron	SLt	01-Sep-14	ENG	MESM	DCEME SULTAN	HMS SULTAN
Coates, Adam J	Lt Cdr	01-Oct-11	ENG	WE	HMS MONTROSE	
Coates, James T	SLt	01-Mar-13	MED	Medical	BLAKE	BRNC DARTMOUTH
Coates, Jonathan R	Lt RN	17-Dec-10	MED	MS	HQ JMC COMD AND ADMIN	LICHFIELD
Coates, Philip J B	Surg Cdr	06-Dec-10	MED	Radiologist	MDHU DERRIFORD	PLYMOUTH
Coates, Thomas M	Lt RN	01-Sep-11	LOGS	L	DES COMLAND	ABBEY WOOD
Coatsworth, Robert W	Lt RN	07-Jan-12	WAR	GSX	MCM2	PORTSMOUTH
Cobbett, James F	Lt Cdr	01-Oct-03	WAR	P SK4	FLEET AV VL	RNAS YEOVILTON
Cobley, Simon D	Mid	01-May-13	WAR	GSX	HMS ENTERPRISE	
Cochrane, Christopher D	Lt Cdr	01-Oct-14	ENG	MESM	HMS VIGILANT	
Cochrane, Matthew	Lt RN	01-Jan-13	ENG	AE	DCEME SULTAN	HMS SULTAN
Cockcroft, Kim M	Lt RN	16-Jun-06	QARNNS	PHC	DPHC OVERSEAS	NAPLES
Cocks, Anthony	Lt RN	01-Oct-07	ENG	AE	DES COMAIR	ARLINGTON USA
Codd, Justin S	Cdr	30-Jun-13	WAR	SM(CQ)	HMS AMBUSH	
Codling, Steven J	Lt RN	20-Oct-06	WAR	C	UK MCC	BAHRAIN
Coe, Ian L	Lt RN	01-Jan-13	ENG	WESM	HMS VENGEANCE	
Coetzee, Rikus H	Surg Cdr	01-Jul-13	MED	Psych	DPHC SW	HMS DRAKE
Coffey, Ralph B D	Lt Cdr	01-Oct-12	ENG	MESM	HMS AMBUSH	
Cogan, Robert	Cdr	30-Jun-14	LOGS	L	FLEET SPT LOGS INFRA	PORTSMOUTH
Cogdell, Michael R	Lt RN	01-Sep-13	ENG	WESM	HMS TRENCHANT	
Coghill, Adrian	Lt Cdr	01-Oct-13	WAR		SCU SHORE	HMS COLLINGWOOD
Colarusso, Barry L	Capt	30-Mar-12	RM	SCC	CDO LOG REGT RM	RMB CHIVENOR
Cole, Michael D	Capt	01-Sep-13	RM	GS	45 CDO RM	DUNDEE
Cole, Simon	Lt Col	30-Jun-14	RM	GS (RES)	MTM DEFAC JSCSC	SHRIVENHAM
Cole, Simon P	Cdr	30-Jun-08	ENG	WE	DCD - MODSAP	LONDON
Coleman, Alexander P G	Lt RN	01-Jul-07	WAR	GSX	MCM2	PORTSMOUTH
Coleman, Gareth W	Lt RN	01-Sep-07	LOGS	L SM	DES COMFLEET	ABBEY WOOD
Coleman, James M	Lt Cdr	01-Oct-14	WAR	P MER CDO	CHF - 846	RAF BENSON
Coleman, Joseph M	SLt	15-Aug-12	WAR	SM(X)	MTM MWS COLLINGWOOD	HMS COLLINGWOOD
Coles, Adam J	Lt Cdr	01-Oct-13	WAR	HM(AS)	HMS GLEANER	
Coles, Andrew L OBE	Cdr	30-Jun-03	WAR	SM(CQ)	COMDEVFLOT	PLYMOUTH

Name	Substantive Rank	Seniority	Branch	Specialisation	Organisation Name	Location Name
Coles, Christopher	Lt Cdr	01-May-08	ENG	AE	DES COMFLEET	ABBEY WOOD
Coles, Christopher J	Cdr	30-Jun-06	ENG	MESM	COMDEVFLOT	PLYMOUTH
Coles, Simon P.	Lt Cdr	01-Oct-10	ENG	TM	RN EXCHANGE USA	WASHINGTON
Coles-Hendry, Frances A.	Lt Cdr	01-Oct-12	LOGS	L	NCHQ - CNLS	PORTSMOUTH
Coles-Hendry, Hamish R	Lt RN	20-Oct-08	WAR	P FW	NO 3 FTS/UAS - JEFTS	GRANTHAM
Collacott, Jonathan S	Cdr	30-Jun-14	LOGS	L SM	DES COMFLEET	ABBEY WOOD
Collen, Sara J	Lt Cdr	01-Dec-09	WAR	MEDIA OPS	FLEET CMR	PORTSMOUTH
Collett, Stuart M	Surg Cdr	14-Dec-09	MED	GMP	DPHC SOUTH	HMS COLLINGWOOD
Colley, Ian P	Lt Cdr	01-Oct-11	ENG	WESM(TWS)	HMS TRIUMPH	
Collie, James A	Lt Cdr	01-Oct-13	WAR	PWO(SM)	HMS VANGUARD	
Collier, David	Lt RN	01-Sep-07	ENG	MESM	HMS VICTORIOUS	
Collin, Martin E	Lt Col	30-Jun-12	RM	GS	COMUKTG	PLYMOUTH
Collings, Antony B	SLt	01-May-13	WAR	C	NATO ACO	NORTHWOOD
Collingwood, Matthew J	Mid	17-Nov-14	WAR	P UT	BRNC	BRNC DARTMOUTH
Collins, Andrew C	Lt Cdr	01-Oct-13	WAR	O WILDCAT	WMF SIM	RNAS YEOVILTON
Collins, Charles A	Lt Cdr	01-Oct-14	WAR	PWO	HMS IRON DUKE	
Collins, Christopher J	Lt RN	09-Apr-12	WAR	SM(X)	HMS VANGUARD	
Collins, Dale A	Lt Cdr	01-Oct-08	ENG	AE	RNAS CULDROSE	HELSTON
Collins, David	Lt Cdr	01-Oct-09	ENG	TM	JFC - DCTS (H)	AYLESBURY
Collins, David I	Lt Cdr	01-Oct-12	LOGS	L	ESG EJSU SHAPE	MONS (CASTEAU)
Collins, Jason D	Lt RN	11-Oct-13	WAR	SM(X)	FLEET COMOPS NSTP30	FAREHAM
Collins, John	Maj	01-Oct-06	RM	GS	EXCHANGE - AUSTRALIA	SALISBURY
Collins, Lorna J	Lt Cdr	01-Oct-14	ENG	TM	FOSNI - CNR	PORTSMOUTH
Collins, Mark	Lt RN	01-May-04	ENG	TM	MWS COLLINGWOOD	HMS COLLINGWOOD
Collins, Paul	Lt Cdr	01-Sep-95	ENG	WESM(SWS)	DES COMFLEET	WASHINGTON
Collins, Peter S	SLt	01-Jul-14	LOGS	L	HMS SULTAN	GOSPORT
Collins, Richard D	Lt RN	07-Aug-13	ENG	ME	HMS DEFENDER	
Collins, Simon H	Lt RN	01-Jan 11	WAR	P UT	MTM RAF CRANWELL	RAFC CRANWELL
Collins, Simon J P	Cdr	30-Jun-14	WAR	O WILDCAT	MTM DEFAC JSCSC	SHRIVENHAM
Collins, Stephen J	Lt RN	01-Nov-08	WAR	P FW	FLEET CSAV	WASHINGTON
Collins, Tamar L	Lt Cdr	01-Oct-07	ENG	IS	FLEET FOST ACOS(Trg)	PORTSMOUTH
Collis, Martin J	Lt Cdr	01-Aug-99	ENG	ME	COMPORFLOT	PORTSMOUTH
Colman, Adam J	Lt RN	01-Apr-12	WAR	GSX	MCM1	FASLANE
Colohan, Sam C	Lt RN	01-Sep-13	WAR	O UT	MTM 750 SQN CULDROSE	RNAS CULDROSE
Colthart, Lee	SLt	01-Apr-12	WAR	O UT	MTM RAF CRANWELL	RAFC CRANWELL
Coltman, Timothy P	Surg Cdr	08-Oct-08	MED	T&O	MDHU PORTSMOUTH	PORTSMOUTH
Colvin, Michael A T	Lt RN	01-May-04	WAR	PWO	HMS DIAMOND	
Concarr, David T	Lt RN	19-Sep-99	CS	CS	FOSNI - NRC NE	NEWCASTLE UPON TYNE
Congreve, Steven C	Maj	01-May-00	RM	GS	SAUDI ARABIA GCT	RIYADH
Conlin, John	Lt Cdr	01-Oct-08	WAR	PWO(U)	MWS COLLINGWOOD	HMS COLLINGWOOD
Connaughton, Mark A	Lt RN	14-Aug-14	ENG	WESM	MTM RALEIGH	HMS RALEIGH
Conneely, Steven A	Lt Cdr	01-Oct-07	ENG	WE	NC REQUIREMENTS MANAGERS	ABBEY WOOD
Connell, Martin J	Capt RN	05-Sep-11	WAR	O LYNX	MTM NELSON	HMS NELSON
Connolly, Christopher J	Cdr	31-Dec-00	WAR	PWO(A)	MTM NELSON	HMS NELSON
Connolly, Sean P	Capt	01-Sep-09	RM	GS	OPTAG HQ - I&STAT	FOLKESTONE
Connor, Daniel J	Surg Cdr	30-Jun-04	MED	Anaes	MDHU PORTSMOUTH	PORTSMOUTH
Conran, Nicholas W D	Lt RN	01-Jan-03	LOGS	L SM	HQ DCLPA & DEEPCUT GAR	CAMBERLEY
Conroy, David A	RN Chpln	24-Sep-00	Ch S	Chaplain	HMS NELSON	PORTSMOUTH
Constable, Thomas	Lt RN	01-Sep-08	ENG	AE	MAA	ABBEY WOOD
Conway, Keith A	Lt Cdr	31-Mar-99	WAR	MW (RES)	FOSNI - NRC	HMS CALEDONIA
Conway, Suzy H	Lt Cdr	01-Mar-07	LOGS	L	ACDS	ABBEY WOOD
Coogan, Thomas	Lt RN	09-Jun-06	ENG	MESM	HMS VANGUARD	
Cook, Benjamin G A	2Lt	25-Aug-14	RM	N/A	CTCRM	EXMOUTH
Cook, Christopher B	Capt RN	02-Jun-14	ENG	IS	NCHQ CNPS	PORTSMOUTH
Cook, Gordon E	Lt Cdr	01-Oct-00	WAR	O LYNX	LHF 815 SQN	RNAS YEOVILTON
Cook, Myles F	Lt Col	30-Jun-07	RM	C	DCDC	SHRIVENHAM
Cook, Paul	Lt	01-Jul-13	RM	SCC	45 CDO RM	DUNDEE
Cook, Timothy A	Lt Col	30-Jun-08	RM	C	NATO - BRUSSELS	BRUSSELS (MONS)
Cooke, Benjamin R	Lt RN	01-Apr-10	ENG	WESM(TWS)	DI - CA	LONDON
Cooke, George E	Mid	01-Feb-14	WAR	GSX	BRNC	BRNC DARTMOUTH
Cooke, Graham S	Lt Cdr	01-Oct-01	WAR	O LYNX	750 SQN	RNAS CULDROSE
Cooke, James R	Lt RN	01-Apr-12	LOGS	L	HMS ARGYLL	

Name	Substantive Rank	Seniority	Branch	Specialisation	Organisation Name	Location Name
Cooke, Joanne M	Surg Lt Cdr	02-Aug-05	MED	GS	MTM INM ALVERSTOKE	GOSPORT
Cooke, Jonathan E	Cdr	30-Jun-12	WAR	PWO(U)	FLEET CAP MARCAP	PORTSMOUTH
Cooke, Stephen N	Lt RN	01-Jan-02	WAR	P LYNX	AWC	BOSCOMBE DOWN
Cooke, Stuart L	SLt	01-Feb-12	WAR	O UT	MTM RAF CRANWELL	RAFC CRANWELL
Cooke-Priest, Nicholas	Capt RN	06-Oct-14	WAR	O LYNX	MTM MWS COLLINGWOOD	HMS COLLINGWOOD
Cooley, Jeannine	Lt RN	01-May-04	WAR	PWO	FLEET MARITIME WARFARE	HMS COLLINGWOOD
Coomber, Jonathan M	Lt Col	30-Jun-14	RM	MLDR	HMS BULWARK	
Coombes, George W T	SLt	01-May-12	LOGS	L	HMS ILLUSTRIOUS	
Coomer, Adam	SLt	01-Nov-14	LOGS	L	HMS OCEAN	
Coope, Philip J	Cdr	30-Jun-14	ENG	WE	MTM DEFAC JSCSC	SHRIVENHAM
Cooper, Charlotte E	Lt RN	01-May-13	LOGS	L	NCHQ CNPERS	PORTSMOUTH
Cooper, Darren T	Lt RN	01-Nov-07	WAR	MCD	MCM2	PORTSMOUTH
Cooper, Edwin	Lt Cdr	01-Oct-13	WAR	O MER	824 SQN	RNAS CULDROSE
Cooper, Hamish S	Mid	08-Sep-14	ENG	WE	BRNC	BRNC DARTMOUTH
Cooper, Jack W	Lt RN	01-Sep-10	WAR	GSX	DCDS PERS TRG	LONDON
Cooper, Janette L	Lt Cdr	01-Oct-11	QARNNS	PHC	DPHC SOUTH REGION HQ	ALDERSHOT
Cooper, John C	Lt RN	09-Apr-09	ENG	MESM	HMS TALENT	
Cooper, John D	Lt RN	09-Apr-09	LOGS	L	HMS ILLUSTRIOUS	
Cooper, Mark A	Capt RN	11-Oct-11	WAR	SM(CQ)	NATO-ACT-HQ	NORFOLK
Cooper, Michael A	Lt RN	01-Feb-09	WAR	P MER	829 SQN	RNAS CULDROSE
Cooper, Michael P	Maj	01-Oct-12	RM	SCC	NCHQ CNPERS	PORTSMOUTH
Cooper, Neil	Maj	01-Oct-05	RM	SCC	CTCRM	EXMOUTH
Cooper-Simpson, Roger J	Lt Col	30-Jun-07	RM	C	MTM NORTHWOOD HQ	NORTHWOOD
Copeland, Stephen N	Cdr	30-Jun-11	ENG	AE	DES COMAIR	ABBEY WOOD
Copinger-Symes, Rory S	Col	14-Sep-09	RM	HW	STRIKFORNATO - LISBON	LISBON
Coppin, Nigel J	Lt RN	01-Jan-03	LOGS	L SM	AIR 22GP	RAF HIGH WYCOMBE
Copsey, Nicholas R B	Maj	01-Oct-10	RM	GS	43 CDO FPGRM	HELENSBURGH
Corbett, Andrew S	Cdr	30-Jun-03	WAR	SM(CQ)	NATO - BRUSSELS	BRUSSELS (MONS)
Corbett, Thomas L	Lt Cdr	01-Oct-05	WAR	AAWO	NC REQUIREMENTS MANAGERS	ABBEY WOOD
Corby, Paul M	Mid	01-Feb-14	ENG	ME	DCEME SULTAN	HMS SULTAN
Corden, Adam	Lt RN	01-Jan-12	WAR	GSX	MCTC (ARMY)	COLCHESTER
Corder, Ian F CB	V Adm	30-May-13	WAR	SM(CQ)	NATO - BRUSSELS	BRUSSELS (MONS)
Corderoy, John	Cdre	02-Sep-13	ENG	MESM	DES COMFLEET	ABBEY WOOD
Core, Emily E	Lt RN	01-Apr-13	WAR	HM	MTM WMO YEOVILTON	RNAS YEOVILTON
Cormack, Andrew	Surg Lt Cdr	01-Jul-10	MED	Occ Med	MTM INM ALVERSTOKE	GOSPORT
Cornell, Jonathan D	Surg Lt RN	07-Aug-13	MED	Medical	BLAKE	BRNC DARTMOUTH
Corness, Andrew S	RN Chpln	06-Sep-04	Ch S	Chaplain	HMS COLLINGWOOD	FAREHAM
Cornford, Marc	Lt Cdr	01-Oct-10	WAR	P LYN7	MAA	ABBEY WOOD
Cornhill, Sharon T	Lt RN	12-Jul-10	QARNNS	Infection C	PCRF	RFA ARGUS
Corps, Stephen	Lt Cdr	11-Nov-98	ENG	WE	COMPORFLOT	PORTSMOUTH
Corrigan, Niall R	Capt RN	30-Jun-06	WAR	PWO(A)	NATO-NCSA-NCSA HQ	BRUSSELS
Corrin, Colby St John	Lt Col	30-Jun-10	RM	MLDR	MTM NELSON	HMS NELSON
Cory, Nicholas J	Lt Cdr	01-Oct-10	WAR	INT	JSSU CH - HQ	CHELTENHAM
Coryton, Oliver C W S	Maj	01-Oct-09	RM	GS	NCHQ CNPERS	PORTSMOUTH
Coryton, Sophie C	Lt Cdr	01-Oct-10	LOGS	L	NCHQ - CNLS	PLYMOUTH
Cosby, Max A I	Lt RN	01-Sep-12	WAR	O UT	MTM LHF 702 SQN YEOVILTON	RNAS YEOVILTON
Costley-White, Benjamin M	Lt RN	01-Jul-11	WAR	GSX	HMS KENT	
Cottee, Benjamin R J	Lt Cdr	01-Sep-06	WAR	ATC	RAF SHAWBURY	SHREWSBURY
Cotterill, Bruce M	Cdr	30-Jun-11	ENG	WESM(TWS)	DES COMLAND	USA
Cottis, Mathew C	Cdr	30-Jun-13	LOGS	L SM	ACDS	LONDON
Cotton, Steven	Capt	18-Jul-08	RM	C (SCC)	42 CDO RM	PLYMOUTH
Cottrell, Ralph	Maj	01-Oct-13	RM	GS	US CENTCOM	USA
Coughlin, Emma J	Lt RN	18-Jan-05	WAR	HM	RNAS CULDROSE	HELSTON
Coughlin, Peter J L	Lt RN	01-Oct-05	WAR	O MER	MTM DEFAC JSCSC	SHRIVENHAM
Coulson, Neil A	RN Chpln	01-Jul-08	Ch S	Chaplain	HMS SULTAN	GOSPORT
Coulson, Peter	Capt RN	18-Oct-11	ENG	WE	COMDEVFLOT	PLYMOUTH
Coultas, Daniel	Lt RN	01-Sep-13	WAR	SM(X)	MTM FLEET HQ	PORTSMOUTH
Coulthard, Adrian J	Cdr	30-Jun-14	ENG	TM	HQ DISC	CHICKSANDS
Court, Matthew R	Lt Cdr	01-Oct-14	WAR	PWO(SM)	HMS LANCASTER	
Court, Nicholas J	Lt RN	01-Jan-09	WAR	MW	MTM DEFAC JSCSC	SHRIVENHAM
Court, Shane J	Lt RN	24-Oct-08	ENG	AE	OCLC PLYMOUTH	BRISTOL
Courtier, Robert N	Capt	01-Mar-11	RM	GS	Op LANSBURY	AFGHANISTAN

Name	Substantive Rank	Seniority	Branch	Specialisation	Organisation Name	Location Name
Courtney, Timothy	Lt RN	01-May-03	ENG	MESM	HMS SULTAN	GOSPORT
Coutts, Maxwell G	Lt RN	22-Mar-10	LOGS	L	FLEET SPT LOGS INFRA	PORTSMOUTH
Coutts, Phoebe H	Lt RN	01-Feb-14	WAR	HM	MTM MWS HMTG (D)	HMS DRAKE
Couzens, Robert F	Lt RN	01-Sep-08	WAR	GSX	HMS WESTMINSTER	
Coventry, Andrew J B	Capt	16-Apr-09	RM	SCC	CTCRM	EXMOUTH
Cowan, Christopher D	Lt RN	01-May-13	WAR	GSX	HMS MERSEY	
Cowan, Peter W	Lt RN	20-Jul-13	WAR	GSX	RN EXCHANGE NETHERLANDS	DEN HELDER
Coward, Suzanne L	Surg Lt Cdr (D)	29-Jun-14	DENTAL	GDP	DEFENCE DENTAL SERVS	PLYMOUTH
Cowie, Andrew D	Lt Cdr	01-Oct-12	ENG	WE	DES COMLAND	ABBEY WOOD
Cowie, Michael	Lt RN	19-Oct-07	WAR	INT	DI - CA - ASUS	WASHINGTON
Cowlishaw, Nicholas D	Lt RN	01-Jul-04	WAR	ATC	FLEET CSAV	RNAS YEOVILTON
Cox, David J	Cdr	30-Jun-09	ENG	WE	DCDS PERS TRG	LONDON
Cox, David W S	Capt	01-Sep-12	RM	GS	CHFHQ	RNAS YEOVILTON
Cox, Mark A MC	Maj	01-Oct-14	RM	GS	NCHQ	PORTSMOUTH
Cox, Mark B	Cdr	30-Jun-13	LOGS	L	NCHQ CNPS	LONDON
Cox, Matthew J	Lt Cdr	01-Oct-13	ENG	WE	FLEET CAP IS	PORTSMOUTH
Cox, Michael	Lt Cdr	01-Oct 10	WAR	INT	JFIG - JT OPS	RAF WYTON
Cox, Nicholas J M	Mid	01-May-14	LOGS	L	BRNC	BRNC DARTMOUTH
Cox, Pieter W S	Cdr	30-Jun-93	ENG	WESM(SWS)	CBRN POL	LONDON
Cox, Rex J	Capt RN	06-Jan-14	WAR	AAWO	HMS DRAGON	
Cox, Sean A J	Lt Cdr	01-Oct-05	WAR	P LYN7	MTM WMO YEOVILTON	RNAS YEOVILTON
Cox, Simon J	Lt Cdr	01-Oct-11	WAR	PWO	FLEET COMOPS NWD	NORTHWOOD
Cox, Simon T	Maj	01-Oct-13	RM	GS	STRIKFORNATO - LISBON	LISBON
Cox, Stephen	Capt	16-Apr-10	RM	SCC	HQ SQN CDO LOG REGT RM	RMB CHIVENOR
Cox, Stephen J	Mid	08-Sep-14	ENG	ME	BRNC	BRNC DARTMOUTH
Coyle, Gavin J	Cdr	30-Jun-12	WAR	PWO(U)	FLEET CAP MARCAP	PORTSMOUTH
Coyle, Ross D	Lt RN	01-May-02	ENG	WE	MTM DEFAC CMT MSC	SHRIVENHAM
Coyne, Paul E	SLt	03-Jan-12	WAR	SM(X)	HMS ECHO	
Cozens, Christopher J	Lt RN	01-Sep-08	ENG	ME	HMS PROTECTOR	
Crabb, Antony J	Lt Cdr	01-Oct-04	WAR	PWO(U)	EU OHQ	NORTHWOOD
Cragg, Richard D	Lt Cdr	01-Oct-04	ENG	MESM	COMDEVFLOT	PLYMOUTH
Craig, Alexander P	Lt RN	01-May-09	WAR	P SK4	845 SQN	RNAS YEOVILTON
Craig, David	Lt RN	19-Oct-07	WAR	C	SVCOPS/DHDOPSPLANS/COR	CORSHAM
Craig, Edward A	Mid	01-Feb-14	WAR	GSX	BRNC	BRNC DARTMOUTH
Craig, John	Cdr	30-Jun-09	WAR	MCD	UKMARBATSTAFF	PORTSMOUTH
Craig, Kenneth M	Maj	01-May-01	RM	HW	NATO-ACT-HQ	NORFOLK
Crallan, Alexander	SLt	01-Sep-14	WAR	GSX	MWS COLLINGWOOD	HMS COLLINGWOOD
Crane, Danielle L	Surg Lt RN	04-Aug-10	MED	GMP	MTM INM ALVERSTOKE	GOSPORT
Crane, Oliver R	Lt RN	01-Oct-98	WAR	P SK4	MTM CHF (MERLIN)	RAF BENSON
Craner, Matthew	Surg Cdr	30-Jun-04	MED	Neurology	MDHU FRIMLEY PARK	FRIMLEY
Craven, Martin W	Lt Cdr	01-Oct-09	WAR	P LYNX	MTM DEFAC JSCSC	SHRIVENHAM
Crawford, Alistair A	Lt RN	01-Nov-07	WAR	P LYNX	LHF 815 SQN HQ	RNAS YEOVILTON
Crawford, Jonathan B	Lt RN	11-Apr-08	WAR	AV	RNAS YEOVILTON	YEOVILTON
Crawford, Valerie E	Lt RN	01-Apr-02	WAR	OP INT	MTM NPT RES MOBILISATION	PORTSMOUTH
Creaney, Anthony P	Capt	16-Apr-10	RM	SCC	MTM NELSON	HMS NELSON
Crease, David A	Lt RN	09-Apr-09	ENG	ME	HMS SCOTT	
Crease, Peter S	Lt RN	01-Apr-13	WAR	P UT	MTM CHF (MERLIN)	RAF BENSON
Creasey, Andrew D	Capt	01-Sep-10	RM	GS	SFSG C COY	RAF ST ATHAN
Cree, Andrew	Capt RN	03-Jan-12	ENG	TM	MTM FLEET HQ	PORTSMOUTH
Cree, Malcolm C	R Adm	07-Oct-13	WAR	PWO(A)	NCHQ	PORTSMOUTH
Creedon, Timothy D	SLt	01-Nov-14	WAR	O UT	MWS COLLINGWOOD	HMS COLLINGWOOD
Creek, Stephen B	Lt RN	01-Jan-02	ENG	WESM(TWS)	NBD COB BASE EXECUTIVE OFFICE	HMS DRAKE
Cresdee, Samuel	SLt	01-Sep-13	WAR	SM(X)	HMS TRIUMPH	
Crewdson, Robert P	Lt RN	01-Feb-09	WAR	O MER	820 SQN	RNAS CULDROSE
Crichton, Gary S	Lt Cdr	01-Oct-11	WAR	PWO	DI - CA	LONDON
Criddle, Gary D J MBE	Cdr	30-Jun-12	WAR	O LYNX	RN EXCHANGE FRANCE	PARIS
Crier, Matthew J	SLt	01-May-12	WAR	O UT	MTM RAF CRANWELL	RAFC CRANWELL
Cripps, Michael J	Lt Cdr	01-Oct-12	ENG	AE	849 SQN	RNAS CULDROSE
Cripps, Nicola	Lt Cdr	01-Oct-14	ENG	TM	JFC - DCTS (H)	AYLESBURY
Crispin, Toby A B	Lt Cdr	01-Apr-94	WAR	O SK6	AWC	BOSCOMBE DOWN
Critchley, Ian J	Lt Cdr	01-Oct-13	WAR	PWO(SM)	HMS CHARGER	
Crockatt, Stephen R J	Cdr	30-Jun-14	WAR	P LYNX	AWC	BOSCOMBE DOWN

Name	Substantive Rank	Seniority	Branch	Specialisation	Organisation Name	Location Name
Crofts, David J	Cdr	30-Jun-14	ENG	WE	HDPROG	CORSHAM
Crombie, Stuart	Lt RN	01-Sep-05	WAR	O LYNX	NATO-ACO-JFC HQ	NAPLES
Cromie, John M	Lt Cdr	01-Oct-08	WAR	AAWO	MCM2	PORTSMOUTH
Crompton, Lynne	Lt Cdr	01-Oct-13	WAR	ATC	MTM DEFAC JSCSC	SHRIVENHAM
Crompton, Philip J	Lt Cdr	01-Oct-14	WAR	P LYNX	LHF HQ	RNAS YEOVILTON
Crook, Daniel S	Lt RN	09-Apr-13	ENG	WE	HMS ST ALBANS	
Crook, Richard	Lt RN	01-Sep-07	ENG	MESM	DES COMFLEET	ABBEY WOOD
Crooks, Charles S	Lt RN	01-Mar-11	ENG	MESM	COMFASFLOT	HELENSBURGH
Cropper, Martin A K	Lt Cdr	16-May-90	LOGS	L SM	CDP PERS TRG	LONDON
Crosbie, Donald E F	Cdr	30-Jun-09	WAR	MCD	FLEET CAP SSM	PORTSMOUTH
Crosby, David W M	Lt Cdr	01-Oct-11	WAR	SM(CQ)	FOST SM SEA	HMNB CLYDE
Cross, Aaron	Lt RN	01-Jun-12	WAR	P SK4	845 SQN	RNAS YEOVILTON
Cross, Alexander L	Lt Cdr	01-Oct-05	ENG	WESM(TWS)	FLEET CAP SSM	PORTSMOUTH
Cross, Andrew G	Maj	01-Oct-08	RM	SCC	1 ASSLT GP RM	PLYMOUTH
Cross, Nicholas	Lt RN	01-Jul-02	ENG	IS	DCCIS CISTU	HMS COLLINGWOOD
Crossey, Matthew D	Lt Cdr	01-Oct-13	ENG	TM	FOST DPORT	PLYMOUTH
Crossley, Heather C	SLt	01-Sep-14	ENG	MESM	DCEME SULTAN	HMS SULTAN
Crosswood, Barry T	Lt RN	01-Jan-12	WAR	GSX	UK MCC	BAHRAIN
Crouch, Benjamin R	Lt RN	01-May-10	LOGS	L	HMS DAUNTLESS	
Crow, Jonathan G	Capt	01-Sep-11	RM	GS	NCHQ	PORTSMOUTH
Crowley, James R	Lt	01-Sep-12	RM	GS	JCTTAT	FOLKESTONE
Crowsley, Francesca C	Lt RN	01-Sep-12	WAR	HM	HMS ECHO	
Crowson, Elizabeth	Surg Cdr	04-Aug-08	MED	GMP	DPHC SCOTLAND & NI	HMNB CLYDE
Crowther, Joshua	Mid	08-Sep-14	ENG	ME	BRNC	BRNC DARTMOUTH
Croxton, Damien P	Lt Cdr	01-Oct-13	LOGS	L	PJHQ (UK)	NORTHWOOD
Crump, Alexander I A	Capt	01-Mar-09	RM	GS	UK MCC	BAHRAIN
Cryar, Timothy M C	Capt RN	22-Jul-14	WAR	AAWO	FLEET CAP MARCAP	PORTSMOUTH
Cuddeford, Jacob W	Mid	17-Nov-14	WAR	TM	BRNC	BRNC DARTMOUTH
Cuff, Samuel H	Lt RN	01-Sep-08	ENG	AE	FLEET CSAV	YEOVIL
Cull, Iain Obe	Cdr	30-Jun-09	WAR	PWO(N)	BRNC	BRNC DARTMOUTH
Cullen, Donna M	Lt RN	01-Sep-08	WAR	GSX	DCSU	RAF HENLOW
Cullen, Matthew R	Lt RN	01-May-13	LOGS	L	NBD NBC HQ	HMS DRAKE
Cullen, Nicola L	Lt Cdr	01-Oct-06	ENG	TM	BRNC	BRNC DARTMOUTH
Cullingford, Richard M	Lt RN	01-Jan-13	WAR	P UT	RAF CONINGSBY	RAF CONINGSBY
Culwick, Peter F	Surg Capt RN (D)	07-Mar-11	DENTAL	GDP(C&S)	DMS WHITTINGTON	LICHFIELD
Cumming, Frazer S	Lt RN	01-Sep-03	WAR	O SKW	NO 3 FTS/UAS - JEFTS	GRANTHAM
Cummings, Alan	Cdr	30-Jun-07	WAR	O SK6	FLEET CSAV	LONDON
Cummings, Darren	Lt Cdr	01-Oct-13	MED	MS(SM)	UK MCC	BAHRAIN
Cummings, David J	Lt Cdr	01-Nov-02	ENG	WE	MTM NELSON	HMS NELSON
Cunane, John R	Lt Cdr	01-Oct-98	LOGS	L SM	DES COMLAND	ABBEY WOOD
Cunnell, Rachael L	Lt Cdr	01-Oct-10	LOGS	L	RNAS YEOVILTON	YEOVILTON
Cunningham, Dexter A	Lt RN	01-Sep-13	ENG	WE	HMS DRAGON	
Cunningham, John	Cdr	30-Jun-03	WAR	O LYNX	UKTI - DSO	LONDON
Cunningham, Matthew S	SLt	01-Sep-14	LOGS	L	RNAS CULDROSE	HELSTON
Curd, Michael C	Lt RN	01-Jan-05	WAR	O LYNX	RN EXCHANGE FRANCE	PARIS
Curnock, Timothy C R	Lt RN	01-Jan-07	WAR	O SKW	849 SQN	RNAS CULDROSE
Curran, Steven J	Lt	01-Jul-13	RM	SCC	CHFHQ	RNAS YEOVILTON
Currass, Timothy	Capt RN	30-Sep-14	ENG	WE	DES COMFLEET	ABBEY WOOD
Currie, Duncan G	Lt Cdr	16-Dec-01	WAR	P SKW	RNAS CULDROSE	HELSTON
Currie, Michael J	Lt Cdr	01-Oct-08	WAR	O MER	FLEET CSAV	PORTSMOUTH
Currie, Stephen	Lt RN	01-Sep-09	ENG	TM	HMS SULTAN	GOSPORT
Currie, Stuart M	Cdr	30-Jun-12	ENG	MESM	COMFASFLOT	HELENSBURGH
Currie, Victor A C	Lt RN	08-Dec-12	WAR	P UT	MTM SHAWBURY	RAF SHAWBURY
Currin, Joseph M	Lt RN	01-Apr-12	WAR	FC	HMS DAUNTLESS	
Curry, Philip D	Lt RN	30-Jun-09	WAR	O SKW	MCM2	PORTSMOUTH
Curry, Robert E	Cdr	30-Jun-11	WAR	PWO(C)	JFC HOC C4ISR	NORTHWOOD
Cursiter, John D	Lt RN	12-Jun-05	WAR	PWO(SM)	RNSMS	HMS RALEIGH
Curtis, Peter J MBE	Maj	01-Oct-14	RM	BS	RM BAND COLLINGWOOD	HMS COLLINGWOOD
Curtis, Suzannah	Cdr	30-Jun-14	LOGS	L	JFLogC	NORTHWOOD
Curwood, Jenny E	Lt Cdr	01-Oct-06	LOGS	L	FOSNI	PORTSMOUTH
Cusack, Michael K	Lt RN	09-Apr-13	WAR	SM(X)	HMS VICTORIOUS	
Cuthbert, Glen	Lt RN	01-May-04	ENG	TM	NAVY CORE TRG HQ	PLYMOUTH

D
34

Name	Substantive Rank	Seniority	Branch	Specialisation	Organisation Name	Location Name
Cutler, Andrew R	Lt Cdr	01-Oct-07	WAR	PWO	MWS COLLINGWOOD	HMS COLLINGWOOD
Cutler, David T	Lt RN	01-May-04	ENG	ME	HMS PROTECTOR	
Cutler, Liam G	Capt	01-Mar-11	RM	GS	SFSG F COY	RAF ST ATHAN
Cutler, Paul A	SLt	01-Oct-13	ENG	WE	MWS COLLINGWOOD	HMS COLLINGWOOD

D

Name	Substantive Rank	Seniority	Branch	Specialisation	Organisation Name	Location Name
Dabell, Guy L	Capt RN	01-Oct-12	ENG	MESM	DES COMFLEET	ABBEY WOOD
Dack, Simon B	Capt	01-Apr-11	RM	SCC	FLEET SPT LOGS INFRA	PORTSMOUTH
Dailey, Paul	Capt RN	27-Aug-10	ENG	WESM(SWS)	DES COMFLEET	ABBEY WOOD
Dainton, Steven CBE	Capt RN	26-Apr-10	WAR	PWO(C)	MWS COLLINGWOOD	HMS COLLINGWOOD
Dale, Alistair	Lt Cdr	01-Feb-06	WAR	ATC	DES COMFLEET	ABBEY WOOD
Dale, Jamie R	Lt RN	01-Apr-07	WAR	ATC	LATCC(MIL) AT SWANWICK	SOUTHAMPTON
Dale, Nathan A	Lt Cdr	01-Oct-13	WAR	P SK4	MTM CHF (MERLIN)	RAF BENSON
Dale, Rebecca A	SLt	01-Sep-13	QARNNS	Nurse Officer	MDHU DERRIFORD	PLYMOUTH
Dale-Smith, Victoria G	Cdr	30-Jun-14	WAR	P SK4	RNAS CULDROSE	HELSTON
Dalgleish, Grant A	Lt Cdr	01-Oct-14	WAR	PWO(N)	HMS ARGYLL	
Dalglish, Kenneth M	Lt Cdr	01-Oct-14	WAR	PWO(C)	JFC HOC C4ISR	NORTHWOOD
Dallamore, Rebecca A	Lt Cdr	01-Oct-14	WAR	INFO OPS	UK MCC	BAHRAIN
Dallas, Lewis I	Lt RN	01-Sep-05	ENG	MESM	HMS VANGUARD	
Dalrymple, James	Lt RN	01-Apr-10	WAR	SM(N)	HMS TORBAY	
Dalton, Ebony	Lt RN	01-May-09	WAR	INT	FLEET COMOPS NWD	HMS COLLINGWOOD
Dalton, Mark F	RN Chpln	12-Jan-03	Ch S	Chaplain	NEPTUNE 2SL/CNH - CHAP	HMNB CLYDE
Dalton, Sally A T	Lt RN	01-Oct-06	ENG	TM	FLEET FOST ACOS(Trg)	ABBEY WOOD
Dalton-Fyfe, Karen S	Lt Cdr	01-Oct-07	WAR	HM(AS)	HMS ENTERPRISE	
Daly, Christopher D	Lt RN	01-Jun-08	WAR	GSX	FOST MPV SEA	HMNB CLYDE
Danbury, Ian G	Cdr	30-Jun-98	ENG	WE	DI - CA	LONDON
Dando, Benjamin J	Lt RN	01-Sep-09	WAR	O LYNX	MWS COLLINGWOOD	HMS COLLINGWOOD
Dando, Jonathon N	Lt Cdr	01-Aug-00	WAR	PWO(A)	FLEET COMOPS NWD	NORTHWOOD
Daniel, Benjamin J E	Lt Cdr	01-Oct-12	WAR	P SK4	RNAS YEOVILTON	YEOVILTON
Daniell, Christopher J	Lt Cdr	01-Oct-95	WAR	O SKW	750 SQN	RNAS CULDROSE
Daniels, Josh	SLt	01-Nov-14	WAR	SM(X)	MWS COLLINGWOOD	HMS COLLINGWOOD
Danks, Jonathan A	SLt	01-Sep-14	ENG	AE	DCEME SULTAN	HMS SULTAN
Darcy, John D	Lt RN	01-Nov-07	WAR	P SK4	845 SQN	RNAS YEOVILTON
D'Arcy, Paul A	Lt Cdr	01-Oct-02	WAR	O LYNX	MOD DEFENCE STAFF	LONDON
Dare, Clifford R S MBE	Maj	16-May-06	RM	GS (RES)	FOSNI - NRC EE	LONDON
Darkins, Colin R	Lt Cdr	01-Oct-10	ENG	TM	NATO-ACO-SHAPE	CASTEAU
Darley, Matthew E	Maj	01-Oct-10	RM	P LYN7	HQ JHC DCOMD	ANDOVER
Darlington, Alan	Lt RN	01-Sep-04	WAR	INT	JSSU CH - SITE 15	GIBRALTAR
Darlow, Paul R	Lt Cdr	01-Oct-02	LOGS	L	MWS COLLINGWOOD	HMS COLLINGWOOD
Dart, Duncan J	Lt RN	01-Sep-04	WAR	P MER CDO	CHF - 846	RAF BENSON
Dart, Michael P	Lt RN	01-Sep-08	WAR	ATC	RAF SHAWBURY	SHREWSBURY
Darwell, Joseph F	SLt	01-Sep-12	WAR	GSX	BRNC	BRNC DARTMOUTH
Dathan, Timothy J	Cdr	30-Jun-08	ENG	ME	DES COMFLEET	WASHINGTON
Daveney, David	Lt Cdr	01-Oct-05	WAR	SM(CQ)	HMS TALENT	
Davey, Alistair J	Lt RN	08-Jul-11	ENG	MESM	MTM DCEME SULTAN	HMS SULTAN
Davey, Andrew J	Lt RN	01-Jan-12	WAR	GSX	MTM NELSON	HMS NELSON
Davey, Kelly L	Surg Lt Cdr	02-Aug-10	MED	GMP	MTM NELSON	HMS NELSON
Davey, Timothy	Lt Cdr	01-Oct-06	WAR	MCD	MCM1	HMNB CLYDE
David, Ian	Lt RN	01-Aug-08	WAR	INT	JFIG - JT IP	RAF WYTON
David, Simon E J MBE	Cdr	30-Jun-03	LOGS	L	2SL CNPT	PORTSMOUTH
Davidson, Edward	Mid	17-Nov-14	LOGS	L	BRNC	BRNC DARTMOUTH
Davidson, Gregor J	Lt RN	01-Jan-08	ENG	ME	CFPS SQUAD	PORTSMOUTH
Davidson, Mark R	RN Chpln	01-May-07	Ch S	Chaplain	45 CDO RM	DUNDEE
Davidson, Matthew J	Capt	31-Aug-14	RM	GS	29 CDO REGT	PLYMOUTH
Davidson, Neil R	Lt Cdr	01-Oct-03	WAR	P MER CDO	CHF - 846	RAF BENSON
Davidson, Serena R	Lt RN	01-Sep-05	WAR	O SKW	857 NAS	RNAS CULDROSE
Davies, Alex	Lt RN	01-Jan-08	ENG	ME	HMS CLYDE	
Davies, Andrew C	Lt RN	15-Apr-11	ENG	ME	COMPORFLOT	PORTSMOUTH
Davies, Christopher R	Lt Col	30-Jun-14	RM	GS	NAVY ICP	PORTSMOUTH
Davies, Darren J	Lt Cdr	01-Oct-11	LOGS	L	JFSp ME	UAE - JOA - MINHAD
Davies, Gary P	Lt RN	12-Aug-90	ENG	MESM	FLEET SPT LOGS INFRA	PORTSMOUTH
Davies, Geraint W T	Lt Cdr	01-Oct-08	WAR	AAWO	FLEET MARITIME WARFARE	HMS COLLINGWOOD

Name	Substantive Rank	Seniority	Branch	Specialisation	Organisation Name	Location Name
Davies, Hazel	Lt Cdr	01-Oct-14	ENG	AE	DES COMJE	ABBEY WOOD
Davies, Huan C A	Lt Col	30-Jun-13	RM	MLDR	BMATT	PRETORIA
Davies, James S A	Lt RN	01-Sep-06	ENG	AE	DES COMJE	YEOVIL
Davies, Jason L	Cdr	16-Jul-12	MED	MS	DCHET DSHT	LICHFIELD
Davies, John P	Lt RN	16-Dec-11	ENG	WE	HMS BULWARK	
Davies, Jonathan R	Mid	17-Nov-14	WAR	GSX	BRNC	BRNC DARTMOUTH
Davies, Julia	Lt RN	01-Apr-10	WAR	P SK4	845 SQN	RNAS YEOVILTON
Davies, Lee	Lt Cdr	01-Jan-02	WAR	P LYNX	DDC	LONDON
Davies, Lloyd R	SLt	19-Sep-14	WAR	GSX	HMS KENT	
Davies, Luke M A	Maj	01-Oct-11	RM	LC	1 ASSLT GP RM	PLYMOUTH
Davies, Mark B	Cdr	30-Jun-06	WAR	O LYNX	NATO-ACO-JFC HQ	NAPLES
Davies, Nathan R	Lt RN	01-Nov-14	WAR	GSX	MWS COLLINGWOOD	HMS COLLINGWOOD
Davies, Neil	Lt RN	08-Feb-13	WAR	C	SVCOPS/DHDOPSPLANS/COR	CORSHAM
Davies, Nicholas M S	Lt Cdr	01-Oct-08	WAR	HM (M CH)	MTM DEFAC JSCSC	SHRIVENHAM
Davies, Ross E	Capt	01-Sep-12	RM	GS	NCHQ CNPERS	PORTSMOUTH
Davies, Sarah J	Lt Cdr	01-Oct-12	WAR	PWO	UK MCC	BAHRAIN
Davies, Warren N	Lt	01-Jul-13	RM	SCC	43 CDO FPGRM	HELENSBURGH
Davis, Carl B	SLt	01-Jul-14	WAR	O UT	MTM RAF CRANWELL	RAFC CRANWELL
Davis, Edward G M CB CBE	Lt Gen	01-Jul-14	RM	GS	NATO-ACO-LC	IZMIR
Davis, Ian Philip	Capt	03-Apr-09	RM	BS	HQ BAND SERVICE	HMS NELSON
Davis, Mark J	Lt RN	01-Sep-08	ENG	AE	DES COMJE	YEOVIL
Davis, Mark S	Lt RN	27-Jul-07	ENG	AE	RNAS YEOVILTON	YEOVILTON
Davis, Peter H	Lt RN	01-Sep-02	ENG	IS	NATO - BRUSSELS	BRUSSELS
Davis, Peter H	Lt Cdr	01-Oct-14	WAR	MCD	SDU 1	HMS DRAKE
Davis, Richard	Lt Cdr	01-Oct-13	ENG	WESM(TWS)	HMS ARTFUL	
Davis, Stephen R	Lt Cdr	01-Oct-05	ENG	WESM(SWS)	FOST SM SEA	HMNB CLYDE
Davison, Warren M	Lt RN	01-Jun-08	WAR	P MER CDO	CHF - 846	RAF BENSON
Davy, Owen E	Mid	17-Nov-14	WAR	GSX	BRNC	BRNC DARTMOUTH
Daw, Arthur B	Lt RN	01-Feb-09	WAR	P MER	820 SQN	RNAS CULDROSE
Daw, Simon J	Lt Cdr	01-Oct-97	WAR	O SK6	771 SQN	RNAS CULDROSE
Dawes, John G J	Mid	08-Sep-14	WAR	HM	BRNC	BRNC DARTMOUTH
Daws, Richard P A	Capt RN	30-Jun-08	ENG	WESM(TWS)	ACDS	NEBRASKA
Dawson, Alan	Lt Cdr	01-Oct-03	ENG	WESM(TWS)	RNSMS	HMS RALEIGH
Dawson, Kris A	Capt	01-Sep-12	RM	GS	40 CDO RM	TAUNTON
Dawson, Nigel J F	Lt Cdr	01-Oct-03	ENG	TM	RNCR BOVINGTON	WAREHAM
Dawson, Paul	Lt Cdr	01-Oct-06	ENG	MESM	HMS CALLIOPE	GATESHEAD
Dawson, William	Lt Cdr	01-Nov-98	WAR	AAWO	BFSAI	FALKLAND ISLANDS
Day, Anthony	Cdr	28-Apr-14	WAR	REG	RNP - HQ PMN	HMS EXCELLENT
Day, Benjamin	Lt Cdr	01-Oct-12	WAR	HM	JFIG - IS	RAF WYTON
Day, George A	Mid	01-Feb-14	WAR	P UT	BRNC	BRNC DARTMOUTH
Day, Michael K	Lt Cdr	01-Oct-06	WAR	P SK4	MTM WMO YEOVILTON	RNAS YEOVILTON
Day, Paul A	Lt RN	27-May-10	WAR	GSX	HMS KENT	
Day, Richard J	Lt RN	21-Dec-09	MED	MS(SM)	COMDEVFLOT	PLYMOUTH
De La Rue, James	Lt RN	01-Sep-13	WAR	SM(X)	HMS TALENT	
De Reya, Anthony L MBE	Lt Col	30-Jun-08	RM	GS	MTM 1 ASSAULT GP RM	PLYMOUTH
De Silva, Oliver A	Lt RN	01-Sep-07	LOGS	L SM	NCHQ - CNLS	PORTSMOUTH
De Velasco, Mari L	Lt Cdr	01-Oct-12	WAR	INT	JFIG - JT IP	RAF WYTON
Deacon, Stephen	Cdr	01-Jun-07	WAR	O MER	HMS OCEAN	
Deakin, Johanna	Cdr	30-Jun-13	ENG	AE	MTM DCEME SULTAN	HMS SULTAN
Deakin, Scott M	Lt Cdr	01-Oct-13	ENG	WE	RN EXCHANGE USA	WASHINGTON
Deal, Charlotte	Lt Cdr	01-Oct-08	ENG	WE	DES COMAIR	ABBEY WOOD
Dean, Adam C	Lt RN	01-Jun-10	WAR	P SK4	845 SQN	RNAS YEOVILTON
Dean, James R OBE	Capt RN	03-Nov-14	LOGS	L	JFLogC	NORTHWOOD
Dean, Natasha C	Surg SLt	21-Jul-14	MED	Medical	BLAKE	BRNC DARTMOUTH
Dean, Simon I R	Maj	01-Oct-09	RM	GS	FMC NAVY	LONDON
Dean, Timothy	Surg Lt Cdr (D)	22-Jul-02	DENTAL	GDP	HMS RALEIGH	TORPOINT
Deaney, Mark N	Capt RN	16-Dec-11	ENG	AE	MAA	ABBEY WOOD
De-Banks, Kyle	Lt RN	01-Sep-12	WAR	GSX	MCM1	FASLANE
Deeks, Peter J	Lt Cdr	01-Oct-06	ENG	MESM	DSEA DNSR	ABBEY WOOD
Deighton, Derek S	Lt Cdr	01-May-92	WAR	AAWO	DEFENCE ATTACHE	SIERRA LEONE
Deighton, Graeme	Lt Cdr	01-Oct-12	WAR	AW (RES)	HMS CALLIOPE	GATESHEAD
Dekker, Barrie J	Surg Cdr	30-Jun-06	MED	Anaes	MDHU PORTSMOUTH	PORTSMOUTH

Name	Substantive Rank	Seniority	Branch	Specialisation	Organisation Name	Location Name
Delahay, Jonathon E	Maj	01-Oct-08	RM	GS	NATO-ACO-LC	IZMIR
Delbridge, Harriet M	Mid	17-Nov-14	LOGS	L	BRNC	BRNC DARTMOUTH
Deller, Mark G OBE	Cdr	30-Jun-05	WAR	P SK6	HMS QUEEN ELIZABETH	
De'Maine, Robert	Lt RN	01-Sep-07	WAR	P MER	824 SQN	RNAS CULDROSE
Dempsey, Sean P	Lt Cdr	01-Feb-06	WAR	PWO(N)	FOST DPORT	PLYMOUTH
Dennard, Kieron J	Lt Cdr	01-Oct-13	ENG	ME	HMS OCEAN	
Denney, James R	Lt Cdr	01-Oct-07	WAR	PWO	DEFENCE ACADEMY	SHRIVENHAM
Denning, Oliver W	Maj	01-Oct-12	RM	GS	COMMANDER FIELD ARMY	PORTSMOUTH
Dennis, Andrew	SLt	01-Aug-13	MED	MS	DCHET DSHT	LICHFIELD
Dennis, James A	Maj	01-Oct-05	RM	C	MTM DEFAC JSCSC	SHRIVENHAM
Dennis, Matthew J	Cdr	30-Jun-12	WAR	SM(CQ)	BDS	WASHINGTON
Dennis, Philip MBE	Cdr	30-Jun-14	WAR	AAWO	HMS DARING	
Denniss, Jack A	Lt	02-Sep-14	RM	GS	CTCRM	EXMOUTH
Denny, Philip M	Lt RN	01-Apr-13	WAR	SM(X)	MTM RALEIGH	HMS RALEIGH
Dent, James I	Lt RN	01-Apr-13	WAR	SM(X)	MTM DEFAC JSCSC	SHRIVENHAM
Denyer, Alistair C	Lt RN	01-Jun-11	WAR	SM(N)	HMS EXPLORER	
Deppe, Garth A	Lt RN	01-Sep-12	WAR	O UT	MTM SHAWBURY	RAF SHAWBURY
Derbyshire, Faye M	Lt RN	01-Mar-13	ENG	TM	MTM NELSON	HMS NELSON
Derrick, Edward J F	Mid	08-Sep-14	WAR	GSX	BRNC	BRNC DARTMOUTH
Derrick, Matthew	Lt RN	01-Dec-99	ENG	TM	FLEET FOST TBTU	HMS COLLINGWOOD
De-Saint-Bissix-Croix, Anna M	Lt RN	13-Apr-10	QARNNS	OT (C&S)	FOSNI - CNR	PORTSMOUTH
Desmond, Jake O	Lt RN	01-Sep-12	WAR	P UT	RAF LINTON-ON-OUSE	RAF LINTON ON OUSE
Despres, Julian A	Lt Cdr	01-Oct-12	QARNNS	EN (C&S)	RCDM	BIRMINGHAM
Devereux, Michael E	Maj	01-Sep-03	RM	P LYN7	854 NAS	RNAS CULDROSE
Devine, Alison	Lt RN	12-Feb-07	QARNNS	OT	MTM 45 CDO RM	DUNDEE
Devine, Edward	Lt RN	09-Apr-13	WAR	O UT	MTM 750 SQN CULDROSE	RNAS CULDROSE
Devlin, Craig	Lt RN	01-Jan-04	ENG	IS	PJHQ (UK)	NORTHWOOD
Devonport, Sean S	Lt RN	01-Sep-10	ENG	AE	HMS SULTAN	GOSPORT
Dew, Anthony M	Surg Cdr	17-Jul-12	MED	GMP (C&S)	NCHQ MEDDIV	PORTSMOUTH
Dewar, Duncan A OBE	Col	31-Aug-09	RM	GS	NCHQ CNPERS	PORTSMOUTH
Dewey, Sarah E	Lt RN	01-Mar-06	QARNNS	EN	MDHU PORTSMOUTH	PORTSMOUTH
Dewing, William T E	Lt RN	01-Sep-14	WAR	GSX	MTM NELSON	HMS NELSON
Dewis, Ben M D	Lt RN	01-Sep-14	ENG	ME	HMS DARING	
Dewynter, Alison	Surg Lt Cdr	06-Aug-09	MED	GMP	DPHC LONDON & SE REGION	NORTHWOOD
Di Maio, Mark D	Lt Cdr	01-Oct-09	LOGS	L CMA	FLEET SPT LOGS INFRA	PORTSMOUTH
Diaper, Kevin S	Lt RN	01-Apr-14	WAR	FC	RNAS YEOVILTON	YEOVILTON
Dible, James	Cdr	30-Jun-04	WAR	P LYNX	SERV ATTACHE/ADVISER	ROME
Dick, Colin M	Lt Cdr	01-Oct-14	WAR	PWO(SM)	HMS ASTUTE	
Dicker, Jeremy	Mid	08-Sep-14	WAR	SM(X)	BRNC	BRNC DARTMOUTH
Dickie, Andrew K	Surg Lt Cdr	02-Aug-11	MED	GMP	DPHC SCOTLAND & NI	HMNB CLYDE
Dickinson, Philip N	Lt Cdr	01-Jul-82	WAR	O SK6	NCHQ - CNLS	PORTSMOUTH
Dickson, Eric	SLt	01-May-12	WAR	SM(X)	HMS NORTHUMBERLAND	
Dickson, James I	Lt Cdr	01-Aug-02	LOGS	L SM	DCDS PERS TRG	LONDON
Dickson, Stuart J	Surg Cdr	30-Jun-07	MED	Med	MDHU DERRIFORD	PLYMOUTH
Dietz, Laura M	Lt RN	01-Sep-08	ENG	AE	DES COMJE	YEOVIL
Dillon, Ben	Lt Cdr	01-Oct-14	ENG	WE	COMPORFLOT	PORTSMOUTH
Dimmock, Guy N	Lt RN	01-Jan-08	ENG	ME	HMS QUEEN ELIZABETH	
Dineen, John M G	Lt Cdr	01-Apr-02	WAR	AAWO	HMS QUEEN ELIZABETH	
Dinsmore, Simon J	Maj	01-Oct-12	RM	HW	HQ 3 CDO BDE RM	PLYMOUTH
Disney, Luke	Capt	01-Sep-09	RM	GS	COMUKAMPHIBFOR	PORTSMOUTH
Disney, Peter W	Lt Cdr	01-Oct-94	WAR	O MER	RNAS CULDROSE	HELSTON
Dix, Caroline P	Lt Cdr	01-Oct-12	ENG	AE	WMF 825 SQN HQ	RNAS YEOVILTON
Dixon, Mark E	Lt RN	01-Jan-04	ENG	MESM	HMS AUDACIOUS	
Dixon, Richard A	Lt RN	01-Jan-01	WAR	P LYNX	LHF 815 SQN	RNAS YEOVILTON
Dixon, Robert	Lt RN	01-Sep-05	WAR	P LYNX	LHF 815 SQN	RNAS YEOVILTON
Dobbins, Stuart J	Lt RN	07-Jul-97	LOGS	L	DNR DAT	PORTSMOUTH
Dobbs, Helen A	Lt RN	01-Sep-13	ENG	AE	849 SQN	RNAS CULDROSE
Dobie, Graham	Capt	18-Jul-08	RM	SCC	NCHQ	PORTSMOUTH
Dobner, Paul C	Capt	30-Mar-12	RM	GS	NCHQ	PORTSMOUTH
Dobson, Richard E	Lt RN	17-Dec-10	WAR	GSX	MTM MWS COLLINGWOOD	HMS COLLINGWOOD
Dobson, William J	Lt RN	01-Nov-14	WAR	SM(X)	MWS COLLINGWOOD	HMS COLLINGWOOD
Docherty, William P	2Lt	25-Aug-14	RM	N/A	CTCRM	EXMOUTH

Name	Substantive Rank	Seniority	Branch	Specialisation	Organisation Name	Location Name
Docherty, Zoe	Lt RN	01-Apr-11	LOGS	L	HMS VENGEANCE	
Dockerty, Neil C	Lt RN	01-Apr-09	WAR	O LYNX	LHF 815 SQN	RNAS YEOVILTON
Dodd, Craig	Lt RN	31-Jul-09	MED	MS	DMS WHITTINGTON	LICHFIELD
Dodd, Nicholas C	Cdr	30-Jun-07	LOGS	L	NAVSEC	HMS EXCELLENT
Dodd, Ryan G	SLt	01-Oct-14	MED	Medical	BLAKE	BRNC DARTMOUTH
Dodd, Shaun	Lt RN	01-Sep-09	WAR	MCD	MCM1	FASLANE
Dodds, Nicholas L	Surg Lt Cdr	01-Nov-11	MED	Anaes	MTM INM ALVERSTOKE	GOSPORT
Dodds, Stephen	Lt RN	12-Aug-05	ENG	WE	OCLC BIRMINGHAM	BIRMINGHAM
Dodson-Wells, Charles	Mid	08-Sep-14	WAR	GSX	BRNC	BRNC DARTMOUTH
Doggart, Adam J	Lt RN	01-Sep-14	WAR	GSX	MWS COLLINGWOOD	HMS COLLINGWOOD
Doherty, Bethany C	SLt	01-Nov-14	WAR	GSX	MWS COLLINGWOOD	HMS COLLINGWOOD
Doherty, David J		25-Aug-14	RM	N/A	CTCRM	EXMOUTH
Doherty, Melanie	Surg Cdr (D)	03-Sep-12	DENTAL	GDP(C&S)	DMS WHITTINGTON	LICHFIELD
Doig, Barry	Lt Cdr	01-Oct-06	WAR	INT	MTM NELSON	HMS NELSON
Dominy, David J D	Capt RN	29-Sep-14	WAR	AAWO	FOST DPORT	PLYMOUTH
Donaghey, Mark	Maj	01-Oct-13	RM	SCC	40 CDO RM	TAUNTON
Donaldson, Andrew M	Cdr	30-Jun-12	ENG	WE	MWS COLLINGWOOD	HMS COLLINGWOOD
Donaldson, Stuart	Lt Cdr	01-Sep-91	WAR	SM(CQ)	RN EXCHANGE USA	WASHINGTON
Donbavand, David W	Lt RN	11-Dec-09	LOGS	L	UK MCC	BAHRAIN
Doney, Nicholas J	Lt RN	01-Mar-13	ENG	MESM	HMS VENGEANCE	
Donohue, Paul	Lt RN	13-Feb-07	WAR	OP INT	DI - SA	LONDON
Donovan, Robin J	Cdr	30-Jun-13	LOGS	L SM	RN EXCHANGE AUSTRALIA	CANBERRA
Donworth, Desmond	Cdr	30-Jun-14	WAR	PWO(N)	MTM NELSON	HMS NELSON
Doran, Catherine M C	Surg Cdr	03-Sep-12	MED	GS	PCRF	RFA ARGUS
Doran, Iain A G	Lt Cdr	01-Oct-04	WAR	AAWO	COMPORFLOT	PORTSMOUTH
Doran, Shane E	Cdr	30-Jun-13	ENG	ME	HMS OCEAN	
Dore, Christopher	Lt RN	01-Sep-07	WAR	SM(N)	MTM RALEIGH	HMS RALEIGH
Dorman, Thomas R	Lt Cdr	01-Oct-14	ENG	IS	FLEET CAP IS	PORTSMOUTH
Dorrington, Benjamin R	Lt RN	01-Oct-10	WAR	GSX	MWS COLLINGWOOD	HMS COLLINGWOOD
Doubleday, Steven	Cdr	30-Jun-14	WAR	P SK4	CHF(MERLIN)	RAF BENSON
Dougan, David S	Lt Cdr	01-Oct-13	WAR	AV	RNAS CULDROSE	HELSTON
Doughty, Stephen W	Lt RN	09-Apr-12	WAR	P UT	MTM SHAWBURY	RAF SHAWBURY
Douglas, Jason	Lt RN	31-Jul-09	ENG	AE	DES COMJE	YEOVIL
Douglas, Patrick J	Capt RN	13-Oct-14	WAR	P SKW	OPS DIR	LONDON
Doull, Donald J M	Capt RN	01-Jul-14	ENG	MESM	DES COMFLEET	USA
Douthwaite, Stuart J	Lt RN	01-Oct-09	WAR	SM(N)	HMS ASTUTE	
Dow, Andrew J R	Maj	01-Oct-11	RM	GS	42 CDO RM	PLYMOUTH
Dow, Clive S	Cdr	30-Jun-10	LOGS	L BAR	FLEET COMMANDER DCNS	PORTSMOUTH
Dowd, Jonathan W	Lt Col	30-Jun-10	RM	GS	RMR MERSEYSIDE	LIVERPOOL
Dowding, Craig	Lt RN	12-Jul-13	LOGS	L SM	HMS TRENCHANT	
Dowell, Paul H N	Cdr	30-Jun-05	ENG	WE	NCHQ CNPS	PORTSMOUTH
Dowlen, Henry T B MBE	Capt	29-Jun-14	RM	GS (RES)	MTM NELSON	SIERRA LEONE
Dowling, Andrew J	Lt Cdr	01-Oct-12	WAR	O LYNX	RNAS YEOVILTON	YEOVILTON
Downie, David R M	Lt Cdr	01-Oct-10	ENG	AE	820 SQN	RNAS CULDROSE
Dowse, Andrew R	Lt RN	01-Sep-09	ENG	WE	MCSU	FLEET HQ
Dowsett, Patrick G	Cdr	30-Jun-09	WAR	PWO(C)	JFHQ	NORTHWOOD
Doyle, Gary	Capt RN	20-Oct-08	WAR	O LYNX	NCHQ CNPS	PORTSMOUTH
Doyle, James R	Lt RN	01-Sep-12	ENG	AE	771 SQN	RNAS CULDROSE
Doyle, Michael J	Lt RN	01-Sep-13	ENG	AE	LHF 702 SQN	RNAS YEOVILTON
Drake, Roderick	Lt Cdr	31-Mar-98	WAR	MTO N (RES)	NATO ACO	NORTHWOOD
Dransfield, Joseph A J	Lt Cdr	01-Oct-09	WAR	O LYNX	NATO-ACT-JWC	STAVANGER
Draper, Mark P	Lt	02-Sep-14	RM	N/A	CTCRM	EXMOUTH
Draper, Stephen	Cdr	30-Jun-08	WAR	PWO(A)	NATO-ACO-JFC HQ	BRUNSSUM
Dray, Jake M	Lt Cdr	01-Oct-09	WAR	PWO(U)	RALEIGH RNSOS	HMS RALEIGH
Dreaves, Christopher R	SLt	01-Sep-14	ENG	MESM	DCEME SULTAN	HMS SULTAN
Dreelan, Michael J	Cdr	30-Jun-07	WAR	PWO(U)	DCDS PERS TRG	LONDON
Drennan, David G	Lt RN	01-Sep-07	WAR	P SK4	DEF HELI FLYING SCH	SHREWSBURY
Drew, Daniel M	Lt RN	21-Mar-13	LOGS	L	NORTHWOOD HQ	NORTHWOOD
Drewett, Brian J H	Lt Cdr	01-Oct-13	WAR	PWO	HMS DUNCAN	
Drewett, Michael J	SLt	01-Sep-13	ENG	WE	BRNC	BRNC DARTMOUTH
Drinkall, Kathryn M	Lt RN	01-Jan-06	ENG	TM	MTM WMO YEOVILTON	RNAS YEOVILTON
Drinkwater, Ross MBE	Maj	01-Oct-12	RM	GS	43 CDO FPGRM	HELENSBURGH

Name	Substantive Rank	Seniority	Branch	Specialisation	Organisation Name	Location Name
Driscoll, Adrian	Lt RN	01-Mar-11	ENG	WE	MTM DEFAC JSCSC	SHRIVENHAM
Driscoll, Robert	Lt Cdr	01-Oct-05	ENG	TM	HMS SULTAN	GOSPORT
Drodge, Andrew P F	Lt Cdr	01-Oct-02	WAR	O SK6	FOST DPORT	PLYMOUTH
Drodge, Kevin N	Lt Cdr	01-Oct-11	WAR	P SKW	FLEET CSAV	PORTSMOUTH
Droog, Sarah J	Surg Lt Cdr	02-Aug-11	MED	Anaes	MTM INM ALVERSTOKE	GOSPORT
Drummond, Anthony S	Lt RN	01-May-08	WAR	SM(N)	MTM RALEIGH	HMS RALEIGH
Drummond, Karl B	Surg Cdr (D)	01-Jul-13	DENTAL	GDP	HMS COLLINGWOOD	FAREHAM
Dry, Ian	Lt Cdr	01-Oct-12	ENG	IS	SVCOPS/DHDOPSPLANS/COR	CORSHAM
Drysdale, Robert T.	Lt RN	01-Mar-14	WAR	SM(X)	MTM MWS COLLINGWOOD	HMS COLLINGWOOD
Drysdale, Steven R	Cdr	30-Jun-06	WAR	SM(CQ)	PJHQ (UK)	NORTHWOOD
D'Silva, Daniel	Cdr	30-Jun-13	ENG	WE	PJHQ (UK)	NORTHWOOD
Dubois, Carina	Lt RN	01-Apr-12	WAR	O MER	814 SQN	RNAS CULDROSE
Duby, Alon	Surg Cdr	30-Jun-07	MED	EM	RCDM	BIRMINGHAM
Duce, Matthew	Lt RN	01-May-01	WAR	PWO(N)	1 ASSLT GP RM	PLYMOUTH
Duckitt, Jack	Maj	01-Oct-11	RM	C	CTCRM	EXMOUTH
Dudley, James	SLt	09-Sep-14	ENG	WE	HMS IRON DUKE	
Dudley, Stephen	Lt Cdr	01-Jan-99	LOGS	L	DCDS PERS TRG	LONDON
Du-Feu, Robert J	Lt RN	01-Sep-12	ENG	AE	847 SQN	RNAS YEOVILTON
Duffell, Glyn T.	Lt RN	01-May-13	WAR	GSX	MCM2	PORTSMOUTH
Duffield, Andrew J	Mid	01-May-14	WAR	P UT	BRNC	BRNC DARTMOUTH
Duffin, Colin J	Lt RN	01-Jul-08	WAR	INT	COMUKAMPHIBFOR	PORTSMOUTH
Duffin, Lee-Anne	Lt RN	01-Jan-05	WAR	MW	MTM MWS COLLINGWOOD	HMS COLLINGWOOD
Duffy, Andrew J	Lt RN	01-Sep-13	WAR	SM(X)	HMS VANGUARD	
Duffy, Henry	Capt RN	06-Dec-11	WAR	PWO(C)	BRNC	BRNC DARTMOUTH
Duffy, James C	Lt Cdr	01-Oct-14	WAR	PWO(SM)	HMS TORBAY	
Duffy, Mark	SLt	01-Sep-12	ENG	WE	MWS COLLINGWOOD	HMS COLLINGWOOD
Dufosee, Sean W MBE	Cdr	30-Jun-14	WAR	P MER CDO	MTM WMO YEOVILTON	RNAS YEOVILTON
Duggan, Louis	2Lt	25-Aug-14	RM	N/A	CTCRM	EXMOUTH
Duke, Adam J	Lt Cdr	01-Oct-14	ENG	AE	1710 NAS	PORTSMOUTH
Duke, Jonathan A	Lt RN	01-Oct-08	WAR	P SK6	854 NAS	RNAS CULDROSE
Duke, Karen D	Lt Cdr	01-Oct-09	MED	MS	NAVY ICP	PORTSMOUTH
Duke, Lee J	SLt	01-Aug-13	ENG	ME	DCEME SULTAN	HMS SULTAN
Dunbar, Ross	Lt RN	01-Sep-08	ENG	AE	FLEET CSAV	PORTSMOUTH
Duncan, Colin J.	Lt RN	01-Sep-93	WAR	P WILDCAT	WMF 825 SQN HQ	RNAS YEOVILTON
Duncan, Giles S	Maj	01-May-04	RM	GS	45 CDO RM	DUNDEE
Duncan, Ian S	Cdr	30-Jun-05	ENG	MESM	DES COMFLEET	ABBEY WOOD
Duncan, Jeremy	Lt Cdr	01-Oct-01	WAR	P MER	824 SQN	RNAS CULDROSE
Duncan, Kathryn C L	Surg Lt Cdr	03-Apr-13	MED	GDMO	MTM WMO YEOVILTON	RNAS YEOVILTON
Duncan, Ross D	Lt RN	01-Sep-10	ENG	WE	HQ JHC DCOMD	ANDOVER
Duncan, Rowan J	SLt	01-Apr-12	WAR	P UT	MTM 847 SQN MIDDLE WALLOP	STOCKBRIDGE
Dunham, Mark W CBE	Brig	21-Apr-08	RM	HW	MTM 40 CDO RM	TAUNTON
Dunham, Thomas W	Lt	02-Sep-14	RM	GS	42 CDO RM	PLYMOUTH
Dunlop, Joanne	Lt Cdr	30-Mar-07	WAR	INFO OPS	FLEET CMR	PORTSMOUTH
Dunn, Anthony	Lt Cdr	01-Oct-08	WAR	AV	NCHQ CNPERS	PORTSMOUTH
Dunn, Ashley J	Lt RN	03-May-13	MED	MS	INM ALVERSTOKE2	GOSPORT
Dunn, Charles R N	Capt	01-Sep-12	RM	GS	DCSU	RAF HENLOW
Dunn, Gary R	Lt Cdr	01-May-98	ENG	WESM(TWS)	D STRAT PROG	ABBEY WOOD
Dunn, Giles	Lt RN	01-Sep-07	ENG	IS	SVCOPS/DHDOPS/COR	CORSHAM
Dunn, Paul E OBE	Capt RN	15-Jul-14	WAR	SM(CQ)	COMFASFLOT	HELENSBURGH
Dunn, Robert P OBE	Cdr	30-Jun-04	WAR	SM(CQ)	BRNC	BRNC DARTMOUTH
Dunn, Thomas J W	Mid	01-Feb-14	WAR	GSX	BRNC	BRNC DARTMOUTH
Dunning, Stephen T O	Lt RN	01-Oct-08	ENG	TM	DMC DMOC	AYLESBURY
Dunning, Timothy J	Lt RN	01-Nov-13	WAR	O UT	MTM 750 SQN CULDROSE	RNAS CULDROSE
Dunthorne, Matthew S	Lt RN	13-Apr-12	ENG	ME	HMS SULTAN	GOSPORT
Durbin, Philip J	Lt Cdr	01-Oct-14	LOGS	L SM	HMS SOMERSET	
Durbin, William J	Lt RN	01-Sep-10	WAR	GSX	HMS SOMERSET	
Durbridge, Joel J	Capt	01-Sep-10	RM	GS	NCHQ	NCHQ
Durham, Paul C L MBE	Lt Cdr	30-Jun-14	ENG	AE	MTM DEFAC JSCSC	SHRIVENHAM
Durkin, Mark T G	Capt RN	19-Oct-09	WAR	MCD	DCD - MODSAP KSA	RIYADH
Durrant, Frederick	Lt RN	01-Oct-11	WAR	P SK4	CHF - 846	RAF BENSON
Durup, Jason M S	Maj	01-Oct-06	RM	LC	MTM NELSON	HMS NELSON
Duthie, Andrew G	Lt Cdr	01-Oct-12	ENG	AE	771 SQN	RNAS CULDROSE

Name	Substantive Rank	Seniority	Branch	Specialisation	Organisation Name	Location Name
Dutt, James E	Lt RN	08-Dec-14	WAR	SM(X)	MTM MWS DDS	PORTSMOUTH
Dutton, David OBE	Cdre	30-Sep-13	WAR	PWO(C)	FLEET ACOS(RP)	PORTSMOUTH
Dutton, James	Capt	01-Sep-09	RM	GS	NCHQ	PORTSMOUTH
Duxbury, Katrina J	SLt	01-Nov-14	WAR	GSX	MWS COLLINGWOOD	HMS COLLINGWOOD
Duxbury, Timothy P	Mid	01-May-14	WAR	GSX	BRNC	BRNC DARTMOUTH
Dyer, Martin L	Lt RN	01-Sep-11	ENG	MESM	HMS VANGUARD	
Dyer, Shani D	Lt Cdr	01-Oct-14	WAR	PWO(N)	COMUKTG	PLYMOUTH
Dyer, Timothy A	2Lt	01-Sep-11	RM	GS	CTCRM	EXMOUTH
Dyke, Christopher	Cdr	30-Jun-03	WAR	PWO(C)	DI - CA - ASUS	WASHINGTON
Dyke, Kenneth A	Lt Cdr	01-Oct-00	ENG	MESM	DES COMFLEET	THURSO
Dymock, Craig H	SLt	01-Sep-14	ENG	WESM	HMS RALEIGH	TORPOINT
Dymond, Justin R M	Lt Cdr	01-Oct-14	ENG	WE	NC REQUIREMENTS MANAGERS	ABBEY WOOD
Dymott, Benjamin C	Mid	01-May-14	WAR	GSX	BRNC	BRNC DARTMOUTH
Dynes, Oliver G	Lt RN	01-May-13	WAR	SM(X)	HMS VANGUARD	

E

Name	Substantive Rank	Seniority	Branch	Specialisation	Organisation Name	Location Name
Eacock, Jason P	Lt Cdr	01-Oct-11	WAR	PWO	HMS DEFENDER	
Eames, Jonathan R	Surg Lt Cdr	01-Dec-12	MED	GMP	HQBF GIBRALTAR	HMS ROOKE
Earland, Daniel	Mid	17-Nov-14	WAR	GSX	BRNC	BRNC DARTMOUTH
Earle-Payne, Gareth E	Lt RN	01-Sep-03	ENG	MESM	CAPTAIN BASE SAFETY CLYDE	HELENSBURGH
Early, Thomas W	Lt	02-Sep-14	RM	GS	LFSS CDO LOG REGT RM	RMB CHIVENOR
Eason, Samuel	Mid	01-May-14	WAR	GSX	BRNC	BRNC DARTMOUTH
Eastaugh, Andrew C	Cdr	30-Jun-06	ENG	IS (RES)	NC PSYA	PORTSMOUTH
Eastburn, Jonathan L	Lt RN	01-May-13	WAR	GSX	MCM2	PORTSMOUTH
Easterbrook, Christopher	Lt RN	01-Sep-04	WAR	P LYNX	MTM MWS COLLINGWOOD	HMS COLLINGWOOD
Easterbrook, Kevin I E	Cdr	30-Jun-13	ENG	WE	FOST DPORT	PLYMOUTH
Easton, Ben S	Mid	08-Sep-14	WAR	GSX	BRNC	BRNC DARTMOUTH
Eaton, Daniel T	Capt	01-Aug-08	RM	GS	NCHQ	PORTSMOUTH
Eaton, David C	Lt RN	01-Jan-02	WAR	ATC	RNAS CULDROSE	HELSTON
Eaton, Max H	SLt	01-May-12	WAR	GSX	HMS RICHMOND	
Eaton, Paul G	Lt Cdr	01-Jun-94	WAR	HM (M CH)	NATO-ACO-SHAPE	CASTEAU
Eatwell, George E	2Lt	25-Aug-14	RM	N/A	CTCRM	EXMOUTH
Ebbitt, Henry	Lt RN	01-Apr-12	WAR	ATC UT	RAF SHAWBURY	SHREWSBURY
Eccles, Matthew P J	Lt RN	01-Sep-11	WAR	O SKW	854 NAS	RNAS CULDROSE
Eddy, Charlotte R	SLt	01-Mar-14	WAR	GSX	HMS SUTHERLAND	
Eden, Christopher J	Capt	01-Sep-06	RM	P SK4	845 SQN	RNAS YEOVILTON
Eden, Jeremy R H	Lt Cdr	01-Oct-13	MED	MS	NCHQ MEDDIV	PORTSMOUTH
Eden, Philip M	Lt RN	08-Dec-13	ENG	MESM	DCEME SULTAN	HMS SULTAN
Edgar, Iain A M M	Surg Lt Cdr	06-Aug-13	MED	EM	MTM INM ALVERSTOKE	GOSPORT
Edge, John H	Cdr	30-Jun-04	LOGS	L SM	DES COMLAND	BOSCOMBE DOWN
Edmonds, Jon S	Lt RN	01-Jun-10	WAR	HM	MTM MWS COLLINGWOOD	HMS COLLINGWOOD
Edmondson, Simon P	Lt Col	30-Jun-13	RM	P GAZ	DIRECTOR (JW)	NORTHWOOD
Edward, Amanda M	Surg Lt Cdr	07-Aug-07	MED	Anaes	MDHU PORTSMOUTH	PORTSMOUTH
Edward, Gavin	Cdr	30-Jun-11	ENG	WE	HMS BULWARK	
Edwards, Andrew	Lt RN	01-Jan-13	WAR	O UT	RNAS CULDROSE	HELSTON
Edwards, Cassandra J	Lt RN	01-Feb-10	WAR	ATC	MTM WMO YEOVILTON	RNAS YEOVILTON
Edwards, Charles J A	Surg Capt RN	01-Jul-14	MED	Anaes	RCDM	BIRMINGHAM
Edwards, Gareth B	Capt	01-Sep-09	RM	GS	30 CDO IX GP RM	PLYMOUTH
Edwards, Gavin R	Lt RN	01-Sep-07	ENG	AE	DES COMAIR	ABBEY WOOD
Edwards, Helen M	Lt RN	08-Feb-13	WAR	ATC	HMS BULWARK	
Edwards, James	Lt Cdr	01-Oct-11	ENG	TM	GIBRALTAR	HMS ROOKE
Edwards, James E	Lt Cdr	01-Oct-05	ENG	WE	MTM DEFAC JSCSC	SHRIVENHAM
Edwards, John D	Lt RN	01-Sep-09	WAR	P SK4	AACEN	STOCKBRIDGE
Edwards, Luke	Lt RN	01-Sep-08	WAR	P LYNX	NO 3 FTS/UAS - JEFTS	GRANTHAM
Edwards, Neal P	Lt RN	17-Dec-10	LOGS	L	30 CDO IX GP RM	PLYMOUTH
Edwards, Rebecca A	Mid	17-Nov-14	ENG	WE	BRNC	BRNC DARTMOUTH
Edwards, Rhydian O	Lt RN	01-Mar-11	WAR	P UT	MTM 815 SQN YEOVILTON	RNAS YEOVILTON
Edwards, Rhys G	Lt RN	01-Sep-13	ENG	AE	MTM 820 SQN CULDROSE	RNAS CULDROSE
Edwards, Sharon P	Lt Cdr	01-Oct-13	QARNNS	EN (C&S)	MDHU PORTSMOUTH	PORTSMOUTH
Edwards, Steven A	Mid	05-May-14	WAR	P UT	BRNC	BRNC DARTMOUTH
Edwards, Tom H H	Lt Cdr	01-Oct-12	WAR	PWO	HMS ST ALBANS	
Edwards-Bannon, William J J	Lt RN	01-Nov-07	WAR	GSX	MTM MWS COLLINGWOOD	HMS COLLINGWOOD

Name	Substantive Rank	Seniority	Branch	Specialisation	Organisation Name	Location Name
Edwins, Mark R	Lt Cdr	01-Oct-07	ENG	ME	NAVY MCTA	PORTSMOUTH
Eedle, Richard	Lt Cdr	01-Mar-91	WAR	SM(AWC)	MTM NEPTUNE	HMNB CLYDE
Eeles, Thomas D	Lt RN	01-Sep-13	ENG	AE	824 SQN	RNAS CULDROSE
Egeland-Jensen, Finn A MBE	Lt Cdr	01-Apr-95	WAR	PWO(N)	FLEET MARITIME WARFARE	HMS COLLINGWOOD
Eglinton, Benjamin R	Lt RN	01-Sep-13	ENG	ME	HMS ARGYLL	
Elder-Dicker, Nicholas	Lt RN	01-Aug-04	WAR	SM(N)	MWS COLLINGWOOD	HMS COLLINGWOOD
Eldridge, Stephen J	Lt Cdr	01-Oct-10	ENG	TM	DCDS PERS TRG	LONDON
Elford, David G	Cdre	01-Jul-13	ENG	AE	DCTT HQ	HMS SULTAN
Ellerton, Paul	Lt Cdr	01-Oct-10	WAR	P LYNX	NO 3 FTS/UAS - JEFTS	GRANTHAM
Ellicott, Matthew J	Lt RN	01-May-06	WAR	FC	HMS DRAGON	
Elliman, Simon	Cdr	30-Jun-07	WAR	PWO(U)	RN EXCHANGE FRANCE	PARIS
Ellingham, Richard E	RN Chpln	17-Apr-96	Ch S	Chaplain	CHAPLAIN OF THE FLEET	PORTSMOUTH
Elliot-Smith, Teilo J	Lt Cdr	01-Oct-09	WAR	AAWO	COMUKTG	PLYMOUTH
Elliott, David J	Lt RN	01-Oct-10	ENG	TM	NCHQ	PORTSMOUTH
Elliott, Jamie A	Lt Cdr	01-Oct-09	ENG	AE	RNAS YEOVILTON	YEOVILTON
Elliott, Mark F	Maj	01-Oct-09	RM	GS	42 CDO RM	PLYMOUTH
Elliott, Stephen P	Lt Cdr	01-Oct-10	ENG	WE	HMS NORTHUMBERLAND	
Elliott, Timothy D	Lt RN	01-Sep-04	WAR	O LYNX	PJHQ (UK)	NORTHWOOD
Ellis, David F	Lt Cdr	01-Oct-05	ENG	IS	DES COMFLEET	ABBEY WOOD
Ellis, James	Lt Cdr	01-Oct-04	ENG	ME	MTM DEFAC JSCSC	SHRIVENHAM
Ellis, James W	Lt	02-Sep-14	RM	GS	45 CDO RM	DUNDEE
Ellis, Nicholas M	Lt Cdr	18-Jul-97	WAR	N/A	NCHQ CNPERS	PORTSMOUTH
Ellis, William J	Lt RN	09-Apr-12	WAR	P UT	MTM SHAWBURY	RAF SHAWBURY
Ellison, Peter J P	Lt RN	01-Jan-06	WAR	PWO	HMS ST ALBANS	
Elmer, Timothy B	Surg Cdr (D)	30-Jun-02	DENTAL	DENTAL CONS	SGD - DSC	LICHFIELD
Elsey, David C	Lt RN	01-Feb-14	LOGS	L	HMS SOMERSET	
Elston, Luke R	Lt RN	13-Apr-12	ENG	AE	CHF(MERLIN)	RAF BENSON
Elvy, Susan D	Lt RN	01-Jun-10	LOGS	L	ESG EJSU SHAPE	MONS (CASTEAU)
Embleton, Alison	Lt RN	09-Jun-06	QARNNS	OT	RCDM	BIRMINGHAM
Emery, Andrew B	Mid	17-Nov-14	WAR	P UT	BRNC	BRNC DARTMOUTH
Emery, Christian S	Lt RN	01-May-03	ENG	WE	MCM1	HMNB CLYDE
Emery, David G	Lt RN	01-Apr-11	WAR	O MER	814 SQN	RNAS CULDROSE
Emmerson, David I	Lt RN	01-Nov-14	WAR	SM(X)	MWS COLLINGWOOD	HMS COLLINGWOOD
Emmett, Robert C	Mid	07-May-14	WAR	P UT	BRNC	BRNC DARTMOUTH
Emptage, Christopher J	Maj	01-Oct-14	RM	GS	COMUKAMPHIBFOR	PORTSMOUTH
Emptage, Daniel J	SLt	01-Aug-13	ENG	AE	RNAS CULDROSE	HELSTON
Emptage, Michael A	Lt RN	01-Sep-10	ENG	AE	LHF 815 SQN HQ	RNAS YEOVILTON
Enever, Shaun A	Lt Cdr	01-Oct-08	WAR	O LYNX	D STRAT PROG	ABBEY WOOD
England, Philip M	Lt Cdr	01-Oct-11	ENG	TM	RNLA	BRNC DARTMOUTH
Entwisle, William N OBE MVO	Cdre	30-Apr-13	WAR	P LYNX	MSP	LONDON
Epps, Matthew	Lt RN	17-Jul-99	ENG	IS	CIO-DSAS	CORSHAM
Erhahiemen, Peter E	Lt RN	01-May-07	LOGS	L	FLEET SPT LOGS INFRA	PORTSMOUTH
Errington, Ridley J B	Lt Cdr	01-Oct-14	ENG	ME	1 ASSLT GP RM	PLYMOUTH
Erskine, Dominic S	Capt	21-Mar-13	RM	GS	NCHQ	PORTSMOUTH
Erskine, Peter	Capt RN	08-Jul-08	ENG	ME	LST AUSTRALIA	AUSTRALIA
Esbensen, Kristoffer P	Lt RN	01-Apr-12	LOGS	L	HMS DEFENDER	
Essenhigh, Angus N P	Cdr	30-Jun-11	WAR	AAWO	IPP	LONDON
Essenhigh, Sir Nigel (Richard) GCB DL	Adm	11-Sep-98				
Ethell, David R	Maj	01-Oct-03	RM	LC	FLEET COMOPS NWD	NORTHWOOD
Etheridge, Anthony C	Lt RN	01-Sep-12	ENG	MESM	HMS TRIUMPH	
Evangelista, Paul G	Lt RN	30-Jul-10	MED	MS	PCRF	RFA ARGUS
Evans, Alexandra C	Mid	17-Nov-14	WAR	HM	BRNC	BRNC DARTMOUTH
Evans, Benjimin G	Lt Cdr	01-Oct-13	WAR	PWO	FLEET COMOPS NWD	NORTHWOOD
Evans, Charles A	Cdr	30-Jun-09	LOGS	L SM	COMDEVFLOT	PLYMOUTH
Evans, Charlotte V	Surg Lt Cdr	01-Aug-12	MED	Psych	MTM INM ALVERSTOKE	GOSPORT
Evans, Christian P	Lt RN	01-Jan-03	ENG	TM	DEF CBRN CENTRE - DNBC	SALISBURY
Evans, Christopher A	Lt RN	01-May-03	WAR	SM(AWC)	MTM DEFAC JSCSC	SHRIVENHAM
Evans, Christopher C	Lt Cdr	01-Oct-11	ENG	MESM	HMS VIGILANT	
Evans, David M M	Brig	03-Sep-13	RM	C	FLEET CAP IS	PORTSMOUTH
Evans, Edward M	Cdr	30-Jun-06	LOGS	L SM	NCHQ CNPERS	PORTSMOUTH
Evans, Gareth C	Surg Cdr	13-Dec-11	MED	GMP	DPHC SCOTLAND & NI	ST ANDREWS
Evans, Giles	Lt Cdr	01-Oct-07	WAR	SM(AWC)	RNSMS	HMS RALEIGH

Name	Substantive Rank	Seniority	Branch	Specialisation	Organisation Name	Location Name
Evans, Helen J	Surg Lt Cdr	01-Aug-10	MED	GMP	MTM NELSON	HMS NELSON
Evans, Joshua J	Lt RN	01-Apr-12	ENG	TM	NCHQ CNPERS (HRTSG)	PORTSMOUTH
Evans, Laura	SLt	01-May-13	WAR	REG	NPM EASTERN	HMS NELSON
Evans, Laura-Jane	Lt RN	01-Sep-02	WAR	O SKW	MTM 824 SQN CULDROSE	RNAS CULDROSE
Evans, Lee S	Lt Cdr	01-Oct-09	WAR	P LYNX	AWC	BOSCOMBE DOWN
Evans, Marc D	Cdr	30-Jun-07	LOGS	L	PJHQ (UK)	NORTHWOOD
Evans, Martin J	Cdr	30-Jun-06	WAR	PWO(U)	HMS EXCELLENT	PORTSMOUTH
Evans, Martin L	RN Chpln	01-Sep-98	Ch S	Chaplain	RNAS YEOVILTON	YEOVILTON
Evans, Peter A	Lt RN	01-May-07	WAR	PWO	HMS DAUNTLESS	
Evans, Robert	Lt Cdr	01-Oct-11	ENG	WE	COMDEVFLOT	PLYMOUTH
Evans, Robert G	Lt Cdr	01-Oct-14	ENG	AE	DES COMAIR	ABBEY WOOD
Evans, Russell F	Lt RN	31-Jul-09	ENG	AE	MASF	RNAS CULDROSE
Evans, Thomas W	Lt RN	01-Sep-06	Ch S	L BAR SM	NATO ACO	NORTHWOOD
Evans, William Q F	Capt RN	08-Jul-13	WAR	PWO(N)	ACNS	HMS NELSON
Evans-Jones, Thomas M	Maj	01-Oct-12	RM	GS	COMUKAMPHIBFOR	PORTSMOUTH
Everard, Paul J	Lt Cdr	01-Oct-14	WAR	C	PJHQ (UK)	NORTHWOOD
Evered, Jonathan F	Lt RN	01-May-06	WAR	P SK4	845 SQN	RNAS YEOVILTON
Everest, Becky	Lt RN	01-May-07	ENG	TM	MTM FLEET HQ	PORTSMOUTH
Everett, Oliver	Lt RN	01-Jun-08	WAR	P SK4	CHFHQ	RNAS YEOVILTON
Evershed, Marcus C	Surg Capt RN	01-Mar-11	MED	GMP (C&S)	DPHC SOUTH WEST REG HQ	HMS DRAKE
Evershed, Rachael E F	Surg Lt Cdr	07-Aug-07	MED	GMP	DPHC SOUTH	HMS NELSON
Every, Michael J D	Lt RN	01-Feb-14	WAR	SM(X)	HMS TORBAY	
Evison, Toby	Lt Cdr	06-Nov-06	ENG	IS	FLEET CAP IS	PORTSMOUTH
Ewen, Andrew P	Cdr	30-Jun-06	ENG	AE	HQ CFC(A)	AFGHANISTAN KABUL
Ewence, Martin W OBE	Cdr	30-Jun-98	WAR	PWO(A)	NCHQ CNPS	PORTSMOUTH
Exworthy, Damian A G MBE	Cdr	30-Jun-13	LOGS	L	FMC NAVY	LONDON
Eyers, Dale S	Lt RN	01-Apr-14	WAR	O SKW	854 NAS	RNAS CULDROSE

F

Name	Substantive Rank	Seniority	Branch	Specialisation	Organisation Name	Location Name
Fabik, Andre N	Lt RN	01-May-01	WAR	HM(AS)	FOST HM	HMS DRAKE
Fagan, Louis Vincent A	Lt RN	01-Mar-11	LOGS	L	AWC	EDWARDS AFB
Fairbairn, Oliver	Lt RN	07-Jun-11	ENG	ME	HMS OCEAN	
Fairweather, Donell	Lt RN	07-Aug-13	WAR	O UT	MTM SHAWBURY	RAF SHAWBURY
Falconer, Paul	Lt RN	24-Oct-08	MED	MS(CDO)	DMS WHITTINGTON	LICHFIELD
Falk, Benedict H G	Cdr	30-Jun-02	WAR	PWO(A)	NATO - BRUSSELS	BRUSSELS
Falla, Lindsay	Surg Lt Cdr (D)	27-Jun-08	DENTAL	GDP	MTM INM ALVERSTOKE	GOSPORT
Fallesen, Lloyd A	Capt	31-Aug-14	RM	GS	29 CDO REGT	PLYMOUTH
Fallows, Lee D	Lt RN	01-Apr-13	WAR	GSX	HMS BULWARK	
Fancy, Robert Obe	Capt RN	01-Mar-10	WAR	SM(CQ)	COMDEVFLOT	PLYMOUTH
Fane-Bailey, Verity M	Lt RN	01-Jun-09	LOGS	L	DCDS PERS - SPA	RAF NORTHOLT
Fanshawe, Edward	Lt Cdr	01-Oct-13	ENG	WESM(TWS)	DEFENCE ACADEMY	SHRIVENHAM
Farley, Emma L	Lt RN	01-Nov-14	WAR	HM	MWS COLLINGWOOD	HMS COLLINGWOOD
Farmer, Gary G	Lt RN	28-Jun-92	WAR	AW (RES)	DNR RCHQ NORTH	HMS CALEDONIA
Farquharson, Craig I	Lt RN	01-Jan-11	WAR	O LYNX	LHF 815 SQN	RNAS YEOVILTON
Farr, Ian R	Lt RN	16-Aug-00	WAR	P MER	MTM DEFAC JSCSC	SHRIVENHAM
Farrage, Michael E CBE	Cdre	07-Nov-11	ENG	TM	NCHQ CNPERS	PORTSMOUTH
Farrant, James D	Lt Cdr	01-Oct-09	LOGS	L BAR	MTM DEFENCE ACADEMY	SHRIVENHAM
Farrant, Sam	Lt RN	01-Nov-05	ENG	WE	COMMANDER OP TRAINING	HMS COLLINGWOOD
Farrington, Richard CBE	Cdre	26-Mar-13	WAR	PWO(C)	COMDEVFLOT	PLYMOUTH
Farthing, Findlay C	Capt	20-Jul-07	RM	SCC	NCHQ	PORTSMOUTH
Faulkner, Julian J	Mid	08-Sep-14	ENG	AE	BRNC	BRNC DARTMOUTH
Faulkner, Sally E	Lt RN	01-Jan-08	LOGS	L BAR	MTM NORTHWOOD HQ	NORTHWOOD
Faulkner, Simon	Lt RN	01-Jan-08	ENG	WESM(SWS)	FLEET COMOPS NWD	NORTHWOOD
Faulkner, Stuart	Lt Cdr	01-Oct-10	ENG	AE	829 SQN	RNAS CULDROSE
Fawcett, Benjamin E	Lt RN	01-Nov-10	WAR	INT	COMUKTG	PLYMOUTH
Fawcett, Stuart	SLt	04-Dec-12	WAR	GSX	MWS COLLINGWOOD	HMS COLLINGWOOD
Faye, Matthew E	Lt Cdr	01-Oct-14	MED	MS	DMS WHITTINGTON	LICHFIELD
Fayers, Samuel R	Lt RN	01-Sep-14	ENG	MESM	DCEME SULTAN	HMS SULTAN
Fear, Richard K	Cdr	30-Jun-99	ENG	WESM(TWS)	NATO - BRUSSELS	BRUSSELS
Fearn, Samuel R	Maj	01-Oct-13	RM	GS	45 CDO RM	DUNDEE
Fearon, David J	Lt Cdr	01-Oct-09	ENG	WE	FOST DPORT	PLYMOUTH
Feasey, Caroline	Lt Cdr	01-Oct-14	LOGS	L	HMS RALEIGH	TORPOINT

Name	Substantive Rank	Seniority	Branch	Specialisation	Organisation Name	Location Name
Feasey, Ian D	Lt Cdr	01-Oct-08	WAR	PWO	FOST DPORT	PLYMOUTH
Feasey, James A	Capt	01-Sep-11	RM	GS	OCLC BIRMINGHAM	BIRMINGHAM
Febbrarro, Luke N	Lt RN	01-Sep-11	WAR	SM(X)	HMS MERSEY	
Feeney, Matthew B	Lt Cdr	01-Apr-08	WAR	INT	NATO-ACO-LC	ISTANBUL
Fellows, Christopher R	Lt RN	01-Jan-07	WAR	O SKW	AWC	BOSCOMBE DOWN
Felton, Jonathan E J	Capt	01-Sep-10	RM	GS	CTCRM	EXMOUTH
Fenn, Christopher J	SLt	01-Feb-14	LOGS	L	LO HMS NEPTUNE	HMNB CLYDE
Fenwick, Steven G	Lt RN	01-Sep-07	ENG	WE	CIO-SPP	LONDON
Fergus-Hunt, Gregory	Lt RN	07-Dec-07	LOGS	L	MTM DRAKE	HMS DRAKE
Ferguson, Calum	Lt RN	01-Jan-11	WAR	GSX	DHU	CHICKSANDS
Ferguson, Simon	Lt RN	08-Jul-12	WAR	GSX	MCM2	PORTSMOUTH
Fergusson, Andrew C	Lt Col	30-Jun-14	RM	GS	DEFENCE ACADEMY	SHRIVENHAM
Fergusson, Iain B	Lt Cdr	01-Oct-12	WAR	SM(AWC)	HMS VIGILANT	
Fergusson, Nigel A	Cdr	30-Jun-10	ENG	WE	FLEET ACOS(RP)	PORTSMOUTH
Ferns, Timothy D	Cdr	30-Jun-07	LOGS	L	HQBF GIBRALTAR	HMS ROOKE
Ferris, Daniel P S	Cdr	30-Jun-04	ENG	WE	FMC JOINT	LONDON
Fickling, James W A	Lt Cdr	01-Oct-12	ENG	WE	DES COMFLEET	ABBEY WOOD
Fiddock, Matthew L	Lt Cdr	01-Oct-12	ENG	ME	HMS KENT	
Fidler, John Q	Maj	01-Oct-09	RM	LC	40 CDO RM	TAUNTON
Fielder, Andrew J	Lt RN	01-Sep-08	ENG	AE	DES COMAIR	ABBEY WOOD
Fields, David	Cdr	30-Jun-03	WAR	PWO(A)	SERV ATTACHE/ADVISER	MOSCOW
Fields, Samuel W R	Lt RN	01-Nov-13	WAR	GSX	HMS DARING	
Fieldsend, Mark	Cdr	30-Jun-03	ENG	ME	RN EXCHANGE FRANCE	PARIS
Figgins, Adam A	SLt	01-Jul-14	WAR	O UT	MTM RAF CRANWELL	RAFC CRANWELL
Filewod, Roger B	Lt RN	01-Aug-08	WAR	GSX	HMS SEVERN	
Filio, Andrew P	Lt RN	01-May-13	WAR	SM(X)	HMS VIGILANT	
Fillmore, Guy M	Capt	01-Sep-12	RM	GS	45 CDO RM	DUNDEE
Fillmore, Raymond J	Lt Cdr	01-Oct-10	WAR	SM(CQ)	FLEET COMOPS NWD	NORTHWOOD
Filshie, Sarah J	Lt Cdr	01-Oct-13	WAR	ATC	HMS OCEAN	
Filtness, David M	Cdr	30-Jun-14	WAR	SM(CQ)	HMS TRIUMPH	
Fincher, Kevin J	Cdr	30-Jun-10	WAR	PWO(C)	JSSU CH - HQ	CHELTENHAM
Findlay, Hamish R	Lt RN	01-Oct-12	WAR	P SK4	857 NAS	RNAS CULDROSE
Finn, Ivan R	Capt RN	03-Jul-14	ENG	AE	FLEET CSAV	PORTSMOUTH
Finn, James S	Lt RN	01-Jan-01	WAR	P MER	MTM WMO YEOVILTON	RNAS YEOVILTON
Finn, Stuart A	Cdr	30-Jun-14	WAR	O MER	814 SQN	RNAS CULDROSE
Finn, Tristan A	Maj	01-Oct-13	RM	MLDR	CTCRM	EXMOUTH
Finnie, Anthony M	Lt RN	01-Jan-12	WAR	O	MTM 815 SQN YEOVILTON	RNAS YEOVILTON
Finnigan, Sebastian	Lt RN	01-Mar-13	ENG	MESM	HMS VANGUARD	
Firth, John S	Lt RN	01-May-00	WAR	PWO(A)	UKMARBATSTAFF	PORTSMOUTH
Firth, Nigel R	Lt Cdr	01-Mar-95	WAR	SM(CQ)	D STRAT PROG	ABBEY WOOD
Fisher, Aaron G	Lt Col	30-Jun-13	RM	LC	CIO-J6	LONDON
Fisher, Cameron S	SLt	01-Sep-14	WAR	GSX	HMS BULWARK	
Fisher, Clayton R A	Capt RN	16-Jul-12	LOGS	L	CDP PERS TRG	LONDON
Fisher, Daniel A MC	Capt	30-Mar-12	RM	GS	NCHQ	
Fisher, Luke I L	SLt	01-May-13	WAR	GSX	HMS MONMOUTH	
Fisher, Mark A	SLt	01-Aug-13	ENG	AE	RNAS YEOVILTON	YEOVILTON
Fitter, Ian S T	Cdr	30-Jun-02	WAR	O SK6	FLEET AV VL	RNAS YEOVILTON
Fitton, Daniel	Lt RN	01-Sep-10	ENG	MESM	MTM DCEME SULTAN	HMS SULTAN
Fitzgibbon, John P	Lt RN	01-Jan-07	WAR	GSX	BRNC	BRNC DARTMOUTH
Fitzpatrick, John A J	Lt Cdr	01-Jul-05	WAR	O LYNX	FLEET CSAV	PORTSMOUTH
Fitzpatrick, Michael J	Lt RN	01-Jul-09	ENG	WESM(TWS)	NAVY MCTA	PORTSMOUTH
Fitzpatrick, Neil	Lt Cdr	01-Oct-12	WAR	PWO	MWS COLLINGWOOD	HMS COLLINGWOOD
Fitzpatrick, Paul S	Maj	01-Oct-06	RM	SCC	NCHQ CNPERS	PORTSMOUTH
Fitzsimmons, Mark B	Cdr	30-Jun-09	WAR	PWO(A)	UKTI - DSO	LONDON
Flaherty, Christopher L	Lt Cdr	01-Oct-12	WAR	MCD	CSF FASLANE	HMNB CLYDE
Flaherty, Thomas P	Mid	17-Nov-14	WAR	GSX	BRNC	BRNC DARTMOUTH
Flanagan, Mark	SLt	01-Aug-13	ENG	ME	FLEET CAP SSM	PORTSMOUTH
Flannagan, Bryan A	Lt RN	01-Sep-13	WAR	SM(X)	HMS VICTORIOUS	
Flannagan, Donna L	Lt Cdr	01-Oct-13	LOGS	L	NCHQ CNPERS	PORTSMOUTH
Flannigan, Aiden	Lt Cdr	01-Oct-14	ENG	MESM	HMS VIGILANT	
Flatman, Timothy D	Lt Cdr	01-Oct-09	WAR	P FW	736 NAS	RNAS CULDROSE
Flatt, Liam B	Lt RN	01-Sep-06	WAR		UK MCC	BAHRAIN

Name	Substantive Rank	Seniority	Branch	Specialisation	Organisation Name	Location Name
Flegg, Kirsty G	Lt Cdr	01-Sep-08	LOGS	L	HMS DEFENDER	
Flegg, Matthew J	Lt Cdr	01-Oct-08	ENG	AE	DES COMJE	YEOVIL
Flegg, William J	Lt RN	01-Nov-06	ENG	TM	NCHQ CNPERS (HRTSG)	PORTSMOUTH
Fleming, Caroline S E	Lt Cdr	01-Oct-14	LOGS	L BAR	NCHQ - CNLS	PLYMOUTH
Fleming, David P	Lt RN	01-Sep-04	WAR	P LYNX	LHF 815 SQN	RNAS YEOVILTON
Fleming, Kevin P	Capt RN	16-May-14	WAR	O LYNX	DEFENCE ACADEMY	SHRIVENHAM
Fleming, Ruth E	Lt Cdr	01-Oct-09	LOGS	L	RNAS YEOVILTON	YEOVILTON
Fletcher, Aled T L	Mid	01-Feb-14	WAR	ATC UT	BRNC	BRNC DARTMOUTH
Fletcher, Andrew S	Lt RN	01-Sep-06	WAR	GSX	MTM MWS COLLINGWOOD	HMS COLLINGWOOD
Fletcher, Christopher P	Lt RN	17-Dec-10	ENG	MESM	FWO FASLANE SEA	HELENSBURGH
Fletcher, Jonathan H G	Lt Cdr	01-Oct-14	WAR	PWO	HMS OCEAN	
Fletcher, Richard	Lt Cdr	01-Oct-14	LOGS	L (RES)	DMLS	HMS RALEIGH
Flewitt, Craig	Capt	01-Sep-12	RM	GS	JFACTSU LEEMING	NORTHALLERTON
Flint, Grahame	Lt RN	01-Sep-07	WAR	FC	FLEET SNMG RN NATO SUP	PORTSMOUTH
Flint, Thomas A	SLt	24-Jan-12	ENG	WESM	HMS ASTUTE	
Flitcroft, Michael	Lt RN	01-Jul-04	ENG	WESM(TWS)	RNSMS	HMS RALEIGH
Flood, Fredrick	Mid	17-Nov-14	ENG	WE	BRNC	BRNC DARTMOUTH
Flower, Neil P	Capt	01-Apr-03	RM	P LYN7	ARF HQ	RNAS YEOVILTON
Flowers, David J	Lt RN	01-Sep-11	ENG	MESM	HMS VICTORIOUS	
Floyd, Robert E	Lt RN	01-Jan-03	ENG	TM	FLEET FOST ACOS(Trg)	ABBEY WOOD
Floyer, Hugo G	Lt RN	01-Nov-07	WAR	GSX	HMS SMITER	OXFORD
Flynn, Andrew	Cdr	30-Jun-14	ENG	AE	MAA	ABBEY WOOD
Flynn, Christopher	Lt RN	01-Jan-10	WAR	O SKW	GANNET SAR FLT	HMS GANNET
Flynn, Luke M	SLt	11-Apr-12	WAR	SM(X)	HMS ENTERPRISE	
Flynn, Michael T	Cdr	30-Jun-03	LOGS	L	DCDS PERS TRG	LONDON
Flynn, Simon J	Lt Cdr	01-Oct-08	WAR	O SKW	RNAS CULDROSE	HELSTON
Fogell, Andrew D	Cdr	30-Jun-11	LOGS	L SM	RNAS CULDROSE	HELSTON
Foley, Thomas R	Lt RN	01-Sep-12	WAR	GSX	MWS COLLINGWOOD	HMS COLLINGWOOD
Follington, Daniel C	Capt RN	06-Oct-14	MED	MS	PCRF	RFA ARGUS
Fomes, Christopher J H	Maj	01-Oct-09	RM	LC	1 ASSLT GP RM	PLYMOUTH
Fooks-Bale, Matthew E	Lt Cdr	01-Oct-14	WAR	P FW	AWC	EDWARDS AFB
Foote, Andrew S	Lt Cdr	01-Oct-09	ENG	ME	NCHQ CNPS	PORTSMOUTH
Forbes, Angela J	Lt Cdr	01-Oct-09	LOGS	L BAR	HMS KENT	
Forbes, Duncan	Lt Col	30-Jun-14	RM	GS	FMC JOINT	LONDON
Forbes, Simon P	Lt RN	01-Feb-14	ENG	WESM	HMS TRENCHANT	
Forbes, Thomas E	Lt RN	01-Sep-12	WAR	GSX	MCM2	PORTSMOUTH
Force, Rory J	Lt RN	01-Mar-14	ENG	MESM	DCEME SULTAN	HMS SULTAN
Ford, Brendan R	Lt RN	01-May-10	ENG	TM	40 CDO RM	TAUNTON
Ford, Christopher R C	Lt RN	01-Apr-12	WAR	O UT	MTM 824 SQN CULDROSE	RNAS CULDROSE
Ford, Jonathan R	Lt RN	01-Aug-09	WAR	ATC	MTM NELSON	HMS NELSON
Ford, Martin J AFC	Lt Cdr	05-Aug-98	WAR	O SK6	GANNET SAR FLT	HMS GANNET
Forde, Rupert J M	Lt RN	01-Jan-15	WAR	GSX	MTM MWS DDS	PORTSMOUTH
Fordham, Phillip J P	SLt	01-Apr-12	WAR	GSX	MCM1	FASLANE
Foreman, John L R	Cdr	30-Jun-01	WAR	PWO(C)	NATO-ACO-JFC HQ	NAPLES
Foreman, Louisa	Lt RN	01-Jun-10	WAR	GSX	MTM NELSON	HMS NELSON
Foreman, Simon M	Cdr	30-Jun-14	ENG	WE	DES COMLAND	ABBEY WOOD
Forer, Duncan A	Cdr	30-Jun-05	ENG	TM	HMS RALEIGH	TORPOINT
Forer, Jonathon T	SLt	01-Jul-14	WAR	GSX	HMS DAUNTLESS	
Forge, Stephen	Lt Cdr	01-Oct-06	LOGS	L	FLEET SPT LOGS INFRA	PORTSMOUTH
Forrest, Adam	Lt RN	13-Jul-12	WAR	C	FLEET CAP IS	PORTSMOUTH
Forrest, David J	Lt RN	01-Jan-08	WAR	P FW	MTM DEFAC JSCSC	SHRIVENHAM
Forrest, Paul M	Maj	01-Oct-12	RM	GS	FLEET COMOPS NWD	NORTHWOOD
Forrester, Michael A	Lt RN	01-Sep-08	ENG	MESM	BRNC	BRNC DARTMOUTH
Forse, Ryan M	Lt RN	01-Sep-14	ENG	WE	MTM NELSON	HMS NELSON
Forster, Christopher R	SLt	14-Dec-13	WAR	GSX	MCM1	FASLANE
Forster, Helen	Lt RN	01-Apr-11	ENG	AE	RNAS CULDROSE	HELSTON
Forster, Robin M	Lt Col	30-Jun-05	RM	GS	CTCRM	EXMOUTH
Forster, Thomas W	Lt RN	01-Apr-14	WAR	GSX	HMS DAUNTLESS	
Forsyth, Adam L	Lt RN	01-Sep-08	ENG	AE	MOD CNS/ACNS	RNAS YEOVILTON
Fortescue, Robert	Cdr	30-Jun-07	WAR	O LYNX	NATO-ACT-HQ	BRUSSELS
Foster, Adrian A	Capt	16-Apr-10	RM	MLDR (SCC)	RMR BRISTOL	BRISTOL
Foster, Alan J	Lt Cdr	01-Oct-11	ENG	MESM	MTM DRAKE	HMS DRAKE

Name	Substantive Rank	Seniority	Branch	Specialisation	Organisation Name	Location Name
Foster, Benjamin	Lt Col	30-Jun-13	RM	GS	MOD DEFENCE STAFF	LONDON
Foster, Darryl E	Lt	01-Jul-13	RM	SCC	42 CDO RM	PLYMOUTH
Foster, Matthew P	SLt	01-Sep-14	WAR	GSX	HMS DARING	
Foster, Nicholas P	Lt Cdr	01-Oct-05	WAR	HM (M CH)	HMS ENTERPRISE	
Foster, Nicholas P	Lt Col	30-Jun-14	RM	GS	OPS DIR	LONDON
Foster, Sebastian J T	Surg Lt RN	04-Aug-10	MED	GDMO	MTM INM ALVERSTOKE	GOSPORT
Fotherby, Stephen J	Mid	17-Nov-14	LOGS	L	BRNC	BRNC DARTMOUTH
Foulger, Thomas E	Surg Cdr (D)	01-Jul-14	DENTAL	GDP	HMS SULTAN	GOSPORT
Foulis, Niall D A	Lt Cdr	01-Mar-03	WAR	HM	RNAS YEOVILTON	YEOVILTON
Fowle, Laura C	Lt RN	01-Sep-04	WAR	INT	FLEET COMOPS NWD	RNAS CULDROSE
Fowler, Gareth S	Lt RN	15-Apr-11	ENG	ME	COMPORFLOT	PORTSMOUTH
Fowler, James E	Lt Cdr	01-Oct-12	MED	MS(CDO)	NCHQ MEDDIV	PORTSMOUTH
Fowler, Remington	Lt RN	01-Sep-06	ENG	WESM(SWS)	CBRN POL	LONDON
Fox, Christopher J	Lt RN	01-Oct-09	WAR	GSX	BRNC	BRNC DARTMOUTH
Fox, David J	Lt Cdr	01-Oct-12	WAR	SM(CQ)	HMS RALEIGH	TORPOINT
Fox, Owen G	SLt	01-Apr-12	WAR	SM(X)	HMS VENGEANCE	
Fox, Trefor M	Lt Cdr	01-Oct-06	WAR	HM (H CH)	DGC(AE) OPS & PLANS	FELTHAM
Fradley, Nicola A	Lt RN	01-Nov-14	WAR	GSX	MCM1	FASLANE
Frame, Wendy	Lt RN	13-Apr-12	ENG	ME	DES COMFLEET	ABBEY WOOD
Frampton, Charles	Lt RN	01-Sep-09	WAR	INT	FLEET COMOPS NWD	NORTHWOOD
Francis, James S	RN Chpln	01-Oct-07	Ch S	Chaplain	HMS NELSON	PORTSMOUTH
Francis, Steven	Col	14-Feb-11	RM	GS	SERV ATTACHE/ADVISER	PAKISTAN
Frankham, Peter J	Cdr	31-Dec-00	ENG	WE	NATO-ACT-JWC	STAVANGER
Franklin, Benjamin J	Cdr	30-Jun-09	WAR	O MER	RNAS CULDROSE	HELSTON
Franklin, Joseph P M	Lt	02-Sep-14	RM	GS	45 CDO RM	DUNDEE
Franks, Christopher S	Lt Cdr	01-Feb-98	ENG	WESM(TWS)	NUCLEAR CAPABILITY	LONDON
Fraser, Callum J	Lt RN	24-Jul-14	ENG	WESM	HMS VICTORIOUS	
Fraser, Gordon A	Lt RN	11-Dec-09	WAR	ATC	RNAS YEOVILTON	YEOVILTON
Fraser, Graeme W	Lt Col	30-Jun-09	RM	LC	JFHQ	NORTHWOOD
Fraser, Ian D	Lt Cdr	01-Jul-02	ENG	AE	NATO-ACT-JWC	STAVANGER
Fraser, Ian E	Lt Cdr	01-Oct-07	WAR	P MER	NCHQ CNPERS	PORTSMOUTH
Fraser, James M	Lt RN	01-Feb-03	WAR	P LYNX	LOANS TO OTHER GOVTS	OMAN
Fraser, Michael	Lt RN	01-Sep-01	WAR	HM(AS)	HMS ECHO	
Fraser, Patrick	Lt Cdr	01-Oct-03	ENG	AE	NATO-ACO-JFC HQ	NAPLES
Fraser, Simon A	Lt RN	01-Sep-13	ENG	WE	HMS PORTLAND	
Fraser, Timothy P	R Adm	16-Jan-12	WAR	PWO(N)	ACDS	LONDON
Fraser-Shaw, Christopher J	Mid	08-Sep-14	WAR	SM(X)	BRNC	BRNC DARTMOUTH
Fraser-Shaw, Dominic A J	SLt	01-Nov-14	LOGS	L	HMS OCEAN	
Fraser-Smith, Sharron A	Lt Cdr	01-Oct-11	QARNNS	T&O	MDHU DERRIFORD	PLYMOUTH
Frater, Rebecca S	Lt Cdr	01-Oct-10	WAR	P LYNX	DEF HELI FLYING SCH	SHREWSBURY
Fredrickson, Charlotte A	Lt RN	01-Sep-06	WAR	O SKW	UKMARBATSTAFF	PLYMOUTH
Free, Andrew S	Lt Cdr	01-Oct-08	ENG	IS	NCHQ CNPS	PORTSMOUTH
Freeman, Abigail A	Mid	17-Nov-14	ENG	TM	BRNC	BRNC DARTMOUTH
Freeman, David R	Cdr	30-Jun-08	WAR	O LYNX	HMS TEMERAIRE	PORTSMOUTH
Freeman, Edmund M R	Lt Cdr	01-Oct-14	WAR	PWO	HMS DRAGON	
Freeman, Mark E	Maj	01-Sep-96	RM	GS	LOAN DSTL	FAREHAM
Freeman, Martin J	Lt Cdr	01-Oct-07	ENG	MESM	HMS AUDACIOUS	
Freeman, Matthew J	Lt RN	01-Mar-14	ENG	WE	MTM FLEET HQ	PORTSMOUTH
Freeman, Nicholas H B	Capt	01-Sep-12	RM	GS	HQ 3 CDO BDE RM	PLYMOUTH
French, Jeremy	Lt Cdr	01-Oct-12	WAR	P SK4	RN EXCHANGE AUSTRALIA	CANBERRA
French, Matthew P	SLt	01-Apr-12	WAR	GSX	MCM1	FASLANE
French, Megan	Surg Lt RN	06-Aug-14	MED	Medical	BLAKE	BRNC DARTMOUTH
French, Paul	Lt Cdr	01-Oct-09	ENG	AE	FLEET CSAV	YEOVIL
French, Rebecca	Lt RN	01-Feb-10	LOGS	L	DES COMLAND	ABBEY WOOD
French, Sophie R	SLt	08-Dec-11	WAR	P UT	RNAS YEOVILTON	YEOVILTON
French, Stephen G	2Lt	25-Aug-14	RM	N/A	CTCRM	EXMOUTH
Freshwater, Dennis A	Surg Cdr	09-Aug-08	MED	Med	RCDM	BIRMINGHAM
Fries, Charles A	Surg Lt Cdr	02-Feb-10	MED	BPS	MTM INM ALVERSTOKE	GOSPORT
Frith, Adele M	Lt Cdr	01-Oct-13	LOGS	L BAR	HMS DUNCAN	
Frith, Ian M	SLt	01-Oct-13	ENG	WE	MWS COLLINGWOOD	HMS COLLINGWOOD
Frost, Laurence J	Lt Cdr	01-Oct-14	ENG	WE	DI - CA	LONDON
Frost, Mark A	Lt Cdr	01-Jan-03	ENG	TM	FLEET FOST ACOS(Trg)	PORTSMOUTH

Name	Substantive Rank	Seniority	Branch	Specialisation	Organisation Name	Location Name
Frost, Oliver A J	Lt	01-Mar-14	RM	GS	45 CDO RM	DUNDEE
Frost, Robert W	Lt RN	01-Oct-09	WAR	GSX	FOST DPORT	PLYMOUTH
Frost, Timothy S	Lt RN	01-May-05	WAR	P SK4	MTM CHF (MERLIN)	RAF BENSON
Frost-Pennington, Fraser R	2Lt	25-Aug-14	RM	N/A	CTCRM	EXMOUTH
Fry, Jonathan M S	Cdre	21-Jan-14	ENG	ME	DCDS PERS TRG	LONDON
Fry, Rebecca L	Surg Lt Cdr	06-Aug-13	MED	Anaes	MTM INM ALVERSTOKE	GOSPORT
Fry, Rohan A	Lt	02-Sep-14	RM	GS	LFSS CDO LOG REGT RM	RMB CHIVENOR
Fry, Stephen P	Surg Lt Cdr	01-May-10	MED	GMP	MTM INM ALVERSTOKE	GOSPORT
Fryer, Adrian C	Cdr	30-Jun-11	WAR	AAWO	HMS DAUNTLESS	
Fryer, Nicholas B	SLt	01-Nov-14	LOGS	L	HMS LANCASTER	
Fulker, Edward P	Lt RN	20-Dec-10	WAR	SM(X)	HMS TORBAY	
Full, Richard J	Lt Cdr	01-Oct-10	WAR	O SKW	849 SQN	RNAS CULDROSE
Fuller, Charles	Lt Cdr	01-Oct-07	WAR	P SK6	GANNET SAR FLT	HMS GANNET
Fuller, Emma J	Lt Cdr	01-Oct-07	LOGS	L	DBS MIL PERS	GLASGOW
Fuller, James A M	Capt	01-Sep-09	RM	GS	45 CDO RM	DUNDEE
Fuller, James B	Maj	01-Oct-05	RM	LC	30 CDO IX GP RM	PLYMOUTH
Fuller, Lucy A J	Lt RN	01-Sep-11	WAR	ATC	RNAS CULDROSE	HELSTON
Fuller, Nicholas M	Lt RN	01-Jan-12	WAR	O SKW	857 NAS	RNAS CULDROSE
Fuller, Richard	Lt RN	01-Jul-03	LOGS	L	MWS COLLINGWOOD	HMS COLLINGWOOD
Fuller, Stephen P	Lt Cdr	01-Oct-09	ENG	AE	BRNC	BRNC DARTMOUTH
Fulton, Craig R	Cdr	31-Dec-09	WAR	SM(CQ)	NOPF DAM NECK	VIRGINIA BEACH
Fulton, David M	Lt RN	01-May-02	ENG	MESM	HMS ARTFUL	
Fulton, Richard C	Mid	17-Nov-14	WAR	GSX	BRNC	BRNC DARTMOUTH
Funnell, Lee C	Lt RN	01-Jun-10	WAR	MCD	MCM2	PORTSMOUTH
Furneaux, James	Lt RN	21-Mar-10	WAR	HM	UK MCC	BAHRAIN
Furniss, Sam	SLt	15-May-14	WAR	GSX	MTM NORTHWOOD HQ	NORTHWOOD
Fyfe, Tobias R M	Surg Lt RN (D)	24-Jul-12	DENTAL	GDP	42 CDO RM	PLYMOUTH
Fyfe-Green, Alexa C	Surg Lt Cdr (D)	09-Jun-10	DENTAL	GDP	DEFENCE DENTAL SERVS	PORTSMOUTH
Fyfe-Green, Ian A	Lt Cdr	01-Oct-08	WAR	ATC	RNAS YEOVILTON	YEOVILTON

G

Name	Substantive Rank	Seniority	Branch	Specialisation	Organisation Name	Location Name
Gabb, John R E	Lt RN	01-Apr-13	WAR	SM(X)	HMS TORBAY	
Gaffney, Benjamin	Maj	01-Oct-11	RM	GS	FLEET CAP LLM & DRM	PORTSMOUTH
Gaffney, Francis	Lt RN	03-Feb-14	WAR	OP INT	DI - FC(A)	RAF WYTON
Gahan, Richard J	Lt Cdr	01-Oct-11	ENG	WESM(SWS)	HMS VIGILANT	
Gaines, Edwin J	Lt RN	28-Jul-06	ENG	WESM(TWS)	D STRAT PROG	ABBEY WOOD
Gale, Crystal V	Lt Cdr	24-Dec-00	LOGS	L	HMS PRESIDENT	LONDON
Gale, Mark A	Capt RN	21-Jan-13	ENG	MESM	DES COMFLEET	BARROW IN FURNESS
Gale, Simon P	Cdr	30-Jun-09	WAR	PWO(U)	LOAN DSTL	FAREHAM
Gall, Michael R C	Surg Capt RN (D)	04-Sep-07	DENTAL	GDP(C&S)	DMS WHITTINGTON	LICHFIELD
Gallagher, James	Mid	01-Feb-14	LOGS	L	HMS BULWARK	
Gallagher, Kieran J D	Capt	01-Sep-11	RM	GS	NC PSYA	NORTHWOOD
Gallagher, Michael V	Lt RN	01-Sep-11	LOGS	L SM	HMS VIGILANT	
Gallagher, Ross C	Lt RN	01-May-13	WAR	GSX	HMS QUEEN ELIZABETH	
Gamble, Phillip	Lt RN	15-May-93	WAR	O SKW	GANNET SAR FLT	HMS GANNET
Gamble, Stephen B	Lt Cdr	01-Oct-10	WAR	P LYNX	WMF 825 SQN HQ	RNAS YEOVILTON
Game, Philip G	Cdr	30-Jun-09	ENG	WE	DES COMFLEET	ABBEY WOOD
Gamwell, Sebastian P	Lt RN	01-Jun-13	WAR	ATC	RNAS CULDROSE	HELSTON
Gannon, Dominic R	Capt	24-Jul-04	RM	GS	NCHQ	PORTSMOUTH
Gardiner, Angus P R	Capt	03-Sep-14	RM	GS	40 CDO RM	TAUNTON
Gardiner, Christopher A	Lt RN	13-Jul-12	LOGS	L	HMS SCOTT	
Gardiner, Christopher I	Mid	08-Sep-14	WAR	GSX	BRNC	BRNC DARTMOUTH
Gardiner, Dermot	Surg Lt Cdr	01-May-09	MED	Occ Med	MTM INM ALVERSTOKE	GOSPORT
Gardner, Christopher R S	Cdre	04-Jan-10	LOGS	L SM	FLEET CAP SSM	PORTSMOUTH
Gardner, John E	Cdr	30-Jun-09	WAR	PWO(A)	COMUKTG	PLYMOUTH
Gardner, Louis C	Lt Cdr	01-Oct-11	WAR	SM(AWC)	HMS TALENT	
Gardner, Michael P	Lt Cdr	01-Oct-08	WAR	PWO	FLEET COMOPS NWD	NORTHWOOD
Gardner, Rachael	Lt RN	01-Apr-11	LOGS	L	MTM NELSON	HMS NELSON
Gardner, Sadie J	Lt RN	09-Apr-09	LOGS	L	OCLC LONDON	LONDON
Gardner-Clark, Suzanne L	Lt Cdr	01-Oct-08	QARNNS	EN (C&S)	RCDM	BIRMINGHAM
Gare, Christopher	Lt Cdr	01-Oct-08	WAR	PWO	RN EXCHANGE CANADA	OTTAWA
Garland, Andrew N	Maj	01-Oct-05	RM	SCC	CTCRM	EXMOUTH

Name	Substantive Rank	Seniority	Branch	Specialisation	Organisation Name	Location Name
Garman, Richard A	Capt	01-Sep-10	RM	GS	CTCRM	EXMOUTH
Garner, Dominic	SLt	01-Nov-14	WAR	GSX	MWS COLLINGWOOD	HMS COLLINGWOOD
Garner, Llyr	Lt RN	01-Jul-12	WAR	O UT	MTM 824 SQN CULDROSE	RNAS CULDROSE
Garner, Michael E	Lt RN	01-Feb-05	WAR	PWO(N)	MTM MWS COLLINGWOOD	HMS COLLINGWOOD
Garner, Robert J	Lt RN	01-Sep-09	WAR	GSX	GIBRALTAR	HMS ROOKE
Garner, Rose E	SLt	01-Oct-14	MED	Medical	BLAKE	BRNC DARTMOUTH
Garner, Sean M	Lt Cdr	01-Aug-06	WAR	ATC	D AIR P	LONDON
Garratt, John K	Cdr	30-Jun-10	WAR	AAWO	DIRECTOR (JW)	NORTHWOOD
Garratt, Mark D	Capt RN	30-Jun-08	WAR	P LYNX	RNAS CULDROSE	HELSTON
Garreta, Carlos E	Lt Cdr	01-Oct-10	WAR	PWO(A)	HMS DARING	
Garside, Robert J K	Maj	01-Oct-14	RM	GS	CDO LOG REGT RM	RMB CHIVENOR
Garth, Lee	Lt RN	15-Apr-11	ENG	AE	MAA	ABBEY WOOD
Garton, Hazelle M	Lt RN	01-Sep-10	ENG	AE	HMS SULTAN	GOSPORT
Gascoigne, Kristina M	SLt	01-Sep-12	ENG	AE	DCEME SULTAN	HMS SULTAN
Gascoigne, Lindsey	SLt	01-Oct-13	LOGS	L	HMS DEFENDER	
Gaskell-Taylor, Hugh M P	Lt RN	01-Oct-10	WAR	GSX	MTM YEOVILTON FCC	RNAS YEOVILTON
Gaskin, Alexander C	2Lt	01-Mar-11	RM	N/A	CTCRM	EXMOUTH
Gatenhy, Daniel	Lt RN	01-May-07	WAR	FC	HMS DARING	
Gates, Nigel S	Lt Cdr	01-Oct-08	WAR	P SK4	MTM CHF (MERLIN)	RAF BENSON
Gates, William C	RN Chpln	06-Sep-05	Ch S	Chaplain	NCHQ	PORTSMOUTH
Gaught, Edwin L	Lt RN	01-Sep-11	ENG	ME	DES COMFLEET	ABBEY WOOD
Gaunt, Amy V	Lt Cdr	01-Oct-14	WAR	O MER	829 SQN	RNAS CULDROSE
Gay, David A T	Surg Cdr	01-Jul-09	MED	Radiologist	PCRF	RFA ARGUS
Gayfer, Mark E	Capt RN	24-Jun-13	ENG	WESM(SWS)	SFM CLYDE	HMNB CLYDE
Gayle, David M	Lt RN	31-May-11	WAR	HM	HMS OCEAN	
Gayson, Christopher P	Lt RN	01-Mar-10	WAR	P SK4	845 SQN	RNAS YEOVILTON
Gaytano, Ronald T M	Lt RN	01-Apr-02	ENG	AE	PJHQ (UK)	NORTHWOOD
Gazzard, Julian H	Cdr	30-Jun-10	WAR	PWO(N)	DCMC	LONDON
Gearing, Richard M	Lt Cdr	01-Oct-12	ENG	AE	DES COMLAND	YEOVIL
Geary, Timothy W	Cdr	30-Jun-05	ENG	ME	DES COMFLEET	ABBEY WOOD
Geddes, Nathaniel C S	Lt RN	01-Sep-11	ENG	ME	HMS SULTAN	GOSPORT
Gee, Mathew	Lt RN	20-Oct-06	LOGS	L	AIB	HMS SULTAN
Geldard, Michael A	Lt Col	30-Jun-09	RM	GS	BMM	KUWAIT
Gell, David M	Lt RN	01-Sep-14	WAR	SM(X)	HMS ARTFUL	
Gell, Thomas	Lt RN	01-Oct-08	WAR	FC	FOST DPORT	PLYMOUTH
Geneux, Nicholas	Lt Cdr	01-Oct-09	ENG	TM	FLEET FOST ACOS(Trg)	PORTSMOUTH
Gennard, Anthony	Cdr	30-Jun-14	LOGS	L	DCDC	SHRIVENHAM
George, Alan P	Cdr	30-Jun-05	WAR	O LYNX	LOAN DSTL	FAREHAM
George, David M	Cdr	30-Jun-09	WAR	PWO(A)	FMC NAVY	LONDON
George, James A	Lt RN	01-Feb-08	WAR	MCD	FDU	PORTSMOUTH
George, Nicholas D	Maj	01-Oct-10	RM	GS	CLR ASG	RNAS YEOVILTON
George, Seth D	Lt Cdr	01-Oct-09	ENG	TM	FLEET FOST ACOS(Trg)	PORTSMOUTH
Gibb, Alexander K B	Maj	01-Oct-09	RM	GS	NCHQ	PORTSMOUTH
Gibbons, Nicholas P	Cdr	30-Jun-12	WAR	O SK6	FLEET COMOPS NWD	NORTHWOOD
Gibbons, Nicola J	Lt RN	01-Jan-13	ENG	WE	HMS BULWARK	
Gibbons, Sean F	Mid	08-Sep-14	ENG	WE	BRNC	BRNC DARTMOUTH
Gibbs, David J	Lt RN	01-Feb-98	WAR	P FW	NO 3 FTS/UAS - 115(R) SQN	RAFC CRANWELL
Gibbs, Emily K	Lt RN	01-Jan-11	ENG	TM	HMS SULTAN	GOSPORT
Gibbs, Mark P	Lt Cdr	01-Apr-10	ENG	ME	MWS EXCELLENT	HMS EXCELLENT
Gibbs, Neil D	Cdr	30-Jun-06	ENG	ME	DES DTECH	ABBEY WOOD
Gibson, Adrian	Lt RN	01-Jan-04	ENG	WE	SCU SHORE	HMS COLLINGWOOD
Gibson, Alastair D	Cdr	30-Jun-06	LOGS	L	ACDS	LONDON
Gibson, Alexander J	Lt Col	30-Jun-14	RM	LC	COMUKTG	PLYMOUTH
Gibson, Andrew	Surg Cdr	30-Jun-07	MED	Ophthal	MDHU NORTHALLERTON	NORTHALLERTON
Gibson, Andrew M	Lt RN	01-Jan-12	LOGS	L	URNU BIRMINGHAM	BIRMINGHAM
Gibson, Scott P	Lt RN	14-Aug-14	ENG	WESM	HMS VANGUARD	
Gibson, Stephen R J	Lt Cdr	31-Mar-94	WAR	P MER	824 SQN	RNAS CULDROSE
Gidney, Raymond S	SLt	01-Feb-12	WAR	SM(X)	HMS MERSEY	
Giffin, Ian	Lt RN	01-Oct-08	WAR	FC	HMS ARCHER	
Gilbert, Mark	Lt Cdr	01-Oct-14	WAR	O MER	MTM MWS COLLINGWOOD	HMS COLLINGWOOD
Gilbert, Peter D	Cdr	30-Jun-03	ENG	ME	DES COMFLEET	ABBEY WOOD
Gilbert, Rachel	Lt RN	01-Jan-05	WAR	O LYNX	750 SQN	RNAS CULDROSE

Name	Substantive Rank	Seniority	Branch	Specialisation	Organisation Name	Location Name
Gilbert, Scott	Lt RN	11-Jul-14	QARNNS	EN (C&S)	DCHET DSHE	BIRMINGHAM
Gilderthorp, Thomas D	Lt RN	01-Feb-12	WAR	GSX	HMS KENT	
Gilding, Douglas	Lt Col	30-Jun-14	RM	HW	DEFENCE ACADEMY	SHRIVENHAM
Giles, David W	Cdr	30-Jun-04	ENG	WE	NATO - BRUSSELS	BRUSSELS
Giles, Gary J	Maj	01-Oct-06	RM	SCC	MTM FLEET HQ	PORTSMOUTH
Giles, Kevin D L	Lt Cdr	01-May-92	WAR	MCD	FLEET MARITIME WARFARE	HMS COLLINGWOOD
Giles, Simon	Maj	01-Oct-10	RM	SCC	45 CDO RM	DUNDEE
Gill, Adam M	Lt RN	08-Feb-13	WAR	C	BATCIS	ABBEY WOOD
Gill, Christopher D	Lt Cdr	01-Jan-08	WAR	SM(CQ)	COMFASFLOT	HELENSBURGH
Gill, Lee	Lt RN	17-Dec-10	WAR	INT	43 CDO FPGRM	HELENSBURGH
Gill, Mark H	Lt Cdr	01-Jul-02	WAR	O SKW	MTM CULDROSE	RNAS CULDROSE
Gill, Martin R	Cdr	30-Jun-07	ENG	MESM	DES COMFLEET	ABBEY WOOD
Gill, Paul S	Lt Cdr	01-Oct-13	ENG	TM	MWS COLLINGWOOD	HMS COLLINGWOOD
Gill, Samuel R	Lt RN	01-Sep-11	ENG	MESM	HMS AUDACIOUS	
Gill, Thomas G	Mid	17-Nov-14	WAR	O UT	BRNC	BRNC DARTMOUTH
Gillespie, Benjamin D	Lt RN	01-Jul-11	WAR	SM(X)	HMS VANGUARD	
Gillett, David A	Lt Cdr	01-Nov-06	WAR	O LYNX	HMS MERSEY	
Gillett, Nathan D	Lt Cdr	01-Oct-10	WAR	AV	HMS QUEEN ELIZABETH	
Gillies, Brett	Lt Cdr	01-Oct-13	ENG	AE P	RNAS YEOVILTON	YFOVILTON
Gillingham, George	Lt RN	01-Jan-07	WAR	O MER	824 SQN	RNAS CULDROSE
Gillman, Robert M	SLt	01-Sep-14	ENG	AE	DCEME SULTAN	HMS SULTAN
Gilmartin, Kieran P	Surg Cdr	26-Aug-14	MED	GMP	DPHC SOUTH	HMS SULTAN
Gilmore, Amy F	Lt RN	01-Sep-08	WAR	O LYNX	LHF 815 SQN	RNAS YEOVILTON
Gilmore, Jeremy E	Lt RN	01-Sep-03	WAR	P SK4	CHFHQ	RNAS YEOVILTON
Gilmore, Martin A	Lt RN	01-Feb-10	WAR	P MER	820 SQN	RNAS CULDROSE
Gilmore, Martin P	Lt Cdr	01-Oct-11	WAR	P LYNX	FLEET AV VL	RNAS YEOVILTON
Gilmore, Steven J	Lt Cdr	01-Oct-09	ENG	WE	DES COMFLEET	ABBEY WOOD
Gilroy, Anthony B	Lt RN	11-Apr-14	ENG	WESM	HMS VANGUARD	
Ginn, Robert D	Maj	01-Oct-12	RM	GS	MTM NELSON	HMS NELSON
Ginty, John A	Lt RN	01-Sep-14	WAR	SM(X)	MTM FLEET HQ	PORTSMOUTH
Girling, Steven P	SLt	01-Sep-14	WAR	GSX	HMS ARGYLL	
Gladwin, Michael D	Lt Cdr	01-Oct-12	WAR	ATC	RNAS CULDROSE	HELSTON
Glanville, Andrew M	Lt	06-Apr-14	RM	SCC	CHFHQ	RNAS YEOVILTON
Gleave, Robert D	Lt RN	01-Nov-07	WAR	P LYNX	WMF 825 SQN HQ	RNAS YEOVILTON
Glendinning, Andreana S	Lt Cdr	01-Oct-09	QARNNS	ITU (C&S)	DMS WHITTINGTON	LICHFIELD
Glendinning, Vicky L	Lt RN	16-Jan-09	QARNNS	PHC	MTM WMO FASLANE	HMNB CLYDE
Glennie, John S	Surg Lt Cdr	05-Aug-14	MED	EM	MTM INM ALVERSTOKE	GOSPORT
Gloak, James	Maj	01-Oct-14	RM	GS	PJHQ (UK)	NORTHWOOD
Glover, Adam	Lt RN	01-Mar-09	ENG	MESM	FOSNI - CNR	PORTSMOUTH
Glover, Daniel	Lt RN	01-Sep-13	ENG	ME	HMS LANCASTER	
Glover, Lee N	Lt RN	13-Apr-12	ENG	AE	824 SQN	RNAS CULDROSE
Glover, Thomas F	Capt	01-Sep-09	RM	GS	40 CDO RM	TAUNTON
Gobbi, Alexander M	Capt	01-Sep-13	RM	GS	43 CDO FPGRM	HELENSBURGH
Gobell, Luke	Capt	01-Sep-12	RM	GS	40 CDO RM	TAUNTON
Gobey, Richard	Lt Cdr	01-Oct-14	WAR	SM(X) (RES)	NCHQ CNPS	PORTSMOUTH
Goddard, Alexander C	Lt RN	06-Apr-07	ENG	ME	HMS SULTAN	GOSPORT
Goddard, David	Lt Cdr	01-Oct-10	Ch S	L BAR SM	MTM NELSON	HMS NELSON
Goddard, James A T	Lt RN	01-Mar-10	ENG	AE	AIB	HMS SULTAN
Goddard, Paul	Lt Cdr	01-Oct-09	ENG	WESM(SWS)	DES COMFLEET	ABBEY WOOD
Godfrey, Matthew F	RN Chpln	03-Jul-04	Ch S	Chaplain	FLEET HM UNIT	PLYMOUTH
Godfrey, Simeon D W	Lt Cdr	01-Oct-07	WAR	SM(AWC)	NATO-ACO-JFC HQ	NAPLES
Godwin, Christopher A	Cdr	30-Jun-08	WAR	P MER	NATO-ACT-HQ	NORFOLK
Godwin, Lee D	Lt RN	07-Apr-06	WAR	AV	RNAS CULDROSE	HELSTON
Gokhale, Stephen G	Surg Lt Cdr	04-Aug-09	MED	GMP	DPHC SW	HMS RALEIGH
Golden, Dominic S C	Lt Cdr	01-Jun-99	WAR	FC	DIRECTOR (JW)	NORTHWOOD
Goldman, Daniel J L	Mid	17-Nov-14	WAR	P UT	BRNC	BRNC DARTMOUTH
Goldman, Paul H L	Lt Cdr	01-Apr-99	ENG	WE	FLEET ACOS(RP)	PORTSMOUTH
Goldsmith, Darran	Cdr	30-Jun-09	WAR	O MER	MTM WMO CULDROSE	RNAS CULDROSE
Goldsmith, David T	Cdr	30-Jun-13	ENG	WE	HMS OCEAN	
Goldsmith, Simon	Lt Cdr	01-May-95	WAR	PWO(C)	DI - CA - ASUS	WASHINGTON
Goldstone, Richard S	Cdr	30-Jun-12	WAR	AAWO	MCM2	PORTSMOUTH
Goldsworthy, Robin	SLt	01-Oct-13	ENG	WESM	MWS COLLINGWOOD	HMS COLLINGWOOD

Name	Substantive Rank	Seniority	Branch	Specialisation	Organisation Name	Location Name
Gomm, Kevin OBE	Cdr	30-Jun-07	WAR	SM(CQ)	RNSMS	HMS RALEIGH
Goodall, Michael A	Lt Cdr	01-May-06	ENG	ME	NCHQ CNPERS	PORTSMOUTH
Goodall, William C	Lt RN	01-Sep-12	WAR	GSX	HMS CLYDE	
Goode, Alun N	Lt Cdr	01-Sep-99	WAR	PWO(A)	FLEET COMOPS NWD	NORTHWOOD
Goode, Lee R	Lt	13-Jan-14	RM	SCC	40 CDO RM	TAUNTON
Goodenough, Rory A	Surg Lt RN	06-Aug-14	MED	Medical	BLAKE	BRNC DARTMOUTH
Goodes, Simon	Lt Cdr	31-Mar-97	WAR	MTO N (RES)	DIRECTOR (JW)	NORTHWOOD
Goodley, Ross	Lt RN	01-Oct-11	WAR	GSX	MTM NELSON	HMS NELSON
Goodman, David F	Lt Cdr	01-Oct-09	WAR	SM(AWC)	HQBF GIBRALTAR	HMS ROOKE
Goodrum, Simon E	Lt Cdr	01-Oct-05	MED	MS	INM ALVERSTOKE2	GOSPORT
Goodsell, Christopher D	Cdr	30-Jun-06	WAR	SM(CQ)	UK MCC	BAHRAIN
Goodwin, Aaron K	Lt RN	01-Sep-11	WAR	GSX	HMS DEFENDER	
Goodwin, Cheryl L	Mid	17-Nov-14	WAR	GSX	BRNC	BRNC DARTMOUTH
Goodwin, Lloyd W	SLt	01-Nov-14	WAR	SM(X)	MWS COLLINGWOOD	HMS COLLINGWOOD
Goodwin, Moss A J	Lt	02-Sep-14	RM	GS	45 CDO RM	DUNDEE
Goodwin, Thomas MBE	RN Chpln	05-May-02	Ch S	Chaplain	CHFHQ	RNAS YEOVILTON
Goose, Samuel J	Lt RN	01-Nov-07	WAR	INT	FLEET COMOPS NWD	NORTHWOOD
Goosen, Richard	Lt Cdr	01-Oct-14	WAR	HM	HMS SCOTT	
Guram, Malcolm	Lt Cdr	31-Mar-04	WAR	ATC (RES)	RNAS YEOVILTON	YEOVILTON
Gordon, Daniel	Lt RN	19-Oct-07	WAR	AV	MASF	RNAS CULDROSE
Gordon, David	Cdr	30-Jun-01	ENG	TM(SM)	AIB	HMS SULTAN
Gordon, David E	Lt Cdr	01-Oct-12	ENG	AE	AWC	BOSCOMBE DOWN
Gordon, David J	Lt Cdr	01-Oct-11	WAR	HM(AS)	LOAN HYDROG DGHR(N)	TAUNTON
Gordon, Emily H	Lt RN	01-Dec-14	WAR	HM	HMS ST ALBANS	
Gordon, John	Lt Cdr	01-Oct-09	WAR	SM(C)	FLEET COMOPS NWD	NORTHWOOD
Gordon, Matthew R	Mid	01-May-14	WAR	P UT	BRNC	BRNC DARTMOUTH
Gorman, Darren A	Lt RN	01-Sep-02	WAR	P SK4	DEF HELI FLYING SCH	HOLYHEAD
Gorman, Glenn K	Lt Cdr	01-Oct-12	WAR	PWO	FOST DPORT	PLYMOUTH
Gorst, Joshua R	Lt RN	01-Jan-13	LOGS	L	FOSNI - NRC NE	LIVERPOOL
Gosling, Jonathan C	Lt	02-Sep-14	RM	GS	2 LANCS	PRESTON
Gosney, Christopher J	Lt Col	30-Jun-14	RM	SCC	HMS OCEAN	
Gotke, Christopher T	Lt Cdr	01-Oct-08	WAR	P FW	RNAS YEOVILTON	YEOVILTON
Goudge, Simon D P	Cdr	30-Jun-12	LOGS	L	FLEET FOST ACOS(Trg)	PORTSMOUTH
Gough, Christopher M	Lt RN	11-Apr-11	ENG	TM	JFC - DCTS (H)	AYLESBURY
Gough, Martyn	RN Prncpl Chpln	01-Jul-14	Ch S	Chaplain	CHAPLAIN OF THE FLEET	PORTSMOUTH
Goulder, Jonathan D	Lt Cdr	01-Oct-06	WAR	AAWO	FOST DPORT	PLYMOUTH
Gow, Peter J	Lt RN	16-Sep-09	LOGS	L SM	HMS ARTFUL	
Gowers, Sarah MBE	Lt Cdr	01-Oct-14	LOGS	L	MTM RALEIGH	HMS RALEIGH
Gowling, Stephen M	Lt RN	01-Dec-13	WAR	GSX	HMS IRON DUKE	
Grace, Nicholas J OBE	Lt Col	30-Jun-09	RM	BS	HQ BAND SERVICE	HMS NELSON
Graddon, Giles J	Lt RN	01-Jan-08	WAR	INT	HQ COMBRITFOR	AFGHANISTAN KABUL
Grafton, Joshua T	Lt RN	01-Feb-14	WAR	SM(X)	HMS VICTORIOUS	
Graham, Alastair N S MVO	Cdr	01-Sep-07	WAR	WESM	JFC HOC C4ISR	NORTHWOOD
Graham, Benjamin R	Lt RN	01-Sep-07	LOGS	L	NBCP CAPTAIN OF THE BASE	PORTSMOUTH
Graham, Elliott T	2Lt	25-Aug-14	RM	N/A	CTCRM	EXMOUTH
Graham, James P	Lt RN	20-Oct-06	WAR	AV	DSTO	RAF ST MAWGAN
Graham, Mark A	Lt Cdr	01-Oct-01	WAR	O LYNX	HANDLING SQN	BOSCOMBE DOWN
Grainger, Natalie	Lt RN	01-Feb-13	WAR	P SK4	CHF - 846	RAF BENSON
Grandy, Mark	Lt RN	01-Sep-10	ENG	WE	NAVY MCTA	PORTSMOUTH
Grant, Anne-Louise	Lt RN	09-Oct-14	MED	MS(EHO)	NCHQ MEDDIV EH	PORTSMOUTH
Grant, Daniel P	SLt	24-Jul-14	WAR	O UT	MTM RAF CRANWELL	RAFC CRANWELL
Grant, David J	Lt Cdr	01-Oct-03	ENG	MESM	NBC CLYDE	HMNB CLYDE
Grant, Elizabeth S A	Lt RN	13-Jul-12	WAR	REG	RNP - HQ PMN	HMS EXCELLENT
Grant, Gary	Lt RN	12-Jul-13	ENG	WESM	MTM RALEIGH	HMS RALEIGH
Grant, Hugo J	Capt	01-Sep-13	RM	GS	30 CDO IX GP RM	PLYMOUTH
Grant, Richard	Lt Cdr	01-Oct-11	ENG	ME	DES COMFLEET	ABBEY WOOD
Grant, Wayne G	Lt Cdr	01-Jun-08	ENG	AE	FLEET CSAV	PORTSMOUTH
Grantham, Guy J	Lt RN	01-Nov-00	ENG	IS	RNEAWC - SNO	LINCOLN
Grantham, Stephen M	Capt RN	01-Jul-13	ENG	MESM	SIT - ABBEYWOOD	LONDON
Gray, Christopher J	Mid	01-May-14	WAR	GSX	BRNC	BRNC DARTMOUTH
Gray, David K	Lt Cdr	01-Apr-95	ENG	WE	FOSNI - YOUTH CCF	PORTSMOUTH
Gray, John A	Cdr	30-Jun-06	WAR	AAWO	FOSNI - NRC	HELENSBURGH

Name	Substantive Rank	Seniority	Branch	Specialisation	Organisation Name	Location Name
Gray, John A	Lt Cdr	01-Oct-06	WAR	SM(CQ)	HMS VENGEANCE	
Gray, Karl D	Maj	01-May-06	RM	C	OPS DIR	LONDON
Gray, Martina E	Lt RN	24-Aug-92	LOGS	L	NCHQ CNPERS	PORTSMOUTH
Gray, Matthew S	Capt	30-Mar-12	RM	SCC	CTCRM	EXMOUTH
Gray, Michael J H	Lt Cdr	01-Oct-08	WAR	INT	FLEET CAP IS	PORTSMOUTH
Gray, Nathan J	Lt Cdr	01-Oct-10	WAR	P FW	AWC	PATUXENT RIVER
Gray, Oliver W	Maj	01-Oct-14	RM	LC	MTM DEFAC JSCSC	SHRIVENHAM
Gray, Paul R	Cdr	30-Jun-12	WAR	P MER	FLEET MARITIME WARFARE	HMS COLLINGWOOD
Gray, Richard G	Lt RN	01-Sep-11	ENG	WESM(SWS)	HMS VIGILANT	
Gray, Richard L	Lt Cdr	01-Oct-12	WAR	PWO	HQ ARRC (JFIB)B	GLOUCESTER
Gray, Samuel D	Lt RN	01-Aug-04	WAR	GSX	MTM RMR MERSEYSIDE	LIVERPOOL
Gray, Simon A N	Maj	01-Oct-08	RM	C	MTM CTCRM	EXMOUTH
Grayland, Andrew	Lt RN	01-Jan-09	ENG	WE	SVCOPS/DHDOPSPLANS/NWD	NORTHWOOD
Grayson, Stephen	Lt Cdr	01-Oct-12	LOGS	L SM	HMS FORWARD	BIRMINGHAM
Greason, Paul A	Lt RN	01-Aug-08	ENG	WE	DCMC	LONDON
Greaves, Michael	Lt RN	01-Sep-08	ENG	WESM(TWS)	RNSMS	HMS RALEIGH
Greaves, Timothy M	Lt RN	01-Sep-06	WAR	ATC	RNAS CULDROSE	HELSTON
Green, Andrew J	Cdr	30-Jun-08	ENG	TM(SM)	NBCP BASE EXEC OFFICER	HMS NELSON
Green, Andrew M	Lt Cdr	12-May-99	ENG	ME	DIO SAPI	PORTSMOUTH
Green, David P	Lt Cdr	13-Aug-93	WAR	SM(AWC)	NCHQ CNPS	PORTSMOUTH
Green, David P S	Capt RN	26-Aug-14	ENG	WESM(TWS)	HDPROG	CORSHAM
Green, Gareth M	Maj	01-Sep-98	RM	GS	STRIKFORNATO - LISBON	LISBON
Green, Gary E	Lt Col	30-Jun-06	RM	SCC	STRIKFORNATO - LISBON	LISBON
Green, Jayne H	Lt Cdr	01-Sep-11	WAR	O LYNX	FOST DPORT	PLYMOUTH
Green, Jeremy D	Lt RN	01-Sep-13	ENG	WESM	MTM DEFAC JSCSC	SHRIVENHAM
Green, Jonathan	Lt Cdr	01-Oct-13	WAR	P SKW	GANNET SAR FLT	HMS GANNET
Green, Jonathan D	SLt	01-Sep-14	ENG	MESM	DCEME SULTAN	HMS SULTAN
Green, Joseph R S	Lt RN	01-Sep-11	WAR	INT	FLEET COMOPS NWD	HMS COLLINGWOOD
Green, Leslie D	Lt Cdr	01-Oct-09	ENG	MESM	FOST SM SEA	HMNB CLYDE
Green, Mark D	Lt RN	09-Apr-10	WAR	O LYNX	LHF 815 SQN HQ	RNAS YEOVILTON
Green, Natalie M	Surg Lt RN	07-Aug-13	MED	Medical	BLAKE	BRNC DARTMOUTH
Green, Nicholas D W	Lt RN	01-Apr-10	WAR	SM(X)	POLICY & COMMITMENTS	LONDON
Green, Peter J	Cdr	30-Jun-05	WAR	SM(CQ)	NUCLEAR CAPABILITY	LONDON
Green, Philip	Capt	18-Jul-07	RM	C (SCC)	FOSNI - YOUTH CCF	PORTSMOUTH
Green, Richard J	Lt RN	01-Apr-14	WAR	P UT	MTM SHAWBURY	RAF SHAWBURY
Green, Steven P	Capt	21-Mar-13	RM	BS	MTM RM SCH MUSIC	HMS NELSON
Green, Timothy C	Cdr	30-Jun-09	WAR	PWO(U)	FLEET CAP SSM	PORTSMOUTH
Green, Timothy J	Cdr	31-Dec-98	WAR	SM(CQ)	UKTI - DSO	LONDON
Greenall, Gilbert E	Surg Lt RN	07-Aug-13	MED	Medical	BLAKE	BRNC DARTMOUTH
Greene, Michael J	Cdr	31-Dec-99	ENG	TM	FOSNI - YOUTH MSCC	PORTSMOUTH
Greener, Carl	Capt RN	17-Nov-14	ENG	WE	DES COMFLEET	ABBEY WOOD
Greenfield, Jennifer	Mid	01-May-14	WAR	HM	BRNC	BRNC DARTMOUTH
Greenfield, Stuart	Lt RN	01-Sep-11	ENG	AE	HMS SULTAN	GOSPORT
Greenhill, Nicholas J	Lt RN	01-May-04	WAR	INT	NATO-ACO-JFC HQ	NAPLES
Greenland, Michael R MVO	Cdr	30-Jun-11	WAR	P LYNX	DDC	LONDON
Greenlees, Iain W	Capt RN	30-Jun-05	WAR	PWO(A)	NBCP DIRECTOR ESTATES & TX	PORTSMOUTH
Greenway, Crendon A L	Lt	01-Sep-12	RM	GS	40 CDO RM	TAUNTON
Greenwood, David R	Lt RN	01-May-10	WAR	GSX	HMS TYNE	
Greenwood, Julia L	Lt RN	01-Feb-10	WAR		UK MCC	BAHRAIN
Greenwood, Peter	Lt Cdr	01-Oct-12	WAR	P MER	824 SQN	RNAS CULDROSE
Gregg, Ryan Lee	Lt RN	01-Sep-11	ENG	AE	DES COMJE	ABBEY WOOD
Gregory, Andrew J	Capt	03-Apr-09	RM	BS	RM BAND SCOTLAND	HMS CALEDONIA
Gregory, Anthony E	Surg Lt Cdr	01-Sep-07	MED	GMP (C&S)	FOST SEA - DMO	PLYMOUTH
Gregory, Daniel P	Lt RN	01-Apr-14	WAR	P	MTM 824 SQN CULDROSE	RNAS CULDROSE
Gregory, Jonathan E	Lt Cdr	01-Oct-14	ENG	TM	FLEET FOST ACOS(Trg)	ABBEY WOOD
Gregory, Samuel G	Lt RN	01-Feb-11	ENG	TM	CTCRM	EXMOUTH
Gregson, Tyler J	Mid	08-Sep-14	ENG	ME	BRNC	BRNC DARTMOUTH
Greig, Ryan A	SLt	01-Mar-14	WAR	GSX	HMS DUNCAN	
Greig, Stuart J	Lt RN	01-May-13	LOGS	L	HMS DRAGON	
Grenfell-Shaw, Mark	Cdr	30-Jun-05	ENG	WESM(TWS)	DES COMFLEET	ABBEY WOOD
Gresswell, Nick A	Lt RN	01-Sep-08	WAR	P LYNX	LHF 815 SQN	RNAS YEOVILTON
Greswell, James S L	Capt	01-Sep-11	RM	GS	1 IG	ALDERSHOT

Name	Substantive Rank	Seniority	Branch	Specialisation	Organisation Name	Location Name
Grey, Amy C	Lt RN	01-Apr-03	WAR	O WILDCAT	FLEET CAP SSM	PORTSMOUTH
Grey, Christopher S	Lt Cdr	01-Oct-09	WAR	O LYNX	RNAS YEOVILTON	YEOVILTON
Grice, Matthew	Lt Cdr	01-Oct-10	ENG	AE	847 SQN	RNAS YEOVILTON
Grice, Sally K	SLt	01-Jun-14	MED	Medical	BLAKE	BRNC DARTMOUTH
Grierson, Andrew D	Lt Cdr	01-Oct-13	ENG	TM	UKMARBATSTAFF	PORTSMOUTH
Griffen, David J	Lt Cdr	01-Oct-10	WAR	PWO MW	RN EXCHANGE USA	WASHINGTON
Griffin, Niall Mbe	Capt RN	01-Jul-13	WAR	P SK4	CHFHQ	RNAS YEOVILTON
Griffin, Stephen	Lt Cdr	01-Oct-09	WAR	AV	MASF	RNAS CULDROSE
Griffith, Phillip B	Lt RN	01-May-14	LOGS	L SM	HMS TORBAY	
Griffiths, Adam M	Surg Lt RN	06-Aug-14	MED	Medical	BLAKE	BRNC DARTMOUTH
Griffiths, Beth	Lt RN	01-Jan-08	ENG	ME	DES COMFLEET	ABBEY WOOD
Griffiths, Charlotte E V	Surg Lt Cdr	01-Aug-12	MED	GMP	MTM INM ALVERSTOKE	GOSPORT
Griffiths, Colin	Lt Cdr	01-Oct-12	WAR	P SK4	CHF - 846	RAF BENSON
Griffiths, David A	Lt RN	01-Jan-15	WAR	GSX	MTM MWS DDS	PORTSMOUTH
Griffiths, David T	Lt Cdr	01-Apr-90	WAR	MCD PWO(U)	CRF HQ POR	PORTSMOUTH
Griffiths, Francis M	Lt Cdr	01-Oct-14	ENG	ME	FLEET CAP SSM	PORTSMOUTH
Griffiths, Gareth	Lt RN	01-Jan-04	WAR	SM(N)	HMS VIGILANT	
Griffiths, Michael O J	Lt Cdr	16-Jan-00	WAR	PWO(U)	RN EXCHANGE NETHERLANDS	DEN HELDER
Griffiths, Neil	Lt Cdr	01-Oct-06	WAR	PWO MW	MTM MWS COLLINGWOOD	HMS COLLINGWOOD
Griffiths, Nicholas A MBE	Lt Col	30-Jun-11	RM	GS	MTM NELSON	HMS NELSON
Griffiths, Richard H	Cdr	30-Jun-12	WAR	SM(CQ)	NUCLEAR CAPABILITY	LONDON
Griggs, James K	Lt RN	30-Jul-10	WAR	ATC	RNAS CULDROSE	HELSTON
Grimes, Keith M	Lt RN	01-Mar-09	ENG	MESM	DES COMFLEET	ABBEY WOOD
Grimley, Timothy P	Lt Cdr	01-Oct-13	LOGS	L SM	HMS ARGYLL	
Grimmer, Nicholas G	Lt RN	01-Jan-10	WAR	P MER	820 SQN	RNAS CULDROSE
Grimshaw, Ernest	RN Chpln	02-May-96	Ch S	Chaplain	HMS SULTAN	GOSPORT
Grindel, David J S	Cdr	30-Jun-02	ENG	TM	DCTT HQ	HMS SULTAN
Grindon, Matthew G	Cdr	30-Jun-09	WAR	P SK4	AWC	BOSCOMBE DOWN
Groom, Ian S MBE	Cdr	30-Jun-07	ENG	ME	FLEET CAP SSM	PORTSMOUTH
Grounsell, Wayne T	Lt	01-Jul-13	RM	SCC	HQ SQN CDO LOG REGT RM	RMB CHIVENOR
Grout, Christopher L	Lt RN	01-Nov-14	ENG	WESM	HMS TORBAY	
Grove, Jeremy J	Lt Cdr	01-Oct-12	WAR	HM (H CH)	FOST HM	HMS DRAKE
Groves, Christopher D	SLt	01-Feb-12	LOGS	L	FOST FAS SHORE	HMNB CLYDE
Groves, Nicholas J	SLt	01-Sep-14	WAR	SM(X)	MCM1	FASLANE
Gruber, James P M	Lt RN	07-Oct-12	ENG	WE	HMS DARING	
Gubby, Adrian W	Lt Cdr	01-May-10	ENG	WE	D CEPP	LONDON
Guest, Craig A	Lt RN	01-Jan-08	WAR	HM	MWS COLLINGWOOD	HMS COLLINGWOOD
Guest, Robert M	Mid	08-Sep-14	ENG	ME	BRNC	BRNC DARTMOUTH
Guest, Ruth E	Surg Lt RN	03-Aug-11	MED	GDMO	MTM NELSON	HMS NELSON
Guild, Ian	Lt Cdr	01-Oct-14	ENG	WE	DES COMFLEET	ABBEY WOOD
Gulley, Trevor J	Capt RN	25-Jan-11	ENG	ME	HMS SULTAN	GOSPORT
Gulliver, Jeff W	Lt Cdr	21-Nov-10	WAR	PWO	HMS ST ALBANS	
Gurmin, Stephen	Cdr	30-Jun-03	WAR	PWO(C)	RN EXCHANGE USA	WASHINGTON
Gurney, Brian D J	2Lt	02-Sep-12	RM	N/A	CTCRM	EXMOUTH
Gurney, Simon R	SLt	01-Jan-14	WAR	AV	MASF	RNAS CULDROSE
Guthrie, Lee D K	Lt RN	17-Dec-10	ENG	WESM(TWS)	FLEET COMOPS NSTP30	FAREHAM
Guy, Charles R	Lt Cdr	01-Oct-07	WAR	AAWO	COMPORFLOT	PORTSMOUTH
Guy, Elizabeth	Lt RN	01-Sep-07	WAR	INT	MTM NORTHWOOD HQ	NORTHWOOD
Guy, Frances L	Lt RN	01-Jan-07	WAR	INT	PJHQ (UK)	NORTHWOOD
Guy, Mark A MBE	Cdr	30-Jun-06	ENG	WE	DES COMFLEET	ABBEY WOOD
Guy, Thomas J	Capt RN	18-Sep-12	WAR	PWO(U)	FLEET SPT FGEN	PORTSMOUTH
Guyver, Paul M	Surg Cdr	03-Nov-14	MED	T&O	MDHU DERRIFORD	PLYMOUTH
Gwatkin, Nicholas J	Lt Cdr	01-Oct-09	WAR	MCD	MTM NELSON	HMS NELSON
Gwilliam, Benjamin	SLt	01-Sep-14	WAR	GSX	MWS COLLINGWOOD	HMS COLLINGWOOD
Gwilliam, Richard J	Lt RN	15-Apr-11	WAR	INT	CHFHQ	RNAS YEOVILTON
Gwinnutt, Oliver F	Lt RN	01-Sep-14	WAR	GSX	HMS OCEAN	
Gymer, Carl A J	Mid	01-Feb-14	WAR	P UT	BRNC	BRNC DARTMOUTH

H

Hackland, Andrew S	Lt RN	01-Apr-03	WAR	ATC	ATM	RNAS YEOVILTON
Hackman, James D	Lt Cdr	01-Oct-10	LOGS	L SM	FLEET SPT LOGS INFRA	PORTSMOUTH
Haddon, Luke D	Mid	08-Sep-14	ENG	ME	BRNC	BRNC DARTMOUTH

Name	Substantive Rank	Seniority	Branch	Specialisation	Organisation Name	Location Name
Hadland, Giles	Lt Cdr	01-Oct-08	WAR	INT	JFC HOC C4ISR	NORTHWOOD
Hadley, Clive M	Lt RN	08-Apr-05	ENG	WESM(TWS)	DES COMFLEET	ABBEY WOOD
Haggo, Jamie R	Lt RN	16-Apr-98	WAR	P FW	FLEET CSAV	PORTSMOUTH
Haigh, Alastair J	Cdr	30-Jun-11	WAR	P LYNX	LHF 815 SQN HQ	RNAS YEOVILTON
Haigh, Julian J	Lt Cdr	01-Oct-05	LOGS	L SM	FLEET SPT LOGS INFRA	PORTSMOUTH
Haigh, Thomas J	Surg Lt RN	06-Aug-14	MED	Medical	BLAKE	BRNC DARTMOUTH
Haines, Paul	OCdt	01-Aug-11	WAR	AW (RES)	MTM NPT RES MOBILISATION	PORTSMOUTH
Haines, Paul R	Cdr	30-Jun-01	ENG	WE	DDC	LONDON
Hains, Justin	Lt Cdr	01-Apr-04	WAR	MCD	JFC HQ	NORTHWOOD
Hairsine, Samuel	Lt	01-Jul-13	RM	BS	CTCRM	HMS NELSON
Hairsine, William	Lt RN	01-Jul-05	WAR	PWO	HMS DIAMOND	
Halahan, Miles D C	Lt RN	01-Feb-14	WAR	GSX	MCM1	FASLANE
Hale, Alexandra L	Surg Lt RN	06-Aug-13	MED	GMP	MTM INM ALVERSTOKE	GOSPORT
Hale, Amanda D	Lt Cdr	01-Oct-14	ENG	TM	DSAE COSFORD	WOLVERHAMPTON
Hale, John N	Maj	27-Apr-02	RM	LC	FOST DPORT	PLYMOUTH
Hale, Stuart D	Lt RN	01-Apr-05	QARNNS	ITU (C&S)	FOSNI - CNR	PORTSMOUTH
Hales, Martin	Lt RN	01-Jan-13	WAR	O LYNX	LHF 815 SQN	RNAS YEOVILTON
Haley, Christopher J	Lt Cdr	01-Oct-11	WAR		UK MCC	BAHRAIN
Halford, John A	Lt RN	01-Mar-13	ENG	AE	CHF - 846	RAF BENSON
Halford, Mark L	Lt RN	01-Jun-09	WAR	P SK4	CHF - 846	RAF BENSON
Halford, Patrick	Capt	01-Sep-12	RM	GS	DCSU	RAF HENLOW
Hall, Allan J	Lt RN	01-Sep-08	LOGS	L	FLEET SPT LOGS INFRA	PORTSMOUTH
Hall, Andrew D F	SLt	01-Aug-13	ENG	AE	RNAS YEOVILTON	YEOVILTON
Hall, Barry J	Cdr	30-Jun-06	ENG	MESM	NUCLEAR CAPABILITY	LONDON
Hall, Christopher	Lt RN	16-Dec-11	WAR	INT	JCU (CH)	CHELTENHAM
Hall, Christopher L	Lt Cdr	01-Oct-10	ENG	MESM	DES COMFLEET	THURSO
Hall, Christopher M I MBE	Maj	01-Oct-07	RM	GS	42 CDO RM	PLYMOUTH
Hall, Daniel	Lt RN	01-Jan-09	ENG	MESM	DES COMFLEET	ABBEY WOOD
Hall, David J	Surg Capt RN (D)	25-Mar-13	DENTAL	GDP(C&S)	DDS PLYMOUTH	HMS DRAKE
Hall, Edward C M	Maj	01-Oct-11	RM	GS	45 CDO RM	DUNDEE
Hall, Graham W R	Lt Cdr	01-Oct-10	WAR	HM (M CH)	URNU GLASGOW	GLASGOW
Hall, James E	Lt Cdr	01-Oct-10	WAR	O SKW	857 NAS	RNAS CULDROSE
Hall, Jessica M	Surg Lt Cdr (D)	14-Jul-13	DENTAL	GDP	NCHQ	PORTSMOUTH
Hall, Kilian J D	Lt RN	01-May-01	WAR	FC	RNAS YEOVILTON	YEOVILTON
Hall, Megan E	Lt RN	01-Apr-12	LOGS	L	COMPORFLOT	PORTSMOUTH
Hall, Nicola E	SLt	01-Nov-14	WAR	GSX	MWS COLLINGWOOD	HMS COLLINGWOOD
Hall, Richard J	Lt RN	22-Oct-12	WAR	O SKW	MWS COLLINGWOOD	HMS COLLINGWOOD
Hall, Richard M	Maj	01-Sep-90	RM	GS	CTCRM	EXMOUTH
Hall, Simon C	Lt RN	01-Jan-12	WAR	P UT	MTM SHAWBURY	RAF SHAWBURY
Hall, Stephen J	Lt RN	01-Apr-09	WAR	SM(N)	CBRN POL	LONDON
Hall, Victoria J	Lt RN	16-Jun-10	ENG	TM	MTM NELSON	HMS NELSON
Hall, William J	Capt	01-Sep-11	RM	GS	43 CDO FPGRM	HELENSBURGH
Hallam, Stuart P	RN Chpln	05-May-02	Ch S	Chaplain	HMS OCEAN	
Hallatt, Nicholas E	Lt RN	01-Sep-08	WAR	P SK4	845 SQN	RNAS YEOVILTON
Hallett, Daniel J	Lt Cdr	01-Oct-13	ENG	TM	TEMP DEP DEF ATTACHE	KIEV
Hallett, Simon J	Cdr	30-Jun-14	LOGS	L	DES COMLAND	ABBEY WOOD
Halliday, Alexander W	Lt RN	08-Dec-12	ENG	AE O	MTM 750 SQN CULDROSE	RNAS CULDROSE
Halliwell, Leon M	SLt	01-Nov-14	WAR	P UT	MWS COLLINGWOOD	HMS COLLINGWOOD
Hallsworth, Kay	Lt Cdr	01-Oct-12	MED	MS	BFGib	HMS ROOKE
Hally, Philip J	Capt RN	02-Sep-14	LOGS	L CMA	CAP JLE	NORTHWOOD
Halsted, Benjamin E MBE	Maj	01-Oct-07	RM	GS	MTM DEFAC JSCSC	SHRIVENHAM
Halton, Paul V OBE	Capt RN	11-Jan-10	WAR	SM(CQ)	DI - FC(A)	LONDON
Hamer, Scott A	Lt RN	01-Feb-10	WAR	MCD	MCM2	PORTSMOUTH
Hamilton, Alex R C	2Lt	25-Aug-14	RM	N/A	CTCRM	EXMOUTH
Hamilton, John R	Lt RN	01-Mar-12	ENG	WE	HMS ALBION	
Hamilton, Mark I	Lt Cdr	01-Oct-08	ENG	ME	DES COMFLEET	ABBEY WOOD
Hamilton, Sean M	Surg Lt Cdr (D)	26-Jun-06	DENTAL	GDP	DDS GERMANY	GUTERSLOH
Hamlyn, Jonathan D	Lt RN	20-Oct-10	WAR	P LYNX	LHF 815 SQN	RNAS YEOVILTON
Hammick, Benjamin J P	Mid	08-Sep-14	WAR	GSX	BRNC	BRNC DARTMOUTH
Hammock, Simon G	Lt Cdr	01-Oct-11	WAR	P SK4	845 SQN	RNAS YEOVILTON
Hammon, Mark A	Lt Cdr	01-Oct-08	WAR	AAWO	NCHQ CNPERS	PORTSMOUTH
Hammond, Christopher R	Lt Cdr	01-Oct-13	LOGS	L	HMS IRON DUKE	

Name	Substantive Rank	Seniority	Branch	Specialisation	Organisation Name	Location Name
Hammond, James A	SLt	09-Apr-12	WAR	SM(X)	HMS AMBUSH	
Hammond, Mark C DFC	Maj	01-May-00	RM	P LYN7	4 REGT AAC	IPSWICH
Hammond, Meirion M	Lt RN	01-Apr-00	WAR	P SKW	GANNET SAR FLT	HMS GANNET
Hammond, Paul	Cdr	30-Jun-12	WAR	PWO(U)	HMS ARGYLL	
Hammond, Paul A	Cdre	19-Jul-12	ENG	AE	DES COMFLEET	ABBEY WOOD
Hammond, Sean J	Lt RN	01-Jun-08	WAR	SM(N)	FLEET COMOPS NWD	NORTHWOOD
Hammond, Tregaron	Lt RN	15-Apr-11	WAR	INT	FOST DPORT	PLYMOUTH
Hampshire, Tony	Lt Cdr	01-Oct-07	WAR	MCD	FOSNI - HQ	HELENSBURGH
Hampson, Alexander G	Lt Cdr	01-Oct-14	WAR	P SK4	CHF(MERLIN)	RAF BENSON
Hanan, William M	Surg Lt RN	07-Aug-13	MED	Medical	BLAKE	BRNC DARTMOUTH
Hancock, Andrew P	Cdr	30-Jun-06	WAR	PWO(U)	SERV ATTACHE/ADVISER	BUENOS AIRES
Hancock, David P	Lt RN	27-Oct-14	ENG	TM	MTM FLEET HQ	PORTSMOUTH
Hancock, James H	Lt Cdr	01-Oct-11	WAR	INT	DCSU	RAF HENLOW
Hancock, Robert T A	Lt Cdr	01-Oct-01	ENG	WE	LOAN DSTL	SALISBURY
Hand, Christopher J	Surg Cdr	30-Jun-03	MED	T&O	MDHU PORTSMOUTH	PORTSMOUTH
Handforth, Riley	Mid	01-May-14	WAR	O UT	BRNC	BRNC DARTMOUTH
Handoll, Guy N G	Lt Cdr	01-Apr-10	ENG	MESM	HMS VANGUARD	
Hands, Anthony J	Surg Cdr (D)	23-Sep-13	DENTAL	GDP	HMS DRAKE	PLYMOUTH
Hands, Edward W	Maj	01-Oct-14	RM	GS	MTM NELSON	HMS NELSON
Hanks, Oliver T	Lt Cdr	01-Oct-12	LOGS	L	PJHQ (UK)	NORTHWOOD
Hanks, Richard M	Lt RN	11-Dec-09	WAR	PWO	HMS LANCASTER	
Hanley, Peter H	Lt RN	01-Nov-12	ENG	MESM	HMS TALENT	
Hannaby, Philippa B	Lt Cdr	01-Oct-14	LOGS	L	MTM DEFAC JSCSC	SHRIVENHAM
Hannah, Edward C	Lt RN	01-Apr-11	LOGS	L SM	MOD CNS/ACNS	LONDON
Hannah, George L	2Lt	25-Aug-14	RM	N/A	CTCRM	EXMOUTH
Hannam, Darrell B	Lt Cdr	01-Oct-12	WAR	O SKW	FLEET MARITIME WARFARE	HMS COLLINGWOOD
Hannigan, Jason D	Lt Cdr	01-Oct-14	WAR	PWO	FLEET CAP SSM	PORTSMOUTH
Hanson, Mark	Mid	01-Feb-14	WAR	P UT	BRNC	BRNC DARTMOUTH
Harcombe, Andrew	Lt Cdr	01-Oct-11	WAR	P LYN7	HQ JHC CAP DIR	ANDOVER
Harcourt, Robert	Cdr	30-Jun-11	WAR	PWO(U)	MOD NSD USA	KEY WEST
Hardern, Simon P	Cdre	01-Jul-13	WAR	PWO(U)	NATO - BRUSSELS	BRUSSELS (MONS)
Hardiman, Nicholas A	Cdr	30-Jun-14	ENG	MESM	NBD NB SAFETY DEVONPORT	HMS DRAKE
Harding, Daniel L	Lt RN	01-Sep-09	WAR	GSX	HMS SUTHERLAND	
Harding, David V	Lt Cdr	01-Oct-12	ENG	WESM(SWS)	HMS VENGEANCE	
Harding, Gary A	Cdr	30-Jun-09	ENG	WE	DES COMFLEET	ABBEY WOOD
Harding, Georgina E	Lt RN	08-Jul-12	WAR	GSX	HMS RICHMOND	
Harding, Ian R	Lt RN	13-Jul-12	ENG	WE	HMS IRON DUKE	
Harding, Matthew J	Lt RN	01-Dec-09	WAR	P SK4	727 NAS	RNAS YEOVILTON
Harding, Russell G CBE	R Adm	28-Feb-11	WAR	O SK6	FLEET COS AVN	PORTSMOUTH
Harding, Scott R	Lt RN	08-Feb-13	WAR	AV	MASF	RNAS CULDROSE
Hardinge, Christopher MBE	Cdr	30-Sep-05	WAR	SM(X) (RES)	NATO-ACO-JFC HQ	BRUNSSUM
Hardman, Matthew J	Lt Cdr	01-Oct-07	WAR	GSX	MTM FLEET HQ	PORTSMOUTH
Hardwick, Mark J	Lt Cdr	01-Oct-05	LOGS	L SM	FLEET SPT LOGS INFRA	NORTHWOOD
Hardy, Lee C	Cdr	30-Jun-02	WAR	AAWO	BF BIOT	DIEGO GARCIA
Hardy, Robert J	Lt Cdr	01-Oct-08	ENG	ME	NC REQUIREMENTS MANAGERS	ABBEY WOOD
Hardy-Hodgson, David N	Lt RN	01-Jul-04	ENG	AE	DES COMFLEET	ABBEY WOOD
Harfield, Sarah J	Lt RN	01-Jan-99	ENG	IS	NC PSYA	PORTSMOUTH
Harkin, James P	Lt RN	01-Feb-08	WAR	PWO	HMS NORTHUMBERLAND	
Harman, Stephen J	Lt Cdr	01-Oct-08	LOGS	L SM	MTM DEFAC JSCSC	SHRIVENHAM
Harmer, Deborah D	Lt RN	01-May-09	ENG	TM	NCHQ CNPERS (HRTSG)	PORTSMOUTH
Harms, James G	Lt Cdr	02-Jun-12	WAR	P FW	MTM RAF VALLEY	
Harper, Jovin H	Lt RN	01-Apr-12	WAR	P UT	RAF SHAWBURY	SHREWSBURY
Harper, Kevan J	Lt RN	01-May-06	WAR	O SKW	849 SQN	RNAS CULDROSE
Harper, Nicholas J	Lt RN	01-Jul-10	WAR	C	FLEET CAP IS	PORTSMOUTH
Harper, Philip R	Cdr	30-Jun-14	WAR	PWO(N)	DEFENCE ACADEMY	SHRIVENHAM
Harradine, Sam A	Lt RN	01-Sep-11	WAR	GSX	HMS TYNE	
Harriman, Peter	Lt Cdr	01-Oct-06	WAR	C	RNLO GULF	DUBAI
Harrington, Lee	Lt Cdr	01-Mar-06	ENG	ME	DCD - MODSAP KSA	SAUDI ARABIA
Harris, Alexandra K	Lt RN	01-Jun-10	WAR	GSX	STRIKFORNATO - LISBON	LISBON
Harris, Andrew I	Capt RN	20-Jul-10	WAR	O LYNX	FLEET CSAV	LONDON
Harris, Carl C Mbe	Lt Col	30-Jun-09	RM	GS	CTCRM	EXMOUTH
Harris, Christopher G W	Lt RN	01-Jun-08	WAR	ATC	RAF MARHAM	KINGS LYNN

Name	Substantive Rank	Seniority	Branch	Specialisation	Organisation Name	Location Name
Harris, Hugh J L	Lt Cdr	01-Oct-12	WAR	PWO(N)	HMS SUTHERLAND	
Harris, Keri J	Capt RN	02-Sep-14	WAR	O SK6	MTM DCLC RN STUDENTS	SHRIVENHAM
Harris, Linda E	Lt Cdr	01-Oct-14	ENG	TM	FLEET FOST ACOS(Trg)	PORTSMOUTH
Harris, Martyn J	Lt RN	01-Jan-15	WAR	GSX	OP VOCATE	LIBYA - TRIPOLI
Harris, Michael B	Lt RN	31-Jul-09	ENG	AE	HMS SULTAN	GOSPORT
Harris, Michael T	Cdr	30-Jun-07	LOGS	L	DSPA	WINCHESTER
Harris, Neil P	Lt RN	13-Apr-12	WAR	AV	RNAS CULDROSE	HELSTON
Harris, Richard A	Lt Cdr	01-Oct-11	ENG	WE	HMS DRAGON	
Harris, Richard P	Cdr	30-Jun-09	LOGS	L	DMLS	HMS RALEIGH
Harris, Robert	Lt RN	01-Sep-06	ENG	AE	1710 NAS	PORTSMOUTH
Harris, Robert C	SLt	01-May-13	WAR	P UT	MTM RAF CRANWELL	RAFC CRANWELL
Harris, Samuel	Lt RN	01-Sep-14	WAR	SM(X)	MCM1	FASLANE
Harris, Tomas G	Mid	08-Sep-14	ENG	ME	BRNC	BRNC DARTMOUTH
Harris, Tristan MBE	Lt Col	30-Jun-10	RM	GS	HQ ISAF	AFGHANISTAN KABUL
Harrison, Anthony	Lt RN	25-Jun-05	WAR	AV	FLEET FOST ACOS(Trg)	PORTSMOUTH
Harrison, Ellen	Lt RN	24-Oct-08	WAR	AV	RNAS CULDROSE	HELSTON
Harrison, Ian	Lt RN	01-Oct-02	WAR	O LYNX	NATO-ACO-JFC HQ	BRUNSSUM
Harrison, James C	Surg Cdr	01-Jul-12	MED	Psych	PCRF	RFA ARGUS
Harrison, Leigh E	Lt Cdr	01-Oct-11	WAR	FC	OCLC MANCH	MANCHESTER
Harrison, Mark A	Cdr	30-Jun-14	ENG	WESM(TWS)	COMDEVFLOT	PLYMOUTH
Harrison, Mark C	Lt RN	01-Jan-13	WAR	O UT	RNAS CULDROSE	HELSTON
Harrison, Matthew S OBE	Cdre	06-May-14	ENG	WE	DES COMFLEET	ABBEY WOOD
Harrison, Paul D MBE	Cdr	30-Jun-12	WAR	O SKW	JFC HQ	NORTHWOOD
Harrison, Peter M	Lt Cdr	26-Mar-12	RNR		DCDC	SHRIVENHAM
Harrison, Richard S MBE	Cdr	30-Jun-11	WAR	P SK4	FLEET CAP LLM & DRM	PORTSMOUTH
Harrison, Thomas A	Lt RN	01-Feb-13	WAR	HM	HMS EXAMPLE	
Harrison, Thomas I	Lt Cdr	01-Oct-06	ENG	TM(SM)	DEF BD SEC	LONDON
Harrison-Jones, Stuart	Lt RN	01-Jan-03	ENG	TM	HMS SULTAN	GOSPORT
Harrisson, Lucas T	SLt	01-Jul-14	WAR	GSX	HMS OCEAN	
Harrocks, Edwina	SLt	01-May-14	QARNNS	Nurse Officer	MDHU DERRIFORD	PLYMOUTH
Harrop, Ian	Cdr	30-Jun-05	ENG	MESM	MTM NELSON	HMS NELSON
Harry, Stephen J	Lt RN	01-Sep-13	WAR	P UT	MTM	WASHINGTON
Harsent, Paul M	SLt	01-Nov-14	WAR	GSX	MWS COLLINGWOOD	HMS COLLINGWOOD
Harsley, Paul	Mid	08-Sep-14	ENG	WE	BRNC	BRNC DARTMOUTH
Hart, Daniel A	Lt RN	01-Mar-09	ENG	WESM(TWS)	MWS COLLINGWOOD	HMS COLLINGWOOD
Hart, Paul A	Lt Cdr	01-Oct-90	WAR	MEDIA OPS	FOST DPORT	PLYMOUTH
Hart, Sarah	Lt RN	08-May-13	WAR	OP INT	UK MCC	BAHRAIN
Hart, Stephen J E	Lt Col	30-Jun-14	RM	GS	DEFENCE ACADEMY	SHRIVENHAM
Hart, Steven D	Lt Cdr	01-Oct-08	WAR	PWO(C)	FLEET CAP IS	PORTSMOUTH
Hartley, David	Capt	16-Apr-10	RM	SCC	RMR MERSEYSIDE	LIVERPOOL
Hartley, James	Lt RN	01-May-98	ENG	TM	DEFENCE ACADEMY	SHRIVENHAM
Hartley, James O	Mid	01-Feb-14	WAR	GSX	BRNC	BRNC DARTMOUTH
Hartley, John L	Lt Cdr	01-Oct-99	WAR	P LYNX	RNAS YEOVILTON	YEOVILTON
Hartley, Solomon J	SLt	24-Jan-12	LOGS	L	814 SQN	RNAS CULDROSE
Hartridge, Roderick A R	Mid	01-Feb-14	WAR	GSX	BRNC	BRNC DARTMOUTH
Harvey, Ben P W	SLt	03-Oct-14	WAR	GSX	MWS COLLINGWOOD	HMS COLLINGWOOD
Harvey, Colin A	Cdr	30-Jun-00	ENG	MESM	SFM CLYDE	HMNB CLYDE
Harvey, Graham A	Lt Cdr	01-Oct-09	ENG	WE	FLEET CAP SSM	PORTSMOUTH
Harvey, Isha S	Lt RN	01-Apr-12	LOGS	L	HMS ECHO	
Harvey, Martin T	Lt	02-Sep-14	RM	GS	42 CDO RM	PLYMOUTH
Harvey, Matthew D H	Lt RN	01-Oct-09	WAR	GSX	HMS DEFENDER	
Harvey, Robert	Cdr	30-Jun-03	WAR	AAWO	MTM DEFENCE ACADEMY	SHRIVENHAM
Harwood, Carl D	Lt RN	27-Jul-07	ENG	AE	1 ASSLT GP RM	PLYMOUTH
Harwood, David P A	Lt RN	01-Jul-11	WAR	P UT	MTM SHAWBURY	RAF SHAWBURY
Haseldine, Stephen G	Lt Cdr	01-Feb-98	WAR	ATC	FLEET AV VL	RNAS YEOVILTON
Haskins, Benjamin S	Lt Cdr	01-Oct-13	WAR	PWO(SM)	HMS ASTUTE	
Hassall, Ian	Lt Cdr	01-Oct-05	ENG	ME	HMS QUEEN ELIZABETH	
Hassett, Justin G	Surg Lt Cdr	01-Jul-10	MED	Occ Med	MTM INM ALVERSTOKE	GOSPORT
Hastings, Craig S	Lt RN	01-Jun-08	LOGS	L	FOSNI - NRC EE	LONDON
Hastings, Thomas	Lt	02-Sep-14	RM	N/A	CTCRM	EXMOUTH
Hastings, Thomas H	Lt RN	01-Jan-12	WAR	GSX	HMS PROTECTOR	
Hatch, Giles W H	Cdr	31-Dec-98	WAR	PWO(A)	FLEET COMOPS NWD	NORTHWOOD

Name	Substantive Rank	Seniority	Branch	Specialisation	Organisation Name	Location Name
Hatchard, Pollyanna	Lt Cdr	01-Oct-07	ENG	AE	MTM WMO YEOVILTON	RNAS YEOVILTON
Hatcher, Rhett S	Capt RN	26-Sep-11	WAR	P LYNX	HMS PROTECTOR	
Hatherall, Joseph S	Mid	01-Feb-14	ENG	MESM	HMS AUDACIOUS	
Hattle, Prideaux M	Lt Cdr	01-Oct-08	WAR	PWO(U)	MWS COLLINGWOOD	HMS COLLINGWOOD
Havers, Luke C D	Lt	02-Sep-14	RM	GS	42 CDO RM	PLYMOUTH
Havis, Gareth J	Capt	01-Sep-09	RM	GS	HQ 3 CDO BDE RM	PLYMOUTH
Haw, Christopher E MC	Lt Col	30-Jun-12	RM	MLDR	CTCRM	EXMOUTH
Haw, David R	SLt	01-Aug-13	ENG	WE	MWS COLLINGWOOD	HMS COLLINGWOOD
Haward, Tom A A	Capt	01-Sep-13	RM	GS	CTCRM	EXMOUTH
Hawkes, Sophie P E	Surg Lt RN	01-Aug-12	MED	GDMO	HMS ARGYLL	
Hawkings, Tom		09-Oct-14	ENG	MESM	HMS AUDACIOUS	
Hawkins, Daniel M	Surg Lt RN	03-Aug-11	MED	GDMO	MASF	RNAS CULDROSE
Hawkins, Emma L	Lt Cdr	01-Oct-14	LOGS	L	MTM RALEIGH	HMS RALEIGH
Hawkins, Martin	Cdr	30-Jun-03	WAR	O SKW	OPS DIR	LONDON
Hawkins, Michael J	Lt RN	01-May-14	LOGS	L	829 SQN	RNAS CULDROSE
Hawkins, Robert MBE	Lt Cdr	01-Oct-91	WAR	MCD	HQ INTER AIR DEF SYS	KUALA LUMPAR
Hawkins, Stephen	Lt Cdr	01-Oct-10	WAR	REG	RNP - IIQ PMN	HMS EXCELLENT
Hawthorn, Simon	SLt	01-Sep-12	ENG	ME	DCEME SULTAN	HMS SULTAN
Hawthorne, Michael J	Capt RN	30-Jun-05	WAR	SM(CQ)	JCU (CH)	CHELTENHAM
Hay, James D	Cdre	21-Dec-11	ENG	WE	HDPROG	CORSHAM
Hay, Michael	Cdr	30-Jun-14	ENG	WE	MTM FLEET HQ	PORTSMOUTH
Hay, Phillip W	Lt RN	30-Jul-10	WAR	INT	JIEDAC	LONDON
Hay, Richard H I	Lt RN	01-Jul-05	WAR	HM	FLEET MARITIME WARFARE	HMS COLLINGWOOD
Hayashi, Luke R	Lt Cdr	01-Oct-07	WAR	AAWO	BFSAI	FALKLAND ISLANDS
Haycock, Timothy P	Cdr	30-Jun-05	WAR	O LYNX	NBD COB BASE EXECUTIVE OFFICE	HMS DRAKE
Hayden, Timothy W	Lt Cdr	01-Oct-08	WAR	P MER	824 SQN	RNAS CULDROSE
Hayes, Brian J	Lt Cdr	01-Oct-05	WAR	GSX (RES)	HMS CAMBRIA	CARDIFF
Hayes, Brian R	Maj	01-Oct-13	RM	MLDR (SCC)	CTCRM	EXMOUTH
Hayes, James V B	Capt RN	01-Aug-08	ENG	WESM(SWS)	CAPTAIN HMS NEPTUNE	HMNB CLYDE
Hayes, Leigh C	Lt RN	01-Aug-08	ENG	WE	NAVY MCTA	PORTSMOUTH
Hayes, Mark A	Lt Cdr	01-Oct-13	WAR	PWO	HMS KENT	
Hayes, Matthew P	Lt RN	12-Jul-13	LOGS	L	JFC HQ	NORTHWOOD
Hayes, Paul	Lt RN	01-May-09	WAR	SM(X)	HMS VANGUARD	
Hayes, Stuart J	Cdr	30-Jun-00	WAR	MCD	DSEA MARITIME	ABBEY WOOD
Hayes, William D	Lt	06-Apr-14	RM	GS	NCHQ	PORTSMOUTH
Hayle, James	Cdr	30-Jun-05	LOGS	L SM	NAVY ICP	PORTSMOUTH
Haynes, Fiona J	Lt Cdr	01-Oct-14	ENG	ME	MTM DRAKE	HMS DRAKE
Haynes, John G	Lt Cdr	01-Oct-13	WAR	HM	FOST DPORT	PLYMOUTH
Haynes, Samuel	Lt RN	01-Apr-08	WAR	O WILDCAT	WMF 815 SQN FLT 201	RNAS YEOVILTON
Haynes, Warren E	Lt RN	18-Dec-08	MED	MS(EHO)	NCHQ MEDDIV	PORTSMOUTH
Hayton, Stephen R C	Lt Cdr	01-Oct-05	WAR	O MER	824 SQN	RNAS CULDROSE
Hayward, Clive R	Lt Cdr	01-Jun-96	WAR	SM(AWC)	FOSNI - HQ	HELENSBURGH
Hayward, Geoffrey MBE	Lt Cdr	01-Oct-03	WAR	O SKW	FLEET MARITIME WARFARE	HMS COLLINGWOOD
Hayward, John W E	Maj	01-Oct-09	RM	GS	30 CDO IX GP RM	PLYMOUTH
Haywood, Andrew J	Lt RN	01-Nov-05	WAR	ATC	3FTS - CMD	RAFC CRANWELL
Haywood, Guy	Cdr	30-Jun-02	WAR	P LYNX	IPP	LONDON
Haywood, Peter	Cdr	30-Jun-14	WAR	P MER	US CENTCOM	USA
Hazard, Lee Mbe	Lt Cdr	01-Oct-10	MED	MS	MTM DEFAC JSCSC	SHRIVENHAM
Hazel, Thomas W T	Lt RN	01-Apr-11	WAR	MCD	MCM2	PORTSMOUTH
Hazell, Emma V	Lt RN	01-May-08	WAR	HM	FOST DPORT	PLYMOUTH
Hazell, Thomas E	SLt	01-Sep-13	WAR	SM(X)	HMS CLYDE	
Hazelwood, Graeme	Lt RN	01-Oct-08	WAR	FC	MTM MWS COLLINGWOOD	HMS COLLINGWOOD
Hazelwood, Steve	Lt Cdr	01-Oct-12	WAR	C	MTM NEPTUNE	HMNB CLYDE
Hazledine, Oliver W C	Lt RN	08-Dec-12	WAR	GSX	HMS SEVERN	
Head, Martin A	Mid	01-May-14	WAR	SM(X)	BRNC	BRNC DARTMOUTH
Head, Matthew A A	Lt RN	01-Feb-14	ENG	ME	MTM NELSON	HMS NELSON
Head, Steven A	Cdr	30-Jun-14	ENG	WE	JFC HOC C4ISR	NORTHWOOD
Headley, Mark J	Lt Cdr	01-Oct-09	WAR	PWO(A)	MCM2	PORTSMOUTH
Heal, Thomas M C	Capt	03-Sep-14	RM	GS	45 CDO RM	DUNDEE
Healey, Mark J	Lt Cdr	01-Oct-07	ENG	AE	DES COMLAND	ABBEY WOOD
Healey, Nicholas J	Surg Lt RN	01-Feb-11	MED	GMP	MTM INM ALVERSTOKE	GOSPORT
Heames, Richard M	Surg Cdr	30-Jun-06	MED	Anaes	MDHU PORTSMOUTH	PORTSMOUTH

Name	Substantive Rank	Seniority	Branch	Specialisation	Organisation Name	Location Name
Heaney, Martin J	Lt Cdr	01-Oct-09	WAR	O MER	UKMARBATSTAFF	PORTSMOUTH
Heap, Graham G	Lt Cdr	01-Oct-10	ENG	MESM	DES COMFLEET	HMS DRAKE
Heap, Matthew J	Lt RN	20-May-09	LOGS	L	OCLC LONDON	LONDON
Heap, Steven A MBE	Lt Cdr	01-Oct-10	ENG	MESM	DES COMFLEET	HMS DRAKE
Hearn, Samuel P	Lt Cdr	01-Oct-14	WAR	MEDIA OPS	NCHQ CNPERS	PORTSMOUTH
Hearnden, Simon T	Lt RN	11-Dec-09	ENG	WE	MWS COLLINGWOOD	HMS COLLINGWOOD
Heath, Benjamin O	Lt RN	01-Jan-12	WAR	FC	UK MCC	BAHRAIN
Heathcote, James E B	Lt RN	08-Jul-13	WAR	SM(X)	HMS VANGUARD	
Heatly, Robert J	Lt Col	31-Dec-95	RM	GS (RES)	FOSNI - NRC	HELENSBURGH
Heaton, Henry G	Lt Cdr	01-Oct-11	WAR	HM(AS)	DI - ICSP	LONDON
Heaton, Oliver H	Lt RN	01-Apr-13	WAR	GSX	HMS WESTMINSTER	
Heaton, Roxane M	Lt Cdr	01-Oct-14	ENG	TM	FLEET FOST ACOS(Trg)	PORTSMOUTH
Heaton, Sean	Lt Cdr	01-Oct-14	WAR	MCD	FDU	PORTSMOUTH
Heaver, John D	Capt	01-Sep-08	RM	GS	CTCRM	EXMOUTH
Hecks, Ian J	Maj	01-Oct-08	RM	GS	45 CDO RM	DUNDEE
Hedgecox, David C	Lt Cdr	01-Jun-04	ENG	WE	MTM DEFAC JSCSC	SHRIVENHAM
Hedgecox, Philip R	Lt RN	08-Dec-11	ENG	AE	DES COMJE	YEOVIL
Hedges, Justin W OBE	Col	27 Aug-13	RM	GS	MOD DEFENCE STAFF	LONDON
Hedworth, Anthony	Lt RN	01-Jun-94	WAR	P LYNX	RN EXCHANGE DENMARK	DENMARK
Heenan, Martyn	Maj	01-Oct-14	RM	SCC	MWS RALEIGH	HMS RALEIGH
Hefford, Christopher	Lt Cdr	01-Oct-05	LOGS	L	HQ ISAF	AFGHANISTAN KABUL
Heil, Kieran	SLt	01-Sep-13	MED	Medical	BLAKE	BRNC DARTMOUTH
Heirs, Gavin G	Lt Cdr	01-Oct-12	WAR	P SKW	RN EXCHANGE USA	WASHINGTON
Heley, David N	Capt RN	30-Jun-08	WAR	PWO(U)	DES COMFLEET	LONDON
Helliwell, Thomas P	Lt RN	01-Dec-08	WAR	P SK4	NCHQ	PORTSMOUTH
Hember, Marcus	Lt Cdr	01-Oct-06	WAR	PWO(C)	MTM MWS COLLINGWOOD	HMS COLLINGWOOD
Hembury, Lawrence	Maj	01-Oct-09	RM	C (SCC)	HQ 3 CDO BDE RM	PLYMOUTH
Hemming, Christopher A S	Mid	01-Feb-14	WAR	SM(X)	BRNC	BRNC DARTMOUTH
Hems, Wendy L	Lt RN	01-Jul-11	WAR	HM	HMS ENTERPRISE	
Henaghen, Stephen J	Lt Cdr	01-Oct-07	WAR	PWO(A)	FOSNI - NRC WWE	BRISTOL
Henaghen, Wayne D	SLt	01-Feb-12	WAR	O UT	MTM RAF CRANWELL	RAFC CRANWELL
Henderson, Andrew G	Lt RN	01-Jan-07	WAR	O LYNX	WMF 825 SQN HQ	RNAS YEOVILTON
Henderson, Arthur H	Surg Lt Cdr	06-Aug-13	MED	ORL	MTM INM ALVERSTOKE	GOSPORT
Henderson, Holly A	Lt RN	01-Nov-07	LOGS	L	2SL CNPT	PORTSMOUTH
Henderson, Katy V	SLt	01-May-13	LOGS	N/A	HMS DEFENDER	
Henderson, Robert A	Mid	08-Sep-14	WAR	GSX	BRNC	BRNC DARTMOUTH
Henderson, Shaun M	Capt	01-Apr-11	RM	SCC	40 CDO RM	TAUNTON
Henderson, Simon A	Lt RN	01-Jun-11	WAR	GSX	HMS NORTHUMBERLAND	
Henderson, Stuart P	Cdr	30-Jun-09	ENG	ME	FMC STRAT MAN	LONDON
Hendra, Allan J	Lt RN	09-Apr-10	ENG	AE	FLEET CSAV	PORTSMOUTH
Hendrickx, Christopher J	Lt Cdr	01-Jan-04	ENG	WE	HDNTA	CORSHAM
Hendrickx, Sarah	Lt RN	01-Feb-08	ENG	TM	FLEET FOST ACOS(Trg)	ABBEY WOOD
Hendry, Alan	SLt	01-May-13	WAR	GSX	HMS ILLUSTRIOUS	
Hennah, Garry	Lt RN	01-Jan-13	WAR	SM(X)	HMS TRIUMPH	
Henning, Daniel C W	Surg Lt Cdr	19-Sep-08	MED	EM	MDHU DERRIFORD	PLYMOUTH
Henrickson, Beau	SLt	01-Feb-12	WAR	GSX	HMS ARGYLL	
Henry, David T	Lt RN	01-Apr-11	WAR	INT	FLEET COMOPS NWD	RAF WYTON
Henry, Mark	Surg Cdr	09-Mar-10	MED	GMP (C&S)	NCHQ CNPERS	PORTSMOUTH
Henry, Timothy M	Capt RN	09-Sep-13	WAR	PWO(U)	HMS OCEAN	
Henton, James M	Lt RN	01-Sep-10	ENG	MESM	NBD NB SAFETY DEVONPORT	HMS DRAKE
Hepplewhite, Mark B	Lt Cdr	01-Oct-09	ENG	AE	HQ JHC DCOMD	ANDOVER
Hepworth, Nicholas P	Lt RN	20-Oct-08	WAR	SM(N)	RN EXCHANGE NETHERLANDS	DEN HELDER
Herbert, Jack A	Lt RN	09-May-13	WAR	SM(X)	HMS TALENT	
Heritage, Francis	Lt RN	01-Jun-10	WAR	FC	MWS COLLINGWOOD	HMS COLLINGWOOD
Hernon, Robert T B	Lt RN	06-Apr-07	ENG	WE	DES COMJE	FAREHAM
Herod, Thomas P	Surg Lt Cdr	01-Aug-12	MED	GMP	MTM INM ALVERSTOKE	GOSPORT
Herridge, Daniel J	Lt Cdr	01-Oct-12	WAR	MCD	MTM MWS COLLINGWOOD	HMS COLLINGWOOD
Herrington, Robert J	Lt Cdr	01-Oct-14	ENG	MESM	HMS AMBUSH	
Herzberg, Mark J	Lt Cdr	01-Oct-14	ENG	WE	NC REQUIREMENTS MANAGERS	ABBEY WOOD
Hesketh, John J	Lt Cdr	01-Oct-12	WAR	O LYNX	FOST DPORT	PLYMOUTH
Hesling, Gary	Cdr	30-Jun-08	WAR	HM (H CH)	FLEET CAP SSM	PORTSMOUTH
Hesse, Peter J L	SLt	01-Feb-12	WAR	SM(X)	HMS DAUNTLESS	

Name	Substantive Rank	Seniority	Branch	Specialisation	Organisation Name	Location Name
Hetherington, Thomas A	Lt RN	01-Dec-03	ENG	ME	HMS QUEEN ELIZABETH	
Heward, Mark G	Lt Cdr	01-Oct-13	WAR	PWO(N)	HMS SOMERSET	
Hewitson, David R	SLt	01-Nov-14	WAR	GSX	BRNC	BRNC DARTMOUTH
Hewitson, Jonathan G A	Lt RN	01-Aug-00	WAR	MW	HMS HIBERNIA	LISBURN
Hewitt, Adrian J	Lt RN	24-Oct-08	ENG	AE	FOSNI - NRC EE	PETERBOROUGH
Hewitt, Clara J	Lt RN	01-Aug-06	WAR	MW	BRNC	BRNC DARTMOUTH
Hewitt, David L	Cdr	30-Jun-07	WAR	AAWO	RNEAWC - SNO	LINCOLN
Hewitt, Lloyd	Cdr	30-Jun-09	LOGS	L	RN EXCHANGE AUSTRALIA	CANBERRA
Hewitt, Mark J	Lt Cdr	01-Oct-07	ENG	ME	NCHQ CNPERS	PORTSMOUTH
Hewitt, Nigel W	Lt RN	08-Apr-05	ENG	AE	MAA CAA GATWICK	CRAWLEY
Hewitt, Richard P	Lt Cdr	01-Oct-10	WAR	PWO(N)	BRNC	BRNC DARTMOUTH
Hewitt, Simon D	SLt	01-Jul-12	WAR	GSX	HMS SOMERSET	
Heywood, Robert H	Lt RN	01-Sep-06	ENG	MESM	HMS VIGILANT	
Hibberd, Nicholas J	Capt RN	12-Sep-14	WAR	SM(CQ)	CABINET OFFICE	LONDON
Hibberd, Sam P	Mid	08-Sep-14	ENG	ME	BRNC	BRNC DARTMOUTH
Higgins, Alex P B	Lt Cdr	01-Oct-13	ENG	WE	HMS KENT	
Higgins, Andrew J N	Lt RN	13-Jun-05	WAR	P MER CDO	CHF - 846	RAF BENSON
Higgins, Carla L	Lt RN	01-Feb-08	WAR	GSX	FASLANE PBS	HMNB CLYDE
Higgins, Edward	Lt RN	01-Sep-09	WAR	MESM	HMS SULTAN	GOSPORT
Higgins, Peter AFC	Lt Cdr	01-Oct-11	WAR	P LYNX	LHF 815 SQN HQ	RNAS YEOVILTON
Higham, James G OBE	Capt RN	07-Mar-11	ENG	WE	DES COMFLEET	ABBEY WOOD
Higham, Stephen	Cdr	30-Jun-14	WAR	AAWO	MTM MWS COLLINGWOOD	HMS COLLINGWOOD
Higson, Glenn R	Lt Cdr	01-Oct-12	WAR	INT	MTM 45 CDO RM	DUNDEE
Higson, Rennie	Lt RN	05-Oct-07	WAR	MTO N (RES)	OCLC PETERBRGH	PETERBOROUGH
Hildreth, Joseph	Mid	01-May-14	WAR	GSX	BRNC	BRNC DARTMOUTH
Hill, Adrian J	Lt Cdr	01-Oct-08	WAR	O SKW	EMBED FRANCE (FW)	TOULON
Hill, Antony P	Maj	01-Oct-13	RM	SCC	40 CDO RM	TAUNTON
Hill, Christopher	Lt Cdr	01-Oct-14	WAR	SM(AWC)	RNSMS	HMS RALEIGH
Hill, Christopher J	Maj	01-Oct-11	RM	SCC	RM NORTON MANOR	TAUNTON
Hill, David	Cdr	30-Jun-07	ENG	AE	FLEET ACOS(RP)	ABBEY WOOD
Hill, David E	Lt RN	01-Mar-12	ENG	ME	HMS SULTAN	GOSPORT
Hill, Giulian F	Capt RN	12-Feb-14	ENG	ME	DES COMFLEET	ABBEY WOOD
Hill, Graham A	Surg Capt RN	01-Jul-11	MED	T&O	PCRF	RFA ARGUS
Hill, Jamie B	Lt RN	01-Mar-11	ENG	MESM	HMS TORBAY	
Hill, Jonathan P	Lt Col	30-Jun-13	RM	GS	JCU (CH)	CHELTENHAM
Hill, Mark R	Lt Cdr	22-Jun-96	WAR	P SK6	ARF HQ	RNAS YEOVILTON
Hill, Michael J	Surg Lt RN	04-Aug-10	MED	EM	MTM INM ALVERSTOKE	GOSPORT
Hill, Nicholas P	Capt	01-Sep-10	RM	GS	CTCRM	EXMOUTH
Hill, Oliver W	Lt RN	01-Sep-11	WAR	P MER	820 SQN	RNAS CULDROSE
Hill, Philip J	Capt RN	15-Aug-11	ENG	WESM(TWS)	HDPROG	CORSHAM
Hill, Rory	SLt	01-Nov-14	WAR	GSX	MWS COLLINGWOOD	HMS COLLINGWOOD
Hill, Ross	Lt RN	01-Sep-08	WAR	O SKW	854 NAS	RNAS CULDROSE
Hill, Thomas	Lt RN	01-May-03	WAR	O SKW	854 NAS	RNAS CULDROSE
Hillard, Christopher	Lt RN	01-Sep-08	ENG	AE	854 NAS	RNAS CULDROSE
Hillier, Andrew	RN Chpln	13-Sep-05	Ch S	Chaplain	RN EXCHANGE USA	WASHINGTON
Hillman, Christopher M	Surg Lt RN	03-Aug-09	MED	EM	MTM INM ALVERSTOKE	GOSPORT
Hills, Anthony A	Lt Cdr	01-Dec-94	WAR	P LYNX	RNAS CULDROSE	HELSTON
Hills, Michael J MBE	RN Chpln	21-Apr-98	Ch S	Chaplain	43 CDO FPGRM	HELENSBURGH
Hilson, Steven M	Lt Cdr	01-Oct-04	WAR	O LYNX	RNAS YEOVILTON	YEOVILTON
Hilton, Michael R C	Lt RN	23-Apr-06	ENG	TM	DES COMJE	ABBEY WOOD
Hilton, Simon T	Lt Cdr	01-Oct-10	WAR	O LYNX	FLEET CSAV	PORTSMOUTH
Hind, Joshua	SLt	01-Sep-14	ENG	ME	DCEME SULTAN	HMS SULTAN
Hindle, Christopher K	SLt	24-Jan-12	WAR	P UT	MTM RAF CRANWELL	RAFC CRANWELL
Hine, Michael J	Lt Cdr	01-Oct-11	LOGS	L SM	ACDS	ABBEY WOOD
Hine, Nicholas W	Cdre	17-Mar-14	WAR	SM(CQ)	FMC STRAT MAN	LONDON
Hine, Thomas P	SLt	01-Sep-14	WAR	GSX	MCM2	PORTSMOUTH
Hinton, Oliver J	Lt RN	05-Aug-11	LOGS	L	FLEET ACOS(RP)	PORTSMOUTH
Hirons, Francis D	Lt Cdr	01-Oct-06	WAR	PWO(C)	MTM DEFAC JSCSC	SHRIVENHAM
Hiscock, Stephen R	Lt Cdr	01-Oct-09	ENG	WE	FLEET CAP SSM	PORTSMOUTH
Hislop, Scott G	Lt RN	28-Jul-06	ENG	AE	MAA MAAIB FARNBOROUGH	ALDERSHOT
Hitchings, Michael J	Lt RN	01-Sep-06	ENG	MESM	HMS ARTFUL	
Hitchman, Stuart M	Capt	18-Jul-08	RM	GS	NCHQ	PORTSMOUTH

Name	Substantive Rank	Seniority	Branch	Specialisation	Organisation Name	Location Name
Hoar, Mark E	Lt RN	01-Apr-11	WAR	P	MTM 815 SQN YEOVILTON	RNAS YEOVILTON
Hoare, Peter J E	Cdr	30-Jun-10	WAR	O LYNX	OPS DIR	LONDON
Hobbs, Thomas P	Lt Cdr	01-Oct-13	WAR	AWO(U)	FOST DPORT	PLYMOUTH
Hobby, David W	Lt RN	01-May-13	WAR	SM(X)	HMS VIGILANT	
Hobin, Daniel C	Lt RN	01-Sep-13	ENG	MESM	HMS VANGUARD	
Hobley, Christopher J	Lt	02-Sep-14	RM	GS	42 CDO RM	PLYMOUTH
Hocking, Mark J	Lt Cdr	01-Oct-07	ENG	WE	HMS ALBION	
Hocking, Roger C	Lt RN	11-Oct-13	WAR	C	SVCOPS/DHDOPSPLANS/COR	CORSHAM
Hockley, Christopher J CBE	R Adm	08-Sep-11	ENG	ME	FOSNI	HELENSBURGH
Hodder, Gregory L P	Lt RN	01-Nov-14	WAR	SM(X)	MWS COLLINGWOOD	HMS COLLINGWOOD
Hodge, Christopher M	Lt Cdr	01-Oct-04	ENG	MESM	DES COMFLEET	ABBEY WOOD
Hodges, Lauren E	Lt RN	17-Nov-12	QARNNS	Nurse Officer	BRNC	BRNC DARTMOUTH
Hodges, Philip R	Lt Cdr	01-Oct-14	ENG	MESM	DCDS PERS TRG	LONDON
Hodgkins, Jonathan M	Cdr	30-Jun-02	WAR	O LYNX	NCHQ - NAVY CMD SEC	PORTSMOUTH
Hodgkinson, Samuel P	Lt RN	01-Sep-04	WAR	P MER CDO	CHF - 846	RAF BENSON
Hodgkiss, James E	Lt RN	01-Apr-12	WAR	GSX	HMS BULWARK	
Hodgson, Katie J	Lt RN	01-Sep-14	ENG	ME	HMS MONTROSE	
Hodgson, Laura	Lt Cdr	01-Oct-11	ENG	ME	HMS MONMOUTH	
Hodgson, Timothy C MBE	Cdre	04-Sep-12	ENG	MESM	DES COMFLEET	ABBEY WOOD
Hodkinson, Christopher B	Capt RN	04-Sep-12	WAR	PWO(A)	FLEET CAP LLM & DRM	PORTSMOUTH
Hofman, Alison J RRC	Cdr	27-Jul-10	QARNNS	Nurse Officer	DMS WHITTINGTON	LONDON
Hogg, Adam J	Lt Cdr	01-Oct-11	WAR	P FW	DES COMAIR	ABBEY WOOD
Hogg, Christopher W	Lt Cdr	01-Mar-97	WAR	PWO(A)	FOST DPORT	PLYMOUTH
Hogg, Theodore J	Capt	01-Sep-13	RM	GS	HMS BULWARK	
Holborn, Lee J	Lt RN	01-Nov-10	WAR	P LYNX	LHF 815 SQN	RNAS YEOVILTON
Holbrook, Simon J	Lt RN	01-Feb-08	WAR	FC	MTM WMO YEOVILTON	RNAS YEOVILTON
Holburt, Richard M	Lt RN	01-Nov-06	LOGS	L	RNAS YEOVILTON	YEOVILTON
Holdcroft, Luke J	Lt RN	01-Aug-14	WAR	SM(X)	MCM1	FASLANE
Holden, Paul A	Lt Cdr	01-Oct-02	ENG	AE	FLEET CSAV	PORTSMOUTH
Holden, Robert J	Lt Cdr	01-Oct-99	WAR	O SKW	750 SQN	RNAS CULDROSE
Holden, Simon W	Lt RN	01-May-13	WAR	GSX	MCM2	PORTSMOUTH
Holder, John	Lt Cdr	01-Oct-09	WAR	P MER	RN EXCHANGE USA	WASHINGTON
Hole, Joseph S I	Lt RN	01-Apr-09	WAR	P	MTM 820 SQN CULDROSE	RNAS CULDROSE
Holford, Kane	Capt	01-Sep-10	RM	GS	COMUKAMPHIBFOR	PORTSMOUTH
Holgate, James A	Lt Cdr	01-Oct-11	ENG	WE	HMS MONMOUTH	
Holland, Amanda	Lt Cdr	01-Nov-04	QARNNS	PHC	DPHC SW	HMS RALEIGH
Holland, Charlotte C	Lt Cdr	01-Oct-08	LOGS	L	RNAS YEOVILTON	YEOVILTON
Holland, Edward R	Lt RN	01-Apr-08	WAR	O MER	829 SQN	RNAS CULDROSE
Holland, Emma E	Surg Lt RN (D)	04-Jul-11	DENTAL	GDP	RNAS CULDROSE	HELSTON
Holland, Fergus W	SLt	14-Aug-12	WAR	GSX	MCM2	PORTSMOUTH
Holland, Paul E	Lt RN	01-Jul-11	LOGS	L	HMS RICHMOND	
Holland, Richard	Lt RN	01-May-08	WAR	SM(X)	FLEET COMOPS NWD	NORTHWOOD
Holland, Steven W	Lt Cdr	01-Oct-13	ENG	AE	DES COMAIR	ABBEY WOOD
Holliehead, Craig	Lt RN	01-Jan-02	WAR	P LYNX	RN EXCHANGE USA	WASHINGTON
Hollinghurst, Philip C	Mid	17-Nov-14	ENG	TM	BRNC	BRNC DARTMOUTH
Hollingworth, Christopher R	Lt Cdr	01-Oct-13	WAR	PWO	UK ACC (83 EAG)	QATAR
Hollingworth, Eleanor	Lt RN	01-Sep-08	WAR	FC	RNAS YEOVILTON	YEOVILTON
Hollins, Rupert	Capt RN	01-Jul-09	LOGS	L BAR	SERV ATTACHE/ADVISER	PEKING
Holloway, Benjamin S V	Lt RN	01-May-07	LOGS	L SM	HQ BFC	EPISKOPI
Holloway, Jonathan T	Capt RN	30-Jun-02	ENG	MESM	FOSNI - YOUTH MSCC	PORTSMOUTH
Holloway, Steven A	Lt Cdr	01-Oct-03	WAR	PWO(U)	LSP OMAN	OMAN
Hollyfield, Peter	Lt Cdr	01-Oct-14	ENG	IS	HDNET	CORSHAM
Holmes, Christopher	Lt Cdr	01-Oct-12	ENG	ME	HMS LANCASTER	
Holmes, Christopher J	Col	01-Dec-14	RM	C	DDC	LONDON
Holmes, Matthew DSO	Brig	19-Mar-13	RM	GS	DCDC	SHRIVENHAM
Holmes, Patrick J M	Lt RN	01-May-02	WAR	P MER	820 SQN	RNAS CULDROSE
Holmes, Robert	Cdr	25-Feb-96	WAR	PWO (RES)	FLEET CMR	PORTSMOUTH
Holroyd, Jason H	Lt RN	27-Jul-07	ENG	WE	OCLC MANCH	MANCHESTER
Holroyd, Jonathon E J	Lt Cdr	01-Oct-08	WAR	O MER	MTM DEFAC JSCSC	SHRIVENHAM
Holt, Christopher J W	Lt RN	01-Sep-14	ENG	AE	MTM WMO CULDROSE	RNAS CULDROSE
Holt, John D	Lt RN	01-May-00	ENG	IS(SM)	NATO-ACT-JWC	STAVANGER
Holt, Joseph	Mid	08-Sep-14	WAR	SM(X)	BRNC	BRNC DARTMOUTH

Name	Substantive Rank	Seniority	Branch	Specialisation	Organisation Name	Location Name
Holt, Justin S MBE	Lt Col	30-Jun-05	RM	LC	DEFENCE ACADEMY	SHRIVENHAM
Holt, Laura	Lt RN	01-Jun-10	LOGS	L	NBCP CAPTAIN OF THE BASE	PORTSMOUTH
Holt, Steven OBE	Capt RN	12-Dec-12	WAR	PWO(N)	MTM FLEET HQ	PORTSMOUTH
Honey Morgan, Janice C	RN Chpln	01-Sep-03	Ch S	Chaplain	CHFHQ	RNAS YEOVILTON
Honnoraty, Mark R OBE	Cdr	30-Jun-05	WAR	SM(CQ)	COMFASFLOT	HELENSBURGH
Hood, Kevin M	Lt Cdr	01-Apr-98	ENG	MESM	DES COMFLEET	ABBEY WOOD
Hook, David A CBE	Maj Gen	26-Oct-11	RM	C	CTCRM	EXMOUTH
Hooper, Christopher C	Surg SLt	22-Jul-14	MED	Medical	BLAKE	BRNC DARTMOUTH
Hooper, Johanna	Cdr	30-Jun-13	LOGS	L	MTM NELSON	HMS NELSON
Hooper, Thomas	Lt RN	01-Jan-05	LOGS	L	NATO-ACT-JWC	STAVANGER
Hooper, William R	Lt RN	01-Jan-06	WAR	P LYNX	DEF HELI FLYING SCH	SHREWSBURY
Hope, Karl	Lt Cdr	01-Sep-96	ENG	IS	DBS MIL PERS	GOSPORT
Hope, William D G	SLt	01-Sep-14	ENG	WE	HMS RICHMOND	
Hoper, Paul R	Lt Cdr	30-Jun-07	WAR	O SKW	FLEET CSAV	PORTSMOUTH
Hopkins, Danielle	SLt	01-Sep-12	ENG	WE	HMS DUNCAN	
Hopkins, Rhys	Maj	01-Oct-07	RM	GS	DHU	CHICKSANDS
Hopkins, Richard M E	Maj	01-Oct-06	RM	GS	NATO-ACT-HQ	MONS (CASTEAU)
Hopkins, Steven D MBE	Lt Cdr	01-Oct-03	WAR	P SK6	771 SQN	RNAS CULDROSE
Hopkinson, Geoffrey A	Lt	01-Sep-12	RM	GS	43 CDO FPGRM	HELENSBURGH
Hopper, Ian	Lt Cdr	09-Apr-02	WAR	PWO(A)	UKMARBATSTAFF	PORTSMOUTH
Hopper, Simon M	Capt RN	29-Sep-14	WAR	PWO(A)	FLEET CAP SSM	PORTSMOUTH
Hopton, Fiona C F	Lt Cdr	01-Oct-13	WAR	HM	HMS MONTROSE	
Hopton, Matthew J	Lt Cdr	01-Oct-13	WAR	PWO(SM)	HMS VANGUARD	
Hopwood, Adrian P	Lt RN	17-Dec-04	WAR	GSX	NBCP BASE EXEC OFFICER	PORTSMOUTH
Horlock, Andrew	Lt Cdr	01-Oct-12	MED	MS(SM)	DES COMFLEET	HMS DRAKE
Horn, Neil R	Lt RN	01-Apr-08	ENG	MESM	DES COMFLEET	ABBEY WOOD
Horn, Peter B MBE	Cdr	30-Jun-99	WAR	PWO(A)	NCHQ CNPS	PORTSMOUTH
Horne, Christopher P	Capt	01-Sep-08	RM	GS	DAT(A) A	AFGHANISTAN KABUL
Horne, Jason	Cdr	30-Jun-10	WAR	PWO(U)	BMM	KUWAIT
Horne, Nicholas	Lt RN	01-Apr-09	WAR	FC	MTM MWS COLLINGWOOD	HMS COLLINGWOOD
Horne, Simon T	RN Chpln	01-Sep-04	Ch S	Chaplain	HMS SULTAN	GOSPORT
Horne, Thomas S	SLt	01-Nov-14	WAR	O UT	MTM 750 SQN CULDROSE	RNAS CULDROSE
Horne, Timothy G	Cdr	30-Jun-97	WAR	PWO(A)	NCHQ CNPS	PORTSMOUTH
Horner, Patrick A	Lt Cdr	01-Aug-94	WAR	AAWO	MTM NELSON	HMS NELSON
Horsted, James A	Lt Cdr	01-Mar-10	ENG	MESM	HMS AMBUSH	
Horton, James R	Lt Cdr	01-Oct-13	WAR	P LYNX	AWC	BOSCOMBE DOWN
Horton, Simon	Lt RN	11-Dec-05	WAR	INT	MTM DRAKE	HMS DRAKE
Hotchkiss, Jonathan J	SLt	01-Sep-14	WAR	GSX	HMS IRON DUKE	
Hougham, Thomas N	Lt RN	01-Sep-05	WAR	P MER	824 SQN	RNAS CULDROSE
Houghton, Ben R	Mid	01-May-14	WAR	P UT	BRNC	BRNC DARTMOUTH
Houghton, Christopher L	Lt RN	01-Nov-13	ENG	WESM	HMS ARTFUL	
Houghton, David G	Lt RN	01-Jun-13	WAR	P SK4	845 SQN	RNAS YEOVILTON
Houghton, James E	Capt	01-Mar-14	RM	GS	43 CDO FPGRM	HELENSBURGH
Houghton, Philip J	Lt Cdr	01-Jul-94	WAR	PWO(U)	COMPORFLOT	PORTSMOUTH
Houlberg, Kenneth M T	Cdr	30-Jun-08	WAR	PWO(A)	COMPORFLOT	PORTSMOUTH
Houlberg, Kristian A N	Surg Cdr	14-Feb-09	MED	Med	PCRF	RFA ARGUS
Houlston, Christopher C	Mid	01-Feb-14	WAR	GSX	BRNC	BRNC DARTMOUTH
Houlston, Ian J E	Lt RN	01-Jan-05	WAR	P LYNX	LHF 702 SQN	RNAS YEOVILTON
Hounslow, Oliver W	Lt RN	24-Jul-14	WAR	SM(X)	HMS LANCASTER	
Hounsom, Timothy	Lt Cdr	01-Apr-05	WAR	PWO(U)	LSP OMAN	MUSCAT
Hounsome, Debra M MBE ARRC	Cdr	01-Jul-13	QARNNS	Nurse Officer	PCRF	RFA ARGUS
Hounsome, Jonathan R	Lt RN	01-Jan-04	WAR	O SK6	771 SQN	RNAS CULDROSE
House, Andrew L	Lt RN	01-Oct-09	WAR	GSX	HMS ST ALBANS	
Houston, Darren J M	Cdr	30-Jun-11	WAR	PWO(N)	RN EXCHANGE USA	WASHINGTON
Howard, Alexander D P	Lt RN	01-Sep-14	ENG	AE	RNAS YEOVILTON	YEOVILTON
Howard, Dale T	Lt RN	01-Sep-13	ENG	WE	HMS ILLUSTRIOUS	
Howard, Daniel G	Cdr	30-Jun-06	WAR	ATC	PERMANENT JOINT HQ - LO-GE	BERLIN
Howard, James W	Lt RN	01-Feb-09	WAR	PWO(SM)	MTM MWS COLLINGWOOD	HMS COLLINGWOOD
Howard, Martin L	Lt RN	01-Sep-07	WAR	O SKW	AWC	BOSCOMBE DOWN
Howard, Nicholas H	Cdr	30-Jun-10	ENG	AE	MTM WMO YEOVILTON	RNAS YEOVILTON
Howarth, John	Maj	01-Oct-05	RM	SCC	CTCRM	EXMOUTH
Howarth, Michael C	Lt Cdr	01-Oct-14	LOGS	L SM	JFC GLOBAL ADMIN UNIT	GLASGOW

Name	Substantive Rank	Seniority	Branch	Specialisation	Organisation Name	Location Name
Howe, Craig M	Lt RN	01-Jul-98	WAR	INT	FLEET COMOPS NWD	RNAS CULDROSE
Howe, David N	Lt RN	05-Aug-11	ENG	WE	DES COMFLEET	ABBEY WOOD
Howe, Jonathan	Lt RN	16-Dec-11	WAR	INT	FLEET COMOPS NWD	HMS COLLINGWOOD
Howe, Jonathan	Lt Cdr	01-Oct-14	ENG	AE	HQ JHC CAP DIR	ANDOVER
Howe, Julian P	Lt Cdr	01-Oct-01	WAR	PWO(A)	NCHQ CNPERS	PORTSMOUTH
Howe, Michael	Lt RN	01-Sep-08	WAR	P MER	UK MCC	BAHRAIN
Howe, Neil D	Lt RN	19-Dec-08	LOGS	L SM	RNAS CULDROSE	HELSTON
Howe, Nicholas E J	Lt RN	01-Nov-14	WAR	GSX	HMS SOMERSET	
Howe, Thomas	Lt Cdr	01-Nov-05	WAR	PWO(N)	MWS COLLINGWOOD	HMS COLLINGWOOD
Howell, Andrew J	Lt RN	01-Aug-08	ENG	WE	COMDEVFLOT	PLYMOUTH
Howell, Michael A	Surg Capt RN	06-May-08	MED	EM	INM ALVERSTOKE2	GOSPORT
Howell, Simon B	Cdr	30-Jun-04	WAR	PWO(A)	NCHQ CNPS	PORTSMOUTH
Howells, Simon M	Lt Cdr	01-Oct-07	WAR	INT	FLEET CAP IS	PORTSMOUTH
Howes, Daniel P	Lt RN	01-Nov-13	WAR	P SK4	845 SQN	RNAS YEOVILTON
Howes, Francis CB, OBE	Maj Gen	08-Feb-10	RM	MLDR	BDS	WASHINGTON
Howes, Richard J	Surg Lt Cdr	02-Aug-11	MED	EM	MTM DEFAC JSCSC	SHRIVENHAM
Howett, Toby C	Mid	17-Nov-14	WAR	GSX	BRNC	BRNC DARTMOUTH
Howie, Ian C	Lt RN	01-Mar-12	WAR	P UT	RAF SHAWBURY	SHREWSBURY
Hoyle, Wayne A	Lt	06-Apr-14	RM	GS	NCHQ	PORTSMOUTH
Hubschmid, Spencer R	Lt Cdr	01-Oct-07	ENG	WESM(SWS)	MOD SSPAG	LONDON
Hucker, Oliver	Lt Cdr	01-Oct-13	WAR	GSX	MTM MWS COLLINGWOOD	HMS COLLINGWOOD
Huckle, Thomas C	Capt	01-Sep-11	RM	GS	45 CDO RM	DUNDEE
Huckstep, Joseph P	SLt	01-Nov-14	WAR	P UT	MWS COLLINGWOOD	HMS COLLINGWOOD
Hudson, Andrew I	Lt Cdr	01-Oct-14	WAR	SM(AWC)	COMDEVFLOT	PLYMOUTH
Hudson, Peter D CB CBE	V Adm	14-Feb-13	WAR	PWO(N)	NATO ACO	NORTHWOOD
Hudson, Richard A	Lt RN	30-Jul-10	ENG	WE	FOST DPORT	PLYMOUTH
Hudson, Tom A J	Lt RN	01-May-04	ENG	TM	MWS COLLINGWOOD	HMS COLLINGWOOD
Huggett, Christopher G	Capt	01-Sep-13	RM	GS	42 CDO RM	PLYMOUTH
Huggins, Michael A	Lt RN	01-Apr-11	WAR	GSX	BFSAI	FALKLAND ISLANDS
Hughes, Adam A	Lt RN	01-Mar-11	ENG	MESM	HMS TIRELESS	
Hughes, Andrew S	Surg Cdre	25-Jul-11	MED	GMP (C&S)	DMS WHITTINGTON	LICHFIELD
Hughes, Benjamin	Lt Cdr	01-Oct-09	LOGS	L CMA	COMPORFLOT	PORTSMOUTH
Hughes, Charlotte L	Surg Lt Cdr	02-Aug-10	MED	GMP	MTM MWS COLLINGWOOD	HMS COLLINGWOOD
Hughes, Christopher B	Lt Cdr	01-Oct-09	WAR	O SKW	MTM DEFAC JSCSC	SHRIVENHAM
Hughes, David M	Lt RN	08-Dec-11	ENG	AE	1710 NAS	PORTSMOUTH
Hughes, Elizabeth E	Lt Cdr	01-Oct-11	ENG	ME	MTM WMO YEOVILTON	RNAS YEOVILTON
Hughes, Gareth D	Lt Cdr	01-Oct-09	ENG	ME	NAVY MCTA	PORTSMOUTH
Hughes, Gareth L	Cdr	31-Dec-00	LOGS	L	NCHQ CNPERS	PORTSMOUTH
Hughes, Garreth J C	Mid	17-Nov-14	LOGS	L	BRNC	BRNC DARTMOUTH
Hughes, Gary A	SLt	01-Sep-14	WAR	GSX	HMS ST ALBANS	
Hughes, Gary E	Lt Cdr	01-Oct-12	WAR	AV	NC REQUIREMENTS MANAGERS	ABBEY WOOD
Hughes, Geoffrey	Lt Cdr	01-Oct-13	LOGS	L	TEMP AIO PLANNING BLB1	ANDOVER
Hughes, John J	Lt Cdr	01-Oct-10	WAR	P SK4	CHFHQ	RNAS YEOVILTON
Hughes, Matthew J	Capt	30-Mar-12	RM	MLDR (SCC)	45 CDO RM	DUNDEE
Hughes, Michael I	SLt	01-Nov-14	WAR	GSX	MWS COLLINGWOOD	HMS COLLINGWOOD
Hughes, Michael S	SLt	01-Aug-13	WAR	SM(X)	MCM1	FASLANE
Hughes, Nicholas D M	SLt	01-Oct-12	MED	MS	NCHQ MEDDIV	PORTSMOUTH
Hughes, Nicholas J	Capt RN	13-Oct-09	WAR	SM(CQ)	MTM NELSON	HMS NELSON
Hughes, Paul A	Surg Capt RN	08-Sep-08	MED	GMP (C&S)	DMRC HEADLEY COURT	EPSOM
Hughes, Peter LVO	Cdr	06-Feb-88	WAR	PWO(N)	NCHQ CNPS	PORTSMOUTH
Hughes, Roger D	Maj	01-Oct-13	RM	SCC	NCHQ CNPERS	PORTSMOUTH
Hughes, Ryan	SLt	01-Sep-12	WAR	GSX	MCM1	FASLANE
Hughes, Samuel E	Capt	01-Aug-07	RM	GS	DEFENCE ACADEMY	SHRIVENHAM
Hughes, Scott M	Lt Cdr	01-Oct-11	WAR	P SKW	RNAS CULDROSE	HELSTON
Hughesdon, Mark D	Cdr	30-Jun-10	ENG	WE	NAVY MCTA	PORTSMOUTH
Hull, Thomas E	SLt	02-May-12	WAR	SM(X)	HMS SOMERSET	
Hulme, Timothy OBE	Cdr	30-Jun-08	WAR	O LYNX	FLEET ACOS(RP)	PORTSMOUTH
Hulse, Anthony W	Maj	01-Oct-07	RM	C	40 CDO RM	TAUNTON
Hulse, Elspeth J	Surg Lt Cdr	06-Aug-08	MED	Anaes	MTM INM ALVERSTOKE	GOSPORT
Hulse, Rebecca J	Lt Cdr	01-Oct-12	LOGS	L	HMS MONMOUTH	
Hulston, Lauren M	Lt Cdr	01-Oct-11	WAR	O MER	829 SQN	RNAS CULDROSE
Hume, James A	Lt RN	01-Apr-12	WAR	O LYNX	MTM 815 SQN YEOVILTON	RNAS YEOVILTON

Name	Substantive Rank	Seniority	Branch	Specialisation	Organisation Name	Location Name
Hume, Kenneth J	Lt RN	01-Mar-99	WAR	HM(AM)	FLEET COMOPS NWD	NORTHWOOD
Hume, Sarah K (ARRC)	Lt RN	01-Nov-03	QARNNS	EN	DMRC HEADLEY COURT	EPSOM
Humphery, Duncan	Lt Cdr	01-Oct-07	ENG	ME	COMDEVFLOT	PLYMOUTH
Humphrey, Darren P	Lt Cdr	01-Oct-14	QARNNS	MH	DPHC SOUTH - DCMH	HMS EXCELLENT
Humphrey, Ivor J	Cdr	30-Jun-11	ENG	WE	D STRAT PROG	LONDON
Humphreys, Rhodri H	Lt RN	08-Jul-09	ENG	TM	RNAS YEOVILTON	YEOVILTON
Humphries, Graham D	Lt RN	01-May-01	WAR	P SK4	CHFHQ	RNAS YEOVILTON
Humphries, Jason E	Lt Cdr	01-Oct-05	WAR	PWO(U)	PJHQ (UK)	NORTHWOOD
Humphries, Mark	Lt Cdr	01-Oct-14	WAR	P FW	AWC	LINCOLN
Hunnibell, John R	Lt Cdr	01-Oct-13	WAR	MCD	HMS COLLINGWOOD	FAREHAM
Hunnybun, Simon P	Lt RN	17-Dec-10	WAR	REG	RNP - HQ PMN	HMS EXCELLENT
Hunt, Ben P	Lt Cdr	01-Oct-14	WAR	P MER	857 NAS	RNAS CULDROSE
Hunt, Darren MBE	Maj	01-Oct-08	RM	P SK4	MONUC CONGO	CONGO
Hunt, Fraser B G	Cdr	30-Jun-14	WAR	P MER	DCDS PERS TRG	LONDON
Hunt, Patrick S	Lt Cdr	01-Jan-07	ENG	WE	DES COMLAND	ABBEY WOOD
Hunt, Rachel E	Lt RN	01-Jan-03	WAR	GSX	FOSNI - CNR	PORTSMOUTH
Hunt, Robert G	Lt RN	01-Feb-09	WAR	P FW	FLEET CSAV	WASHINGTON
Hunt, Robert J C	Lt Cdr	01-Oct 09	LOGS	L BAR	UK MCC	BAHRAIN
Hunt, Stephen	Lt Cdr	01-Oct-03	WAR	AAWO	LOAN DSTL	FAREHAM
Hunt, Steven D	Lt	02-Sep-14	RM	GS	45 CDO RM	DUNDEE
Hunter, Cameron M	Lt RN	03-May-13	ENG	ME	HMS NORTHUMBERLAND	
Hunter, Darran J	Lt RN	01-Sep-07	ENG	MESM	DES COMFLEET	ABBEY WOOD
Hunter, Deryk E	Lt RN	15-Mar-08	WAR	SM(N)	COMFASFLOT	HELENSBURGH
Hunter, Guy M C	Surg Lt RN	03-Aug-11	MED	GDMO	HMS TALENT	
Hunter, Mitchell	Lt RN	01-Sep-12	ENG	MESM	HMS VIGILANT	
Huntingford, Damian J	Lt Col	30-Jun-13	RM	GS	DCDS MIL STRAT OPS	LONDON
Huntington, Simon P OBE	Capt RN	28-Oct-13	WAR	PWO(U)	JFHQ	NORTHWOOD
Huntley, Genevieve E	Lt RN	01-Jan-10	WAR	GSX	MTM NELSON	HMS NELSON
Huntley, Ian	Brig	15-Aug-11	RM	HW	DEFENCE ACADEMY	SHRIVENHAM
Hurdle, Ian	Capt	28-Jul-06	RM	SCC	NCHQ	PORTSMOUTH
Hurley, Karl	Lt Cdr	01-Oct-11	QARNNS	EN	MDHU PORTSMOUTH	PORTSMOUTH
Hurman, Richard N	Lt Cdr	01-Oct-12	WAR	PWO	FLEET COMOPS NWD	NORTHWOOD
Hurry, Andrew P	Lt Cdr	01-Nov-94	WAR	P LYNX	FLEET CSAV	PORTSMOUTH
Hurst, Gareth W	Capt	21-Mar-13	RM	SCC	42 CDO RM	PLYMOUTH
Hurt, Christopher G	Maj	01-Oct-14	RM	GS	MTM DRAKE	HMS DRAKE
Husband, James	Lt Cdr	01-Oct-14	LOGS	L SM	FLEET SPT LOGS INFRA	PORTSMOUTH
Hussain, Shayne MBE	Cdr	30-Jun-07	WAR	METOC	NATO - BRUSSELS	BRUSSELS
Hussey, Steven J MBE	Col	01-Oct-14	RM	P SK4	COMUKAMPHIBFOR	PORTSMOUTH
Hussey, William G	Mid	08-Sep-14	ENG	ME	BRNC	BRNC DARTMOUTH
Hutchings, Justin R	Lt Cdr	01-Oct-07	WAR	SM(CQ)	DI - ICSP	LONDON
Hutchings, Richard	Lt Cdr	01-Dec-05	WAR	PWO	FLEET CAP WARFARE	PORTSMOUTH
Hutchings, Ross	Capt	01-Sep-12	RM	GS	NCHQ	
Hutchings, Sam D	Surg Cdr	14-Jun-11	MED	Anaes	PCRF	RFA ARGUS
Hutchins, Richard F	Cdr	30-Jun-11	ENG	MESM	NCHQ CNPS	PORTSMOUTH
Hutchins, Timothy	Lt Cdr	01-Oct-05	WAR	HM (M CH)	NATO-ACT-HQ	NORFOLK
Hutchinson, Christopher J	Lt Cdr	01-Sep-00	WAR	HM (M CH)	RNAS YEOVILTON	YEOVILTON
Hutchinson, Gillian P	Lt RN	01-Jun-07	LOGS	L	MTM NELSON	HMS NELSON
Hutchinson, Michael R	Lt Cdr	01-Oct-12	WAR	FC	HMS DIAMOND	
Hutchinson, Oliver J P	Cdr	30-Jun-06	WAR	AAWO	UK MCC	BAHRAIN
Hutchinson, Philippa C	Mid	01-Feb-14	WAR	GSX	BRNC	BRNC DARTMOUTH
Hutchinson, Robert	Mid	01-May-14	WAR	GSX	BRNC	BRNC DARTMOUTH
Hutchinson, Thomas D	SLt	01-Sep-14	ENG	MESM	DCEME SULTAN	HMS SULTAN
Hutchison, Paul G	Lt Cdr	01-May-98	ENG	MESM	NBD NB SAFETY DEVONPORT	HMS DRAKE
Hutton, Graham	Lt Cdr	01-Oct-04	WAR	O SKW	HMS QUEEN ELIZABETH	
Hutton, James OBE	Col	30-Jun-07	RM	GS	MTM CTCRM	EXMOUTH
Hutton, Paul R	Lt RN	27-Jul-07	ENG	AE	DES COMJE	YEOVIL
Huxtable, Mark C	SLt	01-Sep-12	WAR	P UT	RAF LINTON-ON-OUSE	RAF LINTON ON OUSE
Huynh, Cuong	Lt Cdr	01-Oct-10	LOGS	L	UK MCC	BAHRAIN
Hyde, James W	Lt Cdr	01-Oct-12	ENG	WE	DES COMLAND	ABBEY WOOD

I

Iliffe, David I	Lt Cdr	01-Oct-08	WAR	INT	DCOG NORTHWOOD	NORTHWOOD

Name	Substantive Rank	Seniority	Branch	Specialisation	Organisation Name	Location Name
Illingworth, Richard A	Lt Cdr	01-Oct-12	WAR	INT	JCU (CH)	CHELTENHAM
Imm, Nicholas D H	Surg Cdr	30-Jul-08	MED	GMP	DPHC SOUTH	HMS NELSON
Imrie, Peter B	Lt Cdr	01-Oct-04	WAR	AV	NCHQ CNPERS	PORTSMOUTH
Imrie, Samantha J	Lt Cdr	01-Oct-11	LOGS	L	DES COMLAND	BICESTER
Ingamells, Stephen D	Lt RN	01-Jan-04	WAR	P SK4	845 SQN	RNAS YEOVILTON
Inge, Daniel J	Lt Cdr	01-Oct-06	WAR	ATC	MTM DEFAC JSCSC	SHRIVENHAM
Ingham, Andrew R	Cdr	30-Jun-13	WAR	AAWO	MTM DEFAC JSCSC	SHRIVENHAM
Ingham, Lee-Anne	Lt RN	01-Sep-01	WAR	HM	RNAS CULDROSE	HELSTON
Ingham, Maryla K	Lt Cdr	01-Oct-08	WAR	PWO(N)	HMS OCEAN	
Inglesby, Paul R	Lt RN	11-Dec-09	WAR	PWO	HMS DEFENDER	
Inglis, David	Surg SLt	15-Jul-14	MED	Medical	BLAKE	BRNC DARTMOUTH
Inglis, David J	Lt RN	01-Jan-02	WAR	P MER CDO	CHF - 846	RAF BENSON
Inglis, Graham D	Lt Cdr	01-Oct-12	WAR	AAWO	HMS DAUNTLESS	
Inglis, William S	Lt RN	01-Jan-07	WAR	SM(N)	UK MCC	BAHRAIN
Ingman, Thomas D	Mid	17-Nov-14	ENG	WE	BRNC	BRNC DARTMOUTH
Ingram, Dean D	Lt RN	20-Jan-07	WAR	PWO(SM)	MOD SSPAG	LONDON
Ingram, Richard	Capt RN	07-Sep-09	WAR	AAWO	LSP OMAN	MUSCAT
Inkley, Simon R	Mid	01-May-14	WAR	GSX	BRNC	BRNC DARTMOUTH
Insley, Carrie A	Lt Cdr	01-Oct-12	LOGS	L	HMS QUEEN ELIZABETH	
Instrell, Christopher B	Lt RN	01-Jan-09	ENG	AE	DES COMLAND	ABBEY WOOD
Ireland, John M	Lt Cdr	01-Oct-02	ENG	MESM	DES COMFLEET	ABBEY WOOD
Irons, Paul A	Lt Cdr	01-Jul-97	WAR	INT	DI - SA	LONDON
Irvine, Oliver	Mid	08-Sep-14	ENG	AE	BRNC	BRNC DARTMOUTH
Irving, Luke V	Capt	01-Sep-10	RM	GS	HQ 3 CDO BDE RM	PLYMOUTH
Irving, Paul J	Lt Cdr	01-Oct-12	WAR	P HELO PWO	HMS RICHMOND	
Irwin, Mark A	Cdr	30-Jun-08	ENG	ME	MTM RMR MERSEYSIDE	LIVERPOOL
Irwin, Matthew	Lt RN	01-Sep-12	WAR	GSX	MCM2	PORTSMOUTH
Irwin, Steven G	Lt RN	01-Oct-11	WAR	P UT	MTM SHAWBURY	RAF SHAWBURY
Irwin, Stuart G	Lt Cdr	01-Oct-11	WAR	P LYNX	AWC	BOSCOMBE DOWN
Isaac, Thomas I	Mid	17-Nov-14	WAR	GSX	BRNC	BRNC DARTMOUTH
Isaacs, Nathan J	Lt Cdr	01-Oct-13	WAR	MCD	FDU	PORTSMOUTH
Isherwood, Carl R	Lt RN	01-May-04	WAR	GSX	CHFHQ	RNAS YEOVILTON
Issitt, Barry D	Lt Cdr	01-Oct-12	WAR	P FW	FLEET CSAV	PORTSMOUTH
Isted, Lee R	Lt RN	01-Sep-07	LOGS	L SM	MTM NELSON	HMS NELSON
Ives, David J	Lt Cdr	25-Oct-12	WAR	HM(AS)	RN EXCHANGE AUSTRALIA	CANBERRA
Ives, Katie M	Lt RN	01-Sep-13	ENG	WE	HMS LANCASTER	
Ivill, Stephen	Lt Cdr	01-Oct-12	WAR	O MER	824 SQN	RNAS CULDROSE
Ivory, Matthew J	Lt RN	01-Sep-11	ENG	ME	BRNC	BRNC DARTMOUTH
Ivory, Thomas J	Lt Cdr	01-Oct-14	ENG	WE	DES COMFLEET	ABBEY WOOD

J

Name	Substantive Rank	Seniority	Branch	Specialisation	Organisation Name	Location Name
Jack, Valencera	Lt RN	01-Jul-09	ENG	ME	HMS OCEAN	
Jackman, Andrew W	Cdr	30-Jun-98	WAR	PWO(C)	BFSAI	FALKLAND ISLANDS
Jacks, Michael J	Lt RN	01-Sep-11	WAR	HM	FLEET HM UNIT	PLYMOUTH
Jackson, Amie R	Lt RN	01-Jan-08	WAR	GSX	HMS BLAZER	
Jackson, Andrew S	Capt RN	29-Sep-14	ENG	MESM	DES COMFLEET	ABBEY WOOD
Jackson, Darren M	Lt RN	15-Mar-07	QARNNS	OT	MDHU PORTSMOUTH	PORTSMOUTH
Jackson, David	Cdr	30-Jun-10	ENG	AE	HQ JHC DCOMD	ANDOVER
Jackson, Howard C	Lt RN	01-May-01	WAR	P SK4	CHFHQ	RNAS YEOVILTON
Jackson, Ian A	Cdr	30-Jun-08	ENG	ME	DES COMFLEET	PORTSMOUTH
Jackson, Mark H	RN Chpln	19-Apr-83	Ch S	Chaplain	RN GIBRALTAR - CHAP	HMS ROOKE
Jackson, Matthew J A DSO	Col	05-Nov-13	RM	GS	DEF BD SEC	LONDON
Jackson, Thomas	Lt RN	10-Nov-14	WAR	GSX	HMS DAUNTLESS	
Jackson-Spence, Nicholas J	SLt	01-May-12	WAR	P UT	MTM RAF CRANWELL	RAFC CRANWELL
Jacob, Andrew W	Lt Cdr	01-Oct-09	WAR	HM (M CH)	NCHQ CNPERS	PORTSMOUTH
Jacobs, Joshua B	SLt	01-Sep-12	WAR	P UT	MTM SHAWBURY	RAF SHAWBURY
Jacques, Kathryn	Lt RN	24-Jan-07	WAR	AW (RES)	HMS SHERWOOD	NOTTINGHAM
Jacques, Marcus J	Cdr	30-Jun-12	WAR	AAWO	BDS	WASHINGTON
Jacques, Michael S	Lt RN	01-Sep-13	ENG	MESM	HMS ASTUTE	
Jacques, Nicholas A	Lt Cdr	01-Oct-02	WAR	O WILDCAT	WMF 825 SQN HQ	RNAS YEOVILTON
Jacques, Sam O	Mid	01-Feb-14	WAR	SM(X)	BRNC	BRNC DARTMOUTH
Jaffrey, Heather B	Lt RN	11-Apr-06	QARNNS	EN	DPHC SOUTH	HMS SULTAN

Name	Substantive Rank	Seniority	Branch	Specialisation	Organisation Name	Location Name
Jaggers, Gary G	Lt Cdr	01-Oct-01	WAR	O MER	824 SQN	RNAS CULDROSE
Jakes, Matthew O	Lt RN	09-Apr-10	ENG	ME	MTM DCEME SULTAN	HMS SULTAN
James, Adam J	Cdr	30-Jun-07	WAR	HM (H CH)	COMDEVFLOT	PLYMOUTH
James, Andrew G	Cdr	30-Jun-14	ENG	MESM	NUCLEAR CAPABILITY	LONDON
James, Christopher I	Lt RN	13-Apr-12	ENG	AE	824 SQN	RNAS CULDROSE
James, Darren B	Lt RN	15-Apr-11	ENG	AE	HMS SULTAN	GOSPORT
James, Gareth C M	Lt Cdr	01-Oct-11	LOGS	L	HMS KENT	
James, Katherine J	Lt Cdr	01-Oct-06	QARNNS	Tutor	DHET - DMS WHITTINGTON	LICHFIELD
James, Mark	Lt Cdr	01-Oct-08	ENG	WE	NC REQUIREMENTS MANAGERS	ABBEY WOOD
James, Oliver N M	Lt RN	01-Jan-13	ENG	WESM	HMS TRIUMPH	
James, Paul M DSO	Col	22-Aug-11	RM	GS	MOD NSD - HDS	LONDON
James, Robert	Lt RN	01-Jul-04	WAR	AV	NATO-ACO-SHAPE	CASTEAU
Jameson, Andrew C	Cdre	01-Jul-11	LOGS	L BAR	FLEET CMR	PORTSMOUTH
Jameson, Andrew J	Lt RN	01-Sep-01	WAR	GSX	CFPS SQUAD	PORTSMOUTH
Jameson, Roger M	Lt Cdr	01-Oct-09	WAR	P LYNX	MTM WMO CULDROSE	RNAS CULDROSE
Jameson, Susan	Cdr	30-Jun-09	WAR	OP INT	FLEET CMR	PORTSMOUTH
Jamieson, Christopher M	Mid	01-Feb-14	WAR	GSX	BRNC	BRNC DARTMOUTH
Jamieson, Paul A	Lt Cdr	01 Oct 13	WAR	SM(AWC)	UK MCC	BAHRAIN
Jamieson, Scott	Surg Lt Cdr	06-Aug-13	MED	GMP	MTM INM ALVERSTOKE	GOSPORT
Jamieson, Scott M	Lt RN	13-Apr-12	MED	MS(CDO)	MDHU DERRIFORD	PLYMOUTH
Jamison, James S	Maj	01-Oct-11	RM	HW	45 CDO RM	DUNDEE
Jane, Samuel C	Lt Cdr	01-Oct-14	WAR	MCD	MTM MWS COLLINGWOOD	HMS COLLINGWOOD
Janzen, Alexander N OBE	Lt Col	30-Jun-10	RM	C	40 CDO RM	TAUNTON
Jaques, Simon C D	Surg Lt Cdr	06-Aug-08	MED	Occ Med	DPHC SW	RNAS CULDROSE
Jardine, Iain	Lt RN	01-May-04	WAR	P MER	BRNC	BRNC DARTMOUTH
Jarman, Paul R	Lt Cdr	01-Oct-08	ENG	WESM(TWS)	COMDEVFLOT	PLYMOUTH
Jarvis, Laurence R	Capt RN	17-Mar-14	ENG	ME	DES COMFLEET	ABBEY WOOD
Jayes, Neil J	Lt Cdr	01-Oct-07	WAR	REG	RNP - HQ PMN	HMS EXCELLENT
Jefferson, Toby S	Cdr	30-Jun-11	ENG	AE	1710 NAS	PORTSMOUTH
Jeffrey, Ben S	Lt RN	01-May-09	WAR	SM(X)	HMS TALENT	
Jeffrey, Joseph S	SLt	01-Sep-14	LOGS	L	43 CDO FPGRM	HELENSBURGH
Jeffreys, Susan	Lt RN	12-Jul-13	QARNNS	ITU	PCRF	RFA ARGUS
Jenkin, Alastair M H	Capt RN	30-Jun-08	ENG	WE	NCHQ CNPS	PORTSMOUTH
Jenkin, Richard H	Lt RN	01-Sep-12	WAR	P UT	MTM SHAWBURY	RAF SHAWBURY
Jenking-Rees, Damian	Lt Cdr	01-Oct-05	LOGS	L	DMLS	HMS RALEIGH
Jenkins, David G	Cdr	30-Jun-14	WAR	SM(CQ)	HMS ASTUTE	
Jenkins, David N	Lt RN	27-Jul-07	ENG	WE	CAP SP CBRN ABW	ABBEY WOOD
Jenkins, Gareth S	Lt	25-Aug-13	RM	N/A	CTCRM	EXMOUTH
Jenkins, Gari Wyn	Cdr	30-Jun-03	ENG	WE	DES COMFLEET	ABBEY WOOD
Jenkins, Gwyn OBE	Col	01-Jul-11	RM	GS	CDS	LONDON
Jenkins, Robert	Lt RN	01-Dec-99	ENG	TM	JFC - DCTS (H)	AYLESBURY
Jenks, Jennifer C B	Surg Lt Cdr (D)	24-Sep-05	DENTAL	GDP	DCPPA	HMS DRYAD
Jepson, Nicholas H M	Lt Col	30-Jun-12	RM	C	MTM NELSON	HMS NELSON
Jermy, Richard	Lt Cdr	31-Mar-04	WAR	HUMINT (RES)	FOSNI - NRC NE	HELENSBURGH
Jerrold, William H	Maj	01-Oct-13	RM	C	COMUKAMPHIBFOR	PORTSMOUTH
Jervis, Christopher	Surg Lt RN	04-Aug-10	MED	GMP	MTM INM ALVERSTOKE	GOSPORT
Jess, Aran E K	Lt Col	30-Jun-13	RM	MLDR	FLEET CAP MARCAP	PORTSMOUTH
Jess, Ian M CBE	R Adm	03-Jul-12	ENG	ME	NCHQ	
Jesson, Christopher M	Capt	20-Jul-07	RM	SCC	HQ 3 CDO BDE RM	PLYMOUTH
Jessop, Paul E	Capt RN	08-Mar-10	ENG	MESM	FLEET CAP SSM	PORTSMOUTH
Jewitt, Charles	Lt Cdr	30-Jun-03	LOGS	L (RES)	FOSNI - YOUTH MSCC	LINCOLN
Jewson, Benjamin D	Lt RN	01-May-04	WAR	O LYNX	MTM RAF CRANWELL	RAFC CRANWELL
Jobin, Wesley N	Mid	01-May-14	WAR	GSX	BRNC	BRNC DARTMOUTH
John, Gareth MBE	Cdr	30-Jun-07	ENG	WE	MOD NSD	CANBERRA
John, James	Lt RN	01-Apr-11	LOGS	L SM	COMFASFLOT	HELENSBURGH
Johns, Andrew W	Cdr	30-Jun-12	WAR	SM(CQ)	HMS TORBAY	
Johns, Michael	Cdr	30-Jun-10	WAR	O MER	AWC	LINCOLN
Johns, Sarah A B	Cdr	30-Jun-07	ENG	TM	FLEET FOST ACOS(Trg)	PORTSMOUTH
Johnson, Andrew S	Cdr	31-Dec-99	WAR	AAWO	NATO-ACO-LC	IZMIR
Johnson, Anthony R	Lt Cdr	01-Oct-05	WAR	O LYNX	LHF 815 SQN	RNAS YEOVILTON
Johnson, Chad C B	Cdr	30-Jun-12	ENG	AE P	CHFHQ	RNAS YEOVILTON
Johnson, Daren	Capt	30-Mar-12	RM	SCC	1 ASSLT GP RM	PLYMOUTH

Name	Substantive Rank	Seniority	Branch	Specialisation	Organisation Name	Location Name
Johnson, Helen E M	Lt RN	01-Sep-05	WAR	O MER	814 SQN	RNAS CULDROSE
Johnson, Isaac	Mid	01-Feb-14	WAR	GSX	BRNC	BRNC DARTMOUTH
Johnson, Jeremy D	Lt RN	01-Jan-98	ENG	TM	HMS SULTAN	GOSPORT
Johnson, Lauren O	Lt Cdr	01-Oct-10	LOGS	L	NBD COB STAFF OFFICER	HMS DRAKE
Johnson, Mark	Lt Col	30-Jun-13	RM	P SK4	OPS DIR	LONDON
Johnson, Matthew D	Lt RN	01-Jun-07	WAR	P SK4	CHF - 846	RAF BENSON
Johnson, Matthew J	Lt RN	01-Apr-14	WAR	P	MTM 815 SQN YEOVILTON	RNAS YEOVILTON
Johnson, Matthew P	Lt RN	01-May-13	WAR	GSX	HMS TYNE	
Johnson, Michael I	Lt RN	09-Apr-12	WAR	GSX	HMS DIAMOND	
Johnson, Oliver B M	Mid	17-Nov-14	LOGS	L	BRNC	BRNC DARTMOUTH
Johnson, Paul R	Lt Cdr	01-Oct-07	ENG	AE	MAA	ABBEY WOOD
Johnson, Roy L	Lt RN	12-Nov-97	ENG	WESM	HMS SULTAN	GOSPORT
Johnson, Scott	Lt Cdr	01-Oct-06	WAR	SM(CQ)	FOST SM SEA	HMNB CLYDE
Johnson, Thomas	Lt RN	01-Sep-08	WAR	PWO	HMS LANCASTER	
Johnson, Tim P	Lt Cdr	01-Oct-13	WAR	INT	JFIG - JT PLANS & FD	RAF WYTON
Johnson, Tobias E	Surg Lt RN	01-Sep-12	MED	GDMO	HMS VICTORIOUS	
Johnston, Andrew I	Lt RN	01-May-04	WAR	P SK4	MTM JTEG - ETPS RN	BOSCOMBE DOWN
Johnston, David R	Lt Cdr	01-Oct-08	LOGS	L SM	DCDS PERS TRG	LONDON
Johnston, David R	Lt RN	11-Apr-08	ENG	WESM(TWS)	DES COMJE	ABBEY WOOD
Johnston, David S	Capt	01-Sep-11	RM	GS	PJHQ (UK)	NORTHWOOD
Johnston, Gregory P	Lt RN	01-Jul-08	ENG	TM	FLEET MARITIME WARFARE	HMS COLLINGWOOD
Johnston, Karl G	Maj	01-Oct-11	RM	GS	42 CDO RM	PLYMOUTH
Johnston, Matthew A	2Lt	25-Aug-14	RM	N/A	CTCRM	EXMOUTH
Johnstone, Clive C C CBE	R Adm	12-Jul-11	WAR	PWO(A)	MOD CNS/ACNS	LONDON
Johnstone, Neil C	Capt	01-Sep-10	RM	GS	MTM NELSON	HMS NELSON
Johnstone-Burt, Charles E	Lt RN	01-Apr-11	LOGS	L	HMS PORTLAND	
Joll, Simon	Cdr	30-Jun-08	LOGS	L SM	MTM RN GLOBAL	USA
Jones, Adam E	Lt RN	01-Nov-02	WAR	P SK4	MTM RAF CRANWELL	RAFC CRANWELL
Jones, Aled L	Surg Lt Cdr	06-Aug-08	MED	GS	MTM INM ALVERSTOKE	GOSPORT
Jones, Alun D	Capt RN	22-Sep-14	WAR	P LYNX	FLEET CSAV	PORTSMOUTH
Jones, Andrew N	Capt	01-Sep-11	RM	GS	MTM 45 CDO RM	DUNDEE
Jones, Benjamin L	Capt	01-Sep-10	RM	GS	SP WPNS SCHOOL	WARMINSTER
Jones, Benjamin P	SLt	09-Oct-14	WAR	SM(X)	BRNC	BRNC DARTMOUTH
Jones, Carolyn	Lt Cdr	01-Oct-14	WAR	MEDIA OPS	NCHQ - NAVY CMD SEC	PORTSMOUTH
Jones, Carolyn J	Surg Lt Cdr	02-Aug-10	MED	GMP	MTM NELSON	HMS NELSON
Jones, Charmody E	Lt Cdr	01-Oct-10	WAR	PWO(C)	FLEET CAP IS	PORTSMOUTH
Jones, Cheryl	Lt RN	01-Sep-06	WAR	O SKW	NCHQ CNPS	PORTSMOUTH
Jones, Christopher	Lt RN	13-Jun-08	WAR	C	MTM FLEET HQ	PORTSMOUTH
Jones, Christopher	Lt RN	01-Sep-10	WAR	O SKW	MTM MWS COLLINGWOOD	HMS COLLINGWOOD
Jones, Christopher D	Lt Cdr	01-Oct-14	ENG	ME	HMS BULWARK	
Jones, Darren P	Lt Cdr	01-Oct-13	ENG	AE	MAA	ABBEY WOOD
Jones, David	Cdr	30-Jun-12	ENG	MESM	DES COMFLEET	ABBEY WOOD
Jones, David K	Lt Cdr	01-Oct-09	LOGS	L	NATO-ACT-HQ	NORFOLK
Jones, David M	Lt Cdr	01-Jul-04	ENG	WE	DES COMFLEET	ABBEY WOOD
Jones, Emmanuel N L	Lt RN	01-Jan-03	WAR	PWO(N)	UK MCC	BAHRAIN
Jones, Gareth D	Lt Cdr	01-Sep-03	ENG	TM	DCOG CIO	LONDON
Jones, Gemma E	Lt RN	01-Oct-09	WAR	GSX	MTM FLEET HQ	PORTSMOUTH
Jones, Gordon	Lt Cdr	01-Oct-14	WAR	HM(AM)	FOST SM SEA	HMNB CLYDE
Jones, Helen C	Lt Cdr	01-Oct-12	ENG	ME	HMS SUTHERLAND	
Jones, Hugh	Capt	28-Jul-06	RM	SCC	ASG RM	RNAS YEOVILTON
Jones, Ian M	Lt Cdr	01-Oct-07	ENG	AE	RNAS CULDROSE	HELSTON
Jones, Jason B	Lt RN	13-Jul-12	ENG	WE	HMS ARGYLL	
Jones, Jason D	SLt	01-Feb-14	MED	Medical	BLAKE	BRNC DARTMOUTH
Jones, Lewis	SLt	01-Sep-14	WAR	SM(X)	HMS PROTECTOR	
Jones, Marc R	Lt RN	01-Jan-07	LOGS	L BAR	DMLS	HMS RALEIGH
Jones, Mark	Lt RN	01-Jul-04	ENG	WE	DES COMJE	ABBEY WOOD
Jones, Mark D	Lt Cdr	01-Oct-10	WAR	O LYNX	LHF HQ	RNAS YEOVILTON
Jones, Mark F	SLt	01-Feb-12	LOGS	L	RNAS CULDROSE	HELSTON
Jones, Mark O	Lt RN	01-Sep-13	ENG	WE	HMS OCEAN	
Jones, Mark R	Lt Cdr	01-Oct-07	ENG	WE	DES COMFLEET	ABBEY WOOD
Jones, Martin C	Cdr	30-Jun-01	WAR	HM (H CH)	C4ISR JT USER	NORTHWOOD
Jones, Martin D	2Lt	25-Aug-14	RM	N/A	CTCRM	EXMOUTH

Name	Substantive Rank	Seniority	Branch	Specialisation	Organisation Name	Location Name
Jones, Morgan	Lt RN	01-Jan-09	WAR	P MER	829 SQN	RNAS CULDROSE
Jones, Nicholas H	Lt Cdr	01-Oct-12	ENG	IS	MCSU	FLEET HQ
Jones, Philip A KCB	V Adm	13-Dec-11	WAR	PWO(C)	FLEET COMMANDER DCNS	PORTSMOUTH
Jones, Richard P M	Lt RN	20-May-12	WAR	GSX	MTM NEPTUNE	HMNB CLYDE
Jones, Robert P	Lt RN	01-Dec-13	ENG	ME	MTM DRAKE	HMS DRAKE
Jones, Robert P M	Maj	01-Sep-09	RM	HW	COMUKAMPHIBFOR	PORTSMOUTH
Jones, Sam D L	Mid	01-Feb-14	WAR	GSX	BRNC	BRNC DARTMOUTH
Jones, Simon A	Lt RN	01-Nov-13	WAR	P SK4	845 SQN	RNAS YEOVILTON
Jones, Stephen	Lt RN	01-May-03	ENG	ME	FOST DPORT	PLYMOUTH
Jones, Steven F	Lt RN	01-Sep-08	LOGS	L	FLEET SPT LOGS INFRA	PORTSMOUTH
Jones, Steven K	Lt RN	15-Apr-11	ENG	WE	MWS COLLINGWOOD	HMS COLLINGWOOD
Jones, Timothy M	Cdr	21-Jul-13	MED	MS	MDHU DERRIFORD	PLYMOUTH
Jones, Toby	Lt RN	01-Feb-07	WAR	INT	JFIG - JT IP	RAF WYTON
Jones, Toby W	Capt	01-Sep-09	RM	LC	NCHQ	PORTSMOUTH
Jones, William A	Lt RN	01-Jun-10	ENG	WE	MWS COLLINGWOOD	HMS COLLINGWOOD
Jones-Thompson, Michael	Lt Cdr	01-Oct-07	WAR	AAWO	MWS COLLINGWOOD	HMS COLLINGWOOD
Jordan, Adrian M	Surg Capt RN (D)	11-Jan-11	DENTAL	GDP(C&S)	DDS RHQ SOUTH	ALDERSHOT
Jordan, Andrew A	Capt RN	25-Sep-13	WAR	PWO(U)	FLEET ACOS(RP)	PORTSMOUTH
Jordan, Catherine E	Cdr	30-Jun-13	WAR	O LYNX	HMS ST ALBANS	
Jordan, Craig	Lt Cdr	01-Oct-05	ENG	IS	CIO-DSAS	CORSHAM
Jordan, Craig D	Lt RN	20-May-09	ENG	AE O	857 NAS	RNAS CULDROSE
Jose, Steven	Cdr	30-Jun-12	ENG	AE P	RNAS CULDROSE	HELSTON
Joshi, Cael R	Lt RN	01-May-14	WAR	GSX	MWS COLLINGWOOD	HMS COLLINGWOOD
Joyce, David A	Cdr	30-Jun-10	ENG	WE	NCHQ CNPS	PORTSMOUTH
Joyce, David J	Lt Cdr	01-Oct-13	ENG	ME	HMS DAUNTLESS	
Joyce, Thomas J	Cdr	30-Jun-11	WAR	P LYNX	FLEET CSAV	PORTSMOUTH
Joynes, Vivienne	Lt RN	01-Apr-08	LOGS	L	DES COMLAND	ABBEY WOOD
Juckes, Martin A	Cdr	30-Jun-06	ENG	AE	CHFHQ	RNAS YEOVILTON
Judd, Oliver J	Lt RN	19-Aug-09	ENG	WE	DES COMFLEET	ABBEY WOOD
Julian, Timothy M	Lt Cdr	01-Oct-04	WAR	P SK6	RNAS CULDROSE	HELSTON

K

Name	Substantive Rank	Seniority	Branch	Specialisation	Organisation Name	Location Name
Kadinopoulos, Benjamin A	Lt Cdr	01-Apr-11	ENG	WE	FLEET CAP MARCAP	PORTSMOUTH
Kain, Matthew J W	SLt	01-Sep-12	MED	Medical	BLAKE	BRNC DARTMOUTH
Kane, Anthony P	Lt RN	01-Sep-12	WAR	GSX	HMS ARGYLL	
Kantharia, Paul	Lt RN	25-Jun-05	ENG	MESM	DES COMFLEET	PLYMOUTH
Kantharia, Richard P	Lt RN	01-Sep-12	WAR	SM(X)	HMS TALENT	
Karavla, Alexandra M I	Lt RN	01-Jan-13	WAR	GSX	EU OHQ	NORTHWOOD
Karsten, Thomas M	R Adm	14-Dec-12	WAR	PWO(U)	LOAN HYDROG DGHR(N)	TAUNTON
Kassapian, David L	Col	16-Feb-11	RM	GS	CTCRM	EXMOUTH
Kavanagh, Craig M	SLt	01-Sep-12	WAR	P UT	MTM SHAWBURY	RAF SHAWBURY
Kay, David	Cdr	01-Jan-02	LOGS	L (RES)	NORTHWOOD HQ	NORTHWOOD
Kay, Paul S	Lt Cdr	01-Oct-08	WAR	SM(CQ)	UKMARBATSTAFF	PLYMOUTH
Kay, Victoria J	Lt RN	15-Mar-06	ENG	WE	MWS COLLINGWOOD	HMS COLLINGWOOD
Keam, Ian	Lt Cdr	01-Oct-10	ENG	AE	DES COMJE	YEOVIL
Keane, Brendan M	Lt Cdr	01-Oct-14	ENG	WE	NC REQUIREMENTS MANAGERS	ABBEY WOOD
Keane, Joseph P	Lt RN	01-May-06	WAR	O LYNX	LHF 815 SQN	RNAS YEOVILTON
Kearsley, Iain P	Lt Cdr	01-Oct-11	LOGS	L	HMS DAUNTLESS	
Keeble, Christopher P	Lt RN	01-May-14	WAR	GSX	MCM2	PORTSMOUTH
Keegan, Amanda C	Lt RN	01-Oct-06	WAR	O MER	820 SQN	RNAS CULDROSE
Keeler, Charlotte L	SLt	14-May-14	LOGS	L	RNAS YEOVILTON	YEOVILTON
Keeling, Megan	Lt RN	01-Sep-11	ENG	ME	HMS SULTAN	GOSPORT
Keenan, Benjamin F	Lt Cdr	01-Oct-14	ENG	MESM	HMS TRIUMPH	
Keenan, Douglas J	Lt RN	01-May-07	WAR	O LYNX	LHF 702 SQN	RNAS YEOVILTON
Keenan, Gregory F	Lt RN	01-Sep-12	ENG	WESM(TWS)	HMS VANGUARD	
Keens, Emma L	Lt RN	07-Oct-11	WAR	HM	FLEET HM UNIT	PLYMOUTH
Keillor, Stuart J	Lt Cdr	01-Oct-12	WAR	SM(AWC)	MTM MWS COLLINGWOOD	HMS COLLINGWOOD
Keith, Benjamin C	Lt Cdr	01-Oct-08	WAR	P LYNX	HMS DEFENDER	
Keith, Charles R	Lt RN	01-Feb-10	WAR	INT	PJHQ (UK)	NORTHWOOD
Kelday, Alexander W	Lt RN	16-Feb-12	ENG	MESM	DCEME SULTAN	HMS SULTAN
Kellett, Andrew	Cdr	30-Jun-13	ENG	ME	COMDEVFLOT	PLYMOUTH
Kelley, Alexandra L	Lt RN	01-Jan-07	WAR	O MER	824 SQN	RNAS CULDROSE

Name	Substantive Rank	Seniority	Branch	Specialisation	Organisation Name	Location Name
Kelly, Grant J	Lt Cdr	01-Oct-09	ENG	TM	FLEET FOST ACOS(Trg)	PORTSMOUTH
Kelly, Howard C	Lt Cdr	01-Apr-02	ENG	MESM	DES COMFLEET	BARROW IN FURNESS
Kelly, John	Cdr	30-Jun-06	ENG	ME	BDS	WASHINGTON
Kelly, Nigel J	RN Chpln	26-May-92	Ch S	Chaplain	HMS NELSON	PORTSMOUTH
Kelly, Patrick J	Lt RN	01-Jun-07	WAR	HM	HMS MERSEY	
Kelly, Philip M	Lt Col	30-Jun-10	RM	P FW	MSP	LONDON
Kelly, Simon P	Lt Cdr	01-Jul-07	WAR	MCD	MCM1	FASLANE
Kelway, Jenna	Lt Cdr	01-Oct-14	ENG	ME	FLEET ACOS(RP)	PORTSMOUTH
Kemp, Gillian J	Surg Lt Cdr (D)	19-Jun-07	DENTAL	GDP	DEFENCE DENTAL SERVS	PLYMOUTH
Kemp, Peter	Lt RN	24-Oct-08	ENG	AE	RNAS CULDROSE	HELSTON
Kemp, Peter G	Surg Lt Cdr	06-Aug-13	MED	GMP	MTM INM ALVERSTOKE	GOSPORT
Kemp, Peter J	Lt Col	30-Jun-10	RM	MLDR	43 CDO FPGRM	HELENSBURGH
Kemp, Richard L	Lt Cdr	01-Oct-14	WAR	GSX	MTM MWS COLLINGWOOD	HMS COLLINGWOOD
Kemp, Thomas A	Lt RN	01-Nov-14	WAR	SM(X)	MWS COLLINGWOOD	HMS COLLINGWOOD
Kempley, Paul S	Lt RN	11-Dec-09	ENG	WE	DIST/DSG	NORTHWOOD
Kenchington, Robin A W	Lt RN	01-Nov-09	WAR	O LYNX	LHF 815 SQN	RNAS YEOVILTON
Kendall-Torry, Guyan C	Lt RN	01-Sep-06	ENG	WESM(SWS)	FOST FAS SHORE	HMNB CLYDE
Kendrick, Alexander M	Lt Cdr	01-Feb-05	ENG	WE	DES COMFLEET	ABBEY WOOD
Kendry, Adam	Lt RN	01-Dec-14	ENG	TM	MTM NELSON	HMS NELSON
Kenneally, Sean J	Maj	01-Oct-06	RM	GS	NCHQ	PORTSMOUTH
Kennedy, Catheryn H	Lt Cdr	01-Oct-12	QARNNS	ITU	MDHU DERRIFORD	PLYMOUTH
Kennedy, Daniel	Lt RN	01-Jan-12	WAR	GSX	MTM WMO YEOVILTON	RNAS YEOVILTON
Kennedy, Elizabeth H	Lt RN	01-Aug-08	WAR	GSX	FOST DPORT	PLYMOUTH
Kennedy, Ian C	Lt Cdr	01-Oct-10	QARNNS	MH	HQ DPHC	LICHFIELD
Kennedy, Ian J A	Capt RN	18-Mar-14	ENG	ME	FLEET ACOS(RP)	PORTSMOUTH
Kennedy, Inga J	Capt RN	21-Nov-11	QARNNS	Nurse Officer	NCHQ MEDDIV	PORTSMOUTH
Kennedy, Roger J	Lt Cdr	01-Oct-07	WAR	O SKW	849 SQN	RNAS CULDROSE
Kennington, Lee A	Lt Cdr	01-Oct-07	WAR	O LYNX	RNAS YEOVILTON	YEOVILTON
Kennon, Stanley	RN Chpln	17-Sep-00	Ch S	Chaplain	BRNC	BRNC DARTMOUTH
Kent, Andrew G	Lt RN	20-Oct-08	WAR	MCD	MCM2	PORTSMOUTH
Kent, Matthew J	Lt Cdr	01-Oct-08	ENG	ME	NCHQ CNPS	PORTSMOUTH
Kent, Robert	Lt RN	12-Feb-08	ENG	WE	LOAN DSTL	FAREHAM
Kent, Thomas W R	Lt RN	14-Aug-14	WAR	SM(X)	MTM MWS COLLINGWOOD	HMS COLLINGWOOD
Kenward, Jonathan C	Lt RN	15-Aug-14	LOGS	L	NATO ACO	NORTHWOOD
Kenyon, Adam M	Lt RN	01-Nov-10	WAR	SM(X)	HMS VANGUARD	
Kenyon, Carolyn M	Lt Cdr	01-Oct-07	LOGS	L BAR	DCDS PERS - SPA	RAF NORTHOLT
Ker, Catherine M	Lt RN	01-Jan-08	WAR	MCD	MTM NELSON	HMS NELSON
Ker, Stuart W	Lt RN	01-Sep-08	ENG	WE	FLEET CAP MARCAP	PORTSMOUTH
Kerley, Benjamin J	Lt RN	01-May-03	WAR	P MER	MTM DEFAC JSCSC	SHRIVENHAM
Kern, Alastair S	Maj	01-Sep-00	RM	GS	FLEET SPT FGEN	PORTSMOUTH
Kerr, Adrian N	Lt Cdr	01-Jan-01	ENG	WESM(TWS)	NC REQUIREMENTS MANAGERS	ABBEY WOOD
Kerr, Jack	Lt Cdr	06-Feb-00	WAR	GSX	MWS COLLINGWOOD	HMS COLLINGWOOD
Kerr, Martin A	Lt RN	22-Mar-09	WAR	P SK4	202 SQN - AFLT	RAF BOULMER
Kerr, William M M	Lt Cdr	09-Apr-90	WAR	MCD	FLEET CAP SSM	PORTSMOUTH
Kerridge, Samuel J	Mid	08-Sep-14	WAR	GSX	BRNC	BRNC DARTMOUTH
Kerrigan, Glen	Lt RN	01-Jan-12	ENG	WE	MWS COLLINGWOOD	HMS COLLINGWOOD
Kershaw, Neville L	Lt RN	08-Oct-12	WAR	SM(X)	HMS AMBUSH	
Kershaw, Richard J	Surg Cdr	07-Jan-14	MED	GMP (C&S)	NCHQ MEDDIV	PORTSMOUTH
Kershaw-Yates, Elizabeth H	Surg Cdr	03-Sep-13	MED	GMP	DPHC SW	HMS RALEIGH
Kershaw-Yates, Simon H C	Surg Lt Cdr (D)	18-Jul-06	DENTAL	GDP	CTCRM	EXMOUTH
Kestle, Mark E	Lt Cdr	01-Oct-09	ENG	ME	DES COMFLEET	ABBEY WOOD
Kestle, Ryan J	Maj	01-Oct-12	RM	MLDR	CTCRM	EXMOUTH
Kew, Nigel	Lt RN	27-Jul-07	ENG	WESM(TWS)	FLEET COMOPS NSTP30	FAREHAM
Key, Andrew D	Mid	08-Sep-14	ENG	WE	BRNC	BRNC DARTMOUTH
Key, Benjamin J	R Adm	29-Apr-13	WAR	O LYNX	FOST DPORT	PLYMOUTH
Key, Matthew P	Lt RN	01-Jan-12	WAR	HM	RNAS CULDROSE	HELSTON
Keyworth, Mark A	Lt RN	01-Aug-08	WAR	C	MWS RALEIGH	HMS RALEIGH
Khan, Mansoor A	Surg Lt Cdr	01-Aug-06	MED	GS	RCDM	BIRMINGHAM
Kidd, Andrew N	Lt RN	01-Aug-07	WAR	SM(N)	HMS TRENCHANT	
Kidd, Matthew A	Mid	17-Nov-14	WAR	HM	BRNC	BRNC DARTMOUTH
Kidson, Adam W B	Capt	03-Sep-14	RM	GS	40 CDO RM	TAUNTON
Kiernan, Colin	Lt Cdr	01-Oct-13	WAR	P LYNX	NATO-ACO-JFC HQ	NAPLES

Name	Substantive Rank	Seniority	Branch	Specialisation	Organisation Name	Location Name
Kierstan, Simon	Lt RN	01-Jan-01	ENG	TM	DEF HELI FLYING SCH	SHREWSBURY
Kies, Lawrence N	Lt Cdr	01-Oct-03	ENG	TM	BRNC	BRNC DARTMOUTH
Kiff, Ian W	Lt Cdr	01-Oct-10	ENG	WE	SCU SHORE	HMS COLLINGWOOD
Kilbane, Liam	Surg Lt RN	07-Aug-13	MED	Medical	BLAKE	BRNC DARTMOUTH
Kilbride, Paul	Lt RN	01-Feb-09	WAR	GSX	MCM1	FASLANE
Kilgallon, Michael J	Mid	01-May-14	LOGS	L	BRNC	BRNC DARTMOUTH
Kilmartin, Steven N	Lt Col	30-Jun-13	RM	GS	MTM NELSON	HMS NELSON
Kimberley, Robert	Lt Cdr	01-Jul-98	WAR	PWO(U)	RN EXCHANGE USA	WASHINGTON
Kime, David	Lt RN	01-May-13	LOGS	L	HMS LANCASTER	
King, Alexander P	SLt	01-Sep-12	WAR	O UT	BRNC	BRNC DARTMOUTH
King, Charles E W	Capt RN	30-Jun-04	LOGS	L	NC PSYA	PORTSMOUTH
King, David A	Lt Cdr	01-Oct-12	WAR	PWO	HMS NORTHUMBERLAND	
King, David L S	Mid	17-Nov-14	WAR	GSX	BRNC	BRNC DARTMOUTH
King, Gordon C	Lt Cdr	01-Oct-03	ENG	MESM	SFM CLYDE	HMNB CLYDE
King, Iain A	Lt RN	01-Sep-02	WAR	P SKW	857 NAS	RNAS CULDROSE
King, Ian J	Lt RN	01-Sep-05	ENG	AE	NC PSYA	PORTSMOUTH
King, Jason M	Lt Cdr	01-Oct-10	ENG	MESM	HMS ARTFUL	
King, Katherine L	Surg Lt Cdr	10-Sep-08	MED	GMP	NCHQ MEDDIV	PORTSMOUTH
King, Matthew	Lt RN	01-Jun-09	WAR	P FW	FLEET CSAV	WASHINGTON
King, Michael A	Lt Cdr	01-Oct-14	ENG	WE	JCU (CH)	CHELTENHAM
King, Paul W	Capt	01-Sep-13	RM	GS	42 CDO RM	PLYMOUTH
King, Richard E	Capt	19-Jul-05	RM	SCC	RNLA	BRNC DARTMOUTH
King, Stratton D	Surg SLt	28-Jul-14	MED	Medical	BLAKE	BRNC DARTMOUTH
King, William R C	Lt Cdr	01-Oct-08	WAR	PWO	MCM1	FASLANE
King, William T P	Lt Cdr	01-Oct-10	ENG	MESM	DES COMFLEET	ABBEY WOOD
Kingdom, Mark A	Cdr	30-Jun-14	ENG	AE	DES COMAIR	ABBEY WOOD
Kingdon, Samuel R	Lt RN	01-Sep-14	ENG	AE	RNAS YEOVILTON	YEOVILTON
Kingdon, Simon J	Lt RN	01-Jan-02	LOGS	L	US CENTCOM	USA
Kingston, Earl A	Lt Cdr	01-Oct-13	WAR	P MER	820 SQN	RNAS CULDROSE
Kingwell, John M L	R Adm	14-Oct-13	WAR	PWO(U)	DCDC	SHRIVENHAM
Kinnear-Mellor, Rex G M	Surg Lt Cdr	01-Dec-09	MED	Anaes	MTM INM ALVERSTOKE	GOSPORT
Kirby, Benjamin P C	Lt RN	01-Apr-08	WAR	GSX	NCHQ CNPERS	PORTSMOUTH
Kirk, Adrian C	Lt Cdr	01-May-05	ENG	AE	DES COMFLEET	ABBEY WOOD
Kirk, David N	Capt	01-Sep-13	RM	GS	45 CDO RM	DUNDEE
Kirkup, John P	Cdr	30-Jun-03	ENG	TM	LSP OMAN	MUSCAT
Kirkwood, James A D	Lt Cdr	25-Oct-91	WAR	PWO(A)	NATO ACO	NORTHWOOD
Kirkwood, Tristram A H	Cdr	30-Jun-13	WAR	PWO(U)	HMS NORTHUMBERLAND	
Kirrage, Charles H D	SLt	01-Sep-14	WAR	SM(X)	MCM2	PORTSMOUTH
Kirton, Daryl	Mid	08-Sep-14	ENG	WE	BRNC	BRNC DARTMOUTH
Kirwan, John A	Lt Cdr	01-Oct-08	LOGS	L	MODSAP COLLINGWOOD	HMS COLLINGWOOD
Kissane, Robert E T	Capt RN	07-May-13	ENG	WE	JFC HOC C4ISR	NORTHWOOD
Kitchen, Bethan	Lt Cdr	01-Oct-10	ENG	AE	HQ AIR HQ 1GP LTNG	MCAS BEAUFORT
Kitching, Paul	Lt RN	01-Sep-12	WAR	GSX	MTM RMR MERSEYSIDE	LIVERPOOL
Klein, Michael E	Lt RN	11-Oct-13	WAR	AV	MASF	RNAS CULDROSE
Klidjian, Michael J	Lt Cdr	01-Oct-08	WAR	AAWO	HMS DAUNTLESS	
Kneller, James	Lt RN	01-Sep-10	ENG	AE	LOAN DSTL	FAREHAM
Knibbs, Mark	Capt RN	30-Jun-07	WAR	PWO(U)	DCDS PERS TRG	LONDON
Knight, Alexander J	Lt RN	01-Feb-09	WAR	GSX	GIBRALTAR	HMS ROOKE
Knight, Andrew R	Lt Cdr	01-Oct-01	WAR	P MER	824 SQN	RNAS CULDROSE
Knight, Anthony R	Lt RN	01-Oct-09	WAR	ATC	RAF SHAWBURY	SHREWSBURY
Knight, Charles E	SLt	01-Jan-13	WAR	O UT	RNAS CULDROSE	HELSTON
Knight, Damon A	Cdr	30-Jun-01	WAR	AAWO	DEFENCE ACADEMY	SHRIVENHAM
Knight, Daniel S	Lt Cdr	01-Oct-05	WAR	SM(CQ)	FLEET COMOPS NWD	NORTHWOOD
Knight, David W	Cdr	30-Jun-14	WAR	AAWO	FLEET CAP SSM	PORTSMOUTH
Knight, James MC	Maj	01-Oct-12	RM	GS	BDS	WASHINGTON
Knight, Jonathan M	Lt RN	01-Jan-06	WAR	ATC	RNAS YEOVILTON	YEOVILTON
Knight, Richard J	Lt RN	01-Sep-08	WAR	P MER	829 SQN	RNAS CULDROSE
Knight, Richard J	Lt RN	01-Oct-09	WAR	P SK4	MTM CHINOOK	RAF ODIHAM
Knock, Gareth P	Cdr	30-Jun-13	LOGS	L SM	LSP OMAN	MUSCAT
Knott, Clive	Lt Cdr	29-May-07	WAR	P LYNX	WMF SIM	RNAS YEOVILTON
Knott, Michael B	Cdr	30-Jun-10	WAR	PWO(N)	FLEET ACOS(RP)	ABBEY WOOD
Knott, Thomas M MBE	Lt Cdr	01-Oct-13	WAR	GSX	MTM MWS COLLINGWOOD	HMS COLLINGWOOD

Name	Substantive Rank	Seniority	Branch	Specialisation	Organisation Name	Location Name
Knowles, Christopher J	Lt Cdr	01-Oct-11	WAR	P MER	FLEET CSAV	PORTSMOUTH
Knowles, David	Lt RN	01-Sep-04	WAR	PWO(N)	HMS MONMOUTH	
Knox, Graeme P	Lt Cdr	01-Oct-06	LOGS	L BAR	NCHQ - CNLS	PORTSMOUTH
Koheeallee, Mohummed C R C	Lt Cdr	01-Oct-14	ENG	AE	HMS SULTAN	GOSPORT
Kohler, Andrew P	Lt Cdr	01-Apr-02	WAR	PWO(A)	DI - CA	LONDON
Kohn, Patricia A	Lt Cdr	01-Jul-08	WAR	PWO	FOST DPORT	PLYMOUTH
Kromolicki, Matthew J	SLt	01-Nov-14	WAR	SM(X)	MWS COLLINGWOOD	HMS COLLINGWOOD
Krosnar-Clarke, Steven M	Cdr	30-Jun-09	ENG	TM	NCHQ CNPERS	PORTSMOUTH
Kubara, Alex M	SLt	01-Sep-14	WAR	HM	HMS KENT	
Kumwenda, Temwa	Lt RN	01-Sep-13	WAR	GSX	HMS PROTECTOR	
Kutarski, Emily A	SLt	01-Sep-14	ENG	ME	DCEME SULTAN	HMS SULTAN
Kyd, Jeremy P	Cdre	24-Feb-14	WAR	PWO(N)	COMUKTG	PLYMOUTH
Kyle, Ryan	Maj	01-Oct-13	RM	GS	COMUKAMPHIBFOR	PORTSMOUTH
Kyrie, Robert	Lt RN	01-Jul-10	WAR	INT	FLEET COMOPS NWD	NORTHWOOD
Kyte, Andrew J	Cdre	26-Aug-14	LOGS	L	ACDS	LONDON

L

Name	Substantive Rank	Seniority	Branch	Specialisation	Organisation Name	Location Name
Lacey, Catherine	Lt Cdr	01-Oct-00	ENG	WE	DEFENCE ACADEMY	SHRIVENHAM
Lacey, Thomas S	Lt RN	01-Sep-12	ENG	WESM(SWS)	DES COMFLEET	ABBEY WOOD
Lacy, Andrew P	Capt	31-Dec-08	RM	LC	1 ASSLT GP RM	PLYMOUTH
Ladds, Grace	Surg SLt	29-Jul-14	MED	Medical	BLAKE	BRNC DARTMOUTH
Ladislaus, Cecil J	Lt RN	01-Jan-02	WAR	HM	HMS ECHO	
Ladlow, Michael I	Lt RN	14-Sep-13	ENG	WESM(SWS)	HMS VANGUARD	
Laidlaw, Jonathan M	Lt RN	01-Jan-05	WAR	P SKW	MTM NEPTUNE	HMNB CLYDE
Laidler, Paul J	Lt Cdr	01-Oct-10	ENG	WE	HMS IRON DUKE	
Lai-Hung, Jeremy J	Lt Cdr	01-Oct-10	LOGS	L SM	DCDS PERS TRG	LONDON
Laing, Iain	Lt Cdr	01-Sep-01	ENG	WE	FLEET CAP IS	PORTSMOUTH
Laird, Douglas A	Lt RN	01-Jul-09	WAR	SM(X)	HMS TRIUMPH	
Laird, Ellen L	Lt RN	01-Feb-10	LOGS	L	DMLS	HMS RALEIGH
Laird, Iain A	Lt RN	01-Sep-07	WAR	GSX	HMS RANGER	
Laird, Joanne E	Surg Lt RN	03-Aug-11	MED	GDMO	MTM DRAKE	HMS DRAKE
Lake, James R F	2Lt	02-Sep-12	RM	GS	CTCRM	EXMOUTH
Lake, Richard J	Capt	18-Jul-08	RM	SCC	42 CDO RM	PLYMOUTH
Lamb, Andrew G OBE	Cdr	30-Jun-10	WAR	PWO(A)	SERV ATTACHE/ADVISER	SINGAPORE
Lamb, Bryce M	Lt RN	07-Aug-13	ENG	WESM	HMS AMBUSH	
Lamb, Robert J F	Lt Cdr	01-Oct-13	WAR	PWO	HMS RICHMOND	
Lambert, Anthony W OBE	Surg Cdr	30-Jun-99	MED	GS	MDHU DERRIFORD	PLYMOUTH
Lambert, Daniel	Lt RN	11-Oct-13	LOGS	L SM	HMS VENGEANCE	
Lambie, Christopher S	SLt	01-Aug-13	WAR	INT	FLEET COMOPS NWD	NORTHWOOD
Lambourne, David J	Lt Cdr	01-Oct-97	WAR	P SK6	771 SQN	RNAS CULDROSE
L'Amie, Christopher A	Lt Cdr	01-Oct-12	WAR	PWO(U)	UKMARBATSTAFF	PORTSMOUTH
Lamont, Calum	Surg Lt RN	01-Mar-14	MED	Medical	BRNC	BRNC DARTMOUTH
Lamont, Neil J	Lt Cdr	01-Oct-05	WAR	SM(CQ)	NCHQ CNPERS	PORTSMOUTH
Lanaghan, Richard	Lt RN	01-Sep-11	ENG	TM(SM)	HMS SULTAN	GOSPORT
Lancashire, Antony C	Maj	01-Oct-05	RM	LC	NAVY ICP	PORTSMOUTH
Lancaster, James H D	Lt Cdr	01-Oct-12	LOGS	L SM	COMFASFLOT	HELENSBURGH
Landrock, Graham J	Cdr	30-Jun-10	WAR	MCD	NATO ACO	NORTHWOOD
Lane, Adam J	Lt RN	19-Aug-09	WAR	P MER	814 SQN	RNAS CULDROSE
Lane, Ashley D	Capt	01-Sep-11	RM	GS	43 CDO FPGRM	HELENSBURGH
Lane, Harry	Capt	01-Sep-11	RM	GS	NCHQ	PORTSMOUTH
Lane, Joseph O	Capt	01-Sep-09	RM	GS	MTM HASLER COY	HMS DRAKE
Lane, Paul V	Lt RN	09-Jul-10	WAR	HM	HMS SCOTT	
Lane, Peter	Lt RN	01-Sep-11	ENG	MESM	HMS VICTORIOUS	
Lane, Roland J	Lt RN	20-Oct-07	ENG	AE	CHFHQ	RNAS YEOVILTON
Lang, Alasdair J M	Lt RN	01-Jan-05	WAR	O LYNX	LHF 815 SQN	RNAS YEOVILTON
Lang, Christopher J	Lt RN	01-May-13	LOGS	L SM	HMS TRIUMPH	
Lang, Lesley A	Lt RN	01-Jan-05	WAR	ATC	RNAS YEOVILTON	YEOVILTON
Langford, Joanna P	Lt RN	01-Feb-06	WAR	GSX	MTM NELSON	HMS NELSON
Langford, Timothy D	Lt Cdr	01-Oct-14	WAR	PWO	HMS ST ALBANS	
Langley, David J	Lt RN	01-Jan-09	WAR	FC	RAF BOULMER - OPSHQ	RAF BOULMER
Langrill, Mark P	Cdr	30-Jun-09	ENG	AE	RNAS YEOVILTON	YEOVILTON
Lanni, Martin N AFC	Lt Cdr	01-Oct-05	WAR	P SK6	GANNET SAR FLT	HMS GANNET

Name	Substantive Rank	Seniority	Branch	Specialisation	Organisation Name	Location Name
Lanning, Roderick M	Lt Cdr	01-Oct-09	WAR	AAWO	HMS QUEEN ELIZABETH	
Lappin, Adam J	Lt RN	09-Apr-09	LOGS	L	HMS DARING	
Large, Stephen A	Cdr	30-Jun-11	ENG	ME	HMS BULWARK	
Lasker, Jonathan A L	Capt	01-Sep-08	RM	GS	OCLC MANCH	MANCHESTER
Lassoued, Alexander N	Lt RN	14-Oct-09	ENG	TM	BRNC	BRNC DARTMOUTH
Latchem, Andrew J	Lt RN	01-Jan-07	WAR	P LYNX	LHF 815 SQN	RNAS YEOVILTON
Latham, Daniel G	Lt RN	01-Sep-07	WAR	P FW	FLEET CSAV	WASHINGTON
Latham, Mark A	Capt	01-Apr-04	RM	SCC	CTCRM	EXMOUTH
Latus, Simon H	Lt Cdr	01-Oct-10	WAR	PWO(N)	RN EXCHANGE AUSTRALIA	CANBERRA
Lauchlan, Robert A	Cdr	30-Jun-08	ENG	WESM(SWS)	NUCLEAR CAPABILITY	LONDON
Laud, Nicola J	Lt RN	01-Apr-11	ENG	ME	RN EXCHANGE NETHERLANDS	DEN HELDER
Laughton, Peter MBE	Cdr	30-Jun-12	WAR	MCD	HMS LANCASTER	
Laurence, Simon T	Lt Cdr	01-Oct-10	WAR	O MER	814 SQN	RNAS CULDROSE
Lauste, William E	Lt Cdr	01-Mar-99	WAR	MEDIA OPS	NCHQ - NAVY CMD SEC	PORTSMOUTH
Laverick, Jonathan R	Lt RN	01-Feb-11	WAR	GSX	BFSAI	FALKLAND ISLANDS
Laverty, Robert E	Lt Cdr	01-Feb-03	WAR	PWO(U)	HMS TYNE	
Law, Benjamin W A	Capt	01-Sep-12	RM	GS	4 SCOTS	FALLINGBOSTEL
Law, Michael J N	Lt RN	01-Sep-14	WAR	ATC UT	MTM SHAWBURY	RAF SHAWBURY
Law, Samuel J	Lt Cdr	01-Oct-09	LOGS	L	EXCHANGE - FRANCE	PARIS
Lawley, Richard J S	Capt	03-Apr-09	RM	C (SCC)	BF BIOT	DIEGO GARCIA
Lawrence, Kevin	Lt RN	01-Sep-10	ENG	AE	MTM DEFAC JSCSC	SHRIVENHAM
Lawrence, Linda J	Lt RN	16-Sep-99	WAR	HM(AM)	RNSMS	HMS RALEIGH
Lawrence, Samuel T	Mid	08-Sep-14	WAR	GSX	BRNC	BRNC DARTMOUTH
Lawrence, Stuart P	Cdr	30-Jun-11	LOGS	L	NCHQ CNPERS	PORTSMOUTH
Lawrence-Archer, Sally E S	Lt RN	07-Sep-07	WAR	O LYNX	I HF 815 SQN	RNAS YEOVILTON
Lawrenson, Timothy A H	Lt Cdr	01-Oct-13	ENG	WE	DCCIS CISTU	HMS COLLINGWOOD
Lawson, James M J	Capt	01-Sep-08	RM	GS	CTG LAND WAR SCHOOL	WARMINSTER
Lawton, Peter MBE	Capt	01-Jan-99	RM	GS	NCHQ	PORTSMOUTH
Lay, Benjamin	Lt RN	01-Aug-14	LOGS	L	NC PSYA	PORTSMOUTH
Lay, Jack	Lt RN	01-Apr-14	WAR	SM(X)	HMS VIGILANT	
Laycock, Antony	Lt Cdr	01-Oct-06	WAR	O LYNX	NCHQ CNPERS	PORTSMOUTH
Layton, Christopher	Lt Cdr	01-Oct-10	ENG	MESM	DSEA DNSR	ABBEY WOOD
Le Gassick, Peter J	Lt Cdr	01-Oct-04	ENG	TM	FLEET FOST ACOS(Trg)	PORTSMOUTH
Le Huray, Jason W	SLt	01-Sep-14	WAR	ATC UT	MTM SHAWBURY	RAF SHAWBURY
Le Poidevin, Ian W	Lt RN	01-Mar-09	ENG	WE	DES COMLAND	ABBEY WOOD
Lea, Chloe	Lt RN	01-Sep-11	WAR	GSX	UK MCC	BAHRAIN
Lea, John	Cdr	30-Jun-08	WAR	O SKW	RNAS CULDROSE	HELSTON
Lea, Oliver D P	Lt RN	01-Apr-11	WAR	SM(N)	Op LANSBURY	AFGHANISTAN
Lea, Thomas G	Capt	01-Mar-13	RM	GS	43 CDO FPGRM	HELENSBURGH
Leadbeater, Mark K	Lt RN	01-Sep-08	ENG	MESM	DES COMFLEET	ABBEY WOOD
Leahy, Sam	SLt	01-Sep-12	ENG	AE	DCEME SULTAN	HMS SULTAN
Leaker, Daniel T	Lt RN	01-May-04	WAR	P SK4	MTM APACHE	IPSWICH
Lear, Stuart F	Lt Cdr	01-Oct-07	LOGS	L	ACDS	LONDON
Leason, Joanna OBE	Surg Cdr	05-Oct-10	MED	Radiologist	PJHQ (UK)	NORTHWOOD
Leathem, Paul J	2Lt	25-Aug-14	RM	N/A	CTCRM	EXMOUTH
Leckey, Elizabeth H	Lt Cdr	01-Oct-14	ENG	AE	MAA MAAIB FARNBOROUGH	ALDERSHOT
Leckey, Timothy	Lt RN	01-Sep-09	ENG	TM	MASF	RNAS CULDROSE
Lee, Daniel C	Lt RN	01-Jun-10	WAR	GSX	MTM MWS COLLINGWOOD	HMS COLLINGWOOD
Lee, David A	Lt Cdr	01-Oct-13	ENG	IS	MTM NELSON	HMS NELSON
Lee, David M	SLt	01-Sep-12	WAR	GSX	MCM1	FASLANE
Lee, Jonathan J E	Lt RN	01-Sep-12	ENG	ME	FOST MPV SEA	HMNB CLYDE
Lee, Martin J	SLt	07-Aug-13	WAR	GSX	MCM2	PORTSMOUTH
Lee, Nicholas F	Lt Cdr	01-Mar-99	WAR	P SK6	RNAS CULDROSE	HELSTON
Lee, Peter A	Lt Cdr	01-Aug-09	WAR	ME	NATO-ACO-JFC HQ	NAPLES
Lee, Raymond A	Lt RN	01-Jan-04	ENG	WESM(TWS)	COMDEVFLOT	PLYMOUTH
Lee, Ross J	Lt RN	01-Apr-09	ENG	ME	HMS ECHO	
Lee, Simon	SLt	01-Sep-12	ENG	WESM	HMS RALEIGH	TORPOINT
Lee, Steven E	Lt Cdr	01-Oct-07	ENG	WE	NCHQ CNPERS	PORTSMOUTH
Lee, Stuart D	Lt RN	01-Apr-12	WAR	GSX	MCM1	FASLANE
Leeder, Timothy R	Lt Cdr	01-Oct-09	WAR	PWO	FOST DPORT	PLYMOUTH
Leek, Joshua R R	Mid	17-Nov-14	WAR	ATC UT	BRNC	BRNC DARTMOUTH
Leeper, James S	Lt Cdr	01-Oct-12	WAR	PWO	FLEET MARITIME WARFARE	HMS COLLINGWOOD

Name	Substantive Rank	Seniority	Branch	Specialisation	Organisation Name	Location Name
Lees, Adrian C S	Lt RN	01-Jan-07	ENG	MESM	DES COMFLEET	ABBEY WOOD
Lees, Christopher M	Lt RN	11-Apr-08	ENG	WE	CTCRM	EXMOUTH
Lees, Claire M F	Lt Cdr	01-Oct-14	LOGS	L	NBD COB BASE EXECUTIVE OFFICE	HMS DRAKE
Lees, Colin A	Capt	01-Apr-11	RM	MLDR (SCC)	30 CDO IX GP RM	PLYMOUTH
Lees, Edward C	Lt Cdr	01-Feb-99	WAR	PWO(C)	DCOG NORTHWOOD	NORTHWOOD
Lees, Rachel H	Lt RN	31-Jul-09	LOGS	L	RNAS YEOVILTON	YEOVILTON
Leeson, Antony R	Lt Cdr	01-Oct-09	WAR	AAWO	HMS DUNCAN	
Legge, William J	Lt RN	26-Aug-12	WAR	P MER	814 SQN	RNAS CULDROSE
Leidig, George	SLt	01-Sep-13	MED	Medical	BLAKE	BRNC DARTMOUTH
Leigh-Smith, Simon J	Surg Cdr	30-Jun-04	MED	EM	PCRF	RFA ARGUS
Leightley, Simon M	Lt Cdr	01-Oct-11	WAR	MCD	UK MCC	BAHRAIN
Leighton, Matthew R	Lt Cdr	01-Oct-07	WAR	P SK4	845 SQN	RNAS YEOVILTON
Leisk, Oliver L A	SLt	01-Jul-14	WAR	P UT	MTM RAF CRANWELL	RAFC CRANWELL
Le-Maistre, Matthew R	Lt RN	03-May-13	ENG	AE	7 AA BN REME	IPSWICH
Lemkes, Paul D	Capt RN	30-Jun-05	WAR	AAWO	SERV ATTACHE/ADVISER	MADRID
Lemmon, Ryan J	SLt	01-Oct-13	LOGS	L	HMS DARING	
Lemon, Christopher J	Lt RN	12-Jul-13	WAR	AV	RNAS CULDROSE	HELSTON
Lennon, Thomas	Lt RN	01-Sep-13	WAR	P UT	MTM SHAWBURY	RAF SHAWBURY
Leonard, John F	Surg Cdr	01-Jul-08	MED	Occ Med	DPHC SCOTLAND & NI	HMNB CLYDE
Leonard, Matthew D	Lt RN	01-Nov-13	WAR	P	MTM 815 SQN YEOVILTON	RNAS YEOVILTON
Leonard, Thomas	Lt RN	01-Jul-07	WAR	GSX	MTM MWS COLLINGWOOD	HMS COLLINGWOOD
Leong, Melvin J Y J	Surg Lt Cdr	06-Feb-13	MED	Anaes	MTM INM ALVERSTOKE	GOSPORT
Leslie, Bruce D	Lt Cdr	01-Oct-13	WAR	O SKW	857 NAS	RNAS CULDROSE
Lester, Rodney L MBE	Lt Cdr	01-Oct-08	WAR	INT	HQ DISC	CHICKSANDS
Lett, Jonathan D	Cdr	30-Jun-10	WAR	PWO(U)	FLEET CAP MARCAP	PORTSMOUTH
Lett, Timothy J	Lt Cdr	01-Oct-14	WAR	INT	NCHQ CNPS	PORTSMOUTH
Lettington, Paul D W	Lt RN	01-Jan-06	ENG	WE	MTM DRAKE	HMS DRAKE
Lever, Thomas J	Lt RN	01-Sep-08	ENG	AE	1710 NAS	PORTSMOUTH
Leveridge, Adam M	Lt RN	01-Mar-14	ENG	WE	MTM NELSON	HMS NELSON
Lewis, Andrew	Cdr	30-Jun-14	ENG	MESM	SFM CLYDE	HMNB CLYDE
Lewis, Angela B	Lt RN	01-Sep-01	WAR	O SK6	GANNET SAR FLT	HMS GANNET
Lewis, Barry M	Maj	01-Oct-10	RM	GS	42 CDO RM	PLYMOUTH
Lewis, Benjamin	Cdr	30-Jun-14	WAR	P SK4	AWC	BOSCOMBE DOWN
Lewis, Daniel	Lt RN	01-Dec-01	ENG	AE P	RNAS YEOVILTON	YEOVILTON
Lewis, David P	Lt	23-Feb-14	RM	GS	42 CDO RM	PLYMOUTH
Lewis, George R	Lt RN	01-May-14	WAR	SM(X)	MTM MWS COLLINGWOOD	HMS COLLINGWOOD
Lewis, Gethin H	Surg SLt	28-Jul-14	MED	Medical	BLAKE	BRNC DARTMOUTH
Lewis, James A E	Maj	01-Oct-11	RM	GS	42 CDO RM	PLYMOUTH
Lewis, Jonathan M	Lt Cdr	01-Oct-13	WAR	SM(AWC)	HMS VIGILANT	
Lewis, Kieran	Lt RN	03-Aug-11	ENG	WE	MWS COLLINGWOOD	HMS COLLINGWOOD
Lewis, Richard P	Mid	01-Feb-14	ENG	ME	BRNC	BRNC DARTMOUTH
Lewis, Richard QVRM	Lt Cdr	31-Mar-01	WAR	O SKW	849 SQN	RNAS CULDROSE
Lewis, Robert G	Lt RN	01-Sep-07	QARNNS	MH	MTM HASLER COY	HMS DRAKE
Lewis, Scott	Lt RN	01-Jul-14	ENG	TM	CTCRM	EXMOUTH
Lewis, Simon	Lt Cdr	31-Mar-04	LOGS	L (RES)	FOST FAS SHORE	HMNB CLYDE
Lewis, Stephen R	Capt	16-Apr-10	RM	SCC	RMR SCOTLAND	HMS CALEDONIA
Lewis, Stuart D	Lt RN	01-Jan-13	WAR	P SK4	845 SQN	RNAS YEOVILTON
Lewis, Thomas R H	Lt RN	01-Feb-14	WAR	GSX	HMS MONTROSE	
Ley, Alastair B	Lt Cdr	01-Nov-03	WAR	SM(AWC)	DI - CA	LONDON
Leyshon, Rhodri	SLt	01-Nov-14	WAR	P UT	MWS COLLINGWOOD	HMS COLLINGWOOD
Leyshon, Robert J	Surg Cdr (D)	09-Jan-09	DENTAL	GDP(C&S)	HQ DPHC	LICHFIELD
Lias, Carl D	Cdr	30-Jun-06	ENG	MESM	DES COMFLEET	ABBEY WOOD
Liddell, Tom H A	2Lt	25-Aug-14	RM	N/A	CTCRM	EXMOUTH
Lifoda, Charlotte	Surg Lt RN (D)	09-Jul-10	DENTAL	GDP	DDS	LONDON
Ligale, Eugene	Lt RN	01-Jan-03	WAR	GSX	MWS COLLINGWOOD	HMS COLLINGWOOD
Lightfoot, Richard A	Lt RN	16-Feb-01	WAR	O SK6	GANNET SAR FLT	HMS GANNET
Lilley, Benjamin D	Lt RN	01-Feb-14	WAR	P UT	MTM RAF CRANWELL	RAFC CRANWELL
Lillington, Claire	SLt	01-Sep-13	MED	Medical	BLAKE	BRNC DARTMOUTH
Lilly, David	Lt RN	01-Dec-98	WAR	P LYNX	MTM WMF 825 SQN YEOVILTON	RNAS YEOVILTON
Lim, Fong Chien	Surg Lt Cdr	01-Sep-10	MED	GMP	MTM DRAKE	HMS DRAKE
Limb, Thomas J	Capt	01-Sep-12	RM	GS	NCHQ	PORTSMOUTH
Linderman, Ian R	Cdr	30-Jun-10	ENG	TM	DCDS PERS TRG	LONDON

Name	Substantive Rank	Seniority	Branch	Specialisation	Organisation Name	Location Name
Lindeyer, Matthew J	Lt Cdr	01-Oct-14	WAR	HM(AS)	COMUKTG	PLYMOUTH
Lindley, Nicholas	Col	15-Dec-08	RM	GS	MTM DEFENCE ACADEMY	SHRIVENHAM
Lindsay, Irvine G OBE	Cdr	30-Jun-06	WAR	SM(CQ)	FOST SM SEA	HMNB CLYDE
Lindsay, James A M	Capt	01-Sep-12	RM	GS	INFANTRY BATTLE SCHOOL	BRECON
Lindsay, Jonathan M	Maj	01-Oct-09	RM	MLDR	CTCRM	EXMOUTH
Lindsay, Michael H	Surg Lt Cdr	06-Aug-08	MED	Occ Med	MTM INM ALVERSTOKE	GOSPORT
Lindsey, Thomas S	Lt RN	01-Sep-14	WAR	GSX	HMS DUNCAN	
Linehan, Paul R	Lt RN	19-Dec-08	LOGS	L SM	FOST NWD (JTEPS)	NORTHWOOD
Lines, James M	Cdre	06-May-14	LOGS		MOD NSD	LONDON
Ling, Christopher	Cdr	30-Jun-12	ENG	AE	MTM DEFAC JSCSC	SHRIVENHAM
Ling, Peter A	Lt RN	20-Oct-09	ENG	WE	NAVY MCTA	PORTSMOUTH
Linn, Byron J	Lt RN	01-Jan-13	WAR	GSX	MCM2	PORTSMOUTH
Lipczynski, Benjamin J	Lt RN	01-Nov-05	ENG	WE	SVCOPS/DHDOPS/COR	CORSHAM
Lippitt, Benjamin J	Lt RN	01-May-09	WAR	ATC	HMS OCEAN	
Lippitt, Simon T	Lt Cdr	01-Apr-10	WAR	ATC	FLEET CSAV	PORTSMOUTH
Lipscomb, Paul	Cdr	30-Jun-07	ENG	MESM	DES COMFLEET	ABBEY WOOD
Lisle, Robert A C	Lt RN	15-Aug-14	WAR	SM(X)	MTM NELSON	HMS NELSON
Lison, Andrew C	Cdre	01-Jul-13	ENG	AE	DES COMJE	YEOVIL
Lister, Mark	Cdr	30-Jun-04	WAR	SM(CQ)	MTM NEPTUNE	HMNB CLYDE
Lister, Matthew J L	Lt Cdr	01-Oct-14	ENG	MESM	HMS ASTUTE	
Lister, Shaun	Lt RN	01-Jan-08	ENG	WE	HMS RALEIGH	TORPOINT
Lister, Simon R CB OBE	V Adm	27-Nov-13	ENG	MESM	DES COMFLEET	ABBEY WOOD
Litchfield, Hannah	SLt	01-Sep-14	ENG	MESM	DCEME SULTAN	HMS SULTAN
Litster, Alan OBE	Col	09-May-11	RM	LC	BDS	WASHINGTON
Little, George J R	Maj	01-Oct-12	RM	GS	NCHQ	PORTSMOUTH
Little, Graeme T OBE	Cdre	17-Jul-12	ENG	ME	NBD NBC HQ	HMS DRAKE
Little, Jonathan I	Lt RN	01-Sep-07	ENG	WE	MCM2	PORTSMOUTH
Little, Matthew I G	Lt Cdr	01-Oct-13	WAR	INT	NATO ACO	NORTHWOOD
Little, Nicola S	Lt RN	01-Jan-05	ENG	TM	FLEET FOST ACOS(Trg)	PORTSMOUTH
Little, Philippa C	SLt	01-May-14	LOGS	L	FOSNI - HQ	PORTSMOUTH
Liva, Anthony J	Maj	01-Oct-08	RM	GS	FLEET CAP LLM & DRM	PORTSMOUTH
Livesey, John E	Cdr	30-Jun-11	WAR	SM(CQ)	MTM NEPTUNE	HMNB CLYDE
Livingstone, Alan J MBE	Col	10-Nov-14	RM	GS	DEFENCE ACADEMY	SHRIVENHAM
Livingstone, Andrew	Lt RN	01-Sep-13	WAR	SM(X)	HMS VIGILANT	
Livingstone, Colin S	Lt RN	06-Apr-07	ENG	ME	HMS ENTERPRISE	
Livingstone, Dana M A	Lt RN	07-Nov-13	WAR	GSX	HMS NORTHUMBERLAND	
Livsey, Andrew E J	Lt Cdr	01-Nov-06	WAR	PWO(U)	MWS COLLINGWOOD	HMS COLLINGWOOD
Lloyd, Jane L	Surg Lt Cdr	02-Aug-10	MED	Occ Med	MTM INM ALVERSTOKE	GOSPORT
Lloyd, Matthew R	Lt RN	01-Sep-02	LOGS	L SM	DES COMLAND	RAF NORTHOLT
Loadman, Dougal R	Lt RN	01-Mar-04	ENG	TM	CTCRM	EXMOUTH
Lock, Andrew G D	Lt Col	30-Jun-10	RM	GS	NCHQ CNPERS	PORTSMOUTH
Lock, William	Lt RN	01-May-02	WAR	O MER	814 SQN	RNAS CULDROSE
Locke, Nicholas M	Lt Cdr	01-Oct-13	ENG	MESM	HMS VIGILANT	
Lockett, Alexander T	Lt RN	13-Feb-08	WAR	P LYN7	771 SQN	RNAS CULDROSE
Lockett, David J	Lt Cdr	01-Apr-04	WAR	PWO(N)	FOST DPORT	PLYMOUTH
Lockhart, John B	Lt Cdr	01-Oct-10	ENG	AE	NCHQ CNPERS	PORTSMOUTH
Lockley, Kelly M	Lt RN	01-Jan-08	WAR	HM(AS)	HMS ENTERPRISE	
Lockley, Simon M	Lt RN	19-Oct-07	LOGS	L	HMS RALEIGH	TORPOINT
Lofthouse, Thomas D	Lt RN	01-Jan-12	WAR	P UT	MTM 845 SQN YEOVILTON	RNAS YEOVILTON
Lofts, Anthony J R	Lt RN	01-Apr-09	ENG	WE	DIST/COR	CORSHAM
Loftus, Andrew L	Surg SLt	23-Jul-14	MED	Medical	BLAKE	BRNC DARTMOUTH
Loftus, Ashley M	SLt	01-Sep-14	WAR	ATC UT	MTM SHAWBURY	RAF SHAWBURY
Logan, Joseph M	Lt Cdr	01-Oct-03	WAR	FC	NC REQUIREMENTS MANAGERS	ABBEY WOOD
Login, Matthew B	Lt	09-Sep-14	RM	GS	43 CDO FPGRM	HELENSBURGH
Lomas, Timothy P	Lt RN	09-Oct-10	WAR	GSX	MTM MWS HMTG (D)	HMS DRAKE
London, Heidi C	Lt Cdr	01-Oct-14	WAR	PWO	MTM MWS COLLINGWOOD	HMS COLLINGWOOD
London, Nicholas J	Lt Cdr	01-Oct-12	ENG	WE	HMS LANCASTER	
Long, Adrian J	Lt RN	31-Jul-12	ENG	ME	HMS MONTROSE	
Long, Adrian M	Capt RN	21-Nov-11	ENG	WE	VCDS	LONDON
Long, Michael	Lt Cdr	01-Apr-08	WAR	INT	HMS COLLINGWOOD	FAREHAM
Long, Richard	Maj	01-Oct-13	RM	BS	HQ BAND SERVICE	HMS NELSON
Long, Simon C	Capt	01-Sep-12	RM	GS	40 CDO RM	TAUNTON

Name	Substantive Rank	Seniority	Branch	Specialisation	Organisation Name	Location Name
Long, Stuart G	Lt Cdr	01-Oct-10	WAR	HM(AS)	HMS SCOTT	
Long, Victoria S	Lt Cdr	01-Oct-13	QARNNS	Tutor	DHET - DMS WHITTINGTON	LICHFIELD
Longia, Sandeep	Lt RN	01-Sep-10	ENG	AE	1710 NAS	PORTSMOUTH
Longley, Richard J	Lt	02-Sep-14	RM	GS	CTCRM	EXMOUTH
Longman, Matthew S	Lt Cdr	01-Oct-13	ENG	ME	HMS RICHMOND	
Longmore, David	Surg Lt Cdr	04-Aug-09	MED	GMP	MTM INM ALVERSTOKE	GOSPORT
Longstaff, Jack B	Mid	01-May-14	ENG	AE	BRNC	BRNC DARTMOUTH
Longstaff, Thomas O M	Lt RN	20-Jul-11	WAR	GSX	MTM FLEET HQ	PORTSMOUTH
Longstaff, Thomas W	Lt Cdr	01-Oct-11	LOGS	L SM	NAVY CORE TRG HQ	PLYMOUTH
Lorenz, Rudi	Lt RN	01-Jun-06	WAR	P LYNX	MTM DEFAC JSCSC	SHRIVENHAM
Loring, Andrew	Cdr	30-Jun-09	ENG	ME	FOSNI - NRC WWE	BRISTOL
Louden, Carl A	Lt Cdr	01-Oct-07	WAR	C	HMS KING ALFRED	PORTSMOUTH
Loudon, Conor J	Mid	01-May-14	WAR	GSX	BRNC	BRNC DARTMOUTH
Loughran, Oliver A G	Lt RN	01-Feb-08	WAR	GSX	GIBRALTAR	HMS ROOKE
Loughrey, Neil C MBE	Lt Cdr	01-Oct-08	ENG	AE	DES COMAIR	ARLINGTON USA
Louis, David R A	Lt Cdr	01-Jul-12	WAR	MCD	HMS BULWARK	
Louw, Len	Lt RN	01-Jan-02	ENG	WESM(SWS)	DES COMFLEET	ABBEY WOOD
Lovatt, Graham J	Cdr	30-Jun-11	WAR	AAWO	MOD NSD	LONDON
Lovatt, Steven	Lt RN	01-Sep-12	ENG	WE	DES COMFLEET	ABBEY WOOD
Love, John J	Lt RN	04-Jun-03	ENG	TM	FOST FAS SHORE	HMNB CLYDE
Love, Richard J	Lt Cdr	01-Oct-05	ENG	AE	MAA	ABBEY WOOD
Love, Tristram S N	Cdr	30-Jun-12	ENG	WESM(TWS)	FLEET CAP SSM	PORTSMOUTH
Lovegrove, Raymond A	Capt RN	03-Dec-13	ENG	WE	MTM FLEET HQ	PORTSMOUTH
Lovell, Alistair	Surg Lt Cdr (D)	25-Jun-08	DENTAL	GDP	FLEET DENPOL	HMS EXCELLENT
Lovell, James E C	Lt Cdr	01-Oct-12	WAR	AWO(U)	FLEET CAP SSM	PORTSMOUTH
Lovell, James H	Lt RN	01-Sep-09	WAR	O MER	824 SQN	RNAS CULDROSE
Lovell, Jonathan	Lt RN	03-May-13	ENG	ME	HMS DAUNTLESS	
Lovell-Smith, Alexandre R	Lt RN	01-Oct-12	WAR	P LYN7	847 SQN	RNAS YEOVILTON
Lovering, Tristan T A MBE	Lt Cdr	01-Oct-04	WAR	INT	NATO-ACT-JWC	STAVANGER
Lowe, Christian T M	Lt RN	01-May-13	WAR	GSX	HMS PORTLAND	
Lowe, Christopher	Lt Cdr	01-Oct-05	ENG	MESM	DI - CA	LONDON
Lowe, Gavin J	Lt RN	01-May-04	WAR	PWO	HMS WESTMINSTER	
Lowe, Julian C	Cdr	30-Jun-10	ENG	ME	HMS QUEEN ELIZABETH	
Lowe, Stuart M	Lt Cdr	01-Dec-00	ENG	WE	FLEET ACOS(RP)	PORTSMOUTH
Lowe, Stuart W R	Lt RN	01-Jan-13	WAR	O UT	RNAS CULDROSE	HELSTON
Lowe, Timothy M	R Adm	17-Sep-12	WAR	PWO(N)	STRIKFORNATO - LISBON	LISBON
Lower, Iain S	Capt RN	10-Sep-12	WAR	AAWO	PJHQ (UK)	NORTHWOOD
Lowery, David	Mid	05-May-14	ENG	TM	BRNC	BRNC DARTMOUTH
Lowndes, Timothy	Lt RN	12-May-14	WAR	MTO N (RES)	RNLO GULF	DUBAI
Lownes, Sarah E	Surg Lt RN	07-Aug-13	MED	Medical	BLAKE	BRNC DARTMOUTH
Lowther, James	Cdr	30-Jun-07	WAR	PWO(N)	NEP	LONDON
Loxton, Thomas C	Lt RN	01-Sep-11	WAR	GSX	HMS SOMERSET	
Lucas, Darren P	Lt Cdr	01-Oct-14	ENG	WE	MWS COLLINGWOOD	HMS COLLINGWOOD
Lucas, Simon U	Maj	01-Oct-06	RM	SCC	CTCRM	EXMOUTH
Lucocq, Nicholas J	Lt Cdr	01-Oct-04	WAR	PWO(N)	MWS COLLINGWOOD	HMS COLLINGWOOD
Lucy, Thomas D	Capt	31-Aug-14	RM	GS	NCHQ	PORTSMOUTH
Lugg, John C	Maj	01-Oct-04	RM	SCC	DES COMFLEET	ABBEY WOOD
Luke, Christopher	Lt RN	01-Jan-08	WAR	O MER	820 SQN	RNAS CULDROSE
Lumsden, Gavin T	Lt RN	05-Aug-11	ENG	TM	HMS SULTAN	GOSPORT
Lundie, Andrew J	Surg Lt Cdr	05-Aug-14	MED	GMP	MTM INM ALVERSTOKE	GOSPORT
Lunn, Adam C	Lt Cdr	01-Jun-94	WAR	P LYNX	NATO-ACO-JFC HQ	NAPLES
Lunn, Darren A	Lt RN	01-Sep-14	ENG	MESM	MTM DCEME SULTAN	HMS SULTAN
Lunn, George R	Mid	17-Nov-14	WAR	P UT	BRNC	BRNC DARTMOUTH
Lupini, James M	Lt RN	01-Oct-02	WAR	GSX	RNLA	HMS COLLINGWOOD
Luscombe, Michael D	Lt Cdr	01-Oct-99	WAR	P SK6	854 NAS	RNAS CULDROSE
Luscombe, Tom M	Mid	01-Feb-14	WAR	GSX	BRNC	BRNC DARTMOUTH
Luxford, Charles A	Lt Cdr	01-Oct-10	WAR	PWO	COMUKTG	PLYMOUTH
L'Vov-Basirov, Nikolai E P	Lt RN	12-Jan-14	ENG	WESM	HMS TRIUMPH	
Lynas, Jonathan F A	Lt RN	01-Sep-00	WAR	P SK6	GANNET SAR FLT	HMS GANNET
Lynch, John S	Capt	01-Sep-10	RM	MLDR	40 CDO RM	TAUNTON
Lynch, Paul P MC	Lt Col	30-Jun-11	RM	GS	30 CDO IX GP RM	PLYMOUTH
Lynch, Stephen	Cdr	30-Jun-11	WAR	O SKW	NC REQUIREMENTS MANAGERS	ABBEY WOOD

Name	Substantive Rank	Seniority	Branch	Specialisation	Organisation Name	Location Name
Lynch, Suzanne	Lt RN	28-Nov-00	LOGS	L (RES)	MTM NPT RES MOBILISATION	UK
Lynn, Ian H OBE	Cdr	30-Jun-10	WAR	PWO(U)	NMIC	FLEET HQ
Lynn, James M	SLt	24-Sep-14	WAR	SM(X)	HMS OCEAN	
Lynn, Sarah L	Lt Cdr	01-Oct-11	WAR	O MER	820 SQN	RNAS CULDROSE
Lynn, Steven R	Cdr	30-Jun-07	ENG	WE	HMS QUEEN ELIZABETH	
Lyons, Michael J	Lt Cdr	01-Jun-04	ENG	MESM	DES COMFLEET	BARROW IN FURNESS
Lyth, Ross A	SLt	01-Oct-13	ENG	WE	MWS COLLINGWOOD	HMS COLLINGWOOD

M

Name	Substantive Rank	Seniority	Branch	Specialisation	Organisation Name	Location Name
Mabbott, Keith I	Lt Cdr	01-Oct-08	WAR	MCD	UKMARBATSTAFF	PORTSMOUTH
Macartney, Simon G	Lt RN	01-May-14	ENG	WESM	HMS VICTORIOUS	
Maccorquodale, Mairi A	Lt Cdr	01-Oct-06	ENG	IS	MTM NELSON	HMS NELSON
Maccrimmon, Stuart	Maj	01-Oct-11	RM	GS	45 CDO RM	DUNDEE
Macdonald, Adam	Lt RN	13-Jul-12	ENG	WESM	HMS TALENT	
Macdonald, Alasdair I	Capt RN	30-Jun-07	ENG	WE	DIO SAPT	HMS COLLINGWOOD
Macdonald, Alastair J	Lt Cdr	01-Sep-02	ENG	WF	CYBER PROG SUPPORT	LONDON
Macdonald, Alastair J	Lt RN	20-May-08	LOGS	L SM	FOSNI - NRC	HMS CALEDONIA
Macdonald, John R	Cdre	22-Jul-13	ENG	WESM(TWS)	CBRN POL	LONDON
Macdonald, Michael	Maj	01-Oct-12	RM	C	30 CDO IX GP RM	PLYMOUTH
Macdonald, Stuart	Lt Cdr	01-Oct-07	LOGS	L	RN EXCHANGE USA	WASHINGTON
Macdonald-Robinson, Nicholas U S	Cdr	30-Jun-08	WAR	PWO(A)	JFHQ	NORTHWOOD
Macdougall, Stewart J	Lt Cdr	01-Oct-03	ENG	WESM(TWS)	DES COMFLEET	ABBEY WOOD
Mace, Stephen J	Lt RN	01-Sep-10	ENG	AE	DES COMLAND	ABBEY WOOD
Macfarlane, Gordon T	Surg Lt Cdr	08-Oct-08	MED	EM	MTM MDHU DERRIFORD	PLYMOUTH
Macfarlane, Iain S D	Lt Cdr	01-Oct-07	WAR	P MER	824 SQN	RNAS CULDROSE
Machin, Matthew P	Lt RN	01-Nov-14	ENG	WE	HMS OCEAN	
Maciejewski, Luke W S	SLt	01-May-13	WAR	O UT	MTM 750 SQN CULDROSE	RNAS CULDROSE
Macindoe, Neil	Lt RN	23-Apr-06	WAR	TM	NATO-ACO-JFC HQ	BRUNSSUM
Mack, Peter E	Lt RN	01-Feb-14	ENG	AE	MTM WMO CULDROSE	RNAS CULDROSE
Mackay, Andrew	Lt Cdr	01-Feb-04	WAR	INT	JFIG - JT OPS	RAF WYTON
Mackay, Fraser R	Lt RN	01-Sep-11	ENG	WE	HDNTA	CORSHAM
Mackay, Graeme A	R Adm	27-May-14	WAR	O SK6	D CEPP	LONDON
Mackay, Peter	Cdr	30-Jun-10	ENG	WE	COMDEVFLOT	PLYMOUTH
Mackay, Richard	Lt RN	01-Sep-10	ENG	AE	DES COMAIR	ABBEY WOOD
Mackay, Shaun A	Lt RN	01-Sep-12	ENG	MESM	HMS VIGILANT	
Mackay, Victor T	Mid	08-Sep-14	WAR	SM(X)	BRNC	BRNC DARTMOUTH
Mackay-Brown, Alan L	Surg Cdr	20-Mar-14	MED	Occ Med	DPHC SW	RNAS YEOVILTON
Mackenow, Helen R	Lt Cdr	01-Oct-13	LOGS	L BAR	HMS NORTHUMBERLAND	
Mackenzie, Ross	Mid	17-Nov-14	WAR	P UT	BRNC	BRNC DARTMOUTH
Mackey, Martin C	Cdr	30-Jun-08	WAR	MCD	OPS DIR	LONDON
Mackie, David F S	Cdr	30-Jun-11	ENG	WE	HDNET	CORSHAM
Mackie, Richard P P	Capt	01-Sep-10	RM	GS	CTCRM	EXMOUTH
Mackie, Scott	Lt RN	01-Jun-14	WAR	GSX	MCM1	FASLANE
Mackie, Simon J	Surg Cdr	01-Dec-10	MED	Urol	MDHU PORTSMOUTH	PORTSMOUTH
Mackinnon, Donald J	Cdr	30-Jun-11	WAR	PWO(U)	MSP	LONDON
Mackley-Heath, Megan A	SLt	01-Sep-14	ENG	MESM	MTM NELSON	HMS NELSON
Maclean, Graeme P	Lt RN	01-Sep-10	ENG	MESM	DES COMFLEET	ABBEY WOOD
Maclean, Shamus	Lt RN	01-Oct-12	WAR	INT	DI - FC(A)	RAF WYTON
Maclennan, Neil R	Lt RN	01-Dec-08	LOGS	L BAR	DCDS PERS - SPA	RAF NORTHOLT
Macleod, Alastair M	Lt RN	01-Jun-07	WAR	P SK4	RNLA	HMS COLLINGWOOD
Macleod, James N	Cdre	14-Nov-14	ENG	WE	NAVY ICP	PORTSMOUTH
Macleod, Mark S	Cdr	30-Jun-11	WAR	P MER	NC REQUIREMENTS MANAGERS	ABBEY WOOD
Macnae, Bridget R	Lt RN	01-Oct-09	WAR	GSX	FOST MPV SEA	HMNB CLYDE
Macphail, Neil M	Lt Cdr	01-Oct-11	MED	MS(SM)	FLEET CAP SSM	PORTSMOUTH
Macpherson, Craig A C	Lt RN	01-Jan-03	WAR	FC	MTM MWS COLLINGWOOD	HMS COLLINGWOOD
Macpherson, William G C	Maj	01-Oct-08	RM	SCC	FLEET CAP SSM	PORTSMOUTH
Macquarrie, Gary A	Lt Cdr	01-Oct-10	ENG	ME	HMS DEFENDER	
Macrae, Kirk	Lt RN	01-Jan-07	WAR	GSX	MTM MWS COLLINGWOOD	HMS COLLINGWOOD
Macsephney, Tracy	Lt Cdr	01-Oct-12	WAR	MTO A (RES)	MWS COLLINGWOOD	HMS COLLINGWOOD
Maddick, James J	Lt RN	27-Nov-12	ENG	MESM	HMS ASTUTE	
Maddick, Mark J	Col	26-Sep-11	RM	LC	UK MISSION TO THE UN NEW YORK	NEW YORK
Maddison, Hugh R	Lt Cdr	01-Oct-12	ENG	ME	HMS ARGYLL	

Name	Substantive Rank	Seniority	Branch	Specialisation	Organisation Name	Location Name
Maddison, Jack M	Mid	08-Sep-14	WAR	SM(X)	BRNC	BRNC DARTMOUTH
Maddison, John D MBE	Lt Col	30-Jun-12	RM	SCC	CTCRM	EXMOUTH
Maddison, Paul	Lt Cdr	01-Oct-12	ENG	WE	MWS COLLINGWOOD	HMS COLLINGWOOD
Madge, Mark R	Mid	01-May-14	ENG	AE	BRNC	BRNC DARTMOUTH
Madgwick, Edward C C	Surg Cdr (D)	14-Oct-08	DENTAL	GDP	HMS DRAKE	PLYMOUTH
Magan, Michael J C	Capt RN	21-Feb-12	ENG	WE	NAVY MCTA	PORTSMOUTH
Magill, Alasdair	Lt RN	01-Jul-07	WAR	MCD	HMS SOMERSET	
Magill, Hal R	Lt RN	09-Apr-09	ENG	ME	HMS ECHO	
Magill, Michael P	SLt	01-Sep-14	WAR	GSX	BRNC	BRNC DARTMOUTH
Magowan, Conor C	Maj	01-Oct-14	RM	GS	NCHQ	PORTSMOUTH
Magowan, Robert A CBE	Brig	18-Mar-13	RM	GS	NCHQ CNPS	PORTSMOUTH
Magzoub, Mohayed	Lt Cdr	01-Oct-14	ENG	ME	OPS DIR	LONDON
Magzoub, Mowafag M M	SLt	01-Nov-14	LOGS	L	HMS DRAGON	
Maher, Michael	Cdr	30-Jun-05	WAR	AAWO	SERV ATTACHE/ADVISER	ANKARA
Mahoney, Andrew	Lt Cdr	01-Oct-14	WAR	PWO	RN EXCHANGE N ZLAND	WELLINGTON
Mahony, David G	Cdr	30-Jun-03	WAR	O SK6	FLEET CSAV	PORTSMOUTH
Mahony, Nicholas J C	Mid	08-Sep-14	ENG	AE	BRNC	BRNC DARTMOUTH
Mailes, Ian R A	Lt Cdr	01-Oct-03	WAR	O MER	FLEET MARITIME WARFARE	HMS COLLINGWOOD
Main, Matthew G	Lt RN	01-Sep-08	ENG	MESM	DES COMFLEET	ABBEY WOOD
Mains, Graham	Lt Cdr	01-Oct-11	WAR	O MER	RN EXCHANGE USA	WASHINGTON
Mair, Barbara I C	Surg Lt RN (D)	21-Jun-11	DENTAL	GDP	PCRF	RFA ARGUS
Mair, Joanna	SLt	01-Apr-12	MED	Medical	BLAKE	BRNC DARTMOUTH
Major, Lee A	Lt RN	01-Sep-13	WAR	GSX	HMS BULWARK	
Major, William	Lt RN	01-Jun-08	WAR	P SK4	RAF ODIHAM	RAF ODIHAM
Makosz, Simon P	SLt	01-Apr-12	WAR	P UT	RNAS CULDROSE	HELSTON
Malcolm, Paul	Lt RN	01-Sep-02	WAR	HM	902 EAW	OMAN - JOA - MUSANNAH
Malkin, Sharon L	Cdr	30-Jun-11	ENG	AE	DES COMAIR	ABBEY WOOD
Mallabone, James J K	Lt Cdr	01-Oct-12	ENG	TM	RNAS YEOVILTON	YEOVILTON
Mallalieu, Harry J	Capt	03-Sep-14	RM	GS	40 CDO RM	TAUNTON
Mallard, James	Capt	01-Sep-13	RM	GS	SFSG C COY	RAF ST ATHAN
Mallin, James D	Mid	08-Sep-14	WAR	HM	BRNC	BRNC DARTMOUTH
Mallinson, Laurence J	Lt Cdr	01-Oct-10	LOGS	L	ACNS	HMS NELSON
Mallinson, Robert	Cdr	30-Jun-05	ENG	AE O	MOD CNS/ACNS	RNAS YEOVILTON
Mallows, Andy	Maj	01-Oct-12	RM	GS	HQ AIR - COS(OPS) - JALO	HIGH WYCOMBE
Malone, Martin T	Lt Cdr	01-Oct-09	LOGS	L	FOST DPORT	PLYMOUTH
Malone, Roger W	Lt Cdr	01-Oct-13	WAR	HM(AS)	FLEET CAP SSM	PORTSMOUTH
Malster, Dudley A	Lt RN	01-May-05	WAR	MW	HMS MONMOUTH	
Maltby, Richard J	Lt Col	30-Jun-12	RM	GS	COMUKAMPHIBFOR	PORTSMOUTH
Manders-Trett, Victoria	Lt Cdr	01-Oct-07	LOGS	L	MTM NELSON	HMS NELSON
Mandley, Philip J	Lt Cdr	01-May-02	ENG	TM	FLEET FOST ACOS(Trg)	PORTSMOUTH
Manger, Garth S C	Col	19-Apr-10	RM	C	MTM DEFAC RCDS	LONDON
Manktelow, Benjamin T	Lt RN	01-Dec-11	WAR	GSX	HMS DIAMOND	
Manning, Christopher L G	Capt	21-Mar-13	RM	SCC	MED SQN CDO LOG REGT RM	RMB CHIVENOR
Manning, David S	Lt RN	08-May-06	ENG	IS	SVCOPS/DHDOPS/COR	CORSHAM
Manning, Gary P	Lt Cdr	01-Oct-07	LOGS	L	MTM DEFAC JSCSC	SHRIVENHAM
Mansfield, Alastair J F	RN Chpln	10-Dec-07	Ch S	Chaplain	RNAS CULDROSE	HELSTON
Manson, Peter D	Maj	01-Sep-99	RM	P SK4	NCHQ CNPERS	PORTSMOUTH
Manson, Robert P	Lt RN	08-Dec-12	ENG	ME	HMS SUTHERLAND	
Manson, Thomas E	Capt RN	02-Jul-13	ENG	AE P	DES COMAIR	ABBEY WOOD
Manwaring, Roy G	Cdr	25-Jul-11	MED	MS	MTM NELSON	HMS NELSON
Maples, Andrew T	Surg Lt Cdr	01-Aug-06	MED	GMP	DPHC SW	HMS DRAKE
Marden, Tony	Lt Cdr	01-Oct-09	ENG	WE	MWS COLLINGWOOD	HMS COLLINGWOOD
Marder, Michael P	Lt	02-Sep-14	RM	N/A	CTCRM	EXMOUTH
Mardlin, Stephen A	Cdr	30-Jun-10	LOGS	L CMA	NAVY ICP	PORTSMOUTH
Marfleet, Adam J	Lt RN	01-Sep-14	ENG	WESM	HMS VIGILANT	
Marin-Ortega, Carl	Lt RN	01-Sep-11	ENG	WE	FOST DPORT	PLYMOUTH
Marjoribanks, Charlotte	Lt Cdr	01-Oct-14	WAR	P MER	MTM DEFENCE ACADEMY	SHRIVENHAM
Mark, Abigail	Lt RN	01-Oct-05	WAR	P (RES)	RAF LINTON-ON-OUSE	RAF LINTON ON OUSE
Marland, Eunice E	Lt Cdr	01-Oct-08	LOGS	L BAR	MTM NELSON	HMS NELSON
Marlor, Andrew	Lt Cdr	01-Oct-12	ENG	WESM(TWS)	DI - CA	LONDON
Marlor, Kirsty L	Lt Cdr	01-Oct-14	ENG	AE	MTM WMO YEOVILTON	RNAS YEOVILTON
Marmont, Kerry L	Cdr	31-Dec-00	ENG	WESM(TWS)	DES COMLAND	ABBEY WOOD

Name	Substantive Rank	Seniority	Branch	Specialisation	Organisation Name	Location Name
Marratt, Richard	Cdr	30-Jun-12	ENG	TM	DEFENCE ACADEMY	SHRIVENHAM
Marriner, Henry M E	SLt	01-Sep-12	WAR	GSX	MCM1	FASLANE
Marriott, Isabella M C	Lt RN	01-Dec-08	WAR	MEDIA OPS	NCHQ CNPS	PORTSMOUTH
Marriott, Matthew J	Lt Cdr	01-Sep-09	WAR	PWO	MOD DEFENCE STAFF	LONDON
Marriott, Neil K	Lt Cdr	01-Oct-05	WAR	MCD	MTM RN GLOBAL	FRANCE
Marrison, Andrew C	Lt RN	16-Dec-11	ENG	WE	MWS COLLINGWOOD	HMS COLLINGWOOD
Marsden, Christopher N	Lt RN	01-Jun-10	LOGS	L	UKMARBATSTAFF	PORTSMOUTH
Marsden, Daniel C	Lt RN	01-Apr-11	WAR	GSX	HMS RICHMOND	
Marsh, Alexander R	Lt RN	01-Aug-12	ENG	MESM	HMS VICTORIOUS	
Marsh, Ceri	Lt Cdr	01-Oct-12	LOGS	L BAR	HMS DIAMOND	
Marsh, James P	SLt	01-Sep-14	WAR	GSX	MWS COLLINGWOOD	HMS COLLINGWOOD
Marsh, Stephen W	Lt Cdr	01-Oct-11	LOGS	L	COMUKAMPHIBFOR	PORTSMOUTH
Marsh, Stuart D	Lt Cdr	01-Oct-14	WAR	HM(AS)	FOST HM	HMS DRAKE
Marshall, Alexander J	Lt RN	01-Sep-11	WAR	SM(X)	HMS VIGILANT	
Marshall, Alistair J	Lt Cdr	01-Oct-08	WAR	SM(CQ)	HMS VANGUARD	
Marshall, Charlotte R	Mid	17-Nov-14	WAR	P UT	BRNC	BRNC DARTMOUTH
Marshall, David S	Lt RN	01-Sep-10	ENG	AE	FLEET CSAV	PORTSMOUTH
Marshall, Fleur T	Surg Capt RN	20-Aug-13	MED	GMP (C&S)	DPHC SOUTH REGION HQ	ALDERSHOT
Marshall, Gavin P	Lt Cdr	01-Oct-09	ENG	ME	NAVY MCTA	PORTSMOUTH
Marshall, Leon	Maj	01-Oct-13	RM	LC	FLEET CAP LLM & DRM	PORTSMOUTH
Marshall, Paul CBE	Capt RN	01-Jul-12	ENG	ME	FLEET CAP SSM	PORTSMOUTH
Marshall, Tracey	Lt Cdr	01-Oct-05	WAR	GSX	DEFENCE ESTATES - DHE	RAF BRAMPTON
Marshall, William E	SLt	01-Nov-14	WAR	P UT	MWS COLLINGWOOD	HMS COLLINGWOOD
Martin, Alan F	Lt RN	01-Jul-10	ENG	TM	NCHQ CNPERS (HRTSG)	PORTSMOUTH
Martin, Andrew J	Lt RN	01-Apr-10	WAR	SM(X)	MTM MWS COLLINGWOOD	HMS COLLINGWOOD
Martin, Antoinette	Surg Lt RN	01-Aug-12	MED	GDMO	MTM INM ALVERSTOKE	GOSPORT
Martin, Ben R	Lt Cdr	01-Oct-14	WAR	PWO	HMS DARING	
Martin, Brian H	Lt RN	11-Dec-09	ENG	WESM(TWS)	HMS ARTFUL	
Martin, Bruce A	Capt RN	08-Apr-14	ENG	MESM	CAPTAIN BASE SAFETY CLYDE	HELENSBURGH
Martin, Dale J	2Lt	25-Aug-14	RM	N/A	CTCRM	EXMOUTH
Martin, David C S	Cdr	30-Jun-13	WAR	PWO	COMPORFLOT	PORTSMOUTH
Martin, David L	Lt RN	01-Sep-06	WAR	MW	MCM1	HMNB CLYDE
Martin, Euan A	Lt RN	01-Apr-12	WAR	GSX	MCM2	PORTSMOUTH
Martin, Harry C	Lt RN	01-Sep-08	ENG	AE	JARTS (RN)	BOSCOMBE DOWN
Martin, James N	Lt RN	01-Jan-06	WAR	GSX	NCHQ CNPERS	PORTSMOUTH
Martin, Jamie M	Lt RN	01-Mar-14	ENG	MESM	DCEME SULTAN	HMS SULTAN
Martin, Nigel	Lt RN	20-Sep-99	WAR	C	NATO-ACO-JFC HQ	BRUNSSUM
Martin, Robert J	Lt Cdr	01-Oct-08	ENG	AE	845 SQN	RNAS YEOVILTON
Martin, Simon J	Cdr	30-Jun-11	ENG	WESM(TWS)	ROYAL BRUNEI ARMED FORCES	SERIA
Martin, Stephanie	Lt RN	01-Nov-14	WAR	HM	HMS IRON DUKE	
Martin, Stuart A R	Lt RN	01-Jul-12	WAR	GSX	MTM NELSON	HMS NELSON
Martyn, Daniel	Cdr	30-Jun-14	WAR	SM(CQ)	HMS VIGILANT	
Martyn, Julie M	Lt Cdr	01-Oct-14	QARNNS	PHC	HQ DPHC	LICHFIELD
Masawi, Sydney K	Lt RN	01-Jul-09	QARNNS	EN	PCRF	RFA ARGUS
Maskell, Bernard M	Lt RN	01-May-04	ENG	WESM(TWS)	FLEET MARITIME WARFARE	HMS COLLINGWOOD
Maslen, David W J	Capt	16-Apr-10	RM	SCC	1 ASSLT GP RM	PLYMOUTH
Mason, Andrew C	Lt Cdr	01-Oct-06	WAR	PWO(A)	MTM DEFAC JSCSC	SHRIVENHAM
Mason, Angus E	Lt RN	01-Oct-07	WAR	SM(N)	HMS VANGUARD	
Mason, Christopher	Lt RN	01-Dec-08	WAR	P SK4	MTM SHAWBURY	RAF SHAWBURY
Mason, Darren J	Lt Cdr	01-Oct-05	WAR	SM(CQ)	HMS VICTORIOUS	
Mason, David	Lt Cdr	01-Oct-13	WAR	MW	MTM MWS COLLINGWOOD	HMS COLLINGWOOD
Mason, Garry	Capt	01-Apr-11	RM	SCC	CHFHQ	RNAS YEOVILTON
Mason, Joe W	Lt RN	01-Apr-13	WAR	P UT	MTM	WASHINGTON
Mason, John	Lt RN	01-Apr-11	WAR	GSX	BRNC	BRNC DARTMOUTH
Mason, Lindsay	Lt Cdr	01-Oct-02	ENG	TM	DEFENCE ACADEMY	SWINDON
Mason, Mark J	Lt Cdr	01-Oct-09	WAR	PWO(U)	HMS DEFENDER	
Mason, Oliver D	Capt	01-Sep-10	RM	GS	CDO LOG REGT RM	RMB CHIVENOR
Mason, Richard H	Lt Cdr	01-May-04	WAR	PWO(SM)	HMS ASTUTE	
Mason, Victoria J	Lt RN	01-Oct-09	LOGS	L	NAVSEC	HMS EXCELLENT
Massey, Benjamin M O	SLt	01-Sep-14	WAR	GSX	HMS DRAGON	
Massey, Paul	Lt Cdr	05-Dec-02	WAR	AV (RES)	CHFHQ	RNAS YEOVILTON
Masson, Neil G	Lt Cdr	01-Oct-10	WAR	SM(AWC)	UK MCC	BAHRAIN

Name	Substantive Rank	Seniority	Branch	Specialisation	Organisation Name	Location Name
Masters, James C	Cdr	30-Jun-06	WAR	AAWO	MTM NELSON	HMS NELSON
Mathers, Fiona C	Lt RN	02-Dec-05	WAR	OP INT	HQ DISC	CHICKSANDS
Matheson, Andrew S M	Surg Lt Cdr	01-Nov-11	MED	GMP	MTM INM ALVERSTOKE	GOSPORT
Mathieson, Neil B	Lt Cdr	01-Oct-08	ENG	AE	DES COMAIR	ABBEY WOOD
Matthams, Paul S	SLt	01-Aug-13	ENG	AE	RNAS CULDROSE	HELSTON
Matthews, Christopher L G	Lt RN	01-Jan-12	LOGS	L	CDO LOG REGT RM	RMB CHIVENOR
Matthews, David W	Capt RN	18-Aug-14	ENG	WESM(TWS)	DES COMFLEET	ABBEY WOOD
Matthews, Garydd R M	Mid	17-Nov-14	ENG	WE	BRNC	BRNC DARTMOUTH
Matthews, Jonathan J	Surg Cdr	01-Sep-09	MED	T&O	MDHU DERRIFORD	PLYMOUTH
Matthews, Justin	Lt Cdr	01-Oct-09	WAR	O SKW	854 NAS	RNAS CULDROSE
Matthews, Kevin A I	Lt RN	13-Jul-12	MED	MS	DES COMFLEET	ABBEY WOOD
Matthews, Lewis J	Mid	17-Nov-14	WAR	GSX	BRNC	BRNC DARTMOUTH
Matthews, Lucy A	Surg Lt Cdr (D)	19-Jun-13	DENTAL	GDP	DDS SCOTLAND	HMNB CLYDE
Matthews, Paul B	Cdr	30-Jun-09	ENG	TM	NATO-ACO-SHAPE	CASTEAU
Matthews, Paul K	Cdr	30-Jun-11	LOGS	L	NATO - BRUSSELS	BRUSSELS
Mattock, Nicholas J	Lt RN	01-Jan-05	WAR	P FW	LOAN DSTL	FAREHAM
Maude, Colin D	Lt Cdr	01-Oct-11	ENG	AE	LHF 815 SQN HQ	RNAS YEOVILTON
Maumy, Jonathan	Lt RN	01-Jan-10	WAR	P MER	MTM DEFAC JSCSC	SHRIVENHAM
Mawdsley, Gareth R	Lt Cdr	01-Oct-07	LOGS	L	STABILISATION UNIT	LONDON
Mawdsley, Owen R	Lt RN	07-Jun-10	WAR	O SKW	8 SQN	RAF WADDINGTON
Mawdsley, Richard J	Capt	01-Sep-13	RM	GS	43 CDO FPGRM	HELENSBURGH
Maxwell, Emma C	Surg SLt	20-Jul-14	MED	Medical	BLAKE	BRNC DARTMOUTH
Maxwell, Hamish	Lt RN	01-Oct-10	WAR	SM(X)	HMS VANGUARD	
May, Connor D W R	Lt RN	03-May-13	ENG	WE	HMS WESTMINSTER	
May, David M	Lt Cdr	01-Oct-08	WAR	REG	RNP SIB EASTERN	HMS NELSON
May, Frederick C	SLt	01-Jul-12	WAR	SM(X)	HMS TORBAY	
May, Nigel P	Cdr	30-Jun-06	WAR	P SKW	NCHQ CNPS	PORTSMOUTH
May, Steven	Lt Cdr	01-Jul-03	ENG	ME	HMS SULTAN	GOSPORT
Maybery, James E	Col	07-Jan-14	RM	GS	MTM DCLC RN STUDENTS	SHRIVENHAM
Mayell, Julie A	Lt Cdr	01-Oct-02	LOGS	L	NATO - BRUSSELS	BRUSSELS
Mayes, David J	SLt	11-Feb-14	WAR	GSX	HMS SUTHERLAND	
Mayger, Martyn	Lt RN	01-Apr-13	WAR	GSX	FOST MPV SEA	HMNB CLYDE
Maynard, Charles I	Lt Cdr	01-Feb-03	WAR	PWO(A)	HMS BULWARK	
Maynard, Paul A	Lt Col	30-Jun-14	RM	GS	OPS DIR	LONDON
Maynard, Sophie D	Mid	17-Nov-14	WAR	GSX	BRNC	BRNC DARTMOUTH
McAll, Benjamin J	Capt	03-Sep-14	RM	GS	40 CDO RM	TAUNTON
McAllister, Andrew W	Lt Cdr	01-Oct-14	ENG	IS	SVCOPS/DHDOPS/COR	CORSHAM
McAllister, Kevin J	Lt RN	17-Dec-10	ENG	WE	OCLC MANCH	MANCHESTER
McAllister, Steven E	Lt Cdr	01-Oct-13	WAR	SM(AWC)	HMS TORBAY	
McAlpine, Martin A	Lt RN	08-Jun-07	WAR	C	CIO-CTO	LONDON
McAlpine, Paul A CBE ADC	Cdre	08-Feb-11	WAR	MCD	COMPORFLOT	PORTSMOUTH
McAlpine, Rory W A	Lt RN	01-Mar-12	WAR	GSX	HMS LANCASTER	
McArdle, Alan D	Surg Lt RN	01-Mar-12	MED	GDMO	45 CDO RM	DUNDEE
McArdle, Christopher J	Capt	01-Sep-09	RM	GS	URNU LIVERPOOL	LIVERPOOL
McArdle, Martin J	Lt RN	01-Jun-08	WAR	ATC	RAF SHAWBURY	SHREWSBURY
McBarnet, Thomas F	Capt RN	30-Jun-06	WAR	PWO(U)	NATO - BRUSSELS	BRUSSELS (MONS)
McBeth, Gary	Lt RN	01-Sep-05	ENG	MESM	HMS AMBUSH	
McBratney, James A G	Lt Cdr	01-Nov-04	WAR	SM(AWC)	NOPF DAM NECK	VIRGINIA BEACH
McBride, Shaun P	SLt	01-Nov-12	WAR	P UT	MTM RAF CRANWELL	RAFC CRANWELL
McBrierty, Craig J	Lt RN	08-Jul-12	ENG	WE	HMS MONMOUTH	
McCafferty, Lesley F	Surg Lt Cdr (D)	23-Jul-12	DENTAL	GDP	DDS SCOTLAND	HMNB CLYDE
McCall, Gary	Lt Cdr	01-Oct-11	WAR	P WILDCAT	FLEET AV VL	RNAS YEOVILTON
McCallum, Malcolm D	Lt Cdr	01-Oct-12	WAR	HM(AS)	HMS OCEAN	
McCallum, Neil	Lt RN	01-Jun-05	ENG	ME	FLEET CAP MARCAP	PORTSMOUTH
McCamphill-Rose, Paul J	Lt Cdr	01-Oct-11	ENG	WE	MWS COLLINGWOOD	HMS COLLINGWOOD
McCann, Andrew G	Lt RN	01-Sep-10	WAR	SM(X)	HMS TRENCHANT	
McCann, Sally J	SLt	24-Jan-12	WAR	HM	HMS PORTLAND	
McCann, Toby	Lt Cdr	01-Dec-06	ENG	AE O	MTM RN GLOBAL	CANADA
McCardle, John A OBE	Col	01-Jul-08	RM	P LYN7	SERV ATTACHE/ADVISER	PRETORIA
McCarthy, Steven	Cdr	30-Jun-09	ENG	ME	FOST DPORT	PLYMOUTH
McCaughan, Christopher J	Lt RN	01-Oct-11	ENG	WE	MWS COLLINGWOOD	HMS COLLINGWOOD
McCaughey, Vincent J	Lt Cdr	01-Oct-05	ENG	IS	DIST/COR	CORSHAM

Name	Substantive Rank	Seniority	Branch	Specialisation	Organisation Name	Location Name
McCaul, Daniel	Surg Lt RN	01-Aug-12	MED	GDMO	HMS DRAGON	
McCavour, Bryan D	Lt Cdr	01-Oct-14	WAR	INT	MTM MWS COLLINGWOOD	HMS COLLINGWOOD
McClaren, Ronni	Lt RN	09-Apr-09	WAR	REG	RNP SIB EASTERN	HMS NELSON
McClean, Stephen	Lt RN	01-Oct-09	ENG	WESM(TWS)	DES COMFLEET	ABBEY WOOD
McCleary, Simon P	Lt Cdr	01-Oct-05	ENG	WESM(SWS)	COMFASFLOT	HELENSBURGH
McClelland, Ian	Lt RN	01-Mar-10	WAR	MCD	MCM1	FASLANE
McClelland, Patrick W	Lt RN	07-Jan-07	WAR	AV	FLEET CSAV	PORTSMOUTH
McClement, Duncan L	Lt Cdr	01-Jan-07	ENG	MESM	CAPTAIN BASE SAFETY CLYDE	HELENSBURGH
McClintock, Lee R	SLt	01-Feb-13	WAR	SM(X)	MTM RALEIGH	HMS RALEIGH
McClurg, Robert J	Lt Cdr	01-Mar-10	ENG	WE	HMS ST ALBANS	
McCombe, John	Lt Cdr	01-Sep-04	ENG	ME	DES COMFLEET	ABBEY WOOD
McConnell, David H P	Surg Lt RN	01-Mar-12	MED	Medical	BRNC	BRNC DARTMOUTH
McConochie, Andrew D	Lt Cdr	16-Apr-96	LOGS	L	NBD COB BASE EXECUTIVE OFFICE	HMS DRAKE
McCormack, Gary	Lt Cdr	01-Oct-10	ENG	ME	FOST DPORT	PLYMOUTH
McCormick, Emma J	Lt RN	01-Jan-05	WAR	GSX	NCHQ - NAVY CMD SEC	PORTSMOUTH
McCrea, Mark J	Lt RN	01-May-05	ENG	ME	DNR N IRELAND	BELFAST
McCreton, Joshua L G	Capt	01-Mar-11	RM	GS	MTM HQ 3 CDO BDE RM	PLYMOUTH
McCrossan, Amy	Lt RN	01-Aug-09	WAR	GSX	HMS MERSEY	
McCue, Duncan	Cdr	30-Jun-06	ENG	ME	NCHQ CNPERS	PORTSMOUTH
McCullagh, Timothy A C	Lt RN	11-Oct-13	LOGS	L	UKMARBATSTAFF	PORTSMOUTH
McCullough, Ian N	Lt Col	30-Jun-14	RM	GS (RES)	NCHQ - NAVY CMD SEC	PORTSMOUTH
McCullough, Karen M	Lt Cdr	01-Oct-14	QARNNS	ITU (C&S)	PCRF	RFA ARGUS
McCurry, Neill I	Capt	01-Sep-09	RM	GS	NCHQ	PORTSMOUTH
McCutcheon, Graeme	Lt Cdr	01-Oct-06	WAR	P LYNX	LHF 815 SQN	RNAS YEOVILTON
McDermott, Owen D	Cdr	30-Jun-10	ENG	WE	NC REQUIREMENTS MANAGERS	ABBEY WOOD
McDonald, Andrew W	Lt Cdr	01-Oct-06	ENG	AE	DES COMAIR	ABBEY WOOD
McDonald, Duncan J	Lt Cdr	01-Oct-08	ENG	ME	DES COMFLEET	ABBEY WOOD
McDonald, Morgan J	Lt RN	01-Jan-05	WAR	MW	FOST MPV SEA	HMNB CLYDE
McDonnell, David	Cdr	30-Jun-11	WAR	HM (M CH)	NATO - BRUSSELS	BRUSSELS
McDonough, Mark	Lt RN	01-Jan-13	ENG	WESM	HMS VICTORIOUS	
McDougall, James N	Lt RN	01-May-13	ENG	MESM	HMS ARTFUL	
McDougall, William	Lt Cdr	02-Oct-10	ENG	MESM	RN EXCHANGE AUSTRALIA	CANBERRA
McDowell, Daniel M	Mid	17-Nov-14	WAR	GSX	BRNC	BRNC DARTMOUTH
McElrath, Calum D	SLt	01-May-13	WAR	REG	RNP - HQ PMN	HMS EXCELLENT
McElroy, Paul J	SLt	01-Sep-14	ENG	MESM	DCEME SULTAN	HMS SULTAN
McElroy-Baker, Lindsey	Lt RN	17-Oct-08	QARNNS		MDHU DERRIFORD	PLYMOUTH
McElwaine, Christopher W	Lt RN	08-Dec-11	ENG	WE	NC REQUIREMENTS MANAGERS	ABBEY WOOD
McEvoy, Jason L	Lt RN	19-Dec-08	ENG	WESM(TWS)	FOST SM SEA	HMNB CLYDE
McEvoy, Thomas P J	Capt	01-Sep-13	RM	GS	45 CDO RM	DUNDEE
McEwan, Rory D	Lt Cdr	01-Oct-10	ENG	WESM(TWS)	FLEET COMOPS NWD	NORTHWOOD
McFadden, Andrew	RN Chpln	01-Sep-98	Ch S	Chaplain	DEFENCE ACADEMY	ANDOVER
McFarlane, Daniel	SLt	11-Apr-12	WAR	SM(X)	MCM1	FASLANE
McFarlane, Gregory T	SLt	02-May-12	LOGS	L	FOST DPORT	PLYMOUTH
McGannity, Colin S	Lt Cdr	01-Oct-08	WAR	O SKW	849 SQN	RNAS CULDROSE
McGhee, Craig	Maj	01-Sep-02	RM	P LYN7	CHFHQ	RNAS YEOVILTON
McGhie, Ian A	Cdre	05-Aug-14	WAR	SM(CQ)	HQBF GIBRALTAR	HMS ROOKE
McGill, Gus	SLt	01-Sep-14	WAR	SM(X)	MCM1	FASLANE
McGill, Ian	Maj	01-Oct-13	RM	MLDR (SCC)	30 CDO IX GP RM	PLYMOUTH
McGinlay, Matthew J	SLt	01-Sep-14	WAR	GSX	HMS RICHMOND	
McGinley, Christopher T	Capt	13-Dec-06	RM	GS (RES)	DNR RCHQ NORTH	HMS CALEDONIA
McGivern, Ryan P	Lt RN	01-Sep-04	WAR	P MER	MTM HASLER COY	HMS DRAKE
McGlory, Stephen J	Cdr	30-Jun-13	WAR	PWO(A)	FLEET COMOPS NWD	NORTHWOOD
McGreal, Benjamin	Lt Cdr	01-Oct-13	WAR	P MER CDO	CHF - 846	RAF BENSON
McGuire, James	Lt Cdr	24-Aug-04	WAR	SM(CQ)	FOST FAS SHORE	HMNB CLYDE
McHugh, Richard H	Lt Cdr	01-Mar-05	ENG	ME	MTM FLEET HQ	PORTSMOUTH
McInerney, Andrew J	Col	31-Mar-11	RM	GS	NCHQ	NCHQ
McInerney, David F	Lt Cdr	01-Oct-13	WAR	C	LOAN DSTL	SALISBURY
McInnes, Allan J	Lt RN	01-Jan-12	WAR	O UT	MTM 849 SQN CULDROSE	RNAS CULDROSE
McInnes, Ian S	SLt	01-Jan-14	ENG	MESM	NBC CLYDE	HMNB CLYDE
McInnes, Stephanie	Lt RN	01-Feb-12	WAR	ATC	RNAS CULDROSE	HELSTON
McIntosh, James D	Surg Cdr	10-Sep-08	MED	GMP (C&S)	MTM DEFAC JSCSC	SHRIVENHAM
McIntosh, Simon J	Surg Lt Cdr	05-Aug-14	MED	GMP	MTM INM ALVERSTOKE	GOSPORT

Name	Substantive Rank	Seniority	Branch	Specialisation	Organisation Name	Location Name
McKay, Thomas W	Lt Cdr	01-Oct-11	WAR	PWO	FOST NWD (JTEPS)	NORTHWOOD
McKechnie, Peter S	Surg Lt Cdr	01-Jun-11	MED	GS	MTM INM ALVERSTOKE	GOSPORT
McKee, Hamish M	Lt Cdr	01-Oct-09	WAR	O MER	824 SQN	RNAS CULDROSE
McKendrick, Andrew M OBE	Capt RN	01-Jun-09	WAR	SM(CQ)	CBRN POL	LONDON
McKenna, Thomas J	Lt RN	01-Sep-12	ENG	WE	DES COMFLEET	ABBEY WOOD
McKibbin, Robert C	Mid	01-Feb-14	ENG	ME	DCEME SULTAN	HMS SULTAN
McKinlay, Jayne A C	Surg Lt Cdr	01-Feb-10	MED	EM	MTM INM ALVERSTOKE	GOSPORT
McKnight, Derek J S	Cdr	30-Jun-14	WAR	MCD	FLEET MARITIME WARFARE	HMS COLLINGWOOD
McLachlan, Andrew C	Lt Cdr	01-Oct-14	ENG	TM	CDP PERS TRG	LONDON
McLaren, James P OBE	Lt Col	30-Jun-07	RM	GS	SERV ATTACHE/ADVISER	NAIROBI
McLauchlan, James M	Lt RN	01-Nov-14	LOGS	L	847 SQN	RNAS YEOVILTON
McLaughlan, Christopher T	Lt RN	01-Mar-08	LOGS	L SM	HMS VANGUARD	
McLaughlin, Ian J	Lt RN	01-Jun-11	ENG	AE	DES COMFLEET	ABBEY WOOD
McLaughlin, Steven	Cdr	30-Jun-14	ENG	TM	MOD NSD	LONDON
McLean, Christopher R	Surg Cdr	01-Jul-10	MED	T&O	PCRF	RFA ARGUS
McLean, David	RN Chpln	18-Sep-96	Ch S	Chaplain	HMS RALEIGH	TORPOINT
McLean, Sean D	Lt RN	01-Jan-13	WAR	GSX	MTM NEPTUNE	HMNB CLYDE
McLellan, James D	Cdr	30-Jun-13	ENG	WE	DES COMFLEET	ABBEY WOOD
McLellan, Moira S	Surg Lt Cdr	03-Aug-11	MED	GDMO	MASF	RNAS CULDROSE
McLeman, William D	Lt RN	01-May-14	LOGS	N/A	HMS DARING	
McLennan, Alexander P	Lt RN	01-Sep-12	ENG	ME	HMS OCEAN	
McLennan, Andrew	Lt Cdr	01-Oct-08	WAR	O MER	PJHQ (UK)	NORTHWOOD
McLocklan, Lee M	Lt Cdr	01-Oct-06	LOGS	L	MOD DEFENCE STAFF	LONDON
McMahon, Christopher T	Mid	17-Nov-14	WAR	GSX	BRNC	BRNC DARTMOUTH
McMahon, Daniel S	Lt RN	01-Jan-04	WAR	HM	RNAS YEOVILTON	YEOVILTON
McManus, Michael K	Mid	01-Feb-14	ENG	MESM	HMS AUDACIOUS	
McMenamin, Diarmaid	Surg Lt Cdr	06-Aug-08	MED	GMP	RMB CHIVENOR	BARNSTAPLE
McMenemy, Louise	Surg Lt RN	03-Aug-11	MED	GDMO	HMS DEFENDER	
McMichael-Phillips, Scott J	Capt RN	30-Jun-08	WAR	HM (H CH)	LOAN HYDROG DGHR(N)	TAUNTON
McMillan, Nelson	Lt Cdr	01-Oct-12	WAR	PWO	UKMARBATSTAFF	PORTSMOUTH
McMillan, Peter F	SLt	17-Nov-13	MED	MS(EHO)	BRNC	BRNC DARTMOUTH
McMonies, Murray J	SLt	01-Feb-12	ENG	MESM	DCEME SULTAN	HMS SULTAN
McMorran, Hannah J	Lt RN	02-May-14	MED	MS(EHO)	NCHQ MEDDIV EH	HMNB CLYDE
McMorrow, Kevin M	Lt RN	01-Jun-09	WAR	ATC	RNAS YEOVILTON	SOUTHAMPTON
McMorrow, Stephen P	SLt	01-Dec-13	WAR	GSX	MCM1	FASLANE
McNair, James OBE	Cdr	30-Jun-11	ENG	AE	HMS SULTAN	GOSPORT
McNally, Barry J	Lt RN	01-Sep-08	LOGS	L SM	FLEET ACOS(RP)	PORTSMOUTH
McNally, Neville	Cdr	30-Jun-10	LOGS	L	DEFENCE ACADEMY	SHRIVENHAM
McNally, Nicholas A	Lt Cdr	01-Oct-13	ENG	ME	HMS NORTHUMBERLAND	
McNally, Peter J A	SLt	01-Sep-14	WAR	GSX	MCM2	PORTSMOUTH
McNaught, Chilton J	Lt RN	13-Jun-08	WAR	REG	HMS SULTAN	GOSPORT
McNicholl, Bruce R	SLt	01-Nov-14	WAR	GSX	MWS COLLINGWOOD	HMS COLLINGWOOD
McPhail, Stuart C	SLt	01-Apr-14	MED	Medical	BLAKE	BRNC DARTMOUTH
McPhail, Thomas C	Lt RN	01-May-04	WAR	PWO	HMS OCEAN	
McPhee, Thomas J	Lt RN	17-Dec-09	WAR	INT	HMS TEMERAIRE	PORTSMOUTH
McQuaid, Ivor T	Lt RN	12-Aug-05	ENG	WESM(TWS)	NAVY MCTA	PORTSMOUTH
McQueen, Jason B	Lt Cdr	01-Oct-03	ENG	TM	JIOTAT	SHRIVENHAM
McQueen, Patrick G	Lt Cdr	01-Oct-13	WAR	MCD	FOST MPV SEA	HMNB CLYDE
McTear, Karen MBE	Capt RN	13-Jan-14	ENG	TM	SERV ATTACHE/ADVISER	KIEV
McWilliams, Adrian R	Lt Cdr	01-Oct-11	WAR	O WILDCAT	WMF 825 SQN HQ	RNAS YEOVILTON
McWilliams, Jacqueline E	Lt Cdr	01-Sep-03	WAR	MW	MASTT	PORTSMOUTH
Meacher, Paul G	Lt Cdr	01-Oct-14	WAR	PWO	HMS DIAMOND	
Meachin, Michael C	RN Chpln	07-Jul-97	Ch S	Chaplain	COMPORFLOT	PORTSMOUTH
Meaden, Alexander P	Lt RN	19-Nov-09	LOGS	L	RNLA	HMS COLLINGWOOD
Meakin, Brian R	Cdr	30-Jun-03	WAR	O SKW	NATO SCHOOL (SHAPE)	OBERAMMERGAU
Mealing, David W	Lt Cdr	30-Jun-13	ENG	AE	DES COMJE	YEOVIL
Mealing, Steven	Lt Cdr	01-Oct-05	ENG	ME	FLEET ACOS(RP)	PORTSMOUTH
Mearns, Craig M	Cdr	30-Jun-05	LOGS	L	HMS QUEEN ELIZABETH	
Mears, Richard J	Lt Col	30-Jun-13	RM	C	MOD NSD - HDS	LONDON
Medlicott, Nicholas	Lt RN	28-Oct-05	WAR	AV	RNAS CULDROSE	HELSTON
Meeds, Kevin	Lt Cdr	16-Dec-95	WAR	O SK6	LSP OMAN	MUSCAT
Meehan, Oliver J P	Lt RN	15-Jul-13	LOGS	L	MTM DOLSU	BEACONSFIELD

Name	Substantive Rank	Seniority	Branch	Specialisation	Organisation Name	Location Name
Meek, Camilla S MBE	Lt Cdr	01-Mar-02	ENG	ME	FLEET CAP SSM	PORTSMOUTH
Mehsen, Samy	Lt RN	01-Sep-13	ENG	WESM	HMS VENGEANCE	
Mehta, Christopher	Lt RN	19-Feb-10	ENG	MESM	FLEET COMOPS NWD	NORTHWOOD
Mehta, Jennifer C K	Lt RN	01-Jan-07	ENG	TM	MTM NELSON	HMS NELSON
Mehta, Kim L	Lt Cdr	01-Oct-06	ENG	TM	NCHQ CNPERS	PORTSMOUTH
Meigh, Peter D	Lt Cdr	01-Oct-14	WAR	AAWO	HMS DIAMOND	
Meldrum, Richard A	Lt RN	01-Mar-09	ENG	MESM	NBC CLYDE	HMNB CLYDE
Melling, Paul G	Lt RN	01-Jun-10	WAR	P LYN7	847 SQN	RNAS YEOVILTON
Mellor, Adrian J	Surg Cdr	30-Jun-03	MED	Anaes	MDHU NORTHALLERTON	NORTHALLERTON
Mellor, Andrew L	Lt RN	16-Dec-11	WAR		UKMARBATSTAFF	PORTSMOUTH
Mellor, Daniel P	Lt RN	01-Sep-05	ENG	MESM	HMS VICTORIOUS	
Mellows, Christopher R	SLt	01-Nov-14	WAR	SM(X)	BRNC	BRNC DARTMOUTH
Melvin, John J	Lt RN	01-Aug-09	LOGS	L	MTM NELSON	HMS NELSON
Mendham, Oliver D	SLt	01-May-14	WAR	GSX	MWS COLLINGWOOD	HMS COLLINGWOOD
Menzies, Bruce	Lt RN	01-Jul-01	WAR	P LYNX	RN XIII SQN REAPER	RAF WADDINGTON
Mercer, Simon	Surg Cdr	02-Aug-11	MED	Anaes	RCDM	BIRMINGHAM
Meredith, Nicholas	Cdr	30-Jun-07	WAR	SM(CQ)	NATO-ACO-SHAPE	CASTEAU
Merewether, Henry A H	Cdr	30-Jun-04	WAR	O LYNX	RNAS YEOVILTON	YEOVILTON
Merrison-Fielder, Nathan R R	Mid	08-Sep-14	WAR	GSX	BRNC	BRNC DARTMOUTH
Merritt, Jonathan J	Cdr	30-Jun-05	ENG	ME	NC REQUIREMENTS MANAGERS	ABBEY WOOD
Messenger, Gordon K DSO* OBE	Lt Gen	14-Jan-13	RM	MLDR	DCDS MIL STRAT OPS	LONDON
Metcalf, Stephen W	Lt Cdr	01-Oct-08	ENG	MESM	SFM CLYDE	HMNB CLYDE
Metcalf, Anthony P W	Lt Cdr	01-Dec-91	WAR	PWO(U)	LOAN DSTL	FAREHAM
Metcalfe, Lauren J	Lt RN	01-Oct-09	LOGS	L	PJHQ (UK)	NORTHWOOD
Metcalfe, Liam M	Maj	01-Oct-09	RM	LC	HQ 3 CDO BDE RM	PLYMOUTH
Metcalfe, Richard J	Lt RN	04-Sep-98	ENG	WE	FOSNI - NRC	HMS CALEDONIA
Methven, Paul	Cdre	24-Feb-14	ENG	MESM	DES COMFLEET	ABBEY WOOD
Meyer, Alexander J	Lt Cdr	01-Oct-06	WAR	PWO(C)	HMS DIAMOND	
Middleditch, Thomas C	Lt RN	01-Sep-09	ENG	ME	COMPORFLOT	PORTSMOUTH
Middleton, Christopher S MBE	Lt Col	30-Jun-10	RM	LC	DIRECTOR (JW)	NORTHWOOD
Middleton, Edward J	Capt	01-Sep-08	RM	GS	EU OHQ	NORTHWOOD
Middleton, John R M	Capt	01-Sep-08	RM	GS	42 CDO RM	PLYMOUTH
Middleton, Mark A	Lt Cdr	01-Oct-12	MED	MS(CDO)	MED SQN CDO LOG REGT RM	RMB CHIVENOR
Middleton, Shane A	Lt RN	30-Jul-10	ENG	WE	DES COMFLEET	ABBEY WOOD
Middleton, Simon W F	Surg Lt Cdr	11-Sep-08	MED	T&O	MTM INM ALVERSTOKE	GOSPORT
Midwinter, Mark CBE	Surg Capt RN	01-Sep-07	MED	GS	RCDM	BIRMINGHAM
Mifflin, Michelle J	Lt RN	01-Jan-05	WAR	PWO	FLEET FOST ACOS(Trg)	PORTSMOUTH
Milburn, Philip K	Capt	04-Nov-09	WAR	AAWO	COMPORFLOT	PORTSMOUTH
Mildener, Lee D	Capt	30-Mar-12	RM	SCC	NCHQ	PORTSMOUTH
Miles, Alexander S	Lt RN	01-Apr-12	WAR	SM(X)	HMS ASTUTE	
Miles, Christopher A	Mid	01-May-14	WAR	GSX	BRNC	BRNC DARTMOUTH
Miles, Emma K	Lt RN	01-Apr-12	ENG	ME	HMS ST ALBANS	
Miles, Gary A MBE	Lt RN	11-Apr-08	ENG	ME	HMS SULTAN	GOSPORT
Miles, Graham J	Lt Cdr	07-Aug-00	ENG	AE	NATO ACO	NORTHWOOD
Miles, Philip	Lt Cdr	01-Oct-06	LOGS	L	DES COMLAND	BICESTER
Miles, Rebecca L	SLt	01-Oct-14	MED	Medical	BLAKE	BRNC DARTMOUTH
Miles, Sean A	Surg Lt Cdr	17-May-07	MED	GMP	HMS OCEAN	
Milkins, Kiel	Lt RN	13-Dec-13	ENG	WE	MTM NELSON	HMS NELSON
Millar, Gary D	Lt RN	01-Nov-14	WAR	GSX	MWS COLLINGWOOD	HMS COLLINGWOOD
Millar, Jennifer A	Surg Lt Cdr	06-Aug-13	MED	GMP	MTM INM ALVERSTOKE	GOSPORT
Millar, Stuart W S	Surg Capt RN	22-Apr-10	MED	GMP (C&S)	DCHET HQ	LICHFIELD
Millard, Jeremy	Lt Cdr	01-Oct-07	ENG	ME	LSP OMAN	MUSCAT
Millen, Stuart C W MBE	Lt Cdr	01-Oct-05	WAR	P SK6	849 SQN	RNAS CULDROSE
Miller, Adam E	Lt RN	09-Apr-10	WAR	AE	CHF - 846	RAF BENSON
Miller, Andrew J G CBE	Capt RN	01-Jun-00	WAR	PWO	FOSNI - NRC WWE	BRISTOL
Miller, Andrew P	Capt	03-Apr-09	RM	GS	NCHQ	PORTSMOUTH
Miller, Colin R	Cdr	30-Jun-07	WAR	O MER	FLEET CSAV	PORTSMOUTH
Miller, David J S	Lt RN	08-Jul-11	ENG	ME	MTM DEFAC CMT MSC	SHRIVENHAM
Miller, Holly M G	Mid	01-May-14	LOGS	L	BRNC	BRNC DARTMOUTH
Miller, Ian	Lt Cdr	01-Jan-08	ENG	MESM	DES COMFLEET	WASHINGTON
Miller, Kevin R	Lt Cdr	01-Oct-10	ENG	WE	COMPORFLOT	PORTSMOUTH
Miller, Paul D	Lt Cdr	01-Feb-01	WAR		UKMARBATSTAFF	PORTSMOUTH

Name	Substantive Rank	Seniority	Branch	Specialisation	Organisation Name	Location Name
Miller, Rosalyn C	Surg Lt RN	01-Aug-12	MED	GDMO	HMS IRON DUKE	
Miller, Ross J	Lt RN	01-Sep-12	ENG	MESM	HMS AMBUSH	
Miller, Sasha L	Lt Cdr	01-Oct-12	WAR	INT	NATO ACO	NORTHWOOD
Miller, Shane R	Lt RN	24-Nov-09	ENG	AE	HMS OCEAN	
Milligan, Robert J	Lt Cdr	01-Oct-08	WAR	O LYNX	MAA	ABBEY WOOD
Milligan, Robert J	Lt RN	19-Jan-14	WAR	SM(X)	MWS COLLINGWOOD	HMS COLLINGWOOD
Milligan, Toby I	Mid	08-Sep-14	ENG	AE	BRNC	BRNC DARTMOUTH
Mills, Gary	Lt Cdr	01-Oct-07	WAR	GSX	RNLA	BRNC DARTMOUTH
Mills, Gregory	SLt	01-Nov-14	WAR	HM	MWS COLLINGWOOD	HMS COLLINGWOOD
Mills, Scott A	Maj	01-Oct-13	RM	SCC	HASLER COY	HMS DRAKE
Mills, William S	Lt RN	01-May-14	WAR	HM	MTM MWS HMTG (D)	HMS DRAKE
Millward, Elliott J	SLt	01-Sep-14	ENG	MESM	MTM DRAKE	HMS DRAKE
Millyard, Matthew	Lt RN	01-Oct-11	WAR	GSX	MWS COLLINGWOOD	HMS COLLINGWOOD
Miln, David	Lt RN	01-May-11	WAR	MCD	MCM2	PORTSMOUTH
Milne, Andre P	Lt Cdr	01-Oct-09	WAR	P LYN7	HQ JHC CAP DIR	ANDOVER
Milne, Anthony	Maj	01-Oct-14	RM	GS	NCHQ	PORTSMOUTH
Milne, Charlotte L	Lt RN	07-Jun-12	ENG	AE	WMF 825 SQN HQ	RNAS YEOVILTON
Milne, Jason R	Maj	01-Oct-10	RM	MLDR (SCC)	CTCRM	EXMOUTH
Milne, Roderick M	Lt RN	01-Mar-10	WAR	GSX	HMS ST ALBANS	
Milner, Lisa D	Lt RN	01-Mar-06	ENG	TM	DEFENCE SCHOOL OF CIS	BLANDFORD FORUM
Milner, Robert A	Surg Cdr	01-Jul-09	MED	Occ Med	HQ 3 CDO BDE RM	PLYMOUTH
Milnes, Grant	Lt RN	01-Feb-14	WAR	GSX	HMS IRON DUKE	
Milsom, Jonathan	Lt Cdr	01-Oct-99	ENG	AE	DSAE COSFORD	WOLVERHAMPTON
Milsom, Matthew L	Lt RN	31-Oct-14	ENG	TM	NETS (OPS)	PORTSMOUTH
Milton, Michael E	SLt	22-Apr-12	WAR	FC	HMS DRAGON	
Mimpriss, Graham D	Cdr	30-Jun-10	WAR	HM (H CH)	NC REQUIREMENTS MANAGERS	ABBEY WOOD
Minall, Paul A	Surg Cdr (D)	24-Jul-06	DENTAL	GDP	DDS SCOTLAND	HMNB CLYDE
Minns, Robert J	SLt	01-May-12	WAR	GSX	HMS ARGYLL	
Minshall, Darren M	Surg Lt Cdr	02-Aug-10	MED	Psych	MTM INM ALVERSTOKE	GOSPORT
Minty, Darren	Lt Cdr	01-Oct-12	ENG	ME	HMS DARING	
Mion, Jonathan J	Lt RN	01-Sep-11	WAR	GSX	MTM DEFAC JSCSC	SHRIVENHAM
Misiak, Anna L	Lt Cdr	10-Apr-12	LOGS	L	HMS EXCELLENT	PORTSMOUTH
Mitchell, Aleesha W	Lt RN	01-Feb-09	ENG	WE	MTM FLEET HQ	PORTSMOUTH
Mitchell, Andrew J	Lt RN	01-Feb-08	WAR	O MER	750 SQN	RNAS CULDROSE
Mitchell, Henry	Cdr	30-Jun-01	WAR	P FW	RNAS YEOVILTON	YEOVILTON
Mitchell, James E	Lt RN	01-Oct-11	WAR	GSX	HMS IRON DUKE	
Mitchell, Jamie	Lt Cdr	01-Oct-08	WAR	SM(CQ)	RNSMS	HMS RALEIGH
Mitchell, Paul J	Lt RN	01-May-03	WAR	HM	FOST HM	HMS DRAKE
Mitchell, Samuel T	Mid	17-Nov-14	WAR	SM(X)	BRNC	BRNC DARTMOUTH
Mitchell, Stephen D	Lt Cdr	01-Oct-01	ENG	MESM	NCHQ CNPERS	PORTSMOUTH
Mitchell, Stuart J	Capt	01-Sep-11	RM	GS	45 CDO RM	DUNDEE
Mitchell-Heggs, Hugo C	Lt RN	07-Jun-12	ENG	MESM	HMS VIGILANT	
Mittins, Simon	Lt Cdr	01-Oct-14	WAR	ATC	RNAS YEOVILTON	SOUTHAMPTON
Moat, Richard	Capt	01-Sep-11	RM	GS	CTCRM	EXMOUTH
Mobbs, Thomas	Capt	01-Sep-08	RM	GS	NCHQ CNPERS	PORTSMOUTH
Moffatt, Neil R	Cdr	30-Jun-02	ENG	MESM	DES COMFLEET	PLYMOUTH
Mole, Andrew J	Lt Cdr	01-Oct-11	ENG	MESM	DES COMFLEET	THURSO
Molnar, Richard M	Lt Cdr	01-Oct-06	WAR	AAWO	FLEET MARITIME WARFARE	HMS COLLINGWOOD
Moloney, Benjamin G	Lt RN	08-Nov-07	WAR	GSX	HMS RICHMOND	
Molyneaux, Dean G OBE	Capt RN	30-Jun-04	ENG	WE	FLEET FOST ACOS(Trg)	PORTSMOUTH
Money, Christopher J	Lt Cdr	01-Oct-10	WAR	HM (M CH)	FLEET COMOPS NWD	NORTHWOOD
Money, John C	RN Chpln	12-Aug-13	Ch S	Chaplain	CTCRM	EXMOUTH
Monger, Paul D	Lt Cdr	21-May-95	WAR	HM	902 EAW	OMAN - JOA - MUSANNAH
Monnox, Jill	Lt Cdr	01-Oct-08	WAR	PWO(A)	MWS COLLINGWOOD	HMS COLLINGWOOD
Montagu, Timothy B E P	Lt RN	01-Jan-07	WAR	GSX	MTM DEFAC JSCSC	SHRIVENHAM
Montgomery, Harvie E	Lt Cdr	01-Oct-13	ENG	TM	HMS QUEEN ELIZABETH	
Moody, Alistair C	Cdr	30-Jun-14	ENG	MESM	DES COMFLEET	ABBEY WOOD
Moody, David C	Cdr	30-Jun-12	ENG	WE	JFCIS(I)	QATAR
Mooney, John	Lt	01-Jul-13	RM	SCC	NCHQ	PORTSMOUTH
Moore, Aimee C	Lt RN	20-Feb-11	LOGS	L	MTM NELSON	HMS NELSON
Moore, Alison L	Lt RN	20-Oct-06	WAR	PWO	MWS COLLINGWOOD	HMS COLLINGWOOD
Moore, Benjamin A	Capt	01-Apr-11	RM	GS	MOD DEFENCE STAFF	LONDON

Name	Substantive Rank	Seniority	Branch	Specialisation	Organisation Name	Location Name
Moore, Christopher I	Cdr	30-Jun-99	WAR	AAWO	FLEET MARITIME WARFARE	HMS COLLINGWOOD
Moore, Jonathan P	Lt RN	01-Jun-06	WAR	P SK4	CHF - 846	RAF BENSON
Moore, Jordan P	SLt	01-Nov-14	WAR	GSX	BRNC	BRNC DARTMOUTH
Moore, Martin	Cdr	30-Jun-12	WAR	PWO(U)	NCHQ CNPS	PORTSMOUTH
Moore, Matthew J	Lt RN	01-Oct-08	WAR	MCD	NCHQ CNPERS	PORTSMOUTH
Moore, Paul	Surg Cdr (D)	10-Jul-07	DENTAL	GDP(C&S)	DMS WHITTINGTON	LICHFIELD
Moore, Piers H G	Cdr	30-Jun-09	WAR	SM(AWC)	NATO-ACO-SHAPE	CASTEAU
Moore, Richard G	Capt	01-Sep-06	RM	P SK4	CHFHQ	PLYMOUTH
Moore, Robert W	Lt RN	01-Apr-11	WAR	FC	MTM MWS COLLINGWOOD	HMS COLLINGWOOD
Moore, Sean	Cdr	30-Jun-12	LOGS	L BAR	NCHQ - CNLS	PORTSMOUTH
Moore, Suzanne K	Cdr	30-Jun-11	WAR	PWO(U)	US CENTCOM	USA
Moore, William I	Capt	01-Sep-04	RM	P LYN7	MTM MWS COLLINGWOOD	HMS COLLINGWOOD
Moorey, Christopher	Cdr	30-Jun-07	WAR	PWO(A)	STRIKFORNATO - LISBON	LISBON
Moorhouse, Edward J	Lt Col	30-Jun-11	RM	GS	BDS	WASHINGTON
Moorhouse, Stephen OBE	Cdr	30-Jun-10	WAR	O SKW	FMC STRAT MAN	LONDON
Moran, Benjamin M	Lt Cdr	01-Oct-13	WAR	SM(AWC)	FLEET CAP SSM	PORTSMOUTH
Moran, Craig A	Cdr	30-Jun-14	WAR	REG	MTM NELSON	HMS NELSON
Moran, John-Paul	Lt Cdr	01-Oct-13	ENG	AE	DES COMJE	RNAS CULDROSE
Moran, Julian T	Maj	01-Oct-06	RM	GS	HQ ARRC COMMAND GROUP	GLOUCESTER
Moran, Russell J	Lt Cdr	01-Oct-08	WAR	PWO	COMDEVFLOT	PLYMOUTH
Moreland, James R M	Lt RN	01-Oct-08	ENG	MESM	DES COMFLEET	ABBEY WOOD
Moreton, Samuel	Capt	01-Sep-13	RM	GS	CTCRM	EXMOUTH
Morey, Kevin N	Lt Cdr	01-Nov-09	WAR	PWO(N)	HMS BULWARK	
Morgan, Ashley K	Lt RN	01-May-10	WAR	O LYNX	WMF 825 SQN HQ	RNAS YEOVILTON
Morgan, Benjamin P	Lt Cdr	01-Oct-14	WAR	P MER	DEF HELI FLYING SCH	SHREWSBURY
Morgan, Christopher W	Lt Cdr	01-Oct-11	WAR	PWO	HMS SUTHERLAND	
Morgan, David H	Cdr	30-Jun-12	WAR	PWO(U)	FOST NWD (JTEPS)	NORTHWOOD
Morgan, Edward J A	Lt Cdr	01-Oct-06	WAR	P SK4	CHFHQ	RNAS YEOVILTON
Morgan, Gareth L	Lt RN	01-Sep-04	WAR	P SK4	CHFHQ	RNAS YEOVILTON
Morgan, Graeme A	SLt	01-Jan-14	WAR	INT	MTM NORTHWOOD HQ	NORTHWOOD
Morgan, Henry L M	Capt	01-Sep-11	RM	GS	HQ BRUNEI GAR	SERIA
Morgan, Hugo N M	Mid	01-May-14	WAR	GSX	BRNC	BRNC DARTMOUTH
Morgan, Huw L MBE	Lt Col	29-Jun-14	RM	GS	NCHQ	NCHQ
Morgan, Hywel R	Lt RN	01-Sep-12	WAR	HM	HMS ENTERPRISE	
Morgan, Kelly	Lt RN	01-Aug-13	QARNNS	Nurse Officer	MDHU PORTSMOUTH	PORTSMOUTH
Morgan, Michael C	Lt RN	31-Jul-09	ENG	AE	RNAS CULDROSE	HELSTON
Morgan, Tony G	Lt RN	01-Sep-12	ENG	WE	NAVY MCTA	PORTSMOUTH
Morgan-Hosey, John N	Lt Cdr	01-Oct-01	ENG	MESM	NBD NB SAFETY DEVONPORT	HMS DRAKE
Morley, Adrian MC	Lt Col	30-Jun-12	RM	LC	FLEET ACOS(RP)	PORTSMOUTH
Morley, David J	Lt RN	11-Dec-09	MED	MS(CDO)	HQ 3 CDO BDE RM	PLYMOUTH
Morley, James	Cdre	13-Oct-14	WAR	PWO(A)	FLEET CAP MARCAP	PORTSMOUTH
Morley, James I	Lt Cdr	01-Nov-05	ENG	ME	COMDEVFLOT	PLYMOUTH
Morphet, Kathryn	Lt RN	01-Jan-01	ENG	TM	NETS (N)	HMNB CLYDE
Morris, Alastair J	Lt RN	27-Feb-11	WAR	INT	DHU	CHICKSANDS
Morris, Alistair J	Surg Lt Cdr	01-Jun-10	MED	GMP	NCHQ	PORTSMOUTH
Morris, Andrew G	Maj	01-Oct-14	RM	GS	NCHQ	NCHQ
Morris, Anthony M	Lt Cdr	01-Oct-07	WAR	P MER	824 SQN	RNAS CULDROSE
Morris, Ashley R	SLt	01-Nov-14	WAR	P UT	BRNC	BRNC DARTMOUTH
Morris, Daniel R	Lt Cdr	01-Oct-11	WAR	MCD	RN EXCHANGE AUSTRALIA	CANBERRA
Morris, David F	Capt	01-Sep-11	RM	GS	42 CDO RM	PLYMOUTH
Morris, Gavin J	Lt RN	01-May-13	WAR	FC	HMS DAUNTLESS	
Morris, Harriet S	Lt Cdr	01-Oct-08	LOGS	L	MTM NELSON	HMS NELSON
Morris, Harry A D	Lt RN	01-Sep-13	WAR	GSX	MTM NELSON	HMS NELSON
Morris, James A J DSO	Col	20-May-10	RM	GS	FMC NAVY	LONDON
Morris, James E D	Maj	01-Oct-13	RM	GS	30 CDO IX GP RM	PLYMOUTH
Morris, Jonothan L	SLt	01-Nov-12	WAR	O UT	RNAS CULDROSE	HELSTON
Morris, Joshua T E	Lt RN	01-Sep-13	WAR	GSX	HMS DRAGON	
Morris, Louisa	Surg Lt Cdr	06-Aug-08	MED	GMP	DMS WHITTINGTON	BIRMINGHAM
Morris, Paul	Lt Col	30-Jun-07	RM	P LYN7	MTM WMO YEOVILTON	RNAS YEOVILTON
Morris, Paul J	Lt Cdr	01-Oct-10	WAR	AAWO	FLEET CAP SSM	PORTSMOUTH
Morris, Paul W	Lt Cdr	01-Oct-13	WAR	AV	MASF	RNAS CULDROSE
Morris, Richard C MBE	Maj	01-Oct-09	RM	GS	NCHQ	NCHQ

Name	Substantive Rank	Seniority	Branch	Specialisation	Organisation Name	Location Name
Morris, Richard J	Cdr	30-Jun-06	WAR	PWO(A)	RNLO GULF	DUBAI
Morris, Simon T	Cdr	30-Jun-06	ENG	WESM(TWS)	DES COMFLEET	ABBEY WOOD
Morris, Thomas O	Lt RN	01-Jun-12	WAR	P SK4	845 SQN	RNAS YEOVILTON
Morrison, Alan P	Lt RN	01-May-13	WAR	SM(X)	HMS VANGUARD	
Morrison, Kevin	Lt RN	13-Apr-12	WAR	AV	MTM WMO CULDROSE	RNAS CULDROSE
Morrison, Mark J	Lt RN	22-Jul-10	WAR	MCD	MCM1	FASLANE
Morrison, Philip C	Lt RN	31-Jul-09	LOGS	L	NATO-ACO-JFC HQ	BRUNSSUM
Morrison, Richard J	Lt RN	01-Apr-07	ENG	TM(SM)	FOST FAS SHORE	HMNB CLYDE
Morrison, Ross	Lt RN	01-Nov-11	ENG	TM	HMS SULTAN	GOSPORT
Morrison, Shaun	Lt Cdr	01-Oct-11	ENG	MESM	DES COMFLEET	BARROW IN FURNESS
Morritt, Dain C	Capt RN	30-Jun-08	ENG	WE	MTM DEFAC RCDS	LONDON
Morrow, Laura	Surg Lt RN	01-Aug-12	MED	GDMO	MTM NEPTUNE	HMNB CLYDE
Morrow, Oliver	Lt RN	01-Jan-07	WAR	PWO(SM)	HMS VANGUARD	
Morse, Andrew C	Lt Cdr	01-Jan-92	WAR	O LYNX	FLEET CSAV	RNAS YEOVILTON
Morse, James	R Adm	28-Aug-12	WAR	PWO(N)	NCHQ	PORTSMOUTH
Mortlock, Philip	Lt Cdr	01-Oct-08	ENG	WESM(SWS)	ACDS	NEBRASKA
Morton, Charles E A	Lt RN	01-Jan-13	WAR	SM(X)	HMS TORBAY	
Morton, David	Lt RN	15-Apr-11	ENG	ME	COMDEVFLOT	PLYMOUTH
Morton, Justin C	Maj	01-Oct-08	RM	SCC	FLEET SPT FGEN	PORTSMOUTH
Morton, Neil	Lt Cdr	01-Oct-13	WAR	INT	DSI	CHICKSANDS
Morton, Nigel P B	Cdr	30-Jun-99	LOGS	L	FOSNI - YOUTH MSCC	BRISTOL
Morton-King, Frederick W H	SLt	01-May-13	WAR	O UT	MTM RAF CRANWELL	RAFC CRANWELL
Moseley, James F	Lt RN	11-Apr-08	WAR	AV	HMS SULTAN	GOSPORT
Moseley, Stephen H	Lt Cdr	01-Oct-11	WAR	P MER	AWC	BOSCOMBE DOWN
Moses, Christopher	Maj	01-Oct-14	RM	GS	MTM DEFAC JSCSC	SHRIVENHAM
Moss, Jonathan	Lt Cdr	01-Oct-13	LOGS	L	HMS LANCASTER	
Moss, Richard A	Cdr	30-Jun-06	WAR	O SK6	RNP TEAM	PORTSMOUTH
Moss, Richard M	Lt RN	01-Jan-02	ENG	TM	DEODS	ANDOVER
Moss, Stephanie	Lt RN	01-Mar-14	WAR	GSX	HMS PORTLAND	
Moss, Stewart J	Lt RN	11-Dec-09	ENG	MESM	HMS VENGEANCE	
Moss, Tyrone J	SLt	01-Nov-12	WAR	P UT	BRNC	BRNC DARTMOUTH
Moss-Ward, Edward G	Lt Cdr	01-Oct-14	WAR	PWO	HMS NORTHUMBERLAND	
Mould, Christopher W	Lt RN	01-Jan-11	WAR	P FW	FLEET CSAV	WASHINGTON
Moulding, Mark D	Lt RN	17-Dec-10	ENG	MESM	HMS ARTFUL	
Moules, Matthew A J	Lt Cdr	01-Aug-04	WAR	PWO	COMDEVFLOT	PLYMOUTH
Moulton, Frederick	Col	23-Sep-13	RM	GS (RES)	FLEET CMR	PORTSMOUTH
Mounsey, Carl A	Lt RN	01-Jan-08	ENG	WE	NAVY MCTA	PORTSMOUTH
Mount, James B	Lt Cdr	01-Oct-12	WAR	P SK6	FLEET AV CU	RNAS YEOVILTON
Mowat, Andrew D J	Lt Cdr	01-Oct-13	LOGS	L	HMS BULWARK	
Mowatt, Patrick	Cdr	30-Jun-13	WAR	HM (H CH)	MTM DEFAC JSCSC	SHRIVENHAM
Mowthorpe, Sarah L	Lt RN	19-Feb-08	WAR	HM	RNAS YEOVILTON	YEOVILTON
Moxham, Glen A	Lt	02-Sep-14	RM	GS	40 CDO RM	TAUNTON
Moyies, Scott A	Capt	03-Apr-08	RM	GS	NCHQ	PORTSMOUTH
Moys, Andrew J	Lt Cdr	01-Oct-97	WAR	HM (M CH)	RNAS CULDROSE	HELSTON
Muddiman, Andrew R	Lt Col	30-Jun-12	RM	GS	FLEET COMOPS NWD	NORTHWOOD
Mudford, Hugh C	Lt Col	30-Jun-99	RM	GS	AIB	HMS SULTAN
Mudge, Adrian M	Cdr	30-Jun-13	WAR	O SKW	UKMARBATSTAFF	PORTSMOUTH
Mudie, Craig A	Lt	13-Jan-14	RM	SCC	45 CDO RM	DUNDEE
Muir, Andrew	Lt RN	01-Feb-06	ENG	ME	NAVY MCTA	PORTSMOUTH
Muir, Katie M	Lt Cdr	01-Oct-13	WAR	PWO	HMS DUNCAN	
Mulcahy, Paul J	Lt RN	01-Jul-12	ENG	WE	HMS NORTHUMBERLAND	
Mules, Anthony J	Lt Cdr	01-Mar-98	WAR	HM(AS)	HMS WILDFIRE	NORTHWOOD
Mullen, Christopher	Mid	01-Feb-14	ENG	ME	DCEME SULTAN	HMS SULTAN
Mullin, Laura E	Lt RN	01-May-14	LOGS	L	MTM RALEIGH	HMS RALEIGH
Mullins, Andrew D	Lt Cdr	01-Dec-04	ENG	MESM	NCHQ CNPS	PORTSMOUTH
Mullis, Geoffrey	Lt Cdr	01-Oct-14	ENG	WESM(TWS)	DI - CA	LONDON
Mulroy, Paul J	Lt RN	18-Feb-05	ENG	MESM	HMS SULTAN	GOSPORT
Mulvaney, Paul A	Cdr	30-Jun-08	ENG	AE	NCHQ CNPERS	PORTSMOUTH
Muncer, Richard	Maj	01-Oct-06	RM	GS	MTM NORTHWOOD HQ	NORTHWOOD
Munday, Stephen W	Lt Cdr	01-Oct-10	ENG	WE	HMS ILLUSTRIOUS	
Mundy, Alan R	Lt Cdr	01-Oct-08	MED	MS(CDO)	DCHET CIC	LICHFIELD
Munn-Bookless, Kerri	Lt RN	01-Feb-08	ENG	TM	BRNC	BRNC DARTMOUTH

Name	Substantive Rank	Seniority	Branch	Specialisation	Organisation Name	Location Name
Munns, Andrew R	Cdr	30-Jun-03	ENG	ME	MOD NSD	RIO DE JANEIRO
Munns, Edward N	Lt RN	01-Sep-06	WAR	GSX	FASLANE PBS	HMNB CLYDE
Munro, Angus R	Lt RN	01-Apr-08	WAR	GSX	MTM MWS COLLINGWOOD	HMS COLLINGWOOD
Munro, Michael	Lt RN	01-Jul-04	ENG	WE	HMS QUEEN ELIZABETH	
Munro-Lott, Peter R J	Cdr	30-Jun-06	WAR	O MER	MTM WMO CULDROSE	RNAS CULDROSE
Munson, Jason S	Lt RN	01-Sep-13	WAR	MCD	MTM MWS DDS	PORTSMOUTH
Munt, James	SLt	01-Aug-13	WAR	INT	MTM MWS COLLINGWOOD	HMS COLLINGWOOD
Murchie, Alistair D	Lt Cdr	01-Oct-03	ENG	ME	NAVY ICP	PORTSMOUTH
Murchison, Ewen A DSO MBE	Col	04-Sep-12	RM	GS	DEFENCE ACADEMY	SHRIVENHAM
Murdoch, Andrew W	Cdr	30-Jun-05	ENG	WESM(SWS)	FLEET CAP SSM	PORTSMOUTH
Murdoch, Hannah	SLt	01-Apr-12	WAR	GSX	MTM DEF SCH OF LANG	BEACONSFIELD
Murgatroyd, Jenna C	Surg Lt Cdr (D)	28-Jul-14	DENTAL	GDP	CDO LOG REGT RM	RMB CHIVENOR
Murgatroyd, Kevin J	Lt Cdr	01-Oct-10	WAR	O MER	824 SQN	RNAS CULDROSE
Murgatroyd, Steven A	Lt RN	31-Jul-09	ENG	AE	HMS SULTAN	GOSPORT
Murphy, Alan J	Lt RN	01-Sep-12	ENG	AE	FLEET CSAV	YEOVIL
Murphy, Caroline R	Lt RN	01-Jul-03	ENG	TM	NCHQ CNPERS (HRTSG)	PORTSMOUTH
Murphy, Dennis E H	Lt RN	01-Jan-12	WAR	SM(X)	MTM RALEIGH	HMS RALEIGH
Murphy, Kian S	Maj	01-Oct-05	RM	GS	EXCHANGE - FRANCE	PARIS
Murphy, Paul A	Cdr	30-Jun-08	Ch S	L CMA SM	FMC NAVY	LONDON
Murphy, Steven R A	Lt Cdr	01-Sep-98	WAR	SM(CQ)	MTM WMO YEOVILTON	RNAS YEOVILTON
Murphy, Thomas C	Lt RN	01-Nov-14	LOGS	L	COMDEVFLOT	PLYMOUTH
Murray, Alister	Cdr	14-Oct-12	MED	MS	NCHQ CNPERS	PORTSMOUTH
Murray, Andrew S AFC	Lt Cdr	01-Oct-99	WAR	P SK6	771 SQN	RNAS CULDROSE
Murray, Audrey R	Lt RN	19-May-09	QARNNS	ITU	RCDM	BIRMINGHAM
Murray, Edward A	Lt RN	01-Sep-13	ENG	MESM	HMS TORBAY	
Murray, Grant M	Cdr	30-Jun-10	ENG	WESM(TWS)	RN EXCHANGE AUSTRALIA	CANBERRA
Murray, Greig M	Lt Cdr	01-Oct-11	WAR	PWO	HMS OCEAN	
Murray, Jamie C	Lt RN	01-May-07	WAR	P SK6	GANNET SAR FLT	HMS GANNET
Murray, Lee S	Capt	01-Apr-11	RM	MLDR (SCC)	LOANS TO OTHER GOVTS	VYSKOV
Murray, Ross S	Mid	08-Sep-14	ENG	AE	BRNC	BRNC DARTMOUTH
Murray, Sara N	Lt RN	15-Apr-11	MED	MS	INM ALVERSTOKE2	GOSPORT
Murray, Simon D	Capt	01-Sep-04	RM	P FW	MTM 736 NAS	RNAS CULDROSE
Murray, Simon O	Lt RN	01-Sep-10	ENG	MESM	FLEET CAP SSM	PORTSMOUTH
Murray, Stephen J OBE	Lt Cdr	02-Nov-89	WAR	O MER	824 SQN	RNAS CULDROSE
Murray, William	Lt RN	01-May-04	WAR	P SK4	RN EXCHANGE GERMANY	BERLIN
Murray, William J	SLt	01-Nov-14	WAR	GSX	MWS COLLINGWOOD	HMS COLLINGWOOD
Murrison, Richard A	Capt RN	16-May-11	LOGS	L	NATO-ACO-JFC HQ	NAPLES
Musgrave, Thomas E	Lt RN	21-Mar-10	WAR	GSX	MTM DEFAC JSCSC	SHRIVENHAM
Musgrove, Christopher	Lt RN	01-Sep-11	WAR	GSX	HMS KENT	
Musgrove, James C	Mid	17-Nov-14	ENG	ME	BRNC	BRNC DARTMOUTH
Musto, Edward C	Lt Col	31-Dec-96	RM	HW	FLEET MARITIME WARFARE	HMS COLLINGWOOD
Muyambo, Nomalanga N	Lt RN	01-Jan-00	WAR	TM	DTR LOGS TTT UPAVON	CAMBERLEY
Myatt, Richard W	Surg Lt RN	01-Aug-12	MED	GDMO	42 CDO RM	PLYMOUTH
Myhill, James E	Lt RN	01-Jan-12	WAR	GSX	HMS PORTLAND	
Myhill, Johnathen J	Lt RN	19-Dec-08	ENG	AE	FLEET CSAV	PORTSMOUTH

N

Name	Substantive Rank	Seniority	Branch	Specialisation	Organisation Name	Location Name
Nadin, Fraser	Mid	01-May-14	WAR	P UT	BRNC	BRNC DARTMOUTH
Najman, Andrew	Surg Lt RN	01-Mar-14	MED	Medical	BRNC	BRNC DARTMOUTH
Napier, Duncan J	Lt RN	01-May-14	WAR	HM	MTM MWS HMTG (D)	HMS DRAKE
Napier, Gary	Lt RN	08-Jul-11	ENG	WESM(TWS)	NBC CLYDE	HMNB CLYDE
Napier, Graham	Cdr	30-Jun-11	ENG	AE	DES COMAIR	WASHINGTON
Nash, Ian D E	SLt	01-Feb-12	LOGS	L	CHF - 846	RAF BENSON
Nash, Philip D	Cdr	30-Jun-10	WAR	O LYNX	HMS DEFENDER	
Nash, Robin D C	Lt Cdr	01-Oct-14	WAR	HM(AS)	HMS PROTECTOR	
Nash, Rubin P	Lt Cdr	01-Oct-14	WAR	PWO	HMS BULWARK	
Nash, Russell F R	Lt Cdr	01-Oct-11	ENG	WESM(TWS)	DES COMFLEET	ABBEY WOOD
Nash, Thomas J	Mid	17-Nov-14	WAR	P UT	BRNC	BRNC DARTMOUTH
Nason, Thomas J	Lt RN	01-Sep-10	WAR	P SK4	845 SQN	RNAS YEOVILTON
Naylor, Andrew J	Lt Cdr	01-Oct-08	WAR	P MER	814 SQN	RNAS CULDROSE
Naylor, James S	Mid	01-Feb-14	WAR	GSX	BRNC	BRNC DARTMOUTH
Neal, Gareth P	Lt RN	01-Sep-12	WAR	O UT	MTM 849 SQN CULDROSE	RNAS CULDROSE

Name	Substantive Rank	Seniority	Branch	Specialisation	Organisation Name	Location Name
Neal, Simon M	Lt Cdr	01-Oct-03	WAR	O MER	NCHQ CNPS	PORTSMOUTH
Neave, Andrew M	Cdr	30-Jun-13	WAR	ATC	FLEET CSAV	PORTSMOUTH
Neave, James R	Lt RN	01-Dec-07	WAR	P SK6	857 NAS	RNAS CULDROSE
Necker, Carl D	Cdr	30-Jun-09	WAR	PWO(N)	NBD COB QUEENS HARBOUR MASTER HMS DRAKE	
Needle, Peter J	Lt RN	01-Sep-11	WAR	MCD	MCM1	FASLANE
Negus, Trystram W	Lt RN	01-Mar-12	WAR	P UT	RAF SHAWBURY	SHREWSBURY
Neil, Alexander G	Lt RN	20-May-08	WAR	MW	MCM1	FASLANE
Neilan, Samuel J J	Lt RN	01-Mar-12	ENG	MESM	MTM NEPTUNE	HMNB CLYDE
Neild, Timothy	Cdr	30-Jun-12	WAR	PWO(C)	FLEET CAP MARCAP	PORTSMOUTH
Neilly, Patrick	Lt RN	01-Sep-12	WAR	SM(N)	FLEET COMOPS NWD	NORTHWOOD
Neilson, Daniel J	Lt RN	22-Jan-13	WAR	MCD	MCM1	FASLANE
Neilson, Robert D	SLt	01-Nov-14	WAR	GSX	BRNC	BRNC DARTMOUTH
Nekrews, Alan N L M QGM	Lt Cdr	01-Oct-10	WAR	MCD	SDU 2	PORTSMOUTH
Nelson, Bartholomew J	Lt RN	01-Sep-09	ENG	MESM	FOSNI	HELENSBURGH
Nelson, Christopher S	Cdr	30-Jun-14	WAR	PWO(N)	HQBF GIBRALTAR	HMS ROOKE
Nelson, Matthew R	Lt Cdr	01-Oct-12	WAR	P LYNX	FLEET CSAV	PORTSMOUTH
Nelson, Paul M	Lt Cdr	01-Oct-05	ENG	TM	HERRICK AMN SEC	MONS (CASTEAU)
Nelstrop, Andrew	Surg Cdr	11-Feb-11	MED	GMP (C&S)	NATO-ACO-JFC HQ	NAPLES
Netherwood, Lyndsey D	Lt Cdr	15-Jan-07	WAR	PWO(U)	HMS IRON DUKE	
Nettleingham, Jamie L	SLt	09-Apr-12	WAR	ATC	RNAS CULDROSE	HELSTON
Neve, Piers	Lt Cdr	11-Feb-94	WAR	SM(CQ)	NCHQ CNPERS	PORTSMOUTH
New, Christopher M	Cdr	30-Jun-10	ENG	ME	NCHQ CNPS	PORTSMOUTH
New, Richard	Lt Cdr	01-Oct-07	LOGS	L SM	HQ DCLPA & DEEPCUT GAR	CAMBERLEY
Newall, Paul J	Lt Cdr	01-Oct-14	ENG	TM	DCDS PERS TRG	LONDON
Newbury, James S	Lt RN	03-May-13	ENG	AE	CHF(MERLIN)	RAF BENSON
Newby, Christopher	Lt RN	01-Jan-05	WAR	O MER	DES COMAIR	ABBEY WOOD
Newby, Ryan	Mid	17-Nov-14	WAR	GSX	BRNC	BRNC DARTMOUTH
Newell, Gary D	Lt Cdr	01-Oct-09	ENG	ME	COMPORFLOT	PORTSMOUTH
Newell, Phillip	Cdr	30-Jun-14	WAR	HM (H CH)	HMS ECHO	
Newlands, Kathryn R	Surg Lt RN	06-Aug-14	MED	Medical	BLAKE	BRNC DARTMOUTH
Newlands, Kristoffer G	SLt	27-Jan-12	WAR	FC	HMS DARING	
Newman, Edmund N	Lt	02-May-13	RM	GS (RES)	GCPSU SOAG	AFGHANISTAN KABUL
Newman, Lee	Lt RN	15-Apr-11	WAR	HM	BRNC	BRNC DARTMOUTH
Newman, Virginia H	Lt Cdr	01-Oct-09	WAR	MEDIA OPS	NATO-ACO-JFC HQ	NAPLES
Newns, Adam D	Lt RN	01-Jul-09	ENG	WE	BRNC	BRNC DARTMOUTH
Newton, Nicholas J P	Surg Lt RN	06-Aug-08	MED	GS	MTM INM ALVERSTOKE	GOSPORT
Newton, Owen	Lt RN	01-Feb-08	WAR	FC	1 ACC	LINCOLN
Neyland, David A	Lt RN	01-Sep-04	WAR	P WILDCAT	WMF 815 SQN FLT 201	RNAS YEOVILTON
Neylen, Serena L	SLt	01-Sep-14	WAR	GSX	HMS DRAGON	
Nguyo, David N	Lt RN	01-Sep-02	ENG	WE	HDNET	CORSHAM
Niblock, Gillian	Lt RN	09-Nov-11	WAR	MTO N (RES)	FOSNI - NRC EE	LONDON
Nicholls, Barry A	Lt Col	30-Jun-11	RM	SCC	FLEET DCS - RNIO	HMS COLLINGWOOD
Nicholls, Edward W	Lt RN	12-Nov-10	WAR	ATC	RNAS YEOVILTON	YEOVILTON
Nicholls, Larry R MBE	Lt Cdr	01-Oct-11	ENG	WE	HMS BULWARK	
Nicholson, Brian H	Lt Cdr	01-Oct-09	ENG	AE	DES COMJE	YEOVIL
Nicholson, Christopher J	Lt RN	31-Jul-09	MED	MS	RNLA	HMS COLLINGWOOD
Nicholson, David P	Lt Col	30-Jun-14	RM	LC	FLEET SPT LOGS INFRA	PORTSMOUTH
Nicholson, Graeme	Surg Capt RN	10-Jun-14	MED	Occ Med	INM ALVERSTOKE2	GOSPORT
Nicholson, Kristin J	Cdr	30-Jun-09	LOGS	L	NCHQ CNPS	PORTSMOUTH
Nicklin, Gareth J E	Lt Cdr	01-Oct-08	ENG	MESM	DES COMFLEET	BARROW IN FURNESS
Nicoll, Mac A	Lt RN	01-Jan-12	WAR	P UT	MTM 824 SQN CULDROSE	RNAS CULDROSE
Nicolson, Vernon	Lt RN	03-May-05	WAR	OP INT	DCSU	RAF HENLOW
Nielsen, Erik M	Maj	01-Oct-13	RM	SCC	30 CDO IX GP RM	PLYMOUTH
Nielsen, Suzi	Lt Cdr	01-Oct-09	LOGS	L	PJHQ (UK)	NORTHWOOD
Nightingale, Christopher J	Capt	01-Sep-11	RM	GS	43 CDO FPGRM	HELENSBURGH
Nightingale, Matthew A	SLt	01-Nov-14	WAR	P UT	MWS COLLINGWOOD	HMS COLLINGWOOD
Nightingale, Samuel	Lt Cdr	01-Oct-14	WAR	PWO	HMS NORTHUMBERLAND	
Nikoufekr, Pejman	SLt	01-Oct-13	WAR	AV	MASF	RNAS CULDROSE
Nimmons, Paul MBE	Lt Cdr	01-Oct-05	ENG	MESM	COMDEVFLOT	PLYMOUTH
Nisbet, James H T	Capt RN	08-Sep-14	WAR	MCD	DDC	LONDON
Nixon, Alexander J	Maj	01-Oct-14	RM	GS	MTM DEFAC JSCSC	SHRIVENHAM
Nixon, Sebastian W	Surg Lt RN	04-Aug-10	MED	GMP	MTM INM ALVERSTOKE	GOSPORT

Name	Substantive Rank	Seniority	Branch	Specialisation	Organisation Name	Location Name
Noakes, Kevin M	Cdr	30-Jun-11	ENG	WE	DES COMFLEET	ABBEY WOOD
Noakes, Mark J	RN Chpln	07-Apr-14	Ch S	Chaplain	FLEET HM UNIT	PLYMOUTH
Noble, Robert	Lt RN	04-Jun-08	WAR	PWO(SM)	FOST FAS SHORE	HMNB CLYDE
Noble, Tom M D	Maj	01-Oct-12	RM	GS	COMUKAMPHIBFOR	PORTSMOUTH
Noblett, Peter G A	Lt Cdr	01-Oct-01	WAR	SM(CQ)	RN EXCHANGE FRANCE	PARIS
Nokes, Oliver	Lt RN	01-Sep-06	WAR	GSX	MTM MWS COLLINGWOOD	HMS COLLINGWOOD
Nolan, Andrew J	Lt RN	03-May-13	ENG	ME	HMS IRON DUKE	
Nolan, Paul E MBE	Maj	01-Oct-08	RM	P LYN7	ARF HQ	RNAS YEOVILTON
Nolan, Samuel T J	Lt RN	01-Jun-13	WAR	INT	857 NAS	RNAS CULDROSE
Noon, David MBE	Lt Cdr	01-Oct-03	LOGS	L	NATO-ACO-JFC HQ	NAPLES
Noonan, Charles D	Lt Cdr	01-Oct-10	WAR	MCD	MTM NEPTUNE	HMNB CLYDE
Norcott, James P	Lt RN	01-Sep-09	ENG	TM	FLEET FOST ACOS(Trg)	ABBEY WOOD
Norcott, William R	Maj	01-Oct-10	RM	HW	SFSG F COY	RAF ST ATHAN
Norgan, David J	Lt Cdr	01-Jul-01	WAR	PWO(C)	MTM NELSON	HMS NELSON
Norgate, Andrew T	Lt Cdr	01-Nov-06	WAR	PWO	MTM MWS HMTG (D)	HMS DRAKE
Norkett, Luke T K	Lt	02-Sep-14	RM	GS	CTCRM	EXMOUTH
Norman, Jaimie M DSO	Lt Col	30-Jun-14	RM	GS	SOFS	LONDON
Normanton, Benedict S	Mid	01-May-14	LOGS	L	BRNC	BRNC DARTMOUTH
Norris, Guy P	Lt Cdr	01-Oct-08	WAR	O SK6	771 SQN	RNAS CULDROSE
Norris, James M W	SLt	10-Nov-13	WAR	GSX	HMS DARING	
Norris, Paul A MBE MC	Capt	30-Mar-12	RM	GS	MOD DEFENCE STAFF	LONDON
Norris, Richard E	Surg Capt RN (D)	26-Oct-04	DENTAL	GDP(C&S)	HQ DPHC	LICHFIELD
North, Adam C	Lt Cdr	01-Oct-12	ENG	AE	FLEET CSAV	PORTSMOUTH
Northcott, Philip J	Lt Cdr	20-Apr-10	ENG	MESM	DES COMFLEET	ABBEY WOOD
Northover, Adam F	Lt Cdr	01-Aug-05	WAR	PWO(N)	MWS COLLINGWOOD	HMS COLLINGWOOD
Norton, Ian A	Lt Cdr	01-Oct-11	ENG	AE	RNAS YEOVILTON	YEOVILTON
Norton, Lee A	Lt RN	01-Oct-08	ENG	TM	RNLA	BRNC DARTMOUTH
Norton, Samuel K	Mid	01-May-14	ENG	MESM	BRNC	BRNC DARTMOUTH
Notley, Edward J	Lt Cdr	01-Oct-14	WAR	SM(AWC)	FOST DPORT	PLYMOUTH
Nottingham, James M	Lt RN	01-Feb-08	WAR	P LYN7	847 SQN	RNAS YEOVILTON
Noyce, Roger MBE	Cdr	30-Jun-13	WAR	INT	PJHQ (UK)	NORTHWOOD
Nutt, William J H	Capt	01-Sep-09	RM	GS	CTCRM	EXMOUTH
Nutting, Christopher J	Capt	01-Sep-13	RM	GS	30 CDO IX GP RM	PLYMOUTH
Nwokora, Dal	Lt RN	01-Mar-09	ENG	AE P	MTM 815 SQN YEOVILTON	RNAS YEOVILTON

O

Name	Substantive Rank	Seniority	Branch	Specialisation	Organisation Name	Location Name
Oakes, Caroline F	Lt RN	01-Sep-11	WAR	O SKW	MASF	RNAS CULDROSE
Oakes, Ian J	Lt Cdr	01-Oct-05	WAR	P LYN7	DEF HELI FLYING SCH	SHREWSBURY
Oakes, Philippe A R	Lt RN	01-Jan-12	WAR	GSX	HMS MERSEY	
Oakey, Dean	Lt Cdr	01-Oct-14	WAR	REG	NPM EASTERN	HMS NELSON
Oakley, Andrew	Lt Cdr	01-Oct-09	ENG	TM	FLEET FOST TBTU	HMS COLLINGWOOD
Oakley, Christopher G	Lt RN	01-Nov-12	WAR	SM(X)	FLEET COMOPS NWD	NORTHWOOD
Oakley, Claire	Lt Cdr	01-Oct-08	WAR	HM(AM)	FOST HM	HMS DRAKE
Oakley, Jonathon	Lt RN	01-Sep-11	WAR	GSX	30 CDO IX GP RM	PLYMOUTH
Oakley, Sarah E	Lt Cdr	01-May-05	WAR	PWO(A)	MTM DEFAC JSCSC	SHRIVENHAM
Oatley, Timothy P	Lt Cdr	01-Oct-05	WAR	O MER	AWC	BOSCOMBE DOWN
O'Boy, Thomas J M	Capt	01-Sep-10	RM	GS	15 POG	SHEFFORD
O'Brien, David J	Surg Lt Cdr	05-Aug-14	MED	Med	MTM INM ALVERSTOKE	GOSPORT
O'Brien, James M	Capt	03-Sep-14	RM	GS	43 CDO FPGRM	HELENSBURGH
O'Brien, Kieran J	Capt RN	14-Jul-14	ENG	AE	DES COMJE	YEOVIL
O'Brien, Patrick M C OBE	Capt RN	24-Aug-10	ENG	IS	DEFENCE ACADEMY	SHRIVENHAM
O'Brien, Thomas P	Lt Cdr	01-Oct-11	ENG	WESM(TWS)	LOAN DSTL	FAREHAM
O'Byrne, Patrick	Cdr	30-Jun-08	WAR	SM(CQ)	ISAT	FREETOWN
O'Callaghan, Lucy B	Lt RN	01-May-13	WAR	GSX	MCM1	FASLANE
O'Callaghan, Patrick	Lt RN	01-May-02	WAR	GSX	HMS EAGLET	LIVERPOOL
O'Callaghan, Philip P	Maj	01-Oct-13	RM	SCC	CTCRM	EXMOUTH
Ochtman-Corfe, Fergus V	Lt Cdr	01-Oct-10	ENG	ME	HMS MONTROSE	
Ockleton, Christopher D	Lt RN	01-Jun-12	WAR	MCD	MCM1	FASLANE
O'Connell, Daniel	Lt RN	01-Nov-10	WAR	GSX	HMS CLYDE	
O'Connell, Heather	Lt RN	01-Jan-10	WAR	HM	HMS ENTERPRISE	
O'Connor, Calum M	Lt RN	01-Sep-14	WAR	P UT	MTM 815 SQN YEOVILTON	RNAS YEOVILTON
O'Connor, David M	Capt	01-Jul-04	RM	C (SCC)	30 CDO IX GP RM	PLYMOUTH

Name	Substantive Rank	Seniority	Branch	Specialisation	Organisation Name	Location Name
O'Connor, David P	Lt Cdr	01-Oct-09	ENG	WESM(SWS)	DES COMFLEET	ABBEY WOOD
O'Connor, Lucy	Lt RN	01-Jul-05	ENG	TM	AIB	HMS SULTAN
O'Dell, Alexander J	Lt RN	01-Apr-14	WAR	SM(X)	HMS AMBUSH	
O'Donnell, Rory	SLt	01-Sep-14	WAR	GSX	MWS COLLINGWOOD	HMS COLLINGWOOD
O'Dooley, Paul	Lt Cdr	01-Oct-14	WAR	INFO OPS	15 POG	SHEFFORD
O'Farrell, Matthew V	Lt RN	01-Sep-12	ENG	WE	FOST DPORT	PLYMOUTH
Offord, Matt	Lt Cdr	01-Apr-02	WAR	MCD	FOST MPV SEA	HMNB CLYDE
Offord, Stephen J J	Lt Cdr	01-Oct-13	ENG	AE	HMS QUEEN ELIZABETH	
O'Flaherty, Christopher P J	Cdr	30-Jun-09	WAR	MCD	FDS HQ	PORTSMOUTH
O'Flaherty, John	Cdr	30-Jun-09	ENG	ME	NAVY MCTA	PORTSMOUTH
O'Hara, Gerard OBE	Maj	01-Sep-03	RM	GS	NATO - BRUSSELS	BRUSSELS
O'Herlihy, Simon I MBE	Lt Col	30-Jun-11	RM	GS	RMR BRISTOL	BRISTOL
O'Kane, Robert J	Lt Cdr	01-Oct-11	WAR	O SK6	FLEET CSAV	PORTSMOUTH
O'Keeffe, Thomas D	Maj	01-Oct-12	RM	GS	HQ 3 (UK) DIV	PORTSMOUTH
Oldfield, Christian	Lt RN	01-Sep-05	ENG	AE P	LOAN VECTOR	GOSPORT
Oldham, David J	Lt RN	09-Apr-09	ENG	WE	MCM2	PORTSMOUTH
Oliphant, Helen	Lt RN	01-Mar-10	WAR	GSX	FOSNI - HQ	PORTSMOUTH
Oliphant, William	Capt RN	29-Aug-13	LOGS	L	NATO-ACO-IFC HQ	NAPLES
Olive, Peter N OBE	Capt RN	02-Oct-12	WAR	PWO(A)	MTM DEFAC RCDS	LONDON
Oliver, Graham	Lt Cdr	01-May-03	WAR	METOC	FLEET COMOPS NWD	NORTHWOOD
Oliver, Kevin	Col	22-Feb-11	RM	MLDR	CTCRM	EXMOUTH
Olmesdahl, Sandra C	Mid	17-Nov-14	WAR	O UT	BRNC	BRNC DARTMOUTH
Olsson, Alexandra	Lt RN	08-Dec-12	ENG	WESM	HMS VIGILANT	
Olver, Thomas A	Lt RN	10-May-13	ENG	MESM	DCEME SULTAN	HMS SULTAN
O'Malley, James P	Lt Cdr	11-Dec-09	MED	MS	EU OHQ	NORTHWOOD
O'Neill, Conor M	Lt Cdr	01-Oct-11	WAR	PWO	MSP	LONDON
O'Neill, Elias P J	Mid	08-Sep-14	WAR	GSX	BRNC	BRNC DARTMOUTH
O'Neill, Harry	Lt RN	01-Jan-03	WAR	P SK4	FLEET MARITIME WARFARE	HMS COLLINGWOOD
O'Neill, James	Lt Cdr	01-Oct-09	WAR	HM (H CH)	JFIG - IS	ABBEY WOOD
O'Neill, Patrick J	Capt RN	30-Jun-06	ENG	WESM(TWS)	NUCLEAR CAPABILITY	LONDON
O'Neill, Paul J	Lt Cdr	01-Oct-03	ENG	MESM	DES COMFLEET	ABBEY WOOD
O'Neill, Timothy J	Lt Cdr	01-Oct-09	WAR	MCD	UKMARBATSTAFF	PORTSMOUTH
Oram, Cemal	Lt RN	01-Jan-11	WAR	P SK4	AACEN	STOCKBRIDGE
Orchard, Adrian P OBE	Capt RN	19-Apr-12	WAR	P FW	MTM MWS COLLINGWOOD	HMS COLLINGWOOD
Orchard, Jonathan J	Lt RN	01-Sep-09	ENG	AE	FOSNI - CNR	PORTSMOUTH
Ord, Dominic	Mid	08-Sep-14	ENG	AE	BRNC	BRNC DARTMOUTH
Ordway, Christopher N M P	Lt Col	30-Jun-12	RM	GS	NCHQ	NCHQ
O'Regan, Kyle	Lt RN	01-Sep-14	WAR	HM	MTM MWS COLLINGWOOD	HMS COLLINGWOOD
O'Reilly, Christopher A	Lt Cdr	01-Oct-11	LOGS	L	NBCP LOGS DEPT UPO	PORTSMOUTH
O'Reilly, Jamie P	Mid	01-Feb-14	ENG	ME	DCEME SULTAN	HMS SULTAN
O'Reilly, Paul A	Lt RN	19-Dec-08	ENG	WESM(TWS)	NAVY MCTA	BARROW IN FURNESS
Ormrod, Ryan	SLt	01-Nov-14	WAR	SM(X)	MWS COLLINGWOOD	HMS COLLINGWOOD
Ormshaw, Martin A	Lt RN	01-Jan-06	WAR	O LYNX	LHF 815 SQN	RNAS YEOVILTON
O'Rourke, Nicholas H	Mid	17-Nov-14	LOGS	L	BRNC	BRNC DARTMOUTH
O'Rourke, Richard M	Lt Cdr	01-Oct-08	LOGS	L	FLEET MARITIME WARFARE	HMS COLLINGWOOD
Orr, Jacqueline M	Lt RN	01-May-14	WAR	GSX	MWS COLLINGWOOD	HMS COLLINGWOOD
Orr, Keith J	Lt Cdr	01-Oct-09	ENG	MESM	NCHQ CNPERS	PORTSMOUTH
Orr, Robert	Lt RN	01-Sep-14	ENG	MESM	DCEME SULTAN	HMS SULTAN
Orton, David M	Cdr	30-Jun-13	ENG	TM(SM)	FLEET FOST ACOS(Trg)	PORTSMOUTH
Orton, Trevellyan	Lt RN	01-Sep-09	ENG	WE	UKMARBATSTAFF	PORTSMOUTH
Orton, Trevor	Lt RN	01-Oct-04	WAR	MCD	MWS DDS	PORTSMOUTH
Osborn, Colvin G	Lt Cdr	01-Jun-02	WAR	INT	FLEET COMOPS NWD	NORTHWOOD
Osborn, Richard	Lt Cdr	01-Feb-99	WAR	AAWO	LSP OMAN	MUSCAT
Osborne, Andrew R	Lt RN	01-May-13	WAR	GSX	HMS ST ALBANS	
Osborne, Connor T	SLt	01-Nov-14	WAR	O UT	MWS COLLINGWOOD	HMS COLLINGWOOD
Osborne, Matthew A	Surg Lt Cdr	05-Aug-14	MED	GMP	MTM INM ALVERSTOKE	GOSPORT
Osborne, Oliver J	Capt	01-Sep-08	RM	GS	FLEET CAP LLM & DRM	PORTSMOUTH
O'Shaughnessy, Paul	Lt Cdr	01-Oct-06	ENG	WE	DIST/COR	CORSHAM
O'Shea, Matthew K	Surg Lt Cdr	06-Sep-09	MED	Med	MTM INM ALVERSTOKE	GOSPORT
Osmond, Justin B	Capt RN	03-Sep-12	ENG	AE	DES COMAIR	ABBEY WOOD
O'Sullivan, Barrie O	Cdr	30-Jun-09	WAR	P SK4	BDS	WASHINGTON
O'Sullivan, Daniel A N	Lt RN	01-Apr-08	ENG	WESM(TWS)	DES COMFLEET	ABBEY WOOD

Name	Substantive Rank	Seniority	Branch	Specialisation	Organisation Name	Location Name
O'Sullivan, Luke A	Lt RN	01-Sep-13	WAR	P	MTM APACHE	IPSWICH
O'Sullivan, Mark	Capt	01-Mar-10	RM	GS	NCHQ	PORTSMOUTH
O'Sullivan, Matthew	Capt	01-Sep-04	RM	P LYN7	RN EXCHANGE USA	WASHINGTON
O'Sullivan, Michael	Cdr	30-Jun-09	WAR	HM (H CH)	SERV ATTACHE/ADVISER	OTTAWA
O'Sullivan, Michael D	2Lt	25-Aug-14	RM	N/A	CTCRM	EXMOUTH
O'Sullivan, Nicholas J	Maj	01-Oct-13	RM	C	42 CDO RM	PLYMOUTH
O'Sullivan, Stephen	Maj	30-Sep-14	RM	SCC	COMUKAMPHIBFOR	PORTSMOUTH
O'Toole, Mathew C	Capt	01-Sep-10	RM	GS	29 CDO REGT	PLYMOUTH
O'Toole, Mathew C	Cdr	30-Jun-14	ENG	MESM	FLEET CAP SSM	PORTSMOUTH
Ottaway, Thomas A	SLt	01-Sep-12	MED	Medical	BLAKE	BRNC DARTMOUTH
Ottewell, Paul S	Cdr	30-Jun-14	WAR	PWO	HQ ARRC (JFIB)B	GLOUCESTER
Ottley, Lucy J	Lt Cdr	01-Oct-10	LOGS	L	UKMARBATSTAFF	PORTSMOUTH
Owen, Christopher R	Lt RN	01-Apr-12	ENG	ME	HMS SOMERSET	
Owen, Douglas P C	Lt Cdr	01-Oct-14	WAR	PWO(N)	FOST DPORT	PLYMOUTH
Owen, Glyn	Cdr	30-Jun-13	WAR	O LYNX	WMF 825 SQN HQ	RNAS YEOVILTON
Owen, Peter C	Lt Cdr	30-Oct-91	WAR	P MER	824 SQN	RNAS CULDROSE
Owen, Robert	Lt RN	01-Jan-13	WAR	O SKW	849 SQN	RNAS CULDROSE
Owen, Samuel T L	Lt Cdr	01-Oct-08	WAR	SM(CQ)	RN EXCHANGE USA	WASHINGTON
Owen, Vincent F	Lt Cdr	01-Oct-12	WAR	O LYNX	PJHQ (UK)	NORTHWOOD
Owen-Hughes, Daniel	Lt RN	01-Apr-12	WAR	GSX	HMS MONMOUTH	
Owens, John W	Lt Cdr	01-Oct-14	LOGS	L	HMS MONTROSE	
Oxley, Angela J	Surg Lt Cdr (D)	27-Jul-14	DENTAL	GDP	HMS EXCELLENT	PORTSMOUTH
Oxley, James D	Lt RN	01-May-08	WAR	MCD	MCM2	PORTSMOUTH

P

Name	Substantive Rank	Seniority	Branch	Specialisation	Organisation Name	Location Name
Packer, Lee J	Lt RN	01-Sep-10	ENG	WE	MTM DEFAC JSCSC	SHRIVENHAM
Packer, Robert	Lt RN	01-Jul-04	WAR	GSX	HMS RALEIGH	TORPOINT
Padden, Gregory M	Lt RN	08-Jul-14	WAR	GSX	UK MCC	BAHRAIN
Paddock, Lee	Lt Cdr	01-Oct-14	WAR	SM(X) (RES)	HQ 42 (NW) BDE	PRESTON
Page, Alexandra J L	Mid	08-Sep-14	ENG	ME	BRNC	BRNC DARTMOUTH
Page, Christopher A	Lt RN	01-Apr-12	WAR	GSX	MTM MWS COLLINGWOOD	HMS COLLINGWOOD
Page, Durward C M	Lt Col	30-Jun-08	RM	GS	MOD NSD USA	WASHINGTON
Page, Mark R	Lt Cdr	01-Oct-14	WAR	O LYNX	UK MCC	BAHRAIN
Page, Martin J	Capt	21-Mar-13	RM	SCC	40 CDO RM	TAUNTON
Page, Michael	Col	30-Jun-07	RM	LC	MTM NELSON	HMS NELSON
Paget, Simon	Lt RN	02-May-00	WAR	GSX	DSTO	RAF ST MAWGAN
Pakenham, Aaron T	SLt	01-Nov-14	MED	Medical	BLAKE	BRNC DARTMOUTH
Palethorpe, Nicholas	Lt Cdr	01-Oct-07	WAR	PWO	FLEET COMOPS NWD	NORTHWOOD
Palin, Giles R	Lt Cdr	01-Oct-05	WAR	PWO(N)	NCHQ CNPERS	PORTSMOUTH
Pallett, Tony S	Lt RN	01-Jan-06	ENG	IS	UK MCC	BAHRAIN
Palmer, Alan C	Surg Cdr	02-Oct-06	MED	GMP	HMS BULWARK	
Palmer, Christopher R	Lt Cdr	01-Oct-07	ENG	MESM	LOAN DSTL	FAREHAM
Palmer, Matthew L	Lt	09-Sep-14	RM	GS	45 CDO RM	DUNDEE
Palmer, Michael C	Lt Cdr	01-Nov-01	ENG	WE	NCHQ CNPERS	PORTSMOUTH
Palmer, Nicholas J C	Lt RN	01-Feb-10	WAR	GSX	HMS WESTMINSTER	
Pandyan, Andrew R	Mid	17-Nov-14	LOGS	L	BRNC	BRNC DARTMOUTH
Panic, Alexander	Lt Cdr	01-Oct-05	ENG	TM(SM)	NCHQ CNPERS (HRTSG)	PORTSMOUTH
Pannell, Jacob L	2Lt	25-Aug-14	RM	N/A	CTCRM	EXMOUTH
Panter, Lawrence G	Mid	08-Sep-14	ENG	ME	BRNC	BRNC DARTMOUTH
Panther, Andrew	Cdr	30-Jun-10	ENG	WE	DEFENCE ACADEMY	SHRIVENHAM
Pariser, Andrew M	Lt Cdr	01-Oct-14	WAR	PWO(SM)	HMS TRIUMPH	
Park, Brian C	Lt Cdr	01-Oct-03	LOGS	L	DES COMLAND	ABBEY WOOD
Park, Ian D	Lt Cdr	01-Oct-09	LOGS	L BAR	NCHQ - CNLS	PORTSMOUTH
Parker, Anthony R	Lt RN	29-Oct-04	LOGS	L	NCHQ CNPS	PORTSMOUTH
Parker, Berron M	Lt RN	01-Oct-06	ENG	IS	HMS SULTAN	GOSPORT
Parker, Daniel J	Lt Cdr	01-Oct-11	LOGS	L SM	FLEET SPT LOGS INFRA	PORTSMOUTH
Parker, Darren S	Lt Cdr	01-Oct-11	MED	MS	CAP SP CBRN ABW	ABBEY WOOD
Parker, Henry H	R Adm	06-Feb-12	ENG	WESM(TWS)	DES COMFLEET	ABBEY WOOD
Parker, John R	Lt RN	01-Sep-12	ENG	WESM(TWS)	HMS AMBUSH	
Parker, Jonathan D	Lt Cdr	01-Oct-14	ENG	WE	DIST/COR	CORSHAM
Parker, Laura M	Lt Cdr	01-Oct-14	LOGS	L	NBC PORTSMOUTH	PORTSMOUTH
Parker, Luke R	Lt RN	01-Sep-11	ENG	AE	DES COMJE	YEOVIL

Name	Substantive Rank	Seniority	Branch	Specialisation	Organisation Name	Location Name
Parker, Neil A	Lt RN	11-Dec-09	WAR	INT	FLEET COMOPS NWD	HMS COLLINGWOOD
Parker, Richard B	Lt RN	01-Nov-10	WAR	P UT	MTM RAF VALLEY	HOLYHEAD
Parker, Sarah E	Lt RN	01-Jan-09	LOGS	L	DES COMFLEET	ABBEY WOOD
Parker, Shaun M	Lt RN	03-May-13	ENG	AE	857 NAS	RNAS CULDROSE
Parker, Simon O	Lt RN	01-Mar-09	ENG	WESM(TWS)	CBRN POL	LONDON
Parker, Timothy S	Lt Cdr	01-Oct-06	ENG	IS	FLEET CAP IS	PORTSMOUTH
Parker-Carn, Rebecca L	Lt RN	17-Apr-08	LOGS	L	COMUKTG	PLYMOUTH
Parkin, Brett A	Lt RN	08-Apr-05	ENG	WESM(TWS)	DES COMFLEET	ABBEY WOOD
Parkin, James M B	Cdr	30-Jun-11	WAR	PWO FC	MOD CNS/ACNS	LONDON
Parkin, Matthew J	Lt RN	01-Aug-06	WAR	INT	FLEET COMOPS NWD	HMS COLLINGWOOD
Parkinson, Henry M L	Lt Cdr	01-Nov-11	ENG	AE P	MTM DCLC RN STUDENTS	SHRIVENHAM
Parkinson, Nicholas	Lt RN	07-Apr-06	WAR	AV	FLEET CSAV	PORTSMOUTH
Parks, Luke J	Lt RN	01-Sep-11	WAR	HM	HMS ECHO	
Parks, Natasha	Lt RN	01-Jun-10	WAR	HM	RNAS YEOVILTON	YEOVILTON
Parmar, Bhavna R	Lt RN	01-Nov-07	ENG	TM	NCHQ CNPERS (HRTSG)	PORTSMOUTH
Parnell, Daniel C	Lt Cdr	01-Oct-13	ENG	ME	COMDEVFLOT	PLYMOUTH
Parr, Matthew J CB	R Adm	02-Dec-11	WAR	SM(CQ)	FLEET COMOPS NWD	NORTHWOOD
Parr, Michael J E	Lt Cdr	02-Feb-05	WAR	HM	UKMARBATSTAFF	PORTSMOUTH
Parri, Eifion L	Lt RN	01-Apr-08	WAR	P LYNX	LHF 815 SQN	RNAS YEOVILTON
Parrock, Neil G	Lt Cdr	01-Oct-09	WAR	P MER	820 SQN	RNAS CULDROSE
Parrott, James P	Lt Cdr	01-Jul-04	WAR	AAWO	UKMARBATSTAFF	PORTSMOUTH
Parrott, Stuart S	Lt RN	01-Apr-06	WAR	INT	FLEET COMOPS NWD	RNAS CULDROSE
Parry, Alexander K I	Capt RN	11-Nov-14	LOGS	L	IPP	LONDON
Parry, Christopher A	Surg Cdr	12-Aug-09	MED	GS	MDHU DERRIFORD	PLYMOUTH
Parry, Eilidh P	SLt	01-May-14	MED	Medical	BLAKE	BRNC DARTMOUTH
Parry, Jonathan A	Maj	01-Oct-04	RM	P LYN7	CHF - 846	RAF BENSON
Parry, Mark	Cdr	30-Jun-13	ENG	AE	NCHQ CNPS	PORTSMOUTH
Parry, Stephen J	Lt RN	01-Jul-06	WAR	ATC	RNAS CULDROSE	HELSTON
Parry, Stuart D	Lt Cdr	01-Oct-09	LOGS	L	COMUKAMPHIBFOR	PORTSMOUTH
Parry-Jones, Alexander J	Lt RN	01-Apr-14	WAR	SM(X)	HMS TIRELESS	
Parsonage, Neil	Lt Cdr	31-Mar-00	WAR	MTO N (RES)	FLEET MARCRT	PORTSMOUTH
Parsons, Andrew D	Cdr	30-Jun-11	WAR	PWO(C)	DCOG JPO	CHELTENHAM
Parsons, Brian R	Cdr	31-Dec-00	ENG	AE	DES COMJE	YEOVIL
Parsons, Jacob W	Capt	31-Aug-14	RM	GS	29 CDO REGT	PLYMOUTH
Parsons, Richard G	Lt RN	01-Apr-11	MED	MS(EHO)	MTM DEFAC JSCSC	SHRIVENHAM
Parsons, Thomas E	SLt	01-Jul-13	WAR	GSX	HMS LANCASTER	
Parsonson, Max E	Lt RN	01-Apr-10	WAR	HM	HMS PROTECTOR	
Parvin, Philip S	Cdr	30-Jun-11	ENG	MESM	DSEA DNSR	ABBEY WOOD
Parvin, Richard A	Lt Col	30-Jun-11	RM	GS	RMR SCOTLAND	HMS CALEDONIA
Pascoe, Christopher	Mid	17-Nov-14	ENG	WE	BRNC	BRNC DARTMOUTH
Pashneh-Tala, Samira	Lt RN	17-Apr-11	WAR	GSX	MWS COLLINGWOOD	HMS COLLINGWOOD
Passey, David W	Capt	01-Apr-11	RM	SCC	HQ SQN CDO LOG REGT RM	RMB CHIVENOR
Paston, William A	Lt Cdr	01-Oct-11	WAR	PWO	MCM1	FASLANE
Pate, Christopher M	Lt Cdr	01-Oct-11	WAR	PWO	PJHQ (UK)	NORTHWOOD
Paterson, James M A	Lt RN	01-Jan-06	WAR	P MER	814 SQN	RNAS CULDROSE
Paterson, Laura	Surg Lt RN	04-Aug-10	MED	GMP	MTM INM ALVERSTOKE	GOSPORT
Paterson, Mark	Capt	18-Jul-08	RM	C (SCC)	HQ 3 CDO BDE RM	PLYMOUTH
Paterson, Matthew	Lt RN	09-Mar-07	WAR	MW (RES)	FOSNI - NRC EE	PORTSMOUTH
Paterson, Michael	Capt RN	20-Nov-12	WAR	PWO(N)	DCDC	SHRIVENHAM
Paterson, Thomas J	Maj	01-Oct-08	RM	MLDR	CAPTAIN BASE SAFETY CLYDE	HELENSBURGH
Paton, Mark W	Lt RN	01-Jan-09	LOGS	L SM	LO HMS NEPTUNE	HMNB CLYDE
Patrick, Christopher M	Lt RN	21-Feb-09	WAR	HM	MTM DRAKE	HMS DRAKE
Patrick, John A	Lt RN	01-Jan-06	WAR	HM	FOST NWD (JTEPS)	NORTHWOOD
Patrick, Thomas D	Capt	31-Aug-14	RM	GS	CTCRM	EXMOUTH
Patterson, David	Cdr	30-Jun-09	ENG	WE	MTM WMO YEOVILTON	RNAS YEOVILTON
Patterson, John D	Cdr	30-Jun-14	WAR	PWO(A)	DES COMFLEET	ABBEY WOOD
Patterson, Pascal X	Lt RN	01-Jan-07	WAR	INT	FLEET COMOPS NWD	NORTHWOOD
Patterson, Paul	Lt RN	01-Feb-10	LOGS	L	RNLA	HMS COLLINGWOOD
Patton, Stephen T L	Lt Cdr	01-Oct-14	ENG	WE	PJHQ (UK)	NORTHWOOD
Pavie, Richard M	Lt RN	01-Jun-10	WAR	P FW	FLEET CSAV	WASHINGTON
Pawley, Ross S	Lt RN	01-Jul-14	WAR	SM(X)	HMS VICTORIOUS	
Pawson, Jonathan R	SLt	01-Feb-13	MED	Medical	BLAKE	BRNC DARTMOUTH

Name	Substantive Rank	Seniority	Branch	Specialisation	Organisation Name	Location Name
Payas, Keith R	Mid	08-Sep-14	ENG	AE	BRNC	BRNC DARTMOUTH
Payling, William A	Lt RN	01-May-13	WAR	GSX	HMS OCEAN	
Payne, Christopher	Maj	01-Oct-12	RM	GS	40 CDO RM	TAUNTON
Payne, John D	Cdr	30-Jun-08	WAR	PWO(U)	FLEET COMOPS NWD	NORTHWOOD
Payne, Mathew J	Lt Cdr	01-Oct-03	WAR	PWO(C)	UKMARBATSTAFF	PORTSMOUTH
Payne, Michael	Lt RN	01-Mar-11	LOGS	L SM	HMS VANGUARD	
Payne, Richard C	Capt RN	01-Jul-09	WAR	P FW	NATO - NADEFCOL ROME	ROME
Peace, Richard W	Lt Cdr	02-Jul-97	ENG	MESM	FLEET COMOPS NWD	NORTHWOOD
Peachey, Neil D	Lt RN	07-Apr-06	ENG	WE	NATO-ACO-JFC HQ	NAPLES
Peachey, Sarah L	Lt RN	01-Apr-08	LOGS	L	MTM NELSON	HMS NELSON
Peacock, Anouchka	Lt RN	01-Dec-05	WAR	OP INT	MTM DOLSU	BEACONSFIELD
Peacock, Joanna R	SLt	01-Sep-14	WAR	GSX	MCM1	FASLANE
Peacock, Laura G J	Lt RN	01-May-07	LOGS	L	FLEET COMOPS NWD	NORTHWOOD
Peacock, Timothy J	Capt RN	10-Dec-12	WAR	P SK6	FLEET FOST ACOS(Trg)	PORTSMOUTH
Peake, Stephen P	Lt RN	01-Jul-04	MED	MS	NCHQ MEDDIV	PORTSMOUTH
Pearce, Christopher J F	Lt RN	01-Mar-14	ENG	AE	CHF(MERLIN)	RAF BENSON
Pearce, Jonathan	Lt Cdr	01 Oct-10	ENG	WE	NCHQ CNPERS	PORTSMOUTH
Pearce, Robert	Lt Cdr	01-Oct-11	WAR	PWO(N)	RN EXCHANGE AUSTRALIA	CANBERRA
Pearce, Sarah L	Lt RN	01-Sep-05	WAR	INT	DI - CDI	LONDON
Pearce, Stephen F	Lt RN	01-Nov-10	WAR	P SK4	845 SQN	RNAS YEOVILTON
Pearch, Sean M	Lt Cdr	01-Oct-10	WAR	ATC	MAA	ABBEY WOOD
Pearmain, Stephanie R	Lt Cdr	01-Oct-10	ENG	TM	HMS SULTAN	GOSPORT
Pears, Ian J Mbe	Cdr	30-Jun-12	WAR	IS	JFC HOC C4ISR	NORTHWOOD
Pearson, Alan J	Lt RN	01-Jan-05	WAR	O SKW	854 NAS	RNAS CULDROSE
Pearson, Andrew C	Lt RN	08-Jun-07	LOGS	L	HQ BFC	EPISKOPI
Pearson, Christopher	Surg Cdr	30-Jun-02	MED	ORL	MDHU FRIMLEY PARK	FRIMLEY
Pearson, Edward T	SLt	01-Sep 13	WAR	GSX	HMS LANCASTER	
Pearson, Ellis	Lt RN	31-Jul-09	ENG	WE	MTM WMO YEOVILTON	RNAS YEOVILTON
Pearson, Ian T	Lt RN	01-Sep-04	ENG	AE P	MTM JTEG - ETPS RN	BOSCOMBE DOWN
Pearson, James C	Lt Cdr	01-Oct-08	WAR	MCD	DCD - MODSAP	HMS COLLINGWOOD
Pearson, Liam M	Lt RN	20-Oct-06	LOGS	L	DES COMLAND	ABBEY WOOD
Pearson, Michael	Lt Cdr	01-Mar-01	WAR	O SK6	DEFENCE ACADEMY	SHRIVENHAM
Pearson, Sarah I	Lt RN	01-Jan-07	LOGS	L	MTM NELSON	HMS NELSON
Pearson, Stephen	Capt RN	07-Jan-11	WAR	O SKW	COMPORFLOT	PORTSMOUTH
Pease, Catherine A	Lt RN	16-Feb-14	LOGS	L	FLEET CSAV	PORTSMOUTH
Peattie, Ian W	Lt Cdr	01-Oct-08	LOGS	L	MTM DEFAC JSCSC	SHRIVENHAM
Peck, Simon R	Lt Cdr	01-Mar-10	ENG	AE	1710 NAS	PORTSMOUTH
Pedler, Mark D	Cdr	30-Jun-13	WAR	P SK4	CHFHQ	RNAS YEOVILTON
Pedre, Robert G	Cdr	30-Jun-10	WAR	PWO(A)	DEFENCE ACADEMY	SWINDON
Pedrick, Amelia	Surg Lt Cdr (D)	11-Jul-13	DENTAL	GDP	RMB STONEHOUSE	PLYMOUTH
Peek, Samuel R	Capt	01-Sep-13	RM	GS	43 CDO FPGRM	HELENSBURGH
Pelham Burn, Alexander	Lt RN	01-Jun-10	LOGS	L SM	DEPT OF THE CGS JSAU (L)	LONDON
Pellecchia, Daniel N	Lt Cdr	01-Oct-14	WAR	INT	JFIG - JT OPS	LONDON
Pelly, Gilbert R	Maj	24-Apr-96	RM	GS	RMB CHIVENOR	BARNSTAPLE
Penfold, Andrew J	Lt RN	01-Sep-08	WAR	MCD	RN EXCHANGE AUSTRALIA	CANBERRA
Penfold, Daniel B	Lt RN	01-May-11	ENG	MESM	HMS TALENT	
Pengelley, Tristan A H	Maj	01-Oct-11	RM	C	MTM 30 CDO IX GP	PLYMOUTH
Pengelly, Michael P	SLt	01-Sep-14	WAR	P UT	MTM RAF CRANWELL	RAFC CRANWELL
Pengelly, Steven P	Surg Lt Cdr	06-Aug-08	MED	GS	MTM INM ALVERSTOKE	GOSPORT
Penkman, William	Maj	01-Sep-04	RM	P LYN7	MTM DEFAC JSCSC	SHRIVENHAM
Pennant, Marcus A	Lt RN	01-Apr-12	WAR	O LYNX	LHF 815 SQN	RNAS YEOVILTON
Penn-Barwell, Jowan G	Surg Lt Cdr	07-Oct-08	MED	T&O	MTM INM ALVERSTOKE	GOSPORT
Pennefather, Douglas C J	Maj	01-Oct-10	RM	GS	NCHQ	NCHQ
Penney, Isobel G	Mid	08-Sep-14	ENG	ME	BRNC	BRNC DARTMOUTH
Pennington, Charles E	Maj	01-Oct-07	RM	GS	NAVY ICP	PORTSMOUTH
Pennington, Matthew J	SLt	01-Dec-13	WAR	SM(X)	MTM RALEIGH	HMS RALEIGH
Pentreath, Jonathan OBE	Cdre	16-Jul-12	WAR	P SK4	MTM DEFAC RCDS	LONDON
Pepper, Nicholas R	Lt RN	01-Sep-07	LOGS	L SM	RNLA	BRNC DARTMOUTH
Pepper, Thomas D C	Surg Lt Cdr (D)	13-Jul-09	DENTAL	GDP	MTM INM ALVERSTOKE	GOSPORT
Peppitt, Christopher J	Lt RN	21-Feb-09	WAR		UKMARBATSTAFF	PLYMOUTH
Percival, Fiona	Cdr	30-Jun-12	LOGS	L	UKMARBATSTAFF	PORTSMOUTH
Percival, Victoria H	Lt Cdr	01-Oct-14	ENG	ME	MTM DCEME SULTAN	HMS SULTAN

Name	Substantive Rank	Seniority	Branch	Specialisation	Organisation Name	Location Name
Percy, Nicolas A	Lt Cdr	01-Apr-11	WAR	MCD	CSF FASLANE	HMNB CLYDE
Perfect, Richard J	SLt	01-Oct-12	LOGS	L	MTM WMO DEVONPORT	DEVONPORT
Perham, Nicholas J	Capt	03-Apr-09	RM	SCC	42 CDO RM	PLYMOUTH
Perigo, Oliver F T	Surg Lt RN	06-Aug-14	MED	Medical	BLAKE	BRNC DARTMOUTH
Perkins, Andora	Surg SLt	28-Jul-14	MED	Medical	BLAKE	BRNC DARTMOUTH
Perkins, George A	Mid	08-Sep-14	ENG	AE	BRNC	BRNC DARTMOUTH
Perkins-Brown, Ben	Lt Cdr	01-Jul-09	ENG	AE	LHF HQ	RNAS YEOVILTON
Perks, Andrew B	Lt Cdr	01-Oct-12	ENG	WESM(TWS)	HMS TORBAY	
Perks, James L OBE	Capt RN	01-Jul-14	WAR	SM(CQ)	FLEET COMOPS NWD	NORTHWOOD
Perks, Matthew D	Lt RN	01-Sep-09	ENG	MESM	DES COMFLEET	ABBEY WOOD
Perks, Matthew N	Capt	01-Sep-10	RM	GS	30 CDO IX GP RM	PLYMOUTH
Perrin, Mark S	Maj	01-Oct-07	RM	GS	JFHQ	NORTHWOOD
Perrins, Sam A	Lt RN	01-Apr-12	WAR	GSX	DCSU	RAF HENLOW
Perry, Carl S L	Lt RN	01-Mar-05	ENG	TM	NCHQ CNPERS (HRTSG)	PORTSMOUTH
Perry, David M	Mid	17-Nov-14	WAR	GSX	BRNC	BRNC DARTMOUTH
Perry, Jonathan N	Surg Cdr	31-Dec-96	MED	Radiologist	RCDM	PETERBOROUGH
Perry, Kit J K	Lt RN	01-Mar-13	ENG	WE	HMS KENT	
Perry, Robert W	Maj	01-Oct-00	RM	SCC	NCHQ CNPERS	PORTSMOUTH
Persheyev, Alistair A	Lt RN	01-Aug-14	WAR	GSX	HMS TYNE	
Persson, Alexandra S	Mid	08-Sep-14	ENG	AE	BRNC	BRNC DARTMOUTH
Peskett, Daniel M	Lt Cdr	01-Oct-10	ENG	ME	MTM DEFAC JSCSC	SHRIVENHAM
Petch, Alan N	Lt Cdr	01-Oct-14	WAR	P SK4	CHF - 846	RAF BENSON
Peters, Matthew T	Lt RN	01-May-12	WAR	ATC	RNAS CULDROSE	HELSTON
Peters, William R	Lt Cdr	01-Mar-04	WAR	PWO(U)	UK MCC	BAHRAIN
Peterson, Keith A	Lt Cdr	01-Oct-14	ENG	WESM(TWS)	DES COMFLEET	BARROW IN FURNESS
Pethick, Ian	Cdr	30-Jun-10	LOGS	L (RES)	FLEET CMR	PORTSMOUTH
Pethick, Thomas G	SLt	01-Sep-12	WAR	P UT	MTM SHAWBURY	RAF SHAWBURY
Pethrick, Jerome F	Lt Cdr	01-Oct-14	ENG	AE	DES COMAIR	ABBEY WOOD
Pethybridge, Alexander R	Mid	17-Nov-14	WAR	GSX	BRNC	BRNC DARTMOUTH
Pethybridge, Richard A	Cdr	30-Jun-07	WAR	PWO(N)	DEFENCE ACADEMY	SHRIVENHAM
Petitt, Simon R	Capt RN	28-May-12	ENG	WE	HMS QUEEN ELIZABETH	
Petken, Alexander G	SLt	01-Sep-14	ENG	MESM	DCEME SULTAN	HMS SULTAN
Pett, Jeremy G	Capt RN	30-Jun-08	ENG	TM	FLEET FOST ACOS(Trg)	PORTSMOUTH
Pettinger, Joseph H	Lt RN	20-Oct-13	WAR	SM(X)	HMS VIGILANT	
Pettitt, Gary W	Capt RN	20-Sep-10	WAR	PWO(U)	NBD COB STAFF OFFICER	HMS DRAKE
Petty, Darren L	SLt	19-Sep-14	WAR	HM	HMS BULWARK	
Peyman, Tracy	Lt Cdr	01-Oct-07	LOGS	L	DEFENCE ACADEMY	SHRIVENHAM
Phelan, Sean C	Lt RN	01-Jan-09	WAR	SM(N)	HMS VICTORIOUS	
Phelps, Alexander M	Lt RN	01-Aug-13	ENG	WE	HMS SOMERSET	
Phelps, Jonathan J	Capt	01-Sep-10	RM	GS	CTCRM	EXMOUTH
Phenna, Andrew	Cdr	30-Jun-01	ENG	WE	HMS COLLINGWOOD	FAREHAM
Philips, Thomas J	Lt RN	01-Jan-06	ENG	ME	DES COMFLEET	ABBEY WOOD
Philipson, Matthew J	Lt RN	01-Sep-06	ENG	WE	DES COMJE	FAREHAM
Phillippo, Duncan G	Lt Cdr	01-Oct-12	ENG	MESM	HMS ASTUTE	
Phillips, Edward H L	Lt RN	01-Feb-07	WAR	GSX	MTM MWS COLLINGWOOD	HMS COLLINGWOOD
Phillips, Ian M	Capt RN	06-Aug-12	MED	MS	NCHQ MEDDIV	PORTSMOUTH
Phillips, James C	Surg Cdr	04-Mar-14	MED	GMP	NCHQ	PORTSMOUTH
Phillips, Jason P OBE	Cdr	30-Jun-09	WAR	O MER	RNAS CULDROSE	HELSTON
Phillips, John R	Lt RN	01-Jan-10	WAR	P LYNX	LHF 815 SQN	RNAS YEOVILTON
Phillips, Lewis P	SLt	11-Feb-14	WAR	ATC UT	RNAS YEOVILTON	YEOVILTON
Phillips, Matthew R	Lt Cdr	01-Oct-13	Ch S	L BAR SM	EU OHQ	NORTHWOOD
Phillips, Paul J	Lt RN	15-Apr-11	ENG	ME	1 ASSLT GP RM	PLYMOUTH
Phillips, Richard E	Lt Cdr	01-Oct-11	WAR	P FW	MTM	WASHINGTON
Phillips, Samuel J	SLt	01-Oct-14	MED	Medical	BLAKE	BRNC DARTMOUTH
Phillips, Simon M	Surg Cdr	01-Jul-09	MED	Occ Med	INM ALVERSTOKE2	GOSPORT
Phillips, Stephen J	Lt Col	30-Jun-04	RM	GS	AIB	HMS SULTAN
Phillips, Thomas	Lt RN	01-Dec-12	WAR	GSX	HMS DEFENDER	
Phillips, Thomas M J	Capt	01-Sep-11	RM	GS	JCTTAT	FOLKESTONE
Philo, Julian G	Cdr	30-Jun-10	ENG	ME	COMPORFLOT	PORTSMOUTH
Philpott, Marcus C	Surg Cdr	01-Jul-12	MED	GMP	DPHC SW	RNAS YEOVILTON
Pickering-Wheeler, Christopher W	Lt Cdr	01-Oct-05	WAR	SM(AWC)	RN EXCHANGE AUSTRALIA	CANBERRA
Pickett, Alexander P	Maj	01-Oct-13	RM	GS (RES)	RMR SCOTLAND	ROSYTH

Name	Substantive Rank	Seniority	Branch	Specialisation	Organisation Name	Location Name
Pickles, David R	Lt Cdr	01-Oct-10	WAR	ATC	RNAS YEOVILTON	YEOVILTON
Pickles, Martin R	Lt Cdr	01-Oct-14	WAR	P LYNX	LHF 815 SQN HQ	RNAS YEOVILTON
Pickles, Richard	Mid	08-Sep-14	ENG	ME	BRNC	BRNC DARTMOUTH
Pickthall, David N	Cdr	31-Dec-97	ENG	WE	NATO - BRUSSELS	BRUSSELS
Pierce, Adrian K M	Cdr	30-Jun-08	WAR	PWO(N)	MWS COLLINGWOOD	HMS COLLINGWOOD
Pierson, Matthew F	Col	07-Dec-10	RM	GS	43 CDO FPGRM	HELENSBURGH
Piggott, Andrew J	Lt RN	08-Jul-11	WAR	P UT	RNAS CULDROSE	HELSTON
Pike, Robin T	Lt Cdr	01-Oct-10	ENG	WESM(TWS)	DES COMFLEET	
Pike, Stuart	Lt Cdr	01-Oct-14	ENG	AE	RNAS CULDROSE	HELSTON
Pilkington, Barry M	Lt RN	01-Feb-07	WAR	P FW	FLEET CSAV	WASHINGTON
Pimm, Anthony R	Lt Cdr	01-Oct-13	WAR	PWO	HMS IRON DUKE	
Pinches, Ben M	2Lt	02-Sep-12	RM	GS	CTCRM	EXMOUTH
Pinder, Aidan O S	Lt RN	01-Feb-14	WAR	GSX	HMS SUTHERLAND	
Pine, Paul M	Lt Cdr	01-Oct-07	ENG	TM	FLEET FOST ACOS(Trg)	HMS RALEIGH
Pink, Simon E	Lt Cdr	01-Jan-02	WAR	PWO(N)	DES DTECH	ABBEY WOOD
Pinney, Jonathan R	Capt	01-Sep-11	RM	GS	NCHQ	NCHQ
Pinney, Richard F	SLt	01-Sep-12	MED	Medical	BLAKE	BRNC DARTMOUTH
Piper, Benjamin J	Lt Cdr	01-Oct-14	WAR	MCD	MTM MWS COLLINGWOOD	HMS COLLINGWOOD
Piper, Lee J	Capt	30-Mar-12	RM	SCC	CTCRM	EXMOUTH
Piper, Neale D ARRC	Cdr	05-Sep-11	QARNNS	Nurse Officer	NCHQ CNPS	PORTSMOUTH
Pipkin, Peter J	Lt Cdr	01-Aug-07	ENG	WE	MTM DEFAC JSCSC	SHRIVENHAM
Pitcher, Paul P	Cdr	30-Jun-10	WAR	PWO(C)	FLEET CAP IS	PORTSMOUTH
Pitcher, Tim C B	Lt	09-Sep-14	RM	GS	42 CDO RM	PLYMOUTH
Pitt, David	Lt RN	13-Apr-12	LOGS	L SM	HMS AMBUSH	
Pitt, Niel	SLt	01-Jan-14	WAR	AV	MASF	RNAS CULDROSE
Pittock, Martin W	Lt RN	01-Apr-12	WAR	O UT	MTM 849 SQN CULDROSE	RNAS CULDROSE
Pizii, Jane V	Lt RN	01-Aug-08	LOGS	L	NCHQ CNPERS (HRTSG)	PORTSMOUTH
Plackett, Andrew J	Lt Cdr	01-Oct-03	WAR	INT	PJHQ (UK)	NORTHWOOD
Plant, Anna L	Lt RN	01-Sep-13	WAR	GSX	HMS ARGYLL	
Plant, Michael J	Lt RN	01-Sep-13	WAR	P UT	MTM RAF CRANWELL	RAFC CRANWELL
Platt, Alexander W	Lt RN	01-Sep-11	WAR	FC	MTM DEFAC JSCSC	SHRIVENHAM
Platt, Maximilian J G	Lt RN	01-Jan-10	ENG	MESM	MTM DEFAC CMT MSC	SHRIVENHAM
Pledger, David	Cdr	30-Jun-10	WAR	AV	DSTO	RAF ST MAWGAN
Plenty, Andrew J	Lt Cdr	01-Oct-14	WAR	ATC	FOST DPORT	PLYMOUTH
Plewes, Andrew B	Maj	27-Apr-02	RM	GS	COMD FDT DGLS&E D EQPT	ANDOVER
Plumer, Stephen J	Lt Cdr	01-Oct-14	LOGS	L	MTM RALEIGH	HMS RALEIGH
Plunkett, Gareth N	Lt RN	01-Sep-06	WAR	P SK4	DEF HELI FLYING SCH	SHREWSBURY
Pocock, Oliver R	Lt RN	01-Jun-12	WAR	P FW	6 SQN TYPHOON	ST ANDREWS
Pollard, Alexandra E	Lt Cdr	01-Oct-07	WAR	AAWO	HMS RICHMOND	
Pollard, Jonathan R	Lt Cdr	01-Oct-07	ENG	WE	DES COMFLEET	ABBEY WOOD
Pollard, Joseph G	Mid	01-Feb-14	WAR	GSX	BRNC	BRNC DARTMOUTH
Polley, Christopher F	Lt RN	01-Sep-09	WAR	SM(X)	HMS VIGILANT	
Pollitt, Alexander W	Lt RN	01-May-06	WAR	P SK6	849 SQN	RNAS CULDROSE
Pollitt, David N A	Lt Cdr	01-Apr-89	WAR	SM(CQ)	FLEET CAP SSM	PORTSMOUTH
Pollock, Barnaby J	Lt RN	01-Nov-05	WAR	PWO	HMS DEFENDER	
Pollock, David J	Capt RN	01-May-12	WAR	SM(CQ)	FLEET CAP SSM	PORTSMOUTH
Pomfrett, Nicholas J	Lt Cdr	01-Apr-95	WAR	SM(CQ)	FOST NWD (JTEPS)	NORTHWOOD
Pons, Michael D	RN Chpln	01-Jul-06	Ch S	Chaplain	MTM DRAKE	HMS DRAKE
Ponsford, Philip K	Cdr	30-Jun-12	WAR	PWO(U)	FLEET MARITIME WARFARE	HMS COLLINGWOOD
Poole, Daniel C	Lt RN	01-Sep-05	LOGS	L BAR	NCHQ - CNLS	PORTSMOUTH
Poole, Jason L	Capt RN	15-Jul-13	WAR	MCD	SERV ATTACHE/ADVISER	TRIPOLI
Poole, Timothy J	Lt Cdr	01-Oct-07	WAR	O MER	FLEET MARITIME WARFARE	HMS COLLINGWOOD
Pooley, Steven W	Lt Cdr	01-Jul-96	ENG	WESM(TWS)	DES COMFLEET	ABBEY WOOD
Pope, Kevin D	Lt RN	01-Jan-05	WAR	P MER	824 SQN	RNAS CULDROSE
Pope, Michelle L	Lt RN	01-Sep-06	ENG	AE P	MTM WMO YEOVILTON	RNAS YEOVILTON
Porteous, Cameron W B	Lt RN	01-Sep-10	ENG	WESM(TWS)	DES COMLAND	ABBEY WOOD
Porter, Matthew E CBE	Brig	21-Jul-14	RM	GS	MOD DEFENCE STAFF	LONDON
Porter, Simon P	Capt RN	13-Jul-09	WAR	AAWO	LOAN DSTL	FAREHAM
Porter, Timothy B	Lt Cdr	07-Jan-14	LOGS	L	FOSNI - YOUTH MSCC	LONDON
Postgate, Michael O	Maj	01-Oct-13	RM	LC	RN EXCHANGE USA	WASHINGTON
Potter, David L	Surg Lt Cdr	04-Aug-10	MED	EM	MTM INM ALVERSTOKE	GOSPORT
Potter, Ian	Lt RN	08-Jun-07	ENG	MESM	CSF FASLANE	HMNB CLYDE

Name	Substantive Rank	Seniority	Branch	Specialisation	Organisation Name	Location Name
Potter, Stephen R	Lt RN	01-Aug-13	WAR	SM(X)	HMS VIGILANT	
Potts, David A	Lt RN	11-Oct-13	LOGS	L SM	OCLC PLYMOUTH	BRISTOL
Potts, Duncan L CB	V Adm	18-Sep-14	WAR	PWO(U)	DEFENCE ACADEMY	SHRIVENHAM
Potts, Kevin M	Lt Cdr	01-Feb-92	WAR	P LYNX	NO 3 FTS/UAS - 115(R) SQN	RAFC CRANWELL
Poulsom, Matthew J O	SLt	01-May-12	LOGS	L	MTM FLEET HQ	PORTSMOUTH
Poulson, Christopher	Lt RN	01-Nov-10	WAR	GSX	HMS OCEAN	
Pound, Alistair	2Lt	25-Aug-14	RM	N/A	CTCRM	EXMOUTH
Poundall, Gareth	SLt	01-Sep-14	WAR	GSX	MCM2	PORTSMOUTH
Pounder, Daryl J	Mid	08-Sep-14	ENG	WE	BRNC	BRNC DARTMOUTH
Pounder, Richard H G	Lt RN	01-Oct-09	WAR	SM(X)	MTM RALEIGH	HMS RALEIGH
Pounds, Alexander N	Maj	01-Oct-13	RM	GS	MTM DEFAC JSCSC	SHRIVENHAM
Powell, Daryl	Lt	01-Jul-13	RM	BS	RM BAND PORTSMOUTH	HMS NELSON
Powell, David A	Lt RN	01-Apr-12	WAR	GSX	MTM NELSON	HMS NELSON
Powell, Gregory M J	Lt Cdr	01-Oct-13	WAR	MCD	MTM DEFAC JSCSC	SHRIVENHAM
Powell, Ian D	Capt	01-Sep-13	RM	GS	CTCRM	EXMOUTH
Powell, Matthew T	Lt RN	17-Jun-14	WAR	SM(X)	HMS TALENT	
Powell, Philip J	Lt RN	01-Jan-07	ENG	TM	FLEET FOST ACOS(Trg)	PORTSMOUTH
Powell, Richard L OBE	Cdre	10-Sep-12	WAR	P LYNX	SERV ATTACHE/ADVISER	CANBERRA
Powell, Robert	Lt RN	01-Jun-10	WAR	P SK4	CHFHQ	RNAS YEOVILTON
Powell, Robert D	SLt	01-Aug-13	ENG	ME	DCEME SULTAN	HMS SULTAN
Powell, Steven R	Lt Cdr	01-Jul-98	WAR	PWO(C)	HQBF GIBRALTAR	HMS ROOKE
Power, Benjamin	Lt Cdr	01-Oct-13	WAR	FC	MTM MWS COLLINGWOOD	HMS COLLINGWOOD
Powles, Derek A	Lt Cdr	01-Feb-04	ENG	ME	MTM DEFAC JSCSC	SHRIVENHAM
Powne, Laura	Lt RN	20-Oct-10	ENG	ME	HMS RALEIGH	TORPOINT
Powney, Lewis	SLt	01-Sep-14	ENG	WESM	HMS RALEIGH	TORPOINT
Pozniak, Alexander R	Mid	01-May-14	WAR	GSX	BRNC	BRNC DARTMOUTH
Prausnitz, Luke	SLt	01-Nov-14	LOGS	L	HMS BULWARK	
Precious, Angus	Maj	01-Oct-11	RM	MLDR	30 CDO IX GP RM	PLYMOUTH
Preece, David G	Cdr	30-Jun-09	LOGS	L SM	COMDEVFLOT	PLYMOUTH
Preece, David J	Lt RN	01-Apr-12	WAR	GSX	HMS SEVERN	
Preece, Simon E	Lt RN	01-Sep-04	WAR	GSX	MTM MWS COLLINGWOOD	HMS COLLINGWOOD
Preece, Timothy M	Lt RN	20-Jul-13	WAR	P UT	MTM RAF VALLEY	HOLYHEAD
Preedy, Helen C	Surg Lt RN	07-Aug-13	MED	Medical	BLAKE	BRNC DARTMOUTH
Prescott, Shaun	Capt RN	22-Apr-13	ENG	WE	DI - CA	LONDON
Pressdee, Simon J	Lt Cdr	01-Oct-06	WAR	MCD	MCM2	PORTSMOUTH
Pressly, James	Lt Col	30-Jun-05	RM	GS	FLEET CAP LLM & DRM	PORTSMOUTH
Prest, Stephen	Cdr	30-Jun-13	ENG	WE	FLEET CAP MARCAP	PORTSMOUTH
Preston, Jacqueline N	Lt RN	30-Jun-06	ENG	TM	URNU NORTHUMBRIA	GATESHEAD
Preston, James M	Lt RN	01-Apr-12	WAR	MCD	MCM1	FASLANE
Prevett, Adam M	Lt RN	01-Apr-09	WAR	O LYNX	LHF 815 SQN	RNAS YEOVILTON
Price, Andrew M	Lt Col	30-Jun-06	RM	C	SERV ATTACHE/ADVISER	MANAMA
Price, David G	Capt	01-Jan-01	RM	P SK4	RAF SHAWBURY	SHREWSBURY
Price, David J	Lt Cdr	01-Apr-93	WAR	AAWO	MWS BRISTOL	PORTSMOUTH
Price, Joseph C	Lt Cdr	01-Oct-08	WAR	MCD	UK MCC	BAHRAIN
Price, Martin J	Lt Col	31-Dec-98	RM	MLDR	NAVAL OUTDOOR CENTRE	SONTHOFEN
Price, Matthew W	Lt RN	01-Jan-08	LOGS	L SM	FLEET ACOS(RP)	ABBEY WOOD
Price, Raymond T	Maj	01-Oct-08	RM	SCC	CTCRM	EXMOUTH
Price, Timothy M	Cdr	30-Jun-07	WAR	AAWO	NCHQ CNPERS	PORTSMOUTH
Prichard, Charles H N M	Lt RN	09-Apr-13	WAR	GSX	MTM NELSON	HMS NELSON
Prideaux, Robert J	Lt Cdr	01-Oct-12	ENG	MESM	COMFASFLOT	HELENSBURGH
Pridham, Kate M	Mid	01-May-14	LOGS	L	BRNC	BRNC DARTMOUTH
Priest, James E	Lt RN	01-Oct-09	WAR	P SK4	NC REQUIREMENTS MANAGERS	ABBEY WOOD
Priest, Rachel E	Lt Cdr	01-Oct-12	ENG	AE	DES COMAIR	ABBEY WOOD
Priestley, Simon M	Mid	01-Feb-14	WAR	GSX	BRNC	BRNC DARTMOUTH
Prince, Mark E	Cdr	30-Jun-09	ENG	MESM	FLEET CAP SSM	PORTSMOUTH
Printie, Christopher J	SLt	01-Sep-12	WAR	GSX	MWS COLLINGWOOD	HMS COLLINGWOOD
Prior, Kate R E J	Surg Cdr	22-Sep-10	MED	Anaes	MDHU FRIMLEY PARK	FRIMLEY
Prior, Robert P E	SLt	01-Sep-12	WAR	P UT	MTM SHAWBURY	RAF SHAWBURY
Pritchard, Christopher W	Lt RN	01-Oct-08	WAR		UK MCC	BAHRAIN
Pritchard, Lloyd D	Maj	01-Oct-12	RM	GS	NCHQ	NCHQ
Pritchard, Simon A	Lt Col	30-Jun-06	RM	HW	FLEET MARITIME WARFARE	HMS COLLINGWOOD
Pritchard, Thomas A	SLt	01-Sep-12	WAR	P UT	MTM SHAWBURY	RAF SHAWBURY

Name	Substantive Rank	Seniority	Branch	Specialisation	Organisation Name	Location Name
Proctor, Paul J R	Lt RN	12-Jul-13	ENG	WE	MTM NELSON	HMS NELSON
Proctor, William J G	Lt Cdr	01-Mar-02	ENG	WE	FLEET CAP IS	PORTSMOUTH
Proffitt, Adrian	Surg Lt Cdr	01-Sep-10	MED	Med	MTM INM ALVERSTOKE	GOSPORT
Proffitt, Julia M M	Lt Cdr	01-Oct-05	ENG	TM	DEFENCE ACADEMY	SHRIVENHAM
Prole, Nicholas M	Cdr	30-Jun-14	WAR	P SK4	JHC HQ LAND	ABBEY WOOD
Prosser, Jason W	Lt RN	01-Aug-08	LOGS	L	CHFHQ	RNAS YEOVILTON
Prosser, Matthew J	Lt RN	01-Aug-01	WAR	MCD	DEMS TRG REGT	BICESTER
Proud, Andrew D	Cdr	30-Jun-09	ENG	AE	DES COMJE	YEOVIL
Proudman, Michael P	Lt RN	01-Aug-06	WAR	FC	MTM MWS COLLINGWOOD	HMS COLLINGWOOD
Prouse, Scott	Lt RN	01-Apr-09	WAR	SM(N)	HMS VENGEANCE	
Prowle, Owen T	SLt	09-Apr-12	LOGS	L	MTM RALEIGH	HMS RALEIGH
Prowse, David G	Lt Cdr	01-Oct-09	ENG	ME	FOST DPORT	PLYMOUTH
Pryce, Alistair M	Mid	01-May-14	WAR	O UT	BRNC	BRNC DARTMOUTH
Pugh, Geoffrey N J	Lt Cdr	01-Oct-14	WAR	ATC	D AIR P	LONDON
Pugh, James	Lt RN	01-Mar-11	ENG	AE	FLEET CSAV	ABBEY WOOD
Pugh, Jonathan	Lt Cdr	08-Mar-00	ENG	WE	DCTT HQ	HMS SULTAN
Pugsley, Andrew	Capt	01-Jan 12	RM	N/A	COMUKTG	PLYMOUTH
Pullan, Keith J	Lt Cdr	01-Oct-05	WAR	HM (H CH)	DGC(AE) OPS & PLANS	FELTHAM
Pulvertaft, Rupert J OBE	Lt Col	30-Jun-03	RM	HW	NATO - BRUSSELS	BRUSSELS
Punch, John M	Lt Cdr	01-Oct-10	WAR	P SK4	MTM CHF (MERLIN)	RAF BENSON
Purdue, Basil H	Lt RN	01-Apr-14	WAR	SM(X)	HMS VANGUARD	
Purdy, Richard	Lt Cdr	01-Oct-11	ENG	AE	ACNS	PORTSMOUTH
Purser, Lloyd J MBE	Maj	01-Oct-08	RM	GS	NCHQ	PORTSMOUTH
Purvis, Christopher	Lt RN	01-May-13	WAR	SM(X)	HMS ARTFUL	
Purvis, David M	Lt Cdr	16-Oct-04	WAR	P LYNX	MAA	ABBEY WOOD
Purvis, Joe D	Mid	17-Nov-14	ENG	TM	BRNC	BRNC DARTMOUTH
Puxley, Michael E	Lt Cdr	01-Sep-04	ENG	WESM(SWS)	NBC CLYDE	HMNB CLYDE
Pye, Paula J	RN Chpln	01-Jul-09	Ch S	Chaplain	NEPTUNE 2SL/CNH - CHAP	HMNB CLYDE
Pyke, Daniel G	Maj	01-Oct-14	RM	C	HQ BFC	EPISKOPI

Q

Name	Substantive Rank	Seniority	Branch	Specialisation	Organisation Name	Location Name
Quade, Nicholas A C	Lt Cdr	01-Oct-05	ENG	MESM	HMS SULTAN	GOSPORT
Quaite, David G	Lt Cdr	01-Oct-13	WAR	HM	BRNC	BRNC DARTMOUTH
Quant, Jacqueline R	Lt RN	20-Oct-06	WAR	INT	DHU	CHICKSANDS
Quantrill, Steven W	Lt Cdr	01-Oct-05	LOGS	L	102 LOG BDE	GUTERSLOH
Quayle, Christopher A	Lt RN	01-Jun-12	WAR	ATC	FOST DPORT	PLYMOUTH
Quekett, Ian P S	Cdr	30-Jun-13	ENG	WE	NCHQ CNPS	PORTSMOUTH
Quick, Benjamin P	Lt RN	01-Jun-06	WAR	MCD	MTM MWS COLLINGWOOD	HMS COLLINGWOOD
Quick, Christopher J	Capt	03-Sep-14	RM	GS	43 CDO FPGRM	HELENSBURGH
Quilter, Gail	Lt RN	01-Nov-10	WAR	GSX	MWS COLLINGWOOD	HMS COLLINGWOOD
Quilter, George	Lt RN	01-Mar-11	WAR	FC	HMS DARING	
Quinn, Antony D	Lt Cdr	01-Oct-10	ENG	TM	FLEET FOST ACOS(Trg)	PORTSMOUTH
Quinn, Bernadette S	Lt RN	10-Oct-14	QARNNS	EN	MTM RCDM	BIRMINGHAM
Quinn, Mark E	Lt Cdr	01-Oct-09	ENG	IS	D STRAT PROG	ABBEY WOOD
Quinn, Martin	Capt RN	01-Jul-14	WAR	MEDIA OPS	FLEET CMR	PORTSMOUTH
Quinn, Michael	Lt RN	12-Dec-14	ENG	TM	MTM NELSON	HMS NELSON
Quinn, Morgan	Surg Lt RN	07-Aug-13	MED	Medical	BLAKE	BRNC DARTMOUTH
Quinn, Shaun A	Lt Cdr	15-May-14	WAR	O MER	MOD NSD	MAITAMA DISTRICT
Quinn, Thomas J	Maj	01-Oct-13	RM	GS	BDS	WASHINGTON
Quirke, Darren L	Lt RN	01-Jul-12	ENG	TM	HMS SULTAN	GOSPORT
Quirke, Fraser J	Lt RN	31-Jul-09	LOGS	L	RNLA	HMS COLLINGWOOD

R

Name	Substantive Rank	Seniority	Branch	Specialisation	Organisation Name	Location Name
Race, Nigel	Cdr	31-Dec-99	WAR	PWO(C)	DEFENCE ACADEMY	SHRIVENHAM
Rackham, Anthony D H	Cdr	30-Jun-10	WAR	PWO(A)	HMS OCEAN	
Radakin, Antony D	R Adm	03-Dec-14	WAR	PWO(U)	UKMARBATSTAFF	PORTSMOUTH
Radcliffe, Albert P	Lt RN	09-Apr-10	ENG	ME	COMDEVFLOT	PLYMOUTH
Radcliffe, Gemma L	Lt RN	01-Jan-09	ENG	TM	MWS COLLINGWOOD	HMS COLLINGWOOD
Radue, Nicholas K	Lt RN	01-Jul-11	WAR	HM	FLEET HM UNIT	PLYMOUTH
Rae, David M	Lt RN	30-Jul-10	ENG	WE	DES COMFLEET	ABBEY WOOD
Rae, Derek G	Cdr	30-Jun-12	WAR	HM (H CH)	MTM NELSON	HMS NELSON

Name	Substantive Rank	Seniority	Branch	Specialisation	Organisation Name	Location Name
Raeburn, Craig	Lt Cdr	01-Sep-08	WAR	PWO(U)	MWS COLLINGWOOD	HMS COLLINGWOOD
Raeburn, Mark	Lt Cdr	01-Jul-02	WAR	PWO(N)	FLEET CAP SSM	PORTSMOUTH
Raeside, Matthew A	Mid	01-Feb-14	WAR	GSX	BRNC	BRNC DARTMOUTH
Raffle, Edward J	Lt RN	01-Sep-10	ENG	ME	DCMC	LONDON
Rainbird, Luke T	Mid	01-Feb-14	ENG	MESM	MTM DRAKE	HMS DRAKE
Raine, Murray S	Lt RN	01-May-13	WAR	SM(X)	HMS AMBUSH	
Raine, Sarah L	Lt Cdr	01-Oct-14	ENG	WE	NCHQ CNPERS	PORTSMOUTH
Rainford, Jayjay	SLt	01-Sep-14	ENG	WESM	MWS COLLINGWOOD	HMS COLLINGWOOD
Raisbeck, Paul T	Lt Cdr	08-Jul-99	WAR	PWO(U)	MWS DDS	PORTSMOUTH
Rake, Rachael	Lt RN	01-Sep-09	ENG	ME	DES COMFLEET	ABBEY WOOD
Ralls, Damien	Lt Cdr	01-Oct-13	ENG	WESM(TWS)	HMS ASTUTE	
Ralston, William A	Lt RN	01-Jan-02	ENG	TM	FLEET FOST ACOS(Trg)	PORTSMOUTH
Ramage, Andrew P P	Lt RN	21-Mar-13	LOGS	L	DES COMLAND	ABBEY WOOD
Ramaswami, Ravi A	Surg Cdr	27-Jul-06	MED	Occ Med	DPHC SOUTH	PORTSMOUTH
Ramsay, Alastair J D	Lt RN	01-Jul-02	ENG	TM(SM)	NETS (W)	HMS DRAKE
Ramsay, Stuart J	Lt RN	01-Mar-13	ENG	WESM	HMS VANGUARD	
Rance, Maxwell G W	Cdr	31-May-01	LOGS	L	STRAT DEF RES	LONDON
Rand, Mark C MBE	Capt	24-Jul-04	RM	GS	NCHQ	PORTSMOUTH
Randall, Richard D	Cdr	30-Jun-03	ENG	MESM	DES COMFLEET	ABBEY WOOD
Randles, Maxwell E S	SLt	01-Jul-14	WAR	GSX	HMS PROTECTOR	
Randles, Steven	Lt Cdr	01-Oct-11	WAR	PWO	OCLC MANCH	MANCHESTER
Rankin, Graham J	Lt Cdr	01-Oct-08	WAR	AAWO	RN EXCHANGE NETHERLANDS	DEN HELDER
Ranscombe, Robert E	Lt RN	01-Jan-12	WAR	P UT	MTM RAF LINTON-ON-OUSE	RAF LINTON ON OUSE
Ransom, Benjamin R J	Lt RN	01-Sep-00	WAR	GSX	MTM NELSON	HMS NELSON
Raper, Daniel S	SLt	01-Nov-12	WAR	P UT	MTM RAF CRANWELL	RAFC CRANWELL
Rason, Stuart P	RN Chpln	01-Jan-12	Ch S	Chaplain	CDO LOG REGT RM	RMB CHIVENOR
Raval, Vivek	Lt RN	01-Feb-08	WAR	INT	MTM	WASHINGTON
Rawlins, Simon	Lt Cdr	01-Oct-10	WAR	P FW	RN EXCHANGE USA	WASHINGTON
Rawlinson, Katherine H	Surg Lt RN	04-Aug-10	MED	EM	MTM INM ALVERSTOKE	GOSPORT
Rawlinson, William G	SLt	19-Sep-14	WAR	SM(X)	HMS OCEAN	
Rawson, Scott M	Cdr	30-Jun-14	ENG	MESM	FLEET COMOPS NWD	NORTHWOOD
Ray, Daniel J A	Lt RN	01-Sep-14	WAR	GSX	MWS COLLINGWOOD	HMS COLLINGWOOD
Ray, Louise B	Lt Cdr	01-Oct-14	WAR	PWO	FOST DPORT	PLYMOUTH
Ray, Steven P	Lt RN	01-Oct-10	ENG	ME	MWS EXCELLENT	HMS EXCELLENT
Raybould, Adrian G	Cdr	30-Jun-01	ENG	WESM(TWS)	HDNET	CORSHAM
Raymont, Edward M	Lt RN	01-Apr-11	WAR	HM	HMS BULWARK	
Rayner, Andrew	Cdr	30-Jun-11	ENG	WE	BDS	WASHINGTON
Rayner, Matthew I	Mid	08-Sep-14	ENG	AE	BRNC	BRNC DARTMOUTH
Read, Alun J	Lt Cdr	01-Oct-04	WAR	P LYNX	LHF 815 SQN	RNAS YEOVILTON
Read, Benjamin	Lt RN	01-May-09	WAR	GSX	HMS SEVERN	
Read, Clinton D	Lt Col	30-Jun-14	RM	GS	MOD NSD	LONDON
Read, Edmund A E	Lt RN	01-Apr-11	WAR	HM	HMS ENTERPRISE	
Read, Jonathon	Surg Cdr	04-Aug-10	MED	Anaes	PCRF	RFA ARGUS
Read, Matthew C	Lt RN	01-Mar-11	ENG	AE	BRNC	BRNC DARTMOUTH
Read, Richard J	Lt Col	30-Jun-11	RM	LC	FLEET CAP LLM & DRM	PORTSMOUTH
Readwin, Roger	Cdr	30-Jun-10	WAR	MCD	MOD NSD USA	WASHINGTON
Reah, Stephen	Lt Cdr	02-May-00	ENG	ME	DES COMFLEET	HMS DRAKE
Reaves, Charles E	Lt Cdr	01-Oct-09	LOGS	L	FOST DPORT	PLYMOUTH
Rebbeck, Christopher	Lt RN	01-Oct-08	WAR	P LYNX	LHF 815 SQN	RNAS YEOVILTON
Reckless, Adam D	SLt	01-Apr-14	MED	Medical	BLAKE	BRNC DARTMOUTH
Redbourn, James	Lt RN	01-Sep-14	ENG	MESM	DCEME SULTAN	HMS SULTAN
Redman, Charles J R	Lt Cdr	23-Nov-98	WAR	GSX	MTM NELSON	HMS NELSON
Redman, Christopher D J	Surg Capt RN (D)	03-Nov-14	DENTAL	GDP(C&S)	DEFENCE DENTAL SERVS	EDINBURGH
Redmayne, Mark E	Lt Cdr	01-Oct-06	WAR	PWO	MCM1	FASLANE
Redpath, Scott D	Lt RN	20-Oct-08	ENG	MESM	DES COMFLEET	ABBEY WOOD
Reece, Nigel D	Cdr	30-Jun-12	ENG	MESM	DES COMFLEET	ABBEY WOOD
Reed, Andrew W OBE	Capt RN	25-Sep-12	WAR	AAWO	FLEET MARITIME WARFARE	HMS COLLINGWOOD
Reed, Christopher G QGM	Capt	16-Apr-10	RM	GS	NCHQ	PORTSMOUTH
Reed, Darren K	Cdr	30-Jun-10	LOGS	L BAR	DCDS PERS - SPA	RAF NORTHOLT
Reed, Mark	Lt Cdr	01-Oct-98	WAR	HM (M CH)	FLEET COMOPS NWD	NORTHWOOD
Reed, Nicholas	Lt Cdr	01-Oct-04	LOGS	L SM	DMLS	HMS RALEIGH
Reed, Peter K MBE	Lt RN	01-Sep-08	ENG	TM	MTM TEMERAIRE	HMS TEMERAIRE

Name	Substantive Rank	Seniority	Branch	Specialisation	Organisation Name	Location Name
Reed, Thomas A H	SLt	01-Nov-14	WAR	GSX	MWS COLLINGWOOD	HMS COLLINGWOOD
Reekie, Fraser C	Lt RN	01-May-13	WAR	SM(X)	HMS VICTORIOUS	
Rees, Adam M	Lt RN	01-Sep-98	ENG	TM	CTCRM	EXMOUTH
Rees, Karen M M	Lt Cdr	01-Oct-07	LOGS	L	FLEET SPT LOGS INFRA	PORTSMOUTH
Rees, Matthew I	Lt Cdr	01-Oct-14	LOGS	L SM	MTM NELSON	HMS NELSON
Rees, Nathan J	Lt RN	01-Feb-12	WAR	ATC	FOST DPORT	PLYMOUTH
Rees, Paul S C	Surg Cdr	28-Dec-11	MED	Med	MDHU FRIMLEY PARK	FRIMLEY
Rees, Richard T	Lt Cdr	01-Dec-03	WAR	PWO(N)	MCM2	PORTSMOUTH
Rees, Simon G	Lt Cdr	01-Oct-13	WAR	PWO(SM)	MTM NEPTUNE	HMNB CLYDE
Reese, David M	Lt Cdr	01-Sep-02	WAR	O LYNX	LHF HQ	RNAS YEOVILTON
Rees-Hughes, Victoria L	Lt RN	01-Sep-10	ENG	TM	HMS SULTAN	GOSPORT
Rees-Swindon, Mikaela J	Lt RN	05-Aug-11	LOGS	L	HMS DIAMOND	
Reeve, Jennifer A	Lt Cdr	01-Oct-14	WAR	INT	PJHQ (UK)	NORTHWOOD
Reeves, Andrew P	Lt Cdr	01-Oct-11	WAR	SM(AWC)	FLEET COMOPS NWD	NORTHWOOD
Reeves, Simon	Maj	01-Oct-14	RM	SCC	DMC DMOC	AYLESBURY
Reeves, Simon J	Lt RN	08-Jul-08	WAR	MCD	MTM NELSON	I IMS NELSON
Regan, Kevin QGM	Lt RN	13-Oct-12	WAR	O UT	MTM LHF 702 SQN YEOVILTON	RNAS YEOVILTON
Reid, Charles I	Capt RN	10-Jan-11	WAR	SM(CQ)	NATO-ACT-HQ	NORFOLK
Reid, Henry J	2Lt	25-Aug-14	RM	N/A	CTCRM	EXMOUTH
Reid, Iain J C	Lt RN	01-Sep-14	WAR	GSX	MTM NELSON	HMS NELSON
Reid, James	Lt RN	07-Feb-08	WAR	SM(N)	FOST FAS SHORE	HMNB CLYDE
Reid, James L	Lt Cdr	01-Oct-09	WAR	PWO	MWS COLLINGWOOD	HMS COLLINGWOOD
Reid, Jason C J	Cdr	30-Jun-12	ENG	WESM(TWS)	DES COMFLEET	ABBEY WOOD
Reid, Jenny E	SLt	24-Jan-12	WAR	GSX	HMS PORTLAND	
Reid, Mark R	Capt	01-Apr-11	RM	SCC	40 CDO RM	TAUNTON
Reid, Martyn	Lt Cdr	01-Apr-07	WAR	PWO(C)	RN EXCHANGE CANADA	OTTAWA
Reid, Philip A	SLt	01-Sep-13	WAR	O UT	MTM 750 SQN CULDROSE	RNAS CULDROSE
Reilly, Scott J	Lt RN	01-Apr-13	WAR	P SK4	CHF(MERLIN)	RAF BENSON
Reindorp, David P	Capt RN	21-Feb-11	WAR	PWO(N)	MTM NORTHWOOD HQ	NORTHWOOD
Renaud, Gavin A R	Lt Cdr	01-Oct-13	WAR	O LYNX	LHF 702 SQN	RNAS YEOVILTON
Rendell, Derrick J	Lt Cdr	01-Oct-05	ENG	MESM	RN GIBRALTAR - PM(NUC)	HMS ROOKE
Renney, Craig E	Maj	01-Oct-12	RM	MLDR (SCC)	NC REQUIREMENTS MANAGERS	ABBEY WOOD
Renney, Rachel A	Lt RN	01-Jan-03	ENG	WE	MTM WMO YEOVILTON	RNAS YEOVILTON
Rennie, Richard A	Surg Lt Cdr	01-Aug-12	MED	GMP	DPHC SW	EXMOUTH
Reston, Samuel C	Surg Cdr	01-Jul-12	MED	T&O	RCDM	PETERBOROUGH
Retallick, Katherine A	Lt RN	01-Apr-09	WAR	HM	MTM MWS HMTG (D)	HMS DRAKE
Revell, Aaron D	Lt RN	30-Sep-08	WAR	GSX	HMS ILLUSTRIOUS	
Rex, Colin	Lt Cdr	01-Oct-10	WAR	P SK4	MTM CHF (MERLIN)	RAF BENSON
Reynolds, Andrew C J	Lt Cdr	01-Oct-12	WAR	ME	NCHQ CNPERS	PORTSMOUTH
Reynolds, Ben K M	Maj	01-Oct-11	RM	GS	LFSS CDO LOG REGT RM	RMB CHIVENOR
Reynolds, Darren P	Lt Cdr	01-Oct-13	ENG	WE	NAVY MCTA	PORTSMOUTH
Reynolds, Huw F	Lt Cdr	01-Mar-14	ENG	AE P	RNAS CULDROSE	HELSTON
Reynolds, James	Lt Cdr	01-Oct-10	WAR	PWO	FOST DPORT	PLYMOUTH
Reynolds, Mark E	Lt Cdr	01-Feb-11	ENG	ME	FOST DPORT	PLYMOUTH
Reynolds, Matthew J	Lt Cdr	01-Oct-10	WAR	PWO(C)	MWS COLLINGWOOD	HMS COLLINGWOOD
Reynolds, Zoe A	Lt RN	01-Dec-03	WAR	INT	DIRECTOR (JW)	NORTHWOOD
Reynolson, Howard B V	Lt Cdr	03-Nov-85	WAR	AV (RES)	CHF - 846	RAF BENSON
Rhodes, Andrew W	Lt Cdr	01-Oct-07	ENG	WE	LOAN DSTL	FARNBOROUGH
Rich, David C	Lt Cdr	20-May-97	WAR	SM(CQ)	FLEET FOST ACOS(Trg)	HMNB CLYDE
Rich, Duncan	Lt RN	19-Feb-08	WAR	SM(N)	MTM RALEIGH	HMS RALEIGH
Richards, Alan D C B	V Adm	19-Jan-12	WAR	P SK6	DI - CDI	LONDON
Richards, Anthony J	Lt Cdr	01-Oct-07	LOGS	L SM	NCHQ CNPS	LONDON
Richards, Gregor I	Lt RN	20-Jul-10	WAR	MW	MCM1	FASLANE
Richards, Guy B	Lt Cdr	01-Oct-14	LOGS	L	HQ ARRC COMMAND GROUP	GLOUCESTER
Richards, Jack P G	Lt	01-Mar-14	RM	GS	42 CDO RM	PLYMOUTH
Richards, James I H	Cdr	30-Jun-13	ENG	WESM(TWS)	SFM CLYDE	HMNB CLYDE
Richards, Jonathan C	Lt RN	01-Jul-11	ENG	MESM	HMS TALENT	
Richards, Natasha K	Mid	08-Sep-14	WAR	GSX	BRNC	BRNC DARTMOUTH
Richards, Paul	Lt Cdr	01-Oct-07	ENG	ME	DG FINANCE	LONDON
Richards, Robert D	Lt RN	01-Sep-07	ENG	WESM(TWS)	FLEET MARITIME WARFARE	HMS COLLINGWOOD
Richards, Simon T	Lt RN	01-Aug-99	WAR	O SKW	AWC	BOSCOMBE DOWN
Richards, Thomas M L	Lt RN	01-Jan-12	WAR	P UT	MTM CHF (MERLIN)	RAF BENSON

Name	Substantive Rank	Seniority	Branch	Specialisation	Organisation Name	Location Name
Richardson, Alexander J M	SLt	01-Nov-14	WAR	O UT	MWS COLLINGWOOD	HMS COLLINGWOOD
Richardson, Benjamin F	Maj	01-Oct-13	RM	GS	CTCRM	EXMOUTH
Richardson, Craig A	Lt RN	01-Sep-14	ENG	WESM	HMS VIGILANT	
Richardson, Gavin A	Cdr	30-Jun-10	WAR	O MER	NCHQ CNPS	PORTSMOUTH
Richardson, Ian H	Lt Cdr	01-Oct-08	WAR	MCD	NCHQ	NCHQ
Richardson, James	Lt RN	01-Jan-09	LOGS	L	RNAS YEOVILTON	YEOVILTON
Richardson, James A	Lt RN	01-May-13	WAR	SM(X)	HMS VANGUARD	
Richardson, John F	Lt RN	01-Sep-04	WAR	PWO(N)	MWS COLLINGWOOD	HMS COLLINGWOOD
Richardson, Peter S M	Cdr	30-Jun-11	ENG	WE	FLEET CAP SSM	PORTSMOUTH
Richardson, Philip	Cdr	30-Jun-14	WAR	P LYNX	MTM FLEET HQ	PORTSMOUTH
Richardson, Simon J	Capt	19-Jul-05	RM	SCC	HQ 3 CDO BDE RM	PLYMOUTH
Richardson, Stuart J	Lt RN	20-Oct-09	ENG	WESM(SWS)	COMFASFLOT	HELENSBURGH
Richardson, William J	2Lt	25-Aug-14	RM	N/A	CTCRM	EXMOUTH
Riches, Ian C OBE	Cdr	30-Jun-04	WAR	SM(CQ)	CAPTAIN HMS NEPTUNE	HMNB CLYDE
Riches, Joanne C	Lt Cdr	01-Oct-13	ENG	TM	NCHQ CNPERS (HRTSG)	PORTSMOUTH
Richmond, David R	Lt	02-Sep-14	RM	GS	45 CDO RM	DUNDEE
Richmond, Iain J M	Capt RN	30-Jun-06	WAR	P SK6	PJHQ (UK)	NORTHWOOD
Richter, Alwyn S B	Lt Cdr	01-Sep-00	ENG	WE	FLEET ACOS(RP)	PORTSMOUTH
Rickard, James J	Lt RN	01-May-10	WAR	SM(X)	HMS AMBUSH	
Rickard, Rory F	Surg Cdr	30-Jun-04	MED	BPS	DMS WHITTINGTON	BIRMINGHAM
Ricketts, Alex F	Lt RN	01-Feb-14	WAR	GSX	HMS RICHMOND	
Ricketts, Simon J	SLt	01-Mar-14	WAR	HM	MTM NELSON	HMS NELSON
Riddett, Adam O	Lt Cdr	01-Oct-10	WAR	PWO	PJHQ (UK)	NORTHWOOD
Rider, John	Lt Cdr	01-Oct-09	WAR	SM(AWC)	DI - CA - ASUS	WASHINGTON
Ridgeway, Adam	Lt RN	01-Apr-12	WAR	GSX	HMS TYNE	
Ridgwell, Daniel R	Lt Cdr	01-Oct-13	ENG	ME	NC REQUIREMENTS MANAGERS	ABBEY WOOD
Ridley, George	Lt RN	01-Apr-09	WAR	P MER	BRNC	BRNC DARTMOUTH
Ridley, Jon	Maj	01-Oct-10	RM	BS	CTCRM	HMS NELSON
Ridley, Nicholas S	Mid	01-May-14	WAR	GSX	BRNC	BRNC DARTMOUTH
Rigby, Jeremy C ADC	Cdre	01-Jul-13	LOGS	L	NBC PORTSMOUTH	PORTSMOUTH
Rigby, Lee A	Lt RN	09-Apr-10	ENG	AE	DES COMJE	YEOVIL
Rignall, William J M	Lt RN	01-Nov-12	WAR	HM	MTM WMO YEOVILTON	RNAS YEOVILTON
Rigsby, David A E	SLt	01-May-12	WAR	SM(X)	HMS BULWARK	
Riley, Neil A	Surg Lt RN	06-Aug-14	MED	Medical	BLAKE	BRNC DARTMOUTH
Riley, Ralph A	Lt Cdr	01-Oct-14	WAR	O MER	MWS COLLINGWOOD	HMS COLLINGWOOD
Rilstone, Nathan	Mid	01-Feb-14	WAR	ATC UT	BRNC	BRNC DARTMOUTH
Rimington, Anthony K	Cdr	30-Jun-11	WAR	P LYNX	UK MCC	BAHRAIN
Rimmer, Heather E	Cdr	30-Jun-10	ENG	TM	MWS COLLINGWOOD	HMS COLLINGWOOD
Rimmer, Owen F	Lt Cdr	01-Oct-12	WAR	SM(AWC)	FLEET COMOPS NWD	NORTHWOOD
Riordan, Shaun	Lt Cdr	01-Oct-12	WAR	WE	DI - CA	LONDON
Ripley, Benjamin E	Cdr	30-Jun-11	WAR	PWO(U)	FLEET ACOS(RP)	PORTSMOUTH
Ripley, Stephen L	Lt Cdr	01-Oct-13	ENG	WE	MTM NELSON	HMS NELSON
Rippingale, Stuart N	Cdr	30-Jun-05	ENG	IS	NATO-ACO-CIS	MONS (CASTEAU)
Risdall, Jane	Surg Cdr	31-Dec-98	MED	Anaes	RCDM	BIRMINGHAM
Risley, James G	Lt Cdr	01-Oct-08	ENG	MESM	DES COMFLEET	ABBEY WOOD
Ritchie, Douglas B	Lt Cdr	01-Oct-14	ENG	MESM	HMS TRENCHANT	
Ritchie, Iain D	Lt Cdr	01-Oct-10	WAR	HM(AM)	FLEET CAP IS	PORTSMOUTH
Ritchie, Luke G	Mid	17-Nov-14	ENG	TM	BRNC	BRNC DARTMOUTH
Ritchie, Stuart D	Lt RN	01-Jun-09	LOGS	L	PJHQ (UK)	NORTHWOOD
Ritson, Jonathan E	Surg Lt Cdr	01-Aug-12	MED	EM	MTM INM ALVERSTOKE	GOSPORT
Rixon, Thomas M	Lt RN	01-Sep-13	WAR	O SKW	849 SQN	RNAS CULDROSE
Roach, Darren J	Lt RN	01-Jun-10	WAR	INT	BRNC	BRNC DARTMOUTH
Roach, Lewis G	Lt RN	24-Nov-14	ENG	AE	LHF 815 SQN HQ	RNAS YEOVILTON
Robbins, Daniel M	SLt	01-Apr-12	WAR	HM	FLEET HM UNIT	PLYMOUTH
Robbins, Harry V	Capt	01-Jan-02	RM	P SK4	771 SQN	RNAS CULDROSE
Roberts, Andrew	Lt RN	16-Feb-07	WAR	SM(X)	FLEET COMOPS NSTP30	FAREHAM
Roberts, Andrew	Lt RN	23-May-10	WAR	ATC	FOST DPORT	PLYMOUTH
Roberts, Andrew	Lt Cdr	01-Oct-12	ENG	AE	RN EXCHANGE AUSTRALIA	CANBERRA
Roberts, Benjamin	Lt Cdr	01-Oct-09	LOGS	L	RN EXCHANGE USA	WASHINGTON
Roberts, Charlotte M	Lt RN	01-Sep-12	ENG	AE	1710 NAS	PORTSMOUTH
Roberts, Christopher S	Lt Cdr	01-Oct-14	WAR	AV	FLEET CSAV	PORTSMOUTH
Roberts, David	Lt RN	01-Nov-06	WAR	FC	MTM NELSON	HMS NELSON

Name	Substantive Rank	Seniority	Branch	Specialisation	Organisation Name	Location Name
Roberts, David G	Lt RN	01-Sep-10	ENG	MESM	FOST SM SEA	HMNB CLYDE
Roberts, Dean	Cdr	30-Jun-11	ENG	WE	DES COMFLEET	ABBEY WOOD
Roberts, Iain G	Lt Cdr	01-Oct-03	ENG	WESM(TWS)	DES COMFLEET	HMS DRAKE
Roberts, Joel	Lt RN	01-Feb-09	WAR	GSX	HMS CLYDE	
Roberts, John A	Lt RN	11-Dec-09	MED	MS(SM)	COMFASFLOT	HELENSBURGH
Roberts, Llion G	SLt	01-Nov-14	WAR	GSX	MWS COLLINGWOOD	HMS COLLINGWOOD
Roberts, Martin A	Lt RN	01-Nov-94	WAR	O SKW	RNAS CULDROSE	HELSTON
Roberts, Nicholas S	Cdre	03-Jan-12	WAR	WE	FMC CAPABILITY PLANS	LONDON
Roberts, Nigel D	Lt Cdr	01-Oct-11	WAR	O WILDCAT	AWC	BOSCOMBE DOWN
Roberts, Patrick D	Mid	01-Feb-14	ENG	ME	DCEME SULTAN	HMS SULTAN
Roberts, Peter N	Lt RN	09-Apr-10	ENG	AE	RNAS YEOVILTON	YEOVILTON
Roberts, Sean L	Mid	01-May-14	LOGS	L	BRNC	BRNC DARTMOUTH
Roberts, Stephen	Lt RN	01-Feb-03	WAR	INFO OPS	EU OHQ	UK
Roberts, Stephen D	Capt RN	11-Aug-14	ENG	WE	DES COMFLEET	ABBEY WOOD
Roberts, Thomas P C	Capt	16-Apr-09	RM	MLDR (SCC)	30 CDO IX GP RM	PLYMOUTH
Roberts, Thomas R J	Lt RN	01-Sep-10	WAR	SM(X)	HMS VICTORIOUS	
Roberts, Timothy J	Capt RN	17-Nov-14	ENG	MESM	DES COMFLEET	PLYMOUTH
Robertson, Adam J	Lt Cdr	01-Oct-13	ENG	WE	FLEET CAP SSM	PORTSMOUTH
Robertson, David C	Capt RN	17-Sep-13	WAR	HM (H CH)	COMDEVFLOT	PLYMOUTH
Robertson, Douglas M	Lt Cdr	01-Oct-93	WAR	ATC	FLEET CSAV	LONDON
Robertson, Jake A	Mid	17-Nov-14	WAR	P UT	BRNC	BRNC DARTMOUTH
Robertson, Keith H	Capt	18-Jul-08	RM	SCC	45 CDO RM	DUNDEE
Robertson, Paul N	Lt Cdr	01-Oct-00	WAR	O SK6	771 SQN	RNAS CULDROSE
Robertson, Sean P	Lt RN	01-Sep-14	ENG	MESM	DCEME SULTAN	HMS SULTAN
Robertson, Stuart T	Lt Cdr	01-Oct-06	LOGS	L SM	JFHQ	NORTHWOOD
Robertson, Thomas A M	Lt RN	01-Apr-12	WAR	GSX	HMS DRAGON	
Robey, James C	Lt Cdr	01-Oct-11	WAR	PWO(N)	FOST DPORT	PLYMOUTH
Robin, Julie I	Surg Cdr	05-Apr-12	MED	Anaes	RCDM	BIRMINGHAM
Robinson, Alan J	Lt RN	16-Dec-11	ENG	MESM	HMS VICTORIOUS	
Robinson, Alex J	SLt	01-Feb-12	WAR	P UT	MTM RAF CRANWELL	RAFC CRANWELL
Robinson, Charles E T	Cdr	30-Jun-99	WAR	PWO(U)	NATO - BRUSSELS	BRUSSELS
Robinson, David	Lt Cdr	01-Oct-08	LOGS	L	NCHQ CNPS	PORTSMOUTH
Robinson, Guy A OBE	Cdre	03-Sep-13	WAR	PWO(A)	FLEET CAP WARFARE	PORTSMOUTH
Robinson, Jennifer A	SLt	01-Jun-14	MED	Medical	BLAKE	BRNC DARTMOUTH
Robinson, John P	Lt RN	10-Nov-13	LOGS	L	MTM RALEIGH	HMS RALEIGH
Robinson, Lee D	Lt Cdr	01-Oct-10	ENG	WESM(SWS)	HMS VANGUARD	
Robinson, Lindsy	Lt RN	11-Oct-13	MED	MS	MDHU DERRIFORD	PLYMOUTH
Robinson, Matthew S	Lt RN	01-May-04	WAR	P MER	824 SQN	RNAS CULDROSE
Robinson, Melanie S	Lt Cdr	07-Jun-04	WAR	GSX	NCHQ CNPERS	PORTSMOUTH
Robinson, Michael P	Cdre	01-Jul-14	ENG	MESM	DSEA DNSR	ABBEY WOOD
Robinson, Michael W	Surg Lt Cdr	06-Aug-13	MED	GS	MTM INM ALVERSTOKE	GOSPORT
Robinson, Nicholas	SLt	01-May-13	ENG	TM(SM)	HMS RALEIGH	TORPOINT
Robinson, Nicholas P	Lt RN	01-Sep-13	LOGS	L	BF BIOT	DIEGO GARCIA
Robinson, Steven L	Lt Cdr	01-Jan-09	ENG	WE	HMS DEFENDER	
Robinson, Timothy	Surg Lt Cdr	02-Aug-10	MED	GMP	MTM WMO CULDROSE	RNAS CULDROSE
Robley, William F	Lt Cdr	01-Oct-06	WAR	P SK6	FLEET CSAV	PORTSMOUTH
Robson, James P	Lt RN	01-Oct-14	LOGS	L	NBD COB LO HMS DRAKE	HMS DRAKE
Robson, Mark A	Capt	16-Apr-10	RM	GS	NCHQ	PORTSMOUTH
Robus, Keith	RN Chpln	27-Aug-07	Ch S	Chaplain	FLEET HM UNIT	PLYMOUTH
Robus, Lucy J	Lt RN	01-Apr-14	WAR	GSX	HMS NORTHUMBERLAND	
Rock, James A	Lt RN	01-Jun-07	WAR	P MER	MTM WMO YEOVILTON	RNAS YEOVILTON
Roddy, Christopher M	Lt RN	31-Jul-09	ENG	AE	MOD CNS/ACNS	PORTSMOUTH
Roden, Ieuan P J	Mid	17-Nov-14	WAR	P UT	BRNC	BRNC DARTMOUTH
Rodgers, Mark A	Lt RN	01-Sep-14	ENG	MESM	DCEME SULTAN	HMS SULTAN
Roe, Roma I	Lt Cdr	01-Oct-11	ENG	AE	824 SQN	RNAS CULDROSE
Roessler, Philippa F	Lt RN	01-Sep-11	WAR	HM	FLEET HM UNIT	PLYMOUTH
Roffey, Kevin D	Lt Cdr	01-Oct-13	ENG	AE	DES COMJE	YEOVIL
Rogers, Alan	Lt Cdr	25-Dec-02	WAR	AV (RES)	MASF	RNAS CULDROSE
Rogers, Alexander T	Lt Cdr	31-Jul-05	WAR	P LYN7	HQ JHC DCOMD	ANDOVER
Rogers, Christopher M	Lt Cdr	01-Jun-00	ENG	WE	ACDS	ABBEY WOOD
Rogers, Clare A	SLt	15-May-13	LOGS	L	HMS SUTHERLAND	
Rogers, Dominic J J	Capt	01-Sep-09	RM	GS	BRNC	BRNC DARTMOUTH

Name	Substantive Rank	Seniority	Branch	Specialisation	Organisation Name	Location Name
Rogers, James	Lt RN	01-Sep-09	ENG	MESM	MTM DEFAC JSCSC	SHRIVENHAM
Rogers, Jennifer C S	Surg Lt RN	01-Aug-12	MED	GDMO	HMS NORTHUMBERLAND	
Rogers, Julia A	Lt Cdr	01-Oct-09	WAR	P SK4	NCHQ CNPS	PORTSMOUTH
Rogers, Julian C E	Lt Cdr	01-Mar-03	WAR	SM(AWC)	COMFASFLOT	HELENSBURGH
Rogers, Philip S	Lt Cdr	01-Oct-06	ENG	TM	MTM DEFAC JSCSC	SHRIVENHAM
Rogers, Phillip R	Lt RN	01-Sep-07	ENG	MESM	HMS VANGUARD	
Rogers, Simon J P	Lt Cdr	01-Oct-06	WAR	PWO(C)	NAVSEC	HMS EXCELLENT
Rogers, Simon M	Maj	01-Oct-08	RM	GS	MTM DEFAC JSCSC	SHRIVENHAM
Rogers, William G	2Lt	25-Aug-14	RM	N/A	CTCRM	EXMOUTH
Roissetter, David	RN Chpln	03-Jan-06	Ch S	Chaplain	HMS RALEIGH	TORPOINT
Rolfe, Conrad	Lt RN	01-Sep-12	WAR	GSX	HMS NORTHUMBERLAND	
Rolls, Edward C	Lt RN	01-Jul-06	WAR	ATC	RNAS YEOVILTON	SOUTHAMPTON
Rolph, Andrew P M	Cdr	30-Jun-04	WAR	PWO(C)	DI - ICSP	LONDON
Roocroft, Nathaniel T	Surg Lt RN	06-Aug-14	MED	Medical	BLAKE	BRNC DARTMOUTH
Rook, Christopher	Lt RN	30-Jul-10	LOGS	L	845 SQN	RNAS YEOVILTON
Ronk, Graeme I	Lt Cdr	01-Apr-98	ENG	WE	NATO-ACT-HQ	MONS (CASTEAU)
Rooke, Adam E	Lt RN	01-Sep-06	ENG	MESM	DES COMFLEET	ABBEY WOOD
Rooke, Mark D	Lt RN	01-Apr-12	ENG	TM	HMS SULTAN	GOSPORT
Roper, Jack H	Capt	01-Sep-13	RM	GS	CTCRM	EXMOUTH
Rose, Alan	Lt Cdr	01-Oct-12	ENG	WESM(TWS)	HMS AMBUSH	
Rose, Andrew D	Cdr	30-Jun-13	WAR	O SKW	MTM DEFAC JSCSC	SHRIVENHAM
Rose, Ian D	Lt RN	01-Jan-10	ENG	MESM	DES COMFLEET	BARROW IN FURNESS
Rose, Marcus E	Lt Cdr	01-Oct-13	ENG	WESM(TWS)	HMS TRENCHANT	
Rose, Matt W	Lt RN	30-Nov-06	WAR	P SK6	GANNET SAR FLT	HMS GANNET
Rose, Matthew L	Surg Lt RN	06-Aug-14	MED	Medical	BLAKE	BRNC DARTMOUTH
Rose, Michael F	Cdr	30-Jun-08	ENG	ME	NCHQ CNPS	PORTSMOUTH
Rose, Simon P	Lt RN	01-Jan-07	ENG	WE	JFCIS(I)	QATAR
Rose, Victoria	Lt RN	01-Nov-09	WAR	O MER	820 SQN	RNAS CULDROSE
Rosenberg, Marcel M G	Lt Cdr	01-Oct-10	ENG	WE	HMS DARING	
Rosen-Nash, William A	Lt RN	01-Sep-12	ENG	WESM(TWS)	HMS TORBAY	
Roskilly, Martyn	Capt	01-May-01	RM	P LYN7	771 SQN	RNAS CULDROSE
Ross, Alison K	SLt	01-Sep-14	ENG	ME	DCEME SULTAN	HMS SULTAN
Ross, David C	Lt RN	31-Jul-08	WAR	SM(C)	NATO ACO	NORTHWOOD
Ross, Jamie M	Lt RN	01-Sep-08	WAR	P SK4	GANNET SAR FLT	HMS GANNET
Ross, Paul W	Lt RN	01-Jan-05	ENG	WESM(TWS)	HMS VANGUARD	
Ross, Phillip D	Lt RN	01-Sep-13	WAR	P UT	771 SQN	RNAS CULDROSE
Ross, Robert A MBE	Surg Capt RN	16-Sep-08	MED	GMP (C&S)	PJHQ (UK)	NORTHWOOD
Ross, Samuel K	Lt RN	01-Jun-12	WAR	ATC	HMS OCEAN	
Ross, Steven	Lt Cdr	01-Oct-14	ENG	WESM(SWS)	MTM RALEIGH	HMS RALEIGH
Roster, Shaun P	Lt Cdr	01-Oct-06	WAR	O LYNX	LOAN VECTOR	GOSPORT
Rostron, David W	Lt Cdr	01-Jan-04	ENG	MESM	HMS TIRELESS	
Rostron, John H	Lt Cdr	01-Oct-09	ENG	WESM(SWS)	DSEA DNSR	ABBEY WOOD
Rotherham, Dominic L	Lt RN	20-Oct-09	WAR	O UT	MTM 824 SQN CULDROSE	RNAS CULDROSE
Rothwell, Christopher D	Lt RN	01-Apr-14	WAR	FC	HMS DARING	
Rouault, Lewis D	SLt	14-Aug-12	WAR	SM(X)	MCM2	PORTSMOUTH
Roughton, Joshua N	Lt	02-Sep-14	RM	GS	40 CDO RM	TAUNTON
Roulston-Eldridge, James W C	Lt RN	01-Jan-08	ENG	ME	HMS SULTAN	GOSPORT
Rounce, George	2Lt	25-Aug-14	RM	N/A	CTCRM	EXMOUTH
Round, Matthew J	Lt Cdr	01-Oct-14	WAR	O SKW	750 SQN	RNAS CULDROSE
Routledge, Ricky J	Lt RN	01-Sep-06	ENG	IS	HMS SULTAN	GOSPORT
Routledge, Rosemary P	Lt RN	01-Nov-09	ENG	TM	HQ EUFOR (SAR)	SARAJEVO
Rowan, Tristian G	Lt RN	01-Sep-12	WAR	P MER CDO	CHF(MERLIN)	RAF BENSON
Rowberry, Adrian G	Lt Cdr	01-Oct-11	WAR	PWO	COMPORFLOT	PORTSMOUTH
Rowbotham, Mark J	Lt Cdr	01-Oct-14	ENG	ME	FDS HQ	PORTSMOUTH
Rowden, Paul C B	Capt	03-Sep-14	RM	GS	LFSS CDO LOG REGT RM	RMB CHIVENOR
Rowe, Antony N	Lt RN	06-Apr-07	ENG	WE	MASF	RNAS CULDROSE
Rowe, Joanne	Lt RN	01-Sep-11	LOGS	L	FOSNI - NRC WWE	BRISTOL
Rowe, Kevin C	Lt RN	04-May-01	WAR	O (RES)	849 SQN	RNAS CULDROSE
Rowe, Richard D	RN Chpln	24-Sep-00	Ch S	Chaplain	COMFASFLOT	HELENSBURGH
Rowe, Warren L	Lt	06-Jan-14	RM	GS	45 CDO RM	DUNDEE
Rowland, Charles	Surg SLt	29-Jul-14	MED	Medical	BLAKE	BRNC DARTMOUTH
Rowland, Justin M	Lt RN	13-Apr-12	ENG	AE	LHF 815 SQN HQ	RNAS YEOVILTON

Name	Substantive Rank	Seniority	Branch	Specialisation	Organisation Name	Location Name
Rowland, Paul N	Cdr	30-Jun-08	ENG	MESM	CBRN POL	LONDON
Rowland, Steven G	Capt	01-Apr-11	RM	SCC	HQ SQN CDO LOG REGT RM	RMB CHIVENOR
Rowlands, Andrew P	Lt RN	01-Jan-10	WAR	GSX	HMS DRAGON	
Rowlands, Andrew R	Cdr	30-Jun-13	ENG	WE	SVCOPS/DHDOPS/COR	CORSHAM
Rowlands, Kevin	Cdr	30-Jun-11	WAR	PWO(A)	JFC HQ	NORTHWOOD
Rowlands, Sarah J	Lt RN	19-Jun-10	ENG	TM	HMS SULTAN	GOSPORT
Rowles, Michael	Lt	01-Jul-13	RM	SCC	45 CDO RM	DUNDEE
Rowley, Thomas P	Lt Cdr	01-Oct-12	WAR	PWO	MWS COLLINGWOOD	HMS COLLINGWOOD
Rowntree, Paul J	Lt RN	01-Jun-07	WAR	INT	HQ ARRC (JFIB)B	GLOUCESTER
Rowson, Marcus J	Lt Cdr	01-Oct-13	WAR	P SK4	MTM CHF (MERLIN)	RAF BENSON
Roy, Christopher A	Lt Cdr	30-Jun-13	WAR	P FW	HQ AIR HQ 1GP LTNG	MCAS CHERRY POINT
Roy, Sudipta K	Surg Lt Cdr	01-Aug-10	MED	GS	MTM INM ALVERSTOKE	GOSPORT
Royce, Roderick H	Lt RN	01-Feb-06	WAR	P LYN7	MTM RAF CRANWELL	RAFC CRANWELL
Roylance, Jaimie F	Col	16-Jul-14	RM	P LYN7	HQ JHC	ANDOVER
Royle, Michael	SLt	01-Feb-12	WAR	GSX	HMS SEVERN	
Royston, James L	Lt Cdr	01-Oct-14	WAR	PWO(SM)	HMS AMBUSH	
Royston, Sarah L	Lt RN	01-Jan-07	ENG	ME	CAPTAIN HMS NEPTUNE	HMNB CLYDE
Royston, Stuart J	Cdr	30-Jun-10	WAR	PWO(C)	UK MCC	BAHRAIN
Ruddock, Gordon W D	Cdr	30-Jun-12	WAR	AAWO	DEFENCE ACADEMY	SHRIVENHAM
Rudkin, Adam L	Lt RN	01-Sep-05	ENG	AE P	RNAS YEOVILTON	YEOVILTON
Ruffell, Lauren	Lt RN	01-Apr-12	WAR	GSX	HMS IRON DUKE	
Rusbridger, Robert C	Capt RN	30-Jun-03	ENG	ME	AIR 22GP	RAF HIGH WYCOMBE
Ruscoe, David I	Lt RN	01-Apr-09	WAR	MW	MCM1	FASLANE
Rushton, Emma V	Lt RN	01-Feb-06	ENG	TM	MTM DEFAC JSCSC	SHRIVENHAM
Rushworth, Benjamin J	Lt Cdr	01-May-06	WAR	PWO(N)	UK MCC	BAHRAIN
Russell, Bruce	Cdr	30-Jun-14	ENG	WESM(TWS)	FLEET CAP MARCAP	PORTSMOUTH
Russell, Katherine E F	Lt Cdr	01-Oct-09	WAR	AAWO	MTM NELSON	HMS NELSON
Russell, Martin S	Lt Cdr	01-Oct-11	WAR	O SKW	814 SQN	RNAS CULDROSE
Russell, Michael J	Surg Lt Cdr	01-Nov-11	MED	GMP	PCRF	RFA ARGUS
Russell, Nigel A D	Lt Cdr	01-Oct-04	WAR	PWO(A)	MWS COLLINGWOOD	HMS COLLINGWOOD
Russell, Paul	Cdr	30-Jun-10	WAR	AAWO	MTM RN GLOBAL	USA
Russell, Philip R	Cdr	30-Jun-05	ENG	ME	DES COMFLEET	ABBEY WOOD
Russell, Thomas	Cdr	30-Jun-07	WAR	MCD	NATO-ACO-SHAPE	CASTEAU
Rutherford, Adam T	Maj	01-Oct-10	RM	MLDR (SCC)	HQ 3 CDO BDE RM	PLYMOUTH
Rutherford, Ian J D	Lt RN	01-Sep-13	ENG	MESM	HMS VIGILANT	
Rutherford, Sarah E	Mid	17-Nov-14	WAR	P UT	BRNC	BRNC DARTMOUTH
Rutter, John C	Lt RN	01-Sep-07	WAR	P SK4	MTM 847 SQN YEOVILTON	RNAS YEOVILTON
Rweyemamu, Anatol M	Lt RN	01-Apr-12	LOGS	L	MTM NELSON	HMS NELSON
Ryall, Thomas A S	Maj	01-Oct-10	RM	GS	NCHQ	PORTSMOUTH
Ryan, John P	Lt Cdr	01-Oct-08	ENG	MESM	DES COMFLEET	HMS DRAKE
Ryan, Kathleen R	Lt RN	12-Jul-10	QARNNS	Infection C	MTM RALEIGH	HMS RALEIGH
Ryan, Paul J	Lt Cdr	01-Oct-13	WAR	P MER	MTM WMO CULDROSE	RNAS CULDROSE
Ryan, Richard M	Cdr	30-Jun-09	WAR	O LYNX	NCHQ CNPERS	PORTSMOUTH
Ryan, Sean J	Cdr	30-Jun-11	WAR	SM(CQ)	MTM DEFAC JSCSC	SHRIVENHAM
Ryde, Emma	Lt RN	14-Aug-14	LOGS	L	COMDEVFLOT	PLYMOUTH
Ryder, Matthew R	Lt Cdr	01-Oct-12	ENG	WE	MTM MWS COLLINGWOOD	HMS COLLINGWOOD
Rydiard, Michael	Lt RN	01-Apr-11	WAR	GSX	HMS DAUNTLESS	
Rylah, Joshua G H	Lt RN	01-Sep-12	WAR	GSX	HMS TYNE	
Rylah, Osgar J A	Surg Lt RN	04-Aug-10	MED	Anaes	MTM INM ALVERSTOKE	GOSPORT
Ryley, Imogen	Mid	01-May-14	WAR	P UT	BRNC	BRNC DARTMOUTH

S

Sabin, Scott M	Lt RN	01-Jul-13	WAR	GSX	HMS SOMERSET	
Saddleton, Andrew D	Lt Col	30-Jun-05	RM	LC	DSP	LONDON
Sadler, Aimee R G	Lt RN	16-May-14	WAR	HM	HMS BULWARK	
Sadler-Smith, Aaron J T	Capt	12-Dec-13	RM	GS	LFSS CDO LOG REGT RM	RMB CHIVENOR
Saffin, James R	Surg Lt Cdr	05-Aug-14	MED	Anaes	MTM INM ALVERSTOKE	GOSPORT
Said, Phillip M	Lt RN	15-Apr-11	ENG	AE	DES COMJE	YEOVIL
Salberg, David G	Lt RN	01-Sep-12	WAR	P UT	RNAS CULDROSE	HELSTON
Sales, Adam	SLt	01-Sep-12	MED	Medical	BLAKE	BRNC DARTMOUTH
Salisbury, David P OBE	Cdr	30-Jun-03	WAR	P LYNX	DEFENCE ACADEMY	SHRIVENHAM
Salisbury, Dominic B A	Lt RN	17-Dec-10	MED	MS	DCHET DSHT	LICHFIELD

Name	Substantive Rank	Seniority	Branch	Specialisation	Organisation Name	Location Name
Salmon, Michael A	Capt RN	01-Jul-13	WAR	O SKW	HQ AIR - COS(CAP)	HIGH WYCOMBE
Salt, Isaac P B	SLt	01-Sep-14	WAR	GSX	MWS COLLINGWOOD	HMS COLLINGWOOD
Salt, Jennifer M	Lt RN	01-May-07	ENG	WE	MTM FLEET HQ	PORTSMOUTH
Salter, Jonas A	Capt	01-Sep-10	RM	GS	1 ASSLT GP RM	PLYMOUTH
Saltonstall, Hugh F R	Lt Cdr	01-Oct-12	WAR	P LYNX	WMF 825 SQN HQ	RNAS YEOVILTON
Salzano, Gerard M MBE	Brig	04-May-10	RM	GS	NAVY CORE TRG HQ	PLYMOUTH
Sampson, Colin G	SLt	01-May-14	QARNNS	Nurse Officer	MDHU DERRIFORD	PLYMOUTH
Sampson, James	Lt Cdr	01-Oct-12	ENG	IS	HMS RICHMOND	
Sampson, James L	Capt	30-Mar-12	RM	GS	NCHQ	PORTSMOUTH
Sampson, Jonathan A	Lt RN	11-Dec-09	WAR	AV	DSTO	RAF ST MAWGAN
Samuel, Ben J	Lt RN	01-Apr-11	LOGS	L SM	PFCS NSCC	HMS EXCELLENT
Samuel, Christopher D R	Maj	01-Oct-07	RM	C	HMAG	AFGHANISTAN
Samuels, Nicholas J	Lt Cdr	01-Oct-09	WAR	SM(AWC)	FOST DSTF - CSST	PLYMOUTH
Sander, Oliver P	Lt RN	01-Jul-12	ENG	ME	HMS QUEEN ELIZABETH	
Sanders, James A	Lt	06-Apr-14	RM	GS	NCHQ	PORTSMOUTH
Sanders, Lee C	Lt RN	19-Apr-12	ENG	AE	MOD CNS/ACNS	RNAS YEOVILTON
Sanderson, Christopher P	Lt Cdr	01-Oct-07	WAR	HM	LOAN HYDROG DGHR(N)	TAUNTON
Sanderson, Mark A	Maj	01-Oct-14	RM	SCC	MTM FLEET HQ	PORTSMOUTH
Sandhu, Jagdeep S	Surg Lt RN	04-Aug-10	MED	GMP	MTM INM ALVERSTOKE	GOSPORT
Sandiford, Aran J	Capt	01-Sep-13	RM	GS	CTCRM	EXMOUTH
Sandle, Neil D	Lt Cdr	01-Aug-03	ENG	ME	FLEET CAP SSM	PORTSMOUTH
Sandy, David J	Lt Cdr	01-Oct-12	WAR	PWO(C)	FOST DPORT	PLYMOUTH
Sankey, Freddie O R	Capt	03-Sep-14	RM	GS	43 CDO FPGRM	HELENSBURGH
Sanocki, Anna M	Lt RN	01-Apr-10	WAR	HM	FLEET HM UNIT	PLYMOUTH
Sansford, Adrian J	Cdr	30-Jun-07	ENG	MESM	DES COMFLEET	ABBEY WOOD
Santrian, Karl	Lt Cdr	01-Oct-05	WAR	AV	RNLA	BRNC DARTMOUTH
Santrian, Mark	Lt RN	21-Feb-09	WAR	AV	CHFHQ	RNAS YEOVILTON
Santrian, Tracey M	Lt RN	26-Oct-09	LOGS	L FS	HMS RALEIGH	TORPOINT
Santry, Paul M	Lt Cdr	01-Oct-07	WAR	C	FLEET CAP IS	PORTSMOUTH
Sargent, David S	Surg Lt Cdr	06-Aug-08	MED	GMP	NCHQ	PORTSMOUTH
Sargent, Lindsay M	Lt Cdr	01-Oct-04	ENG	TM	AIR 22GP	RAF HIGH WYCOMBE
Sargent, Nicholas	Cdr	30-Jun-14	ENG	AE	MAA	ABBEY WOOD
Satterly, Robert J	Lt Cdr	01-Oct-10	ENG	ME	HMS IRON DUKE	
Satterthwaite, Benjamin J	Lt Cdr	01-Oct-06	WAR	INT	DI - FC(A)	LONDON
Saunders, Alexander J	SLt	01-Sep-14	WAR	GSX	MCM2	PORTSMOUTH
Saunders, Alexander M	SLt	01-Sep-13	MED	Medical	BLAKE	BRNC DARTMOUTH
Saunders, Christopher E M MBE	Cdr	30-Jun-12	WAR	PWO(C)	MOD NSD - HDS	LONDON
Saunders, Harry	Mid	17-Nov-14	WAR	P UT	BRNC	BRNC DARTMOUTH
Saunders, Jason	Lt Cdr	01-Oct-06	ENG	TM	HQ DISC	CHICKSANDS
Savage, Alexander F	Lt Cdr	01-Oct-12	LOGS	L	HMS DARING	
Savage, Dominic N	Lt RN	01-Nov-13	WAR	P SK4	845 SQN	RNAS YEOVILTON
Savage, Mark R OBE	Cdr	30-Jun-07	WAR	MCD	FLEET CAP MARCAP	PORTSMOUTH
Saveal, Matthew P	Lt RN	11-Oct-13	MED	MS	DPHC SCOTLAND & NI	HMNB CLYDE
Savery, Stuart L	Lt RN	01-Sep-11	ENG	MESM	HMS VIGILANT	
Savin, David	SLt	01-Sep-12	ENG	WE	HMS OCEAN	
Saw, Stephen	Lt RN	11-Apr-08	ENG	ME	RN EXCHANGE N ZLAND	NEW ZEALAND
Saward, Justin R E	Lt Cdr	01-Oct-06	ENG	AE	DEFENCE ACADEMY	SOUTHAMPTON
Sawers, John R	Lt RN	09-Apr-13	ENG	WESM	MTM DRAKE	HMS DRAKE
Sawyer, Jason L	Lt RN	20-Feb-08	WAR	O SK6	771 SQN	RNAS CULDROSE
Sawyer, Richard C	Lt RN	01-Mar-11	WAR	INT	FLEET COMOPS NWD	HMS COLLINGWOOD
Sawyer, Trevor J	Lt Col	27-Feb-01	RM	GS	FLEET CAP LLM & DRM	PORTSMOUTH
Sawyers, Daniel C	Capt	01-Sep-09	RM	GS	DIRECTOR (JW)	NORTHWOOD
Say, Russell G	Lt RN	01-Jan-04	ENG	WE	MWS COLLINGWOOD	HMS COLLINGWOOD
Sayer, Jamie M	Lt Cdr	01-Oct-05	ENG	AE	DES COMLAND	ABBEY WOOD
Sayer, Russell J E	Maj	01-Oct-13	RM	GS	MSSG ENDURING OP	LUDGERSHALL
Sayer, Timothy J	Capt	01-Mar-14	RM	GS	UK MCC	BAHRAIN
Saywell-Hall, Stephen E	Lt Cdr	01-Oct-06	ENG	AE	FOSNI - CNR	PORTSMOUTH
Scales, Dean R	Lt Cdr	01-Oct-14	WAR	PWO	COMUKAMPHIBFOR	PORTSMOUTH
Scamp, Simon J	Lt RN	01-Oct-10	WAR	FC	HMS DUNCAN	
Scandling, Rachel J	Cdr	30-Jun-11	LOGS	L	JFC HQ	NORTHWOOD
Scanlon, Michael J	Maj	01-Oct-07	RM	GS	CTCRM	EXMOUTH
Scarlett, Christopher J	Lt RN	01-Jan-04	ENG	WESM(SWS)	NBC CLYDE	HMNB CLYDE

Name	Substantive Rank	Seniority	Branch	Specialisation	Organisation Name	Location Name
Schnadhorst, James C	Lt Cdr	01-May-95	WAR	PWO(U)	NATO ACO	NORTHWOOD
Schneider, William	Mid	17-Nov-14	WAR	SM(X)	BRNC	BRNC DARTMOUTH
Schnetler, Simon F	Lt RN	01-Oct-10	WAR	O SKW	857 NAS	RNAS CULDROSE
Schofield, Susan R	Surg Cdr	30-Mar-09	MED	GMP	DPHC SW	HMS DRAKE
Scopes, David	Cdr	30-Jun-12	ENG	AE	DES COMAIR	ARLINGTON USA
Scorer, Thomas G	Surg Lt Cdr	01-Aug-12	MED	Path - Haem	MTM INM ALVERSTOKE	GOSPORT
Scott, Alexander J	Lt Cdr	01-Oct-14	WAR	MCD	MTM MWS COLLINGWOOD	HMS COLLINGWOOD
Scott, Alexandra	Surg Lt Cdr	01-Aug-13	MED	GMP	MTM INM ALVERSTOKE	GOSPORT
Scott, Andrew R D	Lt RN	01-Sep-09	ENG	WE	NCHQ CNPS	PORTSMOUTH
Scott, Elizabeth K	Lt RN	01-Jul-02	ENG	TM	MTM NELSON	HMS NELSON
Scott, James B	Cdr	30-Jun-06	ENG	MESM	DES COMFLEET	ABBEY WOOD
Scott, Jason	Lt RN	08-Jul-11	WAR	ATC	RNAS YEOVILTON	YEOVILTON
Scott, Julian V	Lt Cdr	01-Oct-11	WAR	INT	NCHQ CNPERS	PORTSMOUTH
Scott, Mark R	Cdr	30-Jun-14	WAR	P LYNX	HQ AIR - COS(TRG) - DFT	ABBEY WOOD
Scott, Neil	Lt Cdr	01-Oct-10	WAR	HM	FLEET CAP IS	PORTSMOUTH
Scott, Nigel L J	Capt RN	10-Jan-12	ENG	WESM(TWS)	HDCHG/MSSS	CORSHAM
Scott, Peter D	Lt RN	01-Feb 07	WAR	ATC	RNAS YEOVILTON	YEOVILTON
Scott, Peter J D S OBE	RN Chpln	03-Sep-91	Ch S	Chaplain	HMS DRAKE	PLYMOUTH
Scott, Richard A	Lt Cdr	01-Aug-06	ENG	WE	RNEAWC - SNO	LINCOLN
Scott, Robert J	Lt Cdr	02-Mar-98	WAR	O LYNX	FLEET CSAV	PORTSMOUTH
Scott, Russell B	Lt Cdr	01-Oct-13	ENG	ME	NAVY MCTA	PORTSMOUTH
Scott, Serena C S	Lt RN	01-May-06	ENG	TM	MTM DEFAC JSCSC	SHRIVENHAM
Scott, Simon J OBE	Col	14-Oct-13	RM	LC	FMC JOINT	LONDON
Scott, Thomas	Maj	01-Oct-13	RM	HW(M)	NCHQ CNPERS	PORTSMOUTH
Scott, Thomas L	Capt	01-Sep-13	RM	GS	CTCRM	EXMOUTH
Scott, Timothy E	Surg Cdr	01-Jul-13	MED	Anaes	RCDM	OXFORD
Scott, Victoria	Lt RN	01-Aug-06	QARNNS	OT (C&S)	NCHQ MEDDIV	PORTSMOUTH
Scown, William O	Lt RN	01-Mar-10	WAR	ATC	FOST DPORT	PLYMOUTH
Scraggs, Daniel R	SLt	01-Sep-13	WAR	SM(X)	HMS VIGILANT	
Screaton, Richard M	Cdr	30-Jun-14	ENG	ME	DCMC	LONDON
Screen, James W	Lt Cdr	01-Oct-11	ENG	WE	HMS QUEEN ELIZABETH	
Scutt, Martin J	Surg Lt Cdr	04-Feb-09	MED	GMP	HMS PROTECTOR	
Seabrook, Peter J	Lt RN	01-Nov-13	WAR	SM(X)	FLEET COMOPS NWD	NORTHWOOD
Seager, Daniel	Lt RN	01-Sep-08	ENG	MESM	MTM DEFAC JSCSC	SHRIVENHAM
Seagrave, Suzanna J	Lt Cdr	01-Nov-08	ENG	ME	RN EXCHANGE CANADA	OTTAWA
Seal, Martin R	Lt Cdr	01-Oct-14	WAR	MCD	FDU	PORTSMOUTH
Seal, Michael O	Lt Cdr	01-Oct-13	WAR	PWO(SM)	HMS TORBAY	
Seaman, Alec L	Lt RN	10-Feb-08	LOGS	L	FOSNI - NRC EE	LONDON
Seaman, Gregg P	Lt RN	01-Sep-09	ENG	WE	MTM DEFAC CMT MSC	SHRIVENHAM
Seaman, Joshua J	Mid	01-May-14	WAR	SM(X)	BRNC	BRNC DARTMOUTH
Seaney, Adam D	Lt	13-Jan-14	RM	SCC	CTCRM	EXMOUTH
Sear, Jonathan J	Lt Col	30-Jun-07	RM	GS	FLEET COMOPS NWD	NORTHWOOD
Searight, Mark F C	Maj	01-May-97	RM	GS	6 OPS SQN	PLYMOUTH
Searight, William M C	Capt	01-Sep-10	RM	GS	PJHQ (UK)	NORTHWOOD
Searle, Andrew J A	Lt Cdr	01-Oct-13	ENG	WE	DI - CA	LONDON
Seaton, Samuel	Lt RN	01-Mar-13	ENG	AE	MTM 814 SQN CULDROSE	RNAS CULDROSE
Seddon, Jonathan D	Lt RN	01-Apr-06	WAR	FC	HMS DEFENDER	
Sedgeworth, Alasdair L	Mid	01-Feb-14	WAR	P UT	BRNC	BRNC DARTMOUTH
Sedgwick, Hugo MBE	Lt Cdr	01-Oct-14	WAR	INT	FLEET COMOPS NWD	NORTHWOOD
Selden, John D A	Lt RN	01-Nov-03	ENG	IS(SM)	FLEET CAP SSM	PORTSMOUTH
Sellars, Scott J	Cdr	30-Jun-12	LOGS	L CMA	HMS BULWARK	
Sellen, Thomas J	SLt	01-Jul-14	WAR	SM(X)	HMS MERSEY	
Sellers, Graham	Lt Cdr	01-Feb-01	ENG	WE	LSP OMAN	MUSCAT
Selway, Mark A	Cdr	30-Jun-14	ENG	AE	DES COMJE	YEOVIL
Selwood, Benjamin J	SLt	01-Jan-13	WAR	O UT	MTM 849 SQN CULDROSE	RNAS CULDROSE
Selwood, Peter J	Lt Cdr	01-Oct-08	QARNNS	Tutor	MTM DEFAC JSCSC	SHRIVENHAM
Semple, Brian	Lt Cdr	01-Oct-10	WAR	P FW	FLEET CSAV	WASHINGTON
Senior, Gareth F	Mid	08-Sep-14	ENG	ME	BRNC	BRNC DARTMOUTH
Sercombe, Benjamin	Capt	16-Apr-10	RM	SCC	COMUKAMPHIBFOR	PORTSMOUTH
Sercombe, Daniel	Lt RN	01-May-11	ENG	ME	HMS MONTROSE	
Sergeant, Adam H	Surg Lt RN	06-Aug-14	MED	Medical	BLAKE	BRNC DARTMOUTH
Sewed, Michael A	Lt Cdr	01-Oct-94	WAR	O WILDCAT	WMF SIM	RNAS YEOVILTON

Name	Substantive Rank	Seniority	Branch	Specialisation	Organisation Name	Location Name
Sewell, Lynsey E	Lt RN	01-Jan-11	WAR	GSX	RN EXCHANGE USA	WASHINGTON
Seymour, Kevin W	Capt RN	02-Sep-13	WAR	P FW	BDS	WASHINGTON
Shackleton, Scott	RN Chpln	20-Sep-94	Ch S	Chaplain	CTCRM	EXMOUTH
Shakespeare, Christopher A	Lt Cdr	01-Oct-14	ENG	AE	DES COMJE	YEOVIL
Shallcroft, John E	Lt Cdr	01-Oct-98	WAR	P FW	750 SQN	RNAS CULDROSE
Shanahan, Lloyd A	Lt Cdr	01-Oct-12	WAR	P SK4	GANNET SAR FLT	HMS GANNET
Sharkey, Elton R	Cdr	30-Jun-12	ENG	MESM	DES COMFLEET	ABBEY WOOD
Sharkey, Michael	RN Chpln	01-Oct-90	Ch S	Chaplain	40 CDO RM	TAUNTON
Sharkey, Philip J	Lt Cdr	01-Oct-13	ENG	ME	HMS DIAMOND	
Sharland, Craig J	Lt RN	20-Oct-08	ENG	WE	DES COMFLEET	ABBEY WOOD
Sharland, Simon P	Maj	01-Sep-90	RM	LC	NCHQ CNPS	PORTSMOUTH
Sharman, Max C	Maj	01-Oct-14	RM	GS	43 CDO FPGRM	HELENSBURGH
Sharp, Andrew P MBE	Lt Cdr	01-Oct-11	ENG	MESM	NCHQ CNPS	PORTSMOUTH
Sharp, Christopher A	Lt RN	01-Feb-09	WAR	GSX	MTM MWS COLLINGWOOD	HMS COLLINGWOOD
Sharp, Thomas W	SLt	01-Sep-12	WAR	P UT	RAF LINTON-ON-OUSE	RAF LINTON ON OUSE
Sharp, William M J	Surg Lt Cdr	05-Aug-14	MED	GMP	MTM INM ALVERSTOKE	GOSPORT
Sharpe, Benjamin J D	Surg Lt RN	06-Aug-14	MED	Medical	BLAKE	BRNC DARTMOUTH
Sharpe, Marcus R	Maj	01-Oct-09	RM	SCC	ACDS	LONDON
Sharpe, Thomas G OBE	Cdr	30-Jun-09	WAR	PWO(A)	PJHQ (UK)	NORTHWOOD
Sharples, Joseph H	Lt RN	01-Nov-05	WAR	P LYNX	HMS TEMERAIRE	PORTSMOUTH
Sharpley, John G	Surg Capt RN	01-Jul-10	MED	Psych	DPHC SOUTH - DCMH	HMS EXCELLENT
Sharrott, Christopher	Lt RN	01-Sep-03	WAR	P LYNX	MTM SHAWBURY	RAF SHAWBURY
Shattock, James D	Lt RN	01-Nov-07	WAR	P SK4	AACEN	STOCKBRIDGE
Shaughnessy, Sophie L	Cdr	30-Jun-12	ENG	ME	HMS SULTAN	GOSPORT
Shaughnessy, Toby E	Lt Cdr	01-Oct-05	WAR	AAWO	MTM DEFAC JSCSC	SHRIVENHAM
Shaves, Thomas D L	Lt Cdr	01-Oct-14	LOGS	L	MTM NORTHWOOD HQ	NORTHWOOD
Shaw, Callam R	Lt Cdr	01-Oct-14	ENG	MESM	HMS VANGUARD	
Shaw, Christopher	Lt RN	16-Dec-11	ENG	WE	MWS EXCELLENT	HMS EXCELLENT
Shaw, Hannah K	Lt Cdr	01-Oct-14	LOGS	L	MTM NORTHWOOD HQ	NORTHWOOD
Shaw, Kevin	Capt RN	01-Jul-13	ENG	WE	JFIG	RAF WYTON
Shaw, Mark A	Lt Cdr	01-Oct-13	WAR	MCD	DSEA MARITIME	PORTSMOUTH
Shaw, Mathew J C	Lt RN	17-Dec-10	WAR	HM	MTM MWS HMTG (D)	HMS DRAKE
Shaw, Matthew B	Capt	01-Sep-10	RM	GS	RMR BRISTOL	BRISTOL
Shaw, Ramsay	Lt RN	20-Oct-08	ENG	WESM(TWS)	DES COMFLEET	ABBEY WOOD
Shaw, Simon J	Lt RN	01-Nov-05	WAR	GSX	MTM MWS COLLINGWOOD	HMS COLLINGWOOD
Shaw, Steven M	Cdr	30-Jun-01	LOGS	L	NCHQ CNPS	PORTSMOUTH
Shaw, Stewart	Lt RN	01-Jul-05	WAR	P MER	829 SQN	RNAS CULDROSE
Shawcross, Paul K OBE	Capt RN	01-May-10	WAR	P SK4	DES COMAIR	ABBEY WOOD
Shearn, Matthew A	Lt RN	01-Apr-00	WAR	HM(AM)	FLEET COMOPS NWD	NORTHWOOD
Shears, Alexandra F	Lt Cdr	01-Oct-11	LOGS	L BAR	HMS WESTMINSTER	
Shears, Gary R	Lt RN	01-Sep-03	WAR	ATC	RNAS YEOVILTON	YEOVILTON
Sheehan, Thomas J	Lt RN	01-Oct-04	ENG	WESM(TWS)	NC REQUIREMENTS MANAGERS	ABBEY WOOD
Shelton, James R	Capt	01-Sep-08	RM	GS	45 CDO RM	DUNDEE
Shenton, Calvin L	Lt RN	13-Apr-11	LOGS	L	HMS WESTMINSTER	
Shenton-Brown, William F	Mid	08-Sep-14	ENG	AE	BRNC	BRNC DARTMOUTH
Shephard, Samuel J GC	Capt	01-Sep-13	RM	GS	40 CDO RM	TAUNTON
Shepherd, Anya C	Lt RN	01-Dec-02	WAR	PWO(C)	UKMARBATSTAFF	PORTSMOUTH
Shepherd, Charles S	Cdr	30-Jun-07	WAR	SM(CQ)	FLEET MARITIME WARFARE	HMS COLLINGWOOD
Shepherd, Christopher E	Lt Cdr	01-Oct-12	ENG	WESM(TWS)	HMS TALENT	
Shepherd, Daniel T	Lt RN	07-May-13	WAR	HM	MTM MWS HMTG (D)	HMS DRAKE
Shepherd, Fiona N	Lt Cdr	30-Jun-12	LOGS	L	FLEET SPT LOGS INFRA	PORTSMOUTH
Shepherd, Louise C	Lt RN	01-Sep-13	WAR	GSX	MCM1	FASLANE
Shepherd, Martin P	Cdr	30-Jun-13	WAR	P SK6	DCDC	SHRIVENHAM
Shepherd, Oliver J	Lt RN	01-Sep-09	WAR	MCD	NDG	HELENSBURGH
Shepley, Benjamin J	Lt RN	01-Jan-13	WAR	GSX	HMS DARING	
Sherriff, David A	Cdr	30-Jun-03	WAR	P LYNX	RN EXCHANGE USA	WASHINGTON
Sherriff, Jacqueline MBE	Cdr	30-Jun-14	WAR	MEDIA OPS	EU OHQ	NORTHWOOD
Sherwin, Antony J	Lt RN	01-Jan-05	WAR	O MER	MTM RAF CRANWELL	RAFC CRANWELL
Sherwood, Gideon A F	Lt Cdr	01-Oct-09	WAR	AAWO	HMS DARING	
Shield, Simon J	Cdr	31-Dec-98	WAR	SM(CQ)	FLEET CAP SSM	PORTSMOUTH
Shine, David J	Lt RN	01-Sep-10	LOGS	L	1 ASSLT GP RM	PLYMOUTH
Shipperley, Ian	Cdre	28-Aug-12	ENG	ME	FLEET CAP SSM	PORTSMOUTH

Name	Substantive Rank	Seniority	Branch	Specialisation	Organisation Name	Location Name
Shirley, Benjamin	Lt RN	01-Sep-08	ENG	WE	HDPROG	CORSHAM
Shirley, Christopher I	Capt	01-Sep-11	RM	GS	RMR LONDON	LONDON
Shirtcliff, Justin D J	Mid	17-Nov-14	WAR	GSX	BRNC	BRNC DARTMOUTH
Shirvill, Matthew J	Lt Cdr	01-Oct-14	ENG	ME	FLEET CAP SSM	PORTSMOUTH
Shirvill, Victoria L	Lt Cdr	01-Oct-13	ENG	AE	FLEET CSAV	PORTSMOUTH
Shomuyiwa, Theodore A	Mid	01-May-14	WAR	GSX	BRNC	BRNC DARTMOUTH
Short, John J	Cdr	30-Jun-05	ENG	ME	LSP OMAN	MUSCAT
Shortland, Karen	Lt RN	01-Jan-04	LOGS	L	FLEET SPT LOGS INFRA	PORTSMOUTH
Shortt, Martin	Lt RN	01-Sep-12	ENG	TM	RMB CHIVENOR	BARNSTAPLE
Shouler, Martin	Lt RN	15-Nov-02	WAR	MW (RES)	UK MCC	BAHRAIN
Shrestha, Shekhar	Lt Cdr	01-Oct-13	ENG	ME	HMS SOMERSET	
Shrives, James M	SLt	01-Feb-12	WAR	P UT	MTM RAF CRANWELL	RAFC CRANWELL
Shropshall, Helen L	Lt RN	01-Sep-02	ENG	TM	DES COMFLEET	ABBEY WOOD
Shropshall, Ian	Lt RN	01-Sep-03	WAR	PWO(SM)	HMS VIGILANT	
Shutt, David	SLt	01-Nov-14	WAR	GSX	MWS COLLINGWOOD	HMS COLLINGWOOD
Shuttleworth, Andrew	Maj	01-Oct-13	RM	SCC	30 CDO IX GP RM	PLYMOUTH
Silcock, James S M	Mid	17-Nov-14	WAR	GSX	BRNC	BRNC DARTMOUTH
Simmonds, Daniel D H	Lt Cdr	01-Oct-10	WAR	SM(CQ)	FLEET COMOPS NWD	NORTHWOOD
Simmonds, Zoe N	Lt RN	01-Nov-13	LOGS	L	COMFASFLOT	HELENSBURGH
Simmonite, Gavin I DFC	Cdr	30-Jun-14	WAR	P SK4	845 SQN	RNAS YEOVILTON
Simmons, Nigel D	Cdr	30-Jun-99	ENG	WESM(TWS)	DES DTECH	ABBEY WOOD
Simmons, Paul C	Capt	01-Sep-12	RM	GS	43 CDO FPGRM	HELENSBURGH
Simmons, Robert L	Maj	01-Oct-09	RM	LC	ACDS	LONDON
Simmons, Sarah	Lt RN	01-Sep-10	ENG	AE	HMS QUEEN ELIZABETH	
Simpson, Brett R	Lt RN	31-Jul-09	LOGS	L	HQ JHC COMD JHC	ANDOVER
Simpson, Christopher J	Lt RN	01-Jan-04	WAR	P MER	DEF HELI FLYING SCH	SHREWSBURY
Simpson, Colin C	Lt Cdr	01-Oct-04	WAR	P WILDCAT	WMF SIM	RNAS YEOVILTON
Simpson, Daley G	Lt RN	01-Sep-10	WAR	P UT	MTM DRAKE	HMS DRAKE
Simpson, Daniel J R	Lt RN	01-Oct-11	WAR	GSX	MTM YEOVILTON FCC	RNAS YEOVILTON
Simpson, David J	RN Chpln	07-Mar-05	Ch S	Chaplain	COMPORFLOT	PORTSMOUTH
Simpson, Erin L	Lt RN	15-Mar-06	ENG	WE	MCSU	FLEET HQ
Simpson, Ewan	Mid	01-May-14	WAR	GSX	BRNC	BRNC DARTMOUTH
Simpson, John N	Lt Cdr	01-Oct-13	MED	MS	HQ 2 MED BDE	YORK
Simpson, Jolyon E R	Capt	01-Sep-09	RM	GS	HQ 3 CDO BDE RM	PLYMOUTH
Simpson, Paul G	Lt RN	09-Apr-09	ENG	MESM	FOST SM SEA	HMNB CLYDE
Simpson, Paul N	Capt	20-Jul-07	RM	GS	NCHQ	PORTSMOUTH
Simpson, Scott F	Lt Cdr	01-Oct-10	WAR	O LYNX	LHF 815 SQN HQ	RNAS YEOVILTON
Simpson, William J S	Cdr	30-Jun-14	ENG	MESM	FOST SM SEA	HMNB CLYDE
Sims, Alexander R	Lt Cdr	01-Oct-12	WAR	O LYNX	FLEET MARITIME WARFARE	HMS COLLINGWOOD
Sims, Deborah L	Lt Cdr	02-Nov-13	WAR	FC (RES)	RNAS YEOVILTON	YEOVILTON
Sinclair, Gregory W	Lt RN	15-Aug-14	ENG	WE	HMS DUNCAN	
Sindall, Steven D	Capt	21-Mar-13	RM	GS	NCHQ	PORTSMOUTH
Singleton, Rachel M MBE	Lt Cdr	01-Oct-09	ENG	IS	HMS DIAMOND	
Sitton, John B	Lt Cdr	01-Oct-05	ENG	MESM	DES COMFLEET	ABBEY WOOD
Skeer, Martyn	Cdr	30-Jun-02	WAR	P SK6	DEFENCE ACADEMY	SHRIVENHAM
Skelding, Joshua J	Lt RN	01-Apr-12	WAR	INT	15 POG	SHEFFORD
Skelley, Alasdair N M	Lt Cdr	01-Mar-03	WAR	PWO(U)	AML OP SHADER	NORTHWOOD
Skelley, Julie C	Surg Cdr (D)	30-Jun-05	DENTAL	GDP	DEFENCE DENTAL SERVS	PORTSMOUTH
Skelley, Roger	Lt RN	01-Feb-08	WAR	GSX	HMS DASHER	
Skelton, Richard S	Lt RN	01-Nov-07	WAR	GSX	HMS TYNE	
Skidmore, Christopher M OBE	Capt RN	30-Jun-07	LOGS	L SM	NCHQ CNPS	LONDON
Skinner, Amy L	Lt RN	01-Feb-07	WAR	GSX	OCLC BIRMINGHAM	BIRMINGHAM
Skinner, Jennifer E	Lt RN	13-Oct-12	LOGS	L	HMS KENT	
Skinner, Jonathan J	Lt RN	01-May-06	WAR	MW	HMS COLLINGWOOD	FAREHAM
Skinner, Neil D	Lt RN	01-May-07	WAR	GSX	RNAS YEOVILTON	YEOVILTON
Skirton, Daniel G	Lt RN	01-Apr-12	ENG	WESM(TWS)	FLEET CAP SSM	PORTSMOUTH
Skittrall, Steven	Cdr	30-Jun-14	ENG	AE O	FLEET CSAV	PORTSMOUTH
Skorko, Konrad	Surg Lt RN (D)	20-Jul-11	DENTAL	GDP	40 CDO RM	TAUNTON
Skuse, Matthew	Lt Col	30-Jun-09	RM	MLDR	SERV ATTACHE/ADVISER	OSLO
Slack, Jeremy M	Maj	01-May-97	RM	LC	RN EXCHANGE NETHERLANDS	DEN HELDER
Slater, Benjamin	SLt	01-Sep-12	ENG	WE	MWS COLLINGWOOD	HMS COLLINGWOOD

Name	Substantive Rank	Seniority	Branch	Specialisation	Organisation Name	Location Name
Slater, Sir Jock (John Cunningham Kirkwood)	Adm	29-Jan-91				
GCB LVO DL						
Slater, Louis G	Capt	01-Sep-12	RM	GS	45 CDO RM	DUNDEE
Slater, Ryan A	Mid	01-May-14	WAR	GSX	BRNC	BRNC DARTMOUTH
Slater, William G	SLt	01-Nov-14	ENG	WESM	MWS COLLINGWOOD	HMS COLLINGWOOD
Slattery, Damian J	Lt Cdr	01-Oct-09	WAR	MCD	COMPORFLOT	PORTSMOUTH
Slavin, Max	Surg SLt	29-Jul-14	MED	Medical	BLAKE	BRNC DARTMOUTH
Slayman, Emily	Lt RN	01-Sep-06	LOGS	L	COMUKTG	PLYMOUTH
Sleight, Thomas M	Lt RN	01-Sep-13	WAR	GSX	MCM2	PORTSMOUTH
Slight, Oliver W L	Lt Cdr	01-Oct-13	WAR	PWO	NCHQ CNPERS	PORTSMOUTH
Sloan, Ian A	Lt Cdr	01-Oct-14	WAR	P FW	EMBED FRANCE (FW)	TOULON
Sloan-Murphy, Christian J	Lt Cdr	01-Oct-12	ENG	AE	HQ AIR HQ 1GP LHQ	ABBEY WOOD
Slocombe, Nicholas R	Cdr	30-Jun-11	WAR	ATC	MAA	ABBEY WOOD
Sloper, Max D	Lt RN	01-Apr-14	WAR	P	MTM 820 SQN CULDROSE	RNAS CULDROSE
Slowther, Stuart J	Lt Cdr	01-Oct-08	ENG	WE	FLEET CAP SSM	PORTSMOUTH
Small, Richard	Cdr	30-Jun-09	WAR	SM(CQ)	FLEET COMOPS NWD	NORTHWOOD
Smallbone, Dane	Mid	08-Sep-14	ENG	WE	BRNC	BRNC DARTMOUTH
Smalley, Paul J	Lt RN	01-Jan-08	WAR	P SK4	771 SQN	RNAS CULDROSE
Smallwood, Rachel J MBE	Lt Cdr	01-Oct-10	ENG	TM	NETS (E)	PORTSMOUTH
Smart, Andrew D	Mid	01-May-14	WAR	GSX	BRNC	BRNC DARTMOUTH
Smart, Tyler M	Lt RN	01-Jan-15	WAR	GSX	MCM1	FASLANE
Smedley, Rachel	Lt Cdr	01-Oct-13	LOGS	L	HMS PORTLAND	
Smees, James E	SLt	01-Sep-14	ENG	AE	DCEME SULTAN	HMS SULTAN
Smiles, Simon A	Mid	08-Sep-14	WAR	SM(X)	BRNC	BRNC DARTMOUTH
Smillie, Eleanor J	Lt RN	01-Oct-10	ENG	TM	NETS (OPS)	PORTSMOUTH
Smit, Nathan J	SLt	01-Nov-14	LOGS	L	HMS IRON DUKE	
Smith, Adrian G	Lt Cdr	01-Feb-99	ENG	WE	DES COMFLEET	ABBEY WOOD
Smith, Andrew J E	Lt Cdr	01-Oct-08	WAR	PWO	MCM2	PORTSMOUTH
Smith, Ashley	Lt RN	01-Sep-08	WAR	O MER	RNAS CULDROSE	HELSTON
Smith, Austin B D	Cdr	30-Jun-09	WAR	P SK4	SERV ATTACHE/ADVISER	MUSCAT
Smith, Barry J	Lt RN	31-Jul-09	WAR	AV	FLEET AV PHOT	PORTSMOUTH
Smith, Benjamin	Lt Cdr	01-Oct-12	WAR	PWO(SM)	HMS VANGUARD	
Smith, Benjamin J	SLt	01-Nov-11	WAR	GSX	HMS KENT	
Smith, Brian J	Lt Cdr	01-Dec-99	WAR	AAWO	FLEET CAP SSM	PORTSMOUTH
Smith, Brian S	Surg Cdr (D)	30-Jun-01	DENTAL	GDP(C&S)	FLEET DENPOL	HMS EXCELLENT
Smith, Charles J	Lt Cdr	01-Oct-09	WAR	C	HMS DALRIADA	GLASGOW
Smith, Christian G	SLt	08-Dec-12	WAR	O UT	MTM LHF 702 SQN YEOVILTON	RNAS YEOVILTON
Smith, Christopher A	Capt	01-Sep-10	RM	GS	NCHQ	
Smith, Christopher J	Cdr	30-Jun-06	LOGS	L (RES)	FOSNI - NRC	HELENSBURGH
Smith, Christopher J H	Lt Cdr	01-Oct-04	ENG	WE	DES DTECH	WASHINGTON
Smith, Craig A	Lt RN	01-Feb-06	ENG	WE	NAVY MCTA	PORTSMOUTH
Smith, Dale A	Lt RN	01-Mar-09	ENG	MESM	COMFASFLOT	HELENSBURGH
Smith, David J	Lt Cdr	01-Oct-14	WAR	PWO(SM)	HMS AMBUSH	
Smith, David L	Lt Cdr	01-Oct-04	WAR	AAWO	NC REQUIREMENTS MANAGERS	ABBEY WOOD
Smith, Edwin J	Lt RN	01-Feb-09	WAR	GSX	MWS COLLINGWOOD	HMS COLLINGWOOD
Smith, Gary J	Lt RN	17-Dec-10	LOGS	L	JFSp ME	UAE - JOA - MINHAD
Smith, Graeme D J	Lt Cdr	01-Jan-01	WAR	PWO(C)	FLEET MARITIME WARFARE	HMS COLLINGWOOD
Smith, Gregory C S	Cdr	30-Jun-08	WAR	O SKW	AWC	BOSCOMBE DOWN
Smith, Gregory K	Capt RN	12-May-14	ENG	IS	SVCOPS/DHDOPS/COR	CORSHAM
Smith, James A	Lt RN	01-Jan-08	WAR	FC	HMS BITER	
Smith, James E	Capt	01-Sep-11	RM	GS	RMAS SANDHURST GP	CAMBERLEY
Smith, Jason E	Surg Cdr	30-Jun-05	MED	EM	DMS WHITTINGTON	BIRMINGHAM
Smith, Jason J	Surg Cdr	01-Jul-14	MED	BPS	PCRF	RFA ARGUS
Smith, Jason P	Lt RN	08-Feb-13	ENG	MESM	HMS TRENCHANT	
Smith, Jeff R	Lt RN	01-Jan-15	WAR	P UT	MTM WMO YEOVILTON	RAF LINTON ON OUSE
Smith, Jennifer	Lt RN	01-Apr-11	WAR	HM	MTM DRAKE	HMS DRAKE
Smith, Jennifer C	Lt RN	01-Jan-07	WAR	GSX	FLEET COMOPS NWD	NORTHWOOD
Smith, Karly J	Lt RN	15-May-06	WAR	ATC	RNAS CULDROSE	HELSTON
Smith, Keven J	Lt Cdr	01-Oct-95	WAR	P SK4	845 SQN	RNAS YEOVILTON
Smith, Kim G	Lt RN	01-Sep-12	WAR	SM(X)	MTM RALEIGH	HMS RALEIGH
Smith, Kristian G	Lt RN	30-Jul-10	ENG	WESM(SWS)	FOST FAS SHORE	HMNB CLYDE
Smith, Laurence M	Lt RN	01-Sep-09	WAR	P MER	814 SQN	RNAS CULDROSE

Name	Substantive Rank	Seniority	Branch	Specialisation	Organisation Name	Location Name
Smith, Mark M	Cdr	30-Jun-08	ENG	AE	DES COMJE	YEOVIL
Smith, Mark P	Cdr	26-Mar-12	MED	MS(CDO)	MTM FLEET HQ	PORTSMOUTH
Smith, Martin L MBE	Maj Gen	13-Jun-14	RM	GS	COMUKAMPHIBFOR	PORTSMOUTH
Smith, Martin R K	Cdr	30-Jun-03	WAR	METOC	FLEET COMOPS NWD	NORTHWOOD
Smith, Matthew D	Lt Cdr	01-Oct-13	LOGS	L SM	HMS RICHMOND	
Smith, Matthew J	Mid	08-Sep-14	ENG	WE	BRNC	BRNC DARTMOUTH
Smith, Matthew J P	SLt	01-Mar-14	WAR	GSX	HMS SEVERN	
Smith, Matthew R T	Lt RN	01-Oct-05	WAR	INT	FLEET CAP IS	PORTSMOUTH
Smith, Michael D	Cdr	30-Jun-10	WAR	O LYNX	BDS	WASHINGTON
Smith, Michael J	Lt Cdr	01-May-04	ENG	WESM(SWS)	NCHQ CNPS	PORTSMOUTH
Smith, Nicholas	Lt RN	01-Oct-08	WAR	P FW	FLEET CSAV	WASHINGTON
Smith, Oliver H	Lt RN	01-Sep-12	ENG	MESM	HMS TORBAY	
Smith, Owen J	Lt Cdr	01-Oct-11	ENG	ME	COMPORFLOT	PORTSMOUTH
Smith, Richard J	Lt Cdr	01-Oct-14	LOGS	L	MTM NELSON	HMS NELSON
Smith, Richard W D	Lt RN	01-Jan-12	LOGS	L	NCHQ CNPERS	PORTSMOUTH
Smith, Robert C V	Cdr	30-Jun-10	WAR	O LYNX	MAA	ABBEY WOOD
Smith, Sam R	Mid	01-May-14	WAR	GSX	BRNC	BRNC DARTMOUTH
Smith, Scott A E	Lt RN	01-Jan-12	WAR	GSX	HMS DEFENDER	
Smith, Shelley A	Lt RN	30-Jul-10	LOGS	L	LHF 815 SQN HQ	RNAS YEOVILTON
Smith, Simon J F	Capt	01-Sep-13	RM	GS	CTCRM	EXMOUTH
Smith, Steven R C	Surg Cdr	30-Jun-03	MED	T&O	MDHU DERRIFORD	PLYMOUTH
Smith, Thomas	Lt RN	14-Aug-11	ENG	TM	RNCR BOVINGTON	WAREHAM
Smith, Trevor M MBE	Maj	01-Oct-14	RM	LC (SCC)	1 ASSLT GP RM	PLYMOUTH
Smith, William A	Surg Lt RN	06-Aug-14	MED	Medical	BLAKE	BRNC DARTMOUTH
Smith, William F	Lt RN	01-Feb-11	ENG	TM	42 CDO RM	PLYMOUTH
Smithson, James I	Lt RN	11-Dec-09	MED	MS	UKMARBATSTAFF	PORTSMOUTH
Smithson, Peter E	Capt RN	30-Jun-08	WAR	AE	MTM WMO YEOVILTON	RNAS YEOVILTON
Smye, Malcolm	Lt Cdr	01-Oct-12	ENG	AE	RN EXCHANGE FRANCE	PARIS
Smyth, Daniel	SLt	01-Sep-12	ENG	AE	DCEME SULTAN	HMS SULTAN
Smythe, Sean R	Lt RN	07-Nov-13	WAR	SM(X)	HMS VANGUARD	
Snazell, Matthew A	Lt RN	01-Jan-09	WAR	P MER	814 SQN	RNAS CULDROSE
Sneddon, Russell N	Lt Cdr	01-Oct-01	WAR	P SK6	RAF SHAWBURY	SHREWSBURY
Snelham, Jenny E	SLt	01-Jan-14	WAR	GSX	RNP SIB WESTERN	HMS DRAKE
Snell, Andrew J	Lt Cdr	01-Oct-10	ENG	ME	RN EXCHANGE CANADA	OTTAWA
Snell, Daley A	Lt RN	01-Oct-09	WAR	GSX	HMS EXPLOIT	
Snelling, Paul D	Cdr	30-Jun-12	ENG	MESM	CBRN POL	LONDON
Snook, Mathew	Capt	01-Sep-12	RM	GS	OCLC LONDON	LONDON
Snow, Alexander D	Mid	17-Nov-14	WAR	GSX	BRNC	BRNC DARTMOUTH
Sobers, Scott	Lt Cdr	01-Oct-12	ENG	MESM	HMS VANGUARD	
Soley, Darren S J	Mid	01-Feb-14	WAR	GSX	BRNC	BRNC DARTMOUTH
Sollitt, Victoria A	Lt Cdr	01-Oct-08	LOGS	L	DES COMLAND	ABBEY WOOD
Solly, Matthew M	Cdr	30-Jun-12	ENG	TM(SM)	FLEET FOST ACOS(Trg)	ABBEY WOOD
Soukup, Sebastian A S	Lt	02-Sep-14	RM	GS	43 CDO FPGRM	HELENSBURGH
Soul, Nicholas J	Cdr	30-Jun-14	WAR	P SK4	HQ JHC CAP DIR	ANDOVER
Souter, Alasdair J	Lt RN	01-Sep-14	WAR	SM(X)	MTM NELSON	HMS NELSON
South, David J	Lt Cdr	15-Jun-97	WAR	AAWO	NC REQUIREMENTS MANAGERS	ABBEY WOOD
South, Jack W	Lt	27-Feb-14	RM	GS	43 CDO FPGRM	HELENSBURGH
Southall, Nicholas C J	Lt RN	01-Nov-07	WAR	FC	MTM MWS COLLINGWOOD	HMS COLLINGWOOD
Southorn, Bryony J	Surg Lt Cdr (D)	27-Jun-10	DENTAL	GDP	DEFENCE DENTAL SERVS	PORTSMOUTH
Southorn, Mark D	Cdr	30-Jun-08	WAR	PWO(U)	UKMARBATSTAFF	PORTSMOUTH
Southwood, Shaun C	Lt Cdr	01-Oct-10	ENG	MESM	HMS VENGEANCE	
Southworth, Christopher	Lt RN	01-Jan-06	WAR	P LYNX	LHF 815 SQN	RNAS YEOVILTON
Spacey, Craig D	Lt Cdr	01-Oct-13	ENG	MESM	HMS TRENCHANT	
Spackman, Lucy C	Lt RN	19-May-08	WAR	HM	FLEET HM UNIT	PLYMOUTH
Spalton, Gary	Cdr	11-Jun-93	WAR	PWO(U)	DEFENCE ACADEMY	SHRIVENHAM
Spanner, Paul	Maj	01-May-01	RM	GS	FLEET SPT LOGS INFRA	PORTSMOUTH
Sparkes, Peter J	Capt RN	08-Nov-10	WAR	PWO(C)	NCHQ CNPERS	PORTSMOUTH
Sparrow, Mark	Lt Cdr	01-Oct-09	WAR	P FW	MTM DEFAC JSCSC	SHRIVENHAM
Spear, Toby	SLt	01-Oct-13	ENG	TM	1 ASSLT GP RM	PLYMOUTH
Speck, Ryan C	Mid	08-Sep-14	ENG	ME	BRNC	BRNC DARTMOUTH
Spedding, Joseph J	Mid	01-May-14	WAR	GSX	BRNC	BRNC DARTMOUTH
Speedie, Alan	Maj	01-Oct-11	RM	GS	45 CDO RM	DUNDEE

Name	Substantive Rank	Seniority	Branch	Specialisation	Organisation Name	Location Name
Speller, Nicholas S F.	Lt Cdr	01-May-88	WAR	GSX	FLEET ACOS(RP)	PORTSMOUTH
Spence, Andrei B	Cdre	16-Apr-13	LOGS	L BAR	NCHQ - CNLS	PORTSMOUTH
Spence, Robert G	Lt Cdr	01-Oct-06	WAR	P SK4	847 SQN	RNAS YEOVILTON
Spencer, Ashley C	Lt Cdr	01-Oct-10	WAR	MCD	MCM1	HMS BLYTH
Spencer, Charles M	Capt	01-Sep-11	RM	GS	45 CDO RM	DUNDEE
Spencer, Richard A OBE	Brig	22-Jul-11	RM	C	NAVY ICP	PORTSMOUTH
Spencer, Steven J	Cdr	04-Aug-09	QARNNS	Nurse Officer	NCHQ MEDDIV	PORTSMOUTH
Spike, Adam J	Lt RN	01-May-02	WAR	P SK4	CHF - 846	RAF BENSON
Spillane, Paul W	Lt Cdr	01-Oct-06	WAR	O SKW	MASF	RNAS CULDROSE
Spiller, Stephen N	Lt Cdr	01-Aug-05	ENG	WE	NC REQUIREMENTS MANAGERS	ABBEY WOOD
Spink, David A	Maj	01-Oct-08	RM	GS	PJHQ (UK)	NORTHWOOD
Spink, Gary J	SLt	01-Aug-13	ENG	ME	HMS BULWARK	
Spinks, David	Lt Cdr	01-Aug-05	WAR	AAWO	MWS COLLINGWOOD	HMS COLLINGWOOD
Spinks, Robert J	Lt RN	01-May-01	WAR	P LYN7	845 SQN	RNAS YEOVILTON
Spooner, Ross	Cdr	30-Jun-13	WAR	P MER	820 SQN	RNAS CULDROSE
Spoors, Brendan	Lt Cdr	01-Oct-10	WAR	P MER	824 SQN	RNAS CULDROSE
Spreadborough, Philip J	Surg Lt Cdr	01-Aug-12	MED	GS	MTM INM ALVERSTOKE	GOSPORT
Spreckley, Damian R C	Lt RN	09-Apr-09	LOGS	L	CHF(MERLIN)	RAF BENSON
Spring, Jeremy M	Lt Cdr	03-Aug-97	ENG	AE (RES)	MTM NPT RES MOBILISATION	UK
Springer, Rory J	Lt RN	01-Sep-14	WAR	P UT	MTM 824 SQN CULDROSE	RNAS CULDROSE
Spurdle, Andrew P	Lt Cdr	01-Oct-05	WAR	PWO(A)	NC REQUIREMENTS MANAGERS	ABBEY WOOD
Squires, Jack E	SLt	19-Sep-14	WAR	GSX	MCM2	PORTSMOUTH
Squires, Russell A	Capt	01-Mar-10	RM	GS	COMUKAMPHIBFOR	PORTSMOUTH
St Aubyn, John D E	Lt Cdr	30-Jun-01	ENG	WESM(SWS)	DES COMFLEET	ABBEY WOOD
Stace, Ivan S	Capt RN	28-Aug-12	ENG	WESM(TWS)	DES COMFLEET	ABBEY WOOD
Stacey, Andrew M	Cdr	30-Jun-08	WAR	PWO(A)	PJHQ (UK)	NORTHWOOD
Stacey, Piers	SLt	01-May-13	WAR	INT	FLEET COMOPS NWD	HMS COLLINGWOOD
Stachow, Elizabeth A	Surg Lt RN	03-Aug-11	MED	GDMO	MTM DCEME SULTAN	HMS SULTAN
Stack, Daniel P	Mid	01-Feb-14	WAR	HM	BRNC	BRNC DARTMOUTH
Stack, Eleanor F	Lt Cdr	01-Oct-09	WAR	AAWO	FLEET CAP SSM	PORTSMOUTH
Stackhouse, Martyn C	Lt RN	01-Jan-07	WAR	P MER	824 SQN	RNAS CULDROSE
Stafford, Benedict J C	2Lt	25-Aug-14	RM	N/A	CTCRM	EXMOUTH
Stafford, Benjamin R	Lt Cdr	01-Oct-07	ENG	MESM	MTM DEFAC JSCSC	SHRIVENHAM
Stafford, Derek B MBE	Lt Col	30-Jun-12	RM	P SK4	CHF - 846	RAF BENSON
Stafford, Wayne	Cdr	30-Jun-13	ENG	WESM(TWS)	DES COMFLEET	ABBEY WOOD
Stafford-Shaw, Damian	Lt Cdr	01-Oct-14	ENG	TM	UK MCC	BAHRAIN
Stagg, Antony R	Cdr	30-Jun-14	ENG	AE	MOD NSD	LONDON
Stait, Benjamin G	Lt Cdr	01-Oct-06	WAR	MCD	JFC HQ	NORTHWOOD
Staley, Simon P L	Cdr	30-Jun-07	WAR	O SKW	MOD NSD SEA	TOKYO
Stallard, Samuel C	Mid	01-May-14	WAR	GSX	BRNC	BRNC DARTMOUTH
Stamper, Jonathan C H	Cdr	30-Jun-09	ENG	IS	NBCP MPT	PORTSMOUTH
Stamper, Valerie L	Lt Cdr	01-Oct-14	LOGS	L	FLEET CMR	PORTSMOUTH
Stanbury, David R	Lt RN	19-Oct-07	WAR	MCD	MWS DDS	PORTSMOUTH
Stancliffe, Andrew E	Lt RN	01-Jul-04	ENG	AE	HMS TEMERAIRE	PORTSMOUTH
Standen, Gary D	Lt Cdr	01-Oct-09	ENG	AE	DES COMFLEET	ABBEY WOOD
Stanford, Thomas C	Lt RN	01-Jan-12	ENG	TM	JFC - DCTS (H)	AYLESBURY
Stanhope, Sir Mark GCB OBE	Adm	10-Jul-04				
Stanistreet, Georgina C	Lt Cdr	01-Oct-14	ENG	ME	DCMC	LONDON
Stanley, Nicholas	Capt RN	30-Jun-02	WAR	MCD	NATO - SHAPE - UKNMR	CASTEAU
Stanley, Rebecca F	Mid	01-May-14	WAR	GSX	BRNC	BRNC DARTMOUTH
Stanley-Adams, Tony R	Lt RN	29-Oct-12	ENG	WESM	HMS TALENT	
Stanley-Whyte, Berkeley J OBE	Capt RN	01-Jul-11	ENG	WESM(SWS)	DES COMFLEET	USA
Stannard, Adam	Surg Lt Cdr	02-Aug-05	MED	GS	MTM INM ALVERSTOKE	GOSPORT
Stannard, Joshua N	Lt	02-Sep-14	RM	GS	43 CDO FPGRM	HELENSBURGH
Stannard, Mark	Lt Cdr	01-Aug-97	WAR	GSX	RNLT - KFNA	SAUDI ARABIA
Stanning, Alastair J	Surg Lt Cdr	01-Aug-12	MED	GMP	MTM INM ALVERSTOKE	GOSPORT
Stant, Mark S	Lt RN	01-Apr-07	ENG	WE	HMS QUEEN ELIZABETH	
Stanton, Keith V	Maj	01-Oct-09	RM	SCC	CTCRM	EXMOUTH
Stanton-Brown, Peter J	Lt RN	01-Feb-01	WAR	SM(AWC)	D STRAT PROG	ABBEY WOOD
Stapley, Sarah A	Surg Capt RN	06-May-14	MED	T&O	DMS WHITTINGTON	BIRMINGHAM
Stapley-Bunten, Thomas A	SLt	01-Sep-13	WAR	GSX	HMS RICHMOND	
Stark, Justin R	Lt RN	31-Jul-09	WAR	AV	RNLA	BRNC DARTMOUTH

Name	Substantive Rank	Seniority	Branch	Specialisation	Organisation Name	Location Name
Starkey, David S	Lt RN	01-Feb-06	WAR	MCD	MCM2	PORTSMOUTH
Starling, Christopher M MBE	Maj	01-Oct-12	RM	SCC	MTM DEFAC JSCSC	SHRIVENHAM
Starsmore, Daniel L	Lt RN	01-Dec-09	WAR	P	MTM	WASHINGTON
Staunton, Thomas H	Surg Lt RN	04-Aug-10	MED	GDMO	30 CDO IX GP RM	PLYMOUTH
Staveley, Catherine B B	Lt RN	01-Jun-10	ENG	TM	RNP TEAM	PORTSMOUTH
Stead, Andrew M	Lt Cdr	01-Oct-12	ENG	TM	RNLA	BRNC DARTMOUTH
Steadman, Robert	Cdr	30-Jun-14	WAR	AAWO	FLEET MARITIME WARFARE	HMS COLLINGWOOD
Steadman, Thomas W	SLt	01-Feb-12	ENG	WESM	HMS TALENT	
Steel, David G KBE DL	V Adm	10-Oct-12	LOGS	L BAR	2SL CNPT	PORTSMOUTH
Steele, Alexander M	Mid	08-Sep-14	ENG	WE	BRNC	BRNC DARTMOUTH
Steele, Jason M	Lt RN	31-Jul-09	LOGS	L	ACNS	PORTSMOUTH
Steele, Katie	Lt RN	01-Jun-10	LOGS	L	MTM FLEET HQ	PORTSMOUTH
Steele, Marie L	Lt RN	01-Nov-05	WAR	HM	HMS SOMERSET	
Steele, Matthew E	Lt RN	09-Apr-10	ENG	ME	HMS ENTERPRISE	
Steele, Matthew S	Lt Cdr	01-Oct-13	WAR	HM(AM)	HMS OCEAN	
Steen, Kieron M	Lt Cdr	01-Oct-08	WAR	P FW	RAF LINTON-ON-OUSE	RAF LINTON ON OUSE
Stellon, Christopher	Lt RN	02-Apr-09	WAR	O SKW	854 NAS	RNAS CULDROSE
Stembridge, Daniel P T	Capt RN	20-Jun-14	WAR	P FW	D CEPP	LONDON
Stemp, Justin E	Lt Col	30-Jun-14	RM	GS	PJHQ (UK)	NORTHWOOD
Stent, Mark L	SLt	01-Aug-13	MED	MS	DCHET DSHE	LICHFIELD
Stephen, Barry M	Lt Cdr	01-Mar-02	WAR	PWO(N)	FOST MPV SEA	HMNB CLYDE
Stephen, Cameron E	ENG	01-Sep-07	ENG	AE	MAA	ABBEY WOOD
Stephen, Nicola	Lt RN	01-Feb-11	WAR	GSX	HMS KENT	
Stephens, Brian J	Lt RN	08-Feb-13	WAR	ATC	RNAS YEOVILTON	YEOVILTON
Stephens, Carl W	Lt RN	01-Sep-13	WAR	O MER	814 SQN	RNAS CULDROSE
Stephens, Patrick G	Lt RN	01-Jul-05	WAR	SM(N)	NCHQ CI TEAM	PORTSMOUTH
Stephens, Samuel J R	Lt RN	01-Jan-06	WAR	PWO	HMS PORTLAND	
Stephenson, Christopher J	Lt RN	01-Apr-03	WAR	MCD	HMS OCEAN	
Stephenson, Fiona	Lt RN	01-Sep-11	WAR	FC	HMS DEFENDER	
Stephenson, Gavin	Surg SLt	29-Jul-14	MED	Medical	BLAKE	BRNC DARTMOUTH
Stephenson, John	Lt RN	01-Aug-09	WAR	C	RAF GIBRALTAR - ENG	HMS ROOKE
Stephenson, Keith J M	Cdr	30-Jun-12	ENG	IS	DEF BD SEC	LONDON
Stephenson, Philip G	Lt Cdr	01-Oct-03	LOGS	L	DES COMLAND	BOSCOMBE DOWN
Stephenson, Richard J E	Lt RN	08-Apr-05	LOGS	L	NATO-ACO-JFC HQ	BRUNSSUM
Steven, William G K	Capt	03-Sep-14	RM	GS	45 CDO RM	DUNDEE
Stevens, Anthony J	Cdr	30-Jun-14	ENG	TM(SM)	BRNC	PORTSMOUTH
Stevens, Christopher K	Lt RN	01-Sep-09	WAR	GSX	HMS PUNCHER	
Stevens, Christopher N	Capt	01-Sep-10	RM	GS	CTCRM	EXMOUTH
Stevens, Jonathan A	SLt	01-Oct-14	MED	Medical	BLAKE	BRNC DARTMOUTH
Stevens, Joseph I	Lt Cdr	01-Oct-11	ENG	AE	ACNS	PORTSMOUTH
Stevens, Lisa C	Surg Lt Cdr	02-Aug-10	MED	GMP	MTM CTCRM	EXMOUTH
Stevens, Mark	Lt RN	15-Apr-11	WAR	SM(X)	MTM RALEIGH	HMS RALEIGH
Stevens, Mark J	Lt RN	07-Apr-06	ENG	ME	FOST DPORT	PLYMOUTH
Stevenson, Adam	Lt Cdr	01-Oct-13	WAR	PWO	HMS MONMOUTH	
Stevenson, Alexander N	Lt RN	06-Apr-07	WAR	O SK6	771 SQN	RNAS CULDROSE
Stevenson, Charles D A	Lt RN	01-Mar-14	WAR	GSX	HMS ST ALBANS	
Stevenson, Geoffrey S	Surg Cdr (D)	14-Jan-09	DENTAL	GDP	RN GIBRALTAR - SDS	HMS ROOKE
Stevenson, Helen C	Lt RN	01-Nov-13	ENG	WE	HMS BULWARK	
Stevenson, Julian P	Lt Cdr	01-Nov-05	ENG	MESM	SETT	FORT BLOCKHOUSE
Stevenson, Simon	Lt Cdr	01-Oct-13	WAR	P MER	FOST DPORT	PLYMOUTH
Stevenson, Thomas E J	Surg Lt Cdr	01-Aug-13	MED	GS	MTM INM ALVERSTOKE	GOSPORT
Stewart, Charles H	Lt RN	01-Sep-01	WAR	GSX	NCHQ CNPERS	PORTSMOUTH
Stewart, Christopher J	Mid	17-Nov-14	LOGS	L	BRNC	BRNC DARTMOUTH
Stewart, Gregory	Mid	17-Nov-14	WAR	GSX	BRNC	BRNC DARTMOUTH
Stewart, Lee A	Capt	01-Sep-12	RM	GS	45 CDO RM	DUNDEE
Stewart, Leonie H	SLt	01-Apr-13	DENTAL	DENTAL	BLAKE	BRNC DARTMOUTH
Stewart, Nicholas J	Lt RN	01-May-04	WAR	HM	PJHQ (UK)	NORTHWOOD
Stewart, Rory W	Lt Cdr	01-Jul-91	ENG	MESM	DGHR CS - DBR DEF SY	LONDON
Stewart, Sean T	Lt RN	09-Jun-06	WAR	REG	NPM NORTHERN	HMNB CLYDE
Stewart, Tristan J	Capt	01-Sep-11	RM	GS	MOD CNS/ACNS	LONDON
Stickland, Charles R OBE	Brig	14-Jul-14	RM	LC	HQ 3 CDO BDE RM	PLYMOUTH
Stidston, Ian J	Capt RN	15-Jun-09	ENG	TM	NCHQ - NAVY CMD SEC	PORTSMOUTH

Name	Substantive Rank	Seniority	Branch	Specialisation	Organisation Name	Location Name
Stiles, Maxine K	Lt RN	01-Apr-11	LOGS	L SM	HMS VIGILANT	
Still, James C	SLt	08-Dec-12	WAR	P UT	MTM SHAWBURY	RAF SHAWBURY
Stilwell, James M	Lt Cdr	01-Oct-06	WAR	SM(AWC)	UK MCC	BAHRAIN
Stinchcombe, Mark E	Lt RN	01-Nov-14	WAR	GSX	MWS COLLINGWOOD	HMS COLLINGWOOD
Stinton, George T	Capt	03-Sep-14	RM	GS	45 CDO RM	DUNDEE
Stirling, Andrew C	Lt Cdr	01-Oct-14	WAR	P LYN7	847 SQN	RNAS YEOVILTON
Stitson, Paul	Maj	01-Oct-10	RM	LC	DCBRN CENTRE	SALISBURY
Stock, Christopher M	Cdr	30-Jun-12	WAR	O MER	FLEET ACOS(RP)	PORTSMOUTH
Stockbridge, Antony	Lt Cdr	01-Oct-05	LOGS	L BAR	PJHQ (UK)	NORTHWOOD
Stocker, Jeremy	Capt RN	01-Mar-10	WAR	INFO OPS	FLEET CMR	PORTSMOUTH
Stockley, Sean A	Lt RN	01-Mar-13	ENG	WESM	HMS VIGILANT	
Stockton, Barry G	Lt RN	27-Jul-07	ENG	WESM(TWS)	DES COMLAND	ABBEY WOOD
Stockton, Kevin G	Lt Cdr	19-Nov-00	WAR	MCD	FDS HQ	PORTSMOUTH
Stoffell, David	Cdr	30-Jun-07	LOGS	L SM	NATO-ACT-HQ	NORFOLK
Stokes, Richard	Cdre	25-Jul-11	ENG	WESM(TWS)	NUCLEAR CAPABILITY	LONDON
Stone, James	Lt Cdr	01-Oct-11	WAR	O SKW	849 SQN	RNAS CULDROSE
Stone, Marc D J	Lt RN	20-Aug-12	ENG	AE	845 SQN	RNAS YEOVILTON
Stone, Matthew J	Lt RN	01-Jan-13	ENG	WE	HMS DAUNTLESS	
Stone, Nicholas	Lt Cdr	01-Oct-06	LOGS	L SM	PJHQ (UK)	NORTHWOOD
Stone, Nicholas S	Lt RN	11-Dec-08	WAR	SM(N)	MTM RALEIGH	HMS RALEIGH
Stone-Ward, Robert O	Lt RN	01-Sep-12	WAR	MCD	MCM2	PORTSMOUTH
Storey, Andrew	Lt Cdr	01-Oct-10	WAR	PWO(N)	RN EXCHANGE USA	WASHINGTON
Storey, Helen J	Lt Cdr	01-Oct-08	LOGS	L BAR	MTM NELSON	HMS NELSON
Storey, James I	Lt RN	18-Dec-12	ENG	MESM	MTM WMO FASLANE	HMNB CLYDE
Storey, Kristopher J	Lt RN	01-Sep-12	ENG	AE	814 SQN	RNAS CULDROSE
Storey, William	Lt RN	01-Nov-12	ENG	ME	HMS BULWARK	
Storton, George H	Lt Cdr	01-Oct-13	WAR	PWO(N)	HMS IRON DUKE	
Stow, Adam D	Mid	01-May-14	WAR	ATC UT	BRNC	BRNC DARTMOUTH
Stowell, Perry I M	Cdr	30-Jun-13	WAR	PWO(U)	MWS COLLINGWOOD	HMS COLLINGWOOD
Strachan, Gordon J	SLt	18-Apr-12	WAR	SM(X)	MCM1	FASLANE
Strachan, Robert C M	Surg Lt RN	01-Mar-13	MED	GDMO	HMS LANCASTER	
Stradling, Duncan E	Lt RN	01-Sep-11	WAR	FC	MTM DEF SCH OF LANG	BEACONSFIELD
Straker, Peter D	Lt RN	01-Dec-09	WAR	P SK4	845 SQN	RNAS YEOVILTON
Strange, Jamie L	Lt RN	17-Dec-10	WAR	AV	DSTO	RAF ST MAWGAN
Strange, Steven P	Lt Cdr	01-Oct-05	ENG	WESM(TWS)	OCLC PLYMOUTH	BRISTOL
Strathern, Roderick J	Lt Cdr	01-Oct-98	WAR	PWO(U)	HMS VICTORY	HMNB PORTSMOUTH
Strathie, Gavin S	Lt Cdr	01-Jun-08	WAR	ATC	FLEET CSAV	RNAS YEOVILTON
Stratton, Matthew P	Lt Cdr	01-Oct-08	ENG	WE	FLEET SPT FGEN	PORTSMOUTH
Stratton, Nicholas C	Lt Cdr	01-May-12	WAR		FLEET COMOPS NWD	NORTHWOOD
Stratton, Stuart J	Lt Cdr	01-Oct-09	ENG	MESM	FOST SM SEA	HMNB CLYDE
Strawbridge, Chantal M	Lt RN	01-Sep-04	WAR	GSX	MTM MWS COLLINGWOOD	HMS COLLINGWOOD
Street, Sarah	Lt Cdr	01-Oct-13	LOGS	L	HMS ST ALBANS	
Streeten, Christopher M	Capt RN	01-Jul-13	ENG	WESM(SWS)	NUCLEAR CAPABILITY	LONDON
Streets, Christopher G	Surg Cdr	30-Jun-07	MED	GS	MDHU DERRIFORD	PLYMOUTH
Strickland, Timothy	Lt RN	01-Apr-07	WAR	P MER	829 SQN	RNAS CULDROSE
Stride, James A	Cdr	30-Jun-11	WAR	PWO(A)	FOST DPORT	PLYMOUTH
Stride, Jamieson C	Cdr	30-Jun-13	WAR	O LYNX	FLEET COMOPS NWD	NORTHWOOD
Stringer, Graeme E	Lt Cdr	01-Oct-10	WAR	ATC	RNAS CULDROSE	HELSTON
Stroude, Paul	Cdr	30-Jun-10	WAR	PWO(U)	DOC	LONDON
Strutt, Jason F	Lt Cdr	01-May-00	ENG	WE	FLEET CAP IS	PORTSMOUTH
Stuart, Euan E C	Lt Cdr	01-Oct-04	WAR	AAWO	MTM DEFAC JSCSC	SHRIVENHAM
Stuart, Simon A	Lt RN	01-Sep-04	WAR	O LYNX	LHF 702 SQN	RNAS YEOVILTON
Stubbs, Benjamin D	Lt RN	01-Sep-03	WAR	P FW	MTM DEFAC JSCSC	SHRIVENHAM
Stubbs, Ian	Lt Cdr	01-Oct-11	ENG	TM	FLEET MARITIME WARFARE	HMS COLLINGWOOD
Sturgeon, David M	Lt Cdr	01-Oct-08	LOGS	L SM	ACDS	ABBEY WOOD
Sturgeon, Mark	Lt Cdr	01-Oct-12	ENG	WESM(TWS)	HMS TORBAY	
Sturman, Andrew J	Lt RN	01-Nov-14	WAR	GSX	MWS COLLINGWOOD	HMS COLLINGWOOD
Sturman, Richard W	Lt Cdr	01-Oct-11	WAR	P SK4	CHF(MERLIN)	RAF BENSON
Stuttard, Mark	Cdr	30-Jun-06	WAR	PWO(A)	NATO-ACO-JFC HQ	NAPLES
Suckling, Christopher	Lt RN	01-Jun-09	WAR	P MER	814 SQN	RNAS CULDROSE
Suckling, Robin L	Lt Cdr	01-Oct-02	WAR	O SK6	GANNET SAR FLT	HMS GANNET
Sullivan, Mark N	Lt Cdr	01-Oct-05	ENG	ME	NCHQ CNPS	PORTSMOUTH

Name	Substantive Rank	Seniority	Branch	Specialisation	Organisation Name	Location Name
Summers, James A E	Lt Col	30-Jun-14	RM	GS	DIRECTOR (JW)	NORTHWOOD
Sunderland, Scott A	SLt	01-Apr-12	WAR	P UT	RAF SHAWBURY	SHREWSBURY
Sutcliff, Jonathan D	Lt RN	01-Nov-05	ENG	WE	MWS COLLINGWOOD	HMS COLLINGWOOD
Sutcliffe, Paul	Lt RN	01-Jan-05	WAR	P MER	MTM SHAWBURY	RAF SHAWBURY
Suter, Francis T	Lt RN	01-Jan-02	WAR	O WILDCAT	WMF 825 SQN HQ	RNAS YEOVILTON
Sutherland, Iain	Maj	01-Oct-12	RM	GS	FLEET COMOPS NWD	NORTHWOOD
Sutherland, Neil MBE	Col	05-Aug-14	RM	C	HQ 3 CDO BDE RM	PLYMOUTH
Sutherland, Oliver	SLt	30-Mar-12	WAR	SM(X)	HMS DEFENDER	
Sutherland, Steven	Maj	01-Oct-13	RM	C (SCC)	45 CDO RM	DUNDEE
Suttle, Celia E J	Lt RN	01-Sep-13	WAR	HM	MTM MWS HMTG (D)	HMS DRAKE
Sutton, David MBE	Maj	01-Oct-09	RM	P LYN7	847 SQN	RNAS YEOVILTON
Sutton, Gary B	Cdre	01-Jul-14	WAR	PWO(N)	NCHQ - NAVY CMD SEC	PORTSMOUTH
Sutton, Jonathon	2Lt	25-Aug-14	RM	N/A	CTCRM	EXMOUTH
Suzuki, Hironobu M M	Lt RN	01-Apr-12	ENG	TM	MTM WMO YEOVILTON	RNAS YEOVILTON
Swain, Andrew V MBE	Cdr	30-Jun-05	WAR	HM (H CH)	LSP OMAN	MUSCAT
Swain, Cara S	Surg Lt RN	07-Aug-13	MED	Medical	BLAKE	BRNC DARTMOUTH
Swales, Richard	Lt RN	01-Jan-08	WAR	O MER	771 SQN	RNAS CULDROSE
Swan, Anthony M	Lt	02-Sep-14	RM	GS	43 CDO FPGRM	HELENSBURGH
Swann, Adam P D	Lt RN	02-Dec-14	ENG	TM	MTM NELSON	HMS NELSON
Swann, James J	Lt RN	01-May-14	ENG	WE	HMS DIAMOND	
Swannick, Derek J	Cdr	30-Jun-02	WAR	METOC	UKMO	EXETER
Swarbreck, Cosmo G F	Mid	08-Sep-14	WAR	GSX	BRNC	BRNC DARTMOUTH
Sweeney, Fiona J	Surg SLt	26-Jul-14	MED	Medical	BLAKE	BRNC DARTMOUTH
Sweeney, Keith P M	Cdr	30-Jun-12	ENG	ME	MTM DRAKE	HMS DRAKE
Sweeney, Rachel J	Lt Cdr	01-Oct-13	ENG	AE	MTM DEFAC CMT MBA	SHRIVENHAM
Sweny, Gordon	Maj	01-Oct-12	RM	GS	RN EXCHANGE FRANCE	PARIS
Swift, Jessie J	Mid	01-May-14	WAR	GSX	BRNC	BRNC DARTMOUTH
Swift, Robert D	Lt RN	01-Sep-04	LOGS	L SM	HMS SCOTIA	HMS CALEDONIA
Swindells, Mark	Lt Cdr	01-Oct-10	WAR	P LYNX	WMF SIM	RNAS YEOVILTON
Swire, Barry J	Lt Cdr	01-Oct-14	QARNNS	MH	DPHC SOUTH - DCMH	HMS EXCELLENT
Swithinbank, George R	Lt RN	01-Sep-11	ENG	TM(SM)	HMS TRENCHANT	
Syfret, Matthew J E	Mid	08-Sep-14	ENG	WE	BRNC	BRNC DARTMOUTH
Sykes, Leah D	Lt Cdr	01-Oct-04	QARNNS	PHC	DPHC SW	HMS DRAKE
Sykes, Matthew J	Lt Cdr	01-Sep-10	WAR	PWO	PJHQ (UK)	NORTHWOOD
Sykes, Mitchell C	Lt	01-Sep-12	RM	GS	NCHQ	
Sykes, Robert A	Lt Cdr	01-Oct-96	WAR	O LYNX	DES COMJE	YEOVIL
Sykes-Gelder, Daniel	SLt	01-Aug-13	WAR	GSX	HMS CLYDE	
Sykes-Popham, Christopher	Capt	01-Sep-13	RM	GS	40 CDO RM	TAUNTON
Sylvan, Christopher A	Maj	01-Oct-13	RM	GS	MOD DEFENCE STAFF	LONDON
Syrett, Matthew E	Cdr	30-Jun-10	WAR	HM (H CH)	MOD CNS/ACNS	LONDON
Syson, Carl F	Lt RN	01-Jan-04	WAR	P FW	FLEET AV VL	RNAS YEOVILTON
Szweda, Alexander A	Lt RN	01-Nov-10	WAR	GSX	HMS ILLUSTRIOUS	

T

Name	Substantive Rank	Seniority	Branch	Specialisation	Organisation Name	Location Name
Tabeart, George W	Cdr	30-Jun-10	WAR	HM (H CH)	DI - ICSP	NORTHWOOD
Tabor, James H	RN Chpln	26-Jun-04	Ch S	Chaplain	BRNC	BRNC DARTMOUTH
Taborda, Matthew A	Lt RN	01-Sep-05	WAR	GSX	MTM MWS COLLINGWOOD	HMS COLLINGWOOD
Tacey, Richard	Lt Cdr	01-Dec-07	WAR	PWO(A)	STRIKFORNATO - LISBON	LISBON
Tait, Iain C	Capt	03-Apr-09	RM	SCC	43 CDO FPGRM	HELENSBURGH
Tait, Martyn D	Lt Cdr	27-Aug-14	ENG	TM(SM)	FOST FAS SHORE	HMNB CLYDE
Talbot, Edward T H	Lt	02-Sep-14	RM	GS	45 CDO RM	DUNDEE
Talbot, Liam P	Mid	01-Feb-14	ENG	ME	BRNC	BRNC DARTMOUTH
Talbot, Richard J	Lt Cdr	01-Oct-09	WAR	MCD	FOST DPORT	PLYMOUTH
Talbot, Simon J	Lt RN	01-May-05	WAR	FC	HMS DAUNTLESS	
Talbott, Aidan H	Capt RN	01-Jul-13	LOGS	L	DCDS PERS TRG	LONDON
Tall, Iain T G	Lt Cdr	01-Oct-10	ENG	WE	FOST DPORT	PLYMOUTH
Talmage, Charles R H	Lt RN	01-Apr-08	WAR	P FW	NO 3 FTS/UAS - JEFTS	GRANTHAM
Tamayo, Kieran	Lt RN	01-Oct-14	LOGS	L	HMS ST ALBANS	
Tamlyn, Stephen	Lt Col	30-Jun-14	RM	GS	MTM RN GLOBAL	FRANCE
Tanner, Michael J	Col	16-Dec-13	RM	GS	NBCP CAPTAIN OF THE BASE	PORTSMOUTH
Tanner, Richard	Cdr	30-Jun-13	WAR	SM(CQ)	HMS VIGILANT	
Tantam, Robert J G	Lt Cdr	01-Oct-09	ENG	MESM	FOST SM SEA	HMNB CLYDE

Name	Substantive Rank	Seniority	Branch	Specialisation	Organisation Name	Location Name
Tanzer, William J C E	Surg Lt Cdr	05-Aug-14	MED	GMP	MTM INM ALVERSTOKE	GOSPORT
Tapp, Steven J	Maj	01-Oct-09	RM	P GAZ	COMUKTG	PLYMOUTH
Tappin, Simon J	Lt Cdr	01-Oct-10	WAR	AWO(U)	PJHQ (UK)	NORTHWOOD
Tarbard, Gavin T	Lt RN	01-May-10	ENG	TM	RNCR BOVINGTON	WAREHAM
Targett, Edward G	Lt RN	01-Sep-10	WAR	O LYNX	MTM WMO YEOVILTON	RNAS YEOVILTON
Tarnowski, Tomasz A	Maj	12-Nov-04	RM	LC	RN EXCHANGE FRANCE	TOULON
Tarpey, Richard J	Lt RN	01-Feb-14	WAR	SM(X)	MTM RALEIGH	HMS RALEIGH
Tarrant, Robert K	R Adm	14-Jan-13	WAR	SM(CQ)	NCHQ	PORTSMOUTH
Tasker, Adam M	Lt RN	01-May-05	WAR	O SKW	PJHQ (UK)	NORTHWOOD
Tate, David N	Lt RN	01-Apr-13	WAR	GSX	HMS PROTECTOR	
Tate, Dennis	Lt RN	24-May-14	ENG	MESM	DCEME SULTAN	HMS SULTAN
Tate, Paul A	Lt RN	13-Jul-12	LOGS	L	HQ DCLPA & DEEPCUT GAR	CAMBERLEY
Tayal, Manish	Surg Lt Cdr	01-Aug-09	MED	GMP	DPHC OVERSEAS	NAPLES
Taylor, Alastair B	Lt RN	01-Jan-15	WAR	FC	HMS DRAGON	
Taylor, Alexander I	Lt RN	01-Sep-10	WAR	P SK4	CHF - 846	RAF BENSON
Taylor, Andrew	Lt RN	18-Feb-05	WAR	GSX	NATO ACO	NORTHWOOD
Taylor, Andrew I	Lt Cdr	01-Oct-13	WAR	HM(AM)	MWS COLLINGWOOD	HMS COLLINGWOOD
Taylor, Benjamin G	Lt RN	20-Oct-12	WAR	P SK4	MTM CHF (MERLIN)	RAF BENSON
Taylor, David R	Lt RN	15-Apr-11	ENG	WE	SVCOPS/DHDOPS/COR	CORSHAM
Taylor, Dean A	SLt	01-Nov-14	WAR	GSX	MWS COLLINGWOOD	HMS COLLINGWOOD
Taylor, Dominic	Lt RN	24-Nov-14	WAR	GSX	MCM1	FASLANE
Taylor, Helen M J	Lt RN	01-Apr-11	WAR	GSX	HMS MERSEY	
Taylor, Ian K	Lt Cdr	01-Oct-01	LOGS	L	HMS SULTAN	GOSPORT
Taylor, James E	Lt RN	01-Sep-04	WAR	P MER	824 SQN	RNAS CULDROSE
Taylor, James T	Lt Cdr	01-Oct-13	WAR	O SKW	EMBED FRANCE (FW)	FRANCE
Taylor, Jennifer L	Lt RN	01-May-13	WAR	GSX	MCM1	FASLANE
Taylor, Jonathan P	Lt Cdr	01-Oct-03	WAR	SM(C)	NATO-ACT-JWC	STAVANGER
Taylor, Keith M	Lt Cdr	01-Oct-06	ENG	WE	NCHQ CNPS	PORTSMOUTH
Taylor, Kenneth	Capt RN	30-Jun-07	WAR	O SK6	SERV ADVISER	KUALA LUMPAR
Taylor, Lisa M	Cdr	03-Mar-13	QARNNS	Nurse Officer	MDHU PORTSMOUTH	PORTSMOUTH
Taylor, Marc G	Lt RN	01-Nov-07	WAR	HM	BRNC	BRNC DARTMOUTH
Taylor, Marian C	Lt RN	01-Jan-11	WAR	O SKW	MTM WMO CULDROSE	RNAS CULDROSE
Taylor, Mark A	Cdr	30-Jun-09	WAR	P LYNX	MOD NSD - HDS	LONDON
Taylor, Mark A	Lt RN	11-Apr-08	WAR	ATC	RNAS CULDROSE	HELSTON
Taylor, Matthew R	Lt RN	01-Nov-07	WAR	P SK6	771 SQN	RNAS CULDROSE
Taylor, Matthew R A	Lt RN	01-Nov-10	WAR	GSX	HMS SEVERN	
Taylor, Neil	Lt Cdr	11-Oct-04	ENG	ME	COMUKTG	PLYMOUTH
Taylor, Neil J	Maj	01-Oct-08	RM	GS	NCHQ	PORTSMOUTH
Taylor, Neil R	Lt RN	01-Feb-07	WAR	SM(N)	FLEET COMOPS NWD	NORTHWOOD
Taylor, Nicholas	Lt RN	01-Nov-05	WAR	HM	MTM DRAKE	HMS DRAKE
Taylor, Nicholas F	Lt Cdr	16-Feb-87	WAR	PWO(C)	SVCOPS/COR	CORSHAM
Taylor, Oliver L	Lt RN	01-May-13	WAR	GSX	HMS ST ALBANS	
Taylor, Peter G D OBE	Brig	06-May-14	RM	GS	SERV ATTACHE/ADVISER	MUSCAT
Taylor, Peter J	Surg Cdr	30-Jun-05	MED	GS	RCDM	PETERBOROUGH
Taylor, Peter S	SLt	20-Oct-14	WAR	C	HDNET	CORSHAM
Taylor, Rachel S	Lt RN	01-Sep-12	WAR	GSX	RN EXCHANGE ITALY	ROME
Taylor, Robert	Cdr	30-Jun-10	ENG	WE	COMDEVFLOT	PLYMOUTH
Taylor, Robert J	Lt Cdr	01-Oct-05	WAR	O WILDCAT	AWC	BOSCOMBE DOWN
Taylor, Robert P	Lt RN	01-May-02	WAR	P MER	814 SQN	RNAS CULDROSE
Taylor, Ryan J	2Lt	25-Aug-14	RM	N/A	CTCRM	EXMOUTH
Taylor, Scott A	Lt RN	01-Oct-14	WAR	SM(N)	HMS VICTORIOUS	
Taylor, Spencer A	Capt RN	01-Jul-08	ENG	IS	DBS MIL PERS	GOSPORT
Taylor, Stephen R	Lt RN	01-Jun-07	ENG	ME	COMPORFLOT	PORTSMOUTH
Taylor, Steven	Capt	01-Sep-12	RM	GS	43 CDO FPGRM	HELENSBURGH
Taylor, Stuart D	Maj	01-Oct-04	RM	GS	MTM DEFAC JSCSC	SHRIVENHAM
Tazewell, Matthew R	Lt Cdr	01-Oct-09	WAR	O LYNX	WMF 825 SQN HQ	RNAS YEOVILTON
Tear, Trevor M	Lt RN	15-Apr-11	ENG	AE	RNAS CULDROSE	HELSTON
Teare, Matthew R	Lt RN	01-Jan-10	WAR	MW	MCM2	PORTSMOUTH
Teasdale, David A	Cdr	30-Jun-11	WAR	SM(X) (RES)	RNP - HQ PMN	HMS EXCELLENT
Teasdale, James P	Lt RN	01-Nov-05	ENG	WE	DCCIS CISTU	HMS COLLINGWOOD
Tebbet, Paul	Cdr	30-Jun-07	WAR	PWO(U)	NATO-ACT-HQ	BRUSSELS
Teece, Nicholas J	Lt RN	01-Apr-11	WAR	P UT	MTM CHF (MERLIN)	RAF BENSON

Name	Substantive Rank	Seniority	Branch	Specialisation	Organisation Name	Location Name
Teideman, Ian C	Cdr	30-Jun-09	ENG	WE	FLEET CAP SSM	PORTSMOUTH
Telford, Steven M	Lt RN	15-Apr-11	MED	MS	MTM DEFAC JSCSC	SHRIVENHAM
Tennant, Gareth M	Capt	01-Sep-08	RM	GS	30 CDO IX GP RM	PLYMOUTH
Terry, Judith H	Cdr	30-Jun-14	LOGS	L	PJHQ (UK)	NORTHWOOD
Terry, Michael C G	Surg Cdr	30-Jun-03	MED	GS	MDHU PORTSMOUTH	PORTSMOUTH
Terry, Nigel P	Lt Cdr	01-Oct-10	WAR	P SK6	FLEET CSAV	ABBEY WOOD
Tetchner, David J	Lt RN	01-Nov-05	ENG	WE	FLEET SPT FGEN	PORTSMOUTH
Tetley, Mark	Lt Cdr	01-Oct-03	WAR	O MER	824 SQN	RNAS CULDROSE
Tetlow, Hamish S G	Cdr	30-Jun-08	WAR	SM(AWC)	MOD NSD - HDS	LONDON
Thackray, Penelope D	Lt RN	01-Apr-05	ENG	TM(SM)	NETS (OPS)	HELENSBURGH
Thain-Smith, Julie C	Cdr	01-Apr-08	QARNNS	Nurse Officer	MTM NELSON	HMS NELSON
Thatcher, Geraint L	Capt	01-Sep-11	RM	GS	NCHQ	
Theobold, Daniel	Lt RN	01-Sep-13	ENG	WESM	HMS ASTUTE	
Thicknesse, Thomas R	Lt RN	21-Nov-14	WAR	FC	HMS DEFENDER	
Thomas, Adam J MBE	Lt Cdr	01-Oct-13	ENG	AE	RN EXCHANGE CANADA	OTTAWA
Thomas, Andrew G	I t RN	01-Sep-06	ENG	ME	DES COMFLEET	ABBEY WOOD
Thomas, Charlotte	Lt RN	01-Sep-11	ENG	WE	DHU	CHICKSANDS
Thomas, Daniel G D	Lt RN	01-Jan-12	LOGS	L	BRNC	BRNC DARTMOUTH
Thomas, Daniel H	Lt Cdr	01-Oct-06	WAR	P LYNX	FLEET CAP LLM & DRM	PORTSMOUTH
Thomas, David J	Cdr	30-Jun-13	LOGS	L	DES ACDS	ABBEY WOOD
Thomas, David W	Lt Cdr	01-Oct-11	WAR	P MER	829 SQN	RNAS CULDROSE
Thomas, Duncan J	Lt Cdr	01-Oct-13	WAR	O LYNX	FLEET CSAV	PORTSMOUTH
Thomas, Emma	Lt RN	26-Jul-86	WAR	N/A	NCHQ CNPS	PORTSMOUTH
Thomas, James M	Lt RN	01-Feb-10	WAR	GSX	BRNC	BRNC DARTMOUTH
Thomas, Joseph	Lt RN	01-May-04	WAR	P MER	MWS RALEIGH	HMS RALEIGH
Thomas, Katie J C	Lt RN	01-Sep-07	LOGS	L	MTM NELSON	HMS NELSON
Thomas, Lynn M	Surg Capt RN	01-Jul-10	MED	Med	MTM NELSON	HMS NELSON
Thomas, Mark A	Lt Cdr	01-Oct-11	ENG	WE	COMDEVFLOT	PLYMOUTH
Thomas, Mark P	Lt RN	01-May-06	WAR	O MER	824 SQN	RNAS CULDROSE
Thomas, Matthew	Lt RN	01-Feb-09	WAR	SM(X)	HMS ASTUTE	
Thomas, Michael J	Lt RN	01-Jun-10	WAR	P SK4	MTM CHF (MERLIN)	RAF BENSON
Thomas, Nicholas E	Capt	31-Aug-14	RM	GS	NCHQ	PORTSMOUTH
Thomas, Owen H	Lt Cdr	01-Oct-10	WAR	INT	DI - SA	LONDON
Thomas, Richard	Capt RN	08-Nov-10	WAR	PWO(U)	DEFENCE ACADEMY	SWINDON
Thomas, Richard	Lt RN	01-Mar-10	ENG	MESM	SETT	FORT BLOCKHOUSE
Thomas, Richard D	Lt Cdr	01-Oct-14	LOGS	L	MTM DEFAC JSCSC	SHRIVENHAM
Thomas, Robert L	Surg Lt RN	01-Mar-13	MED	GDMO	MASF	RNAS CULDROSE
Thomas, Ryan C	Surg Lt Cdr	04-Feb-14	MED	GMP	MTM INM ALVERSTOKE	GOSPORT
Thomas, Stephen	Lt RN	30-Jun-14	WAR	P MER	824 SQN	RNAS CULDROSE
Thomas, Stephen	Lt Cdr	01-Jan-01	ENG	ME	UK MCC	BAHRAIN
Thomason, Michael	Cdr	30-Jun-12	LOGS	L (RES)	FLEET CMR	PORTSMOUTH
Thompson, Adam D	Lt RN	07-Aug-13	ENG	WE	HMS DIAMOND	
Thompson, Alastair J	Lt Cdr	01-Oct-14	WAR	P LYNX	LHF 702 SQN	RNAS YEOVILTON
Thompson, Alexander	Lt RN	14-Sep-13	ENG	ME	HMS WESTMINSTER	
Thompson, Andrew R	Lt Cdr	01-Oct-10	WAR	O LYNX	WMF 825 SQN HQ	RNAS YEOVILTON
Thompson, Antony C	2Lt	02-Sep-12	RM	N/A	CTCRM	EXMOUTH
Thompson, Bernard	Cdr	30-Jun-02	WAR	MCD	BMM	KUWAIT
Thompson, Claire F	Lt Cdr	01-Oct-14	WAR	PWO	HMS DRAGON	
Thompson, Daniel P	Mid	01-May-14	WAR	GSX	BRNC	BRNC DARTMOUTH
Thompson, David A	Lt RN	16-Apr-99	WAR	P LYN7	CHFHQ	RNAS YEOVILTON
Thompson, David J	Lt Cdr	01-Oct-11	WAR	AAWO	FOST DPORT	PLYMOUTH
Thompson, Fiona	Cdr	06-Feb-12	QARNNS	Nurse Officer	DMS WHITTINGTON	LICHFIELD
Thompson, George C	Lt RN	01-Sep-06	WAR	P LYNX	DEF HELI FLYING SCH	SHREWSBURY
Thompson, James	Lt RN	01-May-04	WAR	PWO	RN EXCHANGE AUSTRALIA	CANBERRA
Thompson, James N E	Lt RN	01-May-10	WAR	SM(X)	HMS TALENT	
Thompson, Luke C A	Lt RN	01-May-13	WAR	GSX	HMS SEVERN	
Thompson, Matthew	Lt RN	01-Nov-14	WAR	ATC UT	MTM SHAWBURY	RAF SHAWBURY
Thompson, Michael J	Cdr	30-Jun-13	ENG	ME	NCHQ CNPS	PORTSMOUTH
Thompson, Michael W	SLt	01-Sep-14	ENG	MESM	DCEME SULTAN	HMS SULTAN
Thompson, Michelle E	Lt RN	19-Dec-08	WAR	REG	MTM NELSON	HMS DRYAD
Thompson, Neil J OBE	Cdr	30-Jun-06	WAR	P SK4	MTM NELSON	HMS NELSON
Thompson, Penelope M	Lt RN	01-Jul-08	WAR	GSX	MTM DRAKE	HMS DRAKE

Name	Substantive Rank	Seniority	Branch	Specialisation	Organisation Name	Location Name
Thompson, Peter	SLt	01-Sep-12	ENG	AE	DCEME SULTAN	HMS SULTAN
Thompson, Peter W	Lt RN	01-Oct-12	WAR	MCD	MCM1	FASLANE
Thompson, Richard C CBE	Cdre	27-Jul-12	ENG	AE	DES COMAIR	ABBEY WOOD
Thompson, Robert	Cdr	30-Jun-09	WAR	O MER	RN EXCHANGE USA	WASHINGTON
Thompson, Sam D	Lt RN	01-Jun-09	WAR	P SK6	771 SQN	RNAS CULDROSE
Thompson, Samuel C	Lt RN	01-Jan-15	WAR	P UT	MTM WMO YEOVILTON	GRANTHAM
Thompson, Sarah L	Lt RN	01-May-03	WAR	GSX	FLEET COMOPS NWD	NORTHWOOD
Thompson, Simon C	Lt RN	01-Oct-08	WAR	P SK6	857 NAS	RNAS CULDROSE
Thompson, Simon J	Lt RN	01-Jan-09	LOGS	L	ACNS	PORTSMOUTH
Thompson, Stephen J	Capt RN	09-Jan-12	ENG	ME	DES COMFLEET	ABBEY WOOD
Thompson, William A	Lt Cdr	01-Oct-13	WAR	P LYNX	FOST DPORT	PLYMOUTH
Thompson-Pettit, Richard J	Lt RN	31-Jul-09	ENG	WE	DES COMFLEET	ABBEY WOOD
Thomsen-Rayner, Lavinia L	Lt Cdr	01-Oct-06	WAR	PWO(C)	BDS	WASHINGTON
Thomson, Calum M	Surg Lt RN	07-Aug-13	MED	Medical	BLAKE	BRNC DARTMOUTH
Thomson, David G	Lt RN	20-Dec-13	WAR	GSX	MTM NELSON	HMS NELSON
Thomson, James C	Lt Cdr	01-Oct-09	WAR	AAWO	HMS LANCASTER	
Thomson, Jane M	Lt Cdr	01-Oct-13	ENG	TM	EU OHQ	NORTHWOOD
Thomson, Leighton G	Maj	01-Oct-11	RM	C	FLEET COMOPS NWD	NORTHWOOD
Thomson, Luke I	Maj	01-Oct-13	RM	GS	CDO LOG REGT RM	RMB CHIVENOR
Thomson, Michael L	Lt Cdr	01-Oct-08	ENG	ME	DES COMFLEET	ABBEY WOOD
Thomson, Paul A	Lt Cdr	01-Oct-12	ENG	AE	AWC	EDWARDS AFB
Thomson, Paul D	Lt Cdr	01-Oct-06	ENG	IS	FOST DPORT	PLYMOUTH
Thomson, Susie	Lt Cdr	31-Mar-99	WAR	MEDIA OPS	PJHQ (UK)	NORTHWOOD
Thorley, Graham MBE	Lt Cdr	01-Jan-14	WAR	SM(N)	FLEET COMOPS NSTP30	FAREHAM
Thornback, David M	Surg Lt RN	01-Sep-13	MED	Medical	BRNC	BRNC DARTMOUTH
Thorne, Dain MBE	Lt Cdr	01-Mar-05	ENG	AE	FLEET CSAV	PORTSMOUTH
Thorne, Lee J	Lt Cdr	31-Mar-02	WAR	MW (RES)	FOSNI - CNR	PORTSMOUTH
Thornhill, Stephen M	Lt Cdr	01-Oct-11	MED	MS(CDO)	MOD DEFENCE STAFF	LONDON
Thornton, Charles A G	Lt RN	01-Apr-09	WAR	SM(N)	HMS TRIUMPH	
Thornton, William S C	Lt RN	01-Apr-11	WAR	P LYNX	MTM 815 SQN YEOVILTON	RNAS YEOVILTON
Thorp, David B	Lt Cdr	01-Mar-06	ENG	WE	HDNET	CORSHAM
Thorpe, Richard J	Lt RN	01-Sep-08	WAR	O MER	750 SQN	RNAS CULDROSE
Thorpe, Robert M	Maj	01-Oct-09	RM	GS	PJHQ (UK)	NORTHWOOD
Thurgood, Anthony D	Lt RN	13-Jul-12	MED	MS	INM ALVERSTOKE2	GOSPORT
Thurmott, Robert	Lt RN	01-Apr-12	WAR	MEDIA OPS	EU OHQ	NORTHWOOD
Thurstan, Richard W F	Lt Col	30-Jun-07	RM	LC	1 ASSLT GP RM	PLYMOUTH
Thurston, Edward K P	Lt RN	01-Jun-10	WAR	P SK6	854 NAS	RNAS CULDROSE
Thurston, Mark S	Lt Cdr	01-Oct-11	WAR	C	NATO-ACT-HQ	NORFOLK
Thwaites, Lindsey W	Lt RN	01-Jul-04	ENG	WESM(TWS)	HMS AUDACIOUS	
Tibballs, Laura R	Lt RN	01-Jul-04	LOGS	L	JFLogC	NORTHWOOD
Tibbitts, James A	Lt RN	01-Sep-08	WAR	PWO(N)	UKMARBATSTAFF	PORTSMOUTH
Tidball, Ian C	Lt Cdr	01-Oct-04	WAR	P FW	AWC	VALPARAISO
Tidman, Martin D MBE	Capt	10-Sep-01	RM	GS	NCHQ	PORTSMOUTH
Tidswell, Stephen R	Lt RN	13-Apr-12	WAR	AV	RNAS YEOVILTON	YEOVILTON
Tilden, Philip J E	Cdr	30-Jun-14	WAR	PWO(A)	HMS MONMOUTH	
Tilley, Duncan	Cdr	30-Jun-00	WAR	HM (H CH)	LOAN HYDROG DGHR(N)	TAUNTON
Tilley, Eleanor V	Lt RN	01-May-13	WAR	GSX	MTM NELSON	HMS NELSON
Timmins, Paul G	Capt	03-Apr-09	RM	LC (SCC)	HMS BULWARK	
Timpson, Benjamin H	Lt RN	08-Apr-12	ENG	TM	JFC - DCTS (H)	AYLESBURY
Tin, Jennifer M J	Lt RN	01-Jan-09	QARNNS	PHC	DPHC SW	RNAS CULDROSE
Tindal, Nicolas H C	Capt RN	08-Oct-12	WAR	P SK6	MOD NSD USA	HAWAII
Tindle, Jack A	Lt RN	01-Sep-14	ENG	WESM	MTM RALEIGH	HMS RALEIGH
Tingle, Dawn	Lt RN	01-Jan-09	WAR	ATC	RNAS YEOVILTON	YEOVILTON
Tinsley, David	Lt RN	01-Sep-13	ENG	WE	HMS DEFENDER	
Tippetts, Thomas C M	Lt	02-Sep-14	RM	GS	LFSS CDO LOG REGT RM	RMB CHIVENOR
Tipping, Anthony	Lt Cdr	01-Oct-14	MED	MS(CDO)	NCHQ MEDDIV	PORTSMOUTH
Titcombe, Adam J	Lt Cdr	01-Oct-07	LOGS	L CMA	HMS EXCELLENT	PORTSMOUTH
Tite, Matthew W	Lt RN	01-Sep-13	WAR	GSX	HMS MERSEY	
Titerickx, Andrew T	Maj	01-Oct-10	RM	SCC	42 CDO RM	PLYMOUTH
Titherington, Mark E	Lt RN	01-Apr-12	WAR	HM	HMS SCOTT	
Titmuss, Julian F	Cdr	30-Jun-14	LOGS	L CMA	ACDS	ABBEY WOOD
Titterton, Phillip J OBE	Cdre	21-Jul-14	WAR	SM(CQ)	MOD NSD USA	NORFOLK

Name	Substantive Rank	Seniority	Branch	Specialisation	Organisation Name	Location Name
Tobin, Keith M	Lt RN	01-Sep-13	ENG	ME	HMS KENT	
Todd, Oliver J	Maj	01-Oct-06	RM	MLDR	MTM DEFAC JSCSC	SHRIVENHAM
Toft, Michael D	Cdr	30-Jun-04	ENG	WE	DES COMFLEET	ABBEY WOOD
Tolcher, Daniel G	Lt RN	15-Apr-11	WAR	SM(X)	HMS TIRELESS	
Tomasi, Vittorio L	Capt	03-Sep-14	RM	GS	42 CDO RM	PLYMOUTH
Tomlin, Ian S	Lt Cdr	01-Oct-11	ENG	WESM(TWS)	HMS TALENT	
Tomlinson, Amy R	Lt Cdr	01-Oct-11	LOGS	L	UKMARBATSTAFF	PORTSMOUTH
Tomlinson, Luke M	Lt RN	01-Sep-13	WAR	SM(X)	HMS AMBUSH	
Toms, Nicholas J M	Lt RN	01-Jul-11	LOGS	L	HMS ENTERPRISE	
Tonge, Malcolm S	Lt Cdr	01-Oct-09	ENG	ME	FLEET COMOPS NWD	NORTHWOOD
Tonge, Michael	Lt RN	09-Jun-06	ENG	MESM	DES COMFLEET	ABBEY WOOD
Toogood, Mark J	Lt Cdr	01-Oct-14	LOGS	L	HMS DEFENDER	
Toon, Charlotte S	Surg Lt Cdr	02-Aug-11	MED	GMP	DPHC SOUTH	HMS EXCELLENT
Toon, Paul G	Lt Cdr	01-Oct-09	WAR	AV	RNAS CULDROSE	HELSTON
Toone, Stephen A	Lt Cdr	01-Oct-09	ENG	WE	NAVY MCTA	PORTSMOUTH
Toozs-Hobson, Oliver J	Mid	01-Feb-14	WAR	GSX	BRNC	BRNC DARTMOUTH
Topham, Neil F	Lt RN	01-Feb-01	ENG	TM	MTM DEFAC CMT MSC	SHRIVENHAM
Torbet, Linda	Lt RN	01-Jan-04	ENG	AE	OCLC LONDON	LONDON
Torney, Colin J	Lt Cdr	01-Oct-06	ENG		DES COMFLEET	BARROW IN FURNESS
Tortelli, Yasmin	Lt RN	13-Jul-12	LOGS	L	FLEET CMR	PORTSMOUTH
Totten, Philip M MBE	Lt Col	30-Jun-12	RM	GS	HQ 3 CDO BDE RM	PLYMOUTH
Tough, Iain S	Lt Cdr	01-Oct-09	ENG	WESM(SWS)	FOST SM SEA	HMNB CLYDE
Towell, Peter J OBE	Capt RN	04-Mar-14	ENG	ME	COMPORFLOT	PORTSMOUTH
Towler, Alison	Cdr	30-Jun-06	LOGS	L BAR	DCDS PERS - SPA	RAF NORTHOLT
Townend, Henry R	Lt	01-Sep-12	RM	GS	LFSS CDO LOG REGT RM	RMB CHIVENOR
Towner, Stephen D P	Surg Lt Cdr	06-Aug-13	MED	EM	MTM INM ALVERSTOKE	GOSPORT
Townsend, Anna M	Lt RN	22-Mar-08	WAR	HM	RN EXCHANGE USA	WASHINGTON
Townsend, Graham P	Lt Cdr	01-Oct-06	WAR	O SK6	NATO-MOU-NSHQ	CASTEAU
Toy, Malcolm J	Cdre	04-Oct-10	ENG	AE	MAA	ABBEY WOOD
Tracey, Alan D	Cdr	30-Jun-13	ENG	AE	DES COMAIR	ABBEY WOOD
Trafford, Michael	Maj	01-Oct-13	RM	C	PJHQ (UK)	NORTHWOOD
Treanor, Martin A	Cdr	31-Dec-99	ENG	AE	NCHQ CNPS	PORTSMOUTH
Trebilcock, Robert J	Mid	17-Nov-14	WAR	P UT	BRNC	BRNC DARTMOUTH
Tredray, Thomas P	Cdr	30-Jun-13	WAR	AAWO	HMS IRON DUKE	
Tregale, Jamie	Lt RN	01-Apr-04	WAR	HM	FLEET COMOPS NWD	NORTHWOOD
Tregunna, Gary A	Lt Cdr	08-Aug-03	WAR	SM(N)	SETT	FORT BLOCKHOUSE
Tremelling, Paul N	Cdr	30-Jun-14	WAR	P FW	HQ AIR - COS(CAP)	HIGH WYCOMBE
Trent, Thomas	Lt Cdr	01-Oct-11	WAR	PWO	MCM2	PORTSMOUTH
Tretton, Caroline	Lt RN	01-Jan-05	WAR	HM	1 GP MARHAM	KINGS LYNN
Tretton, Joseph E	Lt Cdr	01-Oct-13	WAR	HM(AM)	1 GP MARHAM	KINGS LYNN
Trevethan, Christopher J	Lt Cdr	01-Oct-13	WAR	PWO	MTM NELSON	HMS NELSON
Trevethan, Sean C	Lt Cdr	01-Oct-13	ENG	WE	NC REQUIREMENTS MANAGERS	ABBEY WOOD
Trevor-Harris, George G	SLt	01-Sep-14	WAR	GSX	HMS DRAGON	
Trevorrow, Martyn	Mid	17-Nov-14	WAR	P UT	BRNC	BRNC DARTMOUTH
Trewinnard-Boyle, Robin M	Lt Cdr	01-Oct-10	ENG	AE	DES COMJE	ABBEY WOOD
Triggol, Martin P	Capt	01-Apr-11	RM	SCC	1 ASSLT GP RM	PLYMOUTH
Trim, Brian J	Lt Cdr	01-Jan-07	WAR	PWO(N)	HMS KENT	
Trimble, Andrew P	2Lt	25-Aug-14	RM	N/A	CTCRM	EXMOUTH
Trinder, Stephen	Lt Cdr	01-Oct-08	LOGS	L	DCD - MODSAP KSA	RIYADH
Tristram, Robert E	Lt RN	01-Nov-10	WAR	MCD	FDS HQ	PORTSMOUTH
Tritschler, Edwin L MBE	Capt RN	01-Jul-13	ENG	AE	DES COMJE	YEOVIL
Trowman, Oliver S	Lt RN	01-Sep-09	ENG	AE P	CHF - 846	RAF BENSON
Trubshaw, Christopher	Lt Cdr	01-Oct-04	WAR	P SKW	FLEET AV VL	RNAS YEOVILTON
Trudgian, Martin	Lt RN	01-Apr-12	WAR	HM	HMS ECHO	
Truelove, Samantha	Lt Cdr	01-Oct-08	LOGS	L	MOD NSD	LONDON
Truman, Oliver J	Capt	01-Sep-08	RM	GS	MOD DEFENCE STAFF	LONDON
Tucker, Philip J	Lt RN	01-Sep-04	WAR	P SK4	845 SQN	RNAS YEOVILTON
Tucker, Simon J W	Maj	01-Oct-08	RM	LC	CTCRM	EXMOUTH
Tuckley, Christopher J L	Lt RN	01-Sep-14	ENG	MESM	DCEME SULTAN	HMS SULTAN
Tuckwood, Alex I	Lt RN	19-Nov-09	WAR	O LYNX	LHF 815 SQN	RNAS YEOVILTON
Tuckwood, Neil E	Lt RN	01-Oct-10	WAR	O SKW	854 NAS	RNAS CULDROSE
Tudor, Owen J	Lt RN	01-May-07	LOGS	L	NATO-ACO-JFC HQ	BRUNSSUM

Name	Substantive Rank	Seniority	Branch	Specialisation	Organisation Name	Location Name
Tuhey, James J G	Lt Cdr	01-Oct-14	ENG	WESM(TWS)	PJHQ (UK)	NORTHWOOD
Tulloch, Stuart W	Lt Col	30-Jun-13	RM	SCC	CDO LOG REGT RM	RMB CHIVENOR
Tumilty, Kevin	Lt RN	01-Jan-04	ENG	WE	DES COMFLEET	ABBEY WOOD
Turberville, Christopher T L	Lt Cdr	01-Oct-11	LOGS	L	NATO-ACO-JFC HQ	NAPLES
Turfrey, Matthew	Lt RN	01-Jun-13	ENG	AE	MTM 820 SQN CULDROSE	RNAS CULDROSE
Turley, Richard A	Lt RN	04-Mar-08	WAR	AW (RES)	FLEET CMR	BRNC DARTMOUTH
Turnbull, Graham D	Cdr	30-Jun-02	WAR	HM (H CH)	FOSNI - NRC EE	LONDON
Turnbull, Paul S	Surg Capt RN	15-Jul-14	MED	Occ Med	NCHQ MEDDIV	PORTSMOUTH
Turnbull, Simon J L	Cdr	30-Jun-02	WAR	PWO(U)	FLEET MARITIME WARFARE	HMS COLLINGWOOD
Turner, Antony R	Lt Col	30-Jun-13	RM	GS	COMUKAMPHIBFOR	PORTSMOUTH
Turner, Daniel T	SLt	01-Oct-13	ENG	WE	MWS COLLINGWOOD	HMS COLLINGWOOD
Turner, David J	Cdr	30-Jun-12	LOGS	L SM	COMFASFLOT	HELENSBURGH
Turner, David N	Lt Cdr	01-Oct-08	WAR	P LYNX	FLEET COMOPS NWD	NORTHWOOD
Turner, Duncan L	Lt RN	01-Jan-06	ENG	WE	DES COMFLEET	ABBEY WOOD
Turner, Gareth J	Lt RN	19-Sep-07	LOGS	L	COMMANDER OP TRAINING	HMS COLLINGWOOD
Turner, Gary H	Lt RN	09-Apr-09	LOGS	L	DES COMLAND	ABBEY WOOD
Turner, Kevin P	Lt RN	01-Sep-08	ENG	MESM	CAPTAIN BASE SAFETY CLYDE	HELENSBURGH
Turner, Matthew	Lt Cdr	01-Oct-13	ENG	ME	HMS ST ALBANS	
Turner, Matthew C	Lt RN	01-Sep-14	WAR	GSX	HMS ARGYLL	
Turner, Matthew J	Surg Cdr	04-Jan-11	MED	GMP (C&S)	NCHQ MEDDIV	PORTSMOUTH
Turner, Matthew J	SLt	01-Sep-12	MED	Medical	BLAKE	BRNC DARTMOUTH
Turner, Simon A	Lt Col	30-Jun-13	RM	GS	NCHQ CNPS	PORTSMOUTH
Turrell, Richard D	Lt RN	17-Dec-10	WAR	AV	HMS ILLUSTRIOUS	
Turrell, Shelly S J	Lt RN	08-Dec-12	ENG	ME	HMS RICHMOND	
Tustain, Paul A	Lt RN	09-Jun-06	ENG	MESM	HMS TRENCHANT	
Tutchings, Andrew	Lt Cdr	01-Oct-08	WAR	GSX	RN EXCHANGE GERMANY	PORTSMOUTH
Tweed, Charles S R	Surg Lt RN	01-Jan-14	MED	Medical	BRNC	BRNC DARTMOUTH
Tweed, Jonathan J	Lt RN	01-Sep-08	ENG	ME	HMS SCOTT	
Tweedie, Howard J	Cdr	30-Jun-11	WAR	OP INT	JESC	RAF DIGBY
Twigg, Neil R	Lt Cdr	01-Oct-13	WAR	P FW	MTM	WASHINGTON
Twinn, Richard	Lt RN	01-Mar-11	ENG	MESM	HMS VANGUARD	
Twiselton, Matthew J	Lt Cdr	01-Oct-12	ENG	AE	MAA	ABBEY WOOD
Twist, Martin T	Maj	01-Sep-01	RM	GS	RN EXCHANGE USA	WASHINGTON
Tyack, Terence J	Cdr	30-Jun-07	WAR	P SK4	FLEET ACOS(RP)	PORTSMOUTH
Tyce, David J	Maj	01-Oct-05	RM	SCC	DDC	LONDON
Tyler, Adrian	Lt Cdr	01-Oct-14	WAR		RN EXCHANGE USA	WASHINGTON
Tyler, Ian P.	Capt	03-Apr-09	RM	SCC	RMR LONDON	LONDON
Tyler, Jeremy	Lt Cdr	01-Jul-04	WAR	AAWO	RN EXCHANGE USA	WASHINGTON
Tyler, Joseph J	2Lt	01-Sep-11	RM	GS	43 CDO FPGRM	HELENSBURGH
Tymm, Oliver D	Mid	01-Feb-14	WAR	GSX	BRNC	BRNC DARTMOUTH
Tyrrell-Moore, William E R	2Lt	25-Aug-14	RM	N/A	CTCRM	EXMOUTH
Tysler, Charlotte G	Lt RN	01-Mar-11	WAR	P UT	MTM 824 SQN CULDROSE	RNAS CULDROSE

U

Name	Substantive Rank	Seniority	Branch	Specialisation	Organisation Name	Location Name
Ubhi, Wayne G	Cdr	30-Jun-14	ENG	ME	MTM FLEET HQ	PORTSMOUTH
Uglow, James A	Mid	17-Nov-14	WAR	GSX	BRNC	BRNC DARTMOUTH
Uhrin, Dusan	Capt	01-Sep-12	RM	GS	43 CDO FPGRM	HELENSBURGH
Underwood, Michael R	Lt RN	01-Nov-13	ENG	WE	HMS RALEIGH	TORPOINT
Underwood, Richard	Cdr	30-Jun-14	LOGS	L	MTM DEFAC JSCSC	SHRIVENHAM
Unsworth, Benjamin M	Lt RN	01-Jan-08	WAR	O SKW	849 SQN	RNAS CULDROSE
Unwin, Nicholas R F	Lt Cdr	01-Oct-09	WAR	PWO	MCM1	FASLANE
Uprichard, Andrew J	Maj	01-Oct-10	RM	GS	40 CDO RM	TAUNTON
Upton, Iain D	Cdr	30-Jun-03	ENG	WE	MTM HASLER COY	HMS DRAKE
Urry, Simon R MBE	Lt Col	30-Jun-12	RM	GS	NCHQ	NCHQ
Urwin, Stuart J	Lt Cdr	01-Oct-08	WAR	PWO(C)	PJHQ (UK)	NORTHWOOD
Usborne, Neil V	Lt RN	01-May-13	WAR	GSX	MCM2	PORTSMOUTH
Usher, Brian	Maj	01-Oct-08	RM	SCC	MTM HASLER COY	HMS DRAKE
Ussher, Jeremy H D	Lt Cdr	01-Oct-11	ENG	TM	FLEET FOST ACOS(Trg)	PORTSMOUTH
Utley, Michael K	Capt RN	10-Sep 12	WAR	PWO(A)	MTM MOD CNS/ACNS	LONDON

Name	Substantive Rank	Seniority	Branch	Specialisation	Organisation Name	Location Name

V

Name	Substantive Rank	Seniority	Branch	Specialisation	Organisation Name	Location Name
Vail, David J	Mid	08-Sep-14	WAR	GSX	BRNC	BRNC DARTMOUTH
Vale, Andrew J	Surg Cdr	01-Jul-14	MED	GMP	DPHC OVERSEAS	HMS ROOKE
Valvona, Dominic M MBE	Lt RN	06-Apr-06	ENG	ME	MWS DDS	PORTSMOUTH
Van Der Merwe, F E	Surg Lt Cdr	01-Aug-12	MED	GMP	PCRF	RFA ARGUS
Van Duin, Martin I A	Lt Cdr	01-Oct-14	WAR	P LYNX	MTM WMF 825 SQN YEOVILTON	RNAS YEOVILTON
Vance, Andrew	Lt RN	01-Sep-12	ENG	AE	1710 NAS	PORTSMOUTH
Vanderpump, David J	Capt RN	10-Sep-12	ENG	ME	DES COMFLEET	ABBEY WOOD
Vanstone, Sean M	Surg Lt Cdr	06-Aug-14	MED	Medical	BLAKE	BRNC DARTMOUTH
Varco, Thomas G	SLt	01-Nov-14	LOGS	L	HMS PORTLAND	
Varley, Ian G	Lt Cdr	01-Jan-01	WAR	P MER	824 SQN	RNAS CULDROSE
Vartan, Mark R	Cdr	30-Jun-14	WAR	HM(AS)	HMS ENTERPRISE	
Varty, Jason A	Lt Cdr	01-Oct-07	WAR	HM (H CH)	HMS PROTECTOR	
Vasey, Owen R	Lt RN	01-Jun-09	LOGS	L	MTM NELSON	HMS NELSON
Vassallo, James	Surg Lt RN	04-Aug-10	MED	GDMO	INM ALVERSTOKE2	GOSPORT
Vaughan, Edward A	I t Cdr	01-Oct 13	WAR	P SK4	MTM CHF (MERLIN)	RAF BENSON
Vaughan, James R	Lt RN	01-Jun-03	ENG	MESM	HMS SULTAN	GOSPORT
Vaughan, Jamie B	Lt RN	15-Apr-11	ENG	ME	HMS QUEEN ELIZABETH	
Veacock, Gary T	Maj	01-Oct-13	RM	SCC	42 CDO RM	PLYMOUTH
Veal, Dominic J	Lt RN	01-May-02	WAR	INT	43 CDO FPGRM	HELENSBURGH
Velickovic, Samuel D	Lt RN	01-Apr-12	WAR	GSX	HMS DUNCAN	
Venables, Adrian N	Lt Cdr	01-Dec-00	WAR	CIS (RES)	FLEET CAP IS	PORTSMOUTH
Venables, Daniel M	Maj	01-Oct-09	RM	MLDR	UNMIS SUDAN	SUDAN
Venn, Nicholas S C	Lt Col	30-Jun-12	RM	P LYN7	OPS DIR	LONDON
Vereker, Richard J P	Lt RN	01-Apr-06	WAR	SM(X)	HMS TRENCHANT	
Verney, Kirsty H	Surg Lt Cdr (D)	09-Jul-02	DENTAL	GDP	HMS SULTAN	GOSPORT
Vessey, Lee M	Lt Cdr	01-Oct-12	WAR	PWO	HMS IRON DUKE	
Veti, Mark A	Lt RN	01-Feb-06	WAR	PWO	FLEET MARITIME WARFARE	HMS COLLINGWOOD
Vickers, John OBE	Cdr	30-Jun-06	ENG	AE	DES COMJE	YEOVIL
Vickers, Patrick T	Lt RN	01-Aug-13	ENG	WESM	MTM RALEIGH	HMS RALEIGH
Vickery, Ben R	Lt Cdr	01-Oct-08	WAR	MCD	FOST MPV SEA	HMNB CLYDE
Viggars, Christopher E	Capt	01-Sep-11	RM	GS	HMS OCEAN	
Vijayan, Deepak	Surg Lt Cdr	01-Nov-11	MED	GS	MTM INM ALVERSTOKE	GOSPORT
Vincent, Christopher	Lt RN	01-May-07	WAR	INT	FLEET COMOPS NWD	HMS COLLINGWOOD
Vincent, Daniel	Lt Cdr	01-Oct-04	ENG	TM	MTM DEFAC JSCSC	SHRIVENHAM
Vincent, Fay R	SLt	17-Nov-14	QARNNS	Nurse Officer	BRNC	BRNC DARTMOUTH
Vincent, Peter	Lt RN	01-Mar-12	ENG	MESM	HMS TRIUMPH	
Vincent, Stuart M	Lt RN	01-Jan-07	ENG	TM(SM)	FLEET FOST TBTU	HMS COLLINGWOOD
Vincent-Spall, Richard	Mid	08-Sep-14	ENG	WE	BRNC	BRNC DARTMOUTH
Vines, Adam M	Lt RN	01-Apr-14	WAR	P UT	MTM RAF VALLEY	HOLYHEAD
Vines, Nicholas O	Lt Cdr	01-Oct-09	MED	MS(EHO)	DMS WHITTINGTON	LICHFIELD
Vines, Sarah K	Lt RN	09-Aug-08	ENG	TM	NETS (E)	PORTSMOUTH
Viney, Peter M	Lt Cdr	01-Oct-07	LOGS	L	UKMARBATSTAFF	PORTSMOUTH
Visram, Adrian H	Lt Cdr	01-Oct-13	WAR	PWO	MTM MWS COLLINGWOOD	HMS COLLINGWOOD
Vitali, Robert C	Capt RN	09-Oct-12	WAR	AAWO	MOD NSD	LONDON
Vivian, Michael A	SLt	01-Jul-14	WAR	P UT	MTM RAF CRANWELL	RAFC CRANWELL
Vivian, Philip	Lt Cdr	01-Oct-13	LOGS	L	CHFHQ	RNAS YEOVILTON
Voke, Christen A	Lt RN	01-Aug-02	WAR	SM(X)	RN EXCHANGE USA	WASHINGTON
Vollentine, Lucy	Cdr	30-Jun-10	LOGS	L	COMPORFLOT	PORTSMOUTH
Voudouris, Vangeli	Mid	17-Nov-14	ENG	TM	BRNC	BRNC DARTMOUTH
Vout, Debra K	Lt Cdr	01-Oct-08	WAR	C	HMS COLLINGWOOD	FAREHAM
Vowles, Barnaby J	2Lt	25-Aug-14	RM	N/A	CTCRM	EXMOUTH
Vowles, Iain R	Lt Cdr	01-Apr-14	ENG	WESM(SWS)	MTM RALEIGH	HMS RALEIGH
Vowles, Mitchell J	Lt Cdr	01-Oct-08	WAR	GSX	OCLC BIRMINGHAM	BIRMINGHAM
Voyce, John E	Cdr	30-Jun-09	ENG	ME	DES COMFLEET	ABBEY WOOD

W

Name	Substantive Rank	Seniority	Branch	Specialisation	Organisation Name	Location Name
Waddington, Andrew	SLt	01-Sep-12	ENG	MESM	HMS VIGILANT	
Wade, Frederick O A	Lt RN	01-Aug-14	WAR	GSX	HMS LANCASTER	
Wade, Nicholas J	Lt RN	30-Jul-09	WAR	C	NATO ACO	NORTHWOOD
Wade, Robert J	Lt RN	01-Mar-14	ENG	MESM	DCEME SULTAN	HMS SULTAN

Name	Substantive Rank	Seniority	Branch	Specialisation	Organisation Name	Location Name
Wadsworth, Richard Y	Lt Cdr	01-Oct-09	ENG	ME	NAVY MCTA	PORTSMOUTH
Wafer, Michael J	Mid	17-Nov-14	WAR	GSX	BRNC	BRNC DARTMOUTH
Wagstaff, Michael	RN Chpln	31-Mar-08	Ch S	Chaplain	HMS BULWARK	
Wagstaff, Neil	Capt RN	25-Jun-12	MED	MS	DMS WHITTINGTON	LICHFIELD
Wagstaffe, James N G	Lt RN	01-Sep-11	ENG	WE	MWS COLLINGWOOD	HMS COLLINGWOOD
Wainhouse, Michael J	Cdre	22-Apr-14	WAR	PWO(A)	DEFENCE ACADEMY	SHRIVENHAM
Waite, Matthew T	Maj	01-Oct-08	RM	GS	NCHQ	NCHQ
Waite, Tobias G	Lt Cdr	01-Oct-08	WAR	PWO(U)	MTM DEFAC JSCSC	SHRIVENHAM
Wake, Daniel C	Capt	03-Sep-14	RM	GS	42 CDO RM	PLYMOUTH
Wakefield, Matthew A	Lt RN	01-Sep-11	ENG	AE	DES COMJE	YEOVIL
Waldmeyer, Edward	Maj	01-Oct-10	RM	GS	43 CDO FPGRM	HELENSBURGH
Waldron, James J	Mid	01-May-14	WAR	GSX	BRNC	BRNC DARTMOUTH
Wale, Alexandra J	Lt RN	01-Mar-13	WAR	GSX	HMS DAUNTLESS	
Wales, Benjamin D	Cdr	30-Jun-11	LOGS	L CMA	CDP PERS TRG	LONDON
Walker, Alasdair J OBE	Surg R Adm	29-Jul-14	MED	GS (C&S)	DMS WHITTINGTON	LICHFIELD
Walker, Andrew J	Lt Col	30-Jun-12	RM	GS	NATO-ACT-JWC	STAVANGER
Walker, Daniel H	Lt RN	01-Jan-04	WAR	P FW	736 NAS	RNAS CULDROSE
Walker, Daniel J	SLt	01-May-12	LOGS	L	NCHQ	PORTSMOUTH
Walker, David	Lt Cdr	31-Mar-97	LOGS	L (RES)	NATO-ACO-SHAPE	CASTEAU
Walker, Fergus S	Lt RN	01-Sep-08	ENG	WESM(TWS)	DES COMFLEET	ABBEY WOOD
Walker, Graeme H	Lt RN	01-Sep-07	ENG	AE P	LHF 815 SQN	RNAS YEOVILTON
Walker, Ian M	Lt Cdr	01-Oct-12	ENG	MESM	DES COMFLEET	THURSO
Walker, James J	Lt RN	01-Jan-04	WAR	O LYNX	MOD NSD	LONDON
Walker, Jamie	Lt Cdr	01-Oct-14	ENG	ME	MTM NELSON	HMS NELSON
Walker, John	Lt Cdr	01-Oct-13	WAR	INT	PJHQ (UK)	NORTHWOOD
Walker, Mark	Lt Cdr	01-Oct-02	ENG	TM	DEFENCE ACADEMY	SHRIVENHAM
Walker, Mark	Cdr	30-Jun-07	WAR	P SK4	FLEET CSAV	PORTSMOUTH
Walker, Mark J	Lt Cdr	01-Oct-14	WAR	PWO(SM)	HMS TRIUMPH	
Walker, Mark T	Mid	17-Nov-14	WAR	GSX	BRNC	BRNC DARTMOUTH
Walker, Nicholas J	Capt RN	18-Aug-09	ENG	MESM	DES COMFLEET	ABBEY WOOD
Walker, Nicholas M	Cdr	30-Jun-09	WAR	P FW	FLEET CSAV	PORTSMOUTH
Walker, Peter R	Cdr	30-Jun-07	ENG	IS	LOAN DSTL	SALISBURY
Walker, Richard P	Lt RN	01-Jul-04	WAR	O MER	814 SQN	RNAS CULDROSE
Walker, Robin	Lt Cdr	01-Oct-08	WAR	MCD	RN EXCHANGE CANADA	OTTAWA
Walker, Stephen	Lt Cdr	01-Apr-10	ENG	WESM(TWS)	NBC CLYDE	HMNB CLYDE
Walker, Stephen P	Cdr	30-Jun-08	WAR	SM(CQ)	FLEET COMOPS NWD	NORTHWOOD
Walkley, Kyle J	Lt RN	07-Oct-11	WAR	GSX	MCM2	PORTSMOUTH
Wall, Irene J	Lt Cdr	01-Oct-06	LOGS	L	CHAPLAIN OF THE FLEET	PORTSMOUTH
Wall, John H	Capt	01-Sep-09	RM	GS	1 ASSLT GP RM	PLYMOUTH
Wall, Karl	Lt Cdr	01-Oct-11	WAR	PWO(SM)	NCHQ CNPERS	PORTSMOUTH
Wall, Samuel J	Lt RN	01-Mar-13	ENG	ME	HMS PORTLAND	
Wall, Steven N	Lt Cdr	01-Oct-07	WAR	AAWO	NATO ACO	NORTHWOOD
Wall, Thomas C	Lt RN	01-Feb-08	WAR	MCD	MCM2	PORTSMOUTH
Wallace, Allan OBE	Cdr	30-Jun-01	WAR	PWO(N)	CIO-J6	LONDON
Wallace, Anthony R	Lt Cdr	01-Oct-10	WAR	PWO MW	FOST DPORT	PLYMOUTH
Wallace, Iain S	Lt Cdr	01-Oct-10	ENG	IS	HMS DAUNTLESS	
Wallace, James G	Lt RN	01-Apr-09	WAR	P SK4	845 SQN	RNAS YEOVILTON
Wallace, Josef K E	Surg Lt RN	01-Aug-12	MED	GDMO	HMS VANGUARD	
Wallace, Kirsty E	Lt RN	01-Sep-07	ENG	IS	MTM WMO YEOVILTON	RNAS YEOVILTON
Wallace, Matthew E	Mid	08-Sep-14	ENG	ME	BRNC	BRNC DARTMOUTH
Wallace, Nicola K	Lt RN	19-Dec-08	ENG	AE	1710 NAS	PORTSMOUTH
Wallace, Richard S	Lt Cdr	01-Oct-10	WAR	PWO	FLEET SNMG RN NATO SUP	PORTSMOUTH
Wallace, Richard S	Maj	01-Oct-07	RM	GS	MTM DEFAC JSCSC	SHRIVENHAM
Wallace, Scott P	Maj	01-Oct-08	RM	GS	40 CDO RM	TAUNTON
Wallace, Simon J	Cdr	30-Jun-11	WAR	AAWO	TIO	LONDON
Waller, Bentley R	Surg Lt Cdr	01-Sep-11	MED	Anaes	MTM INM ALVERSTOKE	GOSPORT
Waller, Ramsay	Maj	01-Oct-13	RM	C	NCHQ	
Waller, Robert	Lt RN	01-Mar-13	ENG	MESM	BDS	WASHINGTON
Waller, Steven	Cdr	30-Jun-07	WAR	SM(CQ)	HMS VENGEANCE	
Walliker, Michael J D OBE	Cdre	06-Jan-09	WAR	SM(CQ)	COMFASFLOT	HELENSBURGH
Wallington-Smith, James	Lt RN	01-Sep-09	WAR	GSX	HMS CHARGER	
Wallis, Adrian J	Cdr	30-Jun-02	WAR	PWO(C)	SCU SHORE	HMS COLLINGWOOD

Name	Substantive Rank	Seniority	Branch	Specialisation	Organisation Name	Location Name
Wallis, Michael N A	2Lt	25-Aug-14	RM	N/A	CTCRM	EXMOUTH
Wallis, Thomas D	Capt	03-Sep-14	RM	GS	43 CDO FPGRM	HELENSBURGH
Wallis, Thomas O	Lt RN	01-Mar-11	ENG	AE P	MTM SHAWBURY	RAF SHAWBURY
Walls, Kevin F	Maj	01-May-00	RM	MLDR	CTG LAND WAR SCHOOL	WARMINSTER
Walsh, Kevin M	Lt Cdr	01-Nov-04	WAR	PWO(A)	NC REQUIREMENTS MANAGERS	ABBEY WOOD
Walters, Cameron F	Mid	01-Nov-13	WAR	SM(X)	BRNC	BRNC DARTMOUTH
Walters, Elizabeth	Surg Lt RN	07-Aug-13	MED	Medical	BLAKE	BRNC DARTMOUTH
Walters, Richard	Lt Cdr	31-Mar-04	WAR	MEDIA OPS	MTM NELSON	HMS NELSON
Walton, Darren J	Lt RN	01-Nov-14	LOGS	L	820 SQN	RNAS CULDROSE
Walton, George J	Lt Cdr	01-Oct-11	WAR	AAWO	MTM DRAKE	HMS DRAKE
Walton, Stephen D	Lt Cdr	01-Oct-06	WAR	MW	PJHQ (UK)	NORTHWOOD
Warburton, Alison	Lt Cdr	01-Oct-12	QARNNS	OT (C&S)	DMS WHITTINGTON	BIRMINGHAM
Ward, Alex J	Surg Lt RN	06-Aug-14	MED	Medical	BLAKE	BRNC DARTMOUTH
Ward, Alexander J	Lt Cdr	01-Oct-10	LOGS	L BAR	NCHQ - CNLS	NORTHWOOD
Ward, Andrew E	Lt RN	01-Nov-14	WAR	GSX	MWS COLLINGWOOD	HMS COLLINGWOOD
Ward, Anthony S	Capt	26-May-07	RM	GS (RFS)	RMR MERSEYSIDE	LIVERPOOL
Ward, Antony I	Lt RN	01-Dec-08	WAR	ATC	RNAS YEOVILTON	YEOVILTON
Ward, Douglas J	Lt Cdr	01-Nov-06	Ch S	L BAR SM	NCHQ - CNLS	PORTSMOUTH
Ward, Gareth J	Lt RN	01-Mar-09	ENG	MESM	HMS SULTAN	GOSPORT
Ward, Jared M	Lt Cdr	01-Oct-12	LOGS	L	HMS OCEAN	
Ward, Michelle T	Lt Cdr	01-Oct-14	WAR	PWO	NATO-ACO-JFC HQ	BRUNSSUM
Ward, Nicholas D	Lt RN	01-Sep-14	WAR	GSX	HMS SUTHERLAND	
Ward, Robert A	Lt RN	01-Jul-12	ENG	WESM	HMS VANGUARD	
Ward, Simon	Lt Cdr	01-Sep-05	WAR	P LYNX	RNAS YEOVILTON	YEOVILTON
Ward, Simon	Capt	01-Sep-12	RM	GS	SFSG A COY	RAF ST ATHAN
Ward, Stephen D	Cdr	30-Jun-07	ENG	ME	HMS ALBION	
Ward, Steven I	Capt	30-Mar-12	RM	SCC	CTCRM	EXMOUTH
Ward, Timothy E P	Lt RN	01-Mar-14	ENG	MESM	DCEME SULTAN	HMS SULTAN
Warden, Sophie	Surg SLt (D)	01-Apr-13	DENTAL	GDP(VDP)	BLAKE	BRNC DARTMOUTH
Wardill, George	Lt RN	01-Jan-12	WAR	P UT	MTM 824 SQN CULDROSE	RNAS CULDROSE
Wardle, Daniel J	Lt RN	01-Feb-14	WAR	GSX	HMS MERSEY	
Wardle, Gareth S	Lt RN	21-Feb-09	WAR	P SK4	RN EXCHANGE USA	WASHINGTON
Wardley, Thomas E	Lt Cdr	01-Oct-14	QARNNS	EN (C&S)	MDHU DERRIFORD	PLYMOUTH
Ware, Andrew T	Lt Cdr	01-Oct-12	WAR	INT	FLEET COMOPS NWD	RAF WYTON
Ware, Peter J	Lt Cdr	01-Oct-13	WAR	PWO(N)	FOST DPORT	PLYMOUTH
Wareham, Michael P	R Adm	30-Sep-13	ENG	MESM	DES COMFLEET	ABBEY WOOD
Wareham, Sidney J	Lt Cdr	01-Oct-14	WAR	INT	FLEET COMOPS NWD	NORTHWOOD
Waring, Gavin P	SLt	01-Jan-14	LOGS	L	HMS OCEAN	
Waring, John R	Lt RN	30-Jun-11	ENG	TM	NATO - BRUSSELS	BRUSSELS
Warland, Adam	Lt RN	01-Feb-11	ENG	TM	45 CDO RM	DUNDEE
Warner, Philip C	Lt RN	01-May-14	LOGS	L	RNAS CULDROSE	HELSTON
Warner, Stephen E	Lt RN	01-Jun-09	LOGS	L FS	PFCS HQ	HMS EXCELLENT
Warner, Thomas M	SLt	01-Sep-12	WAR	P UT	RAF LINTON-ON-OUSE	RAF LINTON ON OUSE
Warnock, Christopher	SLt	01-Dec-12	WAR	GSX	HMS DAUNTLESS	
Warr, Richard F	Lt Cdr	01-Oct-02	ENG	WESM(TWS)	D STRAT PROG	ABBEY WOOD
Warren, Matthew J	Lt Cdr	01-Oct-14	WAR	HM	COMDEVFLOT	PLYMOUTH
Warren, Rebecca J	Lt Cdr	01-Oct-13	WAR	HM (M CH)	FLEET HM UNIT	PLYMOUTH
Warren, William J	Lt RN	01-Apr-12	WAR	GSX	MTM MWS DDS	PORTSMOUTH
Warrender, William J	Capt RN	26-Apr-11	WAR	PWO(A)	OPS DIR	LONDON
Warwick, Andrew	Lt RN	01-Nov-12	WAR	SM(X)	HMS TRIUMPH	
Warwick, Francesca R	Surg Lt RN (D)	19-Jul-12	DENTAL	GDP	45 CDO RM	DUNDEE
Warwick, Philip D	Capt RN	06-Jan-09	WAR	PWO(U)	UK MCC	BAHRAIN
Warwick-Brown, Peter R	Mid	01-May-14	WAR	GSX	BRNC	BRNC DARTMOUTH
Washer, Nicholas B J	Capt RN	17-Sep-13	WAR	PWO(C)	FLEET CAP IS	PORTSMOUTH
Waskett, Daniel	Lt RN	01-Jan-07	WAR	O MER	820 SQN	RNAS CULDROSE
Waterfield, Simon	Lt Cdr	01-Jun-02	WAR	INT	FLEET MARITIME WARFARE	HMS COLLINGWOOD
Waterhouse, Phillip	Capt RN	03-Sep-13	LOGS	L	FLEET SPT LOGS INFRA	PORTSMOUTH
Waterman, Matthew L	Lt RN	01-Sep-12	ENG	WE	FLEET CAP SSM	PORTSMOUTH
Waters, Michael R	Lt Cdr	01-Oct-13	WAR	PWO	HMS DRAGON	
Watkin, Paul	Lt RN	01-Sep-10	ENG	WE	HQ JHC	ANDOVER
Watkins, Alun K	Capt	18-Jul-08	RM	SCC	101 LOG BDE	ALDERSHOT
Watkins, Andrew P L	Lt Col	30-Jun-11	RM	GS	MTM MOD CNS/ACNS	LONDON

Name	Substantive Rank	Seniority	Branch	Specialisation	Organisation Name	Location Name
Watkins, Dean T.	Maj	01-Oct-10	RM	SCC	HQ SQN CDO LOG REGT RM	RMB CHIVENOR
Watkins, Jenny	Lt RN	01-Jan-02	ENG	TM	NCHQ CNPS	PORTSMOUTH
Watkins, Kevin J	Lt Cdr	01-Oct-06	ENG	ME	DES COMFLEET	ABBEY WOOD
Watkins, Timothy C	Lt Cdr	01-Oct-00	WAR	P FW	727 NAS	RNAS YEOVILTON
Watkinson, Neil	Lt Col	30-Jun-09	RM	GS (RES)	RMR LONDON	LONDON
Watkis, Andrew N	Lt RN	01-Sep-09	ENG	ME	HMS SULTAN	GOSPORT
Watsham, Richard V	Lt RN	20-May-10	WAR	HM	FLEET COMOPS NWD	NORTHWOOD
Watson, Andrew	Lt Cdr	01-Oct-07	WAR	O MER	HQ JHC CAP DIR	ANDOVER
Watson, Bradley L	Lt Cdr	01-Oct-12	WAR	O SKW	FLEET CSAV	PORTSMOUTH
Watson, Brian R	Capt	01-Jan-02	RM	P LYN7	ARF HQ	RNAS YEOVILTON
Watson, Graham	Maj	01-Oct-10	RM	SCC	HQ 3 CDO BDE RM	ANDOVER
Watson, Ian	Lt Cdr	01-Mar-03	WAR	PWO(A)	MWS COLLINGWOOD	HMS COLLINGWOOD
Watson, James L	Surg Lt RN	01-Aug-12	MED	GDMO	HMS KENT	
Watson, Richard D	Lt Cdr	01-Oct-08	WAR	MCD	DSEA MARITIME	PORTSMOUTH
Watson, Richard I	Maj	01-Oct-04	RM	GS	NCHQ	PORTSMOUTH
Watson, Richard J	Lt Cdr	01-Aug-89	WAR	SM(AWC)	NCHQ CNPS	PORTSMOUTH
Watson, Robin A	Mid	08-Sep-14	WAR	HM	BRNC	BRNC DARTMOUTH
Watson, Simon C	Lt RN	01-Sep-05	ENG	WE	ACNS	PORTSMOUTH
Watson, Stephen P	SLt	01-Oct-13	WAR	AV	CHFHQ	RNAS YEOVILTON
Watt, Anthony J L OBE	Capt RN	18-Jun-13	WAR	PWO(U)	FOST NWD (JTEPS)	NORTHWOOD
Watt, Fraser J	Lt RN	01-Sep-12	WAR	GSX	MCM1	FASLANE
Watt, Nicholas J P	Lt	02-Sep-14	RM	GS	CTCRM	EXMOUTH
Watts, Andrew P	Lt Cdr	01-Oct-93	WAR	O SK6	771 SQN	RNAS CULDROSE
Watts, Nicholas A D	Lt RN	01-May-14	LOGS	L	FOST DPORT	PLYMOUTH
Watts, Nicholas H C	Lt Cdr	01-Oct-14	WAR	AW (RES)	HMS FLYING FOX	BRISTOL
Watts, Robert	Cdr	30-Jun-13	WAR	SM(CQ)	HMS VANGUARD	
Watts, Thomas	Lt RN	10-Oct-10	WAR	AW (RES)	MTM NPT RES MOBILISATION	PORTSMOUTH
Waud, Deborah	Lt RN	14-Apr-11	MED	MS	MDHU DERRIFORD	PLYMOUTH
Waudby, Lindsey	Lt Cdr	01-Oct-14	WAR	MEDIA OPS	RNP TEAM	PORTSMOUTH
Way, Robert A	Lt Cdr	01-Oct-09	WAR	INT	DI - SA	LONDON
Weal, Gregory R	Lt RN	01-Jan-10	WAR	P MER	814 SQN	RNAS CULDROSE
Weale, John S OBE	Cdre	03-Sep-12	WAR	SM(CQ)	FLEET FOST ACOS(Trg)	PORTSMOUTH
Weatherall, Mark	Lt RN	21-Feb-09	WAR	INT	PJHQ (UK)	NORTHWOOD
Weaver, Simon	Lt Cdr	01-Oct-05	WAR	HM(H CH)	MWS COLLINGWOOD	HMS COLLINGWOOD
Weaver, Thomas H	Lt Cdr	01-Oct-10	WAR	PWO	UKMARBATSTAFF	PORTSMOUTH
Webb, Adrian C	Capt	01-Jan-15	RM	SCC	30 CDO IX GP RM	PLYMOUTH
Webb, Eleanor	Lt Cdr	01-Oct-08	LOGS	L	PJHQ (UK)	NORTHWOOD
Webb, John P	Lt Cdr	01-Oct-12	WAR	GSX	HMS SULTAN	GOSPORT
Webb, Keith W	Lt RN	01-Jan-12	WAR	O	MTM 815 SQN YEOVILTON	RNAS YEOVILTON
Webber, Adam A	RN Chpln	02-Sep-13	Ch S	Chaplain	COMFASFLOT	HELENSBURGH
Webber, Christopher A	Capt	01-Sep-11	RM	GS	CDO LOG REGT RM	RMB CHIVENOR
Webber, David J	Lt RN	01-Sep-14	ENG	ME	HMS BULWARK	
Webber, Lauren	SLt	01-Sep-14	WAR	GSX	HMS DEFENDER	
Webber, Richard J	Surg Lt Cdr	01-Jul-09	MED	Occ Med	INM ALVERSTOKE2	GOSPORT
Webster, Andrew J	Lt RN	01-Jan-04	ENG	TM	BRNC	BRNC DARTMOUTH
Webster, David R S	SLt	01-Feb-12	WAR	GSX	HMS SEVERN	
Webster, Mark	Lt RN	01-Apr-07	WAR	GSX	MTM MWS COLLINGWOOD	HMS COLLINGWOOD
Webster, Matthew P	Capt	01-Sep-11	RM	GS	CTCRM	EXMOUTH
Webster, Richard	Lt Cdr	01-Oct-07	WAR	PWO(C)	LSP OMAN	MUSCAT
Webster, Richard J	Lt Cdr	01-Dec-05	LOGS	L	ACDS	LONDON
Weedon, Christopher R	SLt	01-Sep-12	ENG	AE	DCEME SULTAN	HMS SULTAN
Weedon, Grant	Lt RN	01-Dec-11	ENG	ME	HMS DRAGON	
Weetch, Matthew E	Lt RN	21-Feb-09	WAR	AV	MAA	ABBEY WOOD
Weil, Daniel G	Lt Cdr	01-Oct-11	ENG	AE	1710 NAS	PORTSMOUTH
Weir, Scott D	Cdr	29-Mar-11	ENG	WESM(SWS)	CBRN POL	LONDON
Weir, Stewart W A P	SLt	01-Mar-14	WAR	GSX	HMS PORTLAND	
Weites, Matthew G	Capt	21-Mar-13	RM	BS	MTM RM SCH MUSIC	HMS NELSON
Welch, Danielle S	Lt RN	01-Mar-10	WAR	P UT	MTM 815 SQN YEOVILTON	RNAS YEOVILTON
Welch, Harry A	Lt RN	24-Jan-12	WAR	SM(X)	HMS MERSEY	
Welch, James F	Surg Lt Cdr	05-Aug-03	MED	Ophthal	MDHU NORTHALLERTON	NORTHALLERTON
Welch, Joshua J	Lt RN	01-Jul-12	WAR	GSX	HMS SOMERSET	
Welch, Simon	Capt	28-Jul-06	RM	SCC	CTCRM	EXMOUTH

Name	Substantive Rank	Seniority	Branch	Specialisation	Organisation Name	Location Name
Weldon, Dominic R	Capt	01-Sep-12	RM	GS	43 CDO FPGRM	HELENSBURGH
Weller, Jamie K	Lt RN	01-Feb-08	ENG	TM	NCHQ - NAVY CMD SEC	PORTSMOUTH
Wellington, Laura J	Lt Cdr	01-Oct-14	LOGS	L	NBC CLYDE	HMNB CLYDE
Wellington, Stuart	Lt Cdr	01-Feb-98	ENG	WE	FLEET CAP SSM	PORTSMOUTH
Wells, Antony E	Lt RN	01-Sep-09	WAR	P	LHF 815 SQN	RNAS YEOVILTON
Wells, Barry C	Lt Cdr	01-Oct-02	ENG	WESM(SWS)	CBRN POL	LONDON
Wells, Jamie D	Lt Cdr	01-Oct-08	WAR	PWO(N)	HMS DUNCAN	
Wells, John P	Surg Lt Cdr	04-Jul-07	MED	OMFS	MTM INM ALVERSTOKE	GOSPORT
Wells, Jonathan M C	Lt Cdr	01-Aug-97	WAR	P MER	MAA MAAIB FARNBOROUGH	ALDERSHOT
Wells, Matthew L	SLt	01-May-12	WAR	GSX	HMS DAUNTLESS	
Wells, Michael J	Lt RN	01-Sep-08	WAR	P LYN7	847 SQN	RNAS YEOVILTON
Wells, Michael P	Lt Cdr	01-Oct-08	LOGS	L CMA	FLEET SPT LOGS INFRA	NORTHWOOD
Wells, Rory L	Lt	02-Sep-14	RM	GS	42 CDO RM	PLYMOUTH
Welsh, John	Lt Cdr	01-Oct-08	ENG	TM	FLEET FOST ACOS(Trg)	PORTSMOUTH
Welsh, Richard M K	Lt Cdr	01-Oct-09	ENG	AE	CHF(MERLIN)	RAF BENSON
Wesley, Phillipa C	Mid	08-Sep-14	WAR	HM	BRNC	BRNC DARTMOUTH
West, David J	Maj	01-Oct-10	RM	P SK4	FLEET AV VL	RNAS YEOVILTON
West, Hannah R	Lt Cdr	01-Oct-12	ENG	AE	MTM WMO YEOVILTON	RNAS YEOVILTON
West, Jane M	SLt	01-Jan-14	LOGS	L	HMS DARING	
West, the Lord GCB DSC PC	Adm	30-Nov-00				
West, Michael W	Lt Cdr	05-Aug-92	WAR	PWO(A)	RNAS YEOVILTON	YEOVILTON
West, Nicholas K	Lt Cdr	01-Oct-09	LOGS	L CMA	MTM NELSON	HMS NELSON
West, Olivia N	SLt	01-Nov-14	WAR	GSX	BRNC	BRNC DARTMOUTH
West, Rory J	Lt Cdr	01-Jun-02	WAR	O PWO(U)	NCHQ CNPS	PORTSMOUTH
West, Sarah	Cdr	30-Jun-12	WAR	PWO(U)	MTM NELSON	HMS NELSON
Westbrook, Kevin	Lt RN	01-Sep-06	ENG	AE	FLEET CSAV	PORTSMOUTH
Westlake, Simon	Lt RN	20-Oct-09	WAR	SM(X)	HMS VANGUARD	
Westlake, Simon R	Lt Col	30-Jun-13	RM	SCC	COMUKAMPHIBFOR	PORTSMOUTH
Westley, Alexander	Lt RN	01-Sep-06	ENG	WESM(TWS)	FOST FAS SHORE	HMNB CLYDE
Westley, David R	Lt Cdr	01-Oct-01	WAR	P SK4	847 SQN	RNAS YEOVILTON
Westmaas, Timothy J	Lt RN	01-Sep-13	ENG	WE	HMS DEFENDER	
Weston, Antony T	SLt	01-May-12	WAR	GSX	HMS ST ALBANS	
Weston, Karl N N	Lt Cdr	01-Oct-14	WAR	O LYNX	RN EXCHANGE BRAZIL	BRASILIA
Westwood, Amanda J	Surg Lt Cdr (D)	07-Jul-13	DENTAL	GDP	HQ DPHC	LICHFIELD
Westwood, Andrew J	Lt RN	01-Sep-02	WAR	P SK4	DEF HELI FLYING SCH	SHREWSBURY
Westwood, Christopher S	Lt RN	01-Sep-13	ENG	AE	MTM 845 SQN YEOVILTON	RNAS YEOVILTON
Westwood, Mark R	Cdr	30-Jun-11	ENG	MESM	DES COMFLEET	ABBEY WOOD
Westwood, Michelle	Lt Cdr	01-Oct-13	LOGS	L	HMS SUTHERLAND	
Westwood, Thomas P	Lt Cdr	01-Oct-11	WAR	PWO	BRNC	BRNC DARTMOUTH
Wetherfield, Sarah F	Lt RN	01-May-08	ENG	TM	NETS (OPS)	HMS DRAKE
Whalley, Richard J	Cdr	30-Jun-09	LOGS	L CMA	BDS	WASHINGTON
Wharrie, Craig G	Lt Cdr	01-Oct-11	ENG	ME	DES COMFLEET	ABBEY WOOD
Wharry, Douglas F	Lt RN	01-Aug-13	WAR	GSX	HMS DIAMOND	
Wharton, Charles F S	Surg Lt RN	02-Aug-11	MED	GDMO	40 CDO RM	TAUNTON
Whatley, Mark	Lt RN	01-Feb-11	WAR	MEDIA OPS	UK MCC	BAHRAIN
Wheal, Adrian	Cdr	30-Jun-10	ENG	MESM	HMS SULTAN	GOSPORT
Wheatcroft, Ian J	Lt RN	01-Jun-10	LOGS	L SM	DMLS	HMS RALEIGH
Wheatley, George W	Mid	01-Feb-14	LOGS	L	HMS MONMOUTH	
Wheatley, Ian J QHC	Chpln of the Fleet	18-Dec-14	Ch S	Chaplain	CHAPLAIN OF THE FLEET	PORTSMOUTH
Wheatley, Nicola S	Lt Cdr	01-Oct-12	WAR	HM(AM)	MTM NORTHWOOD HQ	NORTHWOOD
Wheaton, Bowden J S	Cdr	30-Jun-12	WAR	O LYNX	FLEET CAP MARCAP	PORTSMOUTH
Wheeler, Luke A J	Capt	01-Mar-10	RM	GS	42 CDO RM	PLYMOUTH
Wheeler, Nicholas J	Cdr	30-Jun-10	WAR	SM(CQ)	MOD NSD	LONDON
Wheeler, Robert J	Lt RN	01-Aug-13	ENG	WE	HMS DARING	
Wheen, Charles	Lt Cdr	01-Oct-12	WAR	MCD	HMS ARGYLL	
Wheldon, Adam J	Lt RN	17-Dec-10	LOGS	L	HMS NORTHUMBERLAND	
Whipp, Ian A	Lt RN	01-Feb-14	WAR	SM(X)	HMS VIGILANT	
Whitby, Oliver	Capt	01-Sep-13	RM	GS	MTM CTCRM	EXMOUTH
White, Alec J	Capt	03-Sep-14	RM	GS	40 CDO RM	TAUNTON
White, Alistair J M	Lt RN	01-May-04	WAR	P MER	820 SQN	RNAS CULDROSE
White, Andrew J	Lt RN	01-Feb-09	WAR	P LYN7	9 REGT	THIRSK
White, Deri T	2Lt	28-Aug-14	RM	N/A	CTCRM	EXMOUTH

Name	Substantive Rank	Seniority	Branch	Specialisation	Organisation Name	Location Name
White, Douglas	Lt Cdr	01-Oct-10	ENG	WESM(SWS)	FOST FAS SHORE	HMNB CLYDE
White, Haydn J	Col	19-Jul-10	RM	LC	JFC HQ	NORTHWOOD
White, Jason P QGM	Lt Cdr	01-Oct-08	WAR	MCD	MCM2	PORTSMOUTH
White, Jonathan A P	Capt RN	13-Dec-10	WAR	SM(CQ)	MTM NELSON	HMS NELSON
White, Jonathan E	Lt Cdr	01-Nov-02	LOGS	L	UK MCC	BAHRAIN
White, Kevin F	Lt Cdr	01-Oct-06	ENG	ME	COMPORFLOT	PORTSMOUTH
White, Kristopher	Lt RN	01-Nov-07	WAR	PWO(SM)	HMS VANGUARD	
White, Mark	Lt RN	01-Feb-09	WAR	HM	NATO-ACO-JFC HQ	NAPLES
White, Maxwell A	SLt	01-Apr-12	WAR	O UT	MTM 824 SQN CULDROSE	RNAS CULDROSE
White, Paul	Lt RN	01-Dec-09	WAR	GSX	RN EXCHANGE SPAIN	MADRID
White, Paul D	Lt RN	01-May-03	WAR	P SK6	771 SQN	RNAS CULDROSE
White, Ross E	Lt RN	01-May-04	WAR	P MER	824 SQN	RNAS CULDROSE
White, Simon H W	Lt Cdr	01-Oct-10	WAR	P MER	820 SQN	RNAS CULDROSE
White, Stephen J	Lt Cdr	06-Oct-09	WAR	C	NATO-ACO-SHAPE	CASTEAU
White, Stephen P	Lt Cdr	01-Oct-11	ENG	IS	JSSU CH - HQ	CHELTENHAM
White, Steven	Lt Cdr	01-Oct-12	WAR	MCD	MTM MWS COLLINGWOOD	HMS COLLINGWOOD
White, Thomas G	Maj	01-Oct-14	RM	GS	CTCRM	EXMOUTH
Whitehall, Sally	Lt Cdr	01-Oct-09	WAR	PWO(C)	JFC HOC C4ISR	NORTHWOOD
Whitehead, Benjamin J	Lt RN	01-Sep-10	WAR	SM(X)	HMS VENGEANCE	
Whitehead, Peter J MBE	Lt Cdr	01-Oct-11	WAR	O SKW	FLEET CAP IS	PORTSMOUTH
Whitehead, Steven J	Lt Cdr	01-Mar-00	ENG	AE	CHFHQ	RNAS YEOVILTON
Whitehouse, Andrew P	Lt RN	01-Sep-05	WAR	P LYN7	847 SQN	RNAS YEOVILTON
Whitehouse, David S	Lt Cdr	01-Oct-08	WAR	SM(AWC)	FLEET MARITIME WARFARE	HMS COLLINGWOOD
Whitehouse, Niall R	Lt Cdr	01-Dec-04	ENG	AE P	DES COMJE	YEOVIL
Whiteley, Peter	Lt RN	01-Mar-14	ENG	MESM	DCEME SULTAN	HMS SULTAN
Whiteman, John W T	Capt	01-Aug-07	RM	GS	HQ 3 CDO BDE RM	PLYMOUTH
Whitfield, Kenneth D	Cdr	30-Jun-08	ENG	AE	FLEET CSAV	PORTSMOUTH
Whitfield, Philip M	Maj	01-Sep-03	RM	GS	DEFENCE ACADEMY	SHRIVENHAM
Whitley, Helen S	Lt RN	01-Apr-02	ENG	IS	FLEET COMOPS NWD	NORTHWOOD
Whitley, Ian D B	Cdr	30-Jun-10	WAR	PWO(C)	FLEET COMOPS NWD	NORTHWOOD
Whitley, Janine F B	Lt RN	08-Feb-13	QARNNS	EN	MED SQN CDO LOG REGT RM	RMB CHIVENOR
Whitmarsh, Adam T	Maj	01-Oct-09	RM	GS	HQ 3 CDO BDE RM	PLYMOUTH
Whitmore, Jennifer S	Lt Cdr	01-Oct-13	LOGS	L BAR	NCHQ - CNLS	PORTSMOUTH
Whitson-Fay, Craig D	Lt Cdr	01-Oct-09	WAR	O SKW	750 SQN	RNAS CULDROSE
Whittaker, Terry J	Lt RN	01-Sep-11	ENG	ME	HMS SULTAN	GOSPORT
Whittington, Christopher C	Lt RN	01-Nov-08	WAR	P SK6	849 SQN	RNAS CULDROSE
Whittles, Gary W	Lt Cdr	01-Oct-12	LOGS	L SM	HMS RALEIGH	TORPOINT
Whitworth, Robert M	Lt Cdr	01-Oct-99	WAR	PWO(U)	LOAN DSTL	FAREHAM
Whybourn, Lesley A	Surg Cdr	01-Jul-10	MED	Occ Med	INM ALVERSTOKE2	GOSPORT
Whyte, Gordon	Lt Cdr	01-Oct-13	ENG	WE	HMS WESTMINSTER	
Whyte, Iain P	Cdr	30-Jun-09	ENG	TM	NATO-ACT-HQ	NORFOLK
Wick, Harry M S	Lt Cdr	01-Sep-12	WAR	GSX	DNR N IRELAND	BELFAST
Wickett, Richard J	Lt RN	01-Mar-02	ENG	ME	DES COMFLEET	ABBEY WOOD
Wickham, Robert J	Lt RN	01-May-01	WAR	PWO(C)	FLEET CAP IS	PORTSMOUTH
Wicking, Geoffrey S	Lt Cdr	01-Oct-03	ENG	AE	MAA MAAIB FARNBOROUGH	ALDERSHOT
Wicks, Sam	Lt RN	01-Apr-13	WAR		UKMARBATSTAFF	PORTSMOUTH
Widdowson, Matthew G	Lt RN	01-Sep-08	ENG	AE	DES COMAIR	ABBEY WOOD
Wielbo, Dominik J	SLt	01-May-12	WAR	O UT	MWS COLLINGWOOD	HMS COLLINGWOOD
Wielopolski, Mark L	Lt RN	01-May-01	WAR	P SK4	FOSNI - NRC	HMS CALEDONIA
Wigan, Thomas J C	Mid	01-May-14	WAR	O UT	BRNC	BRNC DARTMOUTH
Wilcocks, David N	Lt RN	01-Jul-05	WAR	PWO	HMS BULWARK	
Wilcockson, Roy	Capt	07-May-99	CS	CS	OCLC PLYMOUTH	PLYMOUTH
Wilcox, Christopher	Lt RN	01-Sep-06	WAR	O SKW	RN EXCHANGE USA	WASHINGTON
Wild, Gareth	Surg Cdr	10-Sep-12	MED	GMP	MTM INM ALVERSTOKE	GOSPORT
Wild, Richard J	Lt Cdr	01-Oct-09	Ch S	L CMA SM	DES COMFLEET	ABBEY WOOD
Wild, Simon	Lt RN	01-Apr-14	WAR	FC	MTM WMO YEOVILTON	RNAS YEOVILTON
Wildin, Andrew	Cdr	30-Jun-13	ENG	WE	NC REQUIREMENTS MANAGERS	ABBEY WOOD
Wilkins, David P	Lt RN	01-May-01	WAR	SM(AWC)	FLEET MARITIME WARFARE	HMS COLLINGWOOD
Wilkins, Richard R	Lt Cdr	01-Oct-03	ENG	MESM	DES COMFLEET	ABBEY WOOD
Wilkins, Robert L	Lt Cdr	01-Oct-10	ENG	MESM	HMS TORBAY	
Wilkins, Thomas R	SLt	01-May-12	ENG	WE	MWS COLLINGWOOD	HMS COLLINGWOOD
Wilkinson, David H OBE	Cdr	30-Jun-08	WAR	PWO(U)	NCHQ CNPERS	PORTSMOUTH

Name	Substantive Rank	Seniority	Branch	Specialisation	Organisation Name	Location Name
Wilkinson, John	Lt RN	01-Mar-09	ENG	WESM(SWS)	DES COMFLEET	BARROW IN FURNESS
Wilkinson, John R	Lt Cdr	01-Oct-10	WAR	AV	DSTO	RAF ST MAWGAN
Wilkinson, Lloyd J	SLt	01-May-12	LOGS	L	FOST NWD (JTEPS)	NORTHWOOD
Wilkinson, Matthew J MBE	Capt	30-Mar-12	RM	GS	NCHQ	PORTSMOUTH
Wilkinson, Timothy L	RN Chpln	04-Mar-97	Ch S	Chaplain	HQ 3 CDO BDE RM	PLYMOUTH
Williams, Aaron P	Lt RN	20-May-13	WAR	SM(N)	HMS ARTFUL	
Williams, Adam L	Mid	08-Sep-14	WAR	GSX	BRNC	BRNC DARTMOUTH
Williams, Amanda L	Lt RN	20-Jul-10	WAR	ATC	RNAS CULDROSE	HELSTON
Williams, Andrew F	Lt RN	09-Apr-10	WAR	REG	HMS COLLINGWOOD	FAREHAM
Williams, Anthony DSC	Cdr	31-Dec-00	WAR	MCD	LSP OMAN	MUSCAT
Williams, Anthony M	Lt RN	01-Sep-04	WAR	PWO	HMS SOMERSET	
Williams, Anthony S	Cdr	30-Jun-14	WAR	PWO FC	COMPORFLOT	PORTSMOUTH
Williams, Benjamin R	Surg Lt Cdr (D)	27-Jun-05	DENTAL	GDP(C&S)	ROYAL BRUNEI ARMED FORCES	SERIA
Williams, Cassandra L	Lt Cdr	01-Oct-11	ENG	AE	MAA	ABBEY WOOD
Williams, Christopher R D	2Lt	25-Aug-14	RM	N/A	CTCRM	EXMOUTH
Williams, Colin OBE	Cdr	30-Jun-10	WAR	AAWO	FLEET COMOPS NWD	NORTHWOOD
Williams, Daniel L	Lt RN	01-Jan-00	WAR	P LYNX	NO 3 FTS/UAS - JEFTS	GRANTHAM
Williams, David B	Lt RN	08-Dec-11	WAR	INT	HQ DISC	CHICKSANDS
Williams, Dylan S	Surg Lt Cdr (D)	25-Aug-09	DENTAL	GDP	JSU NORTHWOOD	NORTHWOOD
Williams, Edward A D	Capt	01-Sep-11	RM	GS	URNU CAMBRIDGE	CAMBRIDGE
Williams, Gareth	Lt RN	01-Apr-11	ENG	MESM	DEFENCE ACADEMY	SHRIVENHAM
Williams, Gareth	Lt RN	01-Sep-11	ENG	WESM(TWS)	FOST DSTF - CSST	PLYMOUTH
Williams, Graeme T	Lt RN	01-May-13	WAR	SM(X)	HMS VANGUARD	
Williams, Haydn M P	SLt	01-Jan-14	MED	Medical	BLAKE	BRNC DARTMOUTH
Williams, Huw R	Capt	16-Apr-10	RM	BS	CTCRM	EXMOUTH
Williams, James L	Lt RN	01-Feb-07	WAR	INT	NATO - BRUSSELS	BRUSSELS
Williams, James O	Mid	17-Nov-14	WAR	SM(X)	BRNC	BRNC DARTMOUTH
Williams, James P	Lt Cdr	01-Jun-00	WAR	AAWO	FLEET COMOPS NWD	NORTHWOOD
Williams, Jonathan M F	Capt	01-Sep-12	RM	GS	NCHQ	PORTSMOUTH
Williams, Lee J	Lt Cdr	01-Oct-14	ENG	WESM(TWS)	PJHQ (UK)	NORTHWOOD
Williams, Liam S	Lt RN	01-Apr-10	WAR	GSX	HMS PORTLAND	
Williams, Luke	Lt RN	01-Apr-05	WAR	PWO(SM)	HMS ARTFUL	
Williams, Mark A	Cdr	30-Jun-11	WAR	O LYNX	FLEET CAP MARCAP	PORTSMOUTH
Williams, Martyn J	Capt RN	13-Oct-09	ENG	WESM(TWS)	MTM DEFAC RCDS	LONDON
Williams, Matthew R	Capt	01-Sep-10	RM	GS	30 CDO IX GP RM	PLYMOUTH
Williams, Matthew R	Lt RN	01-Oct-09	LOGS	L SM	MTM NELSON	HMS NELSON
Williams, Neil A	Capt	01-Sep-11	RM	GS	42 CDO RM	PLYMOUTH
Williams, Nicola J	Lt RN	01-Jan-13	WAR	O UT	RNAS CULDROSE	HELSTON
Williams, Nigel	Lt RN	17-Dec-09	WAR	SM(C)	FLEET CAP IS	PORTSMOUTH
Williams, Paul A	Lt Cdr	01-Oct-11	ENG	ME	FLEET FOST ACOS(Trg)	PORTSMOUTH
Williams, Paul G	Lt Cdr	01-Oct-10	WAR	INT	JOINT OPERATIONAL STAFF	LISBURN
Williams, Peter L	Capt	01-Sep-08	RM	GS	NCHQ	PORTSMOUTH
Williams, Peter M	Maj	01-Oct-09	RM	GS	DIRECTOR (JW)	NORTHWOOD
Williams, Peter M	Lt Cdr	01-Oct-03	ENG	TM	HMS SULTAN	GOSPORT
Williams, Richard J	Surg Lt Cdr	02-Aug-11	MED	ORL	MTM INM ALVERSTOKE	GOSPORT
Williams, Robert	Lt Cdr	01-Oct-06	WAR	PWO(C)	UKMARBATSTAFF	PORTSMOUTH
Williams, Russell G	Lt RN	16-Feb-07	WAR	GSX	RNLA	BRNC DARTMOUTH
Williams, Simon P	R Adm	17-Sep-12	WAR	PWO(C)	DCDS PERS TRG	LONDON
Williams, Simon R	Mid	17-Nov-14	ENG	TM	BRNC	BRNC DARTMOUTH
Williams, Stephen W L	Cdr	30-Jun-10	LOGS	L	NC REQUIREMENTS MANAGERS	ABBEY WOOD
Williams, Thomas J	Capt	01-Sep-08	RM	GS	MTM CTCRM	EXMOUTH
Williams, Zoe E B	SLt	01-May-13	WAR	GSX	MTM NELSON	HMS NELSON
Williams-Allden, Lucy A	Lt RN	01-Sep-07	ENG	AE	MTM NELSON	HMS NELSON
Williamson, Ben L	SLt	01-Sep-13	MED	Medical	BLAKE	BRNC DARTMOUTH
Williamson, Helen M	Lt RN	31-Oct-14	LOGS	L	MTM FLEET HQ	PORTSMOUTH
Williamson, Peter J	Lt RN	01-Oct-02	WAR	METOC	NATO-ACO-SHAPE	CASTEAU
Williamson, Simon J	Lt RN	01-Oct-04	ENG	TM	FOST DPORT	PLYMOUTH
Williamson, Tobias MVO	Cdre	16-Nov-11	WAR	O SK6	COMMANDER OP TRAINING	HMS COLLINGWOOD
Williford, Susanna J	Lt RN	01-Sep-11	WAR	GSX	HMS LANCASTER	
Willis, Alistair J	Capt RN	07-May-13	LOGS	L	DES COMFLEET	ABBEY WOOD
Willison, Mark G	Capt	01-Sep-11	RM	GS	NCHQ	
Wills, Edward R	RN Chpln	27-Jan-14	Ch S	Chaplain	COMPORFLOT	PORTSMOUTH

Name	Substantive Rank	Seniority	Branch	Specialisation	Organisation Name	Location Name
Wills, Philip	Cdr	30-Jun-12	WAR	O LYNX	DEFENCE ACADEMY	SHRIVENHAM
Wills, Robert H	Lt Cdr	01-Oct-14	ENG	MESM	HMS VENGEANCE	
Wills, Timothy M	Lt RN	01-Jan-12	WAR	P UT	MTM 824 SQN CULDROSE	RNAS CULDROSE
Willsmore, Stuart A	Lt RN	01-Jul-05	WAR	PWO	HMS KENT	
Wilmot, Max A	Lt RN	01-May-09	WAR	MCD	MCM1	FASLANE
Wilmott, Vivian	Mid	01-Feb-14	WAR	O UT	BRNC	BRNC DARTMOUTH
Wilson, Allan J	Cdr	30-Jun-11	WAR	PWO(U)	FMC NAVY	LONDON
Wilson, Bruce R	Capt	01-Sep-13	RM	GS	OCLC ROSYTH	HMS CALEDONIA
Wilson, Charles B	Capt	31-Aug-14	RM	GS	1 PWRR	PADERBORN
Wilson, Charles K	Lt RN	01-Sep-06	LOGS	L	FLEET ACOS(RP)	PORTSMOUTH
Wilson, Christopher J	Cdr	30-Jun-13	ENG	MESM	DES COMFLEET	ABBEY WOOD
Wilson, David J	Lt RN	01-May-04	ENG	TM	NCHQ CNPERS (HRTSG)	PORTSMOUTH
Wilson, David R	Cdr	30-Jun-09	WAR	PWO(A)	FLEET COMOPS NWD	NORTHWOOD
Wilson, David W H	Lt Col	30-Jun-03	RM	GS	NATO-ACT-HQ	NORFOLK
Wilson, Gary P	Lt Cdr	01-Oct-11	WAR	INT	PJHQ (UK)	NORTHWOOD
Wilson, Iain E	Lt RN	19-Dec-08	WAR	INT	JSSU CH - HQ	CHELTENHAM
Wilson, John	Lt Cdr	01-Oct-08	WAR	P MER CDO	CHF - 846	RAF BENSON
Wilson, Kayleigh J	Lt RN	01-Feb-10	LOGS	L	COMFASFLOT	HFI ENSBURGH
Wilson, Lloyd R	Lt RN	01-Sep-14	WAR	GSX	HMS DRAGON	
Wilson, Lorna F	Lt RN	01-Apr-14	WAR	GSX	BRNC	BRNC DARTMOUTH
Wilson, Mark J	Lt RN	08-Jun-07	LOGS	L	MTM DEFAC JSCSC	SHRIVENHAM
Wilson, Matthew J	Surg Lt RN	12-Jul-10	MED	GDMO	MTM INM ALVERSTOKE	GOSPORT
Wilson, Michael J	Mid	01-May-14	LOGS	L	BRNC	BRNC DARTMOUTH
Wilson, Nathan E	SLt	01-Oct-14	MED	Medical	BLAKE	BRNC DARTMOUTH
Wilson, Neil A	Lt Cdr	01-Oct-13	WAR	PWO(SM)	FLEET COMOPS NWD	NORTHWOOD
Wilson, Nicholas C	Lt RN	19-Nov-09	WAR	FC	HQ AIR - COS(OPS) - JFAC	SALISBURY
Wilson, Robert N	Lt RN	01-Jan-13	LOGS	L SM	HMS VANGUARD	
Wilson, Simon A	Lt RN	01-Jan-04	WAR	P LYNX	WMF 825 SQN HQ	RNAS YEOVILTON
Wilson, Thomas E	Lt RN	01-Sep-13	ENG	WESM	HMS VIGILANT	
Wilson, Thomas R D	Lt RN	01-Sep-14	WAR	O LYNX	MTM 815 SQN YEOVILTON	RNAS YEOVILTON
Wilson-Chalon, Louis M	Cdr	30-Jun-09	WAR	P LYNX	LHF HQ	RNAS YEOVILTON
Wilton, Mark	Lt RN	01-Dec-04	WAR	HM	RN EXCHANGE USA	WASHINGTON
Wiltshire, Ross M	Lt RN	01-Mar-12	WAR	P UT	MTM SHAWBURY	RAF SHAWBURY
Winborn, David J	Lt Cdr	01-Oct-12	ENG	MESM	HMS TRIUMPH	
Winch, Joseph A	Maj	01-Oct-10	RM	GS	40 CDO RM	TAUNTON
Winch, Michael T R	Lt RN	01-May-13	LOGS	L	MTM RALEIGH	HMS RALEIGH
Windebank, Stephen J	Cdr	30-Jun-12	WAR	P MER	MAA	ABBEY WOOD
Windle, Christopher M	Mid	17-Nov-14	ENG	WE	BRNC	BRNC DARTMOUTH
Windsor, Christopher J	SLt	01-Sep-12	WAR	O UT	MTM 824 SQN CULDROSE	RNAS CULDROSE
Wingfield, Michael J	Lt Cdr	01-Oct-06	WAR	O WILDCAT	WMF 825 SQN HQ	RNAS YEOVILTON
Winkle, Sean J	Cdr	30-Jun-05	ENG	TM	HMS TEMERAIRE	PORTSMOUTH
Winn, John P	Lt Cdr	01-Oct-09	WAR	HM(AS)	MTM DRAKE	HMS DRAKE
Winning, Robert A M	Lt RN	07-Oct-11	LOGS	L	CTCRM	EXMOUTH
Winsor, James	Lt Cdr	01-Oct-09	WAR	HM(AS)	HMS ECHO	
Winstanley, Mark	Maj	01-Oct-13	RM	SCC	DST	HULL
Winstanley, Robert A J	Capt	03-Apr-09	RM	GS	NCHQ	PORTSMOUTH
Winstone, Nigel P	Lt Cdr	01-Oct-12	ENG	MESM	DES COMFLEET	ABBEY WOOD
Winter, Marcus R	2Lt	25-Aug-14	RM	N/A	CTCRM	EXMOUTH
Winter, Richard J	Capt RN	20-Jan-14	ENG	WE	FLEET CAP SSM	PORTSMOUTH
Winter, Timothy M	Cdr	30-Jun-08	ENG	ME	DCTT HQ	HMS SULTAN
Winterbon, Andrew R	Lt Cdr	01-Oct-10	WAR	AAWO	COMUKAMPHIBFOR	PORTSMOUTH
Winterton, Alexander J	Mid	01-Feb-14	WAR	GSX	BRNC	BRNC DARTMOUTH
Winterton, Gemma	Lt RN	01-Nov-10	WAR	INFO OPS	DEFENCE ACADEMY	SOUTHAMPTON
Winterton, Paul	Lt Cdr	01-Oct-13	WAR	O MER	FLEET AV CU	RNAS CULDROSE
Wintle, Geoffrey L	Cdr	30-Jun-03	LOGS	L SM	BRNC	BRNC DARTMOUTH
Winwood, Matthew R	Lt RN	01-Apr-10	WAR	GSX	HMS TYNE	
Wiseman, Deborah J	Lt RN	01-Mar-12	ENG	TM	JFC - DCTS (H)	AYLESBURY
Wiseman, Hugo	Lt RN	01-Jul-11	WAR	SM(X)	HMS VICTORIOUS	
Wiseman, Ian C	Lt RN	30-Jun-11	WAR	PWO(N)	FOST MPV SEA	HMNB CLYDE
Wiseman, Neil	Lt Cdr	01-Oct-09	WAR	O LYNX	LHF 702 SQN	RNAS YEOVILTON
Witcher, Emily R	SLt	01-Jul-14	WAR	SM(X)	HMS OCEAN	
Witham, Brian M J	Lt RN	01-Sep-13	WAR	O UT	MTM 750 SQN CULDROSE	RNAS CULDROSE

Name	Substantive Rank	Seniority	Branch	Specialisation	Organisation Name	Location Name
Witham, Katharine V	Lt RN	01-Apr-11	WAR	GSX	BRNC	BRNC DARTMOUTH
Witt, Alister K	Cdr	14-Jan-13	MED	MS(EHO)	HQ DPHC	LICHFIELD
Witts, Andrew J	SLt	01-Aug-13	ENG	WESM	HMS RALEIGH	TORPOINT
Woad, Jonathan P R	Lt RN	01-Nov-01	WAR	MW	HMS COLLINGWOOD	FAREHAM
Woliter, Bradley	Mid	08-Sep-14	WAR	SM(X)	BRNC	BRNC DARTMOUTH
Wood, Alexander M	Surg Lt Cdr	01-Aug-07	MED	T&O	MTM INM ALVERSTOKE	GOSPORT
Wood, Andrew G	Lt Cdr	01-Oct-06	ENG	AE	DES COMAIR	ABBEY WOOD
Wood, Christopher R	Lt Cdr	01-Jan-05	WAR	P MER	FLEET CSAV	PORTSMOUTH
Wood, Christopher T	Lt Cdr	01-Oct-12	ENG	TM	NCHQ CNPS	PORTSMOUTH
Wood, Craig	Capt RN	18-Nov-13	WAR	PWO(A)	PJHQ (UK)	NORTHWOOD
Wood, Frederick J	Lt RN	01-Jan-08	MED	MS(EHO)	NCHQ MEDDIV EH	HMS DRAKE
Wood, Graham R	Lt Cdr	01-Oct-05	LOGS	L	DES COMLAND	ABBEY WOOD
Wood, Iain M	Surg Lt Cdr	04-Aug-11	MED	GMP	NCHQ	PORTSMOUTH
Wood, Joanne T	Lt Cdr	01-Oct-14	WAR	ATC	DIRECTOR (JW)	NORTHWOOD
Wood, Joseph A	Lt Cdr	01-Oct-06	WAR	GSX	HMS TEMERAIRE	PORTSMOUTH
Wood, Julian T S	Lt RN	07-Apr-06	ENG	ME	NCHQ	PORTSMOUTH
Wood, Michael J	Surg SLt	29-Jul-14	MED	Medical	BLAKE	BRNC DARTMOUTH
Wood, Michael L	Cdr	30-Jun-14	WAR	PWO(N)	HMS SOMERSET	
Wood, Michael W	Lt RN	01-May-04	WAR	PWO(N)	FOST DPORT	PLYMOUTH
Wood, Nicholas R	Cdr	30-Jun-14	WAR	PWO(U)	COMUKAMPHIBFOR	PORTSMOUTH
Wood, Richard R T	Lt RN	01-Sep-04	WAR	P FW	736 NAS	RNAS CULDROSE
Wood, Robert	Capt RN	22-Feb-11	LOGS	L BAR	NCHQ - CNLS	PORTSMOUTH
Wood, Simon A H	Lt Cdr	01-Oct-11	WAR	P SK4	849 SQN	RNAS CULDROSE
Wood, Thomas D	Lt RN	01-Jan-13	WAR	SM(X)	HMS ASTUTE	
Wood, Uvedale G S	Cdr	30-Jun-13	WAR	P FW	HQ AIR HQ 1GP LFHQ	HIGH WYCOMBE
Woodard, Jolyon	Capt RN	09-Sep-13	WAR	P SK4	HQ JHC	ANDOVER
Woodbridge, Richard G	Lt Cdr	01-Aug-04	ENG	ME	FLEET DCS - RNIO	HMS COLLINGWOOD
Woodcock, Keith	SLt	01-Sep-14	ENG	AE	DCEME SULTAN	HMS SULTAN
Woodcock, Lauren J	Mid	17-Nov-14	WAR	GSX	BRNC	BRNC DARTMOUTH
Woodcock, Simon J OBE	R Adm	11-Sep-12	ENG	ME	NAVSEC	HMS EXCELLENT
Woodley, Stephen L	Lt RN	01-Sep-02	ENG	MESM	COMDEVFLOT	PLYMOUTH
Woodridge, Ryan A	SLt	01-Nov-14	WAR	GSX	MWS COLLINGWOOD	HMS COLLINGWOOD
Woodrow, Kevin	Lt Cdr	01-Oct-03	WAR	SM(C)	JFIG - JT OPS	RAF WYTON
Woods, Anna L	Lt RN	01-Sep-14	WAR	GSX	MWS COLLINGWOOD	HMS COLLINGWOOD
Woods, James D	Lt RN	01-Jan-08	WAR	P WILDCAT	WMF 825 SQN HQ	RNAS YEOVILTON
Woods, Jason S	SLt	01-Oct-13	ENG	TM	MTM NELSON	HMS NELSON
Woods, Jeremy B	Cdr	30-Jun-04	WAR	AAWO	FLEET MARITIME WARFARE	HMS COLLINGWOOD
Woods, Michael J P	Lt Cdr	01-May-09	ENG	WESM(SWS)	HMS VANGUARD	
Woods, Richard K	Mid	01-May-14	WAR	P UT	BRNC	BRNC DARTMOUTH
Woods, Roland P	Cdr	31-Dec-98	WAR	PWO(A)	NC PSYA	NORTHWOOD
Woods, Timothy C	Capt RN	04-Mar-14	ENG	TM(SM)	DCDS PERS TRG	LONDON
Woodward, Alasdair J	Lt RN	01-Feb-08	WAR	P MER	824 SQN	RNAS CULDROSE
Woodward, Guy F	SLt	01-Feb-12	WAR	SM(X)	HMS PROTECTOR	
Woodward, Ian M H	Lt RN	12-Oct-14	LOGS	L	HMS OCEAN	
Woodward, Mark A B	Lt RN	01-Sep-13	WAR	SM(X)	HMS ASTUTE	
Wookey, Mark	Lt Cdr	01-Oct-11	WAR	O WILDCAT	FLEET AV VL	RNAS YEOVILTON
Woolhead, Andrew L	Lt Cdr	30-Jun-14	WAR	PWO(N)	CYBER POLICY	LONDON
Woolhead, Craig M	Lt Cdr	01-Oct-09	WAR	PWO(U)	HMS PORTLAND	
Woollard, Kerry M	SLt	01-Sep-12	WAR	HM	MCM1	FASLANE
Wooller, Louise F V	Lt Cdr	01-Feb-08	WAR	GSX	HMS RALEIGH	TORPOINT
Wooller, Mark A H	Cdr	30-Jun-10	LOGS	L SM	HMS OCEAN	
Woolley, Stephen	Surg Lt RN	04-Aug-10	MED	Path - Micro	MTM INM ALVERSTOKE	GOSPORT
Woollven, Andrew	Cdr	30-Jun-13	WAR	MCD	MWS DDS	PORTSMOUTH
Woollven, Christopher D	Lt Cdr	01-Oct-10	WAR	O LYNX	LHF HQ	RNAS YEOVILTON
Woolsey, Kevin	Lt Cdr	01-May-07	WAR	ATC	MAA	ABBEY WOOD
Woosey, Mark	Maj	01-Jun-04	RM	LC	1 ASSLT GP RM	BIDEFORD
Wordsworth, Joel K	Lt RN	01-Mar-12	ENG	MESM	HMS VICTORIOUS	
Wordsworth, Jonathan D	Lt Cdr	01-Oct-14	WAR	GSX	HMS TRUMPETER	
Workman, Rayner J	Lt RN	01-Sep-03	WAR	HM	FLEET COMOPS NWD	HUNTINGDON
Worley, Thomas F	Lt RN	01-Jan-03	WAR	MW	FLEET CAP WARFARE	PORTSMOUTH
Worrall, Adam C	Lt RN	01-Aug-13	ENG	WESM	HMS VANGUARD	
Wort, Roland S	RN Chpln	28-Jul-89	Ch S	Chaplain	HMS COLLINGWOOD	FAREHAM

Name	Substantive Rank	Seniority	Branch	Specialisation	Organisation Name	Location Name
Worthington, Jonathan M F	Cdr	30-Jun-06	ENG	TM	TIO	LONDON
Wotton, Alan	Lt RN	01-Jul-04	WAR	P LYN7	AACEN	STOCKBRIDGE
Wotton, Ryan J	Lt RN	01-Jan-08	WAR	P LYNX	LHF 815 SQN	RNAS YEOVILTON
Wragg, Gareth T	Lt Cdr	01-Oct-10	WAR	HM	MTM DRAKE	HMS DRAKE
Wraith, Luke	Lt RN	08-Dec-14	WAR	P UT	MTM 824 SQN CULDROSE	RNAS CULDROSE
Wraith, Neil	Lt Col	30-Jun-11	RM	LC	FOST DPORT	PLYMOUTH
Wray, Philip	Lt RN	01-Oct-10	WAR	P SK4	CHFHQ	RNAS YEOVILTON
Wray, Stuart A	Lt RN	08-Jul-14	WAR	P UT	MTM SHAWBURY	RAF SHAWBURY
Wren, Stephen J	Lt Cdr	01-Oct-11	WAR	PWO	FLEET CAP SSM	PORTSMOUTH
Wrennall, Eric P	Lt Cdr	01-Oct-08	ENG	ME	COMDEVFLOT	PLYMOUTH
Wright, Christopher	Lt RN	01-Mar-12	ENG	WE	MWS COLLINGWOOD	HMS COLLINGWOOD
Wright, Daniel J	Lt Cdr	01-Oct-07	WAR	SM(AWC)	FOST FAS SHORE	HMNB CLYDE
Wright, David	Lt Cdr	01-Oct-06	WAR	MCD	DCD - MODSAP KSA	SAUDI ARABIA
Wright, David I	Lt Cdr	01-Sep-04	ENG	WE	NAVY ICP	PORTSMOUTH
Wright, Gabriel J	Lt RN	01-Nov-05	ENG	WE	DES COMFLEET	ABBEY WOOD
Wright, Helen I	Lt RN	13-Aug-04	LOGS	L	NBCP BLC	PORTSMOUTH
Wright, James A C	Mid	17-Nov-14	WAR	O UT	BRNC	BRNC DARTMOUTH
Wright, James A H	Lt RN	01-Jan-08	WAR	GSX	HMS BULWARK	
Wright, James N	Lt RN	01-May-06	LOGS	L SM	JFC HQ	NORTHWOOD
Wright, James P	Lt RN	01-Jan-12	WAR	P UT	MTM SHAWBURY	RAF SHAWBURY
Wright, Joseph R	Lt RN	01-Apr-14	WAR	SM(X)	HMS TIRELESS	
Wright, Justin C	Lt RN	11-Dec-09	ENG	WE	SVCOPS/DHDOPS/COR	CORSHAM
Wright, Lucas H	Mid	08-Sep-14	ENG	ME	BRNC	BRNC DARTMOUTH
Wright, Natalie	Lt RN	11-Jul-14	WAR	HM	MWS COLLINGWOOD	HMS COLLINGWOOD
Wright, Neil D MBE	Lt RN	13-Aug-04	ENG	AE	HQ AIR HQ 1GP LFHQ	HIGH WYCOMBE
Wright, Nigel S	Cdr	30-Jun-09	ENG	ME	CUSTOMER DESIGN	LONDON
Wright, Paul D	Lt RN	01-Jan-08	ENG	IS	MWS EXCELLENT	HMS EXCELLENT
Wright, Stuart H	Cdr	30-Jun-05	LOGS	L BAR	MOD NSD	LONDON
Wright-Jones, Alexandra E M	Lt Cdr	01-Oct-12	QARNNS	PHC	DPHC LONDON & SE REG HQ	LONDON
Wrigley, Alexander J	Surg Lt Cdr	03-Aug-09	MED	GMP	FLEET AV HENLOW	RAF HENLOW
Wyatt, Jason R	Lt RN	01-Sep-12	ENG	WE	MWS COLLINGWOOD	HMS COLLINGWOOD
Wyatt, Julian M	Cdr	30-Jun-03	ENG	MESM	FLEET FOST ACOS(Trg)	PORTSMOUTH
Wyatt, Mark	Cdr	30-Sep-99	WAR	MW (RES)	FLEET DCS - RNIO	PORTSMOUTH
Wylie, David V	RN Chpln	01-Dec-98	Ch S	Chaplain	42 CDO RM	PLYMOUTH
Wylie, Ian C H	Lt Cdr	30-Jun-08	ENG	WESM(TWS)	FLEET ACOS(RP)	ABBEY WOOD
Wylie, Justin J	Lt RN	01-Sep-07	ENG	AE	DES COMJE	YEOVIL
Wylie, Robert D S	Surg Cdr	01-Apr-03	MED	Occ Med	NCHQ MEDDIV	RAF HENLOW
Wyness, Roger S	Lt Cdr	13-Dec-05	WAR	P FW	NO 3 FTS/UAS - JEFTS	GRANTHAM
Wynn, Simon R	Cdr	30-Jun-10	WAR	METOC	FLEET COMOPS NWD	HUNTINGDON
Wyper, James	Cdr	30-Jun-13	WAR	SM(CQ)	HMS VICTORIOUS	

Y

Name	Substantive Rank	Seniority	Branch	Specialisation	Organisation Name	Location Name
Yarker, Sam	Lt RN	01-Jan-11	WAR	O MER	824 SQN	RNAS CULDROSE
Yates, David M	RN Chpln	01-Sep-98	Ch S	Chaplain	BRNC	BRNC DARTMOUTH
Yates, Neal P MBE	Lt Cdr	01-Jun-89	WAR	O LYNX	FLEET CSAV	RNAS YEOVILTON
Yates, Simon P	Lt RN	01-Sep-07	WAR	O LYNX	LHF 815 SQN	RNAS YEOVILTON
Yates, Stuart E	Lt Cdr	01-Oct-06	WAR	AAWO	MCM2	PORTSMOUTH
Yearling, Emma C	Lt RN	24-Nov-14	ENG	WESM	HMS VIGILANT	
Yelland, Christopher B	Lt Cdr	01-Oct-01	WAR	O LYNX	LHF 815 SQN HQ	RNAS YEOVILTON
Yemm, Charlotte P	Lt Cdr	01-Oct-04	WAR	PWO(C)	FLEET COMOPS NWD	NORTHWOOD
Yemm, Matthew A	Lt RN	01-Feb-06	WAR	HM	FLEET COMOPS NWD	NORTHWOOD
Yeomans, Daniel T	Mid	17-Nov-14	ENG	WE	BRNC	BRNC DARTMOUTH
York, George M	Capt	01-Sep-13	RM	GS	43 CDO FPGRM	HELENSBURGH
Young, Andrew J	Lt RN	28-Jul-06	ENG	AE	DES COMJE	YEOVIL
Young, Andrew O G	Lt RN	01-Nov-07	ENG	TM	NETS (OPS)	HMS DRAKE
Young, Christopher K	SLt	01-Aug-13	ENG	AE	RNAS YEOVILTON	YEOVILTON
Young, James A	Lt RN	01-Sep-14	WAR	GSX	MTM NELSON	HMS NELSON
Young, Martin J	SLt	11-Feb-14	WAR	P UT	MTM RAF CRANWELL	RAFC CRANWELL
Young, Martin N W	Lt RN	01-Sep-09	WAR	O MER	824 SQN	RNAS CULDROSE
Young, Michael	Lt RN	20-Oct-08	ENG	WE	DES COMFLEET	ABBEY WOOD
Young, Michael S MBE	Capt RN	03-Dec-13	ENG	TM	NCHQ CNPERS	PORTSMOUTH
Young, Neil	Lt RN	01-Sep-08	ENG	WF	MWS COLLINGWOOD	HMS COLLINGWOOD

Name	Substantive Rank	Seniority	Branch	Specialisation	Organisation Name	Location Name
Young, Sally	Lt Cdr	01-Oct-14	WAR	MEDIA OPS	NCHQ CNPS	PORTSMOUTH
Young, Sean A	Lt RN	17-Mar-13	LOGS	L	HMS IRON DUKE	
Young, William D	Lt Cdr	31-Mar-05	LOGS	L (RES)	ANAOA	AFGHANISTAN KABUL
Youngman, Mitchell C	Lt RN	27-Jul-06	WAR	REG	DCPG	FAREHAM
Youp, Allan	Cdr	30-Jun-13	ENG	TM	FLEET FOST ACOS(Trg)	PORTSMOUTH
Yoxall, William F	Lt RN	01-Jan-12	WAR	GSX	HMS DUNCAN	

Z

Name	Substantive Rank	Seniority	Branch	Specialisation	Organisation Name	Location Name
Zambellas, George M KCB DSC ADC DL	Adm	06-Jan-12	WAR	P LYNX	MOD CNS/ACNS	LONDON
Zauchenberger, Michael J	Lt RN	01-Jan-09	LOGS	L SM	BF BIOT	DIEGO GARCIA
Zdrodowski, Craig A	Lt RN	02-May-14	QARNNS	MH	DPHC SW	HMS DRAKE
Zealey, William	Mid	01-Feb-14	ENG	MESM	HMS AUDACIOUS	
Zitkus, John J	Lt RN	01-May-07	ENG	WE	DES COMJE	ABBEY WOOD

SENIORITY LIST

ADMIRALS OF THE FLEET

Edinburgh, His Royal Highness The Prince Philip, Duke of, KG, KT, OM, GBE, AC, QSO.......15 Jan 53
Ashmore, Sir Edward (Beckwith), GCB, DSC .... 9 Feb 77
Bathurst, Sir (David) Benjamin, GCB, DL ....10 Jul 95
Wales, His Royal Highness The Prince Charles, Prince of, KG, KT, CGB, OM, AK, QSO, PC, ADC ...16 Jun 12
Boyce, the Lord, KG, GCB, OBE, DL...13 Jun 14

ADMIRALS

FORMER CHIEF OF DEFENCE STAFF, FIRST SEA LORD OR VICE CHIEF OF DEFENCE STAFF WHO REMAIN ON THE ACTIVE LIST

Slater, Sir Jock (John Cunningham Kirkwood), GCB, LVO, DL...29 Jan 91
Abbott, Sir Peter (Charles), GBE, KCB, MA .... 3 Oct 95
Essenhigh, Sir Nigel (Richard), GCB, DL .... 11 Sep 98
West, the Lord, GCB, DSC, PC ....30 Nov 00
Band, Sir Jonathon, GCB, DL... 2 Aug 02
Stanhope, Sir Mark, GCB, OBE...10 Jul 04

ADMIRAL

Zambellas, Sir George, KCB, DSC, ADC, DL...6 Jan 12
(CHIEF OF NAVAL STAFF AND FIRST SEA LORD APR 13)

VICE ADMIRALS

Jones, Sir Philip, KCB...13-Dec-11
(FLEET COMMANDER AND DEPUTY CHIEF OF NAVAL STAFF NOV 12)

Steel, Sir David, KBE, DL... 10-Oct-12
(CHIEF OF NAVAL PERSONNEL & TRAINING AND SECOND SEA LORD JUL 10 & CHIEF NAVAL LOGISTICS OFFICER)

Hudson, Peter Derek, CBE... 14-Feb-13
(COMMANDER MARITIME COMMAND FEB 13)

Corder, Ian Fergus, CB 30-May-13
(UK MILITARY REPRESENTATIVE TO NATO & THE EU MAY 13)

Lister, Simon Robert, CB, OBE 27-Nov-13
(CHIEF OF MATERIEL (FLEET) & CHIEF NAVAL ENGINEERING OFFICER NOV 13)

Potts, Duncan Laurence, CB 18-Sep-14
(DIRECTOR GENERAL JOINT FORCE DEVELOPMENT & DIRECTOR DEFENCE ACADEMY SEP 14)

REAR ADMIRALS

Harding, Russell George, CBE.. 01-Mar-11
(ASSISTANT CHIEF OF NAVAL STAFF (AVIATION & CARRIERS) AND REAR ADMIRAL FLEET AIR ARM
SEP12)

Johnstone, Clive Charles Carruthers, CBE.. 12-Jul-11
(ASSISTANT CHIEF OF NAVAL STAFF (POLICY) MAY 13)

Parr, Matthew John, CB 2-Dec-11
(COMMANDER OPERATIONS & REAR ADMIRAL SUBMARINES MAY 13)

Fraser, Timothy Peter.. 16-Jan-12
(ASSISTANT CHIEF OF DEFENCE STAFF (CAPABILITY FORCE DESIGN) JAN 14

Parker, Henry Hardyman 6-Feb-12
(DIRECTOR SHIP ACQUISITION & DEPUTY DIRECTOR SHIPS JUL 14)

Jess, Ian Michael, CBE...3 Jul 12
(ASSISTANT CHIEF OF NAVAL STAFF (SUPPORT) JUL 12)

Beverstock, Mark Alistair.. 23-Jul-12
(ASSISTANT CHIEF OF DEFENCE STAFF NUCLEAR & CHEMICAL, BIOLOGICAL DEC 14)

Morse, James Anthony..28-Aug-12
(ASSISTANT CHIEF OF NAVAL STAFF (CAPABILITY), CHIEF OF STAFF NCHQ, CONTROLLER OF THE
NAVY, SEP 14)

Woodcock, (Simon) Jonathan, OBE 11-Sep-12
(ASSISTANT CHIEF OF NAVAL STAFF (PERSONNEL) AND NAVAL SECRETARY SEP 12)

Williams, Simon Paul..17-Sep-12
ASSISTANT CHIEF OF DEFENCE STAFF (PERSONNEL) & DEFENCE SERVICES SECRETARY SEP 12)

Lowe, Timothy Miles..17-Sep-12
DEPUTY COMMANDER STRIKE FORCE NATO SEP 12)

Karsten, Thomas Michael...14-Dec-12
(NATIONAL HYDROGRAPHER AND DEPUTY CHIEF EXECUTIVE (HYDROGRAPHY) DEC 12)

Bennett, Paul Martin, OBE..04-Feb-13
(CHIEF OF STAFF JOINT FORCES COMMAND SEP 13)

Key, Benjamin John...29-Apr-13
(FLAG OFFICER SEA TRAINING APR 13)

Wareham, Michael Paul 30-Sep-13
(DIRECTOR SUBMARINES SEP 13)

Cree, Malcolm Charles...07-Oct-13
(CHIEF OF STAFF (INTEGRATED CHANGE PROJECT) OCT 13)

Kingwell, John Matthew Leonard..14-Oct-13
(DIRECTOR CONCEPTS & DOCTRINE OCT 13)

Ancona, Simon James 14-Oct-13
(ASSISTANT CHIEF OF DEFENCE STAFF (MILITARY STRATEGY) OCT 13)

Mackay, Graeme Angus 27-May-14
(PROGRAMME DIRECTOR CARRIER STRIKE MAY 14)

Clink, John Robert Hamilton, OBE 26-Aug-14
(FLAG OFFICER SCOTLAND & NORTHERN IRELAND AUG 14)

Beckett, Keith Andrew, CBE 04-Nov-14
(CHIEF STRATEGIC SYSTEMS EXECUTIVE NOV 14)

Radakin, Antony David 03-Dec-14
(COMMANDER UK MARITIME FORCES DEC 14)

Between appointments:

Tarrant, Robert Kenneth (1SL Directed Studies until Jul 15) 14-Jan-13

Since the publication of the last Navy List, the following officers have joined, or will be joining the Retired List:

RAdm Brunton, Steven Buchanan, CBE - to RL 18-Sep-14 ....
RAdm Hockley, Christopher John, CBE - to RL 22-Nov-14 ....
RAdm Williams, Bruce Nicholas Bromley, CBE - to RL 14-Feb-15 ....
RAdm Gower, John Howard James, OBE - to RL 18-Apr-15 ....
VAdm Richards, Alan David, CB - to RL 7-May-15

COMMODORES

2008

Albon, Ross OBE 07-Jul-08

2009

Walliker, Michael J D OBE 06-Jan-09

2010

Gardner, Christopher R S........................04-Jan-10
Brown, Neil L 01-Jul-10
Toy, Malcolm J...04-Oct-10

2011

McAlpine, Paul A CBE ADC....................08-Feb-11
Chivers, Paul A OBE 10-May 11
Jameson, Andrew C.................................01-Jul-11
Stokes, Richard 25-Jul-11
Farrage, Michael E CBE 07-Nov-11
Williamson, Tobias MVO 16-Nov-11
Hay, James D..21-Dec-11

2012

Roberts, Nicholas S 03-Jan-12

Bath, Michael A W................................01-Jul-12	Robinson, Guy A OBE 03-Sep-13
Pentreath, Jonathan OBE 16-Jul-12	Dutton, David OBE................................ 30-Sep-13
Little, Graeme T OBE............................... 17-Jul-12	
Hammond, Paul A................................... 19-Jul-12	
Thompson, Richard C CBE 27-Jul-12	
Shipperley, Ian......................................28-Aug-12	
Weale, John S OBE................................ 03-Sep-12	
Hodgson, Timothy C MBE 04-Sep-12	
Powell, Richard L OBE 10-Sep-12	
Blunden, Jeremy J F LVO 22-Oct-12	
Adams, Alistair J 05-Nov-12	
Alexander, Robert S OBE 04-Dec-12	

2013

Farrington, Richard CBE 26-Mar-13
Spence, Andrei D 16-Apr-13
Entwisle, William N OBE MVO...............30-Apr-13
Allen, Richard M 01-Jul-13
Elford, David G 01-Jul-13
Hardern, Simon P 01-Jul-13
Lison, Andrew C 01-Jul-13
Rigby, Jeremy C ADC 01-Jul-13
Macdonald, John R 22-Jul-13
Blount, Keith E OBE 27-Aug-13
Corderoy, John 02-Sep-13

2014

Bisson, Ian J P 13-Jan-14
Fry, Jonathan M S 21-Jan-14
Kyd, Jeremy P...24-Feb-14
Methven, Paul...24-Feb-14
Hine, Nicholas W 17-Mar-14
Briers, Matthew P 22-Apr-14
Wainhouse, Michael J 22-Apr-14
Harrison, Matthew S OBE..................... 06-May-14
Lines, James M....................................... 06-May-14
Aplin, Adrian T MBE...............................01-Jul-14
Robinson, Michael P...............................01-Jul-14
Sutton, Gary B 01-Jul-14
Titterton, Phillip J OBE 21-Jul-14
McGhie, Ian A.......................................05-Aug-14
Kyte, Andrew J 26-Aug-14
Morley, James.......................................13-Oct-14
Adams, Andrew M 20-Oct-14
Macleod, James N.................................. 14-Nov-14
Betton, Andrew OBE.............................. 01-Dec-14

CAPTAINS

2000

Miller, Andrew J G CBE 01-Jun-00

2002

Holloway, Jonathan T..............................30-Jun-02
Stanley, Nicholas 30-Jun-02

2003

Atherton, Martin J OBE..........................30-Jun-03
Rusbridger, Robert C 30-Jun-03

2004

King, Charles E W....................................30-Jun-04
Molyneaux, Dean G OBE........................30-Jun-04

2005

Greenlees, Iain W....................................30-Jun-05
Hawthorne, Michael J 30-Jun-05
Lemkes, Paul D 30-Jun-05

2006

Baum, Stuart R..30-Jun-06
Corrigan, Niall R......................................30-Jun-06
McBarnet, Thomas F 30-Jun-06
O'Neill, Patrick J 30-Jun-06
Richmond, Iain J M 30-Jun-06

2007

Alcock, Christopher 30-Jun-07
Knibbs, Mark 30-Jun-07
Macdonald, Alasdair I 30-Jun-07
Skidmore, Christopher M OBE.................30-Jun-07
Taylor, Kenneth 30-Jun-07

2008

Abraham, Paul CBE.................................30-Jun-08
Ashcroft, Adam C 30-Jun-08
Daws, Richard P A...................................30-Jun-08
Garratt, Mark D 30-Jun-08
Heley, David N...30-Jun-08
Jenkin, Alastair M H 30-Jun-08
McMichael-Phillips, Scott J 30-Jun-08
Morritt, Dain C 30-Jun-08
Pett, Jeremy G 30-Jun-08
Smithson, Peter E 30-Jun-08
Anderson, Robert G 01-Jul-08
Taylor, Spencer A.....................................01-Jul-08
Erskine, Peter 08-Jul-08
Hayes, James V B 01-Aug-08
Brand, Simon 08-Sep-08
Doyle, Gary...20-Oct-08
Aspden, Andrew M.................................21-Oct-08

2009

Warwick, Philip D....................................06-Jan-09
Chidley, Timothy J...................................08-Jan-09
McKendrick, Andrew M OBE...................01-Jun-09

Stidston, Ian J 15-Jun-09
Bone, Darren N.......................................01-Jul-09
Clarke, Charles M L OBE 01-Jul-09
Hollins, Rupert 01-Jul-09
Payne, Richard C 01-Jul-09
Porter, Simon P 13-Jul-09
Walker, Nicholas J 18-Aug-09
Ingram, Richard 07-Sep-09
Hughes, Nicholas J 13-Oct-09
Williams, Martyn J.................................13-Oct-09
Durkin, Mark T G 19-Oct-09
Milburn, Philip K 04-Nov-09

2010

Halton, Paul V OBE 11-Jan-10
Fancy, Robert Obe 01-Mar-10
Stocker, Jeremy 01-Mar-10
Jessop, Paul E..08-Mar-10
Clough, Christopher R 12-Apr-10
Charlesworth, Graham...........................19-Apr-10
Childs, David G.....................................26-Apr-10
Dainton, Steven CBE.............................26-Apr-10
Shawcross, Paul K OBE......................... 01-May-10
Casson, Paul R OBE............................... 10-May-10
Burke, Paul D OBE................................. 28-May-10
Amphlett, Nigel G..................................07-Jun-10
Harris, Andrew I.....................................20-Jul-10
O'Brien, Patrick M C OBE 24-Aug-10
Dailey, Richard.......................................27-Aug-10
Pettitt, Gary W....................................... 20-Sep-10
Sparkes, Peter J.....................................08-Nov-10
Thomas, Richard 08-Nov-10

CAPTAINS

White, Jonathan A P 13-Dec-10

2011

Pearson, Stephen 07-Jan-11
Borland, Stuart A 10-Jan-11
Reid, Charles I 10-Jan-11
Blackman, Nicholas T OBE 25-Jan-11
Gulley, Trevor J 25-Jan-11
Reindorp, David P 21-Feb-11
Wood, Robert 22-Feb-11
Higham, James G OBE 07-Mar-11
Warrender, William J 26-Apr-11
Murrison, Richard A 16-May-11
Beardall, Michael J D 27-Jun-11
Stanley-Whyte, Berkeley J OBE 01-Jul-11
Hill, Philip J 15-Aug-11
Connell, Martin J 05-Sep-11
Carrick, Richard J 06-Sep-11
Carter, Simon N 07-Sep-11
Hatcher, Rhett S 26-Sep-11
Bellfield, Robert J A 27-Sep-11
Cooper, Mark A 11-Oct-11
Coulson, Peter 18-Oct-11
Kennedy, Inga J 21-Nov-11
Long, Adrian M 21-Nov-11
Duffy, Henry 06-Dec-11
Deaney, Mark N 16-Dec-11

2012

Beard, Hugh D 03-Jan-12
Burns, Andrew P 03-Jan-12
Cree, Andrew 03-Jan-12
Thompson, Stephen J 09-Jan-12
Scott, Nigel L J 10-Jan-12
Magan, Michael J C 21-Feb-12
Burningham, Michael R 12-Mar-12
Orchard, Adrian P OBE 19-Apr-12
Pollock, David J 01-May-12
Petitt, Simon R 28-May-12
Wagstaff, Neil 25-Jun-12
Bartlett, David S G 01-Jul-12
Marshall, Paul CBE 01-Jul-12
Fisher, Clayton R A 16-Jul-12
Phillips, Ian M 06-Aug-12
Stace, Ivan S 28-Aug-12
Osmond, Justin B 03-Sep-12
Hodkinson, Christopher B 04-Sep-12
Lower, Iain S 10-Sep-12
Utley, Michael K 10-Sep-12

Vanderpump, David J 10-Sep-12
Guy, Thomas J 18-Sep-12
Reed, Andrew W OBE 25-Sep-12
Dabell, Guy L 01-Oct-12
Clark, Matthew T 02-Oct-12
Olive, Peter N OBE 02-Oct-12
Tindal, Nicolas H C 08-Oct-12
Vitali, Robert C 09-Oct-12
Cameron, Mark J 06-Nov-12
Paterson, Michael 20-Nov-12
Peacock, Timothy J 10-Dec-12
Holt, Steven OBE 12-Dec-12

2013

Allen, Stephen M 08-Jan-13
Gale, Mark A 21-Jan-13
Betteridge, Carol A OBE 26-Feb-13
Annett, Ian G 11-Mar-13
Prescott, Shaun 22-Apr-13
Kissane, Robert E T 07-May-13
Willis, Alistair J 07-May-13
Watt, Anthony J L OBE 18-Jun-13
Gayfer, Mark E 24-Jun-13
Grantham, Stephen M 01-Jul-13
Griffin, Niall Mbe 01-Jul-13
Salmon, Michael A 01-Jul-13
Shaw, Kevin 01-Jul-13
Streeten, Christopher M 01-Jul-13
Talbott, Aidan H 01-Jul-13
Tritschler, Edwin L MBE 01-Jul-13
Burns, David I 02-Jul-13
Manson, Thomas E 02-Jul-13
Evans, William Q F 08-Jul-13
Poole, Jason L 15-Jul-13
Oliphant, William 29-Aug-13
Seymour, Kevin W 02-Sep-13
Waterhouse, Phillip 03-Sep-13
Bassett, Dean A 09-Sep-13
Henry, Timothy M 09-Sep-13
Woodard, Jolyon 09-Sep-13
Robertson, David C 17-Sep-13
Washer, Nicholas B J 17-Sep-13
Jordan, Andrew A 25-Sep-13
Huntington, Simon P OBE 28-Oct-13
Wood, Craig 18-Nov-13
Lovegrove, Raymond A 03-Dec-13
Young, Michael S MBE 03-Dec-13
Ackland, Heber K MVO 10-Dec-13

2014

Cox, Rex J 06-Jan-14
Breckenridge, Iain G OBE 07-Jan-14
McTear, Karen MBE 13-Jan-14
Winter, Richard J 20-Jan-14
Hill, Giulian F 12-Feb-14
Towell, Peter J OBE 04-Mar-14
Woods, Timothy C 04-Mar-14
Jarvis, Laurence R 17-Mar-14
Kennedy, Ian J A 18-Mar-14
Abernethy, James R G 24-Mar-14
Anstey, Robert J 25-Mar-14
Martin, Bruce A 08-Apr-14
Asquith, Simon P OBE 28-Apr-14
Smith, Gregory K 12-May-14
Fleming, Kevin P 16-May-14
Cook, Christopher B 02-Jun-14
Stembridge, Daniel P T 20-Jun-14
Doull, Donald J M 01-Jul-14
Perks, James L OBE 01-Jul-14
Quinn, Martin 01-Jul-14
Finn, Ivan R 03-Jul-14
O'Brien, Kieran J 14-Jul-14
Dunn, Paul E OBE 15-Jul-14
Cryar, Timothy M C 22-Jul-14
Roberts, Stephen D 11-Aug-14
Matthews, David W 18-Aug-14
Bowbrick, Richard C 26-Aug-14
Green, David P S 26-Aug-14
Hally, Philip J 02-Sep-14
Harris, Keri J 02-Sep-14
Bryan, Rory J L OBE 08-Sep-14
Nisbet, James H T 08-Sep-14
Hibberd, Nicholas J 12-Sep-14
Jones, Alun D 22-Sep-14
Dominy, David J D 29-Sep-14
Hopper, Simon M 29-Sep-14
Jackson, Andrew S 29-Sep-14
Currass, Timothy 30-Sep-14
Carroll, Paul C 06-Oct-14
Cooke-Priest, Nicholas 06-Oct-14
Follington, Daniel C 06-Oct-14
Douglas, Patrick J 13-Oct-14
Dean, James R OBE 03-Nov-14
Beattie, Paul 10-Nov-14
Parry, Alexander K I 11-Nov-14
Greener, Carl 17-Nov-14
Roberts, Timothy J 17-Nov-14
Bowers, John P 08-Dec-14
Bailey, Jeremy J 16-Dec-14

COMMANDERS

1987

Brown, Simon J J 16-Jun-87

1988

Hughes, Peter LVO 06-Feb-88

1993

Spalton, Gary 11-Jun-93

Cox, Pieter W S 30-Jun-93

1994

Chambers, William J 30-Apr-94

1996

Holmes, Robert 25-Feb-96

COMMANDERS

1997

Horne, Timothy G 30-Jun-97
Pickthall, David N 31-Dec-97

1998

Danbury, Ian G 30-Jun-98
Ewence, Martin W OBE 30-Jun-98
Jackman, Andrew W 30-Jun-98
Green, Timothy J 31-Dec-98
Hatch, Giles W H 31-Dec-98
Shield, Simon J 31-Dec-98
Woods, Roland P 31-Dec-98

1999

Barton, Peter G 30-Jun-99
Carden, Peter D 30-Jun-99
Fear, Richard K 30-Jun-99
Horn, Peter B MBE 30-Jun-99
Moore, Christopher I 30-Jun-99
Morton, Nigel P B 30-Jun-99
Robinson, Charles E T 30-Jun-99
Simmons, Nigel D 30-Jun-99
Wyatt, Mark 30-Sep-99
Buckland, Richard J F 31-Dec-99
Chalmers, Donald P 31-Dec-99
Greene, Michael J 31-Dec-99
Johnson, Andrew S 31-Dec-99
Race, Nigel 31-Dec-99
Treanor, Martin A 31-Dec-99

2000

Allibon, Mark C 30-Jun-00
Broadley, Kevin J 30-Jun-00
Harvey, Colin A 30-Jun-00
Hayes, Stuart J 30-Jun-00
Tilley, Duncan 30-Jun-00
Bond, Nigel D MBE 31-Dec-00
Buchan-Steele, Mark A 31-Dec-00
Connolly, Christopher J 31-Dec-00
Frankham, Peter J 31-Dec-00
Fulton, Craig R 31-Dec-00
Hughes, Gareth L 31-Dec-00
Marmont, Kerry L 31-Dec-00
Parsons, Brian R 31-Dec-00
Williams, Anthony DSC 31-Dec-00

2001

Rance, Maxwell G W 31-May-01
Foreman, John L R 30-Jun-01
Gordon, David 30-Jun-01
Haines, Paul R 30-Jun-01
Jones, Martin C 30-Jun-01
Knight, Damon A 30-Jun-01
Mitchell, Henry 30-Jun-01
Phenna, Andrew 30-Jun-01
Raybould, Adrian G 30-Jun-01
Shaw, Steven M 30-Jun-01
St Aubyn, John D E 30-Jun-01

Wallace, Allan OBE 30-Jun-01

2002

Kay, David 01-Jan-02
Barrand, Stuart M 30-Jun-02
Blackmore, Mark S 30-Jun-02
Falk, Benedict H G 30-Jun-02
Fitter, Ian S T 30-Jun-02
Grindel, David J S 30-Jun-02
Hardy, Lee C 30-Jun-02
Haywood, Guy 30-Jun-02
Hodgkins, Jonathan M 30-Jun-02
Moffatt, Neil R 30-Jun-02
Skeer, Martyn 30-Jun-02
Swannick, Derek J 30-Jun-02
Thompson, Bernard 30-Jun-02
Turnbull, Graham D 30-Jun-02
Turnbull, Simon J L 30-Jun-02
Wallis, Adrian J 30-Jun-02

2003

Burlingham, Brett L 30-Jun-03
Clark, Ian D 30-Jun-03
Coles, Andrew L OBE 30-Jun-03
Corbett, Andrew S 30-Jun-03
Cunningham, John 30-Jun-03
David, Simon E J MBE 30-Jun-03
Dyke, Christopher 30-Jun-03
Fields, David 30-Jun-03
Fieldsend, Mark 30-Jun-03
Flynn, Michael T 30-Jun-03
Gilbert, Peter D 30-Jun-03
Gurmin, Stephen 30-Jun-03
Harvey, Robert 30-Jun-03
Hawkins, Martin 30-Jun-03
Jenkins, Gari Wyn 30-Jun-03
Kirkup, John P 30-Jun-03
Mahony, David G 30-Jun-03
Meakin, Brian R 30-Jun-03
Munns, Andrew R 30-Jun-03
Randall, Richard D 30-Jun-03
Salisbury, David P OBE 30-Jun-03
Sherriff, David A 30-Jun-03
Smith, Martin R K 30-Jun-03
Upton, Iain D 30-Jun-03
Wintle, Geoffrey L 30-Jun-03
Wyatt, Julian M 30-Jun-03

2004

Band, James W 30-Jun-04
Bull, Christopher M S 30-Jun-04
Dible, James 30-Jun-04
Dunn, Robert P OBE 30-Jun-04
Edge, John H 30-Jun-04
Ferris, Daniel P S 30-Jun-04
Giles, David W 30-Jun-04
Howell, Simon B 30-Jun-04
Lister, Mark 30-Jun-04
Merewether, Henry A H 30-Jun-04
Riches, Ian C OBE 30-Jun-04

Rolph, Andrew P M 30-Jun-04
Toft, Michael D 30-Jun-04
Woods, Jeremy B 30-Jun-04

2005

Bowen, Nigel T 30-Jun-05
Bower, Nigel S 30-Jun-05
Boyd, Nicholas 30-Jun-05
Buckle, Iain L 30-Jun-05
Cartwright, Darren OBE 30-Jun-05
Chatwin, Nicholas J OBE 30-Jun-05
Clark, Simon 30-Jun-05
Deller, Mark G OBE 30-Jun-05
Dowell, Paul H N 30-Jun-05
Duncan, Ian S 30-Jun-05
Forer, Duncan A 30-Jun-05
Geary, Timothy W 30-Jun-05
George, Alan P 30-Jun-05
Green, Peter J 30-Jun-05
Grenfell-Shaw, Mark 30-Jun-05
Harrop, Ian 30-Jun-05
Haycock, Timothy P 30-Jun-05
Hayle, James 30-Jun-05
Honnoraty, Mark R OBE 30-Jun-05
Maher, Michael 30-Jun-05
Mallinson, Robert 30-Jun-05
Mearns, Craig M 30-Jun-05
Merritt, Jonathan J 30-Jun-05
Murdoch, Andrew W 30-Jun-05
Rippingale, Stuart N 30-Jun-05
Russell, Philip R 30-Jun-05
Short, John J 30-Jun-05
Swain, Andrew V MBE 30-Jun-05
Winkle, Sean J 30-Jun-05
Wright, Stuart H 30-Jun-05
Allen, Elinor J 30-Sep-05
Hardinge, Christopher MBE 30-Sep-05

2006

Albon, Mark 30-Jun-06
Allen, Richard 30-Jun-06
Churcher, Jeremy E 30-Jun-06
Coles, Christopher J 30-Jun-06
Davies, Mark B 30-Jun-06
Drysdale, Steven R 30-Jun-06
Eastaugh, Andrew C 30-Jun-06
Evans, Edward M 30-Jun-06
Evans, Martin J 30-Jun-06
Ewen, Andrew P 30-Jun-06
Gibbs, Neil D 30-Jun-06
Gibson, Alastair D 30-Jun-06
Goodsell, Christopher D 30-Jun-06
Gray, John A 30-Jun-06
Guy, Mark A MBE 30-Jun-06
Hall, Barry J 30-Jun-06
Hancock, Andrew P 30-Jun-06
Howard, Daniel G 30-Jun-06
Hutchinson, Oliver J P 30-Jun-06
Juckes, Martin A 30-Jun-06
Kelly, John 30-Jun-06

COMMANDERS

Lias, Carl D	30-Jun-06
Lindsay, Irvine G OBE	30-Jun-06
Masters, James C	30-Jun-06
May, Nigel P	30-Jun-06
McCue, Duncan	30-Jun-06
Morris, Richard J	30-Jun-06
Morris, Simon T	30-Jun-06
Moss, Richard A	30-Jun-06
Munro-Lott, Peter R J	30-Jun-06
Scott, James B	30-Jun-06
Smith, Christopher J	30-Jun-06
Stuttard, Mark	30-Jun-06
Thompson, Neil J OBE	30-Jun-06
Towler, Alison	30-Jun-06
Vickers, John OBE	30-Jun-06
Worthington, Jonathan M F	30-Jun-06

2007

Deacon, Stephen	01-Jun-07
Ahlgren, Edward G OBE	30-Jun-07
Ashman, Rodney G	30-Jun-07
Boddington, Jeremy D L	30-Jun-07
Bosustow, Antony M	30-Jun-07
Campbell, Robin D H	30-Jun-07
Clarke, Richard	30-Jun-07
Cummings, Alan	30-Jun-07
Dodd, Nicholas C	30-Jun-07
Dreelan, Michael J	30-Jun-07
Elliman, Simon	30-Jun-07
Evans, Marc D	30-Jun-07
Ferns, Timothy D	30-Jun-07
Fortescue, Robert	30-Jun-07
Gill, Martin R	30-Jun-07
Gomm, Kevin OBE	30-Jun-07
Groom, Ian S MBE	30-Jun-07
Hewitt, David L	30-Jun-07
Hill, David	30-Jun-07
Hoper, Paul R	30-Jun-07
Hussain, Shayne MBE	30-Jun-07
James, Adam J	30-Jun-07
John, Gareth MBE	30-Jun-07
Johns, Sarah A B	30-Jun-07
Lipscomb, Paul	30-Jun-07
Lowther, James	30-Jun-07
Lynn, Steven R	30-Jun-07
Meredith, Nicholas	30-Jun-07
Miller, Colin R	30-Jun-07
Moorey, Christopher	30-Jun-07
Pethybridge, Richard A	30-Jun-07
Price, Timothy A	30-Jun-07
Russell, Thomas	30-Jun-07
Sansford, Adrian J	30-Jun-07
Savage, Mark R OBE	30-Jun-07
Shepherd, Charles S	30-Jun-07
Staley, Simon P L	30-Jun-07
Stoffell, David	30-Jun-07
Tebbet, Paul	30-Jun-07
Tyack, Terence J	30-Jun-07
Walker, Mark	30-Jun-07
Walker, Peter R	30-Jun-07
Waller, Steven	30-Jun-07

Ward, Stephen D	30-Jun-07

2008

Thain-Smith, Julie C	01-Apr-08
Allen, Patrick L	30-Jun-08
Asbridge, Jonathan I	30-Jun-08
Atkinson, Mark	30-Jun-08
Bartlett, Ian D	30-Jun-08
Bence, David E	30-Jun-08
Bolton, Matthew T W	30-Jun-08
Bone, Richard C	30-Jun-08
Bower, Andrew J OBE	30-Jun-08
Brady, Sean E	30-Jun-08
Brenchley, Nigel G	30-Jun-08
Brooks, Gary	30-Jun-08
Capes, Stuart G	30-Jun-08
Cole, Simon P	30-Jun-08
Dathan, Timothy J	30-Jun-08
Draper, Stephen	30-Jun-08
Freeman, David R	30-Jun-08
Godwin, Christopher A	30-Jun-08
Green, Andrew J	30-Jun-08
Harris, Michael T	30-Jun-08
Hesling, Gary	30-Jun-08
Houlberg, Kenneth M T	30-Jun-08
Hulme, Timothy OBE	30-Jun-08
Irwin, Mark A	30-Jun-08
Jackson, Ian A	30-Jun-08
Joll, Simon	30-Jun-08
Lauchlan, Robert A	30-Jun-08
Lea, John	30-Jun-08
Macdonald-Robinson, Nicholas U S	30-Jun-08
Mackey, Martin C	30-Jun-08
Mulvaney, Paul A	30-Jun-08
Murphy, Paul A	30-Jun-08
O'Byrne, Patrick	30-Jun-08
Payne, John D	30-Jun-08
Pierce, Adrian K M	30-Jun-08
Rose, Michael F	30-Jun-08
Rowland, Paul N	30-Jun-08
Smith, Gregory C S	30-Jun-08
Smith, Mark M	30-Jun-08
Southorn, Mark D	30-Jun-08
Stacey, Andrew M	30-Jun-08
Tetlow, Hamish S G	30-Jun-08
Walker, Stephen P	30-Jun-08
Whitfield, Kenneth K	30-Jun-08
Wilkinson, David H OBE	30-Jun-08
Winter, Timothy M	30-Jun-08
Wylie, Ian C H	30-Jun-08
Bewley, Geoffrey RD	28-Oct-08

2009

Adam, Ian K	30-Jun-09
Aniyi, Christopher B J	30-Jun-09
Atkins, Ian	30-Jun-09
Balhetchet, Adrian S	30-Jun-09
Blackwell, Richard E	30-Jun-09
Blythe, Paul C	30-Jun-09
Cox, David J	30-Jun-09

Craig, John	30-Jun-09
Crosbie, Donald E F	30-Jun-09
Cull, Iain Obe	30-Jun-09
Dowsett, Patrick G	30-Jun-09
Evans, Charles A	30-Jun-09
Fitzsimmons, Mark B	30-Jun-09
Franklin, Benjamin J	30-Jun-09
Gale, Simon P	30-Jun-09
Game, Philip G	30-Jun-09
Gardner, John E	30-Jun-09
George, David M	30-Jun-09
Goldsmith, Darran	30-Jun-09
Green, Timothy C	30-Jun-09
Grindon, Matthew G	30-Jun-09
Harding, Gary A	30-Jun-09
Harris, Richard P	30-Jun-09
Henderson, Stuart P	30-Jun-09
Hewitt, Lloyd	30-Jun 09
Jameson, Susan	30-Jun-09
Krosnar-Clarke, Steven M	30-Jun-09
Langrill, Mark P	30-Jun-09
Loring, Andrew	30-Jun-09
Matthews, Paul B	30-Jun-09
McCarthy, Steven	30-Jun-09
Moore, Piers H G	30-Jun-09
Necker, Carl D	30-Jun-09
Nicholson, Kristin J	30-Jun-09
O'Flaherty, Christopher P J	30-Jun-09
O'Flaherty, John	30-Jun-09
O'Sullivan, Barrie O	30-Jun-09
O'Sullivan, Michael	30-Jun-09
Patterson, David	30-Jun-09
Phillips, Jason P OBE	30-Jun-09
Preece, David G	30-Jun-09
Prince, Mark E	30-Jun-09
Proud, Andrew D	30-Jun-09
Ryan, Richard M	30-Jun-09
Sharpe, Thomas G OBE	30-Jun-09
Small, Richard	30-Jun-09
Smith, Austin B D	30-Jun-09
Stamper, Jonathan C H	30-Jun-09
Taylor, Mark A	30-Jun-09
Teideman, Ian C	30-Jun-09
Thompson, Robert	30-Jun-09
Voyce, John E	30-Jun-09
Walker, Nicholas M	30-Jun-09
Whalley, Richard J	30-Jun-09
Whyte, Iain P	30-Jun-09
Wilson, David R	30-Jun-09
Wilson-Chalon, Louis M	30-Jun-09
Wright, Nigel S	30-Jun-09
Spencer, Steven J	04-Aug-09
Adams, Peter	01-Sep-09

2010

Baines, David M L	30-Jun-10
Baxter, Iain M	30-Jun-10
Block, Andrew W G	30-Jun-10
Bolton, Jonathan P	30-Jun-10
Bravery, Martin A E	30-Jun-10
Bruford, Robert M C	30-Jun-10

COMMANDERS

Burns, Adrian C OBE 30-Jun-10
Chapman, Charles L 30-Jun-10
Clarke, Ian 30-Jun-10
Dow, Clive S 30-Jun-10
Fergusson, Nigel A.....................30-Jun-10
Fincher, Kevin J 30-Jun-10
Garratt, John K 30-Jun-10
Gazzard, Julian H 30-Jun-10
Hoare, Peter J E..........................30-Jun-10
Horne, Jason 30-Jun-10
Howard, Nicholas H 30-Jun-10
Hughesdon, Mark D 30-Jun-10
Jackson, David 30-Jun-10
Johns, Michael 30-Jun-10
Joyce, David A 30-Jun-10
Knott, Michael R 30-Jun-10
Lamb, Andrew G OBE..................30-Jun-10
Landrock, Graham J 30-Jun-10
Lett, Jonathan D 30-Jun-10
Linderman, Ian R.........................30-Jun-10
Lowe, Julian C 30-Jun-10
Lynn, Ian H OBE 30-Jun-10
Mackay, Peter 30-Jun-10
Mardlin, Stephen A......................30-Jun-10
McDermott, Owen D 30-Jun-10
McNally, Neville...........................30-Jun-10
Mimpriss, Graham D 30-Jun-10
Moorhouse, Stephen OBE............30-Jun-10
Murray, Grant M..........................30-Jun-10
Nash, Philip D 30-Jun-10
New, Christopher M.....................30-Jun-10
Panther, Andrew 30-Jun-10
Pedre, Robert G 30-Jun-10
Pethick, Ian 30-Jun-10
Philo, Julian Q 30-Jun-10
Pitcher, Paul P 30-Jun-10
Pledger, David 30-Jun-10
Rackham, Anthony D H.................30-Jun-10
Readwin, Roger 30-Jun-10
Reed, Darren K 30-Jun-10
Richardson, Gavin A.....................30-Jun-10
Rimmer, Heather E 30-Jun-10
Royston, Stuart J 30-Jun-10
Russell, Paul................................30-Jun-10
Smith, Michael D 30-Jun-10
Smith, Robert C V 30-Jun-10
Stroude, Paul 30-Jun-10
Syrett, Matthew E 30-Jun-10
Tabeart, George W.......................30-Jun-10
Taylor, Robert 30-Jun-10
Vollentine, Lucy...........................30-Jun-10
Wheal, Adrian..............................30-Jun-10
Wheeler, Nicholas J 30-Jun-10
Whitley, Ian D B 30-Jun-10
Williams, Colin OBE 30-Jun-10
Williams, Stephen W L 30-Jun-10
Wooller, Mark A H 30-Jun-10
Wynn, Simon R 30-Jun-10
Hofman, Alison J RRC 27-Jul-10

2011

Weir, Scott D.............................29-Mar-11
Ablett, Eleanor L MBE 30-Jun-11
Aitken, Andrew J 30-Jun-11
Atwill, John W O..........................30-Jun-11
Baggaley, Jason A L 30-Jun-11
Ballard, Mark L 30-Jun-11
Beech, Christopher M 30-Jun-11
Bird, Richard A J..........................30-Jun-11
Borbone, Nicholas........................30-Jun-11
Burge, Roger...............................30-Jun-11
Chapman, Anthony 30-Jun-11
Clarke, Richard 30-Jun-11
Clink, Adam D 30-Jun-11
Copeland, Stephen N....................30-Jun-11
Cotterill, Bruce M.........................30-Jun-11
Curry, Robert E............................30-Jun-11
Edward, Gavin 30-Jun-11
Essenhigh, Angus N P 30-Jun-11
Fogell, Andrew D 30-Jun-11
Fryer, Adrian C 30-Jun-11
Greenland, Michael R MVO...........30-Jun-11
Haigh, Alastair J 30-Jun-11
Harcourt, Robert 30-Jun-11
Harrison, Richard S MBE 30-Jun-11
Houston, Darren J M.....................30-Jun-11
Humphrey, Ivor J 30-Jun-11
Hutchins, Richard F 30-Jun-11
Jefferson, Toby S 30-Jun-11
Joyce, Thomas J 30-Jun-11
Large, Stephen A 30-Jun-11
Lawrence, Stuart P 30-Jun-11
Livesey, John E 30-Jun-11
Lovatt, Graham J..........................30-Jun-11
Lynch, Stephen 30-Jun-11
Mackie, David F S.........................30-Jun-11
Mackinnon, Donald J 30-Jun-11
Macleod, Mark S..........................30-Jun-11
Malkin, Sharon L..........................30-Jun-11
Martin, Simon J 30-Jun-11
Matthews, Paul K..........................30-Jun-11
McDonnell, David 30-Jun-11
McNair, James OBE 30-Jun-11
Moore, Suzanne K 30-Jun-11
Napier, Graham...........................30-Jun-11
Noakes, Kevin M..........................30-Jun-11
Parkin, James M B 30-Jun-11
Parsons, Andrew D 30-Jun-11
Parvin, Philip S 30-Jun-11
Rayner, Andrew 30-Jun-11
Richardson, Peter S M 30-Jun-11
Rimington, Anthony K 30-Jun-11
Ripley, Benjamin E 30-Jun-11
Roberts, Dean 30-Jun-11
Rowlands, Kevin 30-Jun-11
Ryan, Sean J 30-Jun-11
Scandling, Rachel J 30-Jun-11
Slocombe, Nicholas R....................30-Jun-11
Stride, James A 30-Jun-11
Teasdale, David A.........................30-Jun-11
Tweedie, Howard J 30-Jun-11

Wales, Benjamin D.......................30-Jun-11
Wallace, Simon J..........................30-Jun-11
Waring, John R 30-Jun-11
Westwood, Mark R 30-Jun-11
Williams, Mark A 30-Jun-11
Wilson, Allan J 30-Jun-11
Wiseman, Ian C 30-Jun-11
Manwaring, Roy G........................25-Jul-11
Piper, Neale D ARRC....................05-Sep-11

2012

Thompson, Fiona 06-Feb-12
Smith, Mark P..............................26-Mar-12
Barlow, Martin J...........................30-Jun-12
Bonnar, John A 30-Jun-12
Bowden, Matthew T E 30-Jun-12
Burvill, Justin P 30-Jun-12
Carrigan, Jonathan A 30-Jun-12
Chapman, Peter...........................30-Jun-12
Cheshire, Thomas E 30-Jun-12
Clarke, Daniel 30-Jun-12
Cooke, Jonathan E........................30-Jun-12
Coyle, Gavin J 30-Jun-12
Criddle, Gary D J MBE 30-Jun-12
Currie, Stuart M 30-Jun-12
Dennis, Matthew J........................30-Jun-12
Donaldson, Andrew M...................30-Jun-12
Gibbons, Nicholas P 30-Jun-12
Goldstone, Richard S....................30-Jun-12
Goudge, Simon D P 30-Jun-12
Gray, Paul R 30-Jun-12
Griffiths, Richard H 30-Jun-12
Hammond, Paul 30-Jun-12
Harrison, Paul D MBE 30-Jun-12
Jacques, Marcus J 30-Jun-12
Johns, Andrew W 30-Jun-12
Johnson, Chad C B 30-Jun-12
Jones, David................................30-Jun-12
Jose, Steven................................30-Jun-12
Laughton, Peter MBE 30-Jun-12
Ling, Christopher 30-Jun-12
Love, Tristram S N 30-Jun-12
Marratt, Richard...........................30-Jun-12
Moody, David C 30-Jun-12
Moore, Martin 30-Jun-12
Moore, Sean 30-Jun-12
Morgan, David H 30-Jun-12
Neild, Timothy 30-Jun-12
Pears, Ian J Mbe 30-Jun-12
Percival, Fiona 30-Jun-12
Ponsford, Philip K 30-Jun-12
Rae, Derek G 30-Jun-12
Reece, Nigel D 30-Jun-12
Reid, Jason C J 30-Jun-12
Ruddock, Gordon W D...................30-Jun-12
Saunders, Christopher E M MBE.....30-Jun-12
Scopes, David 30-Jun-12
Sellars, Scott J 30-Jun-12
Sharkey, Elton R 30-Jun-12
Shaughnessy, Sophie L 30-Jun-12
Shepherd, Fiona R 30-Jun-12

COMMANDERS

Snelling, Paul D..30-Jun-12
Solly, Matthew M......................................30-Jun-12
Stephenson, Keith J M............................30-Jun-12
Stock, Christopher M...............................30-Jun-12
Sweeney, Keith P M 30-Jun-12
Thomason, Michael 30-Jun-12
Turner, David J 30-Jun-12
West, Sarah 30-Jun-12
Wheaton, Bowden J S.............................30-Jun-12
Wills, Philip 30-Jun-12
Windebank, Stephen J 30-Jun-12
Campbell, Felicity....................................01-Jul-12
Davies, Jason L....................................... 16-Jul-12
Bagnall, Sally-Anne E 06-Aug-12
Murray, Alister 14-Oct-12

2013

Witt, Alister K...................................... 14-Jan-13
Taylor, Lisa M 03-Mar-13
Canale, Andrew J....................................01-Jun-13
Bell, Jeffrey M 24-Jun-13
Atkinson, Richard J 30-Jun-13
Baker, Adrian P 30-Jun-13
Bamforth, Christian J M 30-Jun-13
Barton, Mark A.......................................30-Jun-13
Benfell, Niall A 30-Jun-13
Berry, Ian MBE RD 30-Jun-13
Birse, Gregor J 30-Jun-13
Bolton, Stephen J....................................30-Jun-13
Bowman, Robert......................................30-Jun-13
Boyes, Martyn R......................................30-Jun-13
Buck, James E 30-Jun-13
Byron, James D DSC.................................30-Jun-13
Canning, Christopher P MBE.....................30-Jun-13
Carnie, Manson J 30-Jun-13
Chestnutt, James 30-Jun-13
Codd, Justin S..30-Jun-13
Cottis, Mathew C 30-Jun-13
Cox, Mark B..30-Jun-13
Deakin, Johanna 30-Jun-13
Donovan, Robin J....................................30-Jun-13
Doran, Shane E.......................................30-Jun-13
D'Silva, Daniel..30-Jun-13
Easterbrook, Kevin I E 30-Jun-13
Exworthy, Damian A G MBE.....................30-Jun-13
Goldsmith, David T 30-Jun-13
Hooper, Johanna.....................................30-Jun-13
Ingham, Andrew R...................................30-Jun-13
Jordan, Catherine E..................................30-Jun-13
Kellett, Andrew.......................................30-Jun-13
Kirkwood, Tristram A H............................30-Jun-13
Knock, Gareth P.......................................30-Jun-13
Martin, David C S.....................................30-Jun-13
McGlory, Stephen J..................................30-Jun-13
McLellan, James D 30-Jun-13
Mealing, David W 30-Jun-13
Mowatt, Patrick 30-Jun-13
Mudge, Adrian M....................................30-Jun-13
Neave, Andrew M....................................30-Jun-13
Noyce, Roger MBE 30-Jun-13
Orton, David M..30-Jun-13

Owen, Glyn 30-Jun-13
Parry, Mark 30-Jun-13
Pedler, Mark D 30-Jun-13
Prest, Stephen 30-Jun-13
Quekett, Ian P S......................................30-Jun-13
Richards, James I H 30-Jun-13
Rose, Andrew D.......................................30-Jun-13
Rowlands, Andrew R................................30-Jun-13
Shepherd, Martin P 30-Jun-13
Spooner, Ross 30-Jun-13
Stafford, Wayne......................................30-Jun-13
Stowell, Perry I M....................................30-Jun-13
Stride, Jamieson C 30-Jun-13
Tanner, Richard 30-Jun-13
Thomas, David J.......................................30-Jun-13
Thompson, Michael J 30-Jun-13
Tracey, Alan D 30-Jun-13
Tredray, Thomas P...................................30-Jun-13
Watts, Robert..30-Jun-13
Wildin, Andrew.......................................30-Jun-13
Wilson, Christopher J...............................30-Jun-13
Wood, Uvedale G S..................................30-Jun-13
Woollven, Andrew 30-Jun-13
Wyper, James...30-Jun-13
Youp, Allan...30-Jun-13
Hounsome, Debra M MBE ARRC.............01-Jul-13
Jones, Timothy M....................................21-Jul-13
Charlton, Kevin W 11-Aug-13

2014

Burnett, Paul H 24-Feb-14
Day, Anthony..28-Apr-14
Anderson, Mark E J..................................30-Jun-13
Anderson, Stephen R...............................30-Jun-14
Ballantyne, Craig.....................................30-Jun-14
Bennett, William E 30-Jun-14
Bignell, Stephen......................................30-Jun-14
Bird, Jonathan M 30-Jun-14
Bird, Matthew G J....................................30-Jun-14
Blackburn, Andrew R J.............................30-Jun-14
Blackburn, Stuart J...................................30-Jun-14
Blackmore, James 30-Jun-14
Bollen, Johanna M 30-Jun-14
Bush, Alexander J T..................................30-Jun-14
Caple, Jonathan N 30-Jun-14
Cogan, Robert 30-Jun-14
Collacott, Jonathan S...............................30-Jun-14
Collins, Simon J P 30-Jun-14
Coope, Philip J...30-Jun-14
Coulthard, Adrian J..................................30-Jun-14
Crockatt, Stephen R J...............................30-Jun-14
Crofts, David J 30-Jun-14
Curtis, Suzannah......................................30-Jun-14
Dale-Smith, Victoria G..............................30-Jun-14
Dennis, Philip MBE 30-Jun-14
Donworth, Desmond 30-Jun-14
Doubleday, Steven 30-Jun-14
Dufosee, Sean W MBE 30-Jun-14
Durham, Paul C L MBE 30-Jun-14
Filtness, David M.....................................30-Jun-14
Finn, Stuart A..30-Jun-14

Flynn, Andrew 30-Jun-14
Foreman, Simon M 30-Jun-14
Gennard, Anthony 30-Jun-14
Graham, Alastair N S MVO 30-Jun-14
Hallett, Simon J.......................................30-Jun-14
Hardiman, Nicholas A 30-Jun-14
Harper, Philip R 30-Jun-14
Harrison, Mark A 30-Jun-14
Hay, Michael 30-Jun-14
Haywood, Peter.......................................30-Jun-14
Head, Steven A..30-Jun-14
Higham, Stephen.....................................30-Jun-14
Hunt, Fraser B G 30-Jun-14
James, Andrew G 30-Jun-14
Jenkins, David G 30-Jun-14
Kingdom, Mark A.....................................30-Jun-14
Knight, David W 30-Jun-14
Lewis, Andrew...30-Jun-14
Lewis, Benjamin......................................30-Jun-14
Martyn, Daniel 30-Jun-14
McKnight, Derek J S 30-Jun-14
McLaughlin, Steven..................................30-Jun-14
Moody, Alistair C 30-Jun-14
Moran, Craig A..30-Jun-14
Nelson, Christopher S 30-Jun-14
Newell, Phillip 30-Jun-14
O'Toole, Mathew C 30-Jun-14
Ottewell, Paul S 30-Jun-14
Patterson, John D....................................30-Jun-14
Prole, Nicholas M 30-Jun-14
Rawson, Scott M......................................30-Jun-14
Richardson, Philip....................................30-Jun-14
Russell, Bruce 30-Jun-14
Sargent, Nicholas 30-Jun-14
Scott, Mark R..30-Jun-14
Screaton, Richard M.................................30-Jun-14
Selway, Mark A.......................................30-Jun-14
Sherriff, Jacqueline MBE 30-Jun-14
Simmonite, Gavin I DFC 30-Jun-14
Simpson, William J S 30-Jun-14
Skittrall, Steven 30-Jun-14
Soul, Nicholas J 30-Jun-14
Stagg, Antony R.......................................30-Jun-14
Steadman, Robert....................................30-Jun-14
Stevens, Anthony J...................................30-Jun-14
Terry, Judith H 30-Jun-14
Thomas, James 30-Jun-14
Tilden, Philip J E 30-Jun-14
Titmuss, Julian F......................................30-Jun-14
Tremelling, Paul N 30-Jun-14
Ubhi, Wayne G 30-Jun-14
Underwood, Richard................................30-Jun-14
Vartan, Mark R..30-Jun-14
Williams, Anthony S 30-Jun-14
Wood, Michael L......................................30-Jun-14
Wood, Nicholas R 30-Jun-14
Woolhead, Andrew L 30-Jun-14

LIEUTENANT COMMANDERS

1982

Dickinson, Philip N 01-Jul-82

1985

Buckley, Martin 16-May-85
Reynoldson, Howard B V 03-Nov-85

1987

Taylor, Nicholas F................................... 16-Feb-87

1988

Speller, Nicholas S F............................... 01-May-88

1989

Pollitt, David N A..................................... 01-Apr-89
Yates, Neal P MBE 01-Jun-89
Watson, Richard J................................... 01-Aug-89
Murray, Stephen J OBE........................... 02-Nov-89

1990

Griffiths, David T..................................... 01-Apr-90
Kerr, William M M.................................... 09-Apr-90
Chapman, Nicholas J............................... 01-May 90
Cropper, Martin A K 16-May-90
Hart, Paul A 01-Oct-90

1991

Eedle, Richard 01-Mar-91
Stewart, Rory W...................................... 01-Jul-91
Donaldson, Stuart 01-Sep-91
Hawkins, Robert MBE 01-Oct-91
Kirkwood, James A D............................... 25-Oct-91
Owen, Peter C 30-Oct-91
Bernau, Jeremy C 01-Nov-91
Metcalfe, Anthony P W 01-Dec-91

1992

Morse, Andrew C 01-Jan-92
Potts, Kevin M 01-Feb-92
Deighton, Derek S................................... 01-May-92
Giles, Kevin D L....................................... 01-May-92
Barnes-Yallowley, Jonathan 16-Jul-92
West, Michael W 05-Aug-92

1993

Price, David J.. 01-Apr-93
Bennett, Graham 01-Jul-93
Green, David P.. 13-Aug-93
Robertson, Douglas M 01-Oct-93
Watts, Andrew P...................................... 01-Oct-93

1994

Neve, Piers 11-Feb-94
Gibson, Stephen R J................................ 31-Mar-94
Crispin, Toby A B..................................... 01-Apr-94
Andrews, Paul... 01-Jun-94

Eaton, Paul G.. 01-Jun-94
Lunn, Adam C 01-Jun-94
Houghton, Philip J................................... 01-Jul-94
Horner, Patrick A 01-Aug-94
Disney, Peter W....................................... 01-Oct-94
Sewed, Michael A.................................... 01-Oct-94
Hurry, Andrew P...................................... 01-Nov-94
Hills, Anthony A...................................... 01-Dec-94

1995

Firth, Nigel R.. 01-Mar-95
Egeland-Jensen, Finn A MBE 01-Apr-95
Gray, David K.. 01-Apr-95
Pomfrett, Nicholas J 01-Apr-95
Birley, Jonathan H 01-May-95
Goldsmith, Simon 01-May-95
Schnadhorst, James C 01-May-95
Monger, Paul D....................................... 21-May-95
Brown, Peter S J...................................... 01-Jun-95
Burke, Michael C 01-Sep-95
Collins, Paul... 01-Sep-95
Carter, Robert I 01-Oct-95
Daniell, Christopher J.............................. 01-Oct-95
Smith, Keven J 01-Oct-95
Meeds, Kevin 16-Dec-95
Bath, Edward G 27-Dec-95

1996

McConochie, Andrew D............................ 16-Apr-96
Carter, Jonathon M 01-Jun-96
Hayward, Clive E W 01-Jun-96
Hill, Mark R.. 22-Jun-96
Pooley, Steven W 01-Jul-96
Bark, James S.. 01-Sep-96
Benton, Angus M..................................... 01-Sep-96
Hope, Karl 01-Sep-96
Armstrong, Nicholas P B........................... 01-Oct-96
Biggs, David M.. 01-Oct-96
Sykes, Robert A....................................... 01-Oct-96

1997

Bell, Robert D 01-Mar-97
Hogg, Christopher W............................... 01-Mar-97
Goodes, Simon 31-Mar-97
Walker, David.. 31-Mar-97
Rich, David C 20-May-97
South, David J 15-Jun-97
Irons, Paul A 01-Jul-97
Peace, Richard W 02-Jul-97
Ellis, Nicholas M 18-Jul-97
Stannard, Mark....................................... 01-Aug-97
Wells, Jonathan M C 01-Aug-97
Spring, Jeremy M 03-Aug-97
Daw, Simon J 01-Oct-97
Lambourne, David J 01-Oct-97
Moys, Andrew J 01-Oct-97

1998

Franks, Christopher S.............................. 01-Feb-98

Haseldine, Stephen G............................... 01-Feb-98
Wellington, Stuart................................... 01-Feb-98
Blackburn, Stephen A 01-Mar-98
Mules, Anthony J..................................... 01-Mar-98
Scott, Robert J 02-Mar-98
Drake, Roderick 31-Mar-98
Chapman, Simon J................................... 01-Apr-98
Hood, Kevin M.. 01-Apr-98
Rook, Graeme I 01-Apr-98
Dunn, Gary R 01-May-98
Hutchison, Paul G 01-May-98
Kimberley, Robert.................................... 01-Jul-98
Powell, Steven R 01-Jul-98
Ford, Martin J AFC.................................. 05-Aug-98
Murphy, Steven R A 01-Sep-98
Birbeck, Keith 01-Oct-98
Cunane, John R 01-Oct-98
Reed, Mark... 01-Oct-98
Shallcroft, John E 01-Oct-98
Strathern, Roderick J............................... 01-Oct-98
Dawson, William 01-Nov-98
Corps, Stephen....................................... 11-Nov-98
Redman, Charles J R 23-Nov-98

1999

Dudley, Stephen...................................... 01-Jan-99
Lees, Edward C 01-Feb-99
Osborn, Richard...................................... 01-Feb-99
Smith, Adrian G 01-Feb-99
Bingham, David S..................................... 01-Mar-99
Lauste, William E..................................... 01-Mar-99
Lee, Nicholas F.. 01-Mar-99
Briggs-Mould, Timothy P.......................... 16-Mar-99
Conway, Keith A...................................... 31-Mar-99
Thomson, Susie 31-Mar-99
Goldman, Paul H L................................... 01-Apr-99
Bowhay, Simon 01-May-99
Green, Andrew M.................................... 12-May-99
Golden, Dominic S C................................ 01-Jun-99
Raisbeck, Paul T 08-Jul-99
Collis, Martin J 01-Aug-99
Lee, Peter A 01-Aug-99
Goode, Alun N.. 01-Sep-99
Hartley, John L.. 01-Oct-99
Holden, Robert J 01-Oct-99
Luscombe, Michael D............................... 01-Oct-99
Milsom, Jonathan 01-Oct-99
Murray, Andrew S AFC............................. 01-Oct-99
Whitworth, Robert M............................... 01-Oct-99
Smith, Brian J 01-Dec-99

2000

Griffiths, Michael O J 16-Jan-00
Kerr, Jack 06-Feb-00
Whitehead, Steven J 01-Mar-00
Pugh, Jonathan....................................... 08-Mar-00
Clarke, William 31-Mar-00
Parsonage, Neil 31-Mar-00
Strutt, Jason F... 01-May-00
Reah, Stephen 02-May-00

LIEUTENANT COMMANDERS

Rogers, Christopher M 01-Jun-00	Kelly, Howard C 01-Apr-02	Dawson, Alan 01-Oct-03
Williams, James P 01-Jun-00	Kohler, Andrew P 01-Apr-02	Dawson, Nigel J F 01-Oct-03
Dando, Jonathon N 01-Aug-00	Offord, Matt 01-Apr-02	Fraser, Patrick 01-Oct-03
Miles, Graham J 07-Aug-00	Hopper, Ian 09-Apr-02	Grant, David J 01-Oct-03
Hutchinson, Christopher J 01-Sep-00	Brotherton, John D 16-Apr-02	Hayward, Geoffrey MBE 01-Oct-03
Richter, Alwyn S B 01-Sep-00	Bradley, Matthew 01-May-02	Holloway, Steven A 01-Oct-03
Clarke, Andrew P MBE 01-Oct-00	Mandley, Philip J 01-May-02	Hopkins, Steven D MBE 01-Oct-03
Cook, Gordon E 01-Oct-00	Osborn, Colvin G 01-Jun-02	Hunt, Stephen 01-Oct-03
Dyke, Kenneth A 01-Oct-00	Waterfield, Simon 01-Jun-02	Kies, Lawrence N 01-Oct-03
Lacey, Catherine 01-Oct-00	West, Rory J 01-Jun-02	King, Gordon C 01-Oct-03
Robertson, Paul N 01-Oct-00	Fraser, Ian D 01-Jul-02	Logan, Joseph M 01-Oct-03
Watkins, Timothy C 01-Oct-00	Gill, Mark H 01-Jul-02	Macdougall, Stewart J 01-Oct-03
Stockton, Kevin G 19-Nov-00	Raeburn, Mark 01-Jul-02	Mailes, Ian R A 01-Oct-03
Lowe, Stuart M 01-Dec-00	Dickson, James I 01-Aug-02	McQueen, Jason B 01-Oct-03
Venables, Adrian N 01-Dec-00	Carter, Kevin 27-Aug-02	Murchie, Alistair D 01-Oct-03
Gale, Crystal V 24-Dec-00	Choules, Barrie 01-Sep-02	Neal, Simon M 01-Oct-03
	Macdonald, Alastair J 01-Sep-02	Noon, David MBE 01-Oct-03
2001	Reese, David M 01-Sep-02	O'Neill, Paul J 01-Oct-03
	Barratt, Stephen 01-Oct-02	Park, Brian C 01-Oct-03
Kerr, Adrian N 01-Jan-01	Barry, John P 01-Oct-02	Payne, Mathew J 01-Oct-03
Smith, Graeme D J 01-Jan-01	Brian, Neil 01-Oct-02	Plackett, Andrew J 01-Oct-03
Thomas, Stephen 01-Jan-01	D'Arcy, Paul A 01-Oct-02	Roberts, Iain G 01-Oct-03
Varley, Ian G 01-Jan-01	Darlow, Paul R 01-Oct-02	Stephenson, Philip G 01-Oct-03
Brown, Stephen H 15-Jan-01	Drodge, Andrew P F 01-Oct-02	Taylor, Jonathan P 01-Oct-03
Miller, Paul D 01-Feb-01	Holden, Paul A 01-Oct-02	Tetley, Mark 01-Oct-03
Sellers, Graham 01-Feb-01	Ireland, John M 01-Oct-02	Wicking, Geoffrey S 01-Oct-03
Stanton-Brown, Peter J 01-Feb-01	Jacques, Nicholas A 01-Oct-02	Wilkins, Richard R 01-Oct-03
Chaston, Stephen P 01-Mar-01	Mason, Lindsay 01-Oct-02	Williams, Peter M 01-Oct-03
Pearson, Michael 01-Mar-01	Mayell, Julie A 01-Oct-02	Woodrow, Kevin 01-Oct-03
Bicknell, Richard 31-Mar-01	Suckling, Robin L 01-Oct-02	Ley, Alastair B 01-Nov-03
Lewis, Richard QVRM 31-Mar-01	Walker, Mark 01-Oct-02	Rees, Richard T 01-Dec-03
Norgan, David J 01-Jul-01	Warr, Richard F 01-Oct-02	
Laing, Iain 01-Sep-01	Wells, Barry C 01-Oct-02	**2004**
Brunsden-Brown, Sebastian E 01-Oct-01	Cummings, David J 01-Nov-02	
Cooke, Graham S 01-Oct-01	Jones, Adam E 01-Nov-02	Beadnell, Robert M 01-Jan-04
Duncan, Jeremy 01-Oct-01	White, Jonathan E 01-Nov-02	Hendrickx, Christopher J 01-Jan-04
Graham, Mark A 01-Oct-01	Massey, Paul 05-Dec-02	Rostron, David W 01-Jan-04
Hancock, Robert T A 01-Oct-01	Rogers, Alan 25-Dec-02	Mackay, Andrew 01-Feb-04
Howe, Julian P 01-Oct-01		Powles, Derek A 01-Feb-04
Jaggers, Gary G 01-Oct-01	**2003**	Clark, Michael H 01-Mar-04
Knight, Andrew R 01-Oct-01		Peters, William R 01-Mar-04
Mitchell, Stephen D 01-Oct-01	Allfree, Joseph 01-Jan-03	Goram, Malcolm 31-Mar-04
Morgan-Hosey, John N 01-Oct-01	Frost, Mark A 01-Jan-03	Jermy, Richard 31-Mar-04
Noblett, Peter G A 01-Oct-01	Laverty, Robert E 01-Feb-03	Lewis, Simon 31-Mar-04
Sneddon, Russell N 01-Oct-01	Maynard, Charles I 01-Feb-03	Walters, Richard 31-Mar-04
Taylor, Ian K 01-Oct-01	Foulis, Niall D A 01-Mar-03	Hains, Justin 01-Apr-04
Westley, David R 01-Oct-01	Rogers, Julian C E 01-Mar-03	Lockett, David J 01-Apr-04
Yelland, Christopher B 01-Oct-01	Skelley, Alasdair N M 01-Mar-03	Smith, Michael J 01-May-04
Palmer, Michael E 01-Nov-01	Watson, Ian 01-Mar-03	Hedgecox, David C 01-Jun-04
Castle, Alastair S 01-Dec-01	Oliver, Graham 01-May-03	Lyons, Michael J 01-Jun-04
Currie, Duncan G 16-Dec-01	Jewitt, Charles 30-Jun-03	Robinson, Melanie S 07-Jun-04
	Beacham, Philip R 01-Jul-03	Jones, David M 01-Jul-04
2002	May, Steven 01-Jul-03	Parrott, James P 01-Jul-04
	Bovill, Christopher 31-Jul-03	Tyler, Jeremy 01-Jul-04
Davies, Lee 01-Jan-02	Cahill, Karen A 01-Aug-03	Moules, Matthew A J 01-Aug-04
Pink, Simon E 01-Jan-02	Sandle, Neil D 01-Aug-03	Woodbridge, Richard G 01-Aug-04
Meek, Camilla S MBE 01-Mar-02	Tregunna, Gary A 08-Aug-03	McGuire, James 24-Aug-04
Proctor, William J G 01-Mar-02	Jones, Gareth D 01-Sep-03	McCombe, John 01-Sep-04
Stephen, Barry M 01-Mar-02	McWilliams, Jacqueline E 01-Sep-03	Puxley, Michael E 01-Sep-04
Thorne, Lee J 31-Mar-02	Barrows, David M 01-Sep-03	Wright, David I 01-Sep-04
Childs, John R 01-Apr-02	Cobbett, James F 01-Oct-03	Allen, Paul M 01-Oct-04
Dineen, John M G 01-Apr-02	Davidson, Neil R 01-Oct-03	Armstrong, Scott T 01-Oct-04

LIEUTENANT COMMANDERS

Bance, Nicholas D 01-Oct-04	Spinks, David 01-Aug-05	Weaver, Simon 01-Oct-05
Benstead, Neil 01-Oct-04	Ward, Simon 01-Sep-05	Wood, Graham R..................01-Oct-05
Briggs, Cathryn S 01-Oct-04	Baker, Nicholas..................01-Oct-05	Howe, Thomas..................01-Nov-05
Carpenter, Bryony H..................01-Oct-04	Bing, Neil A..................01-Oct-05	Morley, James I 01-Nov-05
Chadfield, Laurence J..................01-Oct-04	Brayson, Mark..................01-Oct-05	Stevenson, Julian P..................01-Nov-05
Crabb, Antony J..................01-Oct-04	Bryson, Susan 01-Oct-05	Allan, Chris R 01-Dec-05
Cragg, Richard D 01-Oct-04	Clare, Katharine 01-Oct-05	Hutchings, Richard..................01-Dec-05
Doran, Iain A G 01-Oct-04	Corbett, Thomas J..................01-Oct-05	Webster, Richard J..................01-Dec-05
Ellis, James 01-Oct-04	Cox, Sean A J..................01-Oct-05	Wyness, Roger S 13-Dec-05
Hilson, Steven M..................01-Oct-04	Cross, Alexander L 01-Oct-05	
Hodge, Christopher M 01-Oct-04	Daveney, David 01-Oct-05	**2006**
Hutton, Graham 01-Oct-04	Davis, Stephen R..................01-Oct-05	
Imrie, Peter B 01-Oct-04	Driscoll, Robert 01-Oct-05	Dale, Alistair 01-Feb-06
Julian, Timothy M 01-Oct-04	Edwards, James E..................01-Oct-05	Dempsey, Sean P..................01-Feb-06
Le Gassick, Peter J..................01-Oct-04	Ellis, David F..................01-Oct-05	Harrington, Lee..................01-Mar-06
Lovering, Tristan T A MBE 01-Oct-04	Foster, Nicholas P..................01-Oct-05	Thorp, David B 01-Mar-06
Lucocq, Nicholas J..................01-Oct-04	Goodrum, Simon E 01-Oct-05	Brotton, Peter J..................01-Apr-06
Read, Alun J..................01-Oct-04	Haigh, Julian J..................01-Oct-05	Goodall, Michael A 01-May-06
Reed, Nicholas 01-Oct-04	Hardwick, Mark J 01-Oct-05	Rushworth, Benjamin J..................01-May-06
Russell, Nigel A D..................01-Oct-04	Hassall, Ian 01-Oct-05	Garner, Sean M..................01-Aug-06
Sargent, Lindsay M 01-Oct-04	Hayes, Brian J..................01-Oct-05	Scott, Richard A 01-Aug-06
Simpson, Colin C 01-Oct-04	Hayton, Stephen R C..................01-Oct-05	Cottee, Benjamin R J..................01-Sep-06
Smith, Christopher J H 01-Oct-04	Hefford, Christopher..................01-Oct-05	Alexander, Oliver D D 01-Oct-06
Smith, David L..................01-Oct-04	Humphries, Jason E..................01-Oct-05	Ansell, Christopher 01-Oct-06
Stuart, Euan E A..................01-Oct-04	Hutchins, Timothy..................01-Oct-05	Arend, Faye M 01-Oct-06
Sykes, Leah D..................01-Oct-04	Jenking-Rees, Damian 01-Oct-05	Auld, Douglas 01-Oct-06
Tidball, Ian C 01-Oct-04	Johnson, Anthony R..................01-Oct-05	Beaver, Robert M S 01-Oct-06
Trubshaw, Christopher 01-Oct-04	Jordan, Craig 01-Oct-05	Berry, Timothy J 01-Oct-06
Vincent, Daniel 01-Oct-04	Knight, Daniel S 01-Oct-05	Booth, William N..................01-Oct-06
Yemm, Charlotte P..................01-Oct-04	Lamont, Neil J..................01-Oct-05	Boyes, Richard A..................01-Oct-06
Taylor, Neil 11-Oct-04	Lanni, Martin N AFC 01-Oct-05	Brennan, Paul A 01-Oct-06
Purvis, David M..................16-Oct-04	Love, Richard J..................01-Oct-05	Brewer, Christopher E 01-Oct-06
Balletta, Rene J 01-Nov-04	Lowe, Christopher 01-Oct-05	Carter, Paul 01-Oct-06
Holland, Amanda..................01-Nov-04	Marriott, Neil K..................01-Oct-05	Castle, Colin 01-Oct-06
McBratney, James A G 01-Nov-04	Marshall, Tracey..................01-Oct-05	Clague, John J 01-Oct-06
Walsh, Kevin M..................01-Nov-04	Mason, Darren J..................01-Oct-05	Clark, Stephen R..................01-Oct-06
Ankah, Gregory K E 01-Dec-04	McCaughey, Vincent J 01-Oct-05	Cullen, Nicola L..................01-Oct-06
Brown, Andrew..................01-Dec-04	McCleary, Simon P..................01-Oct-05	Curwood, Jenny E..................01-Oct-06
Mullins, Andrew D 01-Dec-04	Mealing, Steven 01-Oct-05	Davey, Timothy..................01-Oct-06
Whitehouse, Niall R..................01-Dec-04	Millen, Stuart C W MBE 01-Oct-05	Dawson, Paul..................01-Oct-06
	Nelson, Paul M..................01-Oct-05	Day, Michael K 01-Oct-06
2005	Nimmons, Paul MBE..................01-Oct-05	Deeks, Peter J 01-Oct-06
	Oakes, Ian J 01-Oct-05	Doig, Barry 01-Oct-06
Boston, Justin 01-Jan-05	Oatley, Timothy P..................01-Oct-05	Forge, Stephen 01-Oct-06
Wood, Christopher R 01-Jan-05	Palin, Giles R..................01-Oct-05	Fox, Trefor M 01-Oct-06
Cleminson, Mark D 01-Feb-05	Panic, Alexander 01-Oct-05	Goulder, Jonathan D 01-Oct-06
Kendrick, Alexander M..................01-Feb-05	Pickering-Wheeler, Christopher W..........01-Oct-05	Gray, John A 01-Oct-06
Parr, Michael J E..................02-Feb-05	Proffitt, Julia M M 01-Oct-05	Griffiths, Neil 01-Oct-06
Armstrong, Katharine L M..................01-Mar-05	Pullan, Keith J 01-Oct-05	Harriman, Peter..................01-Oct-06
McHugh, Richard H..................01-Mar-05	Quade, Nicholas A C 01-Oct-05	Harrison, Thomas I..................01-Oct-06
Thorne, Dain MBE..................01-Mar-05	Quantrill, Steven W..................01-Oct-05	Hember, Marcus..................01-Oct-06
Wells, Michael P..................01-Mar-05	Rendell, Derrick J 01-Oct-05	Hirons, Francis D 01-Oct-06
Young, William D..................31-Mar-05	Santrian, Karl 01-Oct-05	Inge, Daniel J 01-Oct-06
Aird, Pauline 01-Apr-05	Sayer, Jamie M..................01-Oct-05	James, Katherine J 01-Oct-06
Hounsom, Timothy 01-Apr-05	Shaughnessy, Toby E 01-Oct-05	Johnson, Scott 01-Oct-06
Kirk, Adrian C 01-May-05	Sitton, John B 01-Oct-05	Knox, Graeme P..................01-Oct-06
Oakley, Sarah E 01-May-05	Spurdle, Andrew P..................01-Oct-05	Laycock, Antony 01-Oct-06
McCallum, Neil 01-Jun-05	Stockbridge, Antony 01-Oct-05	Maccorquodale, Mairi A..................01-Oct-06
Fitzpatrick, John A J 01-Jul-05	Strange, Steven P 01-Oct-05	Mason, Andrew C..................01-Oct-06
Rogers, Alexander T..................31-Jul-05	Sullivan, Mark N..................01-Oct-05	McCutcheon, Graeme..................01-Oct-06
Northover, Adam F..................01-Aug-05	Taylor, Robert J..................01-Oct-05	McDonald, Andrew W 01-Oct-06
Spiller, Stephen N..................01-Aug-05		McLocklan, Lee M..................01-Oct-06

LIEUTENANT COMMANDERS

Mehta, Kim L 01-Oct-06
Meyer, Alexander J 01-Oct-06
Miles, Philip 01-Oct-06
Molnar, Richard M 01-Oct-06
Morgan, Edward J A 01-Oct-06
O'Shaughnessy, Paul 01-Oct-06
Parker, Timothy S 01-Oct-06
Pressdee, Simon J 01-Oct-06
Redmayne, Mark E 01-Oct-06
Robertson, Stuart T 01-Oct-06
Robley, William F 01-Oct-06
Rogers, Philip S 01-Oct-06
Rogers, Simon J P 01-Oct-06
Roster, Shaun P 01-Oct-06
Satterthwaite, Benjamin J 01-Oct-06
Saunders, Jason 01-Oct-06
Saward, Justin R E 01-Oct-06
Saywell-Hall, Stephen E 01-Oct-06
Spence, Robert G 01-Oct-06
Spillane, Paul W 01-Oct-06
Stait, Benjamin G 01-Oct-06
Stilwell, James M 01-Oct-06
Stone, Nicholas 01-Oct-06
Taylor, Keith M 01-Oct-06
Thomas, Daniel H 01-Oct-06
Thomsen-Rayner, Lavinia L 01-Oct-06
Thomson, Paul D 01-Oct-06
Torney, Colin J 01-Oct-06
Townsend, Graham P 01-Oct-06
Wall, Irene J 01-Oct-06
Walton, Stephen D 01-Oct-06
Watkins, Kevin J 01-Oct-06
White, Kevin F 01-Oct-06
Williams, Robert 01-Oct-06
Wingfield, Michael J 01-Oct-06
Wood, Andrew G 01-Oct-06
Wood, Joseph A 01-Oct-06
Wright, David 01-Oct-06
Yates, Stuart E 01-Oct-06
Gillett, David A 01-Nov-06
Livsey, Andrew E J 01-Nov-06
Norgate, Andrew T 01-Nov-06
Ward, Douglas J 01-Nov-06
Evison, Toby 06-Nov-06
McCann, Toby 01-Dec-06

2007

Hunt, Patrick S 01-Jan-07
McClement, Duncan L 01-Jan-07
Trim, Brian J 01-Jan-07
Netherwood, Lyndsey D 15-Jan-07
Conway, Suzy H 01-Mar-07
Dunlop, Joanne 30-Mar-07
Reid, Martyn 01-Apr-07
Woolsey, Kevin 01-May-07
Knott, Clive 29-May-07
Kelly, Simon P 01-Jul-07
Pipkin, Peter J 01-Aug-07
Abel, Nigel P 01-Oct-07
Anderson, Garry S 01-Oct-07
Armstrong, Stuart M 01-Oct-07

Austin, Peter N 01-Oct-07
Bainbridge, John R 01-Oct-07
Barber, Christopher J H 01-Oct-07
Barritt, Oliver D 01-Oct-07
Beale, Michael D 01-Oct-07
Bell, Scott W 01-Oct-07
Boeckx, Thomas J F 01-Oct-07
Boon, Gareth 01-Oct-07
Clarke, Adam G 01-Oct-07
Clarke, Matthew D 01-Oct-07
Clements, Elizabeth J 01-Oct-07
Collins, Tamar L 01-Oct-07
Conneely, Steven A 01-Oct-07
Cutler, Andrew R 01-Oct-07
Dalton-Fyfe, Karen S 01-Oct-07
Denney, James R 01-Oct-07
Edwins, Mark R 01-Oct-07
Evans, Giles 01-Oct-07
Fraser, Ian E 01-Oct-07
Freeman, Martin J 01-Oct-07
Fuller, Charles 01-Oct-07
Fuller, Emma J 01-Oct-07
Godfrey, Simeon D W 01-Oct-07
Guy, Charles R 01-Oct-07
Hampshire, Tony 01-Oct-07
Hardman, Matthew J 01-Oct-07
Hatchard, Pollyanna 01-Oct-07
Hayashi, Luke R 01-Oct-07
Healey, Mark J 01-Oct-07
Henaghen, Stephen J 01-Oct-07
Hewitt, Mark J 01-Oct-07
Hocking, Mark J 01-Oct-07
Howells, Simon M 01-Oct-07
Hubschmid, Spencer R 01-Oct-07
Humphery, Duncan 01-Oct-07
Hutchings, Justin R 01-Oct-07
Jayes, Neil J 01-Oct-07
Johnson, Paul R 01-Oct-07
Jones, Ian M 01-Oct-07
Jones, Mark R 01-Oct-07
Jones-Thompson, Michael 01-Oct-07
Kennedy, Roger J 01-Oct-07
Kennington, Lee A 01-Oct-07
Kenyon, Carolyn M 01-Oct-07
Lear, Stuart F 01-Oct-07
Lee, Steven E 01-Oct-07
Leighton, Matthew R 01-Oct-07
Louden, Carl A 01-Oct-07
Macdonald, Stuart 01-Oct-07
Macfarlane, Iain S D 01-Oct-07
Manders-Trett, Victoria 01-Oct-07
Manning, Gary P 01-Oct-07
Mawdsley, Gareth R 01-Oct-07
Millard, Jeremy 01-Oct-07
Mills, Gary 01-Oct-07
Morris, Anthony M 01-Oct-07
New, Richard 01-Oct-07
Palethorpe, Nicholas 01-Oct-07
Palmer, Christopher R 01-Oct-07
Peyman, Tracy 01-Oct-07
Pine, Paul M 01-Oct-07

Pollard, Alexandra E 01-Oct-07
Pollard, Jonathan R 01-Oct-07
Poole, Timothy J 01-Oct-07
Rees, Karen M M 01-Oct-07
Rhodes, Andrew W 01-Oct-07
Richards, Anthony J 01-Oct-07
Richards, Paul 01-Oct-07
Sanderson, Christopher P 01-Oct-07
Santry, Paul M 01-Oct-07
Stafford, Benjamin R 01-Oct-07
Titcombe, Adam J 01-Oct-07
Varty, Jason A 01-Oct-07
Viney, Peter M 01-Oct-07
Wall, Steven N 01-Oct-07
Watson, Andrew 01-Oct-07
Webster, Richard 01-Oct-07
Wright, Daniel J 01-Oct-07
Aldous, Benjamin 01-Nov-07
Tacey, Richard 01-Dec-07

2008

Gill, Christopher D 01-Jan-08
Miller, Ian 01-Jan-08
Wooller, Louise F V 01-Feb-08
Barker, Paul D 01-Apr-08
Feeney, Matthew B 01-Apr-08
Long, Michael 01-Apr-08
Coles, Christopher 01-May-08
Grant, Wayne G 01-Jun-08
Strathie, Gavin S 01-Jun-08
Kohn, Patricia A 01-Jul-08
Clark, Russell A 01-Aug-08
Blackburn, Lee R 01-Sep-08
Flegg, Kirsty G 01-Sep-08
Raeburn, Craig 01-Sep-08
Adams, William J MBE 01-Oct-08
Ainsley, Andrew M J 01-Oct-08
Alexander, Amy L 01-Oct-08
Allison, Glenn 01-Oct-08
Bagshaw, James R W 01-Oct-08
Bainbridge, Stuart D 01-Oct-08
Barton, Keith J A 01-Oct-08
Bell, Catriona M 01-Oct-08
Binns, Jon F 01-Oct-08
Bland, Christopher D 01-Oct-08
Brown, Andrew S 01-Oct-08
Buckenham, Peter J 01-Oct-08
Calhaem, Richard T 01-Oct-08
Cameron, Fiona 01-Oct-08
Carne, Richard J P 01-Oct-08
Carroll, Stephen 01-Oct-08
Chadwick, Kara 01-Oct-08
Chapman, Martin S 01-Oct-08
Clay, Toby 01-Oct-08
Cleary, Christopher M 01-Oct-08
Collins, Dale A 01-Oct-08
Conlin, John 01-Oct-08
Cromie, John M 01-Oct-08
Currie, Michael J 01-Oct-08
Davies, Geraint W T 01-Oct-08
Davies, Nicholas M S 01-Oct-08

LIEUTENANT COMMANDERS

Deal, Charlotte	01-Oct-08
Dunn, Anthony	01-Oct-08
Enever, Shaun A	01-Oct-08
Feasey, Ian D	01-Oct-08
Flegg, Matthew J	01-Oct-08
Flynn, Simon J	01-Oct-08
Free, Andrew S	01-Oct-08
Fyfe-Green, Ian A	01-Oct-08
Gardner, Michael P	01-Oct-08
Gardner-Clark, Suzanne L	01-Oct-08
Gare, Christopher	01-Oct-08
Gates, Nigel S	01-Oct-08
Gotke, Christopher T	01-Oct-08
Gray, Michael J H	01-Oct-08
Hadland, Giles	01-Oct-08
Hamilton, Mark I	01-Oct-08
Hammon, Mark A	01-Oct-08
Hardy, Robert J	01-Oct-08
Harman, Stephen J	01-Oct-08
Hart, Steven D	01-Oct-08
Hattle, Prideaux M	01-Oct-08
Hayden, Timothy W	01-Oct-08
Hill, Adrian J	01-Oct-08
Holland, Charlotte C	01-Oct-08
Holroyd, Jonathon E J	01-Oct-08
Iliffe, David I	01-Oct-08
Ingham, Maryla K	01-Oct-08
James, Mark	01-Oct-08
Jarman, Paul R	01-Oct-08
Johnston, David R	01-Oct-08
Kay, Paul S	01-Oct-08
Keith, Benjamin C	01-Oct-08
Kent, Matthew J	01-Oct-08
King, William R C	01-Oct-08
Kirwan, John A	01-Oct-08
Klidjian, Michael J	01-Oct-08
Lester, Rodney L MBE	01-Oct-08
Loughrey, Neil C MBE	01-Oct-08
Mabbott, Keith I	01-Oct-08
Marland, Eunice E	01-Oct-08
Marshall, Alistair J	01-Oct-08
Martin, Robert J	01-Oct-08
Mathieson, Neil B	01-Oct-08
May, David M	01-Oct-08
McDonald, Duncan J	01-Oct-08
McGannity, Colin S	01-Oct-08
McLennan, Andrew	01-Oct-08
Metcalf, Stephen W	01-Oct-08
Milligan, Robert J	01-Oct-08
Mitchell, Jamie	01-Oct-08
Monnox, Jill	01-Oct-08
Moore, Matthew J	01-Oct-08
Moran, Russell J	01-Oct-08
Morris, Harriet S	01-Oct-08
Mortlock, Philip	01-Oct-08
Mundy, Alan R	01-Oct-08
Naylor, Andrew J	01-Oct-08
Nicklin, Gareth J E	01-Oct-08
Norris, Guy P	01-Oct-08
Oakley, Claire	01-Oct-08
O'Rourke, Richard M	01-Oct-08

Owen, Samuel T L	01-Oct-08
Pearson, James C	01-Oct-08
Peattie, Ian W	01-Oct-08
Price, Joseph C	01-Oct-08
Rankin, Graham J	01-Oct-08
Richardson, Ian H	01-Oct-08
Risley, James G	01-Oct-08
Robinson, David	01-Oct-08
Ryan, John P	01-Oct-08
Selwood, Peter J	01-Oct-08
Slowther, Stuart J	01-Oct-08
Smith, Andrew J E	01-Oct-08
Sollitt, Victoria A	01-Oct-08
Steen, Kieron M	01-Oct-08
Storey, Helen J	01-Oct-08
Stratton, Matthew P	01-Oct 08
Sturgeon, David M	01-Oct-08
Thomson, Michael L	01-Oct-08
Trinder, Stephen	01-Oct-08
Truelove, Samantha	01-Oct-08
Turner, David N	01-Oct-08
Tutchings, Andrew	01-Oct-08
Urwin, Stuart J	01-Oct-08
Vickery, Ben R	01-Oct-08
Vout, Debra K	01-Oct-08
Vowles, Mitchell J	01-Oct-08
Waite, Tobias G	01-Oct-08
Walker, Robin	01-Oct-08
Watson, Richard D	01-Oct-08
Webb, Eleanor	01-Oct-08
Wells, Jamie D	01-Oct-08
Welsh, John	01-Oct-08
White, Jason P QGM	01-Oct-08
Whitehouse, David S	01-Oct-08
Wilson, John	01-Oct-08
Wrennall, Eric P	01-Oct-08
Burton, Alex	01-Nov-08
Seagrave, Suzanna J	01-Nov-08

2009

Alexander, Phillip M D	01-Jan-09
Robinson, Steven L	01-Jan-09
Adams, George	01-May-09
Woods, Michael J P	01-May-09
Cantellow, Stuart J	01-Jun-09
Perkins-Brown, Ben	01-Jul-09
Marriott, Matthew J	01-Sep-09
Adams, Edwin S	01-Oct-09
Ainscow, Anthony J	01-Oct-09
Alderton, Paul A	01-Oct-09
Andrews, Christopher	01-Oct-09
Ball, William J E	01-Oct-09
Barrow, Charles M	01-Oct-09
Bass, Emma	01-Oct-09
Bass, Paul W	01-Oct-09
Baverstock, Andrew P	01-Oct-09
Bennett, Christopher	01-Oct-09
Binns, John R	01-Oct-09
Blackburn, Emma C	01-Oct-09
Blois, Simon D	01-Oct-09
Blythe, James	01-Oct-09

Boakes, Philip J	01-Oct-09
Bodman, Simon A	01-Oct-09
Boot, Stephen	01-Oct-09
Bradley, Trevor A	01-Oct-09
Breach, Pamela	01-Oct-09
Brierley, Simon P J	01-Oct-09
Brocklehurst, Judith E	01-Oct-09
Brodie, Stephen D	01-Oct-09
Brooks, Nicholas R	01-Oct-09
Brooks, Paul N	01-Oct-09
Bull, Louis P	01-Oct-09
Carbery, Stephen J	01-Oct-09
Carnell, Richard P	01-Oct-09
Carter Quinn, M G	01-Oct-09
Carthew, Richard J	01-Oct-09
Chang, Christopher J	01-Oct-09
Chapman, James L J	01-Oct-09
Clarkson, Andrew	01-Oct-09
Clear, Nichola J	01-Oct-09
Collins, David	01-Oct-09
Craven, Martin W	01-Oct-09
Di Maio, Mark D	01-Oct-09
Dransfield, Joseph A J	01-Oct-09
Dray, Jake M	01-Oct-09
Duke, Karen D	01-Oct-09
Elliot-Smith, Ieilo J	01-Oct-09
Elliott, Jamie A	01-Oct-09
Evans, Lee S	01-Oct-09
Farrant, James D	01-Oct-09
Fearon, David J	01-Oct-09
Flatman, Timothy D	01-Oct-09
Fleming, Ruth E	01-Oct-09
Foote, Andrew S	01-Oct-09
Forbes, Angela J	01-Oct-09
French, Paul	01-Oct-09
Fuller, Stephen P	01-Oct-09
Geneux, Nicholas	01-Oct-09
George, Seth D	01-Oct-09
Gilmore, Steven J	01-Oct-09
Glendinning, Andreana S	01-Oct-09
Goddard, Paul	01-Oct-09
Goodman, David F	01-Oct-09
Gordon, John	01-Oct-09
Green, Leslie D	01-Oct-09
Grey, Christopher S	01-Oct-09
Griffin, Stephen	01-Oct-09
Gwatkin, Nicholas J	01-Oct-09
Harvey, Graham A	01-Oct-09
Headley, Mark J	01-Oct-09
Heaney, Martin J	01-Oct-09
Hepplewhite, Mark B	01-Oct-09
Hiscock, Stephen R	01-Oct-09
Holder, John	01-Oct-09
Hughes, Benjamin	01-Oct-09
Hughes, Christopher B	01-Oct-09
Hughes, Gareth D	01-Oct-09
Hunt, Robert J C	01-Oct-09
Jacob, Andrew W	01-Oct-09
Jameson, Roger M	01-Oct-09
Jones, David K	01-Oct-09
Kelly, Grant J	01-Oct-09

LIEUTENANT COMMANDERS

Kestle, Mark E	01-Oct-09
Lanning, Roderick M	01-Oct-09
Law, Samuel J	01-Oct-09
Leeder, Timothy R	01-Oct-09
Leeson, Antony R	01-Oct-09
Malone, Martin T	01-Oct-09
Marden, Tony	01-Oct-09
Marshall, Gavin P	01-Oct-09
Mason, Mark J	01-Oct-09
Matthews, Justin	01-Oct-09
McKee, Hamish M	01-Oct-09
Milne, Andre P	01-Oct-09
Newell, Gary D	01-Oct-09
Newman, Virginia H	01-Oct-09
Nicholson, Brian H	01-Oct-09
Nielsen, Suzi	01-Oct-09
Oakley, Andrew	01-Oct-09
O'Connor, David P	01-Oct-09
O'Neill, James	01-Oct-09
O'Neill, Timothy J	01-Oct-09
Orr, Keith J	01-Oct-09
Park, Ian D	01-Oct-09
Parrock, Neil G	01-Oct-09
Parry, Stuart D	01-Oct-09
Priest, James E	01-Oct-09
Prowse, David G	01-Oct-09
Quinn, Mark E	01-Oct-09
Reaves, Charles E	01-Oct-09
Reid, James L	01-Oct-09
Rider, John	01-Oct-09
Roberts, Benjamin	01-Oct-09
Rogers, Julia A	01-Oct-09
Rostron, John H	01-Oct-09
Russell, Katherine E F	01-Oct-09
Samuels, Nicholas J	01-Oct-09
Sherwood, Gideon A F	01-Oct-09
Singleton, Rachel M MBE	01-Oct-09
Slattery, Damian J	01-Oct-09
Smith, Charles J	01-Oct-09
Sparrow, Mark	01-Oct-09
Stack, Eleanor F	01-Oct-09
Standen, Gary D	01-Oct-09
Stratton, Stuart J	01-Oct-09
Talbot, Richard J	01-Oct-09
Tantam, Robert J G	01-Oct-09
Tazewell, Matthew R	01-Oct-09
Thomson, James C	01-Oct-09
Tonge, Malcolm S	01-Oct-09
Toon, Paul G	01-Oct-09
Toone, Stephen A	01-Oct-09
Tough, Iain S	01-Oct-09
Unwin, Nicholas R F	01-Oct-09
Vines, Nicholas O	01-Oct-09
Wadsworth, Richard Y	01-Oct-09
Way, Robert A	01-Oct-09
Welsh, Richard M K	01-Oct-09
West, Nicholas K	01-Oct-09
Whitehall, Sally	01-Oct-09
Whitson-Fay, Craig D	01-Oct-09
Wild, Richard J	01-Oct-09
Winn, John P	01-Oct-09

Winsor, James	01-Oct-09
Wiseman, Neil	01-Oct-09
Woolhead, Craig M	01-Oct-09
White, Stephen J	06-Oct-09
Morey, Kevin N	01-Nov-09
Collen, Sara J	01-Dec-09

2010

Canty, Thomas A	01-Feb-10
Ashton, James	01-Mar-10
Horsted, James A	01-Mar-10
McClurg, Robert J	01-Mar-10
Peck, Simon R	01-Mar-10
Gibbs, Mark P	01-Apr-10
Handoll, Guy N G	01-Apr-10
Lippitt, Simon T	01-Apr-10
Walker, Stephen	01-Apr-10
Northcott, Philip J	20-Apr-10
Alcindor, David J	22-Apr-10
Gubby, Adrian W	01-May-10
Sykes, Matthew J	01-Sep-10
Adey, Joanna L	01-Oct-10
Alder, Mark C	01-Oct-10
Anderson, Andrew E	01-Oct-10
Andrews, Louisa J	01-Oct-10
Bailes, Kenneth	01-Oct-10
Bailey, Ian J	01-Oct-10
Bailey, Michael	01-Oct-10
Baker, James E G	01-Oct-10
Banfield, Steven D	01-Oct-10
Barfoot, Peter M	01-Oct-10
Barrie, Stuart	01-Oct-10
Beanland, Peter L	01-Oct-10
Bennett, Mark A	01-Oct-10
Bevan, Jeffrey R MBE	01-Oct-10
Boon, Simon E	01-Oct-10
Botterill, Hugh W S	01-Oct-10
Botting, Neil A	01-Oct-10
Boughton, Jonathan A L	01-Oct-10
Bowie, Richard	01-Oct-10
Bradley, Rupert	01-Oct-10
Brann, Robert W	01-Oct-10
Breen, John E	01-Oct-10
Brindley, Mark W	01-Oct-10
Brodie, Duncan J	01-Oct-10
Brown, James A	01-Oct-10
Bullock, John B	01-Oct-10
Burbidge, Kay	01-Oct-10
Chambers, Richard	01-Oct-10
Chatterjee, Shatadeep MBE	01-Oct-10
Chawira, Denis	01-Oct-10
Clark, Stephen M	01-Oct-10
Clarkson, Antony M	01-Oct-10
Coackley, Jane	01-Oct-10
Coles, Simon P	01-Oct-10
Cornford, Marc	01-Oct-10
Cory, Nicholas J	01-Oct-10
Coryton, Sophie C	01-Oct-10
Cox, Michael	01-Oct-10
Cunnell, Rachael L	01-Oct-10
Darkins, Colin R	01-Oct-10

Downie, David R M	01-Oct-10
Eldridge, Stephen J	01-Oct-10
Ellerton, Paul	01-Oct-10
Elliott, Stephen P	01-Oct-10
Faulkner, Stuart	01-Oct-10
Fillmore, Raymond J	01-Oct-10
Frater, Rebecca S	01-Oct-10
Full, Richard J	01-Oct-10
Gamble, Stephen B	01-Oct-10
Garreta, Carlos E	01-Oct-10
Gillett, Nathan D	01-Oct-10
Goddard, David	01-Oct-10
Gray, Nathan J	01-Oct-10
Grice, Matthew	01-Oct-10
Griffen, David J	01-Oct-10
Hackman, James D	01-Oct-10
Hall, Christopher L	01-Oct-10
Hall, Graham W R	01-Oct-10
Hall, James E	01-Oct-10
Hawkins, Stephen	01-Oct-10
Hazard, Lee Mbe	01-Oct-10
Heap, Graham G	01-Oct-10
Heap, Steven A MBE	01-Oct-10
Hewitt, Richard P	01-Oct-10
Hilton, Simon T	01-Oct-10
Hughes, John J	01-Oct-10
Huynh, Cuong	01-Oct-10
Johnson, Lauren O	01-Oct-10
Jones, Charmody E	01-Oct-10
Jones, Mark D	01-Oct-10
Keam, Ian	01-Oct-10
Kennedy, Ian C	01-Oct-10
Kiff, Ian W	01-Oct-10
King, Jason M	01-Oct-10
King, William T P	01-Oct-10
Kitchen, Bethan	01-Oct-10
Laidler, Paul J	01-Oct-10
Lai-Hung, Jeremy J	01-Oct-10
Latus, Simon H	01-Oct-10
Laurence, Simon T	01-Oct-10
Layton, Christopher	01-Oct-10
Lockhart, John B	01-Oct-10
Long, Stuart G	01-Oct-10
Luxford, Charles A	01-Oct-10
Macquarrie, Gary A	01-Oct-10
Mallinson, Laurence J	01-Oct-10
Masson, Neil G	01-Oct-10
McCormack, Gary	01-Oct-10
McEwan, Rory D	01-Oct-10
Miller, Kevin R	01-Oct-10
Money, Christopher J	01-Oct-10
Morris, Paul J	01-Oct-10
Munday, Stephen W	01-Oct-10
Murgatroyd, Kevin J	01-Oct-10
Nekrews, Alan N L M QGM	01-Oct-10
Noonan, Charles D	01-Oct-10
Ochtman-Corfe, Fergus V	01-Oct-10
Ottley, Lucy J	01-Oct-10
Pearce, Jonathan	01-Oct-10
Pearch, Sean M	01-Oct-10
Pearmain, Stephanie R	01-Oct-10

LIEUTENANT COMMANDERS

Peskett, Daniel M 01-Oct-10	Bingham, Alexander A J 01-Oct-11	McWilliams, Adrian R 01-Oct-11
Pickles, David R 01-Oct-10	Blethyn, Hugh P 01-Oct-11	Mole, Andrew J 01-Oct-11
Pike, Robin T 01-Oct-10	Bond, Robert D A 01-Oct-11	Morgan, Christopher W 01-Oct-11
Punch, John M 01-Oct-10	Boulind, Matthew A 01-Oct-11	Morris, Daniel R 01-Oct-11
Quinn, Antony D 01-Oct-10	Boyd, Elaine M 01-Oct-11	Morrison, Shaun 01-Oct-11
Rawlins, Simon 01-Oct-10	Brooks, Alexandra L 01-Oct-11	Moseley, Stephen H 01-Oct-11
Rex, Colin 01-Oct-10	Brown, James A 01-Oct-11	Murray, Greig M 01-Oct-11
Reynolds, James 01-Oct-10	Bullock, Robert A 01-Oct-11	Nash, Russell F R 01-Oct-11
Reynolds, Matthew J 01-Oct-10	Burrell, David J 01-Oct-11	Nicholls, Larry R MBE 01-Oct-11
Riddett, Adam O 01-Oct-10	Butler, Jonathon E 01-Oct-11	Norton, Ian A 01-Oct-11
Ritchie, Iain D 01-Oct-10	Coates, Adam J 01-Oct-11	O'Brien, Thomas P 01-Oct-11
Robinson, Lee D 01-Oct-10	Colley, Ian P 01-Oct-11	O'Kane, Robert J 01-Oct-11
Rosenberg, Marcel M G 01-Oct-10	Cooper, Janette L 01-Oct-11	O'Neill, Conor M 01-Oct-11
Satterly, Robert J 01-Oct-10	Cox, Simon J 01-Oct-11	O'Reilly, Christopher A 01-Oct-11
Scott, Neil 01-Oct-10	Crichton, Gary S 01-Oct-11	Parker, Daniel J 01-Oct-11
Semple, Brian 01-Oct-10	Crosby, David W M 01-Oct-11	Parker, Darren S 01-Oct-11
Simmonds, Daniel D H 01-Oct-10	Davies, Darren J 01-Oct-11	Paston, William A 01-Oct-11
Simpson, Scott F 01-Oct-10	Drodge, Kevin N 01-Oct-11	Pate, Christopher M 01-Oct-11
Smallwood, Rachel J MBE 01-Oct-10	Eacock, Jason P 01-Oct-11	Pearce, Robert 01-Oct-11
Snell, Andrew J 01-Oct-10	Edwards, James 01-Oct-11	Phillips, Richard E 01-Oct-11
Southwood, Shaun C 01-Oct-10	England, Philip M 01-Oct-11	Purdy, Richard 01-Oct-11
Spencer, Ashley C 01-Oct-10	Evans, Christopher C 01-Oct-11	Randles, Steven 01-Oct-11
Spoors, Brendan 01-Oct-10	Evans, Robert 01-Oct-11	Reeves, Andrew P 01-Oct-11
Storey, Andrew 01-Oct-10	Foster, Alan J 01-Oct-11	Roberts, Nigel D 01-Oct-11
Stringer, Graeme E 01-Oct-10	Fraser-Smith, Sharron A 01-Oct-11	Robey, James C 01-Oct-11
Swindells, Mark 01-Oct-10	Gahan, Richard J 01-Oct-11	Roe, Roma J 01-Oct-11
Tall, Iain T G 01-Oct-10	Gardner, Louis P 01-Oct-11	Rowberry, Adrian G 01-Oct-11
Tappin, Simon J 01-Oct-10	Gilmore, Martin P 01-Oct-11	Russell, Martin S 01-Oct-11
Terry, Nigel P 01-Oct-10	Gordon, David I 01-Oct-11	Scott, Julian V 01-Oct-11
Thomas, Owen H 01-Oct-10	Grant, Richard 01-Oct-11	Screen, James W 01-Oct-11
Thompson, Andrew R 01-Oct-10	Haley, Christopher J 01-Oct-11	Sharp, Andrew P MBE 01-Oct-11
Trewinnard-Boyle, Robin M 01-Oct-10	Hammock, Simon G 01-Oct-11	Shears, Alexandra F 01-Oct-11
Wallace, Anthony R 01-Oct-10	Hancock, James H 01-Oct-11	Smith, Owen J 01-Oct-11
Wallace, Iain S 01-Oct-10	Harcombe, Andrew 01-Oct-11	Stevens, Joseph I 01-Oct-11
Wallace, Richard S 01-Oct-10	Harris, Richard A 01-Oct-11	Stone, James 01-Oct-11
Ward, Alexander J 01-Oct-10	Harrison, Leigh E 01-Oct-11	Stubbs, Ian 01-Oct-11
Weaver, Thomas H 01-Oct-10	Heaton, Henry G 01-Oct-11	Sturman, Richard W 01-Oct-11
White, Douglas 01-Oct-10	Higgins, Peter AFC 01-Oct-11	Thomas, David W 01-Oct-11
White, Simon H W 01-Oct-10	Hine, Michael J 01-Oct-11	Thomas, Mark A 01-Oct-11
Wilkins, Robert L 01-Oct-10	Hodgson, Laura 01-Oct-11	Thompson, David J 01-Oct-11
Wilkinson, John R 01-Oct-10	Hogg, Adam J 01-Oct-11	Thornhill, Stephen M 01-Oct-11
Williams, Paul G 01-Oct-10	Holgate, James A 01-Oct-11	Thurston, Mark S 01-Oct-11
Winterbon, Andrew R 01-Oct-10	Hughes, Elizabeth E 01-Oct-11	Tomlin, Ian S 01-Oct-11
Woollven, Christopher D 01-Oct-10	Hughes, Scott M 01-Oct-11	Tomlinson, Amy R 01-Oct-11
Wragg, Gareth T 01-Oct-10	Hulston, Lauren M 01-Oct-11	Trent, Thomas 01-Oct-11
McDougall, William 02-Oct-10	Hurley, Karl 01-Oct-11	Turberville, Christopher T L 01-Oct-11
Gulliver, Jeff W 21-Nov-10	Imrie, Samantha J 01-Oct-11	Ussher, Jeremy H D 01-Oct-11
	Irwin, Stuart G 01-Oct-11	Wall, Karl 01-Oct-11
2011	James, Gareth C M 01-Oct-11	Walton, George J 01-Oct-11
	Kearsley, Iain P 01-Oct-11	Weil, Daniel G 01-Oct-11
Reynolds, Mark E 01-Feb-11	Knowles, Christopher J 01-Oct-11	Westwood, Thomas P 01-Oct-11
Kadinopoulos, Benjamin A 01-Apr-11	Leightley, Simon M 01-Oct-11	Wharrie, Craig G 01-Oct-11
Percy, Nicolas A 01-Apr-11	Longstaff, Thomas W 01-Oct-11	White, Stephen P 01-Oct-11
Green, Jayne H 01-Sep-11	Lynn, Sarah L 01-Oct-11	Whitehead, Peter J MBE 01-Oct-11
Abbotts, Michael C 01-Oct-11	Macphail, Neil M 01-Oct-11	Williams, Cassandra L 01-Oct-11
Amorosi, Riccardo G F L 01-Oct-11	Mains, Graham 01-Oct-11	Williams, Paul A 01-Oct-11
Anderson, Neil 01-Oct-11	Marsh, Stephen W 01-Oct-11	Wilson, Gary P 01-Oct-11
Andrews, Justin P 01-Oct-11	Maude, Colin D 01-Oct-11	Wood, Simon A H 01-Oct-11
Bailey, Simon 01-Oct-11	McCall, Gary 01-Oct-11	Wookey, Mark 01-Oct-11
Baillie, Robbie W 01-Oct-11	McCamphill-Rose, Paul J 01-Oct-11	Wren, Stephen J 01-Oct-11
Bainbridge, Paul A 01-Oct-11	McKay, Thomas W 01-Oct-11	Parkinson, Henry M L 01-Nov-11
Baldie, Steven A H 01-Oct-11		

LIEUTENANT COMMANDERS

Bettles, John 25-Nov-11
Weedon, Grant 01-Dec-11

2012

Bayliss, Annabel M 16-Mar-12
Harrison, Peter M 26-Mar-12
Misiak, Anna L 10-Apr-12
Stratton, Nicholas C 01-May-12
Harms, James G 02-Jun-12
Louis, David R A 01-Jul-12
Wick, Harry M S 01-Sep-12
Almond, Nicholas 01-Oct-12
Armstrong, David M 01-Oct-12
Armstrong, Rory J 01-Oct-12
Ashlin, James M 01-Oct-12
Balfour, Ross D 01-Oct-12
Ballard, Adam P V 01-Oct-12
Ballard, Danelle R 01-Oct-12
Bannister, Jonathan 01-Oct-12
Bartram, Gregory J 01-Oct-12
Bartram, Richard 01-Oct-12
Bates, Nicholas 01-Oct-12
Black, Edward J 01-Oct-12
Black, Joanna M 01-Oct-12
Blackett, William P H 01-Oct-12
Bleasdale, Daniel R 01-Oct-12
Blethyn, Catherine 01-Oct-12
Bowen, Richard J 01-Oct-12
Bowers, Keith J 01-Oct-12
Braithwaite, Geoffrey C 01-Oct-12
Brennan, John P 01-Oct-12
Bright, Amanda C 01-Oct-12
Briscoe, James W A 01-Oct-12
Bristow, Paul C 01-Oct-12
Browett, Jon J 01-Oct-12
Brown, Alastair D 01-Oct-12
Bukhory, Hamesh 01-Oct-12
Byron, Douglas C 01-Oct-12
Carpenter, Gary J 01-Oct-12
Clee, James S 01-Oct-12
Coffey, Ralph B D 01-Oct-12
Coles-Hendry, Frances A 01-Oct-12
Collins, David I 01-Oct-12
Cowie, Andrew D 01-Oct-12
Cripps, Michael J 01-Oct-12
Daniel, Benjamin J E 01-Oct-12
Davies, Sarah J 01-Oct-12
Day, Benjamin 01-Oct-12
De Velasco, Mari L 01-Oct-12
Deighton, Graeme 01-Oct-12
Despres, Julian A 01-Oct-12
Dix, Caroline P 01-Oct-12
Dowling, Andrew J 01-Oct-12
Dry, Ian 01-Oct-12
Duthie, Andrew G 01-Oct-12
Edwards, Tom H H 01-Oct-12
Fergusson, Iain B 01-Oct-12
Fickling, James W A 01-Oct-12
Fiddock, Matthew L 01-Oct-12
Fitzpatrick, Neil 01-Oct-12
Flaherty, Christopher L 01-Oct-12

Fowler, James E 01-Oct-12
Fox, David J 01-Oct-12
French, Jeremy 01-Oct-12
Gearing, Richard M 01-Oct-12
Gladwin, Michael D 01-Oct-12
Gordon, David E 01-Oct-12
Gorman, Glenn K 01-Oct-12
Gray, Richard L 01-Oct-12
Grayson, Stephen 01-Oct-12
Greenwood, Peter 01-Oct-12
Griffiths, Colin 01-Oct-12
Grove, Jeremy J 01-Oct-12
Hallsworth, Kay 01-Oct-12
Hanks, Oliver T 01-Oct-12
Hannam, Darrell B 01-Oct-12
Harding, David V 01-Oct-12
Harris, Hugh J L 01-Oct-12
Hazelwood, Steve 01-Oct-12
Heirs, Gavin G 01-Oct-12
Herridge, Daniel J 01-Oct-12
Hesketh, John J 01-Oct-12
Higson, Glenn R 01-Oct-12
Holmes, Christopher 01-Oct-12
Horlock, Andrew 01-Oct-12
Hughes, Gary E 01-Oct-12
Hulse, Rebecca J 01-Oct-12
Hurman, Richard N 01-Oct-12
Hutchinson, Michael R 01-Oct-12
Hyde, James W 01-Oct-12
Illingworth, Richard A 01-Oct-12
Inglis, Graham D 01-Oct-12
Insley, Carrie A 01-Oct-12
Irving, Paul J 01-Oct-12
Issitt, Barry D 01-Oct-12
Ivill, Stephen 01-Oct-12
Jones, Helen C 01-Oct-12
Jones, Nicholas H 01-Oct-12
Keillor, Stuart J 01-Oct-12
Kennedy, Catheryn H 01-Oct-12
King, David A 01-Oct-12
L'Amie, Christopher A 01-Oct-12
Lancaster, James H D 01-Oct-12
Leeper, James S 01-Oct-12
London, Nicholas J 01-Oct-12
Lovell, James E C 01-Oct-12
Maclean, Shamus 01-Oct-12
Macsephney, Tracy 01-Oct-12
Maddison, Hugh R 01-Oct-12
Maddison, Paul 01-Oct-12
Mallabone, James J K 01-Oct-12
Marlor, Andrew 01-Oct-12
Marsh, Ceri 01-Oct-12
McCallum, Malcolm D 01-Oct-12
McMillan, Nelson 01-Oct-12
Middleton, Mark A 01-Oct-12
Miller, Sasha L 01-Oct-12
Minty, Darren 01-Oct-12
Mount, James B 01-Oct-12
Nelson, Matthew R 01-Oct-12
North, Adam C 01-Oct-12
Owen, Vincent F 01-Oct-12

Perks, Andrew B 01-Oct-12
Phillippo, Duncan G 01-Oct-12
Prideaux, Robert J 01-Oct-12
Priest, Rachel E 01-Oct-12
Reynolds, Andrew C J 01-Oct-12
Rimmer, Owen F 01-Oct-12
Riordan, Shaun 01-Oct-12
Roberts, Andrew 01-Oct-12
Rose, Alan 01-Oct-12
Rowley, Thomas P 01-Oct-12
Ryder, Matthew R 01-Oct-12
Saltonstall, Hugh F R 01-Oct-12
Sampson, James 01-Oct-12
Sandy, David J 01-Oct-12
Savage, Alexander F 01-Oct-12
Shanahan, Lloyd A 01-Oct-12
Shepherd, Christopher E 01-Oct-12
Sims, Alexander R 01-Oct-12
Sloan-Murphy, Christian J 01-Oct-12
Smith, Benjamin 01-Oct-12
Smye, Malcolm 01-Oct-12
Sobers, Scott 01-Oct-12
Stead, Andrew M 01-Oct-12
Sturgeon, Mark 01-Oct-12
Thomson, Paul A 01-Oct-12
Twiselton, Matthew J 01-Oct-12
Vessey, Lee M 01-Oct-12
Walker, Ian M 01-Oct-12
Warburton, Alison 01-Oct-12
Ward, Jared M 01-Oct-12
Ware, Andrew T 01-Oct-12
Watson, Bradley L 01-Oct-12
Webb, John P 01-Oct-12
West, Hannah R 01-Oct-12
Wheatley, Nicola S 01-Oct-12
Wheen, Charles 01-Oct-12
White, Steven 01-Oct-12
Whittles, Gary W 01-Oct-12
Winborn, David J 01-Oct-12
Winstone, Nigel P 01-Oct-12
Wood, Christopher T 01-Oct-12
Wright-Jones, Alexandra E M 01-Oct-12
Ives, David J 25-Oct-12

2013

Charnock, Simon J 01-Apr-13
Allen, Jason L 01-Oct-13
Andrews, Dominic M 01-Oct-13
Bane, Nicholas S 01-Oct-13
Barron, Jeremy M 01-Oct-13
Barron, Philip R 01-Oct-13
Bassett, Nicole 01-Oct-13
Bastiaens, Paul A 01-Oct-13
Becker, Robert K 01-Oct-13
Best, Robert M 01-Oct-13
Billings, Andrew J 01-Oct-13
Birch, Peter L 01-Oct-13
Birkby, Christina 01-Oct-13
Blackmore, Andrew M 01-Oct-13
Bouyac, David R L 01-Oct-13
Bray, Andrew 01-Oct-13

LIEUTENANT COMMANDERS

Brettell, Jeremy D 01-Oct-13	Joyce, David J 01-Oct-13	Stevenson, Adam 01-Oct-13
Brockie, Alan F 01-Oct-13	Kiernan, Colin 01-Oct-13	Stevenson, Simon 01-Oct-13
Brown, Lynda E M 01-Oct-13	Kingston, Earl A 01-Oct-13	Storton, George H 01-Oct-13
Browne, Kevin M 01-Oct-13	Knott, Thomas M MBE 01-Oct-13	Street, Sarah 01-Oct-13
Burgess, Philip G 01-Oct-13	Lamb, Robert J F 01-Oct-13	Sweeney, Rachel J 01-Oct-13
Burghall, Rebecca C 01-Oct-13	Lawrenson, Timothy A H 01-Oct-13	Taylor, Andrew I 01-Oct-13
Butler, Philip M 01-Oct-13	Lee, David A 01-Oct-13	Taylor, James T 01-Oct-13
Byrd, Liam 01-Oct-13	Leslie, Bruce D 01-Oct-13	Thomas, Adam J MBE 01-Oct-13
Carr, David J 01-Oct-13	Lewis, Jonathan M 01-Oct-13	Thomas, Duncan J 01-Oct-13
Caswell, Neil C 01-Oct-13	Little, Matthew I G 01-Oct-13	Thompson, William A 01-Oct-13
Ciaravella, Timothy J 01-Oct-13	Locke, Nicholas M 01-Oct-13	Thomson, Jane M 01-Oct-13
Claridge, Alexander M 01-Oct-13	Long, Victoria S 01-Oct-13	Tretton, Joseph E 01-Oct-13
Coghill, Adrian 01-Oct-13	Longman, Matthew S 01-Oct-13	Trevethan, Christopher J 01-Oct-13
Coles, Adam J 01-Oct-13	Mackenow, Helen R 01-Oct-13	Trevethan, Sean C 01-Oct-13
Collie, James A 01-Oct-13	Malone, Roger W 01-Oct-13	Turner, Matthew 01-Oct-13
Collins, Andrew C 01-Oct-13	Mason, David 01-Oct-13	Twigg, Neil R 01-Oct-13
Cooper, Edwin 01-Oct-13	McAllister, Steven E 01-Oct-13	Vaughan, Edward A 01-Oct-13
Cox, Matthew J 01-Oct-13	McGreal, Benjamin 01-Oct-13	Visram, Adrian H 01-Oct-13
Critchley, Ian J 01-Oct-13	McInerney, David F 01-Oct-13	Vivian, Philip 01-Oct-13
Crompton, Lynne 01-Oct-13	McNally, Nicholas A 01-Oct-13	Walker, John 01-Oct-13
Crossey, Matthew D 01-Oct-13	McQueen, Patrick G 01-Oct-13	Ware, Peter J 01-Oct-13
Croxton, Damien P 01-Oct-13	Montgomery, Harvie E 01-Oct-13	Warren, Rebecca J 01-Oct-13
Cummings, Darren 01-Oct-13	Moran, Benjamin M 01-Oct-13	Waters, Michael R 01-Oct-13
Dale, Nathan A 01-Oct-13	Moran, John-Paul 01-Oct-13	Westwood, Michelle 01-Oct-13
Davis, Richard 01-Oct-13	Morris, Paul W 01-Oct-13	Whitmore, Jennifer S 01-Oct-13
Deakin, Scott M 01-Oct-13	Morton, Neil 01-Oct-13	Whyte, Gordon 01-Oct-13
Dennard, Kieron J 01-Oct-13	Moss, Jonathan 01-Oct-13	Wilson, Neil A 01-Oct-13
Dougan, David S 01-Oct-13	Mowat, Andrew D J 01-Oct-13	Winterton, Paul 01-Oct-13
Drewett, Brian J H 01-Oct-13	Muir, Katie M 01-Oct-13	Sims, Deborah L 02-Nov-13
Eden, Jeremy R H 01-Oct-13	Offord, Stephen J J 01-Oct-13	
Edwards, Sharon P 01-Oct-13	Parnell, Daniel C 01-Oct-13	**2014**
Evans, Benjimin G 01-Oct-13	Phillips, Matthew R 01-Oct-13	
Fanshawe, Edward 01-Oct-13	Pimm, Anthony R 01-Oct-13	Thorley, Graham MBE 01-Jan-14
Filshie, Sarah J 01-Oct-13	Powell, Gregory M J 01-Oct-13	Porter, Timothy B 07-Jan-14
Flannagan, Donna L 01-Oct-13	Power, Benjamin 01-Oct-13	Reynolds, Huw F 01-Mar-14
Frith, Adele M 01-Oct-13	Quaite, David G 01-Oct-13	Quinn, Shaun A 15-May-14
Gill, Paul S 01-Oct-13	Ralls, Damien 01-Oct-13	Tait, Martyn D 27-Aug-14
Gillies, Brett 01-Oct-13	Rees, Simon G 01-Oct-13	Adam, Murray W 01-Oct-14
Green, Jonathan 01-Oct-13	Renaud, Gavin A R 01-Oct-13	Allen, Alexander P 01-Oct-14
Grierson, Andrew D 01-Oct-13	Reynolds, Darren P 01-Oct-13	Armand-Smith, Penelope H 01-Oct-14
Grimley, Timothy P 01-Oct-13	Riches, Joanne C 01-Oct-13	Armstrong, Colin D 01-Oct-14
Hallett, Daniel J 01-Oct-13	Ridgwell, Daniel R 01-Oct-13	Attwater, Richard P 01-Oct-14
Hammond, Christopher R 01-Oct-13	Ripley, Stephen L 01-Oct-13	Barker, Peter R 01-Oct-14
Haskins, Benjamin S 01-Oct-13	Robertson, Adam J 01-Oct-13	Barrett, Benjamin T 01-Oct-14
Hayes, Mark A 01-Oct-13	Roffey, Kevin D 01-Oct-13	Bartlett, David L 01-Oct-14
Haynes, John G 01-Oct-13	Rose, Marcus E 01-Oct-13	Beaton, Iain 01-Oct-14
Heward, Mark G 01-Oct-13	Rowson, Marcus J 01-Oct-13	Betchley, James W 01-Oct-14
Higgins, Alex P B 01-Oct-13	Ryan, Paul J 01-Oct-13	Betts, Andrew T J 01-Oct-14
Hobbs, Thomas P 01-Oct-13	Scott, Russell B 01-Oct-13	Betts, Peter R 01-Oct-14
Holland, Steven W 01-Oct-13	Seal, Michael O 01-Oct-13	Bird, Michael P 01-Oct-14
Hollingworth, Christopher R 01-Oct-13	Searle, Andrew J A 01-Oct-13	Boulton, Graham R 01-Oct-14
Hopton, Fiona C F 01-Oct-13	Sharkey, Philip J 01-Oct-13	Brannighan, David M 01-Oct-14
Hopton, Matthew J 01-Oct-13	Shaw, Mark A 01-Oct-13	Brian, Stephen 01-Oct-14
Horton, James R 01-Oct-13	Shirvill, Victoria L 01-Oct-13	Brown, Michael A 01-Oct-14
Hucker, Oliver 01-Oct-13	Shrestha, Shekhar 01-Oct-13	Bryden, David G 01-Oct-14
Hughes, Geoffrey 01-Oct-13	Simpson, John N 01-Oct-13	Campbell-Baldwin, James W 01-Oct-14
Hunnibell, John R 01-Oct-13	Slight, Oliver W L 01-Oct-13	Carey, Trevor 01-Oct-14
Isaacs, Nathan J 01-Oct-13	Smedley, Rachel 01-Oct-13	Carver, Charles A 01-Oct-14
Jamieson, Paul A 01-Oct-13	Smith, Matthew D 01-Oct-13	Cheal, Andrew J 01-Oct-14
Johnson, Tim P 01-Oct-13	Spacey, Craig D 01-Oct-13	Chisholm, Philip J H 01-Oct-14
Jones, Darren P 01-Oct-13	Steele, Matthew S 01-Oct-13	Church, Simon J 01-Oct-14
		Clapham, Grantley T 01-Oct-14

LIEUTENANT COMMANDERS

Clarke, Matthew.................................01-Oct-14	Humphries, Mark..............................01-Oct-14	Piper, Benjamin J.............................01-Oct-14
Claxton, Andrew G D..........................01-Oct-14	Hunt, Ben P.....................................01-Oct-14	Plenty, Andrew J..............................01-Oct-14
Cochrane, Christopher D.....................01-Oct-14	Husband, James................................01-Oct-14	Plumer, Stephen J.............................01-Oct-14
Coleman, James M P...........................01-Oct-14	Ivory, Thomas J.................................01-Oct-14	Pugh, Geoffrey N J............................01-Oct-14
Collins, Charles A...............................01-Oct-14	Jane, Samuel C.................................01-Oct-14	Raine, Sarah L..................................01-Oct-14
Collins, Lorna J...................................01-Oct-14	Jones, Carolyn..................................01-Oct-14	Ray, Louise B....................................01-Oct-14
Court, Matthew R...............................01-Oct-14	Jones, Christopher D..........................01-Oct-14	Rees, Matthew I................................01-Oct-14
Cripps, Nicola....................................01-Oct-14	Jones, Gordon...................................01-Oct-14	Reeve, Jennifer A..............................01-Oct-14
Crompton, Philip J..............................01-Oct-14	Keane, Brendan M.............................01-Oct-14	Richards, Guy B.................................01-Oct-14
Dalgleish, Grant A...............................01-Oct-14	Keenan, Benjamin F...........................01-Oct-14	Riley, Ralph A....................................01-Oct-14
Dalglish, Kenneth M............................01-Oct-14	Kelway, Jenna...................................01-Oct-14	Ritchie, Douglas B.............................01-Oct-14
Dallamore, Rebecca A.........................01-Oct-14	Kemp, Richard L................................01-Oct-14	Roberts, Christopher S.......................01-Oct-14
Davies, Hazel....................................01-Oct-14	King, Michael A..................................01-Oct-14	Ross, Steven.....................................01-Oct-14
Davis, Peter H....................................01-Oct-14	Koheeallee, Mohummed C R C..............01-Oct-14	Round, Matthew J.............................01-Oct-14
Dick, Colin M.....................................01-Oct-14	Langford, Timothy D..........................01-Oct-14	Rowbotham, Mark J...........................01-Oct-14
Dillon, Ben..01-Oct-14	Leckey, Elizabeth H............................01-Oct-14	Royston, James L...............................01-Oct-14
Dorman, Thomas R.............................01-Oct-14	Lees, Claire M F.................................01-Oct-14	Scales, Dean R...................................01-Oct-14
Duffy, James C...................................01-Oct-14	Lett, Timothy J...................................01-Oct-14	Scott, Alexander J..............................01-Oct-14
Duke, Adam J.....................................01-Oct-14	Lindeyer, Matthew J...........................01-Oct-14	Seal, Martin R....................................01-Oct-14
Durbin, Philip J...................................01-Oct-14	Lister, Matthew J L............................01-Oct-14	Sedgwick, Hugo MBE..........................01-Oct-14
Dyer, Shani D.....................................01-Oct-14	London, Heidi C.................................01-Oct-14	Shakespeare, Christopher A................01-Oct-14
Dymond, Justin R M............................01-Oct-14	Lucas, Darren P.................................01-Oct-14	Shaves, Thomas D L...........................01-Oct-14
Errington, Ridley J B............................01-Oct-14	Magzoub, Mohayed............................01-Oct-14	Shaw, Callam R..................................01-Oct-14
Evans, Robert G.................................01-Oct-14	Mahoney, Andrew.............................01-Oct-14	Shaw, Hannah K................................01-Oct-14
Everard, Paul J....................................01-Oct-14	Marjoribanks, Charlotte......................01-Oct-14	Shirvill, Matthew J............................01-Oct-14
Faye, Matthew E.................................01-Oct-14	Marlor, Kirsty L..................................01-Oct-14	Sloan, Ian A......................................01-Oct-14
Feasey, Caroline.................................01-Oct-14	Marsh, Stuart D.................................01-Oct-14	Smith, David J...................................01-Oct-14
Flannigan, Aiden.................................01-Oct-14	Martin, Ben R....................................01-Oct-14	Smith, Richard J.................................01-Oct-14
Fleming, Caroline S E..........................01-Oct-14	Martyn, Julie M..................................01-Oct-14	Stafford-Shaw, Damian.......................01-Oct-14
Fletcher, Jonathan H G.......................01-Oct-14	McAllister, Andrew W.........................01-Oct-14	Stamper, Valerie L..............................01-Oct-14
Fletcher, Richard................................01-Oct-14	McCavour, Bryan D.............................01-Oct-14	Stanistreet, Georgina C......................01-Oct-14
Fooks-Bale, Matthew E........................01-Oct-14	McCullough, Karen M..........................01-Oct-14	Stirling, Andrew C..............................01-Oct-14
Freeman, Edmund M R.........................01-Oct-14	McLachlan, Andrew C..........................01-Oct-14	Swire, Barry J....................................01-Oct-14
Frost, Laurence J................................01-Oct-14	Meacher, Paul G.................................01-Oct-14	Taylor, Scott A...................................01-Oct-14
Gaunt, Amy V.....................................01-Oct-14	Meigh, Peter D...................................01-Oct-14	Thomas, Richard D..............................01-Oct-14
Gilbert, Mark.....................................01-Oct-14	Mittins, Simon...................................01-Oct-14	Thompson, Alastair J..........................01-Oct-14
Gobey, Richard...................................01-Oct-14	Morgan, Benjamin P...........................01-Oct-14	Thompson, Claire F............................01-Oct-14
Goosen, Richard.................................01-Oct-14	Moss-Ward, Edward G.........................01-Oct-14	Tipping, Anthony...............................01-Oct-14
Gowers, Sarah MBE.............................01-Oct-14	Mullis, Geoffrey.................................01-Oct-14	Toogood, Mark J................................01-Oct-14
Gregory, Jonathan E............................01-Oct-14	Nash, Robin D C.................................01-Oct-14	Tuhey, James J G...............................01-Oct-14
Griffiths, Francis M.............................01-Oct-14	Nash, Rubin P....................................01-Oct-14	Tyler, Adrian......................................01-Oct-14
Guild, Ian..01-Oct-14	Newall, Paul J....................................01-Oct-14	Van Duin, Martin I A...........................01-Oct-14
Hale, Amanda D.................................01-Oct-14	Nightingale, Samuel...........................01-Oct-14	Vowles, Iain R...................................01-Oct-14
Hampson, Alexander G.........................01-Oct-14	Notley, Edward J................................01-Oct-14	Walker, Jamie....................................01-Oct-14
Hannaby, Philippa B............................01-Oct-14	Oakey, Dean.....................................01-Oct-14	Walker, Mark J...................................01-Oct-14
Hannigan, Jason D..............................01-Oct-14	O'Dooley, Paul..................................01-Oct-14	Ward, Michelle T................................01-Oct-14
Harris, Linda E...................................01-Oct-14	Owen, Douglas P C.............................01-Oct-14	Wardley, Thomas E............................01-Oct-14
Hawkins, Emma L................................01-Oct-14	Owens, John W..................................01-Oct-14	Wareham, Sidney J.............................01-Oct-14
Haynes, Fiona J..................................01-Oct-14	Paddock, Lee.....................................01-Oct-14	Warren, Matthew J.............................01-Oct-14
Hearn, Samuel P.................................01-Oct-14	Page, Mark R.....................................01-Oct-14	Watts, Nicholas H C............................01-Oct-14
Heaton, Roxane M..............................01-Oct-14	Pariser, Andrew M..............................01-Oct-14	Waudby, Lindsey................................01-Oct-14
Heaton, Sean.....................................01-Oct-14	Parker, Jonathan D.............................01-Oct-14	Wellington, Laura J............................01-Oct-14
Herrington, Robert J...........................01-Oct-14	Parker, Laura M..................................01-Oct-14	Weston, Karl N N...............................01-Oct-14
Herzberg, Mark J................................01-Oct-14	Patton, Stephen T L............................01-Oct-14	Williams, Lee S..................................01-Oct-14
Hill, Christopher.................................01-Oct-14	Pellecchia, Daniel N............................01-Oct-14	Wills, Robert H..................................01-Oct-14
Hodges, Philip R.................................01-Oct-14	Percival, Victoria H............................01-Oct-14	Wood, Joanne T.................................01-Oct-14
Hollyfield, Peter.................................01-Oct-14	Petch, Alan N....................................01-Oct-14	Wordsworth, Jonathan D.....................01-Oct-14
Howarth, Michael C............................01-Oct-14	Peterson, Keith A...............................01-Oct-14	Young, Sally......................................01-Oct-14
Howe, Jonathan.................................01-Oct-14	Pethrick, Jerome F.............................01-Oct-14	
Hudson, Andrew I...............................01-Oct-14	Pickles, Martin R...............................01-Oct-14	
Humphrey, Darren P............................01 Oct-14	Pike, Stuart......................................01-Oct-14	

LIEUTENANTS

1986
Thomas, Emma 26-Jul-86

1990
Davies, Gary P. 12-Aug-90

1992
Farmer, Gary G. 28-Jun-92
Gray, Martina E 24-Aug-92

1993
Gamble, Phillip. 15-May-93
Duncan, Colin J. 01-Sep-93

1994
Hedworth, Anthony 01-Jun-94
Roberts, Martin A 01-Nov-94

1996
Barclay, Alastair J. 21-Jun-96

1997
Dobbins, Stuart J. 07-Jul-97
Johnson, Roy L. 12-Nov-97

1998
Johnson, Jeremy D 01-Jan-98
Gibbs, David J 01-Feb-98
Haggo, Jamie R. 16-Apr-98
Buchan, Sarah R 01-May-98
Hartley, James. 01-May-98
Howe, Craig M 01-Jul-98
Carrick, James P. 01-Sep-98
Rees, Adam M 01-Sep-98
Metcalfe, Richard J. 04-Sep-98
Crane, Oliver R. 01-Oct-98
Lilly, David. 01-Dec-98

1999
Harfield, Sarah J. 01-Jan-99
Butterworth, Leslie MBE 16-Jan-99
Hume, Kenneth J 01-Mar-99
Carter, David. 22-Mar-99
Thompson, David A 16-Apr-99
Ackerman, Richard J 09-May-99
Epps, Matthew 17-Jul-99
Bailey, Sian. 01-Aug-99
Richards, Simon T 01-Aug-99
Lawrence, Linda J. 16-Sep-99
Concarr, David T 19-Sep-99
Martin, Nigel. 20-Sep-99
Derrick, Matthew. 01-Dec-99
Jenkins, Robert 01-Dec-99

2000
Muyambo, Nomalanga N 01-Jan-00

Williams, Daniel L. 01-Jan-00
Hammond, Meirion M 01-Apr-00
Shearn, Matthew A. 01-Apr-00
Firth, John S. 01-May-00
Holt, John D. 01-May-00
Paget, Simon 02-May-00
Hewitson, Jonathan G A 01-Aug-00
Farr, Ian R. 16-Aug-00
Chandler, Philip. 01-Sep-00
Lynas, Jonathan F A 01-Sep-00
Ransom, Benjamin R J 01-Sep-00
Grantham, Guy J. 01-Nov-00
Lynch, Suzanne. 28-Nov-00
Ashby, Maxine 01-Dec-00

2001
Aitken, Steven R 01-Jan-01
Dixon, Richard A. 01-Jan-01
Finn, James S 01-Jan-01
Kierstan, Simon. 01-Jan-01
Morphet, Kathryn 01-Jan-01
Topham, Neil E. 01-Feb-01
Lightfoot, Richard A. 16-Feb-01
Duce, Matthew. 01-May-01
Fabik, Andre N. 01-May-01
Hall, Kilian J D. 01-May-01
Humphries, Graham D 01-May-01
Jackson, Howard C 01-May-01
Spinks, Robert J 01-May-01
Wickham, Robert J. 01-May-01
Wielopolski, Mark L 01-May-01
Wilkins, David P. 01-May-01
Rowe, Kevin C 04-May-01
Menzies, Bruce 01-Jul-01
Bryce-Johnston, Fiona L S 16-Jul-01
Prosser, Matthew J. 01-Aug-01
Andrews, Iain S 01-Sep-01
Booth, Diccon P P 01-Sep-01
Fraser, Michael. 01-Sep-01
Ingham, Lee-Anne 01-Sep-01
Jameson, Andrew J 01-Sep-01
Lewis, Angela B 01-Sep-01
Stewart, Charles H 01-Sep-01
Bennett, Brian. 01-Nov-01
Woad, Jonathan P R 01-Nov-01
Lewis, Daniel. 01-Dec-01

2002
Atwal, Kamaldip 01-Jan-02
Blick, Sarah L 01-Jan-02
Brock, Mathew J 01-Jan-02
Cooke, Stephen N. 01-Jan-02
Creek, Stephen B 01-Jan-02
Eaton, David C. 01-Jan-02
Holliehead, Craig. 01-Jan-02
Inglis, David J 01-Jan-02
Kingdon, Simon C. 01-Jan-02
Ladislaus, Cecil J 01-Jan-02
Louw, Len 01-Jan-02
Moss, Richard M 01-Jan-02

Ralston, William A. 01-Jan-02
Suter, Francis T. 01-Jan-02
Watkins, Jenny. 01-Jan-02
Wickett, Richard J 01-Mar-02
Barr, Derek D 01-Apr-02
Crawford, Valerie E 01-Apr-02
Gaytano, Ronald T M 01-Apr-02
Whitley, Helen S. 01-Apr-02
Baxter, Arran C 01-May-02
Coyle, Ross D. 01-May-02
Fulton, David M 01-May-02
Holmes, Patrick J M. 01-May-02
Lock, William 01-May-02
O'Callaghan, Patrick 01-May-02
Spike, Adam J 01-May-02
Taylor, Robert P 01-May-02
Veal, Dominic J 01-May-02
Cross, Nicholas 01-Jul-02
Ramsay, Alastair J D 01-Jul-02
Scott, Elizabeth K 01-Jul-02
Bullock, James. 01-Aug-02
Chang, Hon W 01-Aug-02
Voke, Christen A. 01-Aug-02
Callis, Gregory J 01-Sep-02
Davis, Peter H 01-Sep-02
Evans, Laura-Jane. 01-Sep-02
Gorman, Darren A 01-Sep-02
King, Iain A. 01-Sep-02
Lloyd, Matthew R. 01-Sep-02
Malcolm, Paul. 01-Sep-02
Nguyo, David N. 01-Sep-02
Shropshall, Helen L 01-Sep-02
Westwood, Andrew J. 01-Sep-02
Woodley, Stephen L 01-Sep-02
Harrison, Ian 01-Oct-02
Lupini, James M 01-Oct-02
Williamson, Peter J. 01-Oct-02
Shouler, Martin 15-Nov-02
Ayrton, Robert E 01-Dec-02
Shepherd, Anya C 01-Dec-02

2003
Bickley, Gary N. 01-Jan-03
Conran, Nicholas W D. 01-Jan-03
Coppin, Nigel J 01-Jan-03
Evans, Christian P. 01-Jan-03
Floyd, Robert E. 01-Jan-03
Harrison-Jones, Stuart 01-Jan-03
Hunt, Rachel E 01-Jan-03
Jones, Emmanuel N L 01-Jan-03
Ligale, Eugene 01-Jan-03
Macpherson, Craig A C 01-Jan-03
O'Neill, Harry 01-Jan-03
Renney, Rachel A 01-Jan-03
Worley, Thomas F. 01-Jan-03
Fraser, James M. 01-Feb-03
Roberts, Stephen 01-Feb-03
Grey, Amy C 01-Apr-03
Hackland, Andrew S 01-Apr-03
Stephenson, Christopher J 01-Apr-03
Chudley, Ian V. 01-May-03

LIEUTENANTS

Courtney, Timothy 01-May-03	Bell, Nicholas A G 01-May-04	McGivern, Ryan P 01-Sep-04
Emery, Christian S 01-May-03	Benbow, James A K 01-May-04	Morgan, Gareth L 01-Sep-04
Evans, Christopher A 01-May-03	Bligh, Sarah L 01-May-04	Neyland, David A 01-Sep-04
Hill, Thomas 01-May-03	Campbell, Alastair 01-May-04	Pearson, Ian T 01-Sep-04
Jones, Stephen 01-May-03	Collins, Mark 01-May-04	Preece, Simon E 01-Sep-04
Kerley, Benjamin J 01-May-03	Colvin, Michael A T 01-May-04	Richardson, John F 01-Sep-04
Mitchell, Paul J 01-May-03	Cooley, Jeannine 01-May-04	Strawbridge, Chantal M 01-Sep-04
Thompson, Sarah L 01-May-03	Cuthbert, Glen 01-May-04	Stuart, Simon A 01-Sep-04
White, Paul D 01-May-03	Cutler, David T 01-May-04	Swift, Robert D 01-Sep-04
Anderson, Kevin 01-Jun-03	Greenhill, Matthew C 01-May-04	Taylor, James E 01-Sep-04
Vaughan, James R 01-Jun-03	Hudson, Tom A J 01-May-04	Tucker, Philip J 01-Sep-04
Love, John J 04-Jun-03	Isherwood, Carl R 01-May-04	Williams, Anthony M 01-Sep-04
Roy, Christopher A 16-Jun-03	Jardine, Iain 01-May-04	Wood, Richard R T 01-Sep-04
Fuller, Richard 01-Jul-03	Jewson, Benjamin D 01-May-04	Orton, Trevor 01-Oct-04
Murphy, Caroline R 01-Jul-03	Johnston, Andrew I 01-May-04	Sheehan, Thomas J 01-Oct-04
Bowers, Mark R 01-Aug-03	Leaker, Daniel T 01-May-04	Williamson, Simon J 01-Oct-04
Burlingham, Alexander C R 01-Aug-03	Lowe, Gavin J 01-May-04	Parker, Anthony R 29-Oct-04
Barber, Mark 01-Sep-03	Maskell, Bernard M 01-May-04	Carman, Felix 01-Dec-04
Caddick, Andrew 01-Sep-03	Mason, Richard J 01-May-04	Wilton, Mark 01-Dec-04
Carnew, Sean F 01-Sep-03	McPhail, Thomas C 01-May-04	Hopwood, Adrian P 17-Dec-04
Cassidy, Stuart M 01-Sep-03	Murray, William 01-May-04	
Cumming, Frazer S 01-Sep-03	Robinson, Matthew S 01-May-04	**2005**
Earle-Payne, Gareth E 01-Sep-03	Stewart, Nicholas J 01-May-04	Barber, Alexander S L 01-Jan-05
Gilmore, Jeremy E 01-Sep-03	Thomas, Joseph 01-May-04	Bulgin, Martin R 01-Jan-05
Sharrott, Christopher 01-Sep-03	Thompson, James 01-May-04	Capps, James A 01-Jan-05
Shears, Gary R 01-Sep-03	White, Alistair J M 01-May-04	Curd, Michael C 01-Jan-05
Shropshall, Ian 01-Sep-03	White, Ross E 01-May-04	Duffin, Lee-Anne 01-Jan-05
Stubbs, Benjamin D 01-Sep-03	Wilson, David J 01-May-04	Gilbert, Rachel 01-Jan-05
Workman, Rayner J 01-Sep-03	Wood, Michael W 01-May-04	Hooper, Thomas 01-Jan-05
Hume, Sarah K (ARRC) 01-Nov-03	Ainsworth, Alan 01-Jul-04	Houlston, Ian J E 01-Jan-05
Selden, John D A 01-Nov-03	Broster, Lee J 01-Jul-04	Laidlaw, Jonathan M 01-Jan-05
Abbott, Katherine Y L 01-Dec-03	Cheema, Sukhdev S 01-Jul-04	Lang, Alasdair J M 01-Jan-05
Hetherington, Thomas A 01-Dec-03	Cowlishaw, Nicholas D 01-Jul-04	Lang, Lesley A 01-Jan-05
Reynolds, Zoe A 01-Dec-03	Flitcroft, Michael 01-Jul-04	Little, Nicola S 01-Jan-05
	Hardy-Hodgson, David N 01-Jul-04	Mattock, Nicholas J 01-Jan-05
2004	James, Robert 01-Jul-04	McCormick, Emma J 01-Jan-05
Barrett, Scott 01-Jan-04	Jones, Mark 01-Jul-04	McDonald, Morgan J 01-Jan-05
Brazenall, Benjamin C 01-Jan-04	Munro, Michael 01-Jul-04	Mifflin, Michelle J 01-Jan-05
Clark, Paul A 01-Jan-04	Packer, Robert 01-Jul-04	Newby, Christopher 01-Jan-05
Devlin, Craig 01-Jan-04	Peake, Stephen P 01-Jul-04	Pearson, Alan J 01-Jan-05
Dixon, Mark E 01-Jan-04	Stancliffe, Andrew E 01-Jul-04	Pope, Kevin D 01-Jan-05
Gibson, Adrian 01-Jan-04	Thwaites, Lindsey W 01-Jul-04	Ross, Paul W 01-Jan-05
Griffiths, Gareth 01-Jan-04	Tibballs, Laura R 01-Jul-04	Sherwin, Antony J 01-Jan-05
Hounsome, Jonathan R 01-Jan-04	Walker, Richard P 01-Jul-04	Sutcliffe, Paul 01-Jan-05
Ingamells, Stephen D 01-Jan-04	Wotton, Alan 01-Jul-04	Tretton, Caroline 01-Jan-05
Lee, Raymond A 01-Jan-04	Elder-Dicker, Nicholas 01-Aug-04	Coughlin, Emma J 18-Jan-05
McMahon, Daniel S 01-Jan-04	Gray, Samuel D 01-Aug-04	Garner, Michael E 01-Feb-05
Say, Russell G 01-Jan-04	Wright, Helen J 13-Aug-04	Carter, Christopher 18-Feb-05
Scarlett, Christopher J 01-Jan-04	Wright, Neil D MBE 13-Aug-04	Mulroy, Paul J 18-Feb-05
Shortland, Karen 01-Jan-04	Attwood, Keith A 01-Sep-04	Taylor, Andrew 18-Feb-05
Simpson, Christopher J 01-Jan-04	Bird, Andrew W 01-Sep-04	Perry, Carl S L 01-Mar-05
Syson, Carl F 01-Jan-04	Blackburn, Craig J 01-Sep-04	Bessant, Matthew 01-Apr-05
Torbet, Linda 01-Jan-04	Brannighan, Ian D 01-Sep-04	Hale, Stuart D 01-Apr-05
Tumilty, Kevin 01-Jan-04	Darlington, Alan 01-Sep-04	Thackray, Penelope D 01-Apr-05
Walker, Daniel H 01-Jan-04	Dart, Duncan J 01-Sep-04	Williams, Luke 01-Apr-05
Walker, James J 01-Jan-04	Easterbrook, Christopher 01-Sep-04	Angliss, Roger J 08-Apr-05
Webster, Andrew J 01-Jan-04	Elliott, Timothy D 01-Sep-04	Blatchford, Timothy P 08-Apr-05
Wilson, Simon A 01-Jan-04	Fleming, David P 01-Sep-04	Hadley, Clive M 08-Apr-05
Black, Charlotte J 01-Mar-04	Fowle, Laura C 01-Sep-04	Hewitt, Nigel W 08-Apr-05
Loadman, Dougal R 01-Mar-04	Hodgkinson, Samuel P 01-Sep-04	Parkin, Brett A 08-Apr-05
Tregale, Jamie 01-Apr-04	Knowles, David 01-Sep-04	Stephenson, Richard J E 08-Apr-05

LIEUTENANTS

Blake, Matthew G.................................01-May-05
Frost, Timothy S.................................01-May-05
Malster, Dudley A.................................01-May-05
McCrea, Mark J.................................01-May-05
Talbot, Simon J.................................01-May-05
Tasker, Adam M.................................01-May-05
Nicolson, Vernon.................................03-May-05
Bowman, Simon K J.................................01-Jun-05
Cursiter, John D.................................12-Jun-05
Higgins, Andrew J N.................................13-Jun-05
Harrison, Anthony.................................25-Jun-05
Kantharia, Paul.................................25-Jun-05
Borrett, John E.................................01-Jul-05
Hairsine, William.................................01-Jul-05
Hay, Richard H I.................................01-Jul-05
O'Connor, Lucy.................................01-Jul-05
Shaw, Stewart.................................01-Jul-05
Stephens, Patrick G.................................01-Jul-05
Wilcocks, David N.................................01-Jul-05
Willsmore, Stuart A.................................01-Jul-05
Dodds, Stephen.................................12-Aug-05
McQuaid, Ivor T.................................12-Aug-05
Armour, Angela B.................................01-Sep-05
Boulton, David S.................................01-Sep-05
Clark, Philip J.................................01-Sep-05
Crombie, Stuart.................................01-Sep-05
Dallas, Lewis I.................................01-Sep-05
Davidson, Serena R.................................01-Sep-05
Dixon, Robert.................................01-Sep-05
Hougham, Thomas N.................................01-Sep-05
Johnson, Helen E M.................................01-Sep-05
King, Ian J.................................01-Sep-05
McBeth, Gary.................................01-Sep-05
Mellor, Daniel P.................................01-Sep-05
Oldfield, Christian.................................01-Sep-05
Pearce, Sarah L.................................01-Sep-05
Poole, Daniel C.................................01-Sep-05
Rudkin, Adam L.................................01-Sep-05
Taborda, Matthew A.................................01-Sep-05
Watson, Simon C.................................01-Sep-05
Whitehouse, Andrew P.................................01-Sep-05
Coughlin, Peter J L.................................01-Oct-05
Mark, Abigail.................................01-Oct-05
Smith, Matthew R T.................................01-Oct-05
Medlicott, Nicholas.................................28-Oct-05
Abel, James A.................................01-Nov-05
Farrant, Sam.................................01-Nov-05
Haywood, Andrew J.................................01-Nov-05
Lipczynski, Benjamin J.................................01-Nov-05
Pollock, Barnaby J.................................01-Nov-05
Sharples, Joseph H.................................01-Nov-05
Shaw, Simon J.................................01-Nov-05
Steele, Marie L.................................01-Nov-05
Sutcliff, Jonathan D.................................01-Nov-05
Taylor, Nicholas.................................01-Nov-05
Teasdale, James P.................................01-Nov-05
Tetchner, David J.................................01-Nov-05
Wright, Gabriel J.................................01-Nov-05
Peacock, Anouchka.................................01-Dec-05
Mathers, Fiona C.................................02-Dec-05
Horton, Simon.................................11-Dec-05

Botham, Adrian M.................................16-Dec-05

2006

Alexander, William A D.................................01-Jan-06
Barnicoat, Karen.................................01-Jan-06
Burton, James H.................................01-Jan-06
Drinkall, Kathryn M.................................01-Jan-06
Ellison, Peter J P.................................01-Jan-06
Hooper, William R.................................01-Jan-06
Knight, Jonathan M.................................01-Jan-06
Lettington, Paul D W.................................01-Jan-06
Martin, James N.................................01-Jan-06
Ormshaw, Martin A.................................01-Jan-06
Pallett, Tony S.................................01-Jan-06
Paterson, James M A.................................01-Jan-06
Patrick, John A.................................01-Jan-06
Philips, Thomas J.................................01-Jan-06
Southworth, Christopher.................................01-Jan-06
Stephens, Samuel J R.................................01-Jan-06
Turner, Duncan L.................................01-Jan-06
Bell, Lewis G.................................01-Feb-06
Langford, Joanna P.................................01-Feb-06
Muir, Andrew.................................01-Feb-06
Royce, Roderick H.................................01-Feb-06
Rushton, Emma V.................................01-Feb-06
Smith, Craig A.................................01-Feb-06
Starkey, David S.................................01-Feb-06
Veti, Mark A.................................01-Feb-06
Yemm, Matthew A.................................01-Feb-06
Bebbington, David M.................................17-Feb-06
Atkinson, James D.................................26-Feb-06
Dewey, Sarah E.................................01-Mar-06
Milner, Lisa D.................................01-Mar-06
Kay, Victoria J.................................15-Mar-06
Simpson, Erin L.................................15-Mar-06
Bond, Robert J.................................01-Apr-06
Parrott, Stuart S.................................01-Apr-06
Seddon, Jonathan D.................................01-Apr-06
Vereker, Richard J P.................................01-Apr-06
Valvona, Dominic M MBE.................................06-Apr-06
Chisholm, David C.................................07-Apr-06
Godwin, Lee D.................................07-Apr-06
Parkinson, Nicholas.................................07-Apr-06
Peachey, Neil D.................................07-Apr-06
Stevens, Mark J.................................07-Apr-06
Wood, Julian T S.................................07-Apr-06
Jaffrey, Heather B.................................11-Apr-06
Hilton, Michael R C.................................23-Apr-06
Macindoe, Neil.................................23-Apr-06
Baker, James K.................................01-May-06
Bell, Richard J.................................01-May-06
Bilson, Gavin.................................01-May-06
Burgoyne, William.................................01-May-06
Cackett, Thomas E R.................................01-May-06
Carlton, Paul D.................................01-May-06
Chisholm, David T.................................01-May-06
Ellicott, Matthew J.................................01-May-06
Evered, Jonathan F.................................01-May-06
Harper, Kevan J.................................01-May-06
Keane, Joseph P.................................01-May-06
Pollitt, Alexander W.................................01-May-06

Scott, Serena C S.................................01-May-06
Skinner, Jonathan J.................................01-May-06
Thomas, Mark P.................................01-May-06
Wright, James N.................................01-May-06
Manning, David S.................................08-May-06
Smith, Karly J.................................15-May-06
Askham, Mathew T.................................01-Jun-06
Bird, Timothy M.................................01-Jun-06
Lorenz, Rudi.................................01-Jun-06
Moore, Jonathan P.................................01-Jun-06
Quick, Benjamin P.................................01-Jun-06
Coogan, Thomas.................................09-Jun-06
Embleton, Alison.................................09-Jun-06
Stewart, Sean T.................................09-Jun-06
Tonge, Michael.................................09-Jun-06
Tustain, Paul A.................................09-Jun-06
Cockcroft, Kim M.................................16-Jun-06
Preston, Jacqueline N.................................30-Jun-06
Bretten, Nicholas J.................................01-Jul-06
Camplisson, Owen G.................................01-Jul-06
Parry, Stephen J.................................01-Jul-06
Rolls, Edward C.................................01-Jul-06
Youngman, Mitchell C.................................27-Jul-06
Brown, Simon J.................................28-Jul-06
Gaines, Edwin J.................................28-Jul-06
Hislop, Scott G.................................28-Jul-06
Young, Andrew J.................................28-Jul-06
Bentley, Grant.................................01-Aug-06
Hewitt, Clara J.................................01-Aug-06
Parkin, Matthew J.................................01-Aug-06
Proudman, Michael P.................................01-Aug-06
Scott, Victoria.................................01-Aug-06
Barham, Edward.................................01-Sep-06
Barnett, Caila.................................01-Sep-06
Becker, Thomas O.................................01-Sep-06
Binns, James B.................................01-Sep-06
Coatalen-Hodgson, Ryan.................................01-Sep-06
Davies, James S A.................................01-Sep-06
Evans, Thomas W.................................01-Sep-06
Flatt, Liam B.................................01-Sep-06
Fletcher, Andrew S.................................01-Sep-06
Fowler, Remington.................................01-Sep-06
Fredrickson, Charlotte A.................................01-Sep-06
Greaves, Timothy M.................................01-Sep-06
Harris, Robert.................................01-Sep-06
Heywood, Robert H.................................01-Sep-06
Hitchings, Michael J.................................01-Sep-06
Jones, Cheryl.................................01-Sep-06
Kendall-Torry, Guyan C.................................01-Sep-06
Martin, David L.................................01-Sep-06
Munns, Edward N.................................01-Sep-06
Nokes, Oliver.................................01-Sep-06
Philipson, Matthew J.................................01-Sep-06
Plunkett, Gareth N.................................01-Sep-06
Pope, Michelle L.................................01-Sep-06
Rooke, Adam E.................................01-Sep-06
Routledge, Ricky J.................................01-Sep-06
Slayman, Emily.................................01-Sep-06
Thomas, Andrew G.................................01-Sep-06
Thompson, George C.................................01-Sep-06
Westbrook, Kevin.................................01-Sep-06

LIEUTENANTS

Westley, Alexander 01-Sep-06	Donohue, Paul......................................13-Feb-07	Barnes, Paul F..14-Aug-07
Wilcox, Christopher 01-Sep-06	Roberts, Andrew...................................16-Feb-07	Andrews, Rick..01-Sep-07
Wilson, Charles K.................................01-Sep-06	Williams, Russell G................................16-Feb-07	Barker, Helen A......................................01-Sep-07
Dalton, Sally A T..................................01-Oct-06	Paterson, Matthew 09-Mar-07	Bartlett, Marie-Claire............................01-Sep-07
Keegan, Amanda C...............................01-Oct-06	Jackson, Darren M 15-Mar-07	Bennett, Ian J..01-Sep-07
Parker, Berron M..................................01-Oct-06	Dale, Jamie R...01-Apr-07	Booth, Alan K..01-Sep-07
Beeching, Lee G...................................20-Oct-06	Morrison, Richard J...............................01-Apr-07	Bowman, Dean E....................................01-Sep-07
Clarke, Richard A.................................20-Oct-06	Stant, Mark S...01-Apr-07	Campbell, Jonathan G 01-Sep-07
Codling, Steven J.................................20-Oct-06	Strickland, Timothy 01-Apr-07	Clarke, James P......................................01-Sep-07
Gee, Mathew.......................................20-Oct-06	Webster, Mark.......................................01-Apr-07	Coleman, Gareth W................................01-Sep-07
Graham, James P..................................20-Oct-06	Anderson, David E A..............................06-Apr-07	Collier, David...01-Sep-07
Moore, Alison L....................................20-Oct-06	Benton, William A J...............................06-Apr-07	Crook, Richard.......................................01-Sep-07
Pearson, Liam M..................................20-Oct-06	Goddard, Alexander C 06-Apr-07	De Silva, Oliver A 01-Sep-07
Quant, Jacqueline R.............................20-Oct-06	Hernon, Robert T B................................06-Apr-07	De'Maine, Robert...................................01-Sep-07
Ayers, Oliver R B..................................01-Nov-06	Livingstone, Colin S...............................06-Apr-07	Dore, Christopher..................................01-Sep-07
Brady, Matthew V.................................01-Nov-06	Rowe, Antony N.....................................06-Apr-07	Drennan, David G..................................01-Sep-07
Flegg, William J....................................01-Nov-06	Stevenson, Alexander N.........................06-Apr-07	Dunn, Giles...01-Sep-07
Holburt, Richard M..............................01-Nov-06	Aitken, Neil D..01-May-07	Edwards, Gavin R...................................01-Sep-07
Roberts, David.....................................01-Nov-06	Anderson, Michael I C............................01-May-07	Fenwick, Steven G 01-Sep-07
Rose, Mark N.......................................30-Nov-06	Beck, Andrew J.......................................01-May-07	Flint, Grahame.......................................01-Sep-07
	Carter, Andrew J M................................01-May-07	Graham, Benjamin R...............................01-Sep-07
2007	Erhahiemen, Peter E..............................01-May-07	Guy, Elizabeth..01-Sep-07
	Evans, Peter A.......................................01-May-07	Howard, Martin J 01-Sep-07
Bakewell, Emma C................................01-Jan-07	Everest, Becky..01-May-07	Hunter, Darran J....................................01-Sep-07
Chatterley-Evans, Dawn A.....................01-Jan-07	Gatenby, Daniel.....................................01-May-07	Isted, Lee R..01-Sep-07
Cheshire, Thomas S 01-Jan-07	Holloway, Benjamin S V..........................01-May-07	Laird, Iain A...01-Sep-07
Curnock, Timothy C R............................01-Jan-07	Keenan, Douglas J 01-May-07	Latham, Daniel G 01-Sep-07
Fellows, Christopher R 01-Jan-07	Murray, Jamie C 01-May-07	Lewis, Robert G 01-Sep-07
Fitzgibbon, John P 01-Jan-07	Peacock, Laura G J.................................01-May-07	Little, Jonathan I....................................01-Sep-07
Gillingham, George...............................01-Jan-07	Salt, Jennifer M......................................01-May-07	Pepper, Nicholas R.................................01-Sep-07
Guy, Frances L......................................01-Jan-07	Skinner, Neil D.......................................01-May-07	Richards, Robert D 01-Sep-07
Henderson, Andrew G 01-Jan-07	Tudor, Owen J..01-May-07	Rogers, Phillip R 01-Sep-07
Inglis, William S....................................01-Jan-07	Vincent, Christopher 01-May-07	Rutter, John C..01-Sep-07
Jones, Marc R.......................................01-Jan-07	Zitkus, John J...01-May-07	Stephen, Cameron E..............................01-Sep-07
Kelley, Alexandra L...............................01-Jan-07	Blenkinsop, Graham J............................02-May-07	Thomas, Katie J C 01-Sep-07
Latchem, Andrew J 01-Jan-07	Berry, David H..01-Jun-07	Walker, Graeme H 01-Sep-07
Lees, Adrian C S....................................01-Jan-07	Breckenridge, Robert J...........................01-Jun-07	Wallace, Kirsty E....................................01-Sep-07
Macrae, Kirk...01-Jan-07	Hutchinson, Gillian P.............................01-Jun-07	Williams-Allden, Lucy A..........................01-Sep-07
Mehta, Jennifer C K..............................01-Jan-07	Johnson, Matthew D..............................01-Jun-07	Wylie, Justin J..01-Sep-07
Montagu, Timothy B E P 01-Jan-07	Kelly, Patrick J.......................................01-Jun-07	Yates, Simon P.......................................01-Sep-07
Morrow, Oliver.....................................01-Jan-07	Macleod, Alastair M...............................01-Jun-07	Lawrence-Archer, Sally E S......................07-Sep-07
Patterson, Pascal X...............................01-Jan-07	Rock, James A..01-Jun-07	Turner, Gareth J 19-Sep-07
Pearson, Sarah I...................................01-Jan-07	Rowntree, Paul J....................................01-Jun-07	Cocks, Anthony......................................01-Oct-07
Powell, Philip J.....................................01-Jan-07	Taylor, Stephen R...................................01-Jun-07	Mason, Angus E......................................01-Oct-07
Rose, Simon P......................................01-Jan-07	McAlpine, Martin A................................08-Jun-07	Higson, Rennie.......................................05-Oct-07
Royston, Sarah L...................................01-Jan-07	Pearson, Andrew C 08-Jun-07	Cleaves, Richard A 19-Oct-07
Smith, Jennifer C..................................01-Jan-07	Potter, Ian...08-Jun-07	Cowie, Michael......................................19-Oct-07
Stackhouse, Martyn C...........................01-Jan-07	Wilson, Mark J.......................................08-Jun-07	Craig, David...19-Oct-07
Vincent, Stuart M.................................01-Jan-07	Coleman, Alexander P G.........................01-Jul-07	Gordon, Daniel......................................19-Oct-07
Waskett, Daniel....................................01-Jan-07	Leonard, Thomas...................................01-Jul-07	Lockley, Simon M...................................19-Oct-07
McClelland, Patrick W............................07-Jan-07	Magill, Alasdair......................................01-Jul-07	Stanbury, David R...................................19-Oct-07
Ingram, Dean D....................................20-Jan-07	Blackbourn, Stephen A 27-Jul-07	Lane, Roland J 20-Oct-07
Jacques, Kathryn..................................24-Jan-07	Bonner, Daniel......................................27-Jul-07	Abbott, Duncan A J...............................01-Nov-07
Boswell, Laura J....................................29-Jan-07	Davis, Mark S...27-Jul-07	Cooper, Darren T...................................01-Nov-07
Jones, Toby..01-Feb-07	Harwood, Carl D....................................27-Jul-07	Crawford, Alistair A................................01-Nov-07
Phillips, Edward H L..............................01-Feb-07	Holroyd, Jason H....................................27-Jul-07	Darcy, John D...01-Nov-07
Pilkington, Barry M...............................01-Feb-07	Hutton, Paul R.......................................27-Jul-07	Edwards-Bannon, William J J...................01-Nov-07
Scott, Peter D.......................................01-Feb-07	Jenkins, David N.....................................27-Jul-07	Floyer, Hugo G.......................................01-Nov-07
Skinner, Amy L......................................01-Feb-07	Kew, Nigel...27-Jul-07	Gleave, Robert D....................................01-Nov-07
Taylor, Neil R..01-Feb-07	Stockton, Barry G..................................27-Jul-07	Goose, Samuel J 01-Nov-07
Williams, James L..................................01-Feb-07	Kidd, Andrew N 01-Aug-07	Henderson, Holly A................................01-Nov-07
Devine, Alison.......................................12-Feb-07		

LIEUTENANTS

Parmar, Bhavna R	01-Nov-07	
Shattock, James D	01-Nov-07	
Skelton, Richard S	01-Nov-07	
Southall, Nicholas C J	01-Nov-07	
Taylor, Marc G	01-Nov-07	
Taylor, Matthew R	01-Nov-07	
White, Kristopher	01-Nov-07	
Young, Andrew O G	01-Nov-07	
Moloney, Benjamin G	08-Nov-07	
Neave, James R	01-Dec-07	
Fergus-Hunt, Gregory	07-Dec-07	

2008

Bayliss, James E L	01-Jan-08
Bennett, Elizabeth C	01-Jan-08
Boothroyd-Gibbs, Adam P	01-Jan-08
Clark, Oliver R	01-Jan-08
Davidson, Gregor J	01-Jan-08
Davies, Alex	01-Jan-08
Dimmock, Guy N	01-Jan-08
Faulkner, Sally E	01-Jan-08
Faulkner, Simon	01-Jan-08
Forrest, David J	01-Jan-08
Graddon, Giles J	01-Jan-08
Griffiths, Beth	01-Jan-08
Guest, Craig A	01-Jan-08
Jackson, Amie R	01-Jan-08
Ker, Catherine M	01-Jan-08
Lister, Shaun	01-Jan-08
Lockley, Kelly M	01-Jan-08
Luke, Christopher	01-Jan-08
Mounsey, Carl A	01-Jan-08
Price, Matthew W	01-Jan-08
Roulston-Eldridge, James W C	01-Jan-08
Smalley, Paul J	01-Jan-08
Smith, James A	01-Jan-08
Swales, Richard	01-Jan-08
Unsworth, Benjamin M	01-Jan-08
Wood, Frederick J	01-Jan-08
Woods, James D	01-Jan-08
Wotton, Ryan J	01-Jan-08
Wright, James A H	01-Jan-08
Wright, Paul D	01-Jan-08
George, James A	01-Feb-08
Harkin, James P	01-Feb-08
Hendrickx, Sarah	01-Feb-08
Higgins, Carla L	01-Feb-08
Holbrook, Simon J	01-Feb-08
Loughran, Oliver A G	01-Feb-08
Mitchell, Andrew J	01-Feb-08
Munn-Bookless, Kerri	01-Feb-08
Newton, Owen	01-Feb-08
Nottingham, James M	01-Feb-08
Raval, Vivek	01-Feb-08
Skelley, Roger	01-Feb-08
Wall, Thomas C	01-Feb-08
Weller, Jamie K	01-Feb-08
Woodward, Alasdair J	01-Feb-08
Reid, James	07-Feb-08
Seaman, Alec L	10-Feb-08
Kent, Robert	12-Feb-08

Lockett, Alexander T	13-Feb-08
Mowthorpe, Sarah L	19-Feb-08
Rich, Duncan	19-Feb-08
Sawyer, Jason L	20-Feb-08
Black, Kenneth J	01-Mar-08
McLaughlan, Christopher T	01-Mar-08
Turley, Richard A	04-Mar-08
Hunter, Deryk J C	15-Mar-08
Townsend, Anna M	22-Mar-08
Adams, Joanne F	01-Apr-08
Benton, Simon A	01-Apr-08
Britton, Gemma L	01-Apr-08
Haynes, Samuel	01-Apr-08
Holland, Edward R	01-Apr-08
Horn, Neil R	01-Apr-08
Joynes, Vivienne	01-Apr-08
Kirby, Benjamin P C	01-Apr-08
Munro, Angus R	01-Apr-08
O'Sullivan, Daniel A N	01-Apr-08
Parri, Eifion L	01-Apr-08
Peachey, Sarah L	01-Apr-08
Talmage, Charles R H	01-Apr-08
Brown, Marc A	11-Apr-08
Clark, David J	11-Apr-08
Crawford, Jonathan B	11-Apr-08
Johnston, David R	11-Apr-08
Lees, Christopher M	11-Apr-08
Miles, Gary A MBE	11-Apr-08
Moseley, James F	11-Apr-08
Saw, Stephen	11-Apr-08
Taylor, Mark A	11-Apr-08
Parker-Carn, Rebecca L	17-Apr-08
Cattanach, James I	01-May-08
Drummond, Anthony S	01-May-08
Hazell, Emma V	01-May-08
Holland, Richard	01-May-08
Oxley, James D	01-May-08
Wetherfield, Sarah F	01-May-08
Spackman, Lucy C	19-May-08
Macdonald, Alastair J	20-May-08
Neil, Alexander G	20-May-08
Beacham, Sophie R	01-Jun-08
Daly, Christopher D	01-Jun-08
Davison, Warren M	01-Jun-08
Everett, Oliver	01-Jun-08
Hammond, Sean J	01-Jun-08
Harris, Christopher G W	01-Jun-08
Hastings, Craig S	01-Jun-08
Major, William	01-Jun-08
McArdle, Martin J	01-Jun-08
Noble, Robert	04-Jun-08
Batsford, Gareth E	13-Jun-08
Boulding, Andrew D	13-Jun-08
Jones, Christopher	13-Jun-08
McNaught, Chilton J	13-Jun-08
Cantillon, Lloyd M	16-Jun-08
Duffin, Colin J	01-Jul-08
Johnston, Gregory P	01-Jul-08
Thompson, Penelope M	01-Jul-08
Reeves, Simon J	08-Jul-08
Ross, David C	31-Jul-08

Akerman, Andrew E	01-Aug-08
Blakeman, Philip M	01-Aug-08
Cane, Jonathan	01-Aug-08
Clarkson, Paul J I	01-Aug-08
David, Ian	01-Aug-08
Filewod, Roger B	01-Aug-08
Greason, Paul A	01-Aug-08
Hayes, Leigh C	01-Aug-08
Howell, Andrew J	01-Aug-08
Kennedy, Elizabeth H	01-Aug-08
Keyworth, Mark A	01-Aug-08
Pizii, Jane V	01-Aug-08
Prosser, Jason W	01-Aug-08
Vines, Sarah K	09-Aug-08
Ashley, Stephen J	01-Sep-08
Beaumont, Richard	01-Sep-08
Betchley, Hannah M	01-Sep-08
Blackwell, Mark E	01-Sep-08
Blatcher, David J	01-Sep-08
Boardman, Andrew	01-Sep-08
Bowmer, Christopher J	01-Sep-08
Britten, Benjamin T	01-Sep-08
Burrows, Thomas G	01-Sep-08
Butcher, Mark W	01-Sep-08
Caddy, Paul D	01-Sep-08
Constable, Thomas	01-Sep-08
Couzens, Robert F	01-Sep-08
Cozens, Christopher J	01-Sep-08
Cuff, Samuel H	01-Sep-08
Cullen, Donna M	01-Sep-08
Dart, Michael P	01-Sep-08
Davis, Mark J	01-Sep-08
Dietz, Laura M	01-Sep-08
Dunbar, Ross	01-Sep-08
Edwards, Luke	01-Sep-08
Fielder, Andrew J	01-Sep-08
Forrester, Michael A	01-Sep-08
Forsyth, Adam L	01-Sep-08
Gilmore, Amy F	01-Sep-08
Greaves, Michael	01-Sep-08
Gresswell, Nick A	01-Sep-08
Hall, Allan J	01-Sep-08
Hallatt, Nicholas E	01-Sep-08
Hill, Ross	01-Sep-08
Hillard, Christopher	01-Sep-08
Hollingworth, Eleanor	01-Sep-08
Howe, Michael	01-Sep-08
Johnson, Thomas	01-Sep-08
Jones, Steven F	01-Sep-08
Ker, Stuart W	01-Sep-08
Knight, Richard J	01-Sep-08
Leadbeater, Mark K	01-Sep-08
Lever, Thomas J	01-Sep-08
Main, Matthew G	01-Sep-08
Martin, Harry C	01-Sep-08
McNally, Barry J	01-Sep-08
Penfold, Andrew J	01-Sep-08
Reed, Peter K MBE	01-Sep-08
Ross, Jamie M	01-Sep-08
Seager, Daniel	01-Sep-08
Shirley, Benjamin	01-Sep-08

LIEUTENANTS

2009

Smith, Ashley	01-Sep-08
Thorpe, Richard J	01-Sep-08
Tibbitts, James A	01-Sep-08
Turner, Kevin P	01-Sep-08
Tweed, Jonathan J	01-Sep-08
Walker, Fergus S	01-Sep-08
Wells, Michael J	01-Sep-08
Widdowson, Matthew G	01-Sep-08
Young, Neil	01-Sep-08
Revell, Aaron D	30-Sep-08
Bye, Ashley	01-Oct-08
Castrinoyannakis, Timothy	01-Oct-08
Duke, Jonathan A	01-Oct-08
Dunning, Stephen T O	01-Oct-08
Gell, Thomas	01-Oct-08
Giffin, Iain	01-Oct-08
Hazelwood, Graeme	01-Oct-08
Moreland, James R M	01-Oct-08
Norton, Lee A	01-Oct-08
Pritchard, Christopher W	01-Oct-08
Rebbeck, Christopher	01-Oct-08
Smith, Nicholas	01-Oct-08
Thompson, Simon C	01-Oct-08
McElroy-Baker, Lindsey	17-Oct-08
Coles-Hendry, Hamish R	20-Oct-08
Hepworth, Nicholas P	20-Oct-08
Kent, Andrew G	20-Oct-08
Redpath, Scott D	20-Oct-08
Sharland, Craig J	20-Oct-08
Shaw, Ramsay	20-Oct-08
Young, Michael	20-Oct-08
Benzie, Andrew	23-Oct-08
Court, Shane J	24-Oct-08
Falconer, Paul	24-Oct-08
Harrison, Ellen	24-Oct-08
Hewitt, Adrian J	24-Oct-08
Kemp, Peter	24-Oct-08
Bratt, James R	01-Nov-08
Clarke, Steven P	01-Nov-08
Collins, Stephen J	01-Nov-08
Whittington, Christopher C	01-Nov-08
Helliwell, Thomas P	01-Dec-08
Maclennan, Neil R	01-Dec-08
Marriott, Isabella M C	01-Dec-08
Mason, Christopher	01-Dec-08
Ward, Antony J	01-Dec-08
Stone, Nicholas S	11-Dec-08
Haynes, Warren E	18-Dec-08
Bond, Ian	19-Dec-08
Charles, Steven R	19-Dec-08
Clough, Warren S	19-Dec-08
Howe, Neil D	19-Dec-08
Linehan, Paul R	19-Dec-08
McEvoy, Jason L	19-Dec-08
Myhill, Johnathen J	19-Dec-08
O'Reilly, Paul A	19-Dec-08
Thompson, Michelle E	19-Dec-08
Wallace, Nicola K	19-Dec-08
Wilson, Iain E	19 Dec-08

Adlam, Charlotte	01-Jan-09
Briscoe, Daniel A	01-Jan-09
Campbell, Colin	01-Jan-09
Carthey, Ben	01-Jan-09
Chambers, Joanne M	01-Jan-09
Charlesworth, Nicholas J	01-Jan-09
Court, Nicholas J	01-Jan-09
Grayland, Andrew	01-Jan-09
Hall, Daniel	01-Jan-09
Instrell, Christopher B	01-Jan-09
Jones, Morgan	01-Jan-09
Langley, David J	01-Jan-09
Parker, Sarah E	01-Jan-09
Paton, Mark W	01-Jan-09
Phelan, Sean C	01-Jan-09
Radcliffe, Gemma L	01-Jan-09
Richardson, James	01-Jan-09
Snazell, Matthew A	01-Jan-09
Thompson, Simon J	01-Jan-09
Tin, Jennifer M J	01-Jan-09
Tingle, Dawn	01-Jan-09
Zauchenberger, Michael J	01-Jan-09
Glendinning, Vicky L	16-Jan-09
Benbow, Melanie	01-Feb-09
Benbow, William	01-Feb-09
Cooper, Michael A	01-Feb-09
Crewdson, Robert P	01-Feb-09
Daw, Arthur B	01-Feb-09
Howard, James W	01-Feb-09
Hunt, Robert G	01-Feb-09
Kilbride, Paul	01-Feb-09
Knight, Alexander J	01-Feb-09
Mitchell, Aleesha W	01-Feb-09
Roberts, Joel	01-Feb-09
Sharp, Christopher A	01-Feb-09
Smith, Edwin J	01-Feb-09
Thomas, Matthew	01-Feb-09
White, Andrew J	01-Feb-09
White, Mark	01-Feb-09
Boaden, Christopher S	19-Feb-09
Clarke, Paul A	21-Feb-09
Patrick, Christopher M	21-Feb-09
Peppitt, Christopher J	21-Feb-09
Santrian, Mark	21-Feb-09
Wardle, Gareth S	21-Feb-09
Weatherall, Mark	21-Feb-09
Weetch, Matthew E	21-Feb-09
Ashley-Smith, R	01-Mar-09
Ashton, Megan E	01-Mar-09
Brown, Rebecca J	01-Mar-09
Curry, Philip D	01-Mar-09
Glover, Adam	01-Mar-09
Grimes, Keith M	01-Mar-09
Hart, Daniel A	01-Mar-09
Le Poidevin, Ian W	01-Mar-09
Meldrum, Richard A	01-Mar-09
Nwokora, Dal	01-Mar-09
Parker, Simon O	01-Mar-09
Smith, Dale A	01-Mar-09
Ward, Gareth J	01-Mar-09

Wilkinson, John	01-Mar-09
Kerr, Martin A	22-Mar-09
Andrews, Alistair J	01-Apr-09
Bayliss, James P	01-Apr-09
Carter, Holly	01-Apr-09
Chandler, Russell S	01-Apr-09
Dockerty, Neil C	01-Apr-09
Hall, Stephen J	01-Apr-09
Hole, Joseph S I	01-Apr-09
Horne, Nicholas	01-Apr-09
Lee, Ross J	01-Apr-09
Lofts, Anthony J R	01-Apr-09
Prevett, Adam M	01-Apr-09
Prouse, Scott	01-Apr-09
Retallick, Katherine A	01-Apr-09
Ridley, George	01-Apr-09
Ruscoe, David I	01-Apr-09
Thornton, Charles A G	01-Apr-09
Wallace, James G	01-Apr-09
Stellon, Christopher	02-Apr-09
Beaumont, Alan J	09-Apr-09
Bicker, Richard E	09-Apr-09
Bower, Dean A MSC	09-Apr-09
Cooper, John C	09-Apr-09
Cooper, John D	09-Apr-09
Crease, David A	09-Apr-09
Gardner, Sadie J	09-Apr-09
Lappin, Adam J	09-Apr-09
Magill, Hal R	09-Apr-09
McClaren, Ronni	09-Apr-09
Oldham, David J	09-Apr-09
Simpson, Paul G	09-Apr-09
Spreckley, Damian R C	09-Apr-09
Turner, Gary H	09-Apr-09
Craig, Alexander P	01-May-09
Dalton, Ebony	01-May-09
Harmer, Deborah D	01-May-09
Hayes, Paul	01-May-09
Jeffrey, Ben S	01-May-09
Lippitt, Benjamin J	01-May-09
Read, Benjamin	01-May-09
Wilmot, Max A	01-May-09
Murray, Audrey R	19-May-09
Heap, Matthew J	20-May-09
Jordan, Craig D	20-May-09
Boyall, Duane R	01-Jun-09
Fane-Bailey, Verity M	01-Jun-09
Halford, Mark L	01-Jun-09
King, Matthew	01-Jun-09
McMorrow, Kevin M	01-Jun-09
Ritchie, Stuart D	01-Jun-09
Suckling, Christopher	01-Jun-09
Thompson, Sam D	01-Jun-09
Vasey, Owen R	01-Jun-09
Warner, Stephen E	01-Jun-09
Bodkin, Lee	01-Jul-09
Fitzpatrick, Michael J	01-Jul-09
Jack, Valencera	01-Jul-09
Laird, Douglas A	01-Jul-09
Masawi, Sydney K	01-Jul-09
Newns, Adam D	01-Jul-09

LIEUTENANTS

Humphreys, Rhodri H	08-Jul-09	
Wade, Nicholas J	30-Jul-09	
Anderson, Martin	31-Jul-09	
Bennett-Smith, Paula	31-Jul-09	
Dodd, Craig	31-Jul-09	
Douglas, Jason	31-Jul-09	
Evans, Russell F	31-Jul-09	
Harris, Michael B	31-Jul-09	
Lees, Rachel H	31-Jul-09	
Morgan, Michael C	31-Jul-09	
Morrison, Philip C	31-Jul-09	
Murgatroyd, Steven A	31-Jul-09	
Nicholson, Christopher J	31-Jul-09	
Pearson, Ellis	31-Jul-09	
Quirke, Fraser J	31-Jul-09	
Roddy, Christopher M	31-Jul-09	
Simpson, Brett R	31-Jul-09	
Smith, Barry J	31-Jul-09	
Stark, Justin R	31-Jul-09	
Steele, Jason M	31-Jul-09	
Thompson-Pettit, Richard J	31-Jul-09	
Ford, Jonathan R	01-Aug-09	
McCrossan, Amy	01-Aug-09	
Melvin, John J	01-Aug-09	
Stephenson, John	01-Aug-09	
Judd, Oliver J	19-Aug-09	
Lanc, Adam J	19-Aug-09	
Clasby, Lorraine	21-Aug-09	
A'Hern, Paul V	01-Sep-09	
Barnes, David C	01-Sep-09	
Bright, Jack MBE	01-Sep-09	
Cambrook, Laura	01-Sep-09	
Currie, Stephen	01-Sep-09	
Dando, Benjamin J	01-Sep-09	
Dodd, Shaun	01-Sep-09	
Dowse, Andrew R	01-Sep-09	
Edwards, John D	01-Sep-09	
Frampton, Charles	01-Sep-09	
Garner, Robert J	01-Sep-09	
Harding, Daniel L	01-Sep-09	
Higgins, Edward	01-Sep-09	
Leckey, Timothy	01-Sep-09	
Lovell, James H	01-Sep-09	
Middleditch, Thomas C	01-Sep-09	
Nelson, Bartholomew J	01-Sep-09	
Norcott, James P	01-Sep-09	
Orchard, Jonathan J	01-Sep-09	
Orton, Trevellyan	01-Sep-09	
Perks, Matthew D	01-Sep-09	
Polley, Christopher F	01-Sep-09	
Rake, Rachael	01-Sep-09	
Rogers, James	01-Sep-09	
Scott, Andrew R D	01-Sep-09	
Seaman, Gregg P	01-Sep-09	
Shepherd, Oliver J	01-Sep-09	
Smith, Laurence M	01-Sep-09	
Stevens, Christopher K	01-Sep-09	
Trowman, Oliver S	01-Sep-09	
Wallington-Smith, James	01-Sep-09	
Watkis, Andrew N	01-Sep-09	
Wells, Antony E	01-Sep-09	

Young, Martin N W	01-Sep-09
Gow, Peter J	16-Sep-09
Bailey, David J	01-Oct-09
Bradshaw, James P	01-Oct-09
Douthwaite, Stuart J	01-Oct-09
Fox, Christopher J	01-Oct-09
Frost, Robert W	01-Oct-09
Harvey, Matthew D H	01-Oct-09
House, Andrew L	01-Oct-09
Jones, Gemma E	01-Oct-09
Knight, Anthony R	01-Oct-09
Knight, Richard J	01-Oct-09
Macnae, Bridget R	01-Oct-09
Mason, Victoria J	01-Oct-09
McClean, Stephen	01-Oct-09
Metcalfe, Lauren J	01-Oct-09
Pounder, Richard H G	01-Oct-09
Snell, Daley A	01-Oct-09
Williams, Matthew R	01-Oct-09
Lassoued, Alexander N	14-Oct-09
Ling, Peter A	20-Oct-09
Richardson, Stuart J	20-Oct-09
Rotherham, Dominic L	20-Oct-09
Westlake, Simon	20-Oct-09
Santrian, Tracey M	26-Oct-09
Kenchington, Robin A W	01-Nov-09
Rose, Victoria	01-Nov-09
Routledge, Rosemary P	01-Nov-09
Meaden, Alexander P	19-Nov-09
Tuckwood, Alex I	19-Nov-09
Wilson, Nicholas C	19-Nov-09
Miller, Shane R	24-Nov-09
Harding, Matthew J	01-Dec-09
Starsmore, Daniel L	01-Dec-09
Straker, Peter D	01-Dec-09
White, Paul	01-Dec-09
Allan, John M	08-Dec-09
Baker, Mark A	08-Dec-09
Allen, Lloyd N	11-Dec-09
Burgess, Maxine J	11-Dec-09
Donbavand, David W	11-Dec-09
Fraser, Gordon A	11-Dec-09
Hanks, Richard M	11-Dec-09
Hearnden, Simon T	11-Dec-09
Inglesby, Paul R	11-Dec-09
Kempley, Paul S	11-Dec-09
Martin, Brian H	11-Dec-09
Morley, David J	11-Dec-09
Moss, Stewart J	11-Dec-09
O'Malley, James P	11-Dec-09
Parker, Neil A	11-Dec-09
Roberts, John A	11-Dec-09
Sampson, Jonathan A	11-Dec-09
Smithson, James I	11-Dec-09
Wright, Justin C	11-Dec-09
Basketfield, Wayne	17-Dec-09
McPhee, Thomas J	17-Dec-09
Williams, Nigel	17-Dec-09
Day, Richard J	21-Dec-09

2010

Breward, Daniel P	01-Jan-10
Flynn, Christopher	01-Jan-10
Grimmer, Nicholas G	01-Jan-10
Huntley, Genevieve E	01-Jan-10
Maumy, Jonathan	01-Jan-10
O'Connell, Heather	01-Jan-10
Phillips, John R	01-Jan-10
Platt, Maximilian J G	01-Jan-10
Rose, Ian D	01-Jan-10
Rowlands, Andrew P	01-Jan-10
Teare, Matthew R	01-Jan-10
Weal, Gregory R	01-Jan-10
Bell, David	01-Feb-10
Edwards, Cassandra J	01-Feb-10
French, Rebecca	01-Feb-10
Gilmore, Martin A	01-Feb-10
Greenwood, Julia L	01-Feb-10
Hamer, Scott A	01-Feb-10
Keith, Charles R	01-Feb-10
Laird, Ellen L	01-Feb-10
Palmer, Nicholas J C	01-Feb-10
Patterson, Paul	01-Feb-10
Thomas, James M	01-Feb-10
Wilson, Kayleigh J	01-Feb-10
Mehta, Christopher	19-Feb-10
Cameron, Sam	01-Mar-10
Clarke, Richard W	01-Mar-10
Gayson, Christopher P	01-Mar-10
Goddard, James A T	01-Mar-10
McClelland, Ian	01-Mar-10
Milne, Roderick M	01-Mar-10
Oliphant, Helen	01-Mar-10
Scown, William O	01-Mar-10
Thomas, Richard	01-Mar-10
Welch, Danielle S	01-Mar-10
Furneaux, James	21-Mar-10
Musgrave, Thomas E	21-Mar-10
Coutts, Maxwell G	22-Mar-10
Calvert, Lauren J	01-Apr-10
Cooke, Benjamin R	01-Apr-10
Dalrymple, James	01-Apr-10
Davies, Julia	01-Apr-10
Green, Nicholas D W	01-Apr-10
Martin, Andrew J	01-Apr-10
Parsonson, Max E	01-Apr-10
Sanocki, Anna M	01-Apr-10
Winwood, Matthew R	01-Apr-10
Allen-Scholey, Spencer G	09-Apr-10
Barr, Simon J C	09-Apr-10
Bean, Edward C	09-Apr-10
Bray, Michael A	09-Apr-10
Cave, Simon J	09-Apr-10
Green, Mark D	09-Apr-10
Hendra, Allan J	09-Apr-10
Jakes, Matthew O	09-Apr-10
Miller, Adam E	09-Apr-10
Radcliffe, Albert P	09-Apr-10
Rigby, Lee A	09-Apr-10
Roberts, Peter N	09-Apr-10
Steele, Matthew E	09-Apr-10

LIEUTENANTS

Williams, Andrew F.....................09-Apr-10	Aston, James A 01-Aug-10	Kenyon, Adam M..........................01-Nov-10
De-Saint-Bissix-Croix, Anna M................13-Apr-10	Bolton, James D...........................01-Aug-10	O'Connell, Daniel............................01-Nov-10
Crouch, Benjamin R.............................01-May-10	Cairns-Holder, Declan P.......................20-Aug-10	Parker, Richard B............................01-Nov-10
Ford, Brendan R.................................01-May-10	Amor, Matthew 01-Sep-10	Pearce, Stephen F 01-Nov-10
Greenwood, David R...........................01-May-10	Boarder, Richard J 01-Sep-10	Poulson, Christopher 01-Nov-10
Morgan, Ashley K................................01-May-10	Bone, Matthew...............................01-Sep-10	Quilter, Gail.....................................01-Nov-10
Rickard, James J.................................01-May-10	Bowler, Thomas 01-Sep-10	Szweda, Alexander A........................01-Nov-10
Tarbard, Gavin T.................................01-May-10	Cooper, Jack W................................01-Sep-10	Taylor, Matthew R A........................01-Nov-10
Thompson, James N E.........................01-May-10	Devonport, Sean S 01-Sep-10	Tristram, Robert E............................01-Nov-10
Bate, Christopher............................20-May-10	Duncan, Ross D...............................01-Sep-10	Winterton, Gemma..........................01-Nov-10
Watsham, Richard V............................20-May-10	Durbin, William J..............................01-Sep-10	Nicholls, Edward W..........................12-Nov-10
Roberts, Andrew.................................23-May-10	Emptage, Michael A..........................01-Sep-10	Cash, Rupert.....................................19-Nov-10
Day, Paul A 27-May-10	Fitton, Daniel 01-Sep-10	Butler, James M................................17-Dec-10
Dean, Adam C...................................01-Jun-10	Garton, Hazelle M.............................01-Sep-10	Coates, Jonathan R..........................17-Dec-10
Edmonds, Jon S 01-Jun-10	Grandy, Mark...................................01-Sep-10	Dobson, Richard E............................17-Dec-10
Elvy, Susan D.....................................01-Jun-10	Henton, James M..............................01-Sep-10	Edwards, Neal P 17-Dec-10
Foreman, Louisa.................................01-Jun-10	Jones, Christopher 01-Sep-10	Fletcher, Christopher P 17-Dec-10
Funnell, Lee C 01-Jun-10	Kneller, James 01-Sep-10	Gill, Lee 17-Dec-10
Harris, Alexandra K.............................01-Jun-10	Lawrence, Kevin 01-Sep-10	Guthrie, Lee D K 17-Dec-10
Heritage, Francis 01-Jun-10	Longia, Sandeep 01-Sep-10	Hunnybun, Simon P 17-Dec-10
Holt, Laura..01-Jun-10	Mace, Stephen J 01-Sep-10	McAllister, Kevin J 17-Dec-10
Jones, William A 01-Jun-10	Mackay, Richard...............................01-Sep-10	Moulding, Mark D 17-Dec-10
Lee, Daniel C 01-Jun-10	Maclean, Graeme P...........................01-Sep-10	Salisbury, Dominic B A......................17-Dec-10
Marsden, Christopher N......................01-Jun-10	Marshall, David S 01-Sep-10	Shaw, Mathew J C 17-Dec-10
Melling, Paul G 01-Jun-10	McCann, Andrew G 01-Sep-10	Smith, Gary J 17-Dec-10
Parks, Natasha 01-Jun-10	Murray, Simon O 01-Sep-10	Strange, Jamie L...............................17-Dec-10
Pavie, Richard M 01-Jun-10	Nason, Thomas J...............................01-Sep-10	Turrell, Richard D..............................17-Dec-10
Pelham Burn, Alexander......................01-Jun-10	Packer, Lee J.....................................01-Sep-10	Wheldon, Adam J.............................17-Dec-10
Powell, Robert 01-Jun-10	Porteous, Cameron W B.....................01-Sep-10	Fulker, Edward P 20-Dec-10
Roach, Darren J..................................01-Jun-10	Raffle, Edward J 01-Sep-10	
Staveley, Catherine B B........................01-Jun-10	Rees-Hughes, Victoria L......................01-Sep-10	**2011**
Steele, Katie......................................01-Jun-10	Roberts, David G...............................01-Sep-10	Best, Alexander.................................01-Jan-11
Thomas, Michael J 01-Jun-10	Roberts, Thomas R J 01-Sep-10	Collins, Simon H 01-Jan-11
Thurston, Edward K P 01-Jun-10	Shine, David J 01-Sep-10	Farquharson, Craig I..........................01-Jan-11
Wheatcroft, Ian J 01-Jun-10	Simmons, Sarah................................01-Sep-10	Ferguson, Calum...............................01-Jan-11
Mawdsley, Owen R 07-Jun-10	Simpson, Daley G..............................01-Sep-10	Gibbs, Emily K...................................01-Jan-11
Hall, Victoria J...................................16-Jun-10	Targett, Edward G.............................01-Sep-10	Mould, Christopher W 01-Jan-11
Rowlands, Sarah J 19-Jun-10	Taylor, Alexander I 01-Sep-10	Oram, Cemal....................................01-Jan-11
Kyme, Robert.....................................01-Jul-10	Watkin, Paul 01-Sep-10	Sewell, Lynsey E 01-Jan-11
Martin, Alan F....................................01-Jul-10	Whitehead, Benjamin J 01-Sep-10	Taylor, Marian C 01-Jan-11
Carter, Laura J....................................08-Jul-10	Abbey, Rachel F.................................07-Sep-10	Yarker, Sam......................................01-Jan-11
Clark, Gordon D 08-Jul-10	Butler, Adam.....................................01-Oct-10	Balmond, Samuel J............................01-Feb-11
Lane, Paul V 09-Jul-10	Dorrington, Benjamin R.......................01-Oct-10	Gregory, Samuel G............................01-Feb-11
Cornhill, Sharon T...............................12-Jul-10	Elliott, David J 01-Oct-10	Laverick, Jonathan R 01-Feb-11
Ryan, Kathleen R 12-Jul-10	Maxwell, Hamish 01-Oct-10	Smith, William F................................01-Feb-11
Richards, Gregor I 20-Jul-10	Ray, Steven P....................................01-Oct-10	Stephen, Nicola.................................01-Feb-11
Williams, Amanda L............................20-Jul-10	Scamp, Simon J.................................01-Oct-10	Warland, Adam.................................01-Feb-11
Morrison, Mark J................................22-Jul-10	Schnetler, Simon F.............................01-Oct-10	Whatley, Mark..................................01-Feb-11
Barlow, Leonard J...............................30-Jul-10	Smillie, Eleanor J 01-Oct-10	Moore, Aimee C 20-Feb-11
Blick, Graham M J...............................30-Jul-10	Tuckwood, Neil E 01-Oct-10	Bray, Matthew 24-Feb-11
Boswell, Emma J 30-Jul-10	Wray, Philip......................................01-Oct-10	Morris, Alastair J 27-Feb-11
Evangelista, Paul G 30-Jul-10	Lomas, Timothy P..............................09-Oct-10	Andrews, Nicholas G.........................01-Mar-11
Griggs, James K..................................30-Jul-10	Watts, Thomas..................................10-Oct-10	Brown, Steven 01-Mar-11
Harper, Nicholas J 30-Jul-10	Hamlyn, Jonathan M..........................20-Oct-10	Clayton, John D 01-Mar-11
Hay, Phillip W....................................30-Jul-10	Powne, Laura....................................20-Oct-10	Crooks, Charles S..............................01-Mar-11
Hudson, Richard A..............................30-Jul-10	Bond, Frances 01-Nov-10	Driscoll, Adrian 01-Mar-11
Middleton, Shane A.............................30-Jul-10	Bowles, Daniel J 01-Nov-10	Edwards, Rhydian O..........................01-Mar-11
Rae, David M.....................................30-Jul-10	Brooksbank, Oliver 01-Nov-10	Fagan, Louis Vincent A 01-Mar-11
Rook, Christopher...............................30-Jul-10	Carver, James D 01-Nov-10	Hill, Jamie B 01-Mar-11
Smith, Kristian G.................................30-Jul-10	Fawcett, Benjamin E..........................01-Nov-10	Hughes, Adam A 01-Mar-11
Smith, Shelley A..................................30-Jul-10	Holborn, Lee J 01-Nov-10	Payne, Michael..................................01-Mar-11

LIEUTENANTS

Pugh, James	01-Mar-11	Said, Phillip M	15-Apr-11	Gill, Samuel R	01-Sep-11
Quilter, George	01-Mar-11	Stevens, Mark	15-Apr-11	Goodwin, Aaron K	01-Sep-11
Read, Matthew C	01-Mar-11	Taylor, David R	15-Apr-11	Gray, Richard G	01-Sep-11
Sawyer, Richard C	01-Mar-11	Tear, Trevor M	15-Apr-11	Green, Joseph R S	01-Sep-11
Twinn, Richard	01-Mar-11	Telford, Steven M	15-Apr-11	Greenfield, Stuart	01-Sep-11
Tysler, Charlotte G	01-Mar-11	Tolcher, Daniel G	15-Apr-11	Gregg, Ryan Lee	01-Sep-11
Wallis, Thomas O	01-Mar-11	Vaughan, Jamie B	15-Apr-11	Harradine, Sam A	01-Sep-11
Bailey, Andrew P	01-Apr-11	Pashneh-Tala, Samira	17-Apr-11	Hill, Oliver W	01-Sep-11
Barber, Christopher J	01-Apr-11	Miln, David	01-May-11	Ivory, Matthew J	01-Sep-11
Bartlett, Simon	01-Apr-11	Penfold, Daniel B	01-May-11	Jacks, Michael J	01-Sep-11
Biddlecombe, Hugh R	01-Apr-11	Sercombe, Daniel	01-May-11	Keeling, Megan	01-Sep-11
Boak, Philip R	01-Apr-11	Gayle, David M	31-May-11	Lanaghan, Richard	01-Sep-11
Bowler, James R	01-Apr-11	Carpenter, James E	01-Jun-11	Lane, Peter	01-Sep-11
Buchan, James	01-Apr-11	Denyer, Alistair C	01-Jun-11	Lea, Chloe	01-Sep-11
Carpenter, Neil P	01-Apr-11	Henderson, Simon A	01-Jun-11	Loxton, Thomas C	01-Sep-11
Docherty, Zoe	01-Apr-11	McLaughlin, Ian J	01-Jun-11	Mackay, Fraser R	01-Sep-11
Emory, David G	01-Apr-11	Fairbairn, Oliver	07-Jun-11	Marin-Ortega, Carl	01-Sep-11
Forster, Helen	01-Apr-11	Behan, Oliver M	01-Jul-11	Marshall, Alexander J	01-Sep-11
Gardner, Rachael	01-Apr-11	Campbell, Edward J	01-Jul-11	Mion, Jonathan J	01-Sep-11
Hannah, Edward C	01-Apr-11	Christie, Laura	01-Jul-11	Musgrove, Christopher	01-Sep-11
Hazel, Thomas W T	01-Apr-11	Costley-White, Benjamin M	01-Jul-11	Needle, Peter J	01-Sep-11
Henry, David T	01-Apr-11	Gillespie, Benjamin D	01-Jul-11	Oakes, Caroline F	01-Sep-11
Hoar, Mark E	01-Apr-11	Harwood, David P A	01-Jul-11	Oakley, Jonathon	01-Sep-11
Huggins, Michael A	01-Apr-11	Hems, Wendy L	01-Jul-11	Parker, Luke R	01-Sep-11
John, James	01-Apr-11	Holland, Paul E	01-Jul-11	Parks, Luke J	01-Sep-11
Johnstone-Burt, Charles E	01-Apr-11	Radue, Nicholas K	01-Jul-11	Platt, Andrew J	01-Sep-11
Laud, Nicola J	01-Apr-11	Richards, Jonathan C	01-Jul-11	Roessler, Philippa F	01-Sep-11
Lea, Oliver D P	01-Apr-11	Toms, Nicholas J M	01-Jul-11	Rowe, Joanne	01-Sep-11
Marsden, Daniel C	01-Apr-11	Wiseman, Hugo	01-Jul-11	Savery, Stuart L	01-Sep-11
Mason, John	01-Apr-11	Davey, Alistair J	08-Jul-11	Stephenson, Fiona	01-Sep-11
Moore, Robert W	01-Apr-11	Miller, David J S	08-Jul-11	Stradling, Duncan E	01-Sep-11
Parsons, Richard G	01-Apr-11	Napier, Gary	08-Jul-11	Swithinbank, George R	01-Sep-11
Raymont, Edward M	01-Apr-11	Piggott, Andrew J	08-Jul-11	Thomas, Charlotte	01-Sep-11
Read, Edmund A E	01-Apr-11	Scott, Jason	08-Jul-11	Wagstaffe, James N G	01-Sep-11
Rydiard, Michael	01-Apr-11	Brooking, Gary N	12-Jul-11	Wakefield, Matthew A	01-Sep-11
Samuel, Ben J	01-Apr-11	Longstaff, Thomas O M	20-Jul-11	Whittaker, Terry J	01-Sep-11
Smith, Jennifer	01-Apr-11	Lewis, Kieran	03-Aug-11	Williams, Gareth	01-Sep-11
Stiles, Maxine K	01-Apr-11	Allen-West, Bart J	05-Aug-11	Williford, Susanna J	01-Sep-11
Taylor, Helen M J	01-Apr-11	Barlow, Jay P	05-Aug-11	Durrant, Frederick	01-Oct-11
Teece, Nicholas J	01-Apr-11	Hinton, Oliver J	05-Aug-11	Gaskell-Taylor, Hugh M P	01-Oct-11
Thornton, William S C	01-Apr-11	Howe, David N	05-Aug-11	Goodley, Ross	01-Oct-11
Williams, Gareth	01-Apr-11	Lumsden, Gavin T	05-Aug-11	Irwin, Steven G	01-Oct-11
Witham, Katharine V	01-Apr-11	Rees-Swindon, Mikaela J	05-Aug-11	McCaughan, Christopher J	01-Oct-11
Gough, Christopher M	11-Apr-11	Christie, Andrew J	14-Aug-11	Millyard, Matthew	01-Oct-11
Shenton, Calvin L	13-Apr-11	Smith, Thomas	14-Aug-11	Mitchell, James E	01-Oct-11
Waud, Deborah	14-Apr-11	Adams, Keith J	01-Sep-11	Simpson, Daniel J R	01-Oct-11
Bernacchi, Jonathan P	15-Apr-11	Arnold, Lee J	01-Sep-11	Keens, Emma L	07-Oct-11
Biddulph, Andrew R	15-Apr-11	Balls, Christopher F	01-Sep-11	Walkley, Kyle J	07-Oct-11
Breen, Paul R	15-Apr-11	Barkey, Barry J	01-Sep-11	Winning, Robert A M	07-Oct-11
Bridge, James G	15-Apr-11	Bateson, Timothy N	01-Sep-11	Morrison, Ross	01-Nov-11
Davies, Andrew C	15-Apr-11	Blackburn, Thomas E	01-Sep-11	Niblock, Gillian	09-Nov-11
Fowler, Gareth S	15-Apr-11	Clark, Matthew H R	01-Sep-11	Manktelow, Benjamin T	01-Dec-11
Garth, Lee	15-Apr-11	Coates, Thomas M	01-Sep-11	Hedgecox, Philip R	08-Dec-11
Gwilliam, Richard J	15-Apr-11	Dyer, Martin L	01-Sep-11	Hughes, David M	08-Dec-11
Hammond, Tregaron	15-Apr-11	Eccles, Matthew P J	01-Sep-11	McElwaine, Christopher W	08-Dec-11
James, Darren B	15-Apr-11	Febbrarro, Luke N	01-Sep-11	Williams, David B	08-Dec-11
Jones, Steven K	15-Apr-11	Flowers, David J	01-Sep-11	Adkins, Paul S	16-Dec-11
Morton, David	15-Apr-11	Fuller, Lucy A J	01-Sep-11	Briggs, Christopher J	16-Dec-11
Murray, Sara N	15-Apr-11	Gallagher, Michael V	01-Sep-11	Davies, John P	16-Dec-11
Newman, Lee	15-Apr-11	Gaught, Edwin L	01-Sep-11	Hall, Christopher	16-Dec-11
Phillips, Paul J	15-Apr-11	Geddes, Nathaniel C S	01-Sep-11	Howe, Jonathan	16-Dec-11

LIEUTENANTS

Marrison, Andrew C 16-Dec-11	Neilan, Samuel J J 01-Mar-12	Dunthorne, Matthew S 13-Apr-12
Mellor, Andrew L 16-Dec-11	Vincent, Peter 01-Mar-12	Elston, Luke R 13-Apr-12
Robinson, Alan J 16-Dec-11	Wiltshire, Ross M 01-Mar-12	Frame, Wendy 13-Apr-12
Shaw, Christopher 16-Dec-11	Wiseman, Deborah J 01-Mar-12	Glover, Lee N 13-Apr-12
	Wordsworth, Joel K. 01-Mar-12	Harris, Neil P 13-Apr-12
2012	Wright, Christopher 01-Mar-12	James, Christopher I 13-Apr-12
	Armstrong, Paul 01-Apr-12	Jamieson, Scott M 13-Apr-12
Ashton, Karl 01-Jan-12	Barnett, Christopher J 01-Apr-12	Morrison, Kevin 13-Apr-12
Bennett, Oliver F 01-Jan-12	Brown, Rebecca K 01-Apr-12	Pitt, David 13-Apr-12
Blackledge, Benjamin P 01-Jan-12	Burrows, James R 01-Apr-12	Rowland, Justin M 13-Apr-12
Boddington, Hannah 01-Jan-12	Callender, James T 01-Apr-12	Tidswell, Stephen R 13-Apr-12
Burns, Natalie J 01-Jan-12	Cardy, Lloyd E 01-Apr-12	Sanders, Lee C 19-Apr-12
Canosa, Luis J 01-Jan-12	Colman, Adam J 01-Apr-12	Peters, Matthew T 01-May-12
Charlton, Andrew R 01-Jan-12	Cooke, James R 01-Apr-12	Jones, Richard P M 20-May-12
Corden, Adam 01-Jan-12	Currin, Joseph M 01-Apr-12	Cross, Aaron 01-Jun-12
Crosswood, Barry T 01-Jan-12	Dubois, Carina 01-Apr-12	Morris, Thomas O 01-Jun-12
Davey, Andrew J 01-Jan-12	Ebbitt, Henry 01-Apr-12	Ockleton, Christopher D 01-Jun-12
Finnie, Anthony M 01-Jan-12	Esbensen, Kristoffer P 01-Apr-12	Pocock, Oliver R 01-Jun-12
Fuller, Nicholas M 01-Jan-12	Evans, Joshua J 01-Apr-12	Quayle, Christopher A 01-Jun-12
Gibson, Andrew M 01-Jan-12	Ford, Christopher R C 01-Apr-12	Ross, Samuel K 01-Jun-12
Hall, Simon C 01-Jan-12	Hall, Megan E 01-Apr-12	Milne, Charlotte L 07-Jun-12
Hastings, Thomas H 01-Jan-12	Harper, Jovin H 01-Apr-12	Mitchell-Heggs, Hugo C 07-Jun-12
Heath, Benjamin O 01-Jan-12	Harvey, Isha S 01-Apr-12	Garner, Llyr 01-Jul-12
Kennedy, Daniel 01-Jan-12	Hodgkiss, James E 01-Apr-12	Martin, Stuart A R 01-Jul-12
Kerrigan, Glen 01-Jan-12	Hume, James A 01-Apr-12	Mulcahy, Oliver J 01-Jul-12
Key, Matthew P 01-Jan-12	Lee, Stuart D 01-Apr-12	Quirke, Darren L 01-Jul-12
Lofthouse, Thomas D 01-Jan-12	Martin, Euan A 01-Apr-12	Sander, Oliver P 01-Jul-12
Matthews, Christopher L G 01-Jan-12	Miles, Alexander S 01-Apr-12	Ward, Robert A 01-Jul-12
McInnes, Allan J 01-Jan-12	Miles, Emma K 01-Apr-12	Welch, Joshua J 01-Jul-12
Murphy, Dennis E H 01-Jan-12	Owen, Christopher R 01-Apr-12	Allen, Nicholas C 08-Jul-12
Myhill, James E 01-Jan-12	Owen-Hughes, Daniel 01-Apr-12	Ferguson, Simon 08-Jul-12
Nicoll, Mac A 01-Jan-12	Page, Christopher A 01-Apr-12	Harding, Georgina E 08-Jul-12
Oakes, Philippe A R 01-Jan-12	Pennant, Marcus A 01-Apr-12	McBrierty, Craig J 08-Jul-12
Ranscombe, Robert E 01-Jan-12	Perrins, Sam A 01-Apr-12	Armstrong, Paul C 13-Jul-12
Richards, Thomas M L 01-Jan-12	Pittock, Martin W 01-Apr-12	Clifford, Stephen D 13-Jul-12
Smith, Richard W D 01-Jan-12	Powell, David A 01-Apr-12	Forrest, Adam 13-Jul-12
Smith, Scott A E 01-Jan-12	Preece, David J 01-Apr-12	Gardiner, Christopher A 13-Jul-12
Stanford, Thomas C 01-Jan-12	Preston, James M 01-Apr-12	Grant, Elizabeth S A 13-Jul-12
Thomas, Daniel G D 01-Jan-12	Ridgeway, Adam 01-Apr-12	Harding, Ian R 13-Jul-12
Wardill, George 01-Jan-12	Robertson, Thomas A M 01-Apr-12	Jones, Jason B 13-Jul-12
Webb, Keith W 01-Jan-12	Rooke, Mark D 01-Apr-12	Macdonald, Adam 13-Jul-12
Wills, Timothy M 01-Jan-12	Ruffell, Lauren 01-Apr-12	Matthews, Kevin A I 13-Jul-12
Wright, James P 01-Jan-12	Rweyemamu, Anatol M 01-Apr-12	Tate, Paul A 13-Jul-12
Yoxall, William F 01-Jan-12	Skelding, Joshua J 01-Apr-12	Thurgood, Anthony D 13-Jul-12
Coatsworth, Robert W 07-Jan-12	Skirton, Daniel G 01-Apr-12	Tortelli, Yasmin 13-Jul-12
Barry, Emma L 31-Jan-12	Suzuki, Hironobu M M 01-Apr-12	Bingham, Edward 15-Jul-12
Brown, Benjamin E 01-Feb-12	Thurmott, Robert 01-Apr-12	Brock, Danny R 20-Jul-12
Gilderthorp, Thomas D 01-Feb-12	Titherington, Mark E 01-Apr-12	Long, Adrian J 31-Jul-12
McInnes, Stephanie 01-Feb-12	Trudgian, Paul 01-Apr-12	Marsh, Alexander R 01-Aug-12
Rees, Nathan J 01-Feb-12	Velickovic, Samuel D 01-Apr-12	Stone, Marc D J 20-Aug-12
Kelday, Alexander W 16-Feb-12	Warren, William J 01-Apr-12	Legge, William J 26-Aug-12
Booth, Anthony R 01-Mar-12	Williams, Liam S 01-Apr-12	Adams, Henry D 01-Sep-12
Brain, Terri 01-Mar-12	Timpson, Benjamin H 08-Apr-12	Adams, Victoria R A 01-Sep-12
Burness-Smith, Oliver N 01-Mar-12	Bacon, David R 09-Apr-12	Baines, Liam P 01-Sep-12
Calder, Thomas A 01-Mar-12	Black, Malcolm DL 09-Apr-12	Ball, Jacob 01-Sep-12
Challans, Benjamin 01-Mar-12	Burnett, Daniel D 09-Apr-12	Barlow, Paul R 01-Sep-12
Chin, Henry R 01-Mar-12	Collins, Christopher J 09-Apr-12	Bekier, Oliver 01-Sep-12
Hamilton, John R 01-Mar-12	Doughty, Stephen W 09-Apr-12	Best, Hannah J 01-Sep-12
Hill, David E 01-Mar-12	Ellis, William J 09-Apr-12	Black, Dominic J 01-Sep-12
Howie, Ian C 01-Mar-12	Johnson, Michael I 09-Apr-12	Blower, Amy 01-Sep-12
McAlpine, Rory W A 01-Mar-12	Chambers, Mark W 13-Apr-12	Burke, Helen E 01-Sep-12
Negus, Trystram W 01-Mar-12		

LIEUTENANTS

Chapman, Christopher	01-Sep-12
Cosby, Max A I	01-Sep-12
Crowsley, Francesca C	01-Sep-12
De-Banks, Kyle	01-Sep-12
Deppe, Garth A	01-Sep-12
Desmond, Jake O	01-Sep-12
Doyle, James R	01-Sep-12
Du-Feu, Robert J	01-Sep-12
Etheridge, Anthony C	01-Sep-12
Foley, Thomas R	01-Sep-12
Forbes, Thomas E	01-Sep-12
Goodall, William C	01-Sep-12
Hunter, Mitchell	01-Sep-12
Irwin, Matthew	01-Sep-12
Jenkin, Richard H	01-Sep-12
Kane, Anthony P	01-Sep-12
Kantharia, Richard P	01-Sep-12
Keenan, Gregory F	01-Sep-12
Kitching, Paul	01-Sep-12
Lacey, Thomas S	01-Sep-12
Lee, Jonathan J E	01-Sep-12
Lovatt, Steven	01-Sep-12
Mackay, Shaun A	01-Sep-12
McKenna, Thomas J	01-Sep-12
McLennan, Alexander P	01-Sep-12
Miller, Ross J	01-Sep-12
Morgan, Hywel R	01-Sep-12
Morgan, Tony G	01-Sep-12
Murphy, Alan J	01-Sep-12
Neal, Gareth P	01-Sep-12
Neilly, Patrick	01-Sep-12
O'Farrell, Matthew V	01-Sep-12
Parker, John R	01-Sep-12
Roberts, Charlotte M	01-Sep-12
Rolfe, Conrad	01-Sep-12
Rosen-Nash, William A	01-Sep-12
Rowan, Tristian G	01-Sep-12
Rylah, Joshua G H	01-Sep-12
Salberg, David G	01-Sep-12
Shortt, Martin	01-Sep-12
Smith, Kim G	01-Sep-12
Smith, Oliver H	01-Sep-12
Stone-Ward, Robert O	01-Sep-12
Storey, Kristopher J	01-Sep-12
Taylor, Rachel S	01-Sep-12
Vance, Andrew	01-Sep-12
Waterman, Matthew L	01-Sep-12
Watt, Fraser J	01-Sep-12
Wyatt, Jason R	01-Sep-12
Findlay, Hamish R	01-Oct-12
Lovell-Smith, Alexandre R	01-Oct-12
Thompson, Peter W	01-Oct-12
Gruber, James P M	07-Oct-12
Kershaw, Neville L	08-Oct-12
Andrews, Steven J	13-Oct-12
Regan, Kevin QGM	13-Oct-12
Skinner, Jennifer E	13-Oct-12
Carrioni-Burnett, Ivana M	20-Oct-12
Taylor, Benjamin G	20-Oct-12
Boast, Rachel	22-Oct-12
Hall, Richard J	22-Oct-12

Stanley-Adams, Tony R	29-Oct-12
Adcock, Markus	01-Nov-12
Barrowclough, William G	01-Nov-12
Clarke, Robert W J	01-Nov-12
Hanley, Peter H	01-Nov-12
Oakley, Christopher G	01-Nov-12
Rignall, William J M	01-Nov-12
Storey, William	01-Nov-12
Warwick, Andrew	01-Nov-12
Hodges, Lauren E	17-Nov-12
Maddick, James J	27-Nov-12
Phillips, Thomas	01-Dec-12
Currie, Victor A C	08-Dec-12
Halliday, Alexander W	08-Dec-12
Hazledine, Oliver W C	08-Dec-12
Manson, Robert P	08-Dec-12
Olsson, Alexandra	08-Dec-12
Turrell, Shelly S J	08-Dec-12
Storey, James I	18-Dec-12

2013

Cochrane, Matthew	01-Jan-13
Coe, Ian L	01-Jan-13
Cullingford, Richard M	01-Jan-13
Edwards, Andrew	01-Jan-13
Gibbons, Nicola J	01-Jan-13
Gorst, Joshua R	01-Jan-13
Hales, Martin	01-Jan-13
Harrison, Mark C	01-Jan-13
Hennah, Garry	01-Jan-13
James, Oliver N M	01-Jan-13
Karavla, Alexandra M I	01-Jan-13
Lewis, Stuart D	01-Jan-13
Linn, Byron J	01-Jan-13
Lowe, Stuart W R	01-Jan-13
McDonough, Mark	01-Jan-13
McLean, Sean D	01-Jan-13
Morton, Charles E A	01-Jan-13
Owen, Robert	01-Jan-13
Shepley, Benjamin J	01-Jan-13
Stone, Matthew J	01-Jan-13
Williams, Nicola J	01-Jan-13
Wilson, Robert N	01-Jan-13
Wood, Thomas D	01-Jan-13
Neilson, Daniel J	22-Jan-13
Bradshaw, Emma R	01-Feb-13
Grainger, Natalie	01-Feb-13
Harrison, Thomas A	01-Feb-13
Davies, Neil	08-Feb-13
Edwards, Helen M	08-Feb-13
Gill, Adam M	08-Feb-13
Harding, Scott R	08-Feb-13
Smith, Jason P	08-Feb-13
Stephens, Brian J	08-Feb-13
Whitley, Janine F B	08-Feb-13
Bending, Shaun P	01-Mar-13
Bolland, Amy	01-Mar-13
Derbyshire, Faye M	01-Mar-13
Doney, Nicholas J	01-Mar-13
Finnigan, Sebastian	01-Mar-13
Halford, John A	01-Mar-13

Perry, Kit J K	01-Mar-13
Ramsay, Stuart J	01-Mar-13
Seaton, Samuel	01-Mar-13
Stockley, Sean A	01-Mar-13
Wale, Alexandra J	01-Mar-13
Wall, Samuel J	01-Mar-13
Waller, Robert	01-Mar-13
Barker, William G	16-Mar-13
Young, Sean A	17-Mar-13
Drew, Daniel M	21-Mar-13
Ramage, Andrew P P	21-Mar-13
Billam, David A	01-Apr-13
Brehaut, John R	01-Apr-13
Core, Emily E	01-Apr-13
Crease, Peter S	01-Apr-13
Denny, Philip M	01-Apr-13
Dent, James I	01-Apr-13
Fallows, Lee D	01-Apr-13
Gabb, John R E	01-Apr-13
Heaton, Oliver H	01-Apr-13
Mason, Joe W	01-Apr-13
Mayger, Martyn	01-Apr-13
Reilly, Scott J	01-Apr-13
Tate, David N	01-Apr-13
Wicks, Sam	01-Apr-13
Crook, Daniel S	09-Apr-13
Cusack, Michael K	09-Apr-13
Devine, Edward	09-Apr-13
Prichard, Charles H N M	09-Apr-13
Sawers, John R	09-Apr-13
Barnes, Thomas M	01-May-13
Bass, Andrew G G	01-May-13
Borland, Kate E	01-May-13
Bugg, Christopher G	01-May-13
Carnie, Christopher	01-May-13
Cooper, Charlotte E	01-May-13
Cowan, Christopher D	01-May-13
Cullen, Matthew R	01-May-13
Duffell, Glyn T	01-May-13
Dynes, Oliver G	01-May-13
Eastburn, Jonathan L	01-May-13
Filio, Andrew P	01-May-13
Gallagher, Ross C	01-May-13
Greig, Stuart J	01-May-13
Hobby, David W	01-May-13
Holden, Simon W	01-May-13
Johnson, Matthew P	01-May-13
Kime, David	01-May-13
Lang, Christopher J	01-May-13
Lowe, Christian T M	01-May-13
McDougall, James N	01-May-13
Morris, Gavin J	01-May-13
Morrison, Alan P	01-May-13
O'Callaghan, Lucy B	01-May-13
Osborne, Andrew R	01-May-13
Payling, William A	01-May-13
Purvis, Christopher	01-May-13
Raine, Murray S	01-May-13
Reekie, Fraser C	01-May-13
Richardson, James A	01-May-13
Taylor, Jennifer L	01-May-13

LIEUTENANTS

Taylor, Oliver L	01-May-13	Burns, Richard J	01-Sep-13	Hocking, Roger C	11-Oct-13

Taylor, Oliver L 01-May-13
Thompson, Luke C A 01-May-13
Tilley, Eleanor V 01-May-13
Usborne, Neil V 01-May-13
Williams, Graeme T 01-May-13
Winch, Michael T R 01-May-13
Beswick, Mark D 03-May-13
Blight, Phillip R R 03-May-13
Clegg, Ross E 03-May-13
Dunn, Ashley J 03-May-13
Hunter, Cameron M 03-May-13
Le-Maistre, Matthew R 03-May-13
Lovell, Jonathan 03-May-13
May, Connor D W R 03-May-13
Newbury, James S 03-May-13
Nolan, Andrew J 03-May-13
Parker, Shaun M 03-May 13
Shepherd, Daniel T 07-May-13
Hart, Sarah 08-May-13
Herbert, Jack A 09-May-13
Olver, Thomas A 10-May-13
Chew, Christopher 20-May-13
Williams, Aaron P 20-May-13
Bryers, Matthew P 01-Jun-13
Gamwell, Sebastian P 01-Jun-13
Houghton, David G 01-Jun-13
Nolan, Samuel T J 01-Jun-13
Turfrey, Matthew 01-Jun-13
Sabin, Scott M 01-Jul-13
Heathcote, James E B 08-Jul-13
Anderson, Bryan A 12-Jul-13
Bicknell, Neil D 12-Jul-13
Dowding, Craig 12-Jul-13
Grant, Gary 12-Jul-13
Hayes, Matthew P 12-Jul-13
Jeffreys, Susan 12-Jul-13
Lemon, Christopher J 12-Jul-13
Proctor, Paul J R 12-Jul-13
Meehan, Oliver J P 15-Jul-13
Cowan, Peter W 20-Jul-13
Preece, Timothy M 20-Jul-13
Astley, William E 23-Jul-13
Morgan, Kelly 01-Aug-13
Phelps, Alexander M 01-Aug-13
Potter, Stephen R 01-Aug-13
Vickers, Patrick T 01-Aug-13
Wharry, Douglas F 01-Aug-13
Wheeler, Robert J 01-Aug-13
Worrall, Adam C 01-Aug-13
Collins, Richard D 07-Aug-13
Fairweather, Donell 07-Aug-13
Lamb, Bryce M 07-Aug-13
Thompson, Adam D 07-Aug-13
Alderson, Stuart J 01-Sep-13
Astley, Daniel 01-Sep-13
Baddeley, James 01-Sep-13
Baker, Kyle L 01-Sep-13
Bassett, Daniel S 01-Sep-13
Bone, Louise 01-Sep-13
Boreham, Daniel J R 01-Sep-13
Brown, Matthew O 01-Sep-13

Burns, Richard J 01-Sep-13
Cary, Matthew R 01-Sep-13
Chandler, Rory G 01-Sep-13
Charters, Emma 01-Sep-13
Clark, Craig S 01-Sep-13
Cogdell, Michael R 01-Sep-13
Colohan, Sam C 01-Sep-13
Coultas, Daniel 01-Sep-13
Cunningham, Dexter A 01-Sep-13
De La Rue, Michael 01-Sep-13
Dobbs, Helen A 01-Sep-13
Doyle, Michael J 01-Sep-13
Duffy, Andrew J 01-Sep-13
Edwards, Rhys G 01-Sep-13
Eeles, Thomas D 01-Sep-13
Eglinton, Benjamin R 01-Sep-13
Flannagan, Bryan A 01-Sep-13
Fraser, Simon A 01-Sep-13
Glover, Daniel 01-Sep-13
Green, Jeremy D 01-Sep-13
Harry, Stephen J 01-Sep-13
Hobin, Daniel C 01-Sep-13
Howard, Dale T 01-Sep-13
Ives, Katie M 01-Sep-13
Jacques, Michael S 01-Sep-13
Jones, Mark O 01-Sep-13
Kumwenda, Temwa 01-Sep-13
Lennon, Thomas 01-Sep-13
Livingstone, Andrew 01-Sep-13
Major, Lee A 01-Sep-13
Mehsen, Samy 01-Sep-13
Morris, Harry A D 01-Sep-13
Morris, Joshua T E 01-Sep-13
Munson, Jason S 01-Sep-13
Murray, Edward A 01-Sep-13
O'Sullivan, Luke A 01-Sep-13
Plant, Anna L 01-Sep-13
Plant, Michael J 01-Sep-13
Rixon, Thomas M 01-Sep-13
Robinson, Nicholas P 01-Sep-13
Ross, Phillip D 01-Sep-13
Rutherford, Ian J D 01-Sep-13
Shepherd, Louise C 01-Sep-13
Sleight, Thomas M 01-Sep-13
Stephens, Carl W 01-Sep-13
Suttle, Celia E J 01-Sep-13
Theobold, Daniel 01-Sep-13
Tinsley, David 01-Sep-13
Tite, Matthew W 01-Sep-13
Tobin, Keith M 01-Sep-13
Tomlinson, Luke M 01-Sep-13
Westmaas, Timothy J 01-Sep-13
Westwood, Christopher S 01-Sep-13
Wilson, Thomas E 01-Sep-13
Witham, Brian M J 01-Sep-13
Woodward, Mark A B 01-Sep-13
Cator, Benjamin H 03-Sep-13
Ladlow, Michael I 14-Sep-13
Thompson, Alexander 14-Sep-13
Cavendish, Gavin W 11-Oct-13
Collins, Jason D 11-Oct-13

Hocking, Roger C 11-Oct-13
Klein, Michael E 11-Oct-13
Lambert, Daniel 11-Oct-13
McCullagh, Timothy A C 11-Oct-13
Potts, David A 11-Oct-13
Robinson, Lindsy 11-Oct-13
Saveal, Matthew P 11-Oct-13
Pettinger, Joseph H 20-Oct-13
Andrews, Liam J R 01-Nov-13
Dunning, Timothy J 01-Nov-13
Fields, Samuel W R 01-Nov-13
Houghton, Christopher L 01-Nov-13
Howes, Daniel P 01-Nov-13
Jones, Simon A 01-Nov-13
Leonard, Matthew D 01-Nov-13
Savage, Dominic N 01-Nov-13
Seabrook, Peter J 01-Nov-13
Simmonds, Zoe N 01-Nov-13
Stevenson, Helen C 01-Nov-13
Underwood, Michael R 01-Nov-13
Livingstone, Dana M A 07-Nov-13
Smythe, Sean R 07-Nov-13
Brindley, Alice E 10-Nov-13
Robinson, John P 10-Nov-13
Gowling, Stephen M 01-Dec-13
Jones, Robert P 01-Dec-13
Eden, Philip M 08-Dec-13
Milkins, Kiel 13-Dec-13
Thomson, David G 20-Dec-13

2014

L'Vov-Basirov, Nikolai E P 12-Jan-14
Milligan, Robert J 19-Jan-14
Alldridge, George M 01-Feb-14
Armitage, David G 01-Feb-14
Barr, Andrew R 01-Feb-14
Benson, Adam D M 01-Feb-14
Bryce, Jenny E 01-Feb-14
Coutts, Phoebe H 01-Feb-14
Elsey, David C 01-Feb-14
Every, Michael J D 01-Feb-14
Forbes, Simon P 01-Feb-14
Grafton, Joshua T 01-Feb-14
Halahan, Miles D C 01-Feb-14
Head, Matthew A A 01-Feb-14
Lewis, Thomas R H 01-Feb-14
Lilley, Benjamin D 01-Feb-14
Mack, Peter E 01-Feb-14
Milnes, Grant 01-Feb-14
Pinder, Aidan O S 01-Feb-14
Ricketts, Alex F 01-Feb-14
Tarpey, Richard J 01-Feb-14
Wardle, Daniel J 01-Feb-14
Whipp, Ian A 01-Feb-14
Gaffney, Francis 03-Feb-14
Pease, Catherine A 16-Feb-14
Blagden, Laura J 01-Mar-14
Drysdale, Robert T 01-Mar-14
Force, Rory J 01-Mar-14
Freeman, Matthew J 01-Mar-14
Leveridge, Adam M 01-Mar-14

LIEUTENANTS

Martin, Jamie M.	01-Mar-14	
Moss, Stephanie	01-Mar-14	
Pearce, Christopher J F	01-Mar-14	
Stevenson, Charles D A	01-Mar-14	
Wade, Robert J	01-Mar-14	
Ward, Timothy E P	01-Mar-14	
Whiteley, Peter	01-Mar-14	
Albon, Joshua G	01-Apr-14	
Aylmer, Matthew A	01-Apr-14	
Bundock, Oliver J	01-Apr-14	
Diaper, Kevin S	01-Apr-14	
Eyers, Dale S	01-Apr-14	
Forster, Thomas W	01-Apr-14	
Green, Richard J	01-Apr-14	
Gregory, Daniel P	01-Apr-14	
Johnson, Matthew J	01-Apr-14	
Lay, Jack	01-Apr-14	
O'Dell, Alexander J	01-Apr-14	
Parry-Jones, Alexander J	01-Apr-14	
Purdue, Basil H	01-Apr-14	
Robus, Lucy J	01-Apr-14	
Rothwell, Christopher D	01-Apr-14	
Sloper, Max D	01-Apr-14	
Vines, Adam M	01-Apr-14	
Wild, Simon	01-Apr-14	
Wilson, Lorna F	01-Apr-14	
Wright, Joseph R	01-Apr-14	
Gilroy, Anthony B	11-Apr-14	
Berridge, Matthew J	01-May-14	
Bowden, Matthew J	01-May-14	
Breaks, James	01-May-14	
Burbidge, Richard L	01-May-14	
Clayton, David H	01-May-14	
Griffith, Phillip B	01-May-14	
Hawkins, Michael J	01-May-14	
Joshi, Cael R	01-May-14	
Keeble, Christopher P	01-May-14	
Lewis, George R	01-May-14	
Macartney, Simon G	01-May-14	
McLeman, William D	01-May-14	
Mills, William S	01-May-14	
Mullin, Laura E	01-May-14	
Napier, Duncan J	01-May-14	
Orr, Jacqueline M	01-May-14	
Swann, James J	01-May-14	
Warner, Philip C	01-May-14	
Watts, Nicholas A D	01-May-14	
McMorran, Hannah J	02-May-14	
Zdrodowski, Craig A	02-May-14	
Lowndes, Timothy	12-May-14	
Sadler, Aimee R G	16-May-14	
Tate, Dennis	24-May-14	
Mackie, Scott	01-Jun-14	
Powell, Matthew T	17-Jun-14	
Lewis, Scott	01-Jul-14	
Pawley, Ross S	01-Jul-14	
Padden, Gregory M	08-Jul-14	
Wray, Stuart A	08-Jul-14	
Gilbert, Scott	11-Jul-14	
Wright, Natalie	11-Jul-14	
Fraser, Callum J	24-Jul-14	

Hounslow, Oliver W	24-Jul-14	
Holdcroft, Luke J	01-Aug-14	
Lay, Benjamin	01-Aug-14	
Persheyev, Alistair A	01-Aug-14	
Wade, Frederick O A	01-Aug-14	
Connaughton, Mark A	14-Aug-14	
Gibson, Scott P	14-Aug-14	
Kent, Thomas W R	14-Aug-14	
Ryde, Emma	14-Aug-14	
Kenward, Jonathan C	15-Aug-14	
Lisle, Robert A C	15-Aug-14	
Sinclair, Gregory W	15-Aug-14	
Andrews, Robert C	01-Sep-14	
Asker, Tristan	01-Sep-14	
Bradshaw, Kieran J	01-Sep-14	
Bray, Michael P	01-Sep-14	
Buttery, Stephanie A	01-Sep-14	
Cave, George	01-Sep-14	
Chenery, Alexander C	01-Sep-14	
Dewing, William T E	01-Sep-14	
Dewis, Ben M D	01-Sep-14	
Doggart, Adam J	01-Sep-14	
Fayers, Samuel R	01-Sep-14	
Forse, Ryan M	01-Sep-14	
Gell, David M	01-Sep-14	
Ginty, John A	01-Sep-14	
Gwinnutt, Oliver F	01-Sep-14	
Harris, Samuel	01-Sep-14	
Hodgson, Katie J	01-Sep-14	
Holt, Christopher J W	01-Sep-14	
Howard, Alexander D P	01-Sep-14	
Kingdon, Samuel R	01-Sep-14	
Law, Michael J N	01-Sep-14	
Lindsey, Thomas S	01-Sep-14	
Lunn, Darren A	01-Sep-14	
Marfleet, Adam J	01-Sep-14	
O'Connor, Calum M	01-Sep-14	
O'Regan, Kyle	01-Sep-14	
Orr, Robert	01-Sep-14	
Ray, Daniel J A	01-Sep-14	
Redbourn, James	01-Sep-14	
Reid, Iain J C	01-Sep-14	
Richardson, Craig A	01-Sep-14	
Robertson, Sean P	01-Sep-14	
Rodgers, Mark A	01-Sep-14	
Souter, Alasdair J	01-Sep-14	
Springer, Rory J	01-Sep-14	
Tindle, Jack A	01-Sep-14	
Tuckley, Christopher J L	01-Sep-14	
Turner, Matthew C	01-Sep-14	
Ward, Nicholas D	01-Sep-14	
Webber, David J	01-Sep-14	
Wilson, Lloyd R	01-Sep-14	
Wilson, Thomas R D	01-Sep-14	
Woods, Anna L	01-Sep-14	
Young, James A	01-Sep-14	
Robson, James P	01-Oct-14	
Grant, Anne-Louise	09-Oct-14	
Quinn, Bernadette S	10-Oct-14	
Woodward, Ian M H	12-Oct-14	
Hancock, David P	27-Oct-14	

Milsom, Matthew L	31-Oct-14	
Williamson, Helen M	31-Oct-14	
Armstrong, Alison C	01-Nov-14	
Bell Williamson, T.	01-Nov-14	
Bowers, Thomas M E	01-Nov-14	
Burbeck, Leslie R L	01-Nov-14	
Campbell, David C	01-Nov-14	
Claringbold, Neill R	01-Nov-14	
Davies, Nathan R	01-Nov-14	
Dobson, William J	01-Nov-14	
Emmerson, David I	01-Nov-14	
Farley, Emma L	01-Nov-14	
Fradley, Nicola A	01-Nov-14	
Grout, Christopher L	01-Nov-14	
Hodder, Gregory L P	01-Nov-14	
Howe, Nicholas E J	01-Nov-14	
Kemp, Thomas A	01-Nov-14	
Machin, Matthew P	01-Nov-14	
Martin, Stephanie	01-Nov-14	
McLauchlan, James M	01-Nov-14	
Millar, Gary D	01-Nov-14	
Murphy, Thomas C	01-Nov-14	
Stinchcombe, Mark E	01-Nov-14	
Sturman, Andrew J	01-Nov-14	
Tamayo, Kieran	01-Nov-14	
Thompson, Matthew	01-Nov-14	
Walton, Darren J	01-Nov-14	
Ward, Andrew E	01-Nov-14	
Beardall-Jacklin, Paul A	03-Nov-14	
Adekoluejo, Gbadebowale A	05-Nov-14	
Jackson, Thomas	10-Nov-14	
Ainscow, Peter D	17-Nov-14	
Thicknesse, Thomas R	21-Nov-14	
Roach, Lewis G	24-Nov-14	
Taylor, Dominic	24-Nov-14	
Yearling, Emma C	24-Nov-14	
Gordon, Emily H	01-Dec-14	
Kendry, Adam	01-Dec-14	
Swann, Adam P D	02-Dec-14	
Dutt, James E	08-Dec-14	
Wraith, Luke	08-Dec-14	
Quinn, Michael	12-Dec-14	

2015

Bowness, Zoe J	01-Jan-15	
Clark, Gary R G	01-Jan-15	
Forde, Rupert J M	01-Jan-15	
Griffiths, David A	01-Jan-15	
Harris, Martyn J	01-Jan-15	
Smart, Tyler M	01-Jan-15	
Smith, Jeff R	01-Jan-15	
Taylor, Alastair B	01-Jan-15	
Thompson, Samuel C	01-Jan-15	
Brereton, Charles	01-Feb-15	

SUB LIEUTENANTS

2011

Smith, Benjamin J 01-Nov-11
French, Sophie R 08-Dec-11

2012

Coyne, Paul E 03-Jan-12
Flint, Thomas A 24-Jan-12
Hartley, Solomon J 24-Jan-12
Hindle, Christopher K 24-Jan-12
McCann, Sally J 24-Jan-12
Reid, Jenny E 24-Jan-12
Welch, Harry A 24-Jan-12
Newlands, Kristoffer G 27-Jan-12
Bambro, Calum A 01-Feb-12
Barley, Andrew G W 01-Feb-12
Beale, Joshua L 01-Feb-12
Cheyne, Rory P 01-Feb-12
Cooke, Stuart L 01-Feb-12
Gidney, Raymond S 01-Feb-12
Groves, Christopher D 01-Feb-12
Henaghen, Wayne D 01-Feb-12
Henrickson, Beau 01-Feb-12
Hesse, Peter J L 01-Feb-12
Jones, Mark F 01-Feb-12
McMonies, Murray J 01-Feb-12
Nash, Ian D E 01-Feb-12
Robinson, Alex J 01-Feb-12
Royle, Michael 01-Feb-12
Shrives, James M 01-Feb-12
Steadman, Thomas W 01-Feb-12
Webster, David R S 01-Feb-12
Woodward, Guy F 01-Feb-12
Sutherland, Oliver 30-Mar-12
Avison, Christopher J 01-Apr-12
Bond, Stuart J 01-Apr-12
Cataffo, Paul J 01-Apr-12
Colthart, Lee 01-Apr-12
Duncan, Rowan J 01-Apr-12
Fordham, Phillip J P 01-Apr-12
Fox, Owen G 01-Apr-12
French, Matthew P 01-Apr-12
Mair, Joanna 01-Apr-12
Makosz, Simon P 01-Apr-12
Murdoch, Hannah 01-Apr-12
Robbins, Daniel M 01-Apr-12
Sunderland, Scott A 01-Apr-12
White, Maxwell A 01-Apr-12
Hammond, James A 09-Apr-12
Nettleingham, Jamie L 09-Apr-12
Prowle, Owen T 09-Apr-12
Flynn, Luke M 11-Apr-12
McFarlane, Daniel 11-Apr-12
Strachan, Gordon J 18-Apr-12
Milton, Michael E 22-Apr-12
Balcam, Jonathan E W 01-May-12
Bryant, Nathan C 01-May-12
Buttar, Daniel M I 01-May-12
Callear, Ben 01-May-12
Carney, Joseph 01-May-12
Clark, Rachael H 01-May-12

Coombes, George W T 01-May-12
Crier, Matthew J 01-May-12
Dickson, Eric 01-May-12
Eaton, Max H 01-May-12
Jackson-Spence, Nicholas J 01-May-12
Minns, Robert J 01-May-12
Poulsom, Matthew J O 01-May-12
Rigsby, David A E 01-May-12
Walker, Daniel J 01-May-12
Wells, Matthew L 01-May-12
Weston, Antony T 01-May-12
Wielbo, Dominik J 01-May-12
Wilkins, Thomas R 01-May-12
Wilkinson, Lloyd J 01-May-12
Hull, Thomas E 02-May-12
McFarlane, Gregory T 02-May-12
Bell, Tristan A 01-Jul-12
Hewitt, Simon D 01-Jul-12
May, Frederick C 01-Jul-12
Holland, Fergus W 14-Aug-12
Rouault, Lewis D 14-Aug-12
Coleman, Joseph M 15-Aug-12
Ball, Liam 01-Sep-12
Boardman, Daniel 01-Sep-12
Brown, Joshua 01-Sep-12
Burns, Amy 01-Sep-12
Burns, Richard 01-Sep-12
Child, William M 01-Sep-12
Clark, Benjamin 01-Sep-12
Clarke, Marcus 01-Sep-12
Darwell, Joseph F 01-Sep-12
Duffy, Mark 01-Sep-12
Gascoigne, Kristina M 01-Sep-12
Hawthorn, Simon 01-Sep-12
Hopkins, Danielle 01-Sep-12
Hughes, Ryan 01-Sep-12
Huxtable, Mark C 01-Sep-12
Jacobs, Joshua B 01-Sep-12
Kain, Matthew J W 01-Sep-12
Kavanagh, Craig M 01-Sep-12
King, Alexander P 01-Sep-12
Leahy, Sam 01-Sep-12
Lee, David M 01-Sep-12
Lee, Simon 01-Sep-12
Marriner, Henry M E 01-Sep-12
Ottaway, Thomas A 01-Sep-12
Pethick, Thomas G 01-Sep-12
Pinney, Richard F 01-Sep-12
Printie, Christopher J 01-Sep-12
Prior, Robert P E 01-Sep-12
Pritchard, Thomas A 01-Sep-12
Sales, Adam 01-Sep-12
Savin, David 01-Sep-12
Sharp, Thomas W 01-Sep-12
Slater, Benjamin 01-Sep-12
Smyth, Daniel 01-Sep-12
Thompson, Peter 01-Sep-12
Turner, Matthew J 01-Sep-12
Waddington, Andrew 01-Sep-12
Warner, Thomas M 01-Sep-12
Weedon, Christopher R 01-Sep-12

Windsor, Christopher J 01-Sep-12
Woollard, Kerry M 01-Sep-12
Hughes, Nicholas D M 01-Oct-12
Perfect, Richard J 01-Oct-12
Ayto, Lydia Jane 08-Oct-12
Bethwaite, Jonathan 18-Oct-12
McBride, Shaun P 01-Nov-12
Morris, Jonothan L 01-Nov-12
Moss, Tyrone J 01-Nov-12
Raper, Daniel S 01-Nov-12
Warnock, Christopher 01-Dec-12
Fawcett, Stuart 04-Dec-12
Aujla, Pavandip S 08-Dec-12
Smith, Christian G 08-Dec-12
Still, James C 08-Dec-12

2013

Clark, James C 01-Jan-13
Knight, Charles E 01-Jan-13
Selwood, Benjamin J 01-Jan-13
McClintock, Lee R 01-Feb-13
Pawson, Jonathan R 01-Feb-13
Coates, James T 01-Mar-13
Barnick, Sebastian G D 08-Mar-13
Stewart, Leonie H 01-Apr-13
Broad, Annabel E 01-May-13
Brown, Oliver G 01-May-13
Collings, Antony B 01-May-13
Evans, Laura 01-May-13
Fisher, Luke I L 01-May-13
Harris, Robert C 01-May-13
Henderson, Katy V B 01-May-13
Hendry, Alan 01-May-13
Maciejewski, Luke W S 01-May-13
McElrath, Calum D 01-May-13
Morton-King, Frederick W H 01-May-13
Robinson, Nicholas 01-May-13
Stacey, Piers 01-May-13
Williams, Zoe E B 01-May-13
Rogers, Clare A 15-May-13
Parsons, Thomas E 01-Jul-13
Clapham, Philip A 03-Jul-13
Clow, Jennifer 24-Jul-13
Brown, Elliot L 01-Aug-13
Chambers, Gary J 01-Aug-13
Dennis, Andrew 01-Aug-13
Duke, Lee J 01-Aug-13
Emptage, Daniel J 01-Aug-13
Fisher, Mark A 01-Aug-13
Flanagan, Mark J 01-Aug-13
Hall, Andrew D F 01-Aug-13
Haw, David R 01-Aug-13
Hughes, Michael S 01-Aug-13
Lambie, Christopher S 01-Aug-13
Matthams, Paul S 01-Aug-13
Munt, James 01-Aug-13
Powell, Robert D 01-Aug-13
Spink, Gary J 01-Aug-13
Stent, Mark L 01-Aug-13
Sykes-Gelder, Daniel 01-Aug-13
Witts, Andrew J 01-Aug-13

SUB LIEUTENANTS

Young, Christopher K.	01-Aug-13
Blunden, Katie L.	07-Aug-13
Lee, Martin J	07-Aug-13
Ball, Ian N	01-Sep-13
Barber, Max A J	01-Sep-13
Brook, Sophie A	01-Sep-13
Butterworth, Chester O	01-Sep-13
Cresdee, Samuel	01-Sep-13
Dale, Rebecca A	01-Sep-13
Drewett, Michael J	01-Sep-13
Hazell, Thomas E	01-Sep-13
Heil, Kieran	01-Sep-13
Leidig, George	01-Sep-13
Lillington, Claire	01-Sep-13
Pearson, Edward T	01-Sep-13
Reid, Philip A	01-Sep-13
Saunders, Alexander M	01-Sep-13
Scraggs, Daniel R	01-Sep-13
Stapley-Bunten, Thomas A	01-Sep-13
Williamson, Ben L	01-Sep-13
Bassett, Karen	14-Sep-13
Brown, Callum J	01-Oct-13
Cutler, Paul A	01-Oct-13
Frith, Ian M	01-Oct-13
Gascoigne, Lindsey	01-Oct-13
Goldsworthy, Robin	01-Oct-13
Lemmon, Ryan J	01-Oct-13
Lyth, Ross A	01-Oct-13
Nikoufekr, Pejman	01-Oct-13
Spear, Toby	01-Oct-13
Turner, Daniel T	01-Oct-13
Watson, Stephen P	01-Oct-13
Woods, Jason S	01-Oct-13
Norris, James M W	10-Nov-13
McMillan, Peter F	17-Nov-13
McMorrow, Stephen P	01-Dec-13
Pennington, Matthew J	01-Dec-13
Forster, Christopher R	14-Dec-13

2014

Aldridge, Rachel	01-Jan-14
Barber, Gregory A	01-Jan-14
Chambers, Lee	01-Jan-14
Gurney, Simon R	01-Jan-14
McInnes, Ian S	01-Jan-14
Morgan, Graeme A	01-Jan-14
Pitt, Niel	01-Jan-14
Snelham, Jenny E	01-Jan-14
Waring, Gavin P	01-Jan-14
West, Jane M	01-Jan-14
Williams, Haydn M P	01-Jan-14
Borthwick, Christopher D	01-Feb-14
Fenn, Christopher J	01-Feb-14
Jones, Jason D	01-Feb-14
Mayes, David J	11-Feb-14
Phillips, Lewis P	11-Feb-14
Young, Martin J	11-Feb-14
Amery, Miles T	01-Mar-14
Broad, James W	01-Mar-14
Eddy, Charlotte R	01-Mar-14
Greig, Ryan A	01-Mar-14

Ricketts, Simon J	01-Mar-14
Smith, Matthew J P	01-Mar-14
Weir, Stewart W A P	01-Mar-14
McPhail, Stuart C	01-Apr-14
Reckless, Adam D	01-Apr-14
Harrocks, Edwina	01-May-14
Little, Philippa C	01-May-14
Mendham, Oliver D	01-May-14
Parry, Eilidh P	01-May-14
Sampson, Colin G	01-May-14
Keeler, Charlotte L	14-May-14
Furniss, Sam	15-May-14
Christie, Rhys L	18-May-14
Berrill, Simon P	19-May-14
Grice, Sally K	01-Jun-14
Robinson, Jennifer A	01-Jun-14
Anderson, Joseph	01-Jul-14
Boak, Charlotte L	01-Jul-14
Collins, Peter S	01-Jul-14
Davis, Carl B	01-Jul-14
Figgins, Adam A	01-Jul-14
Forer, Jonathon T	01-Jul-14
Harrisson, Lucas T	01-Jul-14
Leisk, Oliver L A	01-Jul-14
Randles, Maxwell E S	01-Jul-14
Sellen, Thomas J	01-Jul-14
Vivian, Michael A	01-Jul-14
Witcher, Emily R	01-Jul-14
Grant, Daniel P	24-Jul-14
Allan, Robert C	01-Sep-14
Allen, Benjamin J	01-Sep-14
Anderson, Peter D	01-Sep-14
Benney, Jordon R	01-Sep-14
Blackburn, Ewan J S	01-Sep-14
Brennan, Richard D	01-Sep-14
Brierley, Natalie L	01-Sep-14
Brown, Harry G	01-Sep-14
Burgess, Thomas A	01-Sep-14
Burrows, Oliver R	01-Sep-14
Cameron, Fraser I	01-Sep-14
Clarke, Benjamin J	01-Sep-14
Clayton, Andrew M	01-Sep-14
Coates, Aaron	01-Sep-14
Crallan, Alexander	01-Sep-14
Crossley, Heather C	01-Sep-14
Cunningham, Matthew S	01-Sep-14
Danks, Jonathan A	01-Sep-14
Dreaves, Christopher R	01-Sep-14
Dymock, Craig H	01-Sep-14
Fisher, Cameron S	01-Sep-14
Foster, Matthew P	01-Sep-14
Gillman, Robert M	01-Sep-14
Girling, Steven P	01-Sep-14
Green, Jonathan D	01-Sep-14
Groves, Nicholas J	01-Sep-14
Gwilliam, Benjamin	01-Sep-14
Hind, Joshua	01-Sep-14
Hine, Thomas P	01-Sep-14
Hope, William D G	01-Sep-14
Hotchkiss, Jonathan J	01-Sep-14
Hughes, Gary A	01-Sep-14

Hutchinson, Thomas D	01-Sep-14
Jeffrey, Joseph S	01-Sep-14
Jones, Lewis	01-Sep-14
Kirrage, Charles H D	01-Sep-14
Kubara, Alex M	01-Sep-14
Kutarski, Emily A	01-Sep-14
Le Huray, Jason W	01-Sep-14
Litchfield, Hannah	01-Sep-14
Loftus, Ashley M	01-Sep-14
Mackley-Heath, Megan A	01-Sep-14
Magill, Michael P	01-Sep-14
Marsh, James P	01-Sep-14
Massey, Benjamin M O	01-Sep-14
McElroy, Paul J	01-Sep-14
McGill, Gus	01-Sep-14
McGinlay, Matthew J	01-Sep-14
McNally, Peter J A	01-Sep-14
Millward, Elliott J	01-Sep-14
Neylen, Serena L	01-Sep-14
O'Donnell, Rory	01-Sep-14
Peacock, Joanna R	01-Sep-14
Pengelly, Michael P	01-Sep-14
Petken, Alexander G	01-Sep-14
Poundall, Gareth	01-Sep-14
Powney, Lewis	01-Sep-14
Rainford, Jayjay	01-Sep-14
Ross, Alison K	01-Sep-14
Salt, Isaac P B	01-Sep-14
Saunders, Alexander J	01-Sep-14
Smees, James E	01-Sep-14
Thompson, Michael W	01-Sep-14
Trevor-Harris, George G	01-Sep-14
Webber, Lauren	01-Sep-14
Woodcock, Keith	01-Sep-14
Dudley, James	09-Sep-14
Andrews, David	19-Sep-14
Davies, Lloyd R	19-Sep-14
Petty, Darren L	19-Sep-14
Rawlinson, William G	19-Sep-14
Squires, Jack E	19-Sep-14
Lynn, James M	24-Sep-14
Dodd, Ryan G	01-Oct-14
Garner, Rose E	01-Oct-14
Miles, Rebecca L	01-Oct-14
Phillips, Samuel J	01-Oct-14
Stevens, Jonathan A	01-Oct-14
Wilson, Nathan E	01-Oct-14
Harvey, Ben P W	03-Oct-14
Hawkings, Tom	09-Oct-14
Jones, Benjamin P	09-Oct-14
Taylor, Peter S	20-Oct-14
Aindow, Alice L	01-Nov-14
Alvey, Joshua T D	01-Nov-14
Atkinson, Kevin A	01-Nov-14
Banyard, Adelaide C	01-Nov-14
Bennett, Ashley S	01-Nov-14
Brain, Brandon J	01-Nov-14
Campbell, Scott L	01-Nov-14
Carlisle, Jack C	01-Nov-14
Carr, Stephen A J	01-Nov-14
Coomer, Adam	01-Nov-14

SUB LIEUTENANTS

Creedon, Timothy D...........01-Nov-14	Hughes, Michael I...........01-Nov-14	Pakenham, Aaron T...........01-Nov-14
Daniels, Josh...........01-Nov-14	Kromolicki, Matthew J...........01-Nov-14	Prausnitz, Luke...........01-Nov-14
Doherty, Bethany C...........01-Nov-14	Leyshon, Rhodri...........01-Nov-14	Reed, Thomas A H...........01-Nov-14
Duxbury, Katrina J...........01-Nov-14	Magzoub, Mowafag M M...........01-Nov-14	Richardson, Alexander J M...........01-Nov-14
Fraser-Shaw, Dominic A J...........01-Nov-14	Marshall, William E...........01-Nov-14	Roberts, Llion G...........01-Nov-14
Fryer, Nicholas B...........01-Nov-14	McNicholl, Bruce R...........01-Nov-14	Shutt, David...........01-Nov-14
Garner, Dominic...........01-Nov-14	Mellows, Christopher R...........01-Nov-14	Slater, William G...........01-Nov-14
Goodwin, Lloyd W...........01-Nov-14	Mills, Gregory...........01-Nov-14	Smit, Nathan J...........01-Nov-14
Hall, Nicola E...........01-Nov-14	Moore, Jordan P...........01-Nov-14	Taylor, Dean A...........01-Nov-14
Halliwell, Leon M...........01-Nov-14	Morris, Ashley R...........01-Nov-14	Varco, Thomas G...........01-Nov-14
Harsent, Paul M...........01-Nov-14	Murray, William J...........01-Nov-14	West, Olivia N...........01-Nov-14
Hewitson, David R...........01-Nov-14	Neilson, Robert D...........01-Nov-14	Woodridge, Ryan A...........01-Nov-14
Hill, Rory...........01-Nov-14	Nightingale, Matthew A...........01-Nov-14	Vincent, Fay R...........17-Nov-14
Horne, Thomas S...........01-Nov-14	Ormrod, Ryan...........01-Nov-14	
Huckstep, Joseph P...........01-Nov-14	Osborne, Connor T J...........01-Nov-14	

MIDSHIPMEN

2013

Ball, Samuel P...........01-May-13	
Cobley, Simon D...........01-May-13	
Walters, Cameron F...........01-Nov-13	

2014

Ackers, Simon S...........01-Feb-14	O'Reilly, Jamie P...........01-Feb-14	Longstaff, Jack B...........01-May-14
Adams, Joseph M...........01-Feb-14	Pollard, Joseph G...........01-Feb-14	Loudon, Conor J...........01-May-14
Armitage, John J...........01-Feb-14	Priestley, Simon M...........01-Feb-14	Madge, Mark R...........01-May-14
Bailey, Oliver J...........01-Feb-14	Raeside, Matthew A...........01-Feb-14	Miles, Christopher A...........01-May-14
Brotherton, James M...........01-Feb-14	Rainbird, Luke T...........01-Feb-14	Miller, Holly M G...........01-May-14
Burr, Amapola E...........01-Feb-14	Rilstone, Nathan...........01-Feb-14	Morgan, Hugo N M...........01-May-14
Burton, Joe S...........01-Feb-14	Roberts, Patrick D...........01-Feb-14	Nadin, Fraser...........01-May-14
Cabra Netherton, K...........01-Feb-14	Sedgeworth, Alasdair L...........01-Feb-14	Normanton, Benedict S...........01-May-14
Chowdhury, Devarun...........01-Feb-14	Soley, Darren S J...........01-Feb-14	Norton, Samuel K...........01-May-14
Clark, Steven R...........01-Feb-14	Stack, Daniel P...........01-Feb-14	Pozniak, Alexander R...........01-May-14
Cooke, George E...........01-Feb-14	Talbot, Liam P...........01-Feb-14	Pridham, Kate M...........01-May-14
Corby, Paul M...........01-Feb-14	Toozs-Hobson, Oliver J...........01-Feb-14	Pryce, Alistair M...........01-May-14
Craig, Edward A...........01-Feb-14	Tymm, Oliver D...........01-Feb-14	Ridley, Nicholas S...........01-May-14
Day, George A...........01-Feb-14	Wheatley, George W...........01-Feb-14	Roberts, Sean L...........01-May-14
Dunn, Thomas J W...........01-Feb-14	Wilmott, Vivian...........01-Feb-14	Ryley, Imogen...........01-May-14
Fletcher, Aled T L...........01-Feb-14	Winterton, Alexander J...........01-Feb-14	Seaman, Joshua J...........01-May-14
Gallagher, James...........01-Feb-14	Zealey, William...........01-Feb-14	Shomuyiwa, Theodore A...........01-May-14
Gymer, Carl A J...........01-Feb-14	Adams, Benjamin L...........01-May-14	Simpson, Ewan...........01-May-14
Hanson, Mark...........01-Feb-14	Bees, Thomas D...........01-May-14	Slater, Ryan A...........01-May-14
Hartley, James O...........01-Feb-14	Bhagwan, Gavin S...........01-May-14	Smart, Andrew D...........01-May-14
Hartridge, Roderick A R...........01-Feb-14	Bishop, Alexander N S J...........01-May-14	Smith, Sam R...........01-May-14
Hatherall, Joseph S...........01-Feb-14	Brooks, Daniel...........01-May-14	Spedding, Joseph J...........01-May-14
Hemming, Christopher A S...........01-Feb-14	Buscombe, Leo N P...........01-May-14	Stallard, Samuel C...........01-May-14
Houlston, Christopher C...........01-Feb-14	Chambers, Christopher M...........01-May-14	Stanley, Rebecca F...........01-May-14
Hutchinson, Philippa C...........01-Feb-14	Clarke, Christopher...........01-May-14	Stow, Adam D...........01-May-14
Jacques, Sam O...........01-Feb-14	Clarke, Danny T...........01-May-14	Swift, Jessie J...........01-May-14
Jamieson, Christopher M...........01-Feb-14	Cox, Nicholas J M...........01-May-14	Thompson, Daniel P...........01-May-14
Johnson, Isaac...........01-Feb-14	Duffield, Andrew J...........01-May-14	Waldron, James J...........01-May-14
Jones, Sam D L...........01-Feb-14	Duxbury, Timothy P...........01-May-14	Warwick-Brown, Peter R...........01-May-14
Lewis, Richard P...........01-Feb-14	Dymott, Benjamin C...........01-May-14	Wigan, Thomas J C...........01-May-14
Luscombe, Tom M...........01-Feb-14	Eason, Samuel...........01-May-14	Wilson, Michael J...........01-May-14
McKibbin, Robert C...........01-Feb-14	Gordon, Matthew R...........01-May-14	Woods, Richard K...........01-May-14
McManus, Michael K...........01-Feb-14	Gray, Christopher J...........01-May-14	Babington, James H...........05-May-14
Mullen, Christopher...........01-Feb-14	Greenfield, Jennifer...........01-May-14	Beasley, Samuel C...........05-May-14
Naylor, James S...........01-Feb-14	Handforth, Riley...........01-May-14	Edwards, Steven A...........05-May-14
	Head, Martin A...........01-May-14	Lowery, David...........05-May-14
	Hildreth, Joseph...........01-May-14	Emmett, Robert C...........07-May-14
	Houghton, Ben R...........01-May-14	Abbiss, Jack E C...........08-Sep-14
	Hutchinson, Robert...........01-May-14	Anderson, Richard...........08-Sep-14
	Inkley, Simon R...........01-May-14	Baish, Christopher D...........08-Sep-14
	Jobin, Wesley N...........01-May-14	Bartlett, Kathleen...........08-Sep-14
	Kilgallon, Michael J...........01-May-14	Beardmore A S...........08-Sep-14

MIDSHIPMEN

Brand, James A	08-Sep-14	Richards, Natasha K	08-Sep-14	Leek, Joshua R R	17-Nov-14

Brand, James A 08-Sep-14
Brearley, Nathaniel L 08-Sep-14
Browne, James B 08-Sep-14
Caithness, Julian C 08-Sep-14
Calvert, Charles W A 08-Sep-14
Cooper, Hamish S 08-Sep-14
Cox, Stephen J 08-Sep-14
Crowther, Joshua 08-Sep-14
Dawes, John G J 08-Sep-14
Derrick, Edward J F 08-Sep-14
Dicker, Jeremy 08-Sep-14
Dodson-Wells, Charles 08-Sep-14
Easton, Ben S 08-Sep-14
Faulkner, Julian J 08-Sep-14
Fraser-Shaw, Christopher J 08-Sep-14
Gardiner, Christopher I 08-Sep-14
Gibbons, Sean F 08-Sep-14
Gregson, Tyler J 08-Sep-14
Guest, Robert M 08-Sep-14
Haddon, Luke D 08-Sep-14
Hammick, Benjamin J P 08-Sep-14
Harris, Tomas G 08-Sep-14
Harsley, Paul 08-Sep-14
Henderson, Robert A 08-Sep-14
Hibberd, Sam P 08-Sep-14
Holt, Joseph 08-Sep-14
Hussey, William G 08-Sep-14
Irvine, Oliver 08-Sep-14
Kerridge, Samuel J 08-Sep-14
Key, Andrew D 08-Sep-14
Kirton, Daryl 08-Sep-14
Lawrence, Samuel T 08-Sep-14
Mackay, Victor T 08-Sep-14
Maddison, Jack M 08-Sep-14
Mahony, Nicholas J C 08-Sep-14
Mallin, James D 08-Sep-14
Merrison-Fielder, Nathan R R 08-Sep-14
Milligan, Toby I 08-Sep-14
Murray, Ross S 08-Sep-14
O'Neill, Elias P J 08-Sep-14
Ord, Dominic 08-Sep-14
Page, Alexandra J L 08-Sep-14
Panter, Lawrence G 08-Sep-14
Payas, Keith R 08-Sep-14
Penney, Isobel G 08-Sep-14
Perkins, George A 08-Sep-14
Persson, Alexandra S 08-Sep-14
Pickles, Richard 08-Sep-14
Pounder, Daryl J 08-Sep-14
Rayner, Matthew I 08-Sep-14

Richards, Natasha K 08-Sep-14
Senior, Gareth F 08-Sep-14
Shenton-Brown, William F 08-Sep-14
Smallbone, Dane 08-Sep-14
Smiles, Simon A 08-Sep-14
Smith, Matthew J 08-Sep-14
Speck, Ryan C 08-Sep-14
Steele, Alexander M 08-Sep-14
Swarbreck, Cosmo G F 08-Sep-14
Syfret, Matthew J E 08-Sep-14
Vail, David J 08-Sep-14
Vincent-Spall, Richard 08-Sep-14
Wallace, Matthew E 08-Sep-14
Watson, Robin A 08-Sep-14
Wesley, Phillipa C 08-Sep-14
Williams, Adam L 08-Sep-14
Woliter, Bradley 08-Sep-14
Wright, Lucas H 08-Sep-14
Bhaduri, Thomas 17-Nov-14
Bowe, Alexander B 17-Nov-14
Bradshaw, Matthew P 17-Nov-14
Browne, James M O 17-Nov-14
Butler, Jason N 17-Nov-14
Clouter, Timothy C 17-Nov-14
Collingwood, Matthew J 17-Nov-14
Cuddeford, Jacob W 17-Nov-14
Davidson, Edward 17-Nov-14
Davies, Jonathan R 17-Nov-14
Davy, Owen E 17-Nov-14
Delbridge, Harriet M 17-Nov-14
Earland, Daniel 17-Nov-14
Edwards, Rebecca A 17-Nov-14
Emery, Andrew B 17-Nov-14
Evans, Alexandra C 17-Nov-14
Flaherty, Thomas P 17-Nov-14
Flood, Fredrick 17-Nov-14
Fotherby, Stephen J 17-Nov-14
Freeman, Abigail A 17-Nov-14
Fulton, Richard C 17-Nov-14
Gill, Thomas G 17-Nov-14
Goldman, Daniel J L 17-Nov-14
Goodwin, Cheryl L 17-Nov-14
Hollinghurst, Philip C 17-Nov-14
Howett, Toby C 17-Nov-14
Hughes, Garreth J C 17-Nov-14
Ingman, Thomas D 17-Nov-14
Isaac, Thomas I 17-Nov-14
Johnson, Oliver B M 17-Nov-14
Kidd, Matthew A 17-Nov-14
King, David L S 17-Nov-14

Leek, Joshua R R 17-Nov-14
Lunn, George R 17-Nov-14
Mackenzie, Ross 17-Nov-14
Marshall, Charlotte R 17-Nov-14
Matthews, Garydd R M 17-Nov-14
Matthews, Lewis J 17-Nov-14
Maynard, Sophie D 17-Nov-14
McDowell, Daniel M 17-Nov-14
McMahon, Christopher T 17-Nov-14
Mitchell, Samuel T 17-Nov-14
Musgrove, James C 17-Nov-14
Nash, Thomas J 17-Nov-14
Newby, Ryan 17-Nov-14
Olmesdahl, Sandra C 17-Nov-14
O'Rourke, Nicholas H 17-Nov-14
Pandyan, Andrew R 17-Nov-14
Pascoe, Christopher 17-Nov-14
Perry, David M 17-Nov-14
Pethybridge, Alexander R 17-Nov-14
Purvis, Joe D 17-Nov-14
Ritchie, Luke G 17-Nov-14
Robertson, Jake A 17-Nov-14
Roden, Ieuan P J 17-Nov-14
Rutherford, Sarah E 17-Nov-14
Saunders, Harry 17-Nov-14
Schneider, William 17-Nov-14
Shirtcliff, Justin D J 17-Nov-14
Silcock, James S M 17-Nov-14
Snow, Alexander D 17-Nov-14
Stewart, Christopher J 17-Nov-14
Stewart, Gregory 17-Nov-14
Trebilcock, Robert J 17-Nov-14
Trevorrow, Martyn 17-Nov-14
Uglow, James A 17-Nov-14
Voudouris, Vangeli 17-Nov-14
Wafer, Michael J 17-Nov-14
Walker, Mark T 17-Nov-14
Williams, James O 17-Nov-14
Williams, Simon R 17-Nov-14
Windle, Christopher M 17-Nov-14
Woodcock, Lauren J 17-Nov-14
Wright, James A C 17-Nov-14
Yeomans, Daniel T 17-Nov-14

MEDICAL OFFICERS

SURGEON REAR ADMIRALS

2012
McArthur, Calum J G 08-Oct-12

2014
Walker, Alasdair J OBE 29-Jul-14

SURGEON COMMODORES

2011
Hughes, Andrew S 25-Jul-11
Buxton, Peter OBE.................................15-Aug-11

SURGEON CAPTAINS

2007
Burgess, Andrew J 17-Apr-07
Midwinter, Mark CBE............................ 01-Sep-07

2008
Howell, Michael A................................. 06-May-08
Hughes, Paul A 08-Sep-08
Ross, Robert A MBE 16-Sep-08
Benton, Peter J....................................... 31-Dec-08

2010
Millar, Stuart W S...................................22-Apr-10
Sharpley, John G 01-Jul-10
Thomas, Lynn M 01-Jul-10

2011
Evershed, Marcus C 01-Mar-11
Bree, Stephen E P...................................01-Jul-11
Hill, Graham A..01-Jul-11

2013
Marshall, Fleur T 20-Aug-13

2014
Stapley, Sarah A..................................... 06-May-14
Nicholson, Graeme 10-Jun-14
Edwards, Charles J A.............................. 01-Jul-14
Turnbull, Paul S 15-Jul-14

SURGEON COMMANDERS

1996
Perry, Jonathan N 31-Dec-96

1998
Risdall, Jane 31-Dec-98

1999
Lambert, Anthony W OBE......................30-Jun-99

2001
Birt, David J..30-Jun-01

2002
Clarke, John..30-Jun-02
Pearson, Christopher..............................30-Jun-02

2003
Wylie, Robert D S....................................01-Apr-03
Blair, Duncan G S 30-Jun-03
Hand, Christopher J 30-Jun-03
Mellor, Adrian J.......................................30-Jun-03
Smith, Steven R C 30-Jun-03
Terry, Michael C G...................................30-Jun-03

2004
Connor, Daniel J.....................................30-Jun-04

Craner, Matthew 30-Jun-04
Leigh-Smith, Simon J..............................30-Jun-04
Rickard, Rory F 30-Jun-04

2005
Smith, Jason E...30-Jun-05
Taylor, Peter J 30-Jun-05
Bowie, Alan N..28-Oct-05

2006
Chirnside, Gabriella F.............................30-Jun-06
Dekker, Barrie J 30-Jun-06
Heames, Richard M..................................30-Jun-06
Ramaswami, Ravi A.................................27-Jul-06
Palmer, Alan C 02-Oct-06

2007
Dickson, Stuart J 30-Jun-07
Duby, Alon...30-Jun-07
Gibson, Andrew 30-Jun-07
Streets, Christopher G.............................30-Jun-07
Bland, Steven A..07-Aug-07

2008
Leonard, John F 01-Jul-08
Imm, Nicholas D H 30-Jul-08
Crowson, Elizabeth 04-Aug-08
Freshwater, Dennis A 09-Aug-08

McIntosh, James D...................................10-Sep-08
Coltman, Timothy P.................................08-Oct-08

2009
Houlberg, Kristian A N.............................14-Feb-09
Schofield, Susan R...................................30-Mar-09
Gay, David A T 01-Jul-09
Milner, Robert A.......................................01-Jul-09
Phillips, Simon M 01-Jul-09
Webber, Richard J 01-Jul-09
Parry, Christopher A...............................12-Aug-09
Matthews, Jonathan J 01-Sep-09
Collett, Stuart M......................................14-Dec-09

2010
Henry, Mark...09-Mar-10
Cormack, Andrew.....................................01-Jul-10
McLean, Christopher R.............................01-Jul-10
Whybourn, Lesley A.................................01-Jul-10
Brown, Andrew MBE................................20-Jul-10
Read, Jonathon..04-Aug-10
Prior, Kate R E J.......................................22-Sep-10
Leason, Joanna OBE.................................05-Oct-10
Mackie, Simon J.......................................01-Dec-10
Coates, Philip J B.....................................06-Dec-10

2011
Turner, Matthew J....................................04-Jan-11
Nelstrop, Andrew.....................................11-Feb-11

SURGEON COMMANDERS

Hutchings, Sam D 14-Jun-11	Reston, Samuel C.......................... 01-Jul-12	**2014**
Mercer, Simon............................02-Aug-11	Dew, Anthony M 17-Jul-12	
Evans, Gareth C 13-Dec-11	Doran, Catherine M C.................. 03-Sep-12	Kershaw, Richard J 07-Jan-14
Rees, Paul S C 28-Dec-11	Wild, Gareth 10-Sep-12	Phillips, James C...........................04-Mar-14
		Mackay-Brown, Alan L 20-Mar-14
2012	**2013**	Allcock, Edward C 01-Jul-14
		Smith, Jason J 01-Jul-14
Robin, Julie I 05-Apr-12	Coetzee, Rikus H............................ 01-Jul-13	Vale, Andrew J 01-Jul-14
Harrison, James C 01-Jul-12	Scott, Timothy E 01-Jul-13	Gilmartin, Kieran P 26-Aug-14
Philpott, Marcus C 01-Jul-12	Kershaw-Yates, Elizabeth H 03-Sep-13	Guyver, Paul M 03-Nov-14

SURGEON LIEUTENANT COMMANDERS

2000	**2009**	Russell, Michael J 01-Nov-11
Bedford, Jonathan 01-Jul-00	Scutt, Martin J 04-Feb-09	Vijayan, Deepak 01-Nov-11
	Gardiner, Dermot 01-May-09	**2012**
2003	Tayal, Manish 01-Aug-09	
Welch, James F 05-Aug-03	Hillman, Christopher M 03-Aug-09	Bourn, Sebastian J N 31-Jul-12
	Wrigley, Alexander J.......................03-Aug-09	Evans, Charlotte V 01-Aug-12
2004	Barnard, Edward B G 04-Aug-09	Griffiths, Charlotte E V....................01-Aug-12
	Gokhale, Stephen G........................04-Aug-09	Herod, Thomas P 01-Aug-12
Barton, Sarah J 04-Aug-04	Longmore, David 04-Aug-09	Rennie, Richard A 01-Aug-12
	Dewynter, Alison...........................06-Aug-09	Ritson, Jonathan E 01-Aug-12
2005	O'Shea, Matthew K 06-Sep-09	Scorer, Thomas G...........................01-Aug-12
Cooke, Joanne M 02-Aug-05	Ablett, Daniel J 01-Nov-09	Spreadborough, Philip J....................01 Aug 12
Stannard, Adam...............................02-Aug-05	Kinnear-Mellor, Rex G M 01-Dec-09	Stanning, Alastair J 01-Aug-12
		Van Der Merwe, F E 01-Aug-12
2006	**2010**	Eames, Jonathan R..........................01-Dec-12
Arthur, Calum H C 01-Aug-06	McKinlay, Jayne A C 01-Feb-10	**2013**
Bains, Baldeep S..............................01-Aug-06	Fries, Charles A 02-Feb-10	
Beard, David J 01-Aug-06	Fry, Stephen P............................... 01-May-10	Leong, Melvin J Y J 06-Feb-13
Khan, Mansoor A.............................01-Aug-06	Morris, Alistair J 01-Jun-10	Baker, James O.............................. 01-Mar-13
Maples, Andrew T............................01-Aug-06	Hassett, Justin G 01-Jul-10	Duncan, Kathryn C L.......................03-Apr-13
Bonner, Timothy J 09-Aug-06	Evans, Helen J 01-Aug-10	Scott, Alexandra 01-Aug-13
	Roy, Sudipta K..............................01-Aug-10	Stevenson, Thomas E J 01-Aug-13
2007	Davey, Kelly L 02-Aug-10	Edgar, Iain A M M 06-Aug-13
Miles, Sean A................................. 17-May-07	Hughes, Charlotte L........................02-Aug-10	Fry, Rebecca L 06-Aug-13
Wells, John P 04-Jul-07	Jones, Carolyn J 02-Aug-10	Hale, Alexandra L...........................06-Aug-13
Wood, Alexander M 01-Aug-07	Lloyd, Jane L 02-Aug-10	Henderson, Arthur H.......................06-Aug-13
Edward, Amanda M...........................07-Aug-07	Minshall, Darren M 02-Aug-10	Jamieson, Scott.............................06-Aug-13
Evershed, Rachael E F........................07-Aug-07	Robinson, Timothy 02-Aug-10	Kemp, Peter G 06-Aug-13
Gregory, Anthony E.......................... 01-Sep-07	Stevens, Lisa C 02-Aug-10	Millar, Jennifer A............................06-Aug-13
	Potter, David L...............................04-Aug-10	Robinson, Michael W 06-Aug-13
2008	Lim, Fong Chien............................. 01-Sep-10	Towner, Stephen D P.......................06-Aug-13
Hulse, Elspeth J 06-Aug-08	Proffitt, Adrian.............................. 01-Sep-10	Angus, Donald J C 19-Aug-13
Jaques, Simon C D 06-Aug-08	**2011**	**2014**
Jones, Aled L.................................06-Aug-08		
Lindsay, Michael H 06-Aug-08	McKechnie, Peter S 01-Jun-11	Castledine, Benjamin C 03-Feb-14
McMenamin, Diarmaid 06-Aug-08	Booth, Rachael M 02-Aug-11	Thomas, Ryan C.............................04-Feb-14
Morris, Louisa 06-Aug-08	Brogden, Thomas G 02-Aug-11	Boyes, Georgina K L........................05-Aug-14
Newton, Nicholas J P.........................06-Aug-08	Dickie, Andrew K............................02-Aug-11	Glennie, John S..............................05-Aug-14
Pengelly, Steven P 06-Aug-08	Droog, Sarah J 02-Aug-11	Lundie, Andrew J............................05-Aug-14
Sargent, David S 06-Aug-08	Howes, Richard J............................02-Aug-11	McIntosh, Simon J...........................05-Aug-14
King, Katherine L 10-Sep-08	Toon, Charlotte S...........................02-Aug-11	O'Brien, David J 05-Aug-14
Middleton, Simon W F 11-Sep-08	Williams, Richard J 02-Aug-11	Osborne, Matthew A 05-Aug-14
Henning, Daniel C W 19-Sep-08	Wood, Iain M 04-Aug-11	Saffin, James R..............................05-Aug-14
Penn-Barwell, Jowan G 07-Oct-08	Waller, Bentley R 01-Sep-11	Sharp, William M J 05-Aug-14
Macfarlane, Gordon T........................08-Oct-08	Dodds, Nicholas L 01-Nov-11	Tanzer, William J C E 05-Aug-14
	Matheson, Andrew S M 01-Nov-11	

SURGEON LIEUTENANTS

2010

Wilson, Matthew J	12-Jul-10
Anderson, Timothy J R	04-Aug-10
Butterworth, Sophie	04-Aug-10
Crane, Danielle L	04-Aug-10
Foster, Sebastian J T	04-Aug-10
Hill, Michael J	04-Aug-10
Jervis, Christopher	04-Aug-10
Nixon, Sebastian W	04-Aug-10
Paterson, Laura	04-Aug-10
Rawlinson, Katherine H	04-Aug-10
Rylah, Osgar J A	04-Aug-10
Sandhu, Jagdeep S	04-Aug-10
Staunton, Thomas H	04-Aug-10
Vassallo, James	04-Aug-10
Woolley, Stephen	04-Aug-10

2011

Healey, Nicholas J	01-Feb-11
Wharton, Charles F S	02-Aug-11
Baker, Luke D	03-Aug-11
Bennett, Philippa	03-Aug-11
Guest, Ruth E	03-Aug-11
Hawkins, Daniel M	03-Aug-11
Hunter, Guy M C	03-Aug-11
Laird, Joanne E	03-Aug-11
McLellan, Moira S	03-Aug-11
McMenemy, Louise	03-Aug-11
Stachow, Elizabeth A	03-Aug-11

2012

Adshead, Stephen P	01-Mar-12
McArdle, Alan D	01-Mar-12
McConnell, David H P	01-Mar-12
Arr Woodward, Robert W	01-Aug-12
Ashley, Elizabeth A	01-Aug-12
Bakker-Dyos, Joshua J	01-Aug-12
Booth, Ben	01-Aug-12
Callaghan, John J	01-Aug-12
Hawkes, Sophie P E	01-Aug-12
Martin, Antoinette	01-Aug-12
McCaul, Daniel	01-Aug-12
Miller, Rosalyn C	01-Aug-12
Morrow, Laura	01-Aug-12
Myatt, Richard W	01-Aug-12
Rogers, Jennifer C S	01-Aug-12
Wallace, Josef K E	01 Aug-12
Watson, James L	01-Aug-12
Johnson, Tobias E	01-Sep-12

2013

Clingo, Thomas W	01-Mar-13
Strachan, Robert C M	01-Mar-13
Thomas, Robert L	01-Mar-13
Alberts, Ian	07-Aug-13
Bamford, Alexander	07-Aug-13
Bone, Jonathan D	07-Aug-13
Cornell, Jonathan D	07-Aug-13
Green, Natalie M	07-Aug-13
Greenall, Gilbert E	07-Aug-13

Hanan, William M	07-Aug-13
Kilbane, Liam	07-Aug-13
Lownes, Sarah E	07-Aug-13
Preedy, Helen C	07-Aug-13
Quinn, Morgan	07-Aug-13
Swain, Cara S	07-Aug-13
Thomson, Calum M	07-Aug-13
Walters, Elizabeth	07-Aug-13
Thornback, David M	01-Sep-13

2014

Tweed, Charles S R	01-Jan-14
Birley, Daniel T	01-Mar-14
Clarke, Samuel A S	01-Mar-14
Lamont, Calum	01-Mar-14
Najman, Andrew	01-Mar-14
Chan, Deona Mei Lam	06-Aug-14
French, Megan	06-Aug-14
Goodenough, Rory A	06-Aug-14
Griffiths, Adam M	06-Aug-14
Haigh, Thomas J	06-Aug-14
Newlands, Kathryn R	06-Aug-14
Perigo, Oliver F T	06-Aug-14
Riley, Neil A	06-Aug-14
Roocroft, Nathaniel T	06-Aug-14
Rose, Matthew L	06-Aug-14
Sergeant, Adam H	06-Aug-14
Sharpe, Benjamin J D	06-Aug-14
Smith, William A	06-Aug-14
Vanstone, Sean M	06-Aug-14
Ward, Alex J	06-Aug-14

SURGEON SUB LIEUTENANTS

2014

Inglis, David	15-Jul-14
Maxwell, Emma C	20-Jul-14
Dean, Natasha C	21-Jul-14
Hooper, Christopher C	22-Jul-14
Loftus, Andrew L	23-Jul-14

Adams, Megan A	25-Jul-14
Sweeney, Fiona J	26-Jul-14
Bye, Kyo	28-Jul-14
King, Stratton D	28-Jul-14
Lewis, Gethin H	28-Jul-14
Perkins, Andora	28-Jul-14

Barton, Jenny	29-Jul-14
Ladds, Grace	29-Jul-14
Rowland, Charles	29-Jul-14
Slavin, Max	29-Jul-14
Stephenson, Gavin	29-Jul-14
Wood, Michael J	29-Jul-14

DENTAL OFFICERS

SURGEON CAPTAINS (D)

2004
Norris, Richard E 26-Oct-04

2007
Gall, Michael R C 04-Sep-07

2011
Jordan, Adrian M...............................11-Jan-11

Culwick, Peter F 07-Mar-11

2013
Hall, David J 25-Mar-13

2014
Redman, Christopher D J 03-Nov-14

SURGEON COMMANDERS (D)

1997
Aston, Mark W......................................30-Jun-97

2001
Smith, Brian S 30-Jun-01

2002
Elmer, Timothy B...................................30-Jun-02

2005
Skelley, Julie C.....................................30-Jun-05

2006
Minall, Paul A 24-Jul-06

2007
Moore, Paul 10-Jul-07

2008
Madgwick, Edward C C 14-Oct-08

2009
Leyshon, Robert J.................................09-Jan-09

Stevenson, Geoffrey S............................14-Jan-09

2012
Doherty, Melanie 03-Sep-12

2013
Drummond, Karl B.................................01-Jul-13

Hands, Anthony J...................................23-Sep-13

2014
Foulger, Thomas E.................................01-Jul-14

SURGEON LIEUTENANT COMMANDERS (D)

2002
Verney, Kirsty H.....................................09-Jul-02

Chittick, William 10-Jul-02

Dean, Timothy.......................................22-Jul-02

2005
Williams, Benjamin R 27-Jun-05

Bryce, Graeme E 29-Jun-05

Jenks, Jennifer C B................................24-Sep-05

2006
Hamilton, Sean M.................................26-Jun-06

Kershaw-Yates, Simon H C 18-Jul-06

2007
Kemp, Gillian J.....................................19-Jun-07

2008
Lovell, Alistair.......................................25-Jun-08

Falla, Lindsay 27-Jun-08

2009
Pepper, Thomas D C.............................13-Jul-09

Williams, Dylan S 25-Aug-09

2010
Fyfe-Green, Alexa C 09-Jun-10

Southorn, Bryony J.................................27-Jun-10

2012
Bamber, Michael S 05-Jul-12

McCafferty, Lesley F...............................23-Jul-12

2013
Matthews, Lucy A...................................19-Jun-13

Westwood, Amanda J............................07-Jul-13

Pedrick, Amelia.....................................11-Jul-13

Hall, Jessica M......................................14-Jul-13

2014
Coward, Suzanne L 29-Jun-14

Oxley, Angela J......................................27-Jul-14

Murgatroyd, Jenna C 28-Jul-14

SURGEON LIEUTENANTS (D)

2010
Lifoda, Charlotte...................................09-Jul-10

2011
Mair, Barbara I C...................................21-Jun-11

Holland, Emma E 04-Jul-11

Skorko, Konrad 20-Jul-11

2012
Warwick, Francesca R............................19-Jul-12

Fyfe, Tobias R M....................................24-Jul-12

SURGEON SUB LIEUTENANTS (D)

2013

Warden, Sophie 01-Apr-13

QUEEN ALEXANDRA'S ROYAL NAVAL NURSING SERVICE

CAPTAINS

2011	2013
Kennedy, Inga J.........................21-Nov-11	Betteridge, Carol A OBE.........................26-Feb-13

COMMANDERS

2008	2011	2013
Thain-Smith, Julie C 01-Apr-08	Piper, Neale D ARRC.............................. 05-Sep-11	Taylor, Lisa M 03-Mar-13
2009		Hounsome, Debra M MBE ARRC..............01-Jul-13
Spencer, Steven J 04-Aug-09	**2012**	Charlton, Kevin W 11-Aug-13
2010	Thompson, Fiona 06-Feb-12	
	Campbell, Felicity....................................01-Jul-12	
Hofman, Alison J RRC 27-Jul-10	Bagnall, Sally-Anne E 06-Aug-12	

LIEUTENANT COMMANDERS

2004	Carnell, Richard P.........................01-Oct-09	Wright-Jones, Alexandra E M.................01-Oct-12
	Clarkson, Andrew 01-Oct-09	
Briggs, Cathryn S 01-Oct-04	Glendinning, Andreana S 01-Oct-09	**2013**
Sykes, Leah D...01-Oct-04		
Holland, Amanda................................01-Nov-04	**2010**	Brockie, Alan F.........................01-Oct-13
2006	Kennedy, Ian C.........................01-Oct-10	Claridge, Alexander M 01-Oct-13
		Edwards, Sharon P 01-Oct-13
James, Katherine J 01-Oct-06	**2011**	Long, Victoria S......................................01-Oct-13
2008	Cooper, Janette L.........................01-Oct-11	
	Fraser-Smith, Sharron A 01-Oct-11	**2014**
Gardner-Clark, Suzanne L 01-Oct-08	Hurley, Karl 01-Oct-11	Humphrey, Darren P..............................01-Oct-14
Selwood, Peter J 01-Oct-08	**2012**	Martyn, Julie M......................................01-Oct-14
2009	Despres, Julian A.........................01-Oct-12	McCullough, Karen M.............................01-Oct-14
Brocklehurst, Judith E...........................01-Oct-09	Kennedy, Catheryn H 01-Oct-12	Swire, Barry J 01-Oct-14
Brodie, Stephen D..................................01-Oct-09	Warburton, Alison...................................01-Oct-12	Wardley, Thomas E................................01-Oct-14

LIEUTENANTS

2001	2007	2010
Bryce-Johnston, Fiona L S.......................16-Jul-01	Boswell, Laura J 29-Jan-07	De-Saint-Bissix-Croix, Anna M.................13-Apr-10
	Devine, Alison..12-Feb-07	Cornhill, Sharon T.................................. 12-Jul-10
2003	Jackson, Darren M 15-Mar-07	Ryan, Kathleen R 12-Jul-10
Hume, Sarah K (ARRC)...........................01-Nov-03	Lewis, Robert G 01-Sep-07	
		2011
2005	**2008**	Brooking, Gary N 12-Jul-11
Hale, Stuart D 01-Apr-05	Cantillon, Lloyd M..................................16-Jun-08	
	McElroy-Baker, Lindsey...........................17-Oct-08	**2012**
2006	**2009**	Hodges, Lauren E...................................17-Nov-12
Dewey, Sarah E.......................................01-Mar-06		**2013**
Jaffrey, Heather B...................................11-Apr-06	Tin, Jennifer M J.....................................01-Jan-09	
Embleton, Alison.....................................09-Jun-06	Glendinning, Vicky L 16-Jan-09	Whitley, Janine F B................................08-Feb-13
Cockcroft, Kim M 16-Jun-06	Murray, Audrey R...................................19-May-09	Jeffreys, Susan 12-Jul-13
Scott, Victoria 01-Aug-06	Masawi, Sydney K...................................01-Jul-09	Morgan, Kelly 01-Aug-13

LIEUTENANTS

2014

Zdrodowski, Craig A 02-May-14
Gilbert, Scott 11-Jul-14
Quinn, Bernadette S................................10-Oct-14

SUB LIEUTENANTS

2013

Dale, Rebecca A...................................... 01-Sep-13

2014

Harrocks, Edwina 01-May-14

Sampson, Colin G................................. 01-May-14
Vincent, Fay R.. 17-Nov-14

CHAPLAINS

CHAPLAIN OF THE FLEET & PRINCIPAL ANGLICAN CHAPLAIN

The Venerable Ian Wheatley, QHC...07 August 2012
Chaplain of the Fleet and Archdeacon for the Royal Navy

DEPUTY CHAPLAIN OF THE FLEET

The Reverend Martyn Gough .... 01 September 1998

CHAPLAINS

1992	2005	2010
Kelly NJ.............................26 May 1992	Simpson DJ.................................07 March 2005	Andrew PR.................................04 January 2010
1993	Beardsley NA ....03 May 2005	
	Bridges JM.................................02 July 2005	Horne ST.................................07 October 2010
Beveridge SAR ....28 April 1993	Hillier A.................................13 September 2005	
1998	**2007**	**2012**
	Tabor JH.................................16 April 2007	Rason SP.................................01 January 2012
Hills MJ.............................21 April 1998	Robus K.................................27 August 2007	Pye P.................................17 July 2012
Evans ML.............................01 September 1998	Francis JS.................................01 October 2007	
Wylie DV.............................01 December 1998	Mansfield AJF ....10 December 2007	
	2008	**2013**
2002	Barber RW.................................31 March 2008	Money JC ....12 August 2013
Hallam SP.............................05 May 2002	Wagstaff M.................................31 March 2008	Webber AA.................................02 September 2013
	Allsopp MD.................................02 May 2008	
2004	**2009**	**2014**
Corness AS.............................06 September 2004	Godfrey MF ....01 September 2009	Wills E ....27 January 2014

PRINCIPAL DENOMINATIONAL ROMAN CATHOLIC CHAPLAIN

The Reverend Monsignor Andrew McFadden QHC.. 01 September 1998

CHAPLAINS

1990	1998	2010
Sharkey M.............................01 October 1990	Yates DM.................................01 September 1998	Bruzon CC.................................02 September 2010
1996	**2000**	
Bradbury S.............................18 September 1996		
McLean D.............................18 September 1996	Conroy DA.................................24 September 2000	

CHURCH OF SCOTLAND AND FREE CHURCH CHAPLAINS

The Reverend Timothy Wilkinson QHC .... 04 March 1997

CHAPLAINS

1989
Wort RS .... 28 July 1989

1997
Meachin MC .... 07 July 1997

2000
Ellingham RE .... 17 April 2000
Grimshaw E .... 02 May 2000
Kennon S .... 17 September 2000
Rowe RD .... 24 September 2000

2002
Goodwin T .... 05 May 2002
Botwood TJ .... 09 September 2002

2003
Dalton MF .... 12 January 2003

2005
Gates WC .... 06 September 2005

2006
Roissetter DA .... 03 January 2006

2008
Honey Morgan JC .... 11 August 2008

2009
Allcock AJ .... 05 January 2009

2010
Shackleton SJS .... 20 September 2010

2011
Davidson MR .... 01 May 2011

2012
Pons M .... 02 July 2012
Coulson N .... 10 July 2012

2014
Noakes M .... 07 April 2014

NAVAL CAREERS SERVICE OFFICERS

ROYAL NAVY

LIEUTENANTS

1997	1999
Connolly, MH.................................20-Oct-97	Concarr, DT..19-Sep-99

ROYAL MARINES

LIEUTENANTS

1999	
Wilcockson, R 07-May-99	

ROYAL MARINES

CAPTAIN GENERAL

His Royal Highness The Prince Philip Duke of Edinburgh, KG, KT, OM, GBE, AC, QSO

HONORARY COLONEL

His Majesty King Harald V of Norway, KG, GCVO

COLONELS COMMANDANT

Major General David Wilson, CB, CBE...01-May-12
(Colonel Commandant Royal Marines)

Major General Jeremy Thomas, CB, DSO..18-May-12
(Representative Colonel Commandant Royal Marines)

LIEUTENANT GENERALS

Capewell, Sir David, KCB, OBE...01-Dec-11
(HUDSON FELLOWSHIP OCT 14 - AUG 15)

Messenger, Gordon K, DSO*, OBE 13-Jan-13
(DEPUTY CHIEF OF DEFENCE STAFF (MILITARY STRATEGY & OPERATIONS) JUL 14)

Davis, Edward G M, CB, CBE... 01-Jul-14
(DEPUTY COMMANDER LAND COMMAND IZMIR JAN 13)

MAJOR GENERALS

Howes, Francis H R (Buster), CB, OBE 09-Feb-10
(HEAD OF BRITISH DEFENCE STAFF (WASHINGTON) AND DEFENCE ATTACHE JAN 12)

Smith, Martin L, MBE 13-Jun-14
(COMMANDER UK AMPHIBIOUS FORCES & COMMANDANT GENERAL ROYAL MARINES JUN 14)

Since the publication of the last Navy List, the following officer has joined the Retired List:

Major General D A Hook, CBE – to RL 31 Jul 14

BRIGADIERS

2008		2014
Dunham, Mark W CBE.....................21-Apr-08	Spencer, Richard A OBE.............................22-Jul-11	Taylor, Peter G D OBE............................06-May-14
	Huntley, Ian..15-Aug-11	Cameron, Peter S OBE.........................13-May-14
2010		Stickland, Charles R OBE........................14-Jul-14
Salzano, Gerard M MBE........................04-May-10	**2013**	Porter, Matthew E CBE............................21-Jul-14
	Magowan, Robert A CBE........................18-Mar-13	
2011	Holmes, Matthew DSO...........................19-Mar-13	
Bevis, Timothy J.....................................21-Feb-11	Birrell, Stuart DSO....................................14-Jun-13	
	Evans, David M M....................................03-Sep-13	

COLONELS

2006		2013
Brown, Nigel...30-Jun-06	Morris, James A J DSO.........................20-May-10	Hedges, Justin W ORF 27-Aug-13
	White, Haydn J..19-Jul-10	Moulton, Frederick................................23-Sep-13
2007	Pierson, Matthew F..............................07-Dec-10	Scott, Simon J OBE................................14-Oct-13
Hutton, James OBE.................................30-Jun-07		Jackson, Matthew J A DSO...................05-Nov-13
Page, Michael...30-Jun-07	**2011**	Tanner, Michael J....................................16-Dec-13
	Francis, Steven.......................................14-Feb-11	
2008	Kassapian, David L..................................16-Feb-11	
McCardle, John A OBE............................01-Jul-08	Oliver, Kevin..22-Feb-11	**2014**
Lindley, Nicholas......................................15-Dec-08	McInerney, Andrew J.............................31-Mar-11	Maybery, James E....................................07-Jan-14
	Litster, Alan OBE....................................09-May-11	Hussey, Steven J MBE............................01-Apr-14
2009	Jenkins, Gwyn OBE.................................01-Jul-11	Roylance, Jaimie F...................................16-Jul-14
Dewar, Duncan A OBE...........................31-Aug-09	James, Paul M DSO................................22-Aug-11	Sutherland, Neil MBE..............................05-Aug-14
Copinger-Symes, Rory S.......................14-Sep-09	Maddick, Mark J......................................26-Aug-11	Armour, Graeme A..................................02-Sep-14
		Livingstone, Alan J MBE........................10-Nov-14
2010	**2012**	Holmes, Christopher J............................01-Dec-14
Manger, Garth S C...................................19-Apr-10	Murchison, Ewen A DSO MBE.............04-Sep-12	Burnell, Jeremy.......................................14-Dec-14

LIEUTENANT COLONELS

1995	2004	
Heatly, Robert J..31-Dec-95	Phillips, Stephen J....................................30-Jun-04	Thurstan, Richard W F............................30-Jun-07
		2008
1996	**2005**	Baxendale, Robert F................................30-Jun-08
Musto, Edward C.....................................31-Dec-96	Forster, Robin M......................................30-Jun-05	Cook, Timothy A......................................30-Jun-08
	Holt, Justin S MBE..................................30-Jun-05	De Reya, Anthony L MBE........................30-Jun-08
1998	Pressly, James..30-Jun-05	Page, Durward C M.................................30-Jun-08
Price, Martin J...31-Dec-98	Saddleton, Andrew D..............................30-Jun-05	
		2009
1999	**2006**	Blythe, Tom S..30-Jun-09
Mudford, Hugh C....................................30-Jun-99	Green, Gary E..30-Jun-06	Brown, Leonard A MBE...........................30-Jun-09
	Price, Andrew M......................................30-Jun-06	Bucknall, Robin J W.................................30-Jun-09
2001	Pritchard, Simon A..................................30-Jun-06	Fraser, Graeme W...................................30-Jun-09
Sawyer, Trevor J......................................27-Feb-01		Geldard, Michael A.................................30-Jun-09
	2007	Grace, Nicholas J OBE.............................30-Jun-09
2003	Chapman, Simon OBE.............................30-Jun-07	Harris, Carl C Mbe..................................30-Jun-09
Pulvertaft, Rupert J OBE.........................30-Jun-03	Cook, Myles F...30-Jun-07	Skuse, Matthew......................................30-Jun-09
Wilson, David W H...................................30-Jun-03	Cooper-Simpson, Roger J......................30-Jun-07	Watkinson, Neil.......................................30-Jun-09
	McLaren, James P OBE...........................30-Jun-07	
	Morris, Paul...30-Jun-07	**2010**
	Sear, Jonathan J......................................30-Jun-07	Blanchford, Daniel..................................30-Jun-10

LIEUTENANT COLONELS

Cheesman, Daniel MBE 30-Jun-10	Collin, Martin E................................30-Jun-12	Turner, Antony R................................30-Jun-13
Clark, Paul A.......................................30-Jun-10	Haw, Christopher E MC 30-Jun-12	Turner, Simon A................................30-Jun-13
Corrin, Colby St John..........................30-Jun-10	Jepson, Nicholas H M.........................30-Jun-12	Westlake, Simon R..............................30-Jun-13
Dowd, Jonathan W..............................30-Jun-10	Maddison, John D MBE........................30-Jun-12	
Harris, Tristan MBE 30-Jun-10	Maltby, Richard J................................30-Jun-12	**2014**
Janzen, Alexander N OBE 30-Jun-10	Morley, Adrian MC...............................30-Jun-12	
Kelly, Philip M....................................30-Jun-10	Muddiman, Andrew R.........................30-Jun-12	Morgan, Huw L MBE...........................29-Jun-14
Kemp, Peter J.....................................30-Jun-10	Ordway, Christopher N M P.................30-Jun-12	Alderson, Richard J 30-Jun-14
Lock, Andrew G D 30-Jun-10	Stafford, Derek B MBE 30-Jun-12	Balmer, Guy A....................................30-Jun-14
Middleton, Christopher S MBE..............30-Jun-10	Totten, Philip M MBE..........................30-Jun-12	Cole, Simon 30-Jun-14
	Urry, Simon R MBE 30-Jun-12	Coomber, Jonathan M 30-Jun-14
2011	Venn, Nicholas S C..............................30-Jun-12	Davies, Christopher R..........................30-Jun-14
	Walker, Andrew J................................30-Jun-12	Fergusson, Andrew C..........................30-Jun-14
Bowra, Mark A MBE 30-Jun-11		Forbes, Duncan..................................30-Jun-14
Cantrill, Richard J OBE MC 30-Jun-11	**2013**	Foster, Nicholas P 30-Jun-14
Griffiths, Nicholas A MBE.....................30-Jun-11		Gibson, Alexander J 30-Jun-14
Lynch, Paul P MC 30-Jun-11	Bird, Gary M 30-Jun-13	Gilding, Douglas 30-Jun-14
Moorhouse, Edward J..........................30-Jun-11	Cavill, Niki R D MRF 30-Jun-13	Gosney, Christopher J 30-Jun-14
Nicholls, Barry A.................................30-Jun-11	Davies, Huan C A................................30-Jun-13	Hart, Stephen J E 30-Jun-14
O'Herlihy, Simon I MBE 30-Jun-11	Edmondson, Simon P..........................30-Jun-13	Maynard, Paul A 30-Jun-14
Parvin, Richard A.................................30-Jun-11	Fisher, Aaron G 30-Jun-13	McCullough, Ian N..............................30-Jun-14
Read, Richard J 30-Jun-11	Foster, Benjamin 30-Jun-13	Nicholson, David P..............................30-Jun-14
Watkins, Andrew P L............................30-Jun-11	Hill, Jonathan P..................................30-Jun-13	Norman, Jaimie M DSO........................30-Jun-14
Wraith, Neil 30-Jun-11	Huntingford, Damian J........................30-Jun-13	Read, Clinton D 30-Jun-14
	Jess, Aran E K 30-Jun-13	Stemp, Justin E 30-Jun-14
2012	Johnson, Mark 30-Jun-13	Summers, James A E 30-Jun-14
	Kilmartin, Steven N 30-Jun-13	Tamlyn, Stephen 30-Jun-14
Bakewell, Timothy D 30-Jun-12	Mears, Richard J.................................30-Jun-13	
Brady, Sean P.....................................30-Jun-12	Tulloch, Stuart W 30-Jun-13	
Bubb, Jonathan D 30-Jun-12		

MAJORS

1990	**2001**	Taylor, Stuart D..................................01-Oct-04
		Watson, Richard I................................01-Oct-04
Hall, Richard M 01-Sep-90	Craig, Kenneth M 01-May-01	Campbell, Michael M...........................01-Nov-04
Sharland, Simon P..............................01-Sep-90	Spanner, Paul.....................................01-May-01	Tarnowski, Tomasz A...........................12-Nov-04
	Twist, Martin T...................................01-Sep-01	
1996		**2005**
	2002	
Pelly, Gilbert R....................................24-Apr-96		Baker, Michael 01-Oct-05
Freeman, Mark E................................01-Sep-96	Brighouse, Neil G 24-Apr-02	Cooper, Neil.......................................01-Oct-05
	Hale, John N 27-Apr-02	Dennis, James A..................................01-Oct-05
1997	Plewes, Andrew B...............................27-Apr-02	Fuller, James B....................................01-Oct-05
	McGhee, Craig 01-Sep-02	Garland, Andrew N..............................01-Oct-05
Searight, Mark F C 01-May-97		Howarth, John 01-Oct-05
Slack, Jeremy M 01-May-97	**2003**	Lancashire, Antony C 01-Oct-05
		Murphy, Kian S 01-Oct-05
1998	Devereux, Michael E............................01-Sep-03	Tyce, David J 01-Oct-05
	O'Hara, Gerard OBE............................01-Sep-03	
Green, Gareth M.................................01-Sep-98	Whitfield, Philip M 01-Sep-03	**2006**
	Ethell, David R....................................01-Oct-03	
1999		Atkinson, Neil C 01-May-06
	2004	Gray, Karl D 01-May-06
Manson, Peter D 01-Sep-99		Dare, Clifford R S MBE 16-May-06
	Duncan, Giles S...................................01-May-04	Baines, Alastair C.................................01-Oct-06
2000	Woosey, Mark 01-Jun-04	Brain, William J 01-Oct-06
	Penkman, William 01-Sep-04	Collins, John 01-Oct-06
Congreve, Steven C 01-May-00	Atherton, Bruce W..............................01-Oct-04	Durup, Jason M S................................01-Oct-06
Hammond, Mark C DFC........................01-May-00	Churchward, Matthew J.......................01-Oct-04	Fitzpatrick, Paul S................................01-Oct-06
Walls, Kevin F.....................................01-May-00	Clare, Jonathan F 01-Oct-04	Giles, Gary J 01-Oct-06
Kern, Alastair S 01-Sep-00	Lugg, John C 01-Oct-04	Hopkins, Richard M E...........................01-Oct-06
Bulmer, Renny J MBE...........................01-Oct-00	Parry, Jonathan A................................01-Oct-04	Kenneally, Sean J.................................01-Oct-06
Perry, Robert W...................................01-Oct-00		

MAJORS

Lucas, Simon U 01-Oct-06
Moran, Julian T 01-Oct-06
Muncer, Richard 01-Oct-06
Todd, Oliver J 01-Oct-06
Bowyer, Richard 10-Oct-06

2007

Hall, Christopher M I MBE.......................01-Oct-07
Halsted, Benjamin E MBE 01-Oct-07
Hopkins, Rhys 01-Oct-07
Hulse, Anthony W......................................01-Oct-07
Pennington, Charles E..............................01-Oct-07
Perrin, Mark S 01-Oct-07
Samuel, Christopher D R.........................01-Oct-07
Scanlon, Michael J 01-Oct-07
Wallace, Richard S.....................................01-Oct-07

2008

Alston, Richard 01-Oct-08
Cross, Andrew G...01-Oct-08
Delahay, Jonathon E..................................01-Oct-08
Gray, Simon A N 01-Oct-08
Hecks, Ian J 01-Oct-08
Hunt, Darren MBE......................................01-Oct-08
Liva, Anthony J 01-Oct-08
Macpherson, William G C 01-Oct-08
Morton, Justin C 01-Oct-08
Nolan, Paul E MBE 01-Oct-08
Paterson, Thomas J 01-Oct-08
Price, Raymond T 01-Oct-08
Purser, Lloyd J MBE 01-Oct-08
Rogers, Simon M 01-Oct-08
Spink, David A 01-Oct-08
Taylor, Neil J 01-Oct-08
Tucker, Simon J W......................................01-Oct-08
Usher, Brian 01-Oct-08
Waite, Matthew T 01-Oct-08
Wallace, Scott P 01-Oct-08

2009

Jones, Robert P M 01-Sep-09
Abbott, Grant P 01-Oct-09
Allan, Fraser S..01-Oct-09
Burcham, Jason R.......................................01-Oct-09
Caldwell, Daniel J.......................................01-Oct-09
Clarke, Peter M..01-Oct-09
Coryton, Oliver C W S................................01-Oct-09
Dean, Simon I R 01-Oct-09
Elliott, Mark F 01-Oct-09
Fidler, John Q 01-Oct-09
Fomes, Christopher J H 01-Oct-09
Gibb, Alexander K B...................................01-Oct-09
Hayward, John W E....................................01-Oct-09
Hembury, Lawrence 01-Oct-09
Lindsay, Jonathan M..................................01-Oct-09
Metcalfe, Liam M.......................................01-Oct-09
Morris, Richard C MBE 01-Oct-09
Sharpe, Marcus R.......................................01-Oct-09
Simmons, Robert L....................................01-Oct-09
Stanton, Keith V 01-Oct-09

Sutton, David MBE 01-Oct-09
Tapp, Steven J 01-Oct-09
Thorpe, Robert M 01-Oct-09
Venables, Daniel M 01-Oct-09
Whitmarsh, Adam T...................................01-Oct-09
Williams, Peter M.......................................01-Oct-09

2010

Barden, Paul E..01-Oct-10
Brading, Roland D......................................01-Oct-10
Breach, Charles E M...................................01-Oct-10
Carns, Alistair S MC 01-Oct-10
Catton, Innes C..01-Oct-10
Copsey, Nicholas R B 01-Oct-10
Darley, Matthew E.....................................01-Oct-10
George, Nicholas D 01-Oct-10
Giles, Simon...01-Oct-10
Lewis, Barry M 01-Oct-10
Milne, Jason R..01-Oct-10
Norcott, William R.....................................01-Oct-10
Pennefather, Douglas C J 01-Oct-10
Ridley, Jon 01-Oct-10
Rutherford, Adam T 01-Oct-10
Ryall, Thomas A S 01-Oct-10
Stitson, Paul...01-Oct-10
Titerickx, Andrew T...................................01-Oct-10
Uprichard, Andrew J 01-Oct-10
Waldmeyer, Edward 01-Oct-10
Watkins, Dean T...01-Oct-10
Watson, Graham...01-Oct-10
West, David J 01-Oct-10
Winch, Joseph A...01-Oct-10

2011

Anderson, Bruce W D 01-Oct-11
Davies, Luke M A 01-Oct-11
Dow, Andrew J R 01-Oct-11
Duckitt, Jack 01-Oct-11
Gaffney, Benjamin.....................................01-Oct-11
Hall, Edward C M..01-Oct-11
Hill, Christopher J 01-Oct-11
Jamison, James S 01-Oct-11
Johnston, Karl G 01-Oct-11
Lewis, James A E...01-Oct-11
Maccrimmon, Stuart 01-Oct-11
Pengelley, Tristan A H...............................01-Oct-11
Precious, Angus 01-Oct-11
Reynolds, Ben K M.....................................01-Oct-11
Speedie, Alan...01-Oct-11
Thomson, Leighton G 01-Oct-11

2012

Clarke, David W D 01-Oct-12
Cooper, Michael P......................................01-Oct-12
Denning, Oliver W 01-Oct-12
Dinsmore, Simon J 01-Oct-12
Drinkwater, Ross MBE 01-Oct-12
Evans-Jones, Thomas M 01-Oct-12
Forrest, Paul M...01-Oct-12
Ginn, Robert D...01-Oct-12

Kestle, Ryan J...01-Oct-12
Knight, James MC......................................01-Oct-12
Little, George J R..01-Oct-12
Macdonald, Michael 01-Oct-12
Mallows, Andy..01-Oct-12
Noble, Tom M D..01-Oct-12
O'Keeffe, Thomas D...................................01-Oct-12
Payne, Christopher.....................................01-Oct-12
Pritchard, Lloyd B......................................01-Oct-12
Renney, Craig E..01-Oct-12
Starling, Christopher M MBE...................01-Oct-12
Sutherland, Iain...01-Oct-12
Sweny, Gordon 01-Oct-12

2013

Best, Paul N 01-Oct-13
Burr, Christopher J 01-Oct-13
Carter, Kevin C GM....................................01-Oct-13
Cottrell, Ralph..01-Oct-13
Cox, Simon T 01-Oct-13
Donaghey, Mark 01-Oct-13
Fearn, Samuel R...01-Oct-13
Finn, Tristan A 01-Oct-13
Hayes, Brian R..01-Oct-13
Hill, Antony P...01-Oct-13
Hughes, Roger D..01-Oct-13
Jerrold, William H......................................01-Oct-13
Kyle, Ryan...01-Oct-13
Long, Richard...01-Oct-13
Marshall, Leon 01-Oct-13
McGill, Ian 01-Oct-13
Mills, Scott A 01-Oct-13
Morris, James E D 01-Oct-13
Nielsen, Erik M..01-Oct-13
O'Callaghan, Philip P 01-Oct-13
O'Sullivan, Nicholas J 01-Oct-13
Pickett, Alexander P 01-Oct-13
Postgate, Michael O..................................01-Oct-13
Pounds, Alexander N.................................01-Oct-13
Quinn, Thomas J 01-Oct-13
Richardson, Benjamin F............................01-Oct-13
Sayer, Russell J E..01-Oct-13
Scott, Thomas..01-Oct-13
Shuttleworth, Andrew 01-Oct-13
Sutherland, Steven....................................01-Oct-13
Sylvan, Christopher A................................01-Oct-13
Thomson, Luke I 01-Oct-13
Trafford, Michael.......................................01-Oct-13
Veacock, Gary T 01-Oct-13
Waller, Ramsay...01-Oct-13
Winstanley, Mark 01-Oct-13

2014

Coard, Thomas J 08-May-14
O'Sullivan, Stephen...................................30-Sep-14
Adams, Matthew 01-Oct-14
Apps, Julian C 01-Oct-14
Ashley, Scott M MBE.................................01-Oct-14
Bacon, Thomas G.......................................01-Oct-14
Broadbent, Nicholas J...............................01-Oct-14
Buckley, James D..01-Oct-14

MAJORS

Carty, Michael G 01-Oct-14	Heenan, Martyn 01-Oct-14	Reeves, Simon 01-Oct-14
Cox, Mark A MC 01-Oct-14	Hurt, Christopher G 01-Oct-14	
Curtis, Peter J MBE 01-Oct-14	Magowan, Conor C 01-Oct-14	Sanderson, Mark A 01-Oct-14
Emptage, Christopher J 01-Oct-14	Milne, Anthony 01-Oct-14	
Garside, Robert J K 01-Oct-14	Morris, Andrew G 01-Oct-14	Sharman, Max C 01-Oct-14
Gloak, James 01-Oct-14	Moses, Christopher 01-Oct-14	Smith, Trevor M MBE 01-Oct-14
Gray, Oliver W 01-Oct-14	Nixon, Alexander J 01-Oct-14	
Hands, Edward W 01-Oct-14	Pyke, Daniel G 01-Oct-14	White, Thomas G 01-Oct-14

CAPTAINS

1999

Lawton, Peter MBE 01-Jan-99
Wilcockson, Roy 07-May-99

2001

Price, David G 01-Jan-01
Roskilly, Martyn 01-May-01
Barnwell, Alan F 21-Jul-01
Tidman, Martin D MBE 10-Sep-01

2002

Robbins, Harry V 01-Jan-02
Watson, Brian R 01-Jan-02

2003

Burgess, Mark J 01-Apr-03
Flower, Neil P 01-Apr-03

2004

Latham, Mark A 01-Apr-04
O'Connor, David M 01-Jul-04
Gannon, Dominic R 24-Jul-04
Rand, Mark C MBE 24-Jul-04
Bradford, Malcolm H 01-Sep-04
Moore, William I 01-Sep-04
Murray, Simon D 01-Sep-04
O'Sullivan, Matthew 01-Sep-04

2005

King, Richard E 19-Jul-05
Richardson, Simon J 19-Jul-05

2006

Bridson, Andrew 28-Jul-06
Hurdle, Ian 28-Jul-06
Jones, Hugh 28-Jul-06
Welch, Simon 28-Jul-06
Eden, Christopher J 01-Sep-06
Moore, Richard G 01-Sep-06
McGinley, Christopher T 13-Dec-06

2007

Ward, Anthony S 26-May-07
Green, Philip 18-Jul-07
Farthing, Findlay C 20-Jul-07

Jesson, Christopher M 20-Jul-07
Simpson, Paul N 20-Jul-07
Barlow, Matthew J 01-Aug-07
Beete, Jon E 01-Aug-07
Hughes, Samuel E 01-Aug-07
Whiteman, John W T 01-Aug-07

2008

Moyies, Scott A 03-Apr-08
Cotton, Steven 18-Jul-08
Dobie, Graham 18-Jul-08
Hitchman, Stuart M 18-Jul-08
Lake, Richard J 18-Jul-08
Paterson, Mark 18-Jul-08
Robertson, Keith H 18-Jul-08
Watkins, Alun K 18-Jul-08
Eaton, Daniel T 01-Aug-08
Baylis, Matthew F P 01-Sep-08
Cassells, Benjamin T C 01-Sep-08
Horne, Christopher P 01-Sep-08
Lasker, Jonathan A L 01-Sep-08
Lawson, James M J 01-Sep-08
Middleton, Edward J 01-Sep-08
Middleton, John R M 01-Sep-08
Mobbs, Thomas 01-Sep-08
Osborne, Oliver J 01-Sep-08
Shelton, James R 01-Sep-08
Tennant, Gareth M 01-Sep-08
Truman, Oliver J 01-Sep-08
Williams, Peter L 01-Sep-08
Williams, Thomas J 01-Sep-08
Lacy, Andrew P 31-Dec-08

2009

Brokenshire, Matthew W 01-Mar-09
Crump, Alexander I A 01-Mar-09
Broughton, Jack E 03-Apr-09
Clow, Thomas W 03-Apr-09
Davis, Ian Philip 03-Apr-09
Gregory, Andrew J 03-Apr-09
Lawley, Richard J S 03-Apr-09
Miller, Andrew P 03-Apr-09
Perham, Nicholas J 03-Apr-09
Tait, Iain C 03-Apr-09
Timmins, Paul G 03-Apr-09
Tyler, Ian P 03-Apr-09
Winstanley, Robert A J 03-Apr-09
Coventry, Andrew J B 16-Apr-09

Roberts, Thomas P C 16-Apr-09
Abouzeid, Adam A 01-Sep-09
Armstrong, Christopher T 01-Sep-09
Ashcroft, Benjamin J 01-Sep-09
Bates, Oliver J 01-Sep-09
Bowerman, James W 01-Sep-09
Burns, David M 01-Sep-09
Chambers, Harry 01-Sep-09
Connolly, Sean P 01-Sep-09
Disney, Luke 01-Sep-09
Dutton, James 01-Sep-09
Edwards, Gareth B 01-Sep-09
Fuller, James A M 01-Sep-09
Glover, Thomas F 01-Sep-09
Havis, Gareth J 01-Sep-09
Heaver, John D 01-Sep-09
Jones, Toby W 01-Sep-09
Lane, Joseph O 01-Sep-09
McArdle, Christopher J 01-Sep-09
McCurry, Neill I 01-Sep-09
Nutt, William J H 01-Sep-09
Rogers, Dominic J J 01-Sep-09
Sawyers, Daniel C 01-Sep-09
Simpson, Jolyon E R 01-Sep-09
Wall, John H 01-Sep-09

2010

O'Sullivan, Mark 01-Mar-10
Squires, Russell A 01-Mar-10
Wheeler, Luke A J 01-Mar-10
Bell, Michael H 16-Apr-10
Bowgen, John 16-Apr-10
Cox, Stephen 16-Apr-10
Creaney, Anthony P 16-Apr-10
Foster, Adrian A 16-Apr-10
Hartley, David 16-Apr-10
Lewis, Stephen R 16-Apr-10
Maslen, David W J 16-Apr-10
Reed, Christopher G QGM 16-Apr-10
Robson, Mark A 16-Apr-10
Sercombe, Benjamin 16-Apr-10
Williams, Huw R 16-Apr-10
Addison, Timothy M B 01-Sep-10
Anrude, Jack F 01-Sep-10
Barber, Thomas E 01-Sep-10
Boucher, Jonathan R 01-Sep-10
Chappell, Benjamin J 01-Sep-10
Creasey, Andrew D 01-Sep-10
Durbridge, Joel J 01-Sep-10

CAPTAINS

Felton, Jonathan E J ... 01-Sep-10
Garman, Richard A ... 01-Sep-10
Hill, Nicholas P ... 01-Sep-10
Holford, Kane ... 01-Sep-10
Irving, Luke V ... 01-Sep-10
Johnstone, Neil C ... 01-Sep-10
Jones, Benjamin L ... 01-Sep-10
Lynch, John S ... 01-Sep-10
Mackie, Richard P P ... 01-Sep-10
Mason, Oliver D ... 01-Sep-10
O'Boy, Thomas J M ... 01-Sep-10
O'Toole, Mathew C ... 01-Sep-10
Perks, Matthew N ... 01-Sep-10
Phelps, Jonathan J ... 01-Sep-10
Salter, Jonas A ... 01-Sep-10
Searight, William M C ... 01-Sep-10
Shaw, Matthew B ... 01-Sep-10
Smith, Christopher A ... 01-Sep-10
Stevens, Christopher N ... 01-Sep-10
Williams, Matthew R ... 01-Sep-10

2011

Courtier, Robert N ... 01-Mar-11
Cutler, Liam G ... 01-Mar-11
McCreton, Joshua L G ... 01-Mar-11
Adams, Lee M ... 01-Apr-11
Althorpe, Damian S ... 01-Apr-11
Dack, Simon B ... 01-Apr-11
Henderson, Shaun M ... 01-Apr-11
Lees, Colin A ... 01-Apr-11
Mason, Garry ... 01-Apr-11
Moore, Benjamin A ... 01-Apr-11
Murray, Lee S ... 01-Apr-11
Passey, David W ... 01-Apr-11
Reid, Mark R ... 01-Apr-11
Rowland, Steven G ... 01-Apr-11
Triggol, Martin P ... 01-Apr-11
Baybutt, Thomas J ... 01-Sep-11
Bedford, Daniel J ... 01-Sep-11
Burkin, Craig R ... 01-Sep-11
Crow, Jonathan G ... 01-Sep-11
Feasey, James A ... 01-Sep-11
Gallagher, Kieran J D ... 01-Sep-11
Greswell, James S L ... 01-Sep-11
Hall, William J ... 01-Sep-11
Huckle, Thomas C ... 01-Sep-11
Johnston, David S ... 01-Sep-11
Jones, Andrew N ... 01-Sep-11
Lane, Ashley D ... 01-Sep-11
Lane, Harry ... 01-Sep-11
Mitchell, Stuart J ... 01-Sep-11
Moat, Richard ... 01-Sep-11
Morgan, Henry L M ... 01-Sep-11
Morris, David F ... 01-Sep-11
Nightingale, Christopher J ... 01-Sep-11
Phillips, Thomas M J ... 01-Sep-11
Pinney, Jonathan R ... 01-Sep-11
Shirley, Christopher I ... 01-Sep-11
Smith, James E ... 01-Sep-11
Spencer, Charles M ... 01-Sep-11
Stewart, Tristan J ... 01-Sep-11

Thatcher, Geraint L ... 01-Sep-11
Viggars, Christopher E ... 01-Sep-11
Webber, Christopher A ... 01-Sep-11
Webster, Matthew P ... 01-Sep-11
Williams, Edward A D ... 01-Sep-11
Williams, Neil A ... 01-Sep-11
Willison, Mark G ... 01-Sep-11

2012

Pugsley, Andrew ... 01-Jan-12
Barks, Nicholas ... 30-Mar-12
Colarusso, Barry L ... 30-Mar-12
Dobner, Paul C ... 30-Mar-12
Fisher, Daniel A MC ... 30-Mar-12
Gray, Matthew S ... 30-Mar-12
Hughes, Matthew J ... 30-Mar-12
Johnson, Daren ... 30-Mar-12
Mildener, Lee D ... 30-Mar-12
Norris, Paul A MBE MC ... 30-Mar-12
Piper, Lee J ... 30-Mar-12
Sampson, James L ... 30-Mar-12
Ward, Steven J ... 30-Mar-12
Wilkinson, Matthew J MBE ... 30-Mar-12
Batten, Nicholas J ... 01-Sep-12
Beale, David J ... 01-Sep-12
Bennet, Matthew J ... 01-Sep-12
Bennett, Joseph P G ... 01-Sep-12
Breet, Max W D ... 01-Sep-12
Bruce, Robin P M ... 01-Sep-12
Charnley, David J ... 01-Sep-12
Cox, David W S ... 01-Sep-12
Davies, Ross E ... 01-Sep-12
Dawson, Kris A ... 01-Sep-12
Dunn, Charles R N ... 01-Sep-12
Fillmore, Guy M ... 01-Sep-12
Flewitt, Craig ... 01-Sep-12
Freeman, Nicholas H B ... 01-Sep-12
Gobell, Luke ... 01-Sep-12
Halford, Patrick ... 01-Sep-12
Hutchings, Ross ... 01-Sep-12
Law, Benjamin W A ... 01-Sep-12
Limb, Thomas J ... 01-Sep-12
Lindsay, James A M ... 01-Sep-12
Long, Simon C ... 01-Sep-12
Simmons, Paul C ... 01-Sep-12
Slater, Louis G ... 01-Sep-12
Snook, Mathew ... 01-Sep-12
Stewart, Lee A ... 01-Sep-12
Taylor, Steven ... 01-Sep-12
Uhrin, Dusan ... 01-Sep-12
Ward, Simon ... 01-Sep-12
Weldon, Dominic R ... 01-Sep-12
Williams, Jonathan M F ... 01-Sep-12

2013

Lea, Thomas G ... 01-Mar-13
Atkinson, Andrew W ... 21-Mar-13
Atkinson, David ... 21-Mar-13
Catchpole, Andrew D ... 21-Mar-13
Erskine, Dominic S ... 21-Mar-13

Green, Steven P ... 21-Mar-13
Hurst, Gareth W ... 21-Mar-13
Manning, Christopher L G ... 21-Mar-13
Page, Martin J ... 21-Mar-13
Sindall, Steven D ... 21-Mar-13
Weites, Matthew G ... 21-Mar-13
Arkell, Thomas C ... 01-Sep-13
Attrill, Jonathan D N ... 01-Sep-13
Back, Charles P D ... 01-Sep-13
Berger, Angus E ... 01-Sep-13
Bolam, Samual P P ... 01-Sep-13
Broughton, Arron M ... 01-Sep-13
Bryce, Andrew A ... 01-Sep-13
Cameron, Alastair J ... 01-Sep-13
Carvill, Joe J ... 01-Sep-13
Cole, Michael D ... 01-Sep-13
Gobbi, Alexander M ... 01-Sep-13
Grant, Hugo J ... 01-Sep-13
Haward, Tom A A ... 01-Sep-13
Hogg, Theodore J ... 01-Sep-13
Huggett, Christopher G ... 01-Sep-13
King, Paul W ... 01-Sep-13
Kirk, David N ... 01-Sep-13
Mallard, James ... 01-Sep-13
Mawdsley, Richard J ... 01-Sep-13
McEvoy, Thomas P J ... 01-Sep-13
Moreton, Samuel ... 01-Sep-13
Nutting, Christopher J ... 01-Sep-13
Peek, Samuel R ... 01-Sep-13
Powell, Ian D ... 01-Sep-13
Roper, Jack H ... 01-Sep-13
Sandiford, Aran J ... 01-Sep-13
Scott, Thomas L ... 01-Sep-13
Shephard, Samuel J GC ... 01-Sep-13
Smith, Simon J F ... 01-Sep-13
Sykes-Popham, Christopher ... 01-Sep-13
Whitby, Oliver ... 01-Sep-13
Wilson, Bruce R ... 01-Sep-13
York, George M ... 01-Sep-13
Sadler-Smith, Aaron J T ... 12-Dec-13

2014

Cabot, Thomas L J ... 01-Mar-14
Christie, Tom C ... 01-Mar-14
Houghton, James E ... 01-Mar-14
Sayer, Timothy J ... 01-Mar-14
Dowlen, Henry T B MBE ... 29-Jun-14
Davidson, Matthew J ... 31-Aug-14
Fallesen, Lloyd A ... 31-Aug-14
Lucy, Thomas D ... 31-Aug-14
Parsons, Jacob W ... 31-Aug-14
Patrick, Thomas D ... 31-Aug-14
Thomas, Nicholas E ... 31-Aug-14
Wilson, Charles B ... 31-Aug-14
Adams, Jonathan T ... 03-Sep-14
Ainsley, Alex S ... 03-Sep-14
Bathurst, Benjamin G H ... 03-Sep-14
Bloor, Thomas W ... 03-Sep-14
Buck, Thomas A J ... 03-Sep-14
Cain, John D ... 03-Sep-14
Claxton, Alistair ... 03-Sep-14

CAPTAINS

Gardiner, Angus P R 03-Sep-14	Quick, Christopher J 03-Sep-14	Wake, Daniel C 03-Sep-14
Heal, Thomas M C 03-Sep-14	Rowden, Paul C B 03-Sep-14	Wallis, Thomas D 03-Sep-14
Kidson, Adam W B 03-Sep-14	Sankey, Freddie O R 03-Sep-14	White, Alec J 03-Sep-14
Mallalieu, Harry J 03-Sep-14	Steven, William G K 03-Sep-14	
McAll, Benjamin J 03-Sep-14	Stinton, George T 03-Sep-14	**2015**
O'Brien, James M 03-Sep-14	Tomasi, Vittorio L 03-Sep-14	Webb, Adrian C 01-Jan-15

LIEUTENANTS

2012

Campbell, Thomas C 01-Sep-12	
Crowley, James R 01-Sep-12	
Greenway, Crendon A L 01-Sep-12	
Hopkinson, Geoffrey A 01-Sep-12	
Sykes, Mitchell C 01-Sep-12	
Townend, Henry R 01-Sep-12	

2013

Newman, Edmund N 02-May-13	
Bonin-Casey, Patrick J 01-Jul-13	
Cook, Paul 01-Jul-13	
Curran, Steven J 01-Jul-13	
Davies, Warren N 01-Jul-13	
Foster, Darryl E 01-Jul-13	
Grounsell, Wayne T 01-Jul-13	
Hairsine, Samuel 01-Jul-13	
Mooney, John 01-Jul-13	
Powell, Daryl 01-Jul-13	
Rowles, Michael 01-Jul-13	
Jenkins, Gareth S 25-Aug-13	
Burlton, Patrick 01-Sep-13	

2014

Rowe, Warren L 06-Jan-14

Goode, Lee R 13-Jan-14	Goodwin, Moss A J 02-Sep-14
Mudie, Craig A 13-Jan-14	Gosling, Jonathan C 02-Sep-14
Seaney, Adam D 13-Jan-14	Harvey, Martin T 02-Sep-14
Lewis, David P 23-Feb-14	Hastings, Thomas 02-Sep-14
South, Jack W 27-Feb-14	Havers, Luke C D 02-Sep-14
Brown, Nathan D 01-Mar-14	Hobley, Christopher J 02-Sep-14
Frost, Oliver A J 01-Mar-14	Hunt, Steven D 02-Sep-14
Richards, Jack P G 01-Mar-14	Longley, Richard J 02-Sep-14
Glanville, Andrew M 06-Apr-14	Marder, Michael P 02-Sep-14
Hayes, William D 06-Apr-14	Moxham, Glen A 02-Sep-14
Hoyle, Wayne A 06-Apr-14	Norkett, Luke T K 02-Sep-14
Sanders, James A 06-Apr-14	Richmond, David R 02-Sep-14
Alessandro, Santino S P 02-Sep-14	Roughton, Joshua N 02-Sep-14
Arscott, James S 02-Sep-14	Soukup, Sebastian A S 02-Sep-14
Beaney, Jonathan M 02-Sep-14	Stannard, Joshua N 02-Sep-14
Berry, Thomas P 02-Sep-14	Swan, Anthony M 02-Sep-14
Bomby, Ross A 02-Sep-14	Talbot, Edward T H 02-Sep-14
Boucher, Peter J 02-Sep-14	Tippetts, Thomas C M 02-Sep-14
Brown, Joe H 02-Sep-14	Watt, Nicholas J P 02-Sep-14
Chitty, Jack E 02-Sep-14	Wells, Rory L 02-Sep-14
Denniss, Jack A 02-Sep-14	Login, Matthew B 09-Sep-14
Draper, Mark P 02-Sep-14	Palmer, Matthew L 09-Sep-14
Dunham, Thomas W 02-Sep-14	Pitcher, Tim C B 09-Sep-14
Early, Thomas W 02-Sep-14	
Ellis, James W 02-Sep-14	
Franklin, Joseph P M 02-Sep-14	
Fry, Rohan A 02-Sep-14	

SECOND LIEUTENANTS

2011

Gaskin, Alexander C 01-Mar-11	
Dyer, Timothy A 01-Sep-11	
Tyler, Joseph J 01-Sep-11	

2012

Blake, Jeremy G 02-Sep-12	
Buxton, Joshua L 02-Sep-12	
Gurney, Brian D J 02-Sep-12	
Lake, James R F 02-Sep-12	
Pinches, Ben M 02-Sep-12	
Thompson, Antony C 02-Sep-12	

2014

Adkins, Rhys T 25-Aug-14	
Alexander, Daniel D P 25-Aug-14	
Asplin, Jacob N 25-Aug-14	

Bailey, Angus W C 25-Aug-14	Duggan, Louis 25-Aug-14
Balfour, Andrew J 25-Aug-14	Eatwell, George E 25-Aug-14
Balfour, Daniel M 25-Aug-14	French, Stephen G 25-Aug-14
Barlow, James A 25-Aug-14	Frost-Pennington, Fraser R 25-Aug-14
Bernstein, Khan H 25-Aug-14	Graham, Elliott T 25-Aug-14
Bevan, Hector H 25-Aug-14	Hamilton, Alex R C 25-Aug-14
Blackford, Alexander G 25-Aug-14	Hannah, George L 25-Aug-14
Boorn, Andrew E 25-Aug-14	Johnston, Matthew A 25-Aug-14
Bowman, James A 25-Aug-14	Jones, Martin D 25-Aug-14
Bridger, Callum J 25-Aug-14	Leathem, Paul J 25-Aug-14
Buchanan, Nathan G 25-Aug-14	Liddell, Tom H A 25-Aug-14
Byrne, Christopher J 25-Aug-14	Martin, Dale J 25-Aug-14
Caddick, David 25-Aug-14	O'Sullivan, Michael D 25-Aug-14
Carson, Daniel 25-Aug-14	Pannell, Jacob L 25-Aug-14
Chalk, Martin J 25-Aug-14	Pound, Alistair 25-Aug-14
Clark, William P G 25-Aug-14	Reid, Henry J 25-Aug-14
Cook, Benjamin G A 25-Aug-14	Richardson, William J 25-Aug-14
Docherty, William P 25-Aug-14	Rogers, William G 25-Aug-14
Doherty, David J 25-Aug-14	Rounce, George 25-Aug-14

SECOND LIEUTENANTS

Stafford, Benedict J C...........................25-Aug-14	Tyrrell-Moore, William E R......................25-Aug-14	Winter, Marcus R...................................25-Aug-14
Sutton, Jonathon...................................25-Aug-14	Vowles, Barnaby J..................................25-Aug-14	White, Deri T...28-Aug-14
Taylor, Ryan J..25-Aug-14	Wallis, Michael N A................................25-Aug-14	Chaffe, Sebastian S R G.........................07-Sep-14
Trimble, Andrew P.................................25-Aug-14	Williams, Christopher R D.......................25-Aug-14	

RFA OFFICERS

HONORARY COMMODORE

His Royal Highness Prince Edward, The Earl of Wessex, KG, KCVO, ADC

COMMODORE

Dorey, Robert

COMMODORE (Engineers)

Ian Schumaker

CAPTAINS (Deck)

ALLAN OBE, ROBERT HUGH	MINTER, PAUL BERNARD
BOOTH, SIMON KEIR	NORRIS, STEPHEN JAMES
BUCK, DAVID JOHN	
BUDD, NIGEL ANDREW	PATTERSON, GERARD ANTHONY
CLARKE MBE, CHRISTOPHER GRAHAM	PILLING, IAN NIGEL
DONKERSLEY, STEPHEN PAUL	RIMELL, KEVIN DAVID
EAGLES, DAVID ALEXANDER	
HANTON, PHILIP THOMAS	SELBY, PETER NIGEL
HERBERT, SIMON CHRISTOPHER	SHATTOCK, GARY CHARLES
HUXLEY, JONATHAN PETER	SIMMONS, CHARLES FREDERICK
JONES OBE, SHAUN PETER	
LAMB, DUNCAN LAWRENCE	WATTS, KIM

CAPTAINS (ENGINEER)

AMBROSE, MAURICE OSBON	HILL, MICHAEL SIDNEY
BOWDITCH, ALISTAIR CHARLES	JENKINS, PAUL ADRIAN
BURKE, NIGEL PATRICK	KING, BRIAN ARTHUR
COLLINS, JAMES EDWARD	MADDOCK, RICHARD MARK
DAUNTON, PAUL RALPH	NEW, MICHAEL GEOFFREY
DEAR, PETER RICHARD G	PARNELL, ROGER MARK
EDWARDS, TERENCE JOHN	PETERS, STUART MICHAEL
FOX, NICHOLAS WALKER	PETERSEN, PAUL
GRAHAM, RICHARD STEPHEN	SIM, NIGEL MAYNARD

CAPTAINS (LS)

HOOD, JOHN

SHIPS OF THE ROYAL FLEET AUXILIARY SERVICE

ARGUS, Aviation Training Ship
BFPO 433

BLACK ROVER, Small Fleet Tanker
BFPO 435

CARDIGAN BAY, Bay Class Landing Ship
BFPO 436

DILIGENCE, Forward Repair Ship
BFPO 438

FORT AUSTIN, Fleet Replenishment Ship
BFPO 439

FORT ROSALIE, Fleet Replenishment Ship
BFPO 441

FORT VICTORIA, Fleet Replenishment Ship
BFPO 442

GOLD ROVER, Small Fleet Tanker
BFPO 443

LYME BAY, Bay Class Landing Ship
BFPO 447

MOUNTS BAY, Bay Class Landing Ship
BFPO 448

WAVE RULER, Fast Fleet Tanker
BFPO 431

WAVE KNIGHT, Fast Fleet Tanker
BFPO 432

OFFICERS PRACTISING AS NAVAL BARRISTERS

VICE ADMIRAL

D G Steel KBE DL (David)

COMMODORES

Albon, R OBE
Brown, N L
Jameson, A C
Spence, A B
(Commodore Naval Legal Services)

CAPTAINS

Hollins, R
Wood, R

COMMANDERS

Atwill, J W O
Dow, C S
Moore, S
Reed, D K
Towler, A
Wright, S H

LIEUTENANT COMMANDERS

Barker, P R
Chadwick, K
Farrant, J D
Fleming, C S E

Forbes, A J
Frith, A M
Goddard, D
Hunt, R J C
Kenyon, C M
Knox, G P
Mackenow, H R
Marland, E E
Marsh, C
Park, I D
Phillips, M R
Shears, A F
Stockbridge, A
Storey, H J
Ward, A J
Ward, D J
Whitmore, J S

LIEUTENANTS

Blackwell, M E
Evans, T W
Faulkner, S E
Jones, M R
Maclennan, N R
Poole, D C

HONORARY OFFICERS IN THE MARITIME RESERVES

ROYAL NAVAL RESERVE

Vice Admiral HRH Prince Michael of Kent GCVO

Vice Admiral Sir Donald Gosling KCVO (RNR Air Branch)

Vice Admiral The Right Honourable The Lord Sterling of Plaistow GCVO CBE (HMS President)

Captain Charles Howeson (HMS Vivid)

Captain Robert Woods CBE (HMS President)

Captain Carl Richardson (HMS Forward)

Captain Sir Eric Dancer KCVO CBE JP (HMS Vivid)

Captain The Earl of Dalhousie (HMS Scotia)

Captain Jan Kopernicki CMG (HMS King Alfred)

Captain Adam Gosling (HMS Wildfire)

Captain Dame Mary Peters DBE (HMS Hibernia)

Commander John Billington CBE DL RD* (HMS Eaglet)

Commander Anthony Mason MBE RD* (HMS Cambria)

Commander Peter Moore RD* DL (HMS Sherwood)

Commander Jeremy Greaves (HMS King Alfred)

Commander Dee Caffari MBE (HMS King Alfred)

Commander Christopher Wells (HMS King Alfred)

Commander Anthony Lima MBE RD* (Gibraltar)

Commander Stephen Watson (HMS President)

Commander Simon Bird ((HMS Flying Fox)

Lieutenant Commander Dan Snow (HMS King Alfred)

Lieutenant Commander Sarah Kenny (HMS King Alfred)

Chaplain The Reverend John Williams MBE (HMS Eaglet)

Chaplain The Reverend Canon David Parrott (HMS President)

Chaplain The Reverend Neil Gardner (HMS Scotia)

HONORARY OFFICERS IN THE MARITIME RESERVES

ROYAL MARINE RESERVE

Colonel Mark Hatt-Cook OBE RD* (RMR City of London)

Colonel Paul Jobbins OBE GM RD* (RMR Bristol)

Colonel Phil Loynes (RMR Merseyside)

Colonel David Watt (RMR Scotland)

Lieutenant Colonel David Gosling (1 AGRM)

Lieutenant Colonel Bear Grylls (CTCRM)

OFFICERS OF THE ACTIVE LIST OF THE ROYAL NAVAL RESERVE, ROYAL MARINES RESERVE THE QUEEN ALEXANDRA'S ROYAL NAVAL NURSING RESERVE, SEA CADET CORPS AND COMBINED CADET FORCE

ROYAL NAVAL RESERVE

Name	Rank	Seniority	Brach/Arm/Group	Unit
A				
ACKERMAN, RICHARD J	Lt RN	09-May-99	WAR	HMS CAMBRIA
ADAIR, RICHARD C	Lt RN	05-May-08	WAR	HMS WILDFIRE
ADAM, PAUL J	SLt	20-May-08	WAR	HMS FERRET - RNRIU
AGELOU, RACHEL	Lt Cdr	01-Oct-12	WAR	HMS VIVID
AITCHISON, IAN (H)	Lt Cdr	31-Mar-03	WAR	RNR MEDIA OPERATIONS
AJALA, AHMED R A	Lt Cdr	01-Oct-04	WAR	RNR MEDIA OPERATIONS
ALLAN, NICHOLAS S J	OCdt	01-Oct-13	New Entrant	HMS PRESIDENT
ALLEN, ELINOR J RD	Cdr	30-Sep-05	WAR	HMS VIVID
ALLEN, IAN RD	Cdr	01-May-04	WAR	HMS HIBERNIA
ALLINSON, MICHAEL D	Lt RN	01-Mar-07	WAR	HMS KING ALFRED
ALSOP, SWEYN H	Lt RN	01-Dec-98	WAR	RNR AIR BR VL
ANDERSON, JOHN	Lt Cdr	31-Mar-06	WAR	FLEET CMR
ANDERSON, KERRY	Lt Cdr	17-Nov-04	WAR	HMS HIBERNIA
ANDREW, STEPHEN R	Lt RN	16-Sep-13	WAR	HMS DALRIADA
ANIM, TEKPEKI	OCdt	05-Nov-12	New Entrant	HMS WILDFIRE
ARBEID, MARK	Lt Cdr	01-Oct-09	WAR	HMS FERRET - RNRIU
ARKLE, NICHOLAS J	Lt Cdr	01-Oct-13	WAR	RNR AIR BR VL
ARMOUR, TIMOTHY	Lt RN	20-Sep-10	WAR	RNR MEDIA OPERATIONS
ARMSTRONG, CHRISTOPHER J	Mid	01-Oct-13	New Entrant	HMS CALLIOPE
ASHPOLE, RICHARD	Surg Cdr	30-Sep-04	MED	HMS SHERWOOD
ATKINSON, JAMES D	Lt RN	26-Oct-07	WAR	HMS FERRET - RNRIU
AUSTIN, ELIZABETH J	SLt	10-Feb-11	New Entrant	HMS PRESIDENT
AUSTIN, KEVIN	Cdr	30-Jun-10	WAR	HMS PRESIDENT
B				
BAILEY, ANDREW V	SLt	01-Mar-14	MED	HMS FORWARD
BAILEY, JONATHAN	Lt RN	01-Sep-10	WAR	HMS FERRET - RNRIU
BAILEY, NATASHA	Mid	01-Mar-14	New Entrant	HMS PRESIDENT
BAILEY, TIMOTHY	Lt Cdr	29-Jun-11	ENG	HMS KING ALFRED
BAINES, ANDREW R	Lt Cdr	01-Oct-09	WAR	RNR AIR BR VL
BAINES, MARK D	Lt Cdr	01-Feb-93	WAR	RNR AIR BR VL
BAKEWELL, ROBERT A	Lt RN	14-Sep-07	WAR	HMS KING ALFRED
BALDWIN, CHRISTOPHER	Cdr	30-Jun-11	WAR	FLEET CMR
BALMAIN, STEPHEN	Lt RN	01-Jul-94	WAR	HMS PRESIDENT
BANCROFT, DAVID	Lt Cdr	31-Mar-05	WAR	HMS CALLIOPE
BANNISTER, MARK JAMES	Lt RN	30-Oct-09	LOGS	HMS WILDFIRE
BARKHUYSEN, EDWARD	Lt RN	24-Oct-05	WAR	HMS FLYING FOX
BARNBROOK, JEREMY C	Lt Cdr	16-Dec-96	WAR	RNR AIR BR VL
BARNES, JUDITH	Lt Cdr	01-Oct-08	WAR	HMS EAGLET
BARNES, PATRICK A L	Lt Cdr	01-Oct-14	WAR	RNR AIR BR VL

Name	Rank	Seniority	Brach/Arm/Group	Unit
BARNES, TOSCA M F	Mid	01-Nov-13	New Entrant	HMS PRESIDENT
BARR, LYNNE	Lt RN	30-Nov-12	WAR	HMS DALRIADA
BARRATT, STEPHEN	Lt RN	26-May-07	WAR	HMS FORWARD
BARRY, JACQUELINE	Lt RN	25-Sep-05	LOGS	HMS EAGLET
BARTON, NATASHA M	Lt RN	17-Feb-12	WAR	HMS PRESIDENT
BASSETT, KAREN	SLt	14-Sep-13	LOGS	HMS KING ALFRED
BATHAM, DONALD R	Surg Cdr	01-Sep-04	MED	HMS KING ALFRED
BAYNTUN, DAVID	Lt RN	20-Nov-09	WAR	HMS WILDFIRE
BEATON, IAIN	Lt Cdr	01-Oct-14	WAR	HMS DALRIADA
BEDDING, SIMON W E	Lt Cdr	01-Apr-00	WAR	HMS KING ALFRED
BEIRNE, STEPHEN	Lt Cdr	01-Oct-12	WAR	RNR AIR BR VL
BELLAMY, SIMON	Lt Cdr	01-Oct-14	WAR	RNR MEDIA OPERATIONS
BENBOW, WILLIAM	Lt RN	01-Feb-09	WAR	HMS VIVID
BENMAYOR, DINAH E	Lt RN	24-Feb-08	WAR	HMS FERRET - RNRIU
BENN, PETER	Lt Cdr	31-Mar-06	WAR	RNR MEDIA OPERATIONS
BENNET, NIALL	Lt RN	22-Nov-04	WAR	HMS SCOTIA
BENNETT, GRAHAM	Lt Cdr	01-Jul-93	WAR	HMS VIVID
BENTLEY, DAVID	Lt RN	14-May-04	WAR	HMS SCOTIA
BERRY, DOMINIC	Mid	01-Dec-13	New Entrant	HMS PRESIDENT
BERRY, IAN MBE RD	Cdr	30-Jun-13	WAR	HMS CALLIOPE
BEVAN, ROSS M	OCdt	05-Jul-12	New Entrant	HMS EAGLET
BEVERLEY, ANDREW	Lt RN	01-Feb-03	WAR	HMS PRESIDENT
BEWLEY, GEOFFREY RD	Cdr	30-Jun-08	WAR	HMS KING ALFRED
BHANUMURTHY, SANAPALA	Surg Lt Cdr	03-Jun-03	MED	HMS CAMBRIA
BHATTACHARYA, DEBDASH	Lt Cdr	01-Oct-03	WAR	RNR AIR BR VL
BICKNELL, RICHARD	Lt Cdr	31-Mar-01	WAR	HMS KING ALFRED
BINGHAM, EDWARD	Lt RN	15-Jul-12	WAR	HMS PRESIDENT
BIRCHALL, JAMES	Lt Cdr	01-Oct-08	WAR	RNR MEDIA OPERATIONS
BISHOP, GEORGE C	Lt RN	27-Jul-95	WAR	RNR AIR BR VL
BISHOP, JONATHAN R H	Lt Cdr	31-Mar-96	WAR	RNR AIR BR VL
BISSELL, ROBERT A	Mid	01-Jul-14	New Entrant	HMS KING ALFRED
BLAGDEN, DAVID W	Lt RN	17-Mar-12	WAR	HMS WILDFIRE
BOAL, MICHAEL A	Lt Cdr	02-Jun-06	WAR	HMS HIBERNIA
BOLTON, ADAM R	Lt RN	23-Feb-08	WAR	HMS VIVID
BOTTING, LUKE R	Mid	01-Jul-14	New Entrant	HMS SCOTIA
BOULD, EMMA L	Lt RN	19-Nov-09	WAR	HMS WILDFIRE
BOURNE, DAVID	Mid	01-Nov-13	New Entrant	HMS KING ALFRED
BOWEN, MICHAEL	Surg Cdr	30-Sep-04	MED	HMS PRESIDENT
BOWEN, OLIVER T G	Lt RN	14-Dec-08	WAR	HMS WILDFIRE
BOWN, ANTHONY M	Lt Cdr	08-Mar-91	WAR	HMS CAMBRIA
BOWN, CAROL D RD	Lt Cdr	31-Mar-03	WAR	HMS FERRET - RNRIU
BOYLE, ABIGAIL E	Lt RN	07-Oct-11	WAR	HMS FERRET - RNRIU
BOYLE, KIRK	Lt Cdr	31-Mar-06	WAR	HMS FERRET - RNRIU
BRADBURN, STEPHEN J	Lt Cdr	01-Oct-93	WAR	RNR AIR BR VL
BRADLEY, ALAN C	Lt Cdr	01-Oct-14	WAR	HMS KING ALFRED
BRAILEY, IAN S F	Lt Cdr	24-Jun-07	WAR	RNR AIR BR VL
BRATBY, SIMON P	Lt Cdr	01-Oct-05	WAR	RNR AIR BR VL
BRAYSHAW, TABITHA L	OCdt	04-Jul-12	WAR	HMS FORWARD
BREYLEY, NIGEL P	Lt Cdr	31-Mar-98	WAR	RNR AIR BR VL
BROGAN, GARY	Lt Cdr	01-Oct-09	WAR	HMS PRESIDENT
BROMAGE, KENNETH	RN Chpln	02-Aug-92	RN Chaplaincy Service	HMS DRAKE - CHAP
BROOKS, ALEXANDRA L	Lt Cdr	01-Oct-11	WAR	RNR MEDIA OPERATIONS
BROOKS, RICHARD	Lt RN	19-Apr-06	WAR	HMS KING ALFRED
BROOKSBANK, RICHARD J	Lt Cdr	31-Dec-97	WAR	RNR AIR BR VL
BROOMAN, MARTIN J	Lt RN	16-Aug-95	WAR	RNR AIR BR VL
BROSTER, MARK	Lt Cdr	01-Oct-09	WAR	HMS KING ALFRED
BROTHWOOD, MICHAEL K	Lt Cdr	18-Oct-10	WAR	RNR AIR BR VL
BROUSIL, JAMES	OCdt	01-Jul-09	MED	HMS SHERWOOD
BROWN, ANDREW P	Lt Cdr	13-Aug-06	WAR	RNR AIR BR VL
BROWN, GILLIAN V	Mid	01-Sep-14	New Entrant	HMS DALRIADA
BROWN, SHARON M J	Lt RN	01-Jul-04	LOGS	HMS KING ALFRED
BROWN, TIMOTHY C	Lt Cdr	19-Mar-93	WAR	RNR AIR BR VL

Name	Rank	Seniority	Brach/Arm/Group	Unit
BROWNE, ALASTAIR	Lt RN	31-May-07	WAR	HMS PRESIDENT
BROWNING, EMMA	Lt Cdr	01-Oct-12	QARNNS	HMS HIBERNIA
BROWNING, JAMES	Lt RN	07-Dec-04	WAR	HMS PRESIDENT
BRYNING, CHRISTOPHER J	Lt Cdr	01-Mar-85	WAR	RNR AIR BR VL
BUCHAN, JOHN	Lt Cdr	01-Oct-14	WAR	HMS FERRET - RNRIU
BUCKLEY, JONATHAN	Lt Cdr	05-Oct-10	WAR	HMS CAMBRIA
BUCKNELL, DAVID	Cdr	30-Jun-13	WAR	HMS FLYING FOX
BULLOCK, STEPHANIE J	OCdt	16-Aug-12	New Entrant	HMS EAGLET
BURDETT, RICHARD W	Lt RN	01-May-06	WAR	HMS FLYING FOX
BURNS, ANDREW J	Lt RN	01-Jan-03	WAR	RNR AIR BR VL
BUSH, ROBERT	Mid	28-Jul-09	New Entrant	HMS PRESIDENT
BUTTERWORTH, GRAHAM F A	Mid	01-Jan-14	New Entrant	HMS KING ALFRED
BUTTERWORTH, ROBERT G	OCdt	01-Jul-13	New Entrant	HMS PRESIDENT
BUTTON, EDWARD	Lt RN	01-Jul-10	WAR	HMS FERRET - RNRIU

C

Name	Rank	Seniority	Brach/Arm/Group	Unit
CALHAEM, SARAH	Lt RN	28-Jul-07	WAR	HMS FORWARD
CALLAGHAN, PAUL F.	Lt Cdr	30-Oct-99	WAR	RNR AIR BR VL
CALLISTER, DAVID R	Lt Cdr	24-Nov-95	WAR	RNR AIR BR VL
CAMERON, IAIN	Lt Cdr	01-Sep-99	WAR	RNR AIR BR VL
CAMERON, SHAUN	Lt Cdr	01-Oct-14	WAR	HMS EAGLET
CAMPBELL, GRAHAM	Lt Cdr	31-Mar-05	WAR	HMS FORWARD
CAMPBELL, PETER R	Lt Cdr	01-Oct-12	WAR	RNR AIR BR VL
CAMPBELL-BALCOMBE, ANDRE A	Lt RN	18-Sep-02	WAR	HMS WILDFIRE
CAREY, ANDREW W	Lt RN	05-Sep-04	WAR	HMS WILDFIRE
CARPENTER, PHILIP J	Lt RN	01-Feb-94	WAR	RNR AIR BR VL
CARRETTA, MARK V OBE	Lt Cdr	30-Jun-06	WAR	RNR AIR RR VI
CARTER, DAVID	Lt RN	22-Mar-99	WAR	HMS EAGLET
CARTER, ROBERT I	Lt Cdr	01-Oct-95	WAR	RNR AIR BR VL
CARTER, SIMON P.	Lt Cdr	01-Oct-04	WAR	RNR MEDIA OPERATIONS
CHAMBERS, CHRISTOPHER P	Lt RN	01-Dec-99	WAR	RNR AIR BR VL
CHAMPION, RICHARD	Lt RN	15-Mar-11	WAR	HMS EAGLET
CHAPMAN, ANTHONY	Cdr	30-Jun-11	WAR	FLEET CMR
CHAUVELIN, DAVID C W RD	Lt Cdr	01-Oct-11	WAR	HMS SCOTIA
CHEYNE, STEVEN	Cdr	15-May-04	WAR	RNR AIR BR VL
CHICK, NICHOLAS S	Lt RN	15-Nov-95	WAR	RNR AIR BR VL
CHISHOLM, FELICITY	Lt RN	05-Dec-11	WAR	HMS SCOTIA
CHURCH, ELIZABETH	Lt Cdr	31-Mar-06	WAR	HMS PRESIDENT
CHURCH, STEPHEN C	Lt RN	10-Apr-97	WAR	RNR AIR BR VL
CLARK, SUZANNE B	Lt Cdr	31-Mar-97	WAR	RNR AIR BR VL
CLARKE, BERNARD R MBE, QHC	RN Chpln	30-Jun-81	RN Chaplaincy Service	HMS KING ALFRED
CLARKE, LAURENCE	Lt Cdr	01-Oct-14	WAR	HMS FLYING FOX
CLARKE, ROGER RD	Lt Cdr	31-Mar-96	WAR	HMS VIVID
CLARKE, WILLIAM	Lt Cdr	31-Mar-00	WAR	HMS HIBERNIA
CLEGG, MARTIN L	Lt Cdr	01-Jun-90	WAR	FLEET CMR
CLEGG, TOBY	SLt	13-Nov-09	WAR	HMS PRESIDENT
CLEWS, HARRIET	Lt RN	20-Jun-04	WAR	HMS WILDFIRE
CLINTON, LESLEY	Lt RN	19-Nov-08	WAR	HMS FERRET - RNRIU
CLOKEY, JOHN	Lt RN	04-Feb-08	WAR	HMS PRESIDENT
COAKER, STEWART	Lt RN	02-Nov-02	WAR	HMS FERRET - RNRIU
COATS, MARIA	Surg Lt	23-Jan-12	MED	HMS SCOTIA
CODY, WILLIAM	Lt Cdr	01-Jul-97	WAR	HMS FERRET - RNRIU
COHEN, JAMES S L RD	Cdr	30-Jun-08	WAR	FLEET CMR
COHEN, OLIVER G L	SLt	01-Mar-14	WAR	HMS PRESIDENT
COLEY, JENNIFER	Lt Cdr	01-Oct-12	WAR	RNR MEDIA OPERATIONS
COLLEN, SARA J	Lt Cdr	01-Dec-09	WAR	RNR MEDIA OPERATIONS
COLLIER, ANDREW S.	Cdr	30-Jun-14	WAR	FLEET CMR
COLLIER, DAVID J.	Lt RN	30-Jan-06	WAR	HMS WILDFIRE
COLYER, MICHAEL	Lt Cdr	15-Sep-04	WAR	HMS CALLIOPE
COMPAIN, CRAIG H.	Lt RN	21-Mar-97	WAR	RNR AIR BR VL
CONNORS, LIAM	OCdt	01-May-13	New Entrant	HMS PRESIDENT
CONWAY, KEITH A RD	Lt Cdr	31-Mar-99	WAR	HMS SCOTIA

Name	Rank	Seniority	Brach/Arm/Group	Unit
COOK, SIMON H H	Lt Cdr	01-Oct-08	WAR	HMS WILDFIRE
COOKE, MICHAEL J	Lt Cdr	01-Oct-02	ENG	RNR AIR BR VL
COOPER, ANTHONY	OCdt	01-Nov-12	New Entrant	HMS PRESIDENT
COOPER, DAVID J RD	Lt Cdr	31-Mar-99	WAR	HMS KING ALFRED
COPELAND, NIALL	Lt RN	01-Sep-10	WAR	RNR MEDIA OPERATIONS
COPELAND-DAVIS, TERENCE W	Lt Cdr	31-Mar-03	WAR	RNR AIR BR VL
COSGROVE, ANTHONY	Lt RN	09-Oct-10	WAR	HMS KING ALFRED
COTTAM, SIMON R QVRM RD	Lt Cdr	31-Mar-97	WAR	HMS FLYING FOX
COTTINGHAM, NEIL P S	Cdr	30-Jun-12	WAR	RNR AIR BR VL
COUGHLAN, SCOTT	Lt RN	01-Sep-03	WAR	HMS FERRET - RNRIU
COULING, MATTHEW J	Mid	01-Nov-12	New Entrant	HMS WILDFIRE
COUPLAND, MARK B	Lt RN	01-Mar-89	WAR	RNR AIR BR VL
COURTNEY, KURT	Lt Cdr	01-Oct-13	WAR	HMS FERRET - RNRIU
COWAN, ANDREW	Capt RN	26-Sep-14	WAR	FLEET CMR
COWIN, TIMOTHY J	Lt RN	29-May-99	WAR	RNR AIR BR VL
COX, RHODERICK W	Lt Cdr	01-Dec-88	WAR	RNR AIR BR VL
COYLE, MARK	Lt RN	20-Feb-06	WAR	HMS CALLIOPE
COYNE, JOHN D	Lt RN	17-Dec-93	WAR	RNR AIR BR VL
CRABBE, ROBERT J	Lt Cdr	01-Oct-06	WAR	HMS FLYING FOX
CRAWFORD, ANDREW G	Mid	01-Jun-14	New Entrant	HMS WILDFIRE
CRAWFORD, VALERIE E	Lt RN	01-Apr-02	WAR	HMS FERRET - RNRIU
CRICK, MATTHEW J	Mid	01-Jul-14	New Entrant	HMS KING ALFRED
CUBBAGE, JOANNA	Lt RN	09-Dec-11	LOGS	HMS SCOTIA
CUNNINGHAM, NIGEL J W	Lt Cdr	01-Oct-03	WAR	RNR AIR BR VL
CURTIS, ROGER	Cdr	30-Jun-11	WAR	FLEET CMR

D

Name	Rank	Seniority	Brach/Arm/Group	Unit
DACOMBE, CARL A	Lt RN	01-Sep-04	WAR	RNR AIR BR VL
DADY, SIMON	Lt Cdr	01-Oct-14	WAR	HMS PRESIDENT
DALBY, RUSSELL	Lt Cdr	01-Oct-14	WAR	HMS SHERWOOD
DALLAMORE, REBECCA A	Lt Cdr	01-Oct-14	WAR	HMS KING ALFRED
DANE, RICHARD M H OBE	Lt Cdr	01-Aug-05	WAR	RNR AIR BR VL
DANGERFIELD, CHARLOTTE	Mid	26-Nov-09	New Entrant	HMS PRESIDENT
DARWEN, CLINT	Lt RN	12-Nov-10	WAR	RNR MEDIA OPERATIONS
DAVIES, GEORGE C	Lt Cdr	31-Mar-03	WAR	RNR AIR BR VL
DAVIES, RICHARD M	Lt RN	17-Sep-03	WAR	RNR MEDIA OPERATIONS
DAVIES, SARAH	Lt RN	19-Feb-99	WAR	HMS PRESIDENT
DAVIS, ANDREW R	Lt Cdr	02-Oct-94	WAR	RNR AIR BR VL
DAVIS, SERENA	Lt RN	08-Nov-03	WAR	HMS VIVID
DAWSON, MELISSA	Lt RN	21-Dec-04	WAR	HMS PRESIDENT
DAY, PHILIP O T	Mid	01-Apr-14	New Entrant	HMS FORWARD
DEAN, NICOLA	Surg Lt Cdr	01-Sep-06	MED	HMS CALLIOPE
DEAVIN, MATTHEW J	Lt Cdr	01-Oct-08	WAR	RNR AIR BR VL
DEENEY, STEPHEN J	Lt Cdr	01-Oct-99	WAR	RNR AIR BR VL
DEIGHTON, GRAEME	Lt Cdr	01-Oct-12	WAR	HMS CALLIOPE
DEMUTH, ALICE	OCdt	01-Jul-11	New Entrant	HMS FORWARD
DENT, JOHN	Lt RN	22-Oct-08	WAR	HMS SCOTIA
DEWAR, MICHAEL J	Lt RN	03-Apr-09	WAR	RNR AIR BR VL
DICKENS, CHARLES	Lt Cdr	01-Oct-12	WAR	HMS FERRET - RNRIU
DITTON, NATHAN	Lt Cdr	01-Oct-12	WAR	HMS KING ALFRED
DIXON, SIMON J	Lt RN	01-Jan-05	WAR	RNR AIR BR VL
DODD, KEVIN M	Lt Cdr	01-Apr-99	WAR	RNR AIR BR VL
DONALDSON, JAMES W	OCdt	01-Oct-12	New Entrant	HMS PRESIDENT
DONNELLY, JAMES S OBE	Lt Cdr	28-Jul-98	ENG	RNR AIR BR VL
DONOHUE, PAUL	Lt RN	13-Feb-07	WAR	HMS FERRET - RNRIU
DORMAN, NICHOLAS RD	Capt RN	01-Sep-09	WAR	FLEET CMR
DOVEY, PHILIP A	Lt RN	11-Mar-11	WAR	HMS DALRIADA
DOWDELL, ROBERT E J	Lt Cdr	01-Oct-94	WAR	RNR AIR BR VL
DOWNING, CARL W	Lt Cdr	16-Nov-92	ENG	RNR AIR BR VL
DOWNING, CHARLOTTE	OCdt	22-Oct-09	New Entrant	HMS PRESIDENT
DOWNING, NEIL RD	Lt Cdr	31-Mar-00	WAR	FLEET CMR
DRAKE, RODERICK	Lt Cdr	31-Mar-98	WAR	HMS FLYING FOX

Name	Rank	Seniority	Brach/Arm/Group	Unit
DRODGE, KEVIN N	Lt Cdr	01-Oct-11	WAR	RNR AIR BR VL
DRUMMOND, ANDREW	Surg Lt Cdr	08-Aug-08	MED	HMS CALLIOPE
DUFFIELD, GARY G	Cdr	30-Sep-06	ENG	RNR AIR BR VL
DUFFIELD-SMITH, VICTORIA H S	Mid	01-Oct-13	New Entrant	HMS FORWARD
DUNKLEY, SIMON C	Lt Cdr	01-Oct-08	WAR	RNR AIR BR VL
DUNLOP, JOANNE	Lt Cdr	30-Mar-07	WAR	HMS CAMBRIA
DUNN, EDWARD	Lt RN	11-Dec-11	WAR	HMS WILDFIRE
DUNNE, LAWRENCE J RD	Lt Cdr	31-Mar-04	WAR	HMS FORWARD
DUNNE, VICTORIA	SLt	02-Mar-10	WAR	HMS PRESIDENT
DUSTAN, ANDREW J	Lt Cdr	15-May-04	ENG	RNR AIR BR VL

E

Name	Rank	Seniority	Brach/Arm/Group	Unit
EALEY, NICHOLAS J	Lt Cdr	01-Oct-14	WAR	HMS FLYING FOX
EARLE, GARETH D	OCdt	01-Sep-12	New Entrant	HMS FLYING FOX
EASTAUGH, TIMOTHY C	Lt Cdr	01-Oct-93	WAR	RNR AIR BR VL
EASTERBROOK, HELEN A	Lt RN	19-Jan-11	WAR	HMS WILDFIRE
EASTHAM, ALLAN M RD	Lt Cdr	31 Mar 94	WAR	HMS KING ALFRED
EDWARDS, MATTHEW P	Lt RN	11-Sep-09	WAR	HMS FERRET - RNRIU
EDWARDS, MICHAEL	Surg Cdr	30-Jun-08	MED	HMS SHERWOOD
ELDER-DICKER, NICHOLAS	Lt RN	01-Aug-04	WAR	HMS VIVID
ELLIOTT, LUKE S	Mid	15-Jan-14	New Entrant	HMS VIVID
ELLISON, BRYONY	Lt RN	20-Feb-05	WAR	HMS PRESIDENT
ELMORE, SIMON C	Mid	01-Aug-14	New Entrant	HMS SHERWOOD
ESFAHANI, SHAHROKH	Lt Cdr	31-Mar-02	WAR	HMS WILDFIRE
EVERITT, TOBYN W	Lt Cdr	01-Oct-05	WAR	RNR AIR BR VL

F

Name	Rank	Seniority	Brach/Arm/Group	Unit
FARMER, GARY G RD	Lt Cdr	31-Mar-06	WAR	HMS SCOTIA
FARQUHAR, JAMES	SLt	19-May-12	WAR	HMS CALLIOPE
FEARON, CATHERINE G	Lt RN	02-May-08	WAR	HMS PRESIDENT
FEDOROWICZ, RICHARD	Lt Cdr	16-Oct-00	WAR	RNR AIR BR VL
FEGAN, PAUL	Lt RN	25-Oct-01	WAR	RNR MEDIA OPERATIONS
FERRAN, SIMON H M	Lt RN	17-Jul-07	WAR	HMS HIBERNIA
FERRIE, HEATHER	Lt RN	22-Sep-07	WAR	HMS FERRET - RNRIU
FILOCHOWSKI, KATE	OCdt	01-Jan-13	New Entrant	HMS PRESIDENT
FILTNESS, REBECCA A J	Lt Cdr	01-Oct-14	WAR	HMS DALRIADA
FINCH, STEVEN	Lt Cdr	01-Oct-08	ENG	RNR AIR BR VL
FISHER, ROBERT J	Lt Cdr	01-Oct-09	WAR	RNR AIR BR VL
FITZGERALD, NICHOLAS J	Lt RN	01-Dec-92	WAR	RNR AIR BR VL
FITZPATRICK, DARREN	Lt RN	30-Apr-08	QARNNS	HMS EAGLET
FLANAGAN, MARTIN E A	Lt Cdr	01-Feb-92	WAR	RNR AIR BR VL
FLEMING, SAMUEL	Lt Cdr	01-Nov-04	WAR	HMS KING ALFRED
FLETCHER, CATRIONA	Lt RN	23-Jun-08	WAR	HMS SCOTIA
FLETCHER, RICHARD	Lt Cdr	01-Oct-14	LOGS	HMS VIVID
FLINTOFF, SUSAN E M	Lt RN	29-Jul-02	WAR	HMS DALRIADA
FORBES, PAUL T	Lt RN	16-Jul-96	WAR	RNR AIR BR VL
FOREMAN, TIMOTHY P	Lt Cdr	31-Mar-03	WAR	RNR AIR BR VL
FORSTER, RAYMOND A	Lt Cdr	01-Oct-01	WAR	RNR AIR BR VL
FOSTER, BRUCE M T	Lt Cdr	07-Dec-98	WAR	RNR MEDIA OPERATIONS
FOSTER, NICHOLAS	Lt RN	13-Jun-08	WAR	HMS CALLIOPE
FOX, RICHARD G OBE	Lt Cdr	30-Jun-05	WAR	RNR AIR BR VL
FRANCIS, DEREK E	Lt Cdr	30-Mar-13	WAR	HMS FERRET - RNRIU
FRANCIS, GARRY	Lt RN	05-Apr-08	WAR	HMS FERRET - RNRIU
FRANKS, JASON A	Lt RN	03-Sep-13	WAR	HMS FERRET - RNRIU
FREEMAN, PAUL	Lt RN	13-Jul-12	WAR	HMS CALLIOPE
FRY, STEPHEN M RD	Lt Cdr	31-Mar-05	WAR	HMS CAMBRIA

G

Name	Rank	Seniority	Brach/Arm/Group	Unit
GAFFNEY, FRANCIS	Lt RN	16-Apr-08	WAR	HMS FERRET - RNRIU
GAINSBOROUGH, JONATHAN M	RN Chpln	01-Feb-14	New Entrant	HMS FLYING FOX

Name	Rank	Seniority	Brach/Arm/Group	Unit
GALLIMORE, RICHARD M C	Lt Cdr	01-Oct-00	WAR	RNR AIR BR VL
GARDINER, GEORGE RD	Surg Cdr	30-Sep-04	MED	HMS HIBERNIA
GATENBY, CHRISTOPHER	Lt Cdr	31-Mar-07	WAR	HMS EAGLET
GATER, JAMES C	Lt RN	01-Jan-03	WAR	RNR MEDIA OPERATIONS
GAVEY, STEPHEN RD	Lt Cdr	01-Aug-88	WAR	HMS VIVID
GEARY, MICHAEL D	Lt Cdr	31-Mar-05	WAR	RNR AIR BR VL
GENDER-SHERRY, DANIEL P P	Mid	01-Dec-14	New Entrant	HMS KING ALFRED
GHOST, RICHARD	Lt RN	01-Nov-07	WAR	HMS FERRET - RNRIU
GIBBS, ANTHONY E	Lt RN	08-Apr-01	WAR	RNR AIR BR VL
GIBSON, PHAEDRA	Lt Cdr	01-Oct-07	New Entrant Instructor	HMS VIVID
GILBERT, ANTHONY	Lt RN	26-Aug-06	WAR	HMS FLYING FOX
GLEAVE, JAMES	Lt Cdr	31-Mar-04	WAR	HMS DALRIADA
GOBEY, CHRISTOPHER	Lt Cdr	01-Oct-95	WAR	HMS SCOTIA
GOBEY, RICHARD	Lt Cdr	01-Oct-14	WAR	HMS KING ALFRED
GOLDSWORTHY, ELAINE T	Lt Cdr	01-Oct-04	WAR	RNR MEDIA OPERATIONS
GOOD, GREGORY L	Mid	01-Dec-14	New Entrant	HMS KING ALFRED
GOODES, SIMON RD	Lt Cdr	31-Mar-97	WAR	HMS WILDFIRE
GORAM, MALCOLM	Lt Cdr	31-Mar-04	WAR	RNR AIR BR VL
GOWER, BENJAMIN C S	SLt	01-Mar-14	WAR	HMS PRESIDENT
GRACEY, PETER	Cdr	30-Jun-09	WAR	HMS FORWARD
GRAHAM, RICHARD	Surg Cdr	30-Jun-14	MED	FLEET CMR
GRAY, SAMUEL D	Lt RN	01-Aug-04	WAR	HMS CALLIOPE
GREAVES, CHRISTOPHER J	Lt Cdr	01-Oct-95	WAR	RNR AIR BR VL
GREAVES, MICHAEL J	Lt Cdr	01-Apr-94	WAR	RNR AIR BR VL
GREEN, CHRISTOPHER T	OCdt	23-Feb-11	New Entrant	HMS PRESIDENT
GREENACRE, RICHARD RD	Lt Cdr	31-Mar-97	WAR	HMS VIVID
GREENE, ALISTAIR	Lt RN	04-Jul-03	LOGS	HMS PRESIDENT
GRENNAN, EAMONN F	Lt Cdr	01-Oct-06	WAR	HMS HIBERNIA
GRIFFITHS, CHRISTOPHER P	OCdt	01-Jul-12	New Entrant	HMS CAMBRIA
GRIFFITHS, LINDSAY	Lt RN	01-Mar-13	WAR	HMS FLYING FOX
GRIFFITHS, MICHAEL E RD	Lt Cdr	31-Mar-02	WAR	HMS CAMBRIA
GRIST, DAVID	Lt Cdr	05-Oct-10	QARNNS	HMS KING ALFRED
GUNN, WILLIAM J S	Lt Cdr	01-Nov-94	WAR	RNR AIR BR VL

H

Name	Rank	Seniority	Brach/Arm/Group	Unit
HADDOW, TIMOTHY R	Lt Cdr	01-Mar-05	WAR	HMS SCOTIA
HAFFENDEN, SIMON	Lt Cdr	21-Nov-05	WAR	HMS FLYING FOX
HAIKIN, PETER	Lt RN	02-Feb-96	WAR	HMS FERRET - RNRIU
HAINES, PAUL	OCdt	01-Aug-11	WAR	HMS KING ALFRED
HAINSWORTH, ROBIN	Lt RN	22-Aug-11	WAR	HMS CALLIOPE
HALL, STEPHEN	Lt Cdr	01-Oct-12	WAR	HMS FERRET - RNRIU
HALLIDAY, IAN W	Lt Cdr	01-Sep-90	WAR	RNR AIR BR VL
HAMIDUDDIN, IQBAL	Lt RN	01-Feb-04	WAR	HMS FLYING FOX
HAMILTON, IVAN J	Lt RN	16-Nov-91	WAR	RNR AIR BR VL
HAMILTON, RICHARD	Lt RN	10-Feb-08	WAR	HMS PRESIDENT
HANCOCK, ANGELA M QVRM	Capt RN	15-Oct-12	WAR	HMS VIVID
HAND, NICHOLAS J S	Mid	01-Dec-13	New Entrant	HMS FLYING FOX
HANDLEY, DANE C	Lt Cdr	31-Mar-96	WAR	RNR AIR BR VL
HANKEY, HELEN	Lt RN	14-Dec-01	LOGS	HMS PRESIDENT
HANKEY, MARK RD	Lt Cdr	31-Mar-07	WAR	RNR MEDIA OPERATIONS
HARDINGE, CHRISTOPHER MBE	Cdr	30-Sep-05	WAR	HMS PRESIDENT
HARDINGE, RICHMAL	Lt Cdr	31-Mar-07	WAR	HMS PRESIDENT
HARDWICK, LUCY J	Lt RN	10-Jun-13	WAR	HMS FERRET - RNRIU
HARGREAVES, NEALE MBE	Lt Cdr	23-May-98	WAR	RNR AIR BR VL
HARGREAVES, NICHOLAS	Mid	01-Oct-14	New Entrant	HMS EAGLET
HARGREAVES, SIMON N OBE	Cdr	01-Jul-02	WAR	RNR AIR BR VL
HARPER, ALEC	Lt RN	22-Oct-09	WAR	HMS PRESIDENT
HARPER, JAMES A	Lt Cdr	01-Oct-97	WAR	RNR AIR BR VL
HARPER-ROBERTS, HELENA M	Mid	01-Jul-14	New Entrant	HMS FORWARD
HARRIS, ADAM R L	OCdt	04-Aug-10	New Entrant	HMS PRESIDENT
HARRIS, ADRIAN	Lt Cdr	31-Mar-06	WAR	HMS VIVID
HARRISON, LAURA	Lt RN	20-Jul-07	WAR	RNR MEDIA OPERATIONS

Name	Rank	Seniority	Brach/Arm/Group	Unit
HARRISON, RICHARD W	Surg Lt Cdr	17-May-95	MED	HMS SHERWOOD
HART, PAUL A	Lt Cdr	01-Oct-98	WAR	RNR MEDIA OPERATIONS
HART, SARAH	Lt RN	08-May-13	WAR	HMS FERRET - RNRIU
HAWKINS, CHRISTOPHER R	SLt	01-Mar-14	WAR	HMS SCOTIA
HAWKINS, JOHN	Lt Cdr	16-Oct-12	WAR	HMS KING ALFRED
HAYES, BRIAN J	Lt Cdr	01-Oct-05	WAR	HMS CAMBRIA
HAYHURST, JAMIE	Mid	05-Mar-09	New Entrant	HMS CALLIOPE
HAYWARD-RODGERS, DARREN	Lt Cdr	01-Oct-14	WAR	RNR AIR BR VL
HEARN, SAMUEL P	Lt Cdr	01-Oct-14	WAR	RNR MEDIA OPERATIONS
HEIGHWAY, MARTIN R	Lt RN	08-May-00	WAR	HMS KING ALFRED
HEINOWSKI, THOMAS	Lt RN	20-Jun-04	WAR	HMS SCOTIA
HELSBY, EDWARD	Lt Cdr	31-Mar-96	WAR	RNR AIR BR VL
HERBERT-BURNS, RUPERT H	Lt RN	27-Nov-10	WAR	HMS FERRET - RNRIU
HERMANSON, STEPHEN	Lt RN	23-Mar-06	WAR	HMS FERRET - RNRIU
HERRIMAN, JOHN A	Cdr	30-Jun-14	WAR	HMS PRESIDENT
HERRON, RELTON J P	Mid	01-Sep-14	New Entrant	HMS PRESIDENT
HEWINS, CLIVE	Lt Cdr	20-May-91	WAR	HMS CALLIOPE
HEYWOOD, ANTHONY J	Lt RN	11-Dec-11	WAR	HMS FERRET - RNRIU
HIBBERT, MARTIN	Lt Cdr	01-Nov-96	WAR	HMS VIVID
HICKIN, MARIA	Mid	01-Aug-14	New Entrant	HMS PRESIDENT
HIGSON, RENNIE	Lt RN	05-Oct-07	WAR	HMS SHERWOOD
HILL, PAUL RD	Capt RN	04-Oct-11	WAR	FLEET CMR
HODKINSON-WALKER, KRISTA	Lt RN	18-Nov-05	WAR	HMS CAMBRIA
HOGAN, AMBROSE D	Lt Cdr	01-Oct-13	WAR	HMS WILDFIRE
HOLBORN, CARL	Lt Cdr	31-Mar-03	ENG	RNR AIR BR VL
HOLLAND, OLIVER T P	SLt	22-Sep-14	WAR	HMS PRESIDENT
HOLLEY, STEVEN	Lt Cdr	01-Oct-14	WAR	HMS KING ALFRED
HOLMWOOD, MARK A G	Lt Cdr	01-Aug-11	WAR	HMS EAGLET
HOLOHAN, RUAIRI	SLt	22-Sep-14	WAR	HMS HIBERNIA
HOLVEY, PAUL	Lt RN	01-Apr-01	WAR	HMS VIVID
HORNE, MARTIN	Lt RN	01-Oct-13	WAR	HMS KING ALFRED
HORNER, BENJAMIN	Lt Cdr	01-Oct-13	WAR	HMS PRESIDENT
HORSLEY, JOHN R	Surg Lt Cdr	01-Sep-87	MED	HMS EAGLET
HOWARD-PEARCE, TAMAR A	Lt RN	18-Jun-11	WAR	RNR MEDIA OPERATIONS
HOWITT, SARA	Lt RN	04-Jan-10	WAR	HMS FLYING FOX
HOYLE, STEPHEN	Lt Cdr	31-Mar-03	WAR	HMS EAGLET
HUBBLE, ROBERT S E	Lt Cdr	01-Oct-97	WAR	RNR AIR BR VL
HUGHES, JILL	Lt Cdr	31-Mar-95	WAR	HMS HIBERNIA
HUGHES, SEAN C	Surg Lt Cdr	14-Nov-08	MED	HMS KING ALFRED
HULSE, ROYSTON M	Lt RN	01-Sep-03	WAR	RNR AIR BR VL
HUNWICKS, SARAH E	Lt Cdr	01-Oct-05	ENG	RNR AIR BR VL

I

IRELAND, STEVEN	OCdt	01-Apr-13	New Entrant	HMS HIBERNIA

J

JACKSON, AMIE R	Lt RN	01-Jan-08	WAR	HMS PRESIDENT
JACQUES, KATHRYN	Lt RN	24-Jan-07	WAR	HMS SHERWOOD
JAFFIER, ROBERT RD	Lt Cdr	01-Oct-10	WAR	HMS FORWARD
JAMESON, SUSAN RD	Cdr	30-Jun-09	WAR	HMS FERRET - RNRIU
JERMY, RICHARD	Lt Cdr	31-Mar-04	WAR	HMS FERRET - RNRIU
JEWITT, CHARLES	Lt Cdr	30-Jun-03	LOGS	HMS FORWARD
JOHNSON, ALEX D	Lt Cdr	01-Oct-13	WAR	RNR AIR BR VL
JOHNSON, WILLIAM	Mid	01-Mar-13	New Entrant	HMS PRESIDENT
JONES, ANDREW	Lt Cdr	01-Oct-12	WAR	HMS KING ALFRED
JONES, CAROLYN	Lt Cdr	01-Oct-14	WAR	RNR MEDIA OPERATIONS
JONES, CHARLES	Lt Cdr	31-Mar-00	WAR	HMS SCOTIA
JONES, IAIN	Lt RN	17-Nov-07	WAR	RNR MEDIA OPERATIONS
JONES, KEITH W	Lt Cdr	01-Oct-14	LOGS	HMS FORWARD
JONES, LESLIE	Lt Cdr	11-Sep-93	WAR	HMS FERRET - RNRIU
JONES, PAULINE	Lt Cdr	31-Mar-98	LOGS	HMS CALLIOPE

Name	Rank	Seniority	Brach/Arm/Group	Unit
JONES, SIMON S	Lt Cdr	21-Dec-09	WAR	RNR AIR BR VL
JORDAN, EMMA L	Lt RN	01-May-97	WAR	RNR AIR BR VL

K

KAY, DAVID RD	Cdr	01-Jan-02	LOGS	HMS FLYING FOX
KELYNACK, MARK T	Lt Cdr	01-Oct-05	WAR	RNR AIR BR VL
KEMP, SIMON M	Lt Cdr	31-Mar-99	WAR	HMS FERRET - RNRIU
KENDRICK, KATHERINE	Lt Cdr	01-Oct-13	WAR	HMS PRESIDENT
KENT, THOMAS RD	Cdr	30-Sep-99	WAR	HMS SHERWOOD
KHALEK, ADHAM A A	Surg Lt Cdr	27-May-11	MED	HMS PRESIDENT
KING, CHARLES	Lt Cdr	31-Mar-02	WAR	HMS KING ALFRED
KING, IAN	Lt Cdr	01-Oct-08	WAR	HMS FERRET - RNRIU
KING, KIMBERLEY J	OCdt	01-Mar-11	New Entrant	HMS FLYING FOX
KIRK, WILLIAM	Lt RN	31-Mar-96	WAR	HMS FORWARD
KIRKHAM, SIMON P	Lt Cdr	28-Jan-05	WAR	RNR AIR BR VL
KNOTT, STEPHEN J M	OCdt	01-Nov-12	New Entrant	HMS PRESIDENT
KNOWLES, DONNA	Lt Cdr	31-Mar-01	WAR	HMS HIBERNIA
KNOWLES, THOMAS	Ll Cdr	01-Oct-13	WAR	HMS SCOTIA

L

LACEY, DAVID E	OCdt	01-Apr-13	New Entrant	HMS VIVID
LADISLAUS, PAUL	Lt RN	07-Jul-04	WAR	HMS CALLIOPE
LAMBERT, ALLISON	Lt Cdr	26-Jun-04	WAR	RNR AIR BR VL
LANE, HEATHER J	Lt Cdr	01-Oct-08	WAR	RNR MEDIA OPERATIONS
LANGMEAD, CLIVE F QVRM	Lt Cdr	01-Jul-90	WAR	HMS FORWARD
LAUSTE, WILLIAM E	Lt Cdr	01-Mar-99	WAR	RNR MEDIA OPERATIONS
LAWRENCE, IAN	Lt RN	05-May-08	WAR	HMS KING ALFRED
LEACH, SIMON D	Lt Cdr	31-Mar-06	WAR	RNR AIR BR VL
LEE, AI FAI	SLt	08-May-13	WAR	HMS PRESIDENT
LEE, MATTHEW M	Lt Cdr	31-Jul-94	WAR	HMS FERRET - RNRIU
LEMKES, JAMES	SLt	22-Sep-14	WAR	HMS PRESIDENT
LETTINGTON, PAUL D W	Lt RN	01-Jan-06	ENG	HMS VIVID
LEVINE, ANDREW J	Lt Cdr	31-Mar-06	WAR	RNR AIR BR VL
LEWIN, PHILLIP J	SLt	22-Mar-12	WAR	HMS SHERWOOD
LEWIS, RICHARD QVRM	Lt Cdr	31-Mar-01	WAR	RNR AIR BR VL
LEWIS, SIMON RD	Lt Cdr	31-Mar-04	LOGS	HMS KING ALFRED
LEWIS, THOMAS R	SLt	11-May-13	WAR	HMS FLYING FOX
LINTON, ANDREW	Lt RN	02-Nov-05	WAR	HMS EAGLET
LITTLE, ANDREW J	Mid	01-Jul-14	New Entrant	HMS CALLIOPE
LITTMAN, JON A	Lt RN	17-Jun-12	WAR	HMS WILDFIRE
LLEWELLYN, JONATHAN G	Lt Cdr	01-Oct-12	WAR	RNR AIR BR VL
LLOYD, DAVID	Lt Cdr	31-Mar-99	WAR	HMS KING ALFRED
LLOYD, GARETH RD	Lt Cdr	31-Mar-98	WAR	HMS FERRET - RNRIU
LLOYD, SUSAN J	Lt Cdr	31-Mar-04	WAR	RNR MEDIA OPERATIONS
LOCK, GILBERT J	Mid	01-Jul-14	New Entrant	HMS SHERWOOD
LONG, CHRISTOPHER L	Lt RN	20-Oct-10	WAR	RNR AIR BR VL
LOW, SIMEON A S	Lt RN	01-Nov-05	WAR	HMS WILDFIRE
LOWNDES, TIMOTHY	Lt RN	12-May-14	WAR	HMS PRESIDENT
LUMLEY, RICHARD	Lt RN	03-Apr-10	WAR	HMS FERRET - RNRIU
LUMLEY, SHEILA F	Mid	01-Dec-13	New Entrant	HMS PRESIDENT
LYDON, MICHAEL	Lt RN	30-Sep-96	LOGS	HMS CALLIOPE
LYNAGH, MICHELLE	OCdt	01-Oct-12	New Entrant	HMS DALRIADA
LYNCH, MATTHEW L	Lt RN	29-May-13	WAR	HMS EAGLET
LYNCH, RORY D F	Lt Cdr	14-Apr-00	WAR	RNR AIR BR VL
LYNCH, SUZANNE	Lt RN	28-Nov-00	LOGS	HMS CAMBRIA

M

MACDONALD, JOSEPH B C	OCdt	22-Mar-11	WAR	HMS PRESIDENT
MACKAY, DAVID H	Lt Cdr	01-Oct-93	WAR	RNR AIR BR VL
MACKENZIE, HANNAH	Lt Cdr	01-Oct-12	WAR	HMS WILDFIRE

Name	Rank	Seniority	Brach/Arm/Group	Unit
MACKIE, ROBERT C G	Lt RN	14-Dec-01	WAR	HMS FORWARD
MACLEAN, MARJORY	RN Chpln	25-Nov-04	RN Chaplaincy Service	HMS SCOTIA
MACSEPHNEY, TRACY	Lt Cdr	01-Oct-12	WAR	HMS WILDFIRE
MAHONY, CHRISTOPHER D C	Lt Cdr	12-Apr-96	WAR	RNR AIR BR VL
MALKIN, ROY	Lt Cdr	01-Oct-08	WAR	HMS KING ALFRED
MALLINSON, STUART	Lt RN	31-Dec-95	WAR	HMS PRESIDENT
MANNION, ROBERT	Lt Cdr	01-Jun-95	WAR	HMS VIVID
MANSER, DARREN N.	Lt Cdr	31-Mar-06	WAR	RNR AIR BR VL
MANSERGH, FRANCES A	Lt RN	30-Jan-99	WAR	RNR MEDIA OPERATIONS
MANSFIELD, JAMES	Lt Cdr	01-Oct-06	WAR	HMS PRESIDENT
MARK, ABIGAIL	Lt RN	01-Oct-05	WAR	RAF LINTON-ON-OUSE - BFJT
MARRIOTT, ISABELLA M C	Lt RN	01-Dec-08	WAR	RNR MEDIA OPERATIONS
MARSDEN, SIMON A	Lt RN	25-Nov-11	WAR	HMS PRESIDENT
MARSHALL, COLIN G	Lt RN	01-May-05	WAR	RNR MEDIA OPERATIONS
MARTIN, JAMES H	Lt RN	16-Oct-10	WAR	HMS DALRIADA
MASSEY, PAUL	Lt Cdr	05-Dec-02	WAR	RNR AIR BR VL
MASTERS, SIMON	SLt	14-Sep-13	WAR	HMS FLYING FOX
MATHER, ROBIN A	Mid	01-Jun-14	New Entrant	HMS FLYING FOX
MATHERS, FIONA C	Lt RN	02-Dec-05	WAR	HMS FERRET - RNRIU
MAWHINNEY, ABIGAIL	Surg Lt Cdr	16-Jun-13	MED	HMS HIBERNIA
MCARDELL, STEVEN J	Lt Cdr	31-Mar-04	WAR	RNR AIR BR VL
MCDADE, CHRISTOPHER G.	SLt	19-Nov-09	WAR	HMS DALRIADA
MCEVOY, LEE P	Lt Cdr	01-Oct-03	WAR	HMS FERRET - RNRIU
MCHALE, GARETH J	Lt Cdr	01-Dec-91	WAR	RNR AIR BR VL
MCINTYRE, ALASTAIR W	Lt Cdr	01-Oct-04	WAR	HMS FERRET - RNRIU
MCKEATING, JOHN	Surg Cdr	31-Dec-99	MED	HMS SHERWOOD
MCKEE, ROBERT W	Lt RN	01-May-04	WAR	RNR AIR BR VL
MCKENZIE, GARY	Lt Cdr	01-Oct-09	WAR	HMS CAMBRIA
MCKINLEY, MAIRI	Lt Cdr	01-Oct-13	QARNNS	HMS SCOTIA
MCKINTY, GARETH	Lt RN	12-Jun-07	WAR	HMS FERRET - RNRIU
MCLAVERTY, KAREN	Lt Cdr	17-Mar-99	WAR	HMS HIBERNIA
MCLEAN, DANIEL J	Mid	01-Nov-14	New Entrant	HMS KING ALFRED
MCLUNDIE, WILLIAM M	SLt	18-Feb-12	WAR	HMS FORWARD
MCMURRAN, ROBERT C	Lt Cdr	17-Nov-04	WAR	HMS HIBERNIA
MCNAUGHT, EDWARD RD	Cdr	30-Jun-08	WAR	FLEET CMR
MCVICAR, CRAIG	Mid	01-Nov-14	WAR	HMS SCOTIA
MCWILLIAMS, BARRY J	SLt	22-Sep-14	WAR	HMS HIBERNIA
MEHARG, NEIL RD	Lt Cdr	31-Mar-06	WAR	HMS HIBERNIA
MEIKLE, STUART A	Lt Cdr	01-Oct-07	ENG	RNR AIR BR VL
MELHUISH, DAVID R	Lt RN	04-Jul-14	WAR	HMS SCOTIA
MEROPOULOS, JOHN	Lt Cdr	01-Oct-14	WAR	HMS FERRET - RNRIU
MESTON, JOHN M	Lt Cdr	10-Apr-00	WAR	RNR AIR BR VL
MILLER, DAVID S	Lt Cdr	01-Apr-95	WAR	RNR AIR BR VL
MILLER, IAN	Lt RN	11-Aug-13	WAR	HMS CAMBRIA
MILLER, ROY	Lt RN	04-Dec-07	LOGS	HMS EAGLET
MILLIKEN, JAMES W	RN Chpln	01-Jun-14	RN Chaplaincy Service	HMS DALRIADA
MILLS, ANDREW	Lt Cdr	01-May-95	WAR	RNR MEDIA OPERATIONS
MILLS, SYDNEY D G	Lt Cdr	01-Oct-12	WAR	RNR AIR BR VL
MOMBRU, ALEIX D	SLt	22-Sep-14	WAR	HMS PRESIDENT
MONK, STEPHEN R	Lt Cdr	17-Mar-10	WAR	HMS KING ALFRED
MOORE, CHRISTOPHER	Lt RN	24-Sep-05	WAR	HMS FORWARD
MOORTHY, ROHAN M	Lt RN	02-Jul-00	WAR	HMS PRESIDENT
MORAN, SIMON D	Lt Cdr	31-Mar-05	WAR	RNR AIR BR VL
MORDAUNT, PENELOPE M	OCdt	19-Jan-12	New Entrant	HMS KING ALFRED
MORGAN, EUGENE P	Cdr	30-Jun-11	WAR	HMS FERRET - RNRIU
MORGAN, GARETH W	Lt Cdr	31-Mar-01	LOGS	HMS SHERWOOD
MORGAN, PHILLIP D J	Lt RN	26-Sep-11	WAR	RNR MEDIA OPERATIONS
MORGANS, DANIEL J	Lt Cdr	01-Oct-08	WAR	HMS FERRET - RNRIU
MORLEY, DIETMAR	Lt Cdr	31-Mar-06	WAR	HMS SHERWOOD
MORRISON, JOSEPH	OCdt	01-Jun-13	New Entrant	HMS HIBERNIA
MORSE, JEREMY	Lt Cdr	01-Oct-09	WAR	RNR AIR BR VL
MOSELEY, ALLISON	Lt RN	29-Apr-04	WAR	HMS CALLIOPE

Name	Rank	Seniority	Brach/Arm/Group	Unit
MOULTON, SIMON J	Lt RN	01-Jan-92	WAR	RNR AIR BR VL
MULLOWNEY, PAUL	Lt Cdr	01-Oct-10	WAR	RNR AIR BR VL
MUNSON, EILEEN P RD	Lt Cdr	01-Oct-08	QARNNS	HMS CAMBRIA
MURPHY, DICCON A	Lt Cdr	01-Oct-12	WAR	RNR AIR BR VL
MURPHY, STEPHEN M	Lt Cdr	13-Jan-06	ENG	FLEET CMR
MURRAY, ANITA MAY	Lt Cdr	01-Oct-09	LOGS	HMS VIVID
MURRISON, ANDREW	Surg Cdr	31-Dec-97	MED	HMS PRESIDENT
MURRISON, MARK RD	Cdr	06-Nov-06	WAR	HMS PRESIDENT

N

Name	Rank	Seniority	Brach/Arm/Group	Unit
NEWALL, JEREMY A	Lt Cdr	03-Jun-95	WAR	RNR AIR BR VL
NEWMAN, VIRGINIA H	Lt Cdr	01-Oct-09	WAR	RNR MEDIA OPERATIONS
NEWTON, JAMES L DFC	Lt Cdr	11-Feb-03	WAR	RNR AIR BR VL
NIBLOCK, GILLIAN	Lt RN	09-Nov-11	WAR	HMS WILDFIRE
NICHOLAS, BRYAN J MBE	Lt Cdr	01-Oct-01	WAR	RNR AIR BR VL
NICHOLSON, JOHN K	Lt RN	01-Apr-06	WAR	HMS WILDFIRE
NICOLSON, VERNON	Lt RN	03-May-05	WAR	HMS FERRET - RNRIU
NISBET, JAMES T	Lt Cdr	01-Oct-14	WAR	HMS FERRET - RNRIU
NOAKES, DAVID RD	Lt Cdr	01-Oct-12	LOGS	HMS CALLIOPE
NOBLE, ALEXANDER	Lt RN	02-Feb-06	WAR	HMS KING ALFRED
NOBLE, ROBERT H	Lt Cdr	31-Mar-97	WAR	HMS SHERWOOD
NOLAN, GRAEME A R	OCdt	06-Feb-12	New Entrant	HMS KING ALFRED
NORTHCOTT, JOHN	Cdr	30-Jun-13	LOGS	FLEET CMR
NOTLEY, CLAIRE A	SLt	19-May-12	WAR	RNR MEDIA OPERATIONS
NOTLEY, RICHARD M	Lt RN	04-Aug-10	WAR	HMS PRESIDENT
NOYCE, NIGEL	Lt Cdr	15-Jan-97	WAR	HMS FERRET - RNRIU

O

Name	Rank	Seniority	Brach/Arm/Group	Unit
OARTON, JAMIE C	Mid	01-Mar-10	WAR	HMS FERRET - RNRIU
OATES, EDWARD P	Lt Cdr	16-Feb-93	WAR	RNR AIR BR VL
O'DOOLEY, PAUL	Lt Cdr	01-Oct-14	WAR	HMS SHERWOOD
ODRISCOLL, EDWARD H	Lt RN	25-Jan-03	WAR	HMS FERRET - RNRIU
OKUKENU, DELE	Lt Cdr	01-Oct-08	WAR	RNR AIR BR VL
OLVER, JEREMY	Lt RN	01-Mar-10	WAR	RNR MEDIA OPERATIONS
ORD, ELIZABETH	Lt Cdr	01-Oct-09	WAR	HMS FERRET - RNRIU
ORMSHAW, ANDREW P	Cdr	15-Jul-04	WAR	RNR AIR BR VL
OVENS, JEREMY J	Lt Cdr	01-Dec-91	WAR	RNR AIR BR VL

P

Name	Rank	Seniority	Brach/Arm/Group	Unit
PACKHAM, CRAIG N R	Lt RN	01-Mar-96	WAR	RNR AIR BR VL
PADDOCK, LEE	Lt Cdr	01-Oct-14	WAR	HMS EAGLET
PARKER, JEREMY C S	Lt Cdr	01-Jan-09	WAR	HMS FLYING FOX
PARKHOUSE, MARK J	Lt RN	04-Oct-09	WAR	HMS FERRET - RNRIU
PARNELL, TERENCE A MBE	Lt RN	24-Oct-08	WAR	RNR AIR BR VL
PARRY, CHRISTOPHER MBE MA	Lt Cdr	05-Oct-10	WAR	HMS VIVID
PARSONAGE, NEIL	Lt Cdr	31-Mar-00	WAR	HMS EAGLET
PARTRIDGE, RICHARD W	Lt RN	01-Sep-12	WAR	HMS KING ALFRED
PATEMAN, JASON E	Lt RN	15-Apr-11	WAR	HMS CALLIOPE
PATERSON, MATTHEW	Lt RN	09-Mar-07	WAR	HMS WILDFIRE
PATTEN, MARK	Surg Lt Cdr	29-Mar-96	MED	HMS WILDFIRE
PEACHEY, RICHARD M	Lt RN	01-Nov-94	WAR	RNR AIR BR VL
PEACOCK, ANOUCHKA	Lt RN	01-Dec-05	WAR	HMS FERRET - RNRIU
PEARSON, CRAIG	Lt RN	02-Nov-10	WAR	HMS KING ALFRED
PEARSON, ROBERT J	Lt RN	01-Jun-05	WAR	HMS KING ALFRED
PEDLEY, MICHAEL E	Lt Cdr	01-Oct-13	WAR	HMS WILDFIRE
PEPPER, DANIEL J	Lt RN	01-Sep-09	WAR	HMS PRESIDENT
PERREN, ROBERT	Mid	01-Nov-14	New Entrant	HMS PRESIDENT
PERRETT, CHARLES H R	Mid	01-Aug-14	New Entrant	HMS PRESIDENT
PETHICK, IAN	Cdr	30-Jun-10	LOGS	HMS VIVID
PHILLIPS, JACOB	Mid	25-Nov-08	WAR	HMS PRESIDENT

Name	Rank	Seniority	Brach/Arm/Group	Unit
PHILLIPS, JAMES	Lt RN	20-Jun-11	WAR	HMS VIVID
PHILPOT, DAVID	Lt Cdr	18-Jul-00	WAR	HMS VIVID
PIKE, STUART	Lt Cdr	31-Mar-05	WAR	RNR AIR BR VL
PINFOLD, THOMAS D	OCdt	25-Mar-13	New Entrant	HMS EAGLET
PING, MICHELLE QVRM	Mid	01-Feb-14	New Entrant	HMS KING ALFRED
PIPE, DIANA	Lt RN	01-Jan-03	WAR	HMS PRESIDENT
POGSON, ANDREW D	Lt RN	10-Nov-08	WAR	HMS FERRET - RNRIU
POLLOCK, MALCOLM P	Lt Cdr	03-Aug-03	WAR	RNR AIR BR VL
POSNETT, DICKON W	Lt Cdr	31-Mar-99	WAR	RNR AIR BR VL
POULTON-WATT, ANDREW	Lt Cdr	01-Oct-09	WAR	HMS SCOTIA
POWELL, WILLIAM R	Lt Cdr	31-Mar-99	ENG	RNR AIR BR VL
POYSER, ROBIN Z M	Mid	01-Jul-14	New Entrant	HMS SCOTIA
PRATT, IAN	Lt Cdr	06-Oct-93	WAR	RNR MEDIA OPERATIONS
PRITCHARD, GWYN H	Mid	01-Jun-14	New Entrant	HMS FLYING FOX
PUGH, NEIL	Lt Cdr	31-Mar-06	LOGS	HMS CAMBRIA
PYKE, THOMAS F P	RN Chpln	13-Jun-07	RN Chaplaincy Service	HMS PRESIDENT

Q

QUINN, MARTIN	Capt RN	01-Jul-14	WAR	FLEET CMR

R

RAE, ALISTAIR L	Lt Cdr	01-Apr-05	WAR	HMS FERRET - RNRIU
RAMSAY, BRIAN	Lt Cdr	31-Mar-01	WAR	FLEET CMR
RANDLES, PHILIP	Lt Cdr	01-Oct-14	WAR	HMS CALLIOPE
RANKIN, CHRISTOPHER	Lt RN	01-Mar-04	QARNNS	HMS PRESIDENT
RANSOM, BENJAMIN R J	Lt RN	01-Sep-00	WAR	HMS FLYING FOX
RASOR, ANDREW M	Lt Cdr	01-Oct-12	WAR	RNR AIR BR VL
READ, DAVID A RD	Lt Cdr	31-Mar-97	WAR	HMS FERRET - RNRIU
READ, SIMON	Mid	01-Oct-14	WAR	HMS CAMBRIA
REDMOND, ROBERT	Lt Cdr	01-Nov-07	WAR	HMS KING ALFRED
REID, DOUGLAS R	Lt RN	01-Jul-04	WAR	RNR AIR BR VL
REILLY, REBECCA	Mid	06-Sep-14	New Entrant	HMS EAGLET
RENAUD, NEIL	Mid	01-Nov-13	New Entrant	HMS PRESIDENT
RENNELL, IAN	Lt Cdr	31-Mar-06	WAR	HMS EAGLET
RENOUF, ROBERT	Lt RN	24-Apr-05	WAR	HMS SCOTIA
RHODES, MARTIN J	Lt Cdr	01-Oct-04	WAR	HMS FLYING FOX
RICHARDS, GREGORY B	Lt RN	13-Oct-06	WAR	RNR MEDIA OPERATIONS
RICHARDS, GUY	Lt Cdr	01-Apr-03	WAR	HMS CAMBRIA
RICHARDSON, GEOFFREY L	Lt Cdr	01-Oct-02	WAR	RNR AIR BR VL
ROBERT, IAIN A	Lt RN	23-Dec-01	ENG	RNR AIR BR VL
ROBERTS, MARTYN	Lt Cdr	19-Jan-03	WAR	RNR AIR BR VL
ROBERTS, PHILIP E	SLt	01-Mar-14	WAR	HMS EAGLET
ROBERTS, ROBERT	Lt RN	27-May-05	WAR	HMS SCOTIA
ROBERTS, STEPHEN	Lt RN	01-Feb-03	WAR	HMS VIVID
ROBERTS, STUART A G	Surg Lt Cdr	12-Feb-14	MED	HMS FORWARD
ROBERTSON, LORNE THOMAS RD	Cdr	30-Jun-09	WAR	FLEET CMR
ROBERTSON, STUART	Lt Cdr	08-Nov-99	WAR	HMS SCOTIA
ROBINSON, ANDREW	Lt Cdr	01-Oct-11	WAR	FLEET CMR
ROBINSON, JAMES	Lt RN	24-Feb-90	WAR	HMS FERRET - RNRIU
ROGERS, ALAN	Lt Cdr	25-Dec-02	WAR	RNR AIR BR VL
ROGERS, VICTORIA A	Mid	01-Dec-14	New Entrant	HMS SHERWOOD
ROLL, SUSAN	Lt Cdr	31-Mar-01	WAR	HMS FLYING FOX
ROSINDALE, PHILIP RD	Lt Cdr	31-Mar-06	WAR	HMS VIVID
ROSS, JONATHAN A D RD	Cdr	30-Sep-06	WAR	FLEET CMR
ROSSITER, CLAIRE A	SLt	07-Oct-14	WAR	RNR MEDIA OPERATIONS
ROURKE, KEVIN H	Surg Lt Cdr	05-Feb-08	MED	HMS EAGLET
ROWE, KEVIN C	Lt RN	04-May-01	WAR	849 SQN
ROWLANDS, GEOFFREY A	Lt Cdr	16-Nov-85	WAR	RNR AIR BR VL
RUSS, PHILIP J RD	Cdr	30-Sep-05	WAR	HMS EAGLET
RUTHERFORD, KEVIN J	Lt RN	01-Oct-93	WAR	RNR AIR BR VL
RYAN, DENNIS G	Lt Cdr	01-Mar-93	ENG	RNR AIR BR VL

Name	Rank	Seniority	Brach/Arm/Group	Unit
RYAN, PATRICK	Lt RN	07-Feb-03	WAR	HMS PRESIDENT
RYAN, PETER A	Lt RN	18-Jan-03	WAR	HMS PRESIDENT

S

Name	Rank	Seniority	Brach/Arm/Group	Unit
SAINTCLAIR-ABBOTT, SIMON	Lt Cdr	01-Jun-92	WAR	HMS FERRET - RNRIU
SAIR, MARK	Surg Lt Cdr	26-Jul-98	MED	HMS VIVID
SALT, HEDLEY S	Lt Cdr	01-Oct-09	WAR	RNR AIR BR VL
SAMPSON-JONES, CHRISTOPHER J	Mid	18-Jul-12	New Entrant	HMS EAGLET
SAN, HOWARD	Lt Cdr	31-Mar-06	WAR	HMS PRESIDENT
SANDERSON, JENNIFER P RD	Lt Cdr	31-Mar-05	WAR	HMS FERRET - RNRIU
SAUNDERS, ALICE C	Lt Cdr	01-Oct-09	WAR	RNR AIR BR VL
SAUNDERS, BRENDAN R	Mid	01-Dec-13	New Entrant	HMS WILDFIRE
SCARTH, MARTIN	Lt RN	18-Jan-01	WAR	RNR MEDIA OPERATIONS
SCOTT, ANTHONY	Lt Cdr	01-Oct-13	WAR	HMS PRESIDENT
SCOTT, DEBRA J	OCdt	02-Aug-11	New Entrant	HMS PRESIDENT
SCRIMGEOUR, JOHN	SLt	23-Jun-07	WAR	HMS VIVID
SCRIVEN, DUNCAN G	Mid	01-Jul-14	New Entrant	HMS FLYING FOX
SEABORN, ADAM	Lt RN	01-Jan-92	WAR	RNR AIR BR VL
SEARLE, GEOFFREY D RD	Lt Cdr	31-Mar-00	WAR	HMS KING ALFRED
SETON, JAMES	Lt Cdr	01-Oct-14	WAR	HMS PRESIDENT
SEVERS, ANTHONY D	Lt Cdr	01-Apr-06	WAR	RNR AIR BR VL
SHAKESPEARE, MARTIN	Lt Cdr	31-Mar-97	WAR	HMS FERRET - RNRIU
SHAMMAS-ESFAHANI, KATHY	Mid	01-Jan-14	New Entrant	HMS PRESIDENT
SHAYLER, STEPHEN A	Lt RN	12-Jul-10	WAR	HMS FERRET - RNRIU
SHELLEY, JAMES	Surg Lt Cdr	05-May-08	MED	FLEET CMR
SHEPHERD, PAUL R	Lt Cdr	01-Oct-02	WAR	RNR AIR BR VL
SHEPHERD, STEPHEN	Lt RN	22-Aug-02	LOGS	HMS KING ALFRED
SHERRIFF, JACQUELINE MBE	Lt Cdr	31-Mar-06	WAR	RNR MEDIA OPERATIONS
SHINNER, PATRICK A RD	Lt Cdr	31-Mar-99	WAR	HMS PRESIDENT
SHINNER, STEPHANIE K F	Cdr	30-Jun-13	WAR	HMS WILDFIRE
SHINNER, THOMAS	Lt RN	20-Feb-12	WAR	HMS WILDFIRE
SHIPLEY, JOANNE	Lt Cdr	05-Oct-10	WAR	RNR MEDIA OPERATIONS
SHORT, KEVIN	Lt RN	01-Feb-08	WAR	HMS VIVID
SHORT, MATTHEW	Lt RN	05-Dec-09	WAR	HMS FERRET - RNRIU
SHOULER, MARTIN	Lt RN	15-Nov-02	WAR	HMS PRESIDENT
SHOULER, MATTHEW F	Lt RN	30-Aug-07	WAR	HMS FERRET - RNRIU
SIGLEY, ARTHUR	Lt Cdr	01-Oct-14	WAR	HMS SCOTIA
SIMMS, DAVID M	Lt Cdr	01-Oct-12	WAR	RNR AIR BR VL
SIMONIS, DOMINIC V	SLt	01-Mar-14	WAR	HMS FLYING FOX
SIMS, DEBORAH L	Lt Cdr	02-Nov-13	WAR	RNAS YEOVILTON - RNFS
SINGH, NEEL	Lt RN	16-Feb-10	WAR	RNR MEDIA OPERATIONS
SKELLY, ANDREW	Lt RN	06-Jun-08	LOGS	HMS HIBERNIA
SKELTON, MICHAEL G	Lt RN	18-Apr-13	WAR	HMS KING ALFRED
SKINNER, NIGEL G	Lt RN	15-Nov-99	WAR	HMS VIVID
SLONECKI, ADAM T	Lt RN	05-Apr-08	WAR	HMS FERRET - RNRIU
SMALL, CATHERINE	Mid	01-Aug-14	New Entrant	HMS SCOTIA
SMALL, PAULINE	Lt Cdr	31-Mar-05	QARNNS	FLEET CMR
SMALL, PETER	Surg Cdr	30-Sep-97	MED	HMS CALLIOPE
SMITH, DAVID T	Lt RN	08-Sep-93	WAR	RNR AIR BR VL
SMITH, GORDON S	Lt Cdr	31-Mar-01	WAR	RNR AIR BR VL
SMITH, JAMIE R	OCdt	01-Oct-12	New Entrant	HMS KING ALFRED
SMITH, PETER G	Lt Cdr	01-Oct-98	WAR	RNR AIR BR VL
SMITH, SIMON R F	Lt Cdr	02-Jan-08	WAR	RNAS YEOVILTON - AS
SMITH, STEPHEN AE	Lt Cdr	31-Mar-07	WAR	HMS WILDFIRE
SMITH, WILLIAM	Lt RN	26-Feb-02	LOGS	HMS SCOTIA
SNOSWELL, JANE L C	OCdt	01-Sep-12	New Entrant	HMS PRESIDENT
SPACEY, CRAIG D	Lt Cdr	01-Oct-13	ENG	HMS KING ALFRED
SPARKE, PHILIP R W	Lt Cdr	01-Mar-00	WAR	RNR MEDIA OPERATIONS
SPEAKE, JONATHAN	Lt Cdr	01-Oct-08	WAR	RNR AIR BR VL
SPENCER, MICHAEL D	Lt RN	25-Nov-03	WAR	HMS FERRET - RNRIU
SPENCER, PHILIP E	SLt	10-Aug-14	WAR	HMS PRESIDENT
SPRING, JEREMY M	Lt Cdr	03-Aug-97	ENG	RNR AIR BR VL

Name	Rank	Seniority	Brach/Arm/Group	Unit
SPRINGETT, SIMON P	RN Chpln	10-Sep-91	RN Chaplaincy Service	HMS VIVID
SQUIRE, ELIZABETH J C	Lt Cdr	01-Oct-08	WAR	HMS FERRET - RNRIU
STANFORD, GEORGE N	Mid	01-Sep-14	New Entrant	HMS FLYING FOX
STANLEY, NICHOLAS J	Lt RN	16-Sep-93	WAR	RNR AIR BR VL
STARR, THOMAS W	Lt RN	11-Oct-07	WAR	HMS PRESIDENT
STEPHEN, LESLEY RD	Lt Cdr	01-Oct-08	LOGS	HMS DALRIADA
STEPHENSON, MICHAEL	Lt RN	25-Jul-05	WAR	HMS KING ALFRED
STEVENSON, PAUL M	Lt RN	01-Sep-04	WAR	HMS FLYING FOX
STICKLAND, ANTHONY RD	Lt Cdr	31-Mar-98	WAR	HMS KING ALFRED
STIDSTON, DAVID	Lt Cdr	01-Oct-94	WAR	FLEET CMR
STOBO, ALEXANDER P	Lt RN	02-Oct-00	WAR	RNR AIR BR VL
STOCK, CHRISTOPHER G	Mid	01-Nov-14	New Entrant	HMS WILDFIRE
STOCKER, JEREMY	Capt RN	01-Mar-10	WAR	FLEET CMR
STONE, PAUL C J	Lt Cdr	01-Oct-98	WAR	RNR AIR BR VL
STOREY, NAOMI A	Lt Cdr	01-Jan-09	WAR	HMS WILDFIRE
STRONG, JAMES	Mid	09-Oct-07	New Entrant	HMS HIBERNIA
STUBBS, GARY A	Lt Cdr	01-Oct-08	WAR	RNR AIR BR VL
STUBBS, IAN	Lt Cdr	01-Oct-09	WAR	RNR AIR BR VL
STYLES, SARAH	Lt RN	29-Oct-02	WAR	HMS PRESIDENT
SUTTON, RICHARD M MBE	Lt Cdr	01-Oct-02	WAR	RNR AIR BR VL
SYMCOX, CHARLES M	Lt RN	01-Jan-08	WAR	RNR AIR BR VL

T

Name	Rank	Seniority	Brach/Arm/Group	Unit
TATHAM, STEPHEN A	Cdr	30-Jun-10	WAR	HMS KING ALFRED
TAYLOR, JAMES E H	Lt Cdr	01-Oct-14	WAR	HMS FLYING FOX
TAYLOR, LESLIE	Lt Cdr	01-Oct-94	WAR	RNR AIR BR VL
TAYLOR, NEIL	Lt Cdr	11-Oct-04	WAR	HMS VIVID
TAYLOR, RUPERT	Lt Cdr	31-Mar-99	WAR	HMS KING ALFRED
TAYLOR, TIMOTHY J	Lt Cdr	01-Oct-00	WAR	RNR AIR BR VL
TEASDALE, DAVID A	Capt RN	24-Nov-14	WAR	FLEET CMR
TEMPLE, MILES	Lt Cdr	31-Mar-06	WAR	HMS FERRET - RNRIU
TENNANT, MICHAEL I	Surg Cdr	29-Jun-09	MED	HMS CALLIOPE
THOM, MATHEW F	Lt RN	22-Jul-06	WAR	HMS FERRET - RNRIU
THOMAS, ANDREW	Lt RN	19-Jun-05	WAR	HMS PRESIDENT
THOMAS, DAVID	Lt RN	04-May-07	WAR	HMS CAMBRIA
THOMAS, DAVID	Lt Cdr	01-Oct-09	WAR	HMS KING ALFRED
THOMAS, KEVIN I	Lt Cdr	01-Oct-92	WAR	RNR AIR BR VL
THOMASON, MICHAEL	Cdr	30-Jun-12	LOGS	HMS EAGLET
THOMSON, ANNA C	Mid	01-Aug-14	New Entrant	HMS FLYING FOX
THOMSON, COLIN	Lt RN	28-Oct-11	WAR	HMS DALRIADA
THOMSON, FRED D	Lt RN	23-Jan-05	WAR	HMS KING ALFRED
THOMSON, LAUREN K	Mid	01-Feb-14	New Entrant	HMS PRESIDENT
THOMSON, SUSIE	Lt Cdr	31-Mar-99	WAR	RNR MEDIA OPERATIONS
THORNLEY, JEREMY G C	Lt Cdr	01-Oct-11	WAR	HMS SHERWOOD
THORNTON, PHILIP J	Lt Cdr	01-Oct-93	WAR	RNR AIR BR VL
THURMOTT, ROBERT	Lt RN	01-Apr-12	WAR	RNR MEDIA OPERATIONS
TONG, STEVEN	Lt RN	12-Jun-08	WAR	HMS FERRET - RNRIU
TOOR, JEEVAN J S	Lt Cdr	01-Sep-98	WAR	HMS FERRET - RNRIU
TOOTH, MARK C	SLt	29-Oct-11	WAR	HMS KING ALFRED
TOPPING, MARK	Lt Cdr	31-Mar-97	WAR	HMS CAMBRIA
TRELAWNY, CHRISTOPHER C RD	Lt Cdr	31-Mar-06	WAR	HMS PRESIDENT
TRIBE, JEREMY D	Lt RN	16-Oct-87	WAR	RNR AIR BR VL
TRIGG, MARK A W	Lt RN	28-Jan-13	WAR	HMS SHERWOOD
TRIMMER, PATRICK D M RD	Lt Cdr	31-Mar-96	WAR	HMS FERRET - RNRIU
TROMANHAUSER, KERRY	Lt RN	23-Nov-11	WAR	RNR MEDIA OPERATIONS
TROTT, CRAIG M J	Lt Cdr	31-Mar-05	WAR	RNR AIR BR VL
TULETT, MATTHEW B	OCdt	31-May-14	New Entrant	HMS KING ALFRED
TURLEY, RICHARD A	Lt RN	04-Mar-08	WAR	HMS EAGLET
TURNBULL, CHRISTOPHER P	Mid	01-Feb-14	New Entrant	HMS EAGLET
TURNER, JONATHAN S	Lt RN	02-Aug-00	WAR	RNR AIR BR VL
TURNER, PHILIP C	Mid	14-Nov-13	New Entrant	HMS SCOTIA
TURNER, SIMON	Lt Cdr	11-Mar-99	WAR	HMS VIVID

Name	Rank	Seniority	Brach/Arm/Group	Unit
TURNER, THOMAS W	Lt RN	29-Apr-12	WAR	JSSU HQ
TWEEDIE, HOWARD J	Lt Cdr	22-Oct-97	WAR	FLEET CMR
TWIGG, KELLY A	Lt RN	01-Aug-05	WAR	RNR AIR BR VL

U

URE, FIONA	Lt RN	03-Oct-06	WAR	HMS HIBERNIA
URQUHART, RODERICK	Lt RN	19-Sep-06	WAR	HMS PRESIDENT

V

VALENTE, ANTONIO E	Mid	01-Jul-14	New Entrant	HMS EAGLET
VALLANCE, MICHAEL S	Lt RN	16-Jun-98	WAR	RNR AIR BR VL
VAN DEN BERGH, MARK	Lt Cdr	05-Oct-10	LOGS	HMS PRESIDENT
VAN HOORN, LUCY A	Mid	01-Oct-14	New Entrant	HMS PRESIDENT
VANSON, THOMAS D R	Mid	01-Jun-14	New Entrant	HMS PRESIDENT
VENABLES, ADRIAN N	Lt Cdr	01-Dec-00	WAR	FLEET CMR
VERSALLION, MARK A G	Lt RN	30-Mar-05	WAR	HMS WILDFIRE
VICKERS, MARK	Lt RN	13-Aug-09	WAR	HMS PRESIDENT
VINCENT, PETER H	Lt Cdr	01-Dec-12	WAR	RNR AIR BR VL
VITALI, JULIE	Lt Cdr	31-Mar-05	WAR	HMS FERRET - RNRIU

W

WAINWRIGHT, BARNABY G	Lt Cdr	01-Sep-89	WAR	RNR AIR BR VL
WALES, FREDERICK	Lt Cdr	31-Mar-98	WAR	HMS KING ALFRED
WALKER, DAVID	Lt Cdr	31-Mar-97	LOGS	HMS DALRIADA
WALTERS, RICHARD	Lt Cdr	31-Mar-04	WAR	RNR MEDIA OPERATIONS
WARD, EMMA J	Lt RN	01-Jan-01	WAR	RNR AIR BR VL
WARD, KRISTIAN N	Lt Cdr	01-Oct-07	WAR	RNR AIR BR VL
WAREING, LAURA	SLt	02-Mar-14	WAR	HMS KING ALFRED
WARNOCK, GAVIN	Lt Cdr	01-Oct-95	WAR	RNR AIR BR VL
WATERWORTH, ANGELA	SLt	01-Mar-14	WAR	HMS KING ALFRED
WATERWORTH, STEPHEN	Lt Cdr	31-Mar-06	WAR	HMS KING ALFRED
WATSON, CATHERINE J RD	Cdr	30-Jun-08	WAR	HMS EAGLET
WATSON, LLOYD J	Lt Cdr	01-Oct-94	WAR	RNR AIR BR VL
WATTERS, OWEN P	SLt	01-Mar-14	WAR	HMS SCOTIA
WATTS, NICHOLAS H C	Lt Cdr	01-Oct-14	WAR	HMS FLYING FOX
WATTS, THOMAS	Lt RN	10-Oct-10	WAR	HMS VIVID
WAUDBY, LINDSEY	Lt Cdr	01-Oct-14	WAR	RNR MEDIA OPERATIONS
WAUGH, GILLIAN N	Lt RN	10-Sep-12	WAR	HMS FERRET - RNRIU
WEBB, CHRISTOPHER	Cdr	30-Jun-08	LOGS	FLEET CMR
WEBBER, CHRISTOPHER J	Lt Cdr	05-May-98	WAR	RNR AIR BR VL
WEBBER, STEVEN J A M	Capt RN	01-Dec-09	LOGS	HMS FLYING FOX
WEBSTER, ANDREW J E	Lt Cdr	05-May-99	WAR	RNR AIR BR VL
WEDGWOOD, JONATHAN	Surg Lt Cdr	26-Nov-98	MED	HMS SCOTIA
WEIGHTMAN, NICHOLAS E	Lt Cdr	29-Feb-04	WAR	RNR AIR BR VL
WEST, JEFFREY	Lt Cdr	01-Oct-14	WAR	HMS FERRET - RNRIU
WHATLEY, MARK	Lt RN	01-Feb-11	WAR	RNR MEDIA OPERATIONS
WHEATLEY, WENDY J	Lt Cdr	04-Oct-97	WAR	RNR AIR BR VL
WHEELER, ROBERT	Lt RN	19-Aug-06	WAR	HMS KING ALFRED
WHEELER, SOPHIA	Lt Cdr	01-Oct-14	WAR	HMS KING ALFRED
WHITE, IAN	Cdr	30-Jun-08	WAR	HMS CALLIOPE
WHITE, MICHAEL L	Lt Cdr	31-Mar-06	WAR	HMS VIVID
WHITEHEAD, KEITH S RD	Lt Cdr	31-Mar-00	WAR	HMS FERRET - RNRIU
WHITEHOUSE, DOMINIC P	Surg Lt Cdr	01-Feb-03	MED	HMS KING ALFRED
WHITFIELD, JOE A	Lt Cdr	01-Oct-03	WAR	RNR AIR BR VL
WHITING, MARK	Lt RN	11-Oct-07	WAR	HMS FLYING FOX
WILCOCKSON, ALASTAIR	Surg Cdr	01-Apr-05	MED	HMS KING ALFRED
WILCOCKSON, MOIRA	Lt Cdr	31-Mar-05	QARNNS	HMS KING ALFRED
WILKINSON, DOUGLAS	Surg Lt Cdr	28-Oct-04	MED	HMS PRESIDENT
WILKINSON, MICHAEL C P	Surg Lt Cdr	01-Jul-99	MED	HMS PRESIDENT
WILKINSON, RICHARD T M	Lt RN	03-Aug-14	WAR	RNR MEDIA OPERATIONS

Name	Rank	Seniority	Brach/Arm/Group	Unit
WILLIAMS, JULIAN	Lt RN	11-Apr-08	WAR	RNR AIR BR VL
WILLIAMS, KEVIN	Lt RN	01-Feb-06	WAR	HMS FLYING FOX
WILLIAMS, TIMOTHY	Lt Cdr	31-Mar-07	WAR	HMS WILDFIRE
WILLIAMS, TIMOTHY R	SLt	05-Oct-13	WAR	HMS CAMBRIA
WILLING, NIGEL P	Lt RN	16-Aug-93	WAR	RNR AIR BR VL
WILSON, PETER N	Lt Cdr	07-Sep-99	WAR	RNR AIR BR VL
WILSON, ROLAND D	Lt RN	03-Feb-13	WAR	HMS SCOTIA
WINDOW, STEPHEN	Lt Cdr	01-Sep-95	WAR	HMS KING ALFRED
WINKEL VON HESSE-NASSAU, FRIEDRICH W C	Lt Cdr	01-Oct-11	WAR	HMS KING ALFRED
WINTERTON, GEMMA	Lt RN	01-Nov-10	WAR	HMS KING ALFRED
WOLSTENCROFT, PAUL	Lt Cdr	01-Oct-11	LOGS	HMS KING ALFRED
WOOD, JUSTIN N A	Cdr	30-Sep-06	WAR	RNR AIR BR VL
WOOD, SUZANNE	Lt RN	05-Apr-93	WAR	HMS PRESIDENT
WOODARD, MATILDA J	Lt RN	14-Dec-04	WAR	RNR AIR BR VL
WOODMAN, CLARE F J	Lt Cdr	31-Mar-07	WAR	RNR MEDIA OPERATIONS
WRAY, RONALD RD	Cdr	30-Jun-12	WAR	FLEET CMR
WRIGGLESWORTH, PETER J	Surg Lt Cdr	02-Aug-88	MED	HMS FLYING FOX
WRIGHT, ANTONY	Lt Cdr	01 Oct 97	WAR	RNR AIR BR VL
WRIGHT, DOUGLAS	Lt Cdr	31-Mar-05	WAR	HMS FERRET - RNRIU
WRIGHT, NICHOLAS A	Mid	01-Aug-14	New Entrant	HMS SCOTIA
WRIGHT, STEPHEN	Lt Cdr	01-Nov-04	WAR	HMS KING ALFRED
WRIGHT, STEPHEN W	Lt Cdr	31-Mar-01	WAR	RNR AIR BR VL
WRING, MATTHEW RD	Lt Cdr	31-Mar-03	WAR	HMS FLYING FOX
WYATT, MARK RD	Capt RN	08-Mar-09	WAR	FLEET CMR
WYLIE, DAVID	Lt RN	02-Aug-02	WAR	RNR MEDIA OPERATIONS

Y

Name	Rank	Seniority	Brach/Arm/Group	Unit
YATES, STEVEN RD	Lt Cdr	31-Mar-00	WAR	HMS FLYING FOX
YEE, SOU YAN SAMUEL	SLt	14-Sep-13	WAR	HMS KING ALFRED
YIBOWEI, CHRISTOPHE	Lt RN	02-Feb-09	LOGS	HMS PRESIDENT
YONG, ANDREW	Lt RN	21-Mar-09	WAR	HMS PRESIDENT
YOUNG, CARL	Lt Cdr	31-Mar-98	WAR	RNR AIR BR VL
YOUNG, COLIN S	Lt RN	24-Apr-12	WAR	HMS DALRIADA
YOUNG, DUNCAN	Lt Cdr	31-Mar-98	WAR	HMS CALLIOPE
YOUNG, GREGORY	Lt Cdr	01-Oct-09	WAR	RNR MEDIA OPERATIONS
YOUNG, JOSEPHINE	Lt RN	28-Apr-07	WAR	RNR MEDIA OPERATIONS
YOUNG, SALLY	Lt Cdr	01-Oct-14	WAR	RNR MEDIA OPERATIONS
YOUNG, WILLIAM D	Lt Cdr	31-Mar-05	LOGS	HMS KING ALFRED

ROYAL MARINES RESERVE

Name	Rank	Seniority	Branch	Unit

A

| ADAMS, MARTYN F J | Capt | 18-Jul-08 | RN Royal Marines GS | RMR BRISTOL |

B

BIRD, PETER J	Lt	05-Jan-15	RN Royal Marines GS	RMR BRISTOL
BOURNE, ASHLEY E	Capt	03-Apr-09	RN Royal Marines GS	RMR LONDON
BOWYER, RICHARD	Maj	01-Oct-06	RN Royal Marines GS	HMS PRESIDENT
BROWN, ROGER F RD	Maj	16-Jul-04	RN Royal Marines GS	RMR MERSEYSIDE
BROWNRIGG, ANDREW M	Lt	01-Mar-13	RN Royal Marines GS	RMR MERSEYSIDE
BRUCE, RORY M	Col	01-Mar-11	RN Royal Marines GS	FLEET CMR
BUCKLAND, CHRISTOPHER S	Capt	17-Apr-12	RN Royal Marines GS	RMR MERSEYSIDE
BURNHAM, PAUL	Capt	01-Jun-10	RN Royal Marines GS	RMR MERSEYSIDE

C

| COARD, THOMAS J | Maj | 08-May-14 | RN Royal Marines GS | RMR SCOTLAND |
| COLE, SIMON | Lt Col | 30-Jun-14 | RN Royal Marines GS | RMR BRISTOL |

D

DARE, CLIFFORD R S MBE	Maj	16-May-06	RN Royal Marines GS	HMS FLYING FOX
DOWLEN, HENRY T B MBE	Capt	29-Jun-14	RN Royal Marines GS	RMR LONDON
DYER, ANDREW R	Lt	15-Sep-05	RN Royal Marines GS	RMR SCOTLAND

E

| EDGAR, ALASTAIR W L | Capt | 01-Jun-10 | RN Royal Marines GS | RMR MERSEYSIDE |

F

FENWICK, ROBIN J	Maj	01-Oct-04	RN Warfare FAA	RNR AIR BR VL
FIELDER, DAVID A	Maj	10-Apr-99	RN Royal Marines GS	RNR MEDIA OPERATIONS
FODEN, JONATHAN B	Capt	03-Apr-09	RN Royal Marines GS	RMR SCOTLAND
FOREMAN, NEIL A	Capt	21-Sep-05	RN Royal Marines GS	RMR SCOTLAND

G

| GOLDSMITH, ANDREW G | Capt | 01-Sep-05 | RN Royal Marines GS | RMR SCOTLAND |
| GRIFFITHS, NICHOLAS W | Capt | 17-Jun-08 | RN Royal Marines GS | RMR BRISTOL |

H

HALE, WILLIAM	Maj	01-Apr-14	RN Royal Marines GS	RMR LONDON
HALL, DAVID	Capt	29-Dec-00	RN Royal Marines GS	RMR SCOTLAND
HAMILTON, CORMAC	Capt	29-Mar-06	RN Royal Marines GS	RMR MERSEYSIDE
HAMILTON, STUART J D	Capt	02-Feb-06	RN Royal Marines GS	RMR SCOTLAND
HESTER, JAMES F W	Maj	25-Oct-03	RN Royal Marines GS	RMR SCOTLAND
HILLMAN, DAVID	Maj	29-Oct-02	RN Royal Marines GS	HMS DALRIADA
HILLS, MATTHEW	Capt	01-Aug-07	RN Royal Marines GS	RMR LONDON

K

| KEDWARD, CHRISTOPHER J | Maj | 01-Apr-14 | RN Royal Marines GS | RMR BRISTOL |
| KENNEDY, ROBERT L | Capt | 04-Dec-13 | RN Royal Marines GS | RMR SCOTLAND |

L

| LAW, DUNCAN J F | Capt | 01-Aug-07 | RN Royal Marines GS | RMR LONDON |
| LEE, ADAM J | Capt | 17-Sep-14 | RN Royal Marines GS | RMR LONDON |

Name	Rank	Seniority	Branch	Unit

M

MAROK, JANI	Col	08-Oct-13	RN Royal Marines GS	FLEET CMR
MASON, ANDREW C	Maj	30-Apr-04	RN Royal Marines GS	
MCCULLOUGH, IAN N	Lt Col	30-Jun-14	RN Royal Marines GS	NCHQ - NAVY CMD SEC
MCGINLEY, CHRISTOPHER T	Capt	13-Dec-06	RN Royal Marines GS	RMR SCOTLAND
MCGOVERN, JAMES N	Capt	30-Jul-12	RN Royal Marines GS	HMS FERRET - RNRIU
MCLEISH, ROBIN N	Capt	31-Mar-01	RN Royal Marines GS	
MOULTON, FREDERICK	Col	23-Sep-13	RN Royal Marines GS	FLEET CMR

N

NEWMAN, EDMUND N	Lt	02-May-13	RN Royal Marines GS	RMR BRISTOL

P

PICKETT, ALEXANDER P	Maj	01-Oct-13	RN Royal Marines GS	RMR SCOTLAND

R

ROBERTS, JOHN	Lt Col	30-Jun-09	RN Royal Marines GS	FLEET CMR
ROCHESTER, ANDREW D	Maj	01-Jun-12	RN Royal Marines GS	RMR BRISTOL

S

SHAW, ANDREW P	Capt	01-Aug-07	RN Royal Marines GS	RMR LONDON
SMITH, FRASER RD	Lt Col	01-Jul-14	RN Royal Marines GS	FLEET CMR
STEVENS, GREGORY	2Lt	29-Apr-09	RN Royal Marines GS	RMR LONDON

T

TAYLOR, ROBERT A P	Capt	01-Sep-10	RN Royal Marines GS	RMR LONDON
TELFORD, JONATHAN	Capt	01-Aug-14	RN Royal Marines GS	RMR MERSEYSIDE
THOMAS, JEFFREY G	Capt	22-Jul-03	RN Royal Marines GS	RMR BRISTOL
TOTTENHAM, TIMOTHY W	Capt	04-Jul-07	RN Royal Marines GS	RMR LONDON

W

WADDELL, IAN S RD	Maj	01-Oct-08	RN Royal Marines GS	RMR LONDON
WARD, ANTHONY S	Capt	26-May-07	RN Royal Marines GS	RMR MERSEYSIDE
WATKINSON, NEIL	Lt Col	30-Jun-09	RN Royal Marines GS	FLEET CMR
WILLIAMS, MATTHEW C	Maj	01-Apr-14	RN Royal Marines GS	RMR BRISTOL
WISEMAN, GEORGE R	Maj	01-Oct-05	RN Royal Marines GS	RMR BRISTOL

SEA CADET CORPS

Name	Rank	Seniority	Name	Rank	Seniority
A			BELL, Fred	Ch RNR	15-Sep-2010
			BELL, Joseph	Lt (SCC) RNR	13-Sep-2001
ABLETT, Michael	SLt (SCC) RNR	14-May-2007	BELL, Kenneth	A/SLt (SCC) RNR	07-Oct-2014
ACKERMAN, David	Ch RNR	09-Jun-2014	BELL, Ruth	A/Lt Cdr (SCC) RNR	01-Jun-2013
ADEY, Kay	Lt (SCC) RNR	14-May-2010	BELL, Veronica	Lt Cdr (SCC) RNR	01-Jan-2008
AIREY, Robert	Ch RNR	17-Aug-2005	BENNETT, Samuel	Mid (SCC) RNR	
ALLAM, John	Lt (SCC) RNR	25-May-1994	BENNETT, Stephen	Lt (SCC) RNR	01-Dec-2008
ALLEN, Leslie	Lt Cdr (SCC) RNR	01-Jan-1999	BERRIDGE, Grahame	Ch RNR	02-May-2000
ALLISON, Neil	SLt (SCC) RNR	16-May-2010	BEVAN, Mark	A/SLt (SCC) RNR	07-Mar-2010
ANDERSON, Alex	Lt Cdr (SCC) RNR	18-Feb-2013	BICKLE, Margaret	Lt (SCC) RNR	01-Mar-2013
ANDERSON, Kevin	A/Lt (SCC) RNR	20-Nov-2011	BILES, Kathleen	Ch RNR	14-Oct-2009
ANDREWS, James Edward	Ch RNR	06-Sep-2013	BILVERSTONE, Brian	Lt Cdr (SCC) RNR	22-Nov-2005
ANDREWS, Steven	A/SLt (SCC) RNR	17-Nov-2014	BINGHAM, Keith	Cdr (SCC) RNR	01-Aug-2009
APPLEBY, Gary	A/SLt (SCC) RNR	03-Jun-2013	BISHOP, Peter	Lt (SCC) RNR	01-Nov-1995
APPLEBY, Keith	Lt (SCC) RNR	21-Feb-1998	BISSON, Keith	Lt (SCC) RNR	16-Nov-2006
AQUILINA, Rene	A/Lt (SCC) RMR	20 Mar 2012	BLACK, Karen	Lt (SCC) RNR	06-Nov-2012
ARCHBOLD, Dennis	Lt Cdr (SCC) RNR	11-Aug-1999	BLACKBURN, Alan	Lt (SCC) RNR	15-Jun-2004
ARCHBOLD, Theresa	Lt (SCC) RNR	20-Nov-1997	BLUMENTHAL, Adrian	SLt (SCC) RNR	08-Aug-2014
ARCHER, Dudley Ian	Ch RNR	03-Mar-1998	BONFIELD, Christopher	Lt (SCC) RNR	06-Nov-1996
ARMSTRONG, Leslie	Ch RNR	08-May-2010	BONJOUR, Andre	Lt (SCC) RNR	27-May-1992
ARNOLD, Bernard	Ch RNR	18-Sep-2013	BOOKLESS, Andrew	Ch RNR	25-Jan-2014
ASHFORD-OKAI, Fred	Ch RNR	13-Jan-2014	BOORMAN, Nicholas	Lt (SCC) RNR	01-Dec-1988
ASHLEY, Victoria	Ch RNR	04-Dec-2012	BOSTEL, Claire	A/SLt (SCC) RNR	23-Nov-2014
ASHWORTH, John	SLt (SCC) RNR	26-Jun-2011	BOSTOCK, Beverley	A/SLt (SCC) RNR	15-Jun-2014
ASTON, Courtney	Mid (SCC) RNR	09-Sep-2012	BOSWELL, Robert	Lt (SCC) RNR	01-Jan-2007
ATKINS, Doreen	Lt (SCC) RNR	08-Apr-1992	BOURNE, Jack	Lt (SCC) RNR	23-Nov-2012
ATKINSON, Terence	Ch RNR	06-Sep-2006	BOURNE, Nigel	Ch RNR	13-Dec-2008
ATLING, Brian	Ch RNR	15-Nov-2011	BOWDITCH, Michael	Ch RNR	11-Mar-2014
AVILL, Fraser	Lt (SCC) RNR	25-Sep-2010	BOWEN-DAVIES, Alison	A/Lt Cdr (SCC) RNR	01-Jan-2015
AVILL, Jennifer	SLt (SCC) RNR	07-Nov-2010	BOWMAN, John	SLt (SCC) RNR	28-Jun-2009
AVILL, Susan	Lt (SCC) RNR	01-Nov-1989	BOWSKILL, Michael	Lt Cdr (SCC) RNR	01-Jul-2002
			BOYD, Frank	Lt (SCC) RNR	17-Feb-2008
B			BOYES, Stephen	Lt (SCC) RNR	25-Feb-1999
			BOYLE, Robert	Ch RNR	04-Feb-2014
BAGSHAWE, Allen	Ch RNR	01-Feb-1989	BRADBURY, David	Lt (SCC) RNR	07-Sep-1985
BAILEY, Arthur	Lt (SCC) RNR	03-Oct-2010	BRADFORD, David	Lt Cdr (SCC) RNR	01-Nov-2000
BAKER, Mark	Ch RNR	31-Jan-2013	BRATLEY, Charles	Lt (SCC) RNR	25-Jul-2005
BALL, Alan	Ch RNR	18-May-1998	BRAZIER, Colin	Lt Cdr (SCC) RNR	01-Feb-2003
BALL, Philip	Ch RNR	16-Sep-2008	BRENNAN-WRIGHT, Alison	Lt (SCC) RNR	25-Jan-2009
BANNER, Tamsin	Mid (SCC) RNR	23-Mar-2014	BRIGGS, Donald	Lt Cdr (SCC) RNR	01-Sep-1977
BARBER, Anthony	Lt (SCC) RNR	12-Mar-1991	BRISTER, Andrew	Ch RNR	30-Nov-2009
BARBER, Martyn	SLt (SCC) RNR	26-Jun-2011	BRISTOW, Roger	Ch RNR	18-Apr-2006
BARKER, David	Lt (SCC) RNR	21-Jun-1999	BROADBENT, Graham	Lt Cdr (SCC) RNR	01-Aug-1984
BARKER, Paul	Lt (SCC) RNR	18-Sep-2014	BROCKWELL, Graham	Lt (SCC) RNR	31-Mar-2006
BARKER, Robert	Ch RNR	07-Sep-2010	BROUGHTON, James	Ch RNR	29-Aug-2000
BARLOW, Steuart	SLt (SCC) RNR	07-Feb-2011	BROWN, Damien	Lt Cdr (SCC) RNR	01-Feb-2013
BARR, William	Lt (SCC) RNR	15-Feb-2000	BROWN, Jordan	A/SLt (SCC) RNR	15-Jun-2014
BARRAS, Hugh	Cdr (SCC) RNR	01-Aug-2009	BROWN, John	Lt Cdr (SCC) RNR	04-Jul-1978
BARTHOLOMEW, Julia	Ch RNR	24-Apr-2004	BROWN, Michael	Ch RNR	12-Apr-2000
BASSETT, Gary	A/Lt Cdr (SCC) RNR	31-Mar-2014	BROWNING, Martin	Lt (SCC) RNR	02-Aug-2002
BASSETT, Karen	Ch RNR	12-Apr-2010	BROWNING, Tony	Lt (SCC) RNR	19-Dec-1993
BASSETT, Lindsay	SLt (SCC) RNR	24-Mar-2013	BROXHAM, Roy	Lt (SCC) RNR	21-Sep-1990
BATTLE, Stephen	Ch RNR	02-Feb-2005	BRYANT, Charles	Lt (SCC) RNR	19-Feb-1987
BAXTER, Grant	Capt (SCC) RMR	01-Nov-2012	BUCKELS, Emma	SLt (SCC) RNR	01-Apr-2010
BAYLEY, George	Lt Cdr (SCC) RNR	01-Jan-2011	BUCKETT, Vivienne	SLt (SCC) RNR	01-Nov-2009
BAYLISS, John	Lt Cdr (SCC) RNR	14-Feb-1987	BUCKINGHAM, Buck	SLt (SCC) RNR	28-Mar-2010
BEARNE, Jeremy	Cdr (SCC) RNR	01-Aug-2009	BUDDEN, Paul	Capt (SCC) RNR	25-Jan-2009
BEDDOW, Jay	Lt Cdr (SCC) RNR	02-Jan-2013	BULLOCK, Lynn	Lt (SCC) RNR	01-Dec-1984
BEECH, Nicholas	A/Lt (SCC) RMR	25-Mar-2012	BULMAN, JAMES	A/SLt (SCC) RNR	30-Aug-2014
BELL, David	Ch RNR	12-Apr-2010			

Name	Rank	Seniority	Name	Rank	Seniority
BUNDOCK, Anthony	Ch RNR	08-Nov-2004	CLYBURN, Timothy	SLt (SCC) RNR	01-Jun-2013
BURGON, Vivienne	A/SLt (SCC) RNR	15-Jun-2014	COAST, Philip	Lt Cdr (SCC) RNR	09-Jul-1990
BURNS, Cliff	A/Lt Cdr (SCC) RNR	01-Jan-2013	COATES, Margaret	Lt Cdr (SCC) RNR	30-Jun-2008
BURNS, Desmond	Lt (SCC) RNR	18-Feb-1978	COCKELL, Lynn	SLt (SCC) RNR	07-Nov-2010
BURNS, Philip	Lt (SCC) RNR	14-Feb-2003	COCKELL, Richard	Lt Cdr (SCC) RNR	04-Dec-1996
BURT, Christopher	Lt (SCC) RNR	20-Aug-1999	COLES, Jane	SLt (SCC) RNR	02-Jun-2014
BURTON, Martyn	Lt (SCC) RNR	31-Mar-2014	COLES, Thomas	Lt Cdr (SCC) RNR	19-Dec-1987
BUTCHER, Colin	Lt (SCC) RNR	26-Nov-2002	COLLIER, Billy	Lt (SCC) RMR	25-Mar-2012
BUTCHER, Sarah	SLt (SCC) RNR	29-Mar-2009	COLLINS, David	Lt Cdr (SCC) RNR	01-Feb-1982
BUTTERFIELD, Peter	Ch RNR	23-Jan-2013	COLLINS, Timothy	Lt (SCC) RNR	27-Jan-2007
BUTTERWORTH, John	Lt (SCC) RNR	23-Mar-1987	COMER, Kieran	SLt (SCC) RNR	10-Oct-2014
			CONNOR, Christopher	Lt (SCC) RMR	09-Aug-2013
C			CONWAY, Paul	Lt (SCC) RMR	27-Mar-2011
CADDICK, David	Lt (SCC) RMR	10-Nov-2013	COOK, Richard	Ch RNR	11-May-2012
CADDICK, Keith	A/Lt (SCC) RMR	02-Jun-2013	COOKE, John	Ch RNR	20-Apr-1998
CADDICK, Natalie	SLt (SCC) RNR	11-May-2010	COOMBES, Peter	Ch RNR	11-Nov-2010
CADMAN, John	Lt Cdr (SCC) RNR	26-Nov-1986	COOPER, Tristan	SLt (SCC) RNR	31-Jan-2013
CAINES, Danny	SLt (SCC) RNR	29-Mar-2009	COPELIN, Maureen	Lt Cdr (SCC) RNR	01-Feb-2005
CALVER, Russell	SLt (SCC) RNR	28-Jun-2009	CORMACK, Raymond	Lt (SCC) RNR	25-Apr-2000
CAMILLERI, Carmel Lino	Lt Cdr (SCC) RNR	12-Oct-1997	CORNELL, Helga	Ch RNR	03-May-2010
CAMPBELL, Donald	Ch RNR	30-Jul-2010	CORNISH, Rachel	Ch RNR	12-Dec-2013
CAMPBELL, Gordon	Ch RNR	20-Apr-2001	COSTERD, David	Lt (SCC) RNR	06-Dec-2000
CARLILL, Adam	Ch RNR	01-Mar-2005	COTTERILL, Victoria	Lt (SCC) RNR	29-Apr-2012
CARR, Barry	Lt (SCC) RNR	25-Mar-2005	COUSINS, Karen	SLt (SCC) RNR	23-Mar-2013
CARR, Helen	Ch RNR	10-Mar-2011	COX, Donald	Lt (SCC) RMR	07-Aug-2006
CARR, Leonard	Lt Cdr (SCC) RNR	13-Oct-1977	COX, Jon	Lt (SCC) RNR	16-Jan-2009
CARROLL, Kenneth	Capt (SCC) RMR	13-Oct-2012	COX, Simon	Ch RNR	25-Sep-1995
CARTER, David	Lt Cdr (SCC) RNR	06-Nov-2006	CRAIG, Neil	Lt (SCC) RNR	01-Apr-1986
CARTER, Marion	Ch RNR	24-Aug-2011	CRAWLEY, Stephen	Maj (SCC) RMR	01-Jan-2009
CARTER, Rebecca	SLt (SCC) RNR	24-Jun-2012	CREIGHTON, Edward	Lt (SCC) RNR	26-Nov-1992
CARTWRIGHT, Michael	A/Maj (SCC) RMR	01-Feb-2013	CRICK, Philip	Ch RNR	11-May-2004
CARVER, Steven	A/SLt (SCC) RNR	24-Sep-2013	CRITCHLOW, Jonathan	Lt (SCC) RNR	19-Feb-1989
CASHMORE, Matthew	Lt (SCC) RNR	09-May-2009	CROWE, Keith	Capt (SCC) RMR	15-Jun-2009
CASLAW, Paul	Lt (SCC) RNR	01-Aug-1994	CROWTHER, Jonathan	SLt (SCC) RNR	19-Nov-2013
CAVLAN, Rebecca	Lt (SCC) RMR	29-May-2014	CRUICKSHANK, Jonathan	Ch RNR	24-Aug-1989
CEA, Franklin	Lt Cdr (SCC) RNR	01-Jan-2002	CRUMP, Adam	Lt (SCC) RNR	02-Nov-2013
CEA, Katrina	SLt (SCC) RNR	29-Mar-2009	CUSH, Martin	A/SLt (SCC) RNR	25-Apr-2013
CHALLIS, Stewart	Lt (SCC) RNR	09-May-2009			
CHAMBERS, Joanne	A/Lt (SCC) RNR	18-Aug-2014	**D**		
CHAMBERS, Oliver	A/SLt (SCC) RNR	15-Jun-2014	DADE, Jason	A/SLt (SCC) RNR	28-Jun-2014
CHAPMAN, Paul	Lt (SCC) RMR	25-Mar-2012	DALY, Shane	Lt (SCC) RNR	29-Aug-2012
CHARD, Michael	Lt (SCC) RNR	14-Apr-2013	DANIELS, Roger	Lt Cdr (SCC) RNR	14-Jan-1991
CHEEK, Ronald	Lt (SCC) RNR	23-Mar-2005	DANIELS, Steven	Lt (SCC) RNR	02-Nov-2013
CHEETHAM, Mark	SLt (SCC) RNR	07-Nov-2010	DARGIE, David	A/SLt (SCC) RNR	31-Aug-2014
CHESWORTH, Howard	Lt (SCC) RNR	03-Dec-1991	DAVIES, Aled	Mid (SCC) RNR	25-Jun-2013
CHINN, John	Lt Cdr (SCC) RNR	01-Jan-1983	DAVIES, Gareth	A/SLt (SCC) RNR	31-Aug-2014
CHITTOCK, Michael	Lt Cdr (SCC) RNR	01-Jan-2008	DAVIES, Helen	Lt (SCC) RNR	02-Oct-2012
CHRISTIE, Randall	Lt (SCC) RNR	21-Jan-2014	DAVIES, John	SLt (SCC) RNR	07-Nov-2010
CIOMA, Antoni	Lt Cdr (SCC) RNR	01-Jul-1990	DAVIES, Natalie	A/SLt (SCC) RNR	15-Jun-2014
CLAMMER, Thomas	Ch RNR	18-Mar-2009	DAVIES, Peter	Lt (SCC) RNR	01-Jul-2003
CLAPHAM, Stephen	Ch RNR	27-Jun-2009	DAVIES, William	Lt Cdr (SCC) RNR	01-Jul-2004
CLARK, Anne	Lt Cdr (SCC) RNR	02-Feb-2007	DAVIS, Daniel	SLt (SCC) RNR	27-Mar-2011
CLARK, David	Lt (SCC) RNR	18-Jun-2012	DAVIS, Samantha	A/Maj (SCC) RMR	17-Oct-2012
CLARK, Daniel	A/SLt (SCC) RNR	20-Jan-2014	DAVISON, Henry	Lt Cdr (SCC) RNR	01-Jan-2011
CLARK, Steven	SLt (SCC) RNR	13-Apr-2013	DAW, Nicholas William	Ch RNR	12-Dec-2013
CLARKE, Aaron	Lt (SCC) RNR	03-Aug-2011	DAWSON, Craig	Lt (SCC) RNR	29-Jan-2012
CLARKE, Lee	A/SLt (SCC) RNR	27-Oct-2014	DAWSON, David	Ch RNR	17-Nov-2007
CLARKE, Nigel	SLt (SCC) RNR	29-Mar-2009	DAY, Scott	SLt (SCC) RNR	09-Sep-2012
CLAY, Paul	A/Lt Cdr (SCC) RNR	01-Aug-2012	DAY, Trevor	Ch RNR	15-Feb-2011
CLEWORTH, Dean	Lt Cdr (SCC) RNR	01-Jan-2011	DEACON, Andrew	Lt Cdr (SCC) RNR	16-Jan-2014
CLIFFORD, Ian	Lt (SCC) RNR	11-Feb-1999	DEAN, Janice	A/SLt (SCC) RNR	23-Nov-2014
CLUNAS, William	A/Lt (SCC) RNR	08-Dec-2005	DEBRUYNE, Jacquelyn	Lt (SCC) RNR	21-Aug-1995

Name	Rank	Seniority	Name	Rank	Seniority
DEE, Graham	Ch RNR	27-Mar-2014	FLETCHER, Suzanne	Ch RNR	20-Jan-2012
DELACOUR, Michael	Lt (SCC) RMR	09-Sep-2012	FLUDE, Mark	Lt (SCC) RMR	03-Jun-2014
DEMANUELE, Raymond	Lt (SCC) RNR	05-Nov-2011	FORD, Joseph	SLt (SCC) RNR	02-Jun-2013
DEMUTH, Alice	A/Lt (SCC) RNR	14-Sep-2013	FOREMAN, Waleria	Lt (SCC) RNR	22-Sep-1995
DENYER, Philip	Ch RNR	25-Apr-2009	FOSTER, James	Capt (SCC) RMR	12-Dec-2012
DERBYSHIRE, David	Lt (SCC) RNR	03-Jun-1992	FOWLER, Alison	Lt Cdr (SCC) RNR	01-Mar-2006
DERHAM, Peter	Ch RNR	14-May-1996	FOX, Jane	Lt (SCC) RNR	11-Sep-2011
DEVENISH, Ian	Maj (SCC) RMR	01-Oct-2006	FRANCIS, Rebecca	Lt (SCC) RNR	11-Sep-2007
DEVEREUX, Edwin	Lt Cdr (SCC) RNR	01-May-1987	FRASER, Sean	SLt (SCC) RNR	27-Mar-2011
DEVEREUX, Helen	A/SLt (SCC) RNR	14-Feb-2014	FREESTONE, Andrew	Lt (SCC) RNR	07-Nov-1995
DIAPER, Kevin	SLt (SCC) RNR	14-Apr-2011	FRITH, Michael	Lt (SCC) RNR	26-Sep-2003
DIBBEN, Michael	Lt (SCC) RNR	03-Nov-1988	FROOM, Ian	Ch RNR	27-Mar-2000
DICKINSON, Keith	Lt Cdr (SCC) RNR	01-Jan-2010	FULCHER, Diane	Lt Cdr (SCC) RNR	24-Jul-2009
DICKSON, John	Lt (SCC) RMR	10-Nov-2013	FULCHER, Scott	A/Lt (SCC) RNR	22-Apr-2013
DIXIE, Colin	Lt (SCC) RNR	15-Oct-2000	FULLER, Andrew	Capt (SCC) RMR	14-May-2010
DONNELLY, James	SLt (SCC) RNR	30-Oct-2005	FULTON, Karen	Lt Cdr (SCC) RNR	01-May-2005
DREW, Garry	Lt (SCC) RNR	08-Jan-2014			
DRYDEN, Graeme	Lt (SCC) RNR	26-Mar-2002	**G**		
DRYDEN, Stephen	Lt (SCC) RNR	01-Mar-1981	GALLAGHER, Eamonn	Lt (SCC) RNR	23-Jun-1992
DUCKETT, Raphael	Ch RNR	16-Jul-2012	GAMBELL, Mark	Lt Cdr (SCC) RNR	01-Jan-2011
DUXBURY, MEGAN	SLt (SCC) RNR	10-Feb-2014	GAMBLE, David	Ch RNR	01-May-2004
DYER, Roger	Lt (SCC) RNR	07-Jun-1997	GARRINGTON, Malcolm	Lt (SCC) RNR	30-Jan-2013
			GATHERGOOD, John	Lt (SCC) RNR	17-Apr-1998
E			GEARING, Robert	Lt Cdr (SCC) RNR	01-Sep-1977
EALES, Geoffrey	Ch RNR	11-Jul-2001	GENTILELLA, BARBARA		
EARL, David	Ch RNR	01-Jun-1998	GIBSON, Lynne	Ch RNR	28-Mar-2013
EDGE, Christopher	SLt (SCC) RNR	10-Nov-2013	GILBERT, Robin	Maj (SCC) RMR	01-Jun-1999
EDMONDS, Annette	Lt (SCC) RNR	12-Jun-2010	GILBERT-JONES, Hilary	Lt (SCC) RNR	23-Nov-2008
EDMUNDS, Roger	SLt (SCC) RNR	07-Nov-2010	GILBERT-JONES, Robert	Lt (SCC) RNR	30-Oct-2011
EDWARDS, Mark	Capt (SCC) RMR	01-Dec-2013	GILES, Andrew	Cdr (SCC) RNR	28-Jun-2013
EDWARDS, Paul	Lt (SCC) RMR	28-Mar-2010	GILKS, Nicholas	SLt (SCC) RNR	30-Oct-2011
EIVERS, David	A/SLt (SCC) RNR	15-Jun-2014	GILL, Jacqueline	Lt (SCC) RNR	28-Feb-1995
ELLIOTT, Philip	Ch RNR	17-Jun-2014	GILLARD, Terence	Lt Cdr (SCC) RNR	01-Jan-1995
ELLIOTT, William	SLt (SCC) RNR	29-Mar-2009	GILLERT, Valerie	Lt (SCC) RNR	19-Oct-1991
ELLIS, Christopher	Ch RNR	21-Feb-2012	GILLIAM, Kevin	Lt (SCC) RNR	01-Jul-1993
ELLIS, Hugh	Ch RNR	07-Jul-2014	GILLINGHAM, Michael	Ch RNR	07-Sep-1999
ERB-SMITH, Darren	A/Capt (SCC) RMR	05-Nov-2012	GIRLING, Craig	SLt (SCC) RNR	28-Jun-2009
ERSKINE, Richard	Lt (SCC) RNR	23-Nov-2003	GITTENS, Adrian	Lt (SCC) RNR	23-Jan-2009
EVANS, Janet	Cdr (SCC) RNR	01-Aug-2009	GITTINS, Susan	Lt (SCC) RNR	07-Dec-2002
EVANS, John	Lt (SCC) RNR	28-Sep-2000	GLANVILLE, Debra	Lt Cdr (SCC) RNR	01-Jan-2011
EXCELL, Timothy	SLt (SCC) RNR	28-Mar-2010	GLEAVE, Anthony	SLt (SCC) RNR	28-Mar-2010
EYDMANN, Eileen	Ch RNR	05-Jul-1993	GLOVER, Stuart	Lt (SCC) RNR	12-Jun-2010
EYNON, David	Ch RNR	04-Aug-2003	GODDARD, Myan	2nd Lt (SCC) RMR	23-Mar-2014
			GODFREY, Simon	Ch RNR	24-Jan-2011
F			GODWIN, Timothy	A/Lt (SCC) RMR	05-Dec-2013
FARNWORTH, Tom	SLt (SCC) RNR	17-Sep-2012	GOODCHILD, Joanne	SLt (SCC) RNR	28-Jun-2009
FARRELL, Michael	Lt (SCC) RNR	05-May-2007	GOODCHILD, Matthew	SLt (SCC) RNR	07-Feb-2012
FAULKNER, Shelley-Ann	Lt Cdr (SCC) RNR	04-Apr-2007	GOODE, Victoria	Lt (SCC) RNR	08-Nov-2000
FAULKNER, Shane	SLt (SCC) RNR	26-Jun-2011	GOODING, Peter	Lt Cdr (SCC) RNR	01-Jan-1981
FENN, Paul	Lt (SCC) RNR	06-Sep-2007	GOODLEFF, Deborah	Lt (SCC) RNR	04-Jun-2012
FENTON, Keith	Ch RNR	18-Oct-2011	GORDON, Andrew	Lt (SCC) RNR	19-Feb-1989
FIELD, Jeremy	Ch RNR	12-Jul-2014	GORMAN, Jacqueline	Lt Cdr (SCC) RNR	01-Mar-2014
FIELD, Kevin	Lt (SCC) RMR	20-Nov-2012	GRAINGE, Andrew	Lt Cdr (SCC) RNR	01-Jan-2009
FIELDS, Dawn	SLt (SCC) RNR	27-Mar-2011	GRAINGER, Steven	SLt (SCC) RNR	27-Jun-2011
FINLAY, David	Lt Cdr (SCC) RNR	01-Jan-2008	GRANT, Malcolm	Lt Cdr (SCC) RNR	01-Jan-2009
FIRTH, Peter	Ch RNR	04-Jul-2014	GRANT, Steven	Mid (SCC) RNR	10-Nov-2013
FISHER, Stephanie	A/SLt (SCC) RNR	22-Mar-2014	GRAY, Brian	Lt (SCC) RNR	12-Dec-1987
FITCH, Michael	Lt (SCC) RNR	28-Feb-2003	GRAYLESS, Edward	A/SLt (SCC) RNR	23-Mar-2014
FLEET, Gordon	Maj (SCC) RMR	18-Dec-2005	GREAR, Hugh	Ch RNR	03-Jul-2014
FLEMING, Alan	Lt Cdr (SCC) RNR	01-Jan-2008	GREAVES, Charles	A/Lt (SCC) RNR	31-Aug-2014
FLETCHER, Malcolm	Lt (SCC) RNR	20-Feb-1984	GREEN, Alison	Ch RNR	04-Jul-2014
			GREEN, Christopher	Mid (SCC) RNR	18-Nov-2012

Name	Rank	Seniority	Name	Rank	Seniority
GREEN, Derek	SLt (SCC) RNR	26-Jun-2011	HILL, Edward	SLt (SCC) RNR	18-Nov-2012
GREEN, Malcolm	Lt (SCC) RNR	16-Aug-1997	HILL, Monica	A/Lt Cdr (SCC) RNR	18-Jul-2014
GREENFIELD, Stephen	Capt (SCC) RMR	09-Apr-2012	HILLIER, Barbara	Lt (SCC) RNR	04-Sep-2003
GREENFIELD(SEYMOUR), Diana	Ch RNR	26-Jul-2012	HISCOX, Lee	A/Lt (SCC) RNR	13-Dec-2013
GREENHALGH, Peter	Lt Cdr (SCC) RNR	01-Apr-2007	HITCHINS, Graham	Ch RNR	14-Jul-2010
GREGORY, Dominic	Lt (SCC) RNR	14-Jan-2013	HITHERSAY, John	Lt (SCC) RNR	28-Oct-1978
GRESTY, Stephen	Lt (SCC) RNR	07-Oct-1998	HOBBINS, Raymond	Ch RNR	23-Jul-1998
GREY, Roger	Ch RNR	02-Dec-2009	HOEY, David	Lt Cdr (SCC) RNR	10-Jul-2012
GRIBBLE, Michael	SLt (SCC) RNR	25-Mar-2012	HOEY, Richard	Capt (SCC) RMR	30-Nov-2013
GRIEVE, Derek	Lt (SCC) RNR	01-Jan-2007	HOFBAUER, Andrea	Ch RNR	22-Feb-2011
GRIFFITHS, Alexander	A/SLt (SCC) RNR	15-Jun-2014	HOLDER, John	Ch RNR	15-Aug-2002
GRIFFITHS, Martyn	Ch RNR	03-Jul-2008	HOLLAND, Donald	Lt (SCC) RNR	15-Sep-1984
GRIFFITHS, Thomas	SLt (SCC) RNR	25-Jul-2010	HOLLIDAY, Anthony	Lt Cdr (SCC) RNR	01-Jan-2001
GROGAN, Kenneth	Lt (SCC) RNR	16-Sep-1978	HOLLOWAY, Pamela	SLt (SCC) RNR	25-Jul-2010
GROSS, Lucy	Lt (SCC) RNR	23-Jun-2007	HOOKINS, Eric	Ch RNR	09-Jun-2007
GROVES, Richard	Lt Cdr (SCC) RNR	29-Aug-1986	HOPKINS, Henry	Ch RNR	18-Apr-2007
GUISHARD, Mark	SLt (SCC) RNR	04-Dec-2000	HORNE, Allan	Lt (SCC) RNR	16-Sep-1989
GUPPY, Graham	Maj (SCC) RMR	01-Jul-1999	HORTON, Paul	Capt (SCC) RMR	18-Apr-2013
GYI, Stephen	SLt (SCC) RNR	13-Dec-2009	HOULDEN, Wendy	Lt (SCC) RNR	30-Sep-2001
			HOWARD, Jon	Ch RNR	28-Feb-2008
H			HOWES, Alan	Ch RNR	18-Jun-1997
HACKETT, Clive	Lt Cdr (SCC) RNR	12-Oct-1990	HOWIE, Thomas	Lt Cdr (SCC) RNR	01-Nov-1988
HAGAN, George	Lt (SCC) RNR	09-Apr-2006	HUGHES, Rachel	Ch RNR	01-Apr-2014
HAINES, Linda	Lt (SCC) RNR	01-Nov-1989	HUGHES, Sharon	Ch RNR	01-Aug-2006
HALL, Christopher	Ch RNR	10-Jan-2006	HULONCE, Michael	Lt Cdr (SCC) RNR	01-Mar-1982
HALL, Derek	Lt Cdr (SCC) RNR	19-Feb-1998	HUMPHREYS, Lewis	Mid (SCC) RNR	09-Sep-2012
HALL, John	Ch RNR	27-Nov-2009	HUNT, Helen	SLt (SCC) RNR	07-Nov-2010
HALLAS, Jeanette	Lt (SCC) RNR	17-Jun-2005	HUNT, James	SLt (SCC) RNR	24-Mar-2013
HALLIDAY, Angela	Lt (SCC) RNR	11-May-2000	HUNT, Kevin		
HAMILTON, Francis Craig	A/Capt (SCC) RMR	27-Aug-2013	HUNTER, Philip	Lt (SCC) RNR	01-Feb-2002
HAMILTON, Gary	A/Lt (SCC) RNR	01-Jan-2015	HURST, Thomas	Lt Cdr (SCC) RNR	01-Jun-1985
HANKEY, Carolyne	Lt (SCC) RNR	30-Sep-1999	HUTCHINGS, Andrew	Lt (SCC) RNR	22-Jun-2004
HANLEY, David	Lt Cdr (SCC) RNR	01-Apr-2005	HUTCHINSON, John	Lt (SCC) RNR	20-Jun-2014
HANLON, Scott	SLt (SCC) RNR	30-Apr-2011			
HANN, Peter	Ch RNR	19-Dec-2010	**I**		
HANSON, Neil	Lt (SCC) RNR	11-Nov-2006	INGHAM, Anthony	SLt (SCC) RNR	24-Feb-1999
HARMER, Robert	Lt (SCC) RNR	28-Oct-1999	INGHAM, Mark	SLt (SCC) RNR	22-Nov-2000
HARRIS, Duncan	Ch RNR	27-Jun-2009	IRVING, Douglas	Ch RNR	05-Feb-2002
HARRIS, Geoffrey	Ch RNR	03-May-2012	IZZARD, Michael	Lt (SCC) RNR	25-Jun-1998
HARRIS, Kenneth	A/SLt (SCC) RNR	05-May-2012			
HARRIS, Rachel	A/Lt (SCC) RNR	16-Jul-2013	**J**		
HARRIS, Trevor	Lt (SCC) RNR	05-Dec-2001	JABLONSKI, Christopher	SLt (SCC) RNR	04-Nov-2009
HARTFIELD, John	Ch RNR	25-Jan-2010	JACKSON, Margaret Elizabeth	Ch RNR	02-Nov-2013
HARTWELL, Neil	Lt (SCC) RNR	26-Mar-2002	JAMES, Robert	Lt Cdr (SCC) RNR	01-Jan-1995
HARVEY, Brian	Lt (SCC) RNR	09-Jan-2007	JANNER-BURGESS, Mark	Lt (SCC) RNR	21-Jan-2006
HARVEY, Stephen	A/Lt Cdr (SCC) RNR	01-Nov-2014	JEFFRIES, Leila	Lt (SCC) RNR	25-Jun-2010
HATHERLEY, David	Lt (SCC) RNR	22-Nov-2006	JELLIS, Josephine	Ch RNR	28-Jan-2008
HAWKINS, Leslie	A/Lt (SCC) RNR	22-Apr-2010	JENNINGS, Mark	Ch RNR	13-Jan-2014
HAY, Robert	Lt (SCC) RNR	14-Oct-2010	JENNINGS, Pamela	Ch RNR	20-Sep-2004
HAZELDON, Donald	SLt (SCC) RNR	28-Apr-1993	JENNINGS, William	Lt Cdr (SCC) RNR	01-Jan-2007
HAZZARD, Michael	A/Lt (SCC) RNR	13-Jun-2011	JEZZARD, Michael	Ch RNR	02-Apr-2004
HEAD, Gareth	SLt (SCC) RNR	10-Nov-2013	JOHNS, Bevan	Lt Cdr (SCC) RNR	06-Jan-2014
HEALEY, Stephen	Lt (SCC) RNR	15-May-1984	JOHNS, Gareth	SLt (SCC) RNR	27-Mar-2011
HEALY, Christopher	A/Lt Cdr (SCC) RNR	14-Oct-2014	JOHNSON, Peter	Ch RNR	09-Sep-2010
HEARD, Steven	A/SLt (SCC) RNR	15-Jun-2014	JOHNSON-PAUL, David	Lt (SCC) RNR	23-Feb-2012
HEARL, James	Lt Cdr (SCC) RNR	01-Dec-2004	JOHNSTONE, Geoffrey	Capt (SCC) RMR	01-Jul-2012
HEARL, James	Lt (SCC) RNR	07-Nov-2014	JONES, Christopher	Lt Cdr (SCC) RNR	11-Aug-1999
HEEKS, Theresa	Lt (SCC) RNR	02-Nov-2013	JONES, Clive	Ch RNR	01-Oct-2005
HEMSWORTH, John	Ch RNR	04-Jan-2008	JONES, Dorothy	Lt (SCC) RNR	22-Nov-1994
HERSANT, Michael	Ch RNR	08-Jan-2003	JONES, Ian	A/Capt (SCC) RMR	12-Dec-2012
HIBBINS, Neil	Ch RNR	12-Dec-2005	JONES, Jonathan	A/SLt (SCC) RNR	26-Jun-2013
HIDE, Brenda	Lt (SCC) RNR	17-Jul-1986			

Name	Rank	Seniority	Name	Rank	Seniority
JONES, Kelvin	Lt (SCC) RNR	07-Apr-1997	LISTER, Richard	A/Lt Cdr (SCC) RNR	01-Jan-2013
JONES, Mark	Lt (SCC) RNR	06-Nov-1996	LOCKE, David	Lt Cdr (SCC) RNR	01-Jan-2005
JONES, Mark	SLt (SCC) RNR	28-Jun-2009	LOGIN, Brenda	Lt Cdr (SCC) RNR	01-Oct-2002
JONES, Nicholas	Lt (SCC) RNR	02-Apr-2010	LOGIN, Craig	SLt (SCC) RNR	28-Mar-2010
JONES, Sian	Ch RNR	20-Jan-2012	LOGIN, Derek	Cdr (SCC) RNR	01-Aug-2009
JORDAN, Sheila	Lt (SCC) RNR	26-Jul-1990	LOGIN, Susan	SLt (SCC) RNR	09-Sep-2011
JOREY, Richard	SLt (SCC) RNR	12-Feb-2014	LONDON, Phillip	SLt (SCC) RNR	31-Oct-2005
JUBB, Elizabeth	Lt (SCC) RNR	21-Aug-2009	LOUCH, Stephen	Lt (SCC) RNR	21-Nov-2009
JUNIPER, James	Capt (SCC) RMR	22-Jun-2007	LOVERIDGE, Anthony	Lt Cdr (SCC) RNR	01-Dec-1989
JUNIPER, Stephanie	Lt (SCC) RNR	11-Nov-2006	LOVERIDGE, Jillian	A/SLt (SCC) RNR	23-Nov-2014
JUPE, Paul	Lt (SCC) RNR	02-Mar-1988	LOW, Peter	Ch RNR	16-Apr-2007
			LOWE, David	Lt (SCC) RNR	23-Jul-1977
K			LOXTON, LINDA	Ch RNR	21-Oct-2014
KAY, Anne	Lt (SCC) RNR	21-Jan-2006	LUCAS, Peter	Lt (SCC) RNR	24-Mar-1999
KAYE, Timothy	Ch RNR	01-Aug-2000	LUCKMAN, Bruce	Lt (SCC) RNR	01-Oct-1992
KEERY, William	Lt Cdr (SCC) RNR	01-Jan-1983	LUXTON, Phillip	Lt (SCC) RNR	05-Nov-2000
KEETON, Craig	A/SLt (SCC) RNR	22-Mar-2014	LYNCH, Matthew	A/Lt (SCC) RNR	23-Sep-2013
KENDALL, George	SLt (SCC) RNR	01-Jul-2007	LYSTER, Cody	Lt (SCC) RNR	27-Nov-2009
KENRICK, Peter	Lt (SCC) RNR	23-Nov-1994			
KEOWN, Paul	Ch RNR	17-Feb-2014	**M**		
KERRIGAN, Gareth	SLt (SCC) RNR	24-Jun-2012	MACEY, Mark	Lt Cdr (SCC) RNR	01-Sep-2003
KERSLAKE, Adrian	Lt (SCC) RNR	06-Apr-2011	MACHIN, Ian	Maj (SCC) RMR	01-Jul-1999
KETTLEBOROUGH, Thomas	SLt (SCC) RNR	07-Nov-2010	MACKAY, Charles	SLt (SCC) RNR	01-Dec-1997
KILLICK, Peter	Lt (SCC) RNR	08-Oct-1987	MACKAY, Colin	Ch RNR	30-May-2013
KING, Leslie	Lt Cdr (SCC) RNR	15-Mar-1998	MACKAY, David	Lt (SCC) RNR	01-Jul-1984
KINGHORN, Jason	Lt Cdr (SCC) RNR	01-Jan-2008	MACKINLAY, Colin	Lt (SCC) RNR	08-Apr-1992
KINGSHOTT, Andrew	A/SLt (SCC) RNR	31-Aug-2014	MACLENNAN, Glenn	Lt (SCC) RMR	30-Oct-2011
KNIGHT, Robert	Lt Cdr (SCC) RNR	01-Jun-2008	MACLENNAN, Robert	Lt (SCC) RNR	21-Nov-2009
KRISTIANSEN, Karen	Lt Cdr (SCC) RNR	10-Aug-2007	MACLEOD, Ronald	A/Lt (SCC) RNR	24-Jun-2012
			MACNAUGHTON, Diana	Ch RNR	07-Feb-2012
L			MAIR, Brian	Lt Cdr (SCC) RNR	01-Jan-2002
LAMPERT, Brian	Lt Cdr (SCC) RNR	01-Dec-1984	MALM, Alexander	SLt (SCC) RNR	25-Mar-2013
LAMPERT, Mark	Lt (SCC) RNR	25-Jan-2009	MANNOUCH, John	Lt (SCC) RNR	14-May-1990
LAMPERT, Susan	Lt Cdr (SCC) RNR	01-Apr-2006	MARK, Nicholas	Ch RNR	10-Aug-2010
LANCASTER, Jonathan	Lt (SCC) RNR	25-Mar-2012	MARLBOROUGH, Andrew	SLt (SCC) RNR	29-Mar-2009
LANE, Roy	Ch RNR	03-Aug-1992	MARLOWE, Bernard	A/Lt (SCC) RNR	08-Mar-2010
LAWES, Sonia	Lt Cdr (SCC) RNR	01-Jan-2007	MARSHALL, Dean	SLt (SCC) RNR	26-Jun-2011
LAWRENCE, Kevin	Lt (SCC) RNR	01-May-2001	MARSHALL, Keith	SLt (SCC) RNR	25-Nov-2012
LE-BASSE, Myles	A/Capt (SCC) RNR	08-Feb-2012	MARSON, Victoria	Lt Cdr (SCC) RNR	01-Feb-2005
LEAPER, Richard	Ch RNR	05-Jan-1999	MARTIN, Kevin	Lt Cdr (SCC) RNR	01-Jan-2008
LEAVER, Carl	SLt (SCC) RNR	27-Mar-2011	MASON, Edward	Lt Cdr (SCC) RNR	01-Jan-1978
LECKIE, Alexander	A/Maj (SCC) RMR	01-Jan-2013	MATTHEWS, John	A/Lt Cdr (SCC) RNR	12-Jul-2012
LECKIE, Lesley	Lt (SCC) RNR	01-Oct-2011	MATTHEWS, Phillip	Lt Cdr (SCC) RNR	01-Feb-1989
LEE, Philip	Lt (SCC) RNR	04-Oct-2013	MATTHEWS, Ronald	Lt (SCC) RNR	14-Jan-1997
LEEVES, Luke	SLt (SCC) RNR	10-Aug-2012	MATTHIAS, Paul	Ch RNR	12-Apr-2010
LEGGATE, Colin	Ch RNR	20-Oct-2011	MAY, John (Iain)	Ch RNR	26-Apr-2013
LEIGH-PEARSON, Michael	Ch RNR	09-Aug-2012	MAYLAM, Nicholas	A/SLt (SCC) RNR	22-Nov-2013
LEVERETT, Colin	SLt (SCC) RNR	01-Jul-2007	MCCUISH, Ewan	Lt (SCC) RNR	05-Oct-2011
LEVERETT, Rosamund	SLt (SCC) RNR	07-Apr-2007	MCDERMOTT, Keith	SLt (SCC) RNR	28-Jun-2009
LEWIS, Clifford	Lt Cdr (SCC) RNR	23-Feb-2009	MCDONALD, LESLEY Mary	Lt (SCC) RNR	05-May-1998
LEWIS, David	Lt Cdr (SCC) RNR	01-Jan-2007	MCDONALD, PETER	Lt (SCC) RNR	29-Jun-1992
LEWIS, Deirdre	Lt (SCC) RNR	03-Nov-2014	MCGARRY, George	Lt (SCC) RNR	08-Aug-2006
LEWIS, Eleanor	Lt (SCC) RNR	23-Nov-1994	MCGLONE, Fergus	SLt (SCC) RNR	10-Aug-2010
LEWIS, John	Capt (SCC) RMR	01-Jul-1999	MCKEE, David	Lt Cdr (SCC) RNR	27-Sep-1987
LEWIS, John	Ch RNR	10-Jul-1998	MCKENDREY, Susan	Ch RNR	08-Apr-2014
LEWIS, Peter	Lt Cdr (SCC) RNR	01-Jan-2004	MCKENNA, Paul	Lt Cdr (SCC) RNR	01-Jun-2007
LEWIS, Stephen	A/SLt (SCC) RNR	15-Jun-2014	MCKEOWN, Glenda	Lt (SCC) RNR	24-Apr-1996
LEWIS, Walter	Lt (SCC) RNR	06-May-1979	MCNAUGHTAN-OWEN, James	Ch RNR	20-Apr-1998
LINCOLN, David	Lt Cdr (SCC) RNR	01-Jan-2006	MCSWEENEY, Denis	Ch RNR	02-Mar-2014
LINDLEY, James	Lt (SCC) RNR	16-May-2012	MCVEAGH, Paul	Ch RNR	31-Aug-2004
LINDSEY, Helen	SLt (SCC) RNR	10-Nov-2012	MCVINNIE, Elizabeth	Lt (SCC) RNR	06-Nov-2000
			MEADOWS, Paul	Lt Cdr (SCC) RNR	01-Apr-2008

Name	Rank	Seniority
MEADOWS, Sharon	SLt (SCC) RNR	01-Nov-2009
MEEK, Caroline	Lt (SCC) RNR	06-May-2006
MENDRYS, Adam	Lt (SCC) RNR	10-Jul-2014
MENHAMS, Angela	Lt Cdr (SCC) RNR	01-Jan-2009
MERRICK, Charles	Ch RNR	21-Oct-2014
MERRIN, Roy	Ch RNR	02-Feb-2012
MERRY, Andrew	Capt (SCC) RMR	29-Oct-2011
MILLER, Kerensa	A/SLt (SCC) RNR	23-Mar-2014
MILLER, Luke	Ch RNR	11-May-2009
MILLER, Martin	Ch RNR	08-Nov-2006
MILLER, Richard	A/SLt (SCC) RNR	23-Jul-2009
MILLIGAN, Kevin	A/Lt Cdr (SCC) RNR	30-Mar-2012
MILLIGAN, Victoria	Lt (SCC) RNR	01-May-1998
MILLS, John	Lt (SCC) RNR	04-Oct-2004
MILLS, William	Lt (SCC) RNR	23-Jun-1993
MILNE, Janet	Lt Cdr (SCC) RNR	18-Sep-1987
MITCHELL, Alec	Ch RNR	01-Mar-2000
MITCHELL, Barry	Lt (SCC) RNR	19-Jan-2008
MITCHELL, Craig	SLt (SCC) RNR	19-Jan-2011
MITCHELL, Jane	Lt (SCC) RNR	01-Jun-2000
MITCHELL, Ray	Lt Cdr (SCC) RNR	05-Jan-2005
MITCHISON, Maria	SLt (SCC) RNR	06-Apr-2008
MITCHISON, Robert	Lt (SCC) RNR	12-Jun-2010
MOIR, Brian	Lt Cdr (SCC) RNR	01-Jan-2009
MOLLART, Oliver	SLt (SCC) RNR	06-Dec-2013
MONKCOM, Susan	Lt (SCC) RNR	01-Jan-1998
MONTEITH, William	A/Lt (SCC) RMR	23-Mar-2014
MONTGOMERY, Nina	SLt (SCC) RNR	30-Oct-2011
MOODY, Roger	Lt Cdr (SCC) RNR	01-Jan-1985
MOONEY, Paul	Lt (SCC) RMR	26-Jun-2011
MOORE, Brian	Lt (SCC) RNR	23-Nov-2008
MOORE, Geoffrey	Ch RNR	18-Oct-2007
MORGAN, Angus	SLt (SCC) RNR	25-Jul-2010
MORGAN, John	Lt (SCC) RNR	10-Feb-1988
MORGAN, Norman John	Lt Cdr (SCC) RNR	23-Jul-2004
MORRELL, Michael	A/SLt (SCC) RNR	15-Jun-2014
MORRIS, Angela	Lt (SCC) RNR	01-Jul-2007
MORRIS, Kevin	A/Lt Cdr (SCC) RNR	01-Sep-2013
MORTON, Rita	Lt (SCC) RNR	13-May-1998
MOSLEY, E Peter	Ch RNR	10-Sep-2012
MOULTON, Nicholas	Lt Cdr (SCC) RNR	21-Nov-1998
MOWATT, Marleen	SLt (SCC) RNR	02-Jul-2006
MOYSE, David	Ch RNR	13-Nov-1998
MULHOLLAND, Ross	Lt Cdr (SCC) RNR	08-Jan-2007
MULLIN, William	Lt (SCC) RNR	10-Nov-1986
MUSSELWHITE, Ruth	Lt (SCC) RNR	19-Dec-2002

N

Name	Rank	Seniority
NAGGS, Darren	A/Lt (SCC) RNR	15-Feb-2010
NASH, Benjamin	SLt (SCC) RNR	28-Jun-2009
NEEDHAM, Peter	Ch RNR	26-Aug-2008
NEWMAN, Raymond	Lt (SCC) RNR	20-Jul-1982
NEWTON, Robert	Ch RNR	24-Sep-2012
NICHOL, David	SLt (SCC) RNR	28-Mar-2010
NICHOLLS, David	Lt (SCC) RNR	25-Jul-2001
NIMMO, Alexander	Ch RNR	03-Jan-1990
NIXON, Joseph	Lt (SCC) RNR	30-Jun-1984
NORRIS, Anthony	Lt Cdr (SCC) RNR	01-Nov-2002
NORRIS, Peter	Ch RNR	20-Mar-2007
NORTHEAST, Lindsay	A/SLt (SCC) RNR	07-May-2014
NORWOOD, Paul	Ch RNR	24-Jun-2011
NUNN, Jacqui	SLt (SCC) RNR	10-Aug-2013

O

Name	Rank	Seniority
O'DONNELL, Adrian	Lt (SCC) RNR	06-Nov-1990
O'DONNELL, David	Lt (SCC) RNR	02-Oct-2012
O'DONNELL, Wendy	SLt (SCC) RNR	01-Feb-2005
O'DONOGHUE, Amanda	A/Lt Cdr (SCC) RNR	01-Jul-2013
O'KEEFFE, Richard	Lt Cdr (SCC) RNR	01-May-2002
O'SULLIVAN, Michael	SLt (SCC) RNR	29-Mar-2009
OGLESBY, Simon	Lt (SCC) RNR	08-Dec-2005
ORCHARD, Richard	Ch RNR	25-Nov-2011
ORR, Jake	Lt (SCC) RNR	30-Apr-2012
ORR, Robert	Lt (SCC) RNR	26-Mar-2002
ORTON, Adrian	Capt (SCC) RMR	01-Jan-1999
OSBORNE, Brian	Lt (SCC) RNR	01-Jan-1987
OSBORNE, Dawn	Lt (SCC) RNR	01-Feb-1986
OWEN, William	Lt (SCC) RNR	05-Jun-1996
OWENS, Christopher	A/Lt Cdr (SCC) RNR	11-Nov-2013
OWENS, Christopher	Ch RNR	17-Jul-2009

P

Name	Rank	Seniority
PAGETT, Marie	SLt (SCC) RNR	27-Mar-2011
PAINE, Peter	Ch RNR	01-Aug-2000
PAINTER, Lorretta	Lt (SCC) RNR	28-Jan-1993
PALMER, Alan	Capt (SCC) RMR	20-Nov-2001
PARK, Peter	Ch RNR	30-Jul-2010
PARKER, Andrew	Ch RNR	07-Nov-2014
PARRIS, Stephen	Capt (SCC) RMR	01-Jul-1999
PARSONS, Jack	SLt (SCC) RNR	04-Sep-2013
PARTINGTON, Kenneth	Ch RNR	23-May-2013
PASCOE, William	Lt (SCC) RNR	26-Jul-1984
PASK, Thomas	Lt (SCC) RNR	25-Sep-2010
PASSANT, Keith	Ch RNR	11-Feb-1998
PATERSON, Debbie	A/Lt Cdr (SCC) RNR	
PATERSON, Gordon	A/Lt (SCC) RNR	01-Dec-1999
PATTERSON, Phillip	Cdr (SCC) RNR	01-May-2010
PAYNE, Derek	Lt Cdr (SCC) RNR	01-Jan-2001
PEAKE, Christopher	A/SLt (SCC) RNR	10-Nov-2013
PEARCE, Gaynor	SLt (SCC) RNR	24-Mar-2014
PEEL, Tracy	A/Lt (SCC) RNR	06-Oct-2014
PENNY, Carl	Capt (SCC) RMR	17-Sep-2005
PERCHARD, Ronald	Lt (SCC) RNR	08-Sep-2005
PERKIN, Simon	Ch RNR	13-Dec-2012
PERKINS, Douglas	Ch RNR	16-Apr-2010
PERKINS, Jonathon	Lt (SCC) RNR	09-Mar-2003
PERKINS, Kevin	Lt (SCC) RNR	05-Nov-1997
PERRY, Paul	Lt Cdr (SCC) RNR	04-Feb-1994
PETERS, Adam	A/Lt Cdr (SCC) RNR	18-Feb-2013
PETERS-JONES, Lauren	SLt (SCC) RNR	28-Jun-2009
PETHER, Marc	Lt (SCC) RMR	13-Jun-2011
PETHER, Phillip	Lt (SCC) RNR	02-Dec-1972
PHILIP, Charles	Ch RNR	20-Jul-2011
PHILLIPS, Mark	Ch RNR	16-Oct-2014
PHILLIPS, Niyall	Mid (SCC) RNR	23-Nov-2014
PHILPOT, David	Lt (SCC) RMR	09-May-2004
PHILPOTT, Matthew	2nd Lt (SCC) RMR	02-Nov-2008
PICKERING, Jean	Lt (SCC) RNR	03-Jul-1990
PIERCY, Peter	Lt Cdr (SCC) RNR	25-Oct-1986
PIKE, John	Lt (SCC) RNR	31-May-1996
PITSIKAS, Anastasios	SLt (SCC) RNR	09-Sep-2012
PLUMMER, Thomas	Lt (SCC) RNR	24-May-1991
POKE, David	A/Lt Col(SCC) RMR	11-Nov-2013
POLLARD, Colin	SLt (SCC) RNR	10-Oct-2007

Name	Rank	Seniority	Name	Rank	Seniority
POOLTON, Martin	Ch RNR	01-Aug-2001	RUSSELL, James	A/Lt Cdr (SCC) RNR	05-Aug-2013
POPE, Darren	Lt (SCC) RNR	22-Apr-1993	RUSSELL, Robert	Lt (SCC) RNR	14-Jan-2013
PORTER, John	Lt Cdr (SCC) RNR	01-Jan-2002	RUST, Darren	A/SLt (SCC) RNR	02-Jun-2013
POWELL, Diane	Ch RNR	06-May-1998	RUTHERFORD, Sarah	SLt (SCC) RNR	08-Oct-2010
POWELL, Robert	Capt (SCC) RMR	24-Sep-2001	RYCROFT, Louise	Lt (SCC) RNR	25-Sep-2010
POWELL, Terry	Lt (SCC) RNR	09-Feb-2013	RYCROFT, Paul	Lt Cdr (SCC) RNR	09-Aug-1989
POWNALL, Edwin	Capt (SCC) RMR	23-May-2014	RYDER, Emma	Lt (SCC) RNR	03-Jul-2012
PREECE, Colin	Ch RNR	16-Dec-1998			
PRENTICE, Paul	Ch RNR	20-Jun-2012	**S**		
PRIEST, Richard	A/SLt (SCC) RNR	23-Nov-2014			
PRIOR-SANKEY, Adrian	Ch RNR	08-Feb-2007	SADLER, Simonetta	SLt (SCC) RNR	28-Jun-2009
PRITCHARD, Carol	Lt Cdr (SCC) RNR	05-Oct-2008	SALISBURY, Linda	Lt (SCC) RNR	02-Apr-1999
PRITCHARD, David	Lt Cdr (SCC) RNR	01-Jan-1995	SAMIEC, George	Ch RNR	15-May-2005
PROCTER, Michael	SLt (SCC) RNR	25-Jul-2009	SAMUELS, Patrick	Ch RNR	19-May-2011
PROLLINS, Mark	Capt (SCC) RMR	19-Jan-2014	SANDERS, James	SLt (SCC) RNR	29-May-2014
PUGH, Heather	Lt Cdr (SCC) RNR	28-Apr-1998	SANDILANDS, James	A/Capt (SCC) RMR	06-Jul-2013
PURCELL, Mark	A/SLt (SCC) RNR	23-Mar-2014	SANDISON, Michael	Ch RNR	08-Dec-2008
			SAUPE, Peter	Lt (SCC) RNR	01-Jul-1987
Q			SAWYER, Keith	Ch RNR	15-Jul-2014
			SCHOFIELD, Hannah	SLt (SCC) RNR	09-Sep-2012
QUINN, David	Lt (SCC) RMR	17-Aug-2013	SCHOLES, Aaron	A/SLt (SCC) RNR	31-Aug-2014
			SCHOLES, David	Capt (SCC) RMR	01-Jul-1999
R			SCHOLES, Peter	SLt (SCC) RNR	08-Aug-2013
			SCHOLES, Sian	Lt (SCC) RMR	18-Nov-2013
RADCLIFFE, Brian	Lt Cdr (SCC) RNR	29-Oct-1995	SCHUMAN, Andrew	Ch RNR	23-Aug-2005
RAINE, David	Ch RNR	13-Jan-2014	SCOTT, Guy	Ch RNR	10-Oct-2011
RANKLIN, Adam	Lt (SCC) RNR	01-Jan-2012	SEABURY, Paul	Lt (SCC) RNR	16-Aug-1997
RASHLEIGH, Carol	Lt (SCC) RNR	04-Dec-2014	SEARLES, Andrew	Lt Cdr (SCC) RNR	30-Mar-2013
RAWCLIFFE, Michael	Lt (SCC) RNR	17-Apr-1998	SEDGWICK, Mark	Lt (SCC) RNR	03-Jun-2000
RAYSON, Trevor	Lt Cdr (SCC) RNR	01-Jan-2001	SEEX, Lucy-Anne	SLt (SCC) RNR	25-Mar-2012
READ, Christopher	Lt Cdr (SCC) RNR	01-Apr-2012	SEGGIE, Andrew	Lt (SCC) RNR	26-Jun-2009
READ, Clare	Lt (SCC) RNR	26-Oct-2007	SEYCHELL, Charles	Lt (SCC) RNR	01-Jan-1990
REDHEAD, Julie	Lt (SCC) RNR	13-Jun-2002	SHAW, David	Lt (SCC) RNR	14-May-1984
REDVERS-HARRIS, Jonathan	Ch RNR	23-Apr-2003	SHAW, Margaret	Ch RNR	30-Jul-2009
REEVES, Angela	Lt Cdr (SCC) RNR	01-Jan-2001	SHEEHAN, Joshua	A/Lt (SCC) RNR	13-May-2014
REEVES, Mark	Lt (SCC) RNR	11-May-2001	SHELTON, Clive	Lt Cdr (SCC) RNR	24-Apr-1998
REID, Jeffery	Lt (SCC) RNR	04-Nov-2003	SHELTON, John	Lt (SCC) RNR	07-Oct-1989
REYNOLDS, Lee	SLt (SCC) RNR	02-Jun-2013	SHIELS, Robert	Lt Cdr (SCC) RNR	08-Sep-1986
REYNOLDS, Nicola	Ch RNR	07-Oct-2004	SHIELS, Suzanne	Lt Cdr (SCC) RNR	01-Apr-2006
RHODES, Adrian	Capt (SCC) RMR	05-Feb-2014	SHINTON, Bertram	Ch RNR	11-Jan-2011
RIDGWAY, Paul	Lt Cdr (SCC) RNR	21-Feb-2000	SHONE, Michael	Lt Cdr (SCC) RNR	03-Feb-2014
RILEY, Paul	A/Lt (SCC) RMR	23-Nov-2014	SHORT, Keith	Lt Cdr (SCC) RNR	06-Apr-1986
RINDL, Anthony	Ch RNR	04-Apr-2014	SHUTTLEWORTH, James	SLt (SCC) RNR	28-Mar-2010
ROAF, Alistair	SLt (SCC) RNR	07-Jun-1996	SHUTTLEWORTH, Tye	Lt Cdr (SCC) RNR	27-Jan-2013
ROBBINS, Allan	Lt Cdr (SCC) RNR	01-Oct-2001	SICKELMORE, Barry	Lt Cdr (SCC) RNR	05-Apr-1999
ROBERTS, Euphemia	Lt Cdr (SCC) RNR	27-Nov-2003	SIDWELL, Victoria	Lt (SCC) RNR	09-Jun-2010
ROBERTS, Tammy	SLt (SCC) RNR	01-Nov-2009	SILK, Ian	Ch RNR	24-Apr-2008
ROBERTSON, Robbie	SLt (SCC) RNR	23-Mar-2009	SILVER, Barry-John	Lt (SCC) RNR	30-May-2008
ROBINSON, Charlotte	Lt (SCC) RNR	09-Oct-2013	SILVER, Yolanda C	A/SLt (SCC) RNR	15-Jun-2014
ROBINSON, Hannah	A/SLt (SCC) RNR	31-Aug-2014	SILVERTHORNE, Robert	Lt (SCC) RNR	31-Oct-1991
ROBINSON, John	Lt (SCC) RNR	24-Feb-2014	SIMISTER, Alan	Lt (SCC) RNR	14-Sep-2003
ROBINSON, Paul	Lt (SCC) RNR	11-Mar-2003	SIMM, John	A/SLt (SCC) RNR	16-Jan-2012
ROCK, William	Lt (SCC) RNR	12-Nov-2000	SIMMONS, Melvyn	Lt (SCC) RNR	10-Apr-1993
ROCKEY, David	SLt (SCC) RNR	11-Mar-1998	SIMPSON, Alfred	Lt Cdr (SCC) RNR	08-Feb-1984
ROGERS, Carol	Lt (SCC) RNR	26-Feb-2010	SIMS, Bernard	Ch RNR	01-Nov-1994
ROGERS, Neil	Lt (SCC) RNR	30-Sep-2000	SIMS, Martin	SLt (SCC) RNR	02-Jun-2014
ROGERS, Sally-Anne	Lt (SCC) RNR	22-Nov-1997	SINCLAIR, Derek	Lt (SCC) RNR	30-Aug-2011
ROOTS, Joseph	Lt (SCC) RNR	21-Sep-2001	SINDEN, Daniel-Paul	Lt Cdr (SCC) RNR	01-Nov-2010
ROSS, David	Lt (SCC) RNR	13-Oct-1990	SKINGLE, Stephen	Lt (SCC) RNR	05-May-2003
ROWLAND, Sebastian	Lt (SCC) RNR	25-Jul-2010	SKINNER, Michael	Ch RNR	26-May-2007
ROWLES, David	Lt Cdr (SCC) RNR	03-May-1974	SMALL, Stephen	Lt Cdr (SCC) RNR	28-Feb-2014
RUSHTON, Steven	Lt (SCC) RNR	15-Mar-1995	SMEDLEY, Monty	SLt (SCC) RNR	21-Aug-2004
RUSSELL, John	Lt (SCC) RNR	01-Nov-1989	SMEETON, Karen	Ch RNR	27-Nov-2009

Name	Rank	Seniority	Name	Rank	Seniority
SMITH, Adrian	Lt (SCC) RNR	21-Nov-1994	THEOBALD, Robert	Lt (SCC) RNR	11-Sep-1990
SMITH, Angela	A/Lt (SCC) RMR	31-Aug-2014	THOMAS, Alan	Lt (SCC) RNR	14-Apr-1998
SMITH, Deborah	Lt (SCC) RNR	30-Jan-2007	THOMAS, Christopher	Ch RNR	12-Sep-2005
SMITH, Don	Ch RNR	03-Jul-2011	THOMAS, Michael	Lt (SCC) RNR	19-Jul-1980
SMITH, Frank	SLt (SCC) RNR	30-Oct-2011	THOMAS, Nancy	Ch RNR	12-Apr-2000
SMITH, Graham	Lt (SCC) RNR	05-Apr-1997	THOMAS, Stephen	Lt (SCC) RNR	03-Jul-2012
SMITH, Janet	Lt (SCC) RMR	29-Mar-2009	THOMPSON, David	Lt (SCC) RMR	18-Jun-2010
SMITH, Lee	SLt (SCC) RNR	01-Nov-2012	THOMPSON, Mark	SLt (SCC) RNR	30-Oct-2011
SMITH, Noel	SLt (SCC) RNR	25-Jun-2013	THOMSON, Andrew	Lt (SCC) RNR	07-Apr-1995
SMITH, Sally	SLt (SCC) RNR	24-Mar-2013	THOMSON, Robert	Lt (SCC) RNR	17-Mar-1971
SMITH, Sean	Capt (SCC) RMR	12-Jun-2011	THORN, Simon	Ch RNR	18-Nov-2010
SMITH, Tamsin	SLt (SCC) RNR	13-Nov-2014	THURGOOD, Anthony	Lt (SCC) RNR	08-Feb-2013
SNEDDEN, David	Lt (SCC) RNR	01-Sep-2014	THURLAND, Joseph	SLt (SCC) RNR	14-Jul-2014
SOMERVILLE, Lesley	A/SLt (SCC) RNR	23-Mar-2014	TILLBROOK, Richard	Ch RNR	18-Mar-2009
SOMERVILLE, Neal	A/SLt (SCC) RNR	23-Nov-2014	TIMOTHY, Emile	Maj (SCC) RMR	01-Jul-1999
SPEAR, Keith	Lt (SCC) RNR	06-Jul-2012	TITLEY, John	Lt (SCC) RNR	04-May-1993
SPICER, David	Lt (SCC) RNR	23-Feb-1987	TOBIN, Richard	Ch RNR	27-Feb-2006
SPICER, Janice	Lt (SCC) RNR	01-Jul-1987	TOLLEY, George	SLt (SCC) RNR	27-Sep-2010
SPINK, James	Lt Cdr (SCC) RNR	01-Apr-2007	TOWNSEND, Graham	Lt Cdr (SCC) RNR	01-Jan-2011
SPINKS, Sally	Lt (SCC) RNR	16-Jul-2014	TOWNSEND, Stephen	SLt (SCC) RNR	30-Mar-2003
SQUIRE, Richard	A/SLt (SCC) RNR	24-Oct-2009	TOWNSEND, William	A/Lt (SCC) RMR	23-Nov-2014
SQUIRES, Anna	Lt (SCC) RNR	23-Feb-2013	TRAHAIR, Estella	Lt Cdr (SCC) RNR	01-Apr-2006
SQUIRES, John	Lt Cdr (SCC) RNR	01-Jan-2007	TRAIL, Craig	A/SLt (SCC) RNR	31-Aug-2014
STAFFORD, Craig Richard	A/Lt (SCC) RMR	03-Sep-2014	TRANTER, John	Ch RNR	22-Feb-2007
STAPLES, Jeffrey	Ch RNR	16-Dec-2013	TRICK, Matthew	Ch RNR	08-Oct-2012
STEGGALL, Mark	Lt Cdr (SCC) RNR	01-Jan-2011	TROJAN, Margaret	Lt (SCC) RNR	30-Nov-1999
STEPHEN, Kenneth	Ch RNR	04-Oct-2007	TROTT, Dwayne	A/Lt Cdr (SCC) RNR	01-Jul-2000
STEPHENS, Mark	A/Lt (SCC) RNR	24-Jun-2012	TRUELOVE, Gary	Lt (SCC) RNR	01-Jul-2004
STEPHENSON, Claire	SLt (SCC) RNR	01-Nov-2009	TRUSCOTT, Gary	Lt Cdr (SCC) RNR	01-Jan-1996
STEVENSON, David	A/SLt (SCC) RNR	13-Feb-2013	TRUSWELL, Jacqueline	Lt (SCC) RNR	03-Nov-2007
STEWART, Alan	Lt Cdr (SCC) RNR	01-Jun-2007	TRUSWELL, Simon	SLt (SCC) RNR	01-Nov-2009
STEWART, Keith	Ch RNR	11-Aug-2004	TSANG, Wing	Ch RNR	15-Mar-2010
STINTON, Douglas	SLt (SCC) RNR	23-Mar-2014	TUDOR, Simon	Lt (SCC) RNR	28-Sep-2012
STOKER, Andrew	Ch RNR	05-Sep-2005	TURNER, Ian	Lt Cdr (SCC) RNR	01-Jan-2007
STONE, Kathleen	SLt (SCC) RNR	21-Nov-2004	TURNER, Mark	SLt (SCC) RNR	28-Jun-2009
STONE, Terence	Lt (SCC) RNR	26-Feb-1991	TWEED, Alan	Lt (SCC) RNR	06-Jan-1993
STONEMAN, Allan	SLt (SCC) RNR	10-Nov-2013	TYSON, Michael	Lt (SCC) RNR	22-Mar-1983
STREET, Steven	Lt (SCC) RNR	14-Apr-1999			
STYLES, Marc	Lt (SCC) RNR	21-Nov-2009	**U**		
SUMNER, Robert	Lt (SCC) RNR	06-Dec-1999			
SUMPTER, Clive	Lt (SCC) RNR	10-Jul-2011	UMFREVILLE, Robert	SLt (SCC) RNR	10-Dec-2013
SURREY, Elizabeth	Lt (SCC) RNR	29-Oct-2014	UNSWORTH, John	Lt (SCC) RNR	11-May-2008
SUTTON, Ryan	A/Lt (SCC) RMR	03-Dec-2007	URQUHART, John	Lt Cdr (SCC) RNR	01-Nov-2004
SVENDSEN, Peter	Lt Cdr (SCC) RNR	01-May-2002	UTTING, Joseph	A/Lt Cdr (SCC) RNR	01-Jan-2014
SWAIN, David	Lt (SCC) RNR	06-Sep-2014	UTTING, Susan	Mid (SCC) RNR	15-Jun-2014
SWARBRICK, David	Lt (SCC) RNR	15-Jan-1999			
SWATTON, Jennifer	SLt (SCC) RNR	01-Feb-2011	**V**		
SWEETING, Peter	Ch RNR	18-Jun-2003			
			VALENTINE, Andrew	SLt (SCC) RNR	26-Jun-2011
			VANDENBERGH, Victor	Ch RNR	07-Nov-2005
T			VANDERLELY, Jan	Ch RNR	18-Sep-2013
			VANNS, Jonathan	Lt Cdr (SCC) RNR	06-Nov-2006
TAIT, Graham	Lt Cdr (SCC) RNR	01-Jul-2008	VANNS, Matthew	A/SLt (SCC) RNR	23-Mar-2014
TANNER, Roland	Lt Cdr (SCC) RNR	21-Jul-1987	VOKES, Simon	Lt (SCC) RNR	27-Jan-2007
TAPP, Maria	Lt (SCC) RNR	23-Oct-1995			
TAYLOR, Ashleigh	SLt (SCC) RNR	24-Mar-2013	**W**		
TAYLOR, Alex	Lt (SCC) RNR	09-Aug-2013			
TAYLOR, Fay	Lt (SCC) RNR	21-Jan-2006	WADDINGTON, Janet	Ch RNR	01-Nov-1992
TAYLOR, Roy	A/Lt (SCC) RNR	14-Feb-2011	WAGSTAFF, Paul	A/Maj (SCC) RMR	09-Aug-2013
TAYLOR, Sheila	Lt (SCC) RNR	03-May-2011	WAGSTAFF, Voirrey	Lt (SCC) RNR	28-Mar-2010
TEBBY, Christine	Lt (SCC) RNR	05-Sep-1989	WALES, Stephen Francis	Ch RNR	30-Aug-2013
TEMPLE, Edward	Lt Cdr (SCC) RNR	14-Oct-1991	WALFORD, Jolyon	Ch RNR	07-Mar-2014
TEMPLETON, James	Ch RNR	14-Aug-1998	WALKER, Keith	Lt (SCC) RNR	05-Feb-1988
THACKERY, Richard	Lt Cdr (SCC) RNR	01-Jan-2008			

Name	Rank	Seniority	Name	Rank	Seniority
WALKER, Pamela	Lt (SCC) RNR	01-Jun-2007	WHITEHEAD, Michael	SLt (SCC) RNR	11-Nov-2014
WALKER, Stanley	Ch RNR	01-Feb-1989	WHITLEY, Glenda	Lt (SCC) RNR	08-May-1987
WALLACE, Douglas	Ch RNR	24-Aug-2006	WHITLEY, Roger	Lt (SCC) RNR	14-Apr-1999
WALLACE, Thomas	Lt (SCC) RNR	01-Apr-2006	WHITTLESEA, Grahame	Ch RNR	09-Oct-2001
WALLDER, Max	A/Lt (SCC) RMR	15-Jun-2014	WHORWOOD, Julia	Lt (SCC) RNR	07-May-1997
WALSH, Joshua	Mid (SCC) RNR	10-Nov-2013	WICKENDEN, Frances	Lt (SCC) RNR	14-Oct-2000
WALSH, Richard	SLt (SCC) RNR	28-Mar-2010	WILKES, Robert	Ch RNR	28-Jun-2011
WANLISS, Hector	Lt (SCC) RNR	21-Jan-2013	WILKINSON, Graeme	SLt (SCC) RNR	29-Mar-2009
WARD, Allison	A/SLt (SCC) RNR	23-Nov-2014	WILKINSON, Laura	SLt (SCC) RNR	07-Dec-2011
WARD, Christopher	Mid (SCC) RNR	24-Mar-2013	WILKS, Stephen	Lt (SCC) RNR	27-Jul-2001
WARD, John	Lt Cdr (SCC) RNR	01-Oct-2003	WILLETT, Marion	Lt (SCC) RNR	21-Dec-1988
WARD, June	Ch RNR	18-Aug-2011	WILLIAMS, Alan	Lt Cdr (SCC) RNR	01-May-1984
WARE-JARRETT, David	Ch RNR	17-Jun-2008	WILLIAMS, David	Lt (SCC) RNR	15-Mar-2000
WARING, Peter	Lt Cdr (SCC) RNR	01-Jan-2009	WILLIAMS, Deborah	Lt (SCC) RNR	04-Nov-1992
WARNER, Derrick	Lt (SCC) RNR	01-May-2013	WILLIAMS, David Neil	SLt (SCC) RNR	06-Mar-2003
WARWICK, Stephen	Lt (SCC) RNR	12-Mar-1998	WILLIAMS, John	Ch RNR	13-Oct-2000
WASLEY, John	Ch RNR	01-Feb-2001	WILLIAMS, Susan	Lt (SCC) RNR	26-Mar-2002
WATERFIELD, Robert	SLt (SCC) RNR	27-Mar-2011	WILLIS, David	Ch RNR	01-Dec-2011
WATERS, Scott	Lt (SCC) RNR	21-Apr-1994	WILSON, Ethel	Lt (SCC) RNR	01-Nov-1998
WATKINS, Colin	Lt Cdr (SCC) RNR	17-Nov-2003	WILSON, George	Lt Cdr (SCC) RNR	01-Jan-2011
WATSON, Adrian	Lt (SCC) RNR	06-May-2006	WILSON, Ian	Cdr (SCC) RNR	17-Nov-2012
WATSON, Sheila	Lt (SCC) RNR	04-Feb-2000	WINCHESTER, John	Lt (SCC) RMR	25-Oct-2008
WAYLETT, Graham	Lt Cdr (SCC) RNR	01-Apr-2001	WISHART, Michael	Ch RNR	18-Aug-2012
WAYLETT, Matthew	A/Lt Cdr (SCC) RNR	01-Aug-2011	WITHAM, Susan	Ch RNR	22-May-2013
WEBB, Colin	Lt (SCC) RNR	17-Nov-1995	WOOD, Norman	Lt Cdr (SCC) RNR	01-Mar-1990
WEBB, John	Lt Cdr (SCC) RNR	09-Nov-1985	WOODBURN, Brian	Ch RNR	15-Nov-2014
WEBB, John	Lt Cdr (SCC) RNR	28-Aug-2003	WOODS, Martina	SLt (SCC) RNR	20-Mar-2013
WEBSTER, John	Lt Cdr (SCC) RNR	14-Dec-1990	WOODWARD, Stewart	Lt Cdr (SCC) RNR	26-Oct-1984
WEIGHT, Maurice	A/SLt (SCC) RNR	24-Jan-2014	WOOLGAR, Victor	Lt Cdr (SCC) RNR	01-Apr-1988
WELSH, Michelle	Lt Cdr (SCC) RNR	01-Jan-2009	WORSLEY, Madeline	A/SLt (SCC) RNR	05-Jul-2014
WEOBLEY, Malcolm	Maj (SCC) RMR	23-Aug-1986	WRIGHT, Alan	Lt (SCC) RNR	29-Apr-2012
WEST, Phil	SLt (SCC) RNR	29-Jun-2008	WYLIE, William	Lt Cdr (SCC) RNR	05-Dec-1983
WEST, Timothy	A/Lt (SCC) RNR	01-Nov-2012	WYNNE, David	Lt (SCC) RNR	21-Apr-1993
WESTON, Mark	Lt Cdr (SCC) RNR	01-Jan-2010			
WESTOVER, Robert	Lt (SCC) RNR	09-Jun-1978	**Y**		
WHATMOUGH, Mark	Lt (SCC) RMR	25-Sep-2010	YATES, Daniel	Lt (SCC) RNR	03-Apr-2009
WHEATLEY, Noel	Cdr (SCC) RNR	01-Aug-2009	YORKE, Barrie	Lt (SCC) RNR	01-Jul-1987
WHITE, David	Lt (SCC) RNR	29-Nov-2002	YOUNG, Barry	Lt (SCC) RNR	17-Feb-2013
WHITE, Robert	Lt Cdr (SCC) RNR	01-May-2008	YOUNG, Craig	A/SLt (SCC) RNR	29-Jul-2013
WHITEAR, Colin	A/Lt Cdr (SCC) RNR	01-Jan-2015	YOUNG, Rosalyn	Ch RNR	24-Jun-2010
WHITEHEAD, Adam	SLt (SCC) RNR	02-Jun-2014	YUILLE, Benjamin	2nd Lt (SCC) RMR	24-Mar-2013

YACHT CLUBS USING A SPECIAL ENSIGN

Yachts belonging to members of the following Yacht Clubs may, subject to certain conditions, obtain a Warrant to wear a Special Ensign.

Club	Address (where applicable)

WHITE ENSIGN

Royal Yacht Squadron .... Royal Yacht Squadron, The Castle, Cowes, Isle of Wight PO31 7QT

BLUE ENSIGN

Hornet Services Sailing Club .... Haslar Road, Gosport, Hants. PO12 2AQ

Royal Naval Club & Royal Albert Yacht Club .... 17 Pembroke Road, Portsmouth PO1 2NT

Royal Brighton Yacht Club .... 253 The Esplanade, Middle Brighton, Victoria 3186, Australia

Royal Cinque Ports Yacht Club .... 5 Waterloo Crescent, Dover CT16 1LA

Royal Cruising Club .... C/O Royal Thames Yacht Club, 60 Knightsbridge, London SW1X 7LF

Royal Dorset Yacht Club .... 11 Custom House Quay, Weymouth DT4 8BG

Royal Engineer Yacht Club .... BATCIS DT, Yew 0 1039, MOD Abbeywood, Bristol BS36 8JH

Royal Geelong Yacht Club .... P.O. Box 156, Geelong, Victoria 3220, Australia

Royal Gourock Yacht Club .... Ashton, Gourock PA19 1DA

Royal Highland Yacht Club .... Achavraid, Clachan, Tarbert PA29 6XN

Royal Marines Sailing Club ....

Royal Melbourne Yacht Squadron .... P.O. Box 2001, St Kilda West, Victoria 3182, Australia

Royal Motor Yacht Club .... Panorama Road, Sandbanks, Poole BH13 7RN

Royal Naval Sailing Association .... 10 Haslar Marina, Haslar Road, Gosport PO12 1NU

Royal Naval Volunteer Reserve Yacht Club .... The Naval Club, 38 Hill Street, Mayfair, London W1X 8DB

Royal New Zealand Yacht Squadron .... P.O. Box 46 182, Herne Bay, Auckland 1147, New Zealand

Royal Northern and Clyde Yacht Club .... Rhu, By Helensburgh G84 8NG

Royal Perth Yacht Club of Western Australia ................P.O. Box 5, Nedlands, Western Australia 6909

Royal Port Nicholson Yacht Club....................................Clyde Quay Boat Harbour, P.O. Box 9674,
Wellington, New Zealand

Royal Queensland Yacht Squadron ................................P.O. Box 5021, Manly, Queensland 4179,
Australia

Royal Scottish Motor Yacht Club ....35 Brueacre Drive, Wemyss Bay PA18 6HA

Royal Solent Yacht Club ....The Square, Yarmouth,
Isle of Wight PO41 0NS

Royal South Australian Yacht Squadron .......................P.O. Box 1066, North Haven,
South Australia 5018

Royal Southern Yacht Club..Rope Walk, Hamble, Southampton SO31 4HB

Royal Sydney Yacht Squadron ....P.O. Box 484, Milson's Point,
New South Wales 1565

Royal Temple Yacht Club...6 Westcliff Mansions, Ramsgate CT11 9HY

Royal Thames Yacht Club..60 Knightsbridge, London SW1X 7LF

Royal Victorian Motor Yacht Club ....260 Nelson Place, Williamstown,
Victoria 3016, Australia

Royal Western Yacht Club of England ....Queen Anne's Battery, Plymouth PL4 0TW

Royal Western Yacht Club of Scotland...........................Shandon, Helensburgh G84 8NP

Royal Yacht Club of Tasmania.......................................Marieville Esplanade, Sandy Bay,
Tasmania 7005, Australia

Royal Yacht Club of Victoria...120 Nelson Place, Williamstown,
Victoria 3016, Australia

Sussex Motor Yacht Club ....Medina House, Brighton Marina, Brighton.

BLUE ENSIGN DEFACED BY BADGE OF CLUB

Aldeburgh Yacht Club...Slaughden Road, Aldeburgh IP15 5NA

Army Sailing Association ....Clayton Barracks, Thornhill Road,
Aldershot GU11 2BG

Bar Yacht Club..47 Tower Bridge Wharf, 86 St Katharines Way,
London E1W 1UR

City Livery Yacht Club ....

Conway Club Cruising Association.................................

Cruising Yacht Club of Australia....................................New Beach Road, Darling Point,
New South Wales 2027, Australia

Household Division Yacht Club .... RHQ Scots Guards, Wellington Barracks,
Birdcage Walk, London SW1E 6HQ

Little Ship Club .... Bell Wharf Lane, Upper Thames Street,
London EC4R 3TB

Little Ship Club (Queensland Squadron) .... P.O. Box 8036, Cleveland 4183, Queensland,
Australia

Medway Cruising Club .... Anchorage Yard, Waterside Lane,
Gillingham ME7 2SE

Old Worcesters Yacht Club .... 21 Brunel Quays, Lostwithiel, PL22 0JB

Parkstone Yacht Club .... Pearce Avenue, Parkstone, Poole BH14 8EH

Rochester Cruising Yacht Club .... 10 The Esplanade, Rochester ME1 1QN

Royal Air Force Yacht Club .... Riverside House, Rope Walk, Hamble,
Southampton SO31 4HD

Royal Akarana Yacht Club .... P.O. Box 42-004, Orakei, Auckland,
New Zealand

Royal Anglesey Yacht Club .... 6-7 Green Edge, Beaumaris LL58 8BY

Royal Armoured Corps Yacht Club .... Kings Royal Hussars, Aliwall Barracks,
Tidworth SP9 7BB

Royal Artillery Yacht Club ....

Royal Australian Navy Sailing Association .... Edgecliffe, New South Wales 2027, Australia

Royal Bermuda Yacht Club .... P.O. Box 894, Hamilton HM DX, Bermuda

Royal Bombay Yacht Club .... P.O. Box 206, Apollo Bunder, Fort Bombay,
400 001, Mumbai, India

Royal Burnham Yacht Club .... The Quay, Burnham-on-Crouch, CM0 8AU

Royal Channel Islands Yacht Club .... Le Mont du Boulevard, St Brelade,
Jersey JE3 8AD

Royal Corinthian Yacht Club .... The Quay, Burnham-on-Crouch, CM0 8AX

Royal Cornwall Yacht Club .... Greenbank, Falmouth TR11 2SP

Royal Dee Yacht Club .... Siglen, Pulford, Chester CH4 9EL

Royal Forth Yacht Club .... Middle Pier, Granton Harbour,
Edinburgh EH5 1HF

Royal Freshwater Bay Yacht Club of Western Australia ... Keanes Point, Peppermint Grove, 6011,
Western Australia, Australia

Royal Gibraltar Yacht Club .... 26 Queensway, Gibraltar

Royal Hamilton Yacht Club...Foot of McNab Street North, Hamilton, Ontario, Canada

Royal Harwich Yacht Club ....Wolverstone, Ipswich IP9 1AT

Royal Hong Kong Yacht Club ....Kellett Island, Causeway Bay, Hong King

Royal Irish Yacht Club ....Harbour Road, Dun Laoghaire, County Dublin, Eire

Royal Jamaica Yacht Club...Norman Manly International Airport, Palisadoes Park, Kingston, Jamaica

Royal London Yacht Club ....The Parade, Cowes, Isle of Wight PO31 7QS

Royal Malta Yacht Club...Couvre Point, Fort Manoel, Manoel Island, Gzira, Malta

Royal Mersey Yacht Club..Bedford Road East, Rock Ferry, Birkenhead CH42 1LS

Royal Motor Yacht Club of New South Wales.................Wunulla Road, Point Piper 2027, New South Wales, Australia

Royal Nassau Sailing Club ....P.O. Box SS 6891, Nassau, Bahamas

Royal Natal Yacht Club...P.O. Box 2946, Durban 4000, South Africa

Royal North of Ireland Yacht Club ....7 Seafront Road, Holywood, County Down BT18 0BB

Royal Northumberland Yacht Club ....South Harbour, Blyth NE24 3PB

Royal Ocean Racing Club ....20 St James' Place, London SW1A 1NN

Royal Plymouth Corinthian Yacht Club ....Madeira Road, The Barbican, Plymouth PL1 2NY

Royal Prince Alfred Yacht Club ....P.O. Box 99, Newport Beach 2106, New South Wales, Australia

Royal Prince Edward Yacht Club.....................................P.O. Box 2502 Bondi Junction, New South Wales 1355, Australia

Royal Southampton Yacht Club.......................................1 Channel Way, Ocean Village, Southampton SO14 3QF

Royal Suva Yacht Club ....P.O. Box 335 Suva, Republic of Fiji

Royal Torbay Yacht Club...12 Beacon Terrace, Torquay TQ1 2BH

Royal Ulster Yacht Club..101 Clifton Road, Bangor, County Down BT20 5HY

Royal Welsh Yacht Club ....Porth Yr Aur Caernarfon LL55 1SN

Royal Yorkshire Yacht Club...1-3 Windsor Crescent, Bridlington YO15 3HX

Severn Motor Yacht Club ....Bath Road, Broomhall, Worcester WR5 3HR

Sussex Yacht Club ....85-89 Brighton Road, Shoreham-by-Sea
BN43 6RE

Thames Motor Yacht Club..............................The Green, Hampton Court, Surrey KT8 9BW

The Cruising Association ....CA House, 1 Northey Street, Limehouse Basin,
London E14 8BT

The House of Lords Yacht Club ....Overseas Office, House of Lords,
London SW1A 0PW

The Medway Yacht Club ....Lower Upnor, Rochester ME2 4XB

The Poole Harbour Yacht Club ....

The Poole Yacht Club...................................The Yacht Haven, New Harbour Road West,
Hamworthy, Poole, BH15 4AQ

RED ENSIGN DEFACED BY BADGE OF CLUB

Brixham Yacht Club ....Overgang, Brixham TQ5 8AR

House of Commons Yacht Club ....C/O RYA, RYA House, Ensign Way, Hamble,
Southampton SO31 4YA

Lloyd's Yacht Club.......................................

Royal Dart Yacht Club ....Priory Street, Kingswear, Dartmouth TQ6 0AB

Royal Fowey Yacht Club.................................Whitford Yard, Fowey PL23 1BH

Royal Hamilton Amateur Dinghy Club .............P.O. Box 298 Paget PG BX, Bermuda

Royal Lymington Yacht Club...........................Bath Road, Lymington SO41 3SE

Royal Norfolk and Suffolk Yacht Club.............Royal Plain, Lowestoft NR33 0AQ

Royal St George Yacht Club ....Dun Laoghaire, County Dublin, Eire

Royal Victoria Yacht Club ....91 Fishbourne Lane, Ryde, Isle of Wight
PO33 4EU

Royal Windermere Yacht Club........................Fallbarrow Road, Bowness-on-Windermere
LA33 3DJ

St Helier Yacht Club ....South Pier, St Helier, Jersey JE2 3NB

West Mersea Yacht Club................................116 Coast Road, West Mersea, Colchester
CO5 8PB

DEFACED RAF ENSIGN

The RAF Sailing Association.............................HQ Air Command, RAF High Wycombe,
HP14 4UE

ROYAL NAVAL RESERVE AND OTHER VESSELS AUTHORISED TO FLY THE BLUE ENSIGN IN MERCHANT VESSELS (FOREIGN OR HOME TRADE ARTICLES) AND FISHING VESSELS

1. A list of Royal Naval Reserve and other vessels authorised to fly the Blue Ensign will no longer be published in the Navy List.

2. Its inclusion was intended for the information of Captains of Her Majesty's Ships with reference to provisions of Article 9153 of the Queen's Regulations for the Royal Navy under which they are authorised to ascertain whether British Merchant Ships (including Fishing Vessels) flying the Blue Ensign of Her Majesty's Fleet are legally entitled to do so.

3. However, the usefulness of this list serves only a limited purpose as the list of vessels that could fly the Blue Ensign can change frequently. British merchant ships and fishing vessels are allowed to wear the plain Blue Ensign under the authority of a special Warrant, subject to certain conditions being fulfilled, and which are outlined below.

4. Vessels registered on the British Registry of Shipping or the Registry of a relevant British possession may wear a plain Blue Ensign providing the master or skipper is in possession of a warrant issued by the Commander Maritime Reserves under the authority of the Secretary of State for Defence, and the additional conditions outlined below are fulfilled. The Blue Ensign is to be struck if the officer to whom the warrant was issued relinquishes command, or if the ship or vessel passes into foreign ownership and ceases to be a British ship as defined in Part 1 of the Merchant Shipping Act 1995 (MSA 1995).

   a. Vessels on Parts I, II and IV of the Register. The master must be an officer of the rank of lieutenant RN/RNR or Captain RM/RMR or above in the Royal Fleet Reserve or the maritime forces of a United Kingdom Overseas Territory or Commonwealth country of which Her Majesty is Head of State, or an officer on the Active or Retired Lists of any branch of the maritime reserve forces of these countries or territories.

   b. Vessels on Part II of the Register. This part of the Register is reserved for fishing vessels. The skipper must comply with the same criteria as for sub-clause 4.a. above, however the crew must contain at least four members, each of whom fulfils at least one of the following criteria:

   Royal Naval or Royal Marine reservists or pensioner Reservists or pensioners from a Commonwealth monarchy or United Kingdom Overseas Territory, Ex-ratings or Royal Marines who have completed twenty years service in the Reserves, members of the Royal Fleet Reserve.

5. Action on sighting a merchant ship wearing a Blue Ensign: The Commanding Officer of one of HM ships on meeting a vessel wearing the Blue Ensign may, in exercise of powers conferred by sections 5, 7 and 257 MSA 1995, send on board a commissioned officer to confirm that the criteria outlined above are being met in full. If it is found that the ship is wearing a Blue Ensign, without authority of a proper warrant, the ensign is to be seized, taken away and forfeited to the Sovereign and the circumstances reported to the Commander Maritime Reserves, acting on behalf of the Chief of Naval Personnel and Training/Second Sea Lord, who maintains the list of persons authorised to hold such warrants.

   However, if it is found that, despite the warrant being sighted, the ship is failing to comply with the criteria in some other particular, the ensign is not to be seized but the circumstances are to be reported to the Commander Maritime Reserves.

HM SHIPS BFPO NUMBERS

ALBION (Albion) BFPO 204	**DARING (Type 45)** BFPO 270
AMBUSH (Astute) BFPO 205	**DASHER (P2000)** BFPO 271
ARCHER (Patrol) BFPO 208	**DAUNTLESS (Type 45)** BFPO 272
ARGYLL (Type 23) BFPO 210	**DEFENDER (Type 45)** BFPO 267
ARTFUL (Astute) BFPO 213	**DIAMOND (Type 45)** BFPO 273
ASTUTE (Astute) BFPO 214	**DRAGON (Type 45)** BFPO 268
ATHERSTONE (Hunt) BFPO 215	**DUNCAN (Type 45)** BFPO 269
AUDACIOUS (Astute) BFPO 216	**ECHO (SVHO)** BFPO 275
BANGOR (Sandown) BFPO 222	**ENTERPRISE (SVHO)** BFPO 276
BITER (Patrol) BFPO 229	**EXAMPLE (Patrol)** BFPO 281
BLAZER (Patrol) BFPO 231	**EXPLOIT (Patrol)** BFPO 285
BLYTH (Sandown) BFPO 221	**EXPLORER (Patrol)** BFPO280
BROCKLESBY (Hunt) BFPO 241	**EXPRESS (Patrol)** BFPO 282
BULWARK (Albion) BFPO 243	**GLEANER (CSV)** BFPO 288
CATTISTOCK (Hunt) BFPO 251	**GRIMSBY (Sandown)** BFPO 292
CHARGER (Patrol) BFPO 252	**HURWORTH (Hunt)** BFPO 300
CHIDDINGFOLD (Hunt) BFPO 254	**ILLUSTRIOUS (Invincible)** BFPO 305
CLYDE (River) BFPO 255	**IRON DUKE (Type 23)** BFPO 309

KENT (Type 23) BFPO 318	**RAMSEY (Sandown)** BFPO 368
LANCASTER (Type 23) BFPO 323	**RANGER (Patrol)** BFPO 369
LEDBURY (Hunt) BFPO 324	**RICHMOND (Type 23)** BFPO 375
MERSEY (River) BFPO 334	**SABRE (Fast Patrol)** BFPO 378
MIDDLETON (Hunt) BFPO 335	**SCIMITAR (Fast Patrol)** BFPO 384
MONMOUTH (Type 23) BFPO 338	**SCOTT (OSV)** BFPO 381
MONTROSE (Type 23) BFPO 339	**SEVERN (River)** BFPO 382
NORTHUMBERLAND (Type 23) BFPO 345	**SHOREHAM (Sandown)** BFPO 386
OCEAN (LPH) BFPO 350	**SMITER (Patrol)** BFPO 387
PEMBROKE (Sandown) BFPO 357	**SOMERSET (Type 23)** BFPO 395
PENZANCE (Sandown) BFPO 358	**ST ALBANS (Type 23)** BFPO 399
PORTLAND (Type 23) BFPO 361	**SUTHERLAND (Type 23)** BFPO 398
PROTECTOR (Antarctic Patrol Ship) BFPO 367	**TALENT (Trafalgar)** BFPO 401
PUNCHER (Patrol) BFPO 362	**TIRELESS (Trafalgar)** BFPO 402
PURSUER (P2000) BFPO 363	**TORBAY (Trafalgar)** BFPO 403
QUEEN ELIZABETH (Carrier) BFPO 365	**TRACKER (Patrol)** BFPO 409
QUORN (Hunt) BFPO 366	**TRENCHANT (Trafalgar)** BFPO 405
RAIDER (Patrol) BFPO 377	**TRIUMPH (Trafalgar)** BFPO 406

TRUMPETER (Patrol)
BFPO 407

TURBULENT (Trafalgar)
BFPO 408

TYNE (River)
BFPO 412

VANGUARD (Vanguard)
BFPO 418

VENGEANCE (Vanguard)
BFPO 421

VICTORIOUS (Vanguard)
BFPO 419

VIGILANT (Vanguard)
BFPO 420

WESTMINSTER (Type 23)
BFPO 426

SHIPS OF THE ROYAL FLEET AUXILIARY SERVICE BFPO NUMBERS

ARGUS, Aviation Training Ship
BFPO 433

BLACK ROVER, Small Fleet Tanker
BFPO 435

CARDIGAN BAY, Bay Class Landing Ship
BFPO 436

DILIGENCE, Forward Repair Ship
BFPO 438

FORT AUSTIN, Fleet Replenishment Ship
BFPO 439

FORT ROSALIE, Fleet Replenishment Ship
BFPO 441

FORT VICTORIA, Fleet Replenishment Ship
BFPO 442

GOLD ROVER, Small Fleet Tanker
BFPO 443

LYME BAY, Bay Class Landing Ship
BFPO 447

MOUNTS BAY, Bay Class Landing Ship
BFPO 448

RFA ORANGELEAF, Support Tanker
BFPO 449

WAVE KNIGHT, Fast Fleet Tanker
BFPO 432

WAVE RULER, Fast Fleet Tanker
BFPO 431

ABBREVIATIONS OF RANKS USED BY JPA

A/ .... Acting
Adm .... Admiral
Adm of Fleet.. Admiral of The Fleet
Brig..Brigadier
Capt ....Captain, Royal Marines
Capt, RN..Captain, Royal Navy
Cdr ....Commander
Cdre ....Commodore
Chpln of The Fleet ....Chaplain of The Fleet
Col .... Colonel
FTRS .... Full Time Reserve Service
Gen .... General
Lt..Lieutenant, Royal Marines
Lt Cdr ....Lieutenant Commander
Lt Col.. Lieutenant Colonel
Lt Gen .... Lieutenant General
Lt RN .... Lieutenant, Royal Navy
Maj.. Major
Maj Gen .... Major General
Mid.. Midshipman
OCdt ....Officer Cadet
R Adm .... Rear Admiral
RN Chpln.. Chaplain, Royal Navy
RN Prncpl Chpln .... Principal Chaplain, Royal Navy
RNR Chaplain.. Royal Naval Reserve Chaplain
SLt..Sub-Lieutenant
Surg.. Surgeon
Surg (D) .... Surgeon (Dental)
V Adm ....Vice Admiral
2Lt.. Second Lieutenant, Royal Marines

LIST OF BRANCH ABBREVIATIONS

CS .... Careers Service
Ch S ....Chaplaincy Service
DENTAL .... Dental
ENG..Engineering
LOGS .... Logistics
MED .... Medical
QARNNS..Queen Alexandra's Royal Naval Nursing Service
RM ....Royal Marines
RMR .... Royal Marines Reserve
RNR .... Royal Naval Reserve
WAR..Warfare

LIST OF MAIN TRADE ABBREVIATIONS

AE .... Air Engineer
AE O...Air Engineer Observer
AE P..Air Engineer Pilot
ATC .... Air Traffic Controller
AV ....Aviation
BAR ....Barrister
BS.. Royal Marines Band Service
C .... Communications
CIS...Communication Information Specialist
CMA ....Management Accountant
CONSULTANT.. Consultant
FAA ....Fleet Air Arm
FC..Fighter Controller
FS ....Family Services
GDP...General Dental Practitioner
GD (RES) ....General Duties (Reserves)
GMP ....General Medical Practitioner
GS ....General Service
GSX .... General Service Warfare
L... Logistics
LC... Landing Craft
MCD... Mine Warfare Clearance Diver
ME.. Marine Engineering
MESM..Marine Engineering Submariner
METOC ....Meteorology & Oceanography
MLDR ....Mountain Leader
MS.. Medical Services
MTM .... Manning & Training Margins
MW .... Mine Warfare
O ....Observer
O LYNX..Observer Lynx
O MER ....Observer Merlin
O SK6 .... Observer Sea King 6
O SKW...Observer Sea King AEW
OTSPEC .... Operating Theatre Specialist
O UT .... Observer Under Training
P..Pilot
P GAZ... Pilot Gazelle
P HELO .... Pilot Helicopter
P LYN7 ....Pilot Lynx 7
P LYNX..Pilot Lynx
P MER..Pilot Merlin
P SK4.. Pilot Sea King 4
P SK6.. Pilot Sea King 6

P SKW ....Pilot Sea King AEW
P UT... Pilot Under Training
PWO..Principal Warfare Officer
PWO(A) ....Principal Warfare Officer (Above Water)
PWO(C) ....Principal Warfare Officer (Communications)
PWO(N) .... Principal Warfare Officer (Navigator)
PWO(U) ....Principal Warfare Officer (Underwater)
REG .... Regulator
SCC ....Senior Corps Commission
SM ....Submariner
TM... Training Management
UT ....Under Training
WE ....Weapons Engineering
WESM ....Weapons Engineer Submarines

ABBREVIATIONS OF ORGANISATIONS WHERE OFFICERS SERVE WHEN NOT AT SEA

1 ACC ....1 Air Control Centre
1 ASSLT GP RM...1 Assault Group Royal Marines
1 IG .... 1st Battalion Irish Guards
1 PWRR .... 1st Battalion Princess of Wales Royal Regiment
1 REGT AAC ....1 Regiment Army Air Corps
1 RIFLES.. 1st Battalion the Rifles
10 TRG SQN 1 ASSLT GP RM.................. 10 Training Squadron, 1 Assault Group Royal Marines
11 (ATT) SQN....................................11 (Amphibious Trials & Training) Squadron, Royal Marines
101 LOG BDE...101 Logistics Brigade
102 LOG BDE...102 Logistics Brigade
148 FO BTY RA .... 148 (Meiktila) Commando Forward Observation Battery Royal Artillery
15 POG.. 15 Psychological Operations Group
1SL/CNS.. First Sea Lord & Chief of Naval Staff
202 SQN – E FLT .... E Flight, 202 Squadron Royal Air Force
26 REGT RA...26 Regiment, Royal Artillery
29 CDO REGT.. 29 Commando Regiment
3 CDO BDE RM... 3 Commando Brigade Royal Marines
3 FTS .... 3 Flying Training School
3 REGT AAC ....3 Regiment Army Air Corps
30 CDO IX GP RM......................30 Commando Information Exploitation Group Royal Marines
4 REGT AAC ....4 Regiment Army Air Corps
40 CDO RM ....40 Commando Royal Marines
42 CDO RM..42 Commando Royal Marines
45 CDO RM ....45 Commando Royal Marines
5 REGT AAC ....5 Regt Army Air Corps
5 SCOTS .... 5th Battalion the Royal Regiment of Scotland
539 ASSLT SQN RM .... 539 Assault Squadron Royal Marines
6 OPS SQN...6 Operations Squadron
6 SQN TYPHOON ....6 Squadron TYPHOON

7 AA BN REME............................7 Air Assault Battalion Royal Electrical & Mechanical Engineers
AACen.. Army Aviation Centre
ACHQ..Air Command Headquarters
ACDS(Nuc & Chem, Bio)..........Assistant Chief of Defence Staff (Nuclear & Chemical, Biological)
ACNS(A&C) ....Assistant Chief of Naval Staff (Aviation & Carriers)
ACNS(Cap) .... Assistant Chief of Naval Staff (Capability)
ACNS(Pers)/NAVSEC........................ Assistant Chief of Naval Staff (Personnel) & Naval Secretary
ACNS(Pol)..Assistant Chief of Naval Staff (Policy)
AFCC .... Armed Forces Chaplaincy Centre
AIB .... Admiralty Interview Board
ARF... Aviation Reconnaissance Force
ARRC..Allied Rapid Reaction Corps
ASG RM.. Armoured Support Group, Royal Marines
AWC .... Air Warfare Centre
BDS ....British Defence Section
BF BIOT.. British Forces British Indian Ocean Territory
BF C...British Forces Cyprus
BF G .... British Forces Germany
BF GIBRALTAR ....British Forces Gibraltar
BFSAI.. British Forces South Atlantic Islands
BFPO...British Forces Post Office
BMATT.. British Military Attache
BMM ....British Military Mission
BRNC... Britannia Royal Naval College
CATCS ....Central Air Traffic Control School
CATD...Combined Arms Tactics Division
CDI...Chief of Defence Intelligence
CDO LOG REGT RM .... Commando Logistics Regiment Royal Marines
CFPS ....Commander, Fishery Protection Squad
CGRM ....Commandant General Royal Marines
CHF HQ ....Commando Helicopter Force, Headquarters
CJO ....Chief of Joint Operations
CNP&T/2SL ....Chief of Naval Personnel & Training and Second Sea Lord
CoM(Fleet)/CFS........................... Chief of Materiel (Fleet) and Chief of Fleet Support
COM(Ops) .... Commander, Operations
COMPORFLOT .... Commodore, Portsmouth Flotilla
COMUKAMPHIBFOR .... Commander UK Amphibious Forces
COMUKMARFOR..Commander UK Maritime Forces
COMUKTG ....Commander United Kingdom Task Group
COS CC MAR FOR .... Chief of Staff to the Commander, Allied Naval Forces, Southern Europe
COS (Ops) PJHQ.................. Chief of Staff (Operations) Permanent Joint Headquarters
COS SACT .... Chief of Staff to Supreme Allied Commander, Transformation
CSSE.. Chief Strategic Systems Executive
CTCRM.. Commando Training Centre Royal Marines
DCAE... Defence College of Aeronautical Engineering
DCBRNC ....Defence Chemical, Biological, Radiological & Nuclear Centre
DCCIS............................. Defence College of Communications & Information Systems

DCDS...Deputy Chief of Defence Staff
DCEME ....Defence College of Electro-Mechanical Engineering
DCLPA .... Defence College of Logistics & Personnel Administration
DCMH ....Department of Community Mental Health
DCNS.. Deputy Chief of Naval Staff
DCOS Force Readiness .... Deputy Chief of Staff, Force Readiness
DCPG .... Defence College of Police & Guarding
DCSU...Defence Cultural Specialist Unit
DDG EUMS ....Deputy Director General, European Union Military Staff
DDS ....Defence Dental Services
DE&S .... Defence Equipment & Support
DEFENCE ACADEMY...Defence Academy of the United Kingdom
Def Reform (Mar) ITL.........................Defence Reform (Maritime) Implementation Team Leader
DEMSS...................................Defence Explosive Ordnance Disposal Munitions & Search School
DEPCOMSTRIKFORNATO.. Deputy Commander Strike Force NATO
DHFS ....Defence Helicopter Flying School
DIO.. Defence Infrastructure Organisation
DISC .... Defence Intelligence & Security Centre
D(MarCap & Transformation) /CofN ....Director (Maritime Capability & Transformation) and
Controller of the Navy
DMLS...Defence Maritime Logistics School
DMOC ....Defence Media Operations Centre
DMRC.. Defence Medical Rehabilitation Centre
DMS ....Defence Medical Services
DMSTG...Defence Medical Services Training Group
DPMD...Defence Post-Graduate Medical Deanery
DSAS ....Defence Security & Assurance Services
DSEA ....Defence Safety and Environment Authority
DSL..Defence School of Languages
DST..Defence School of Transport
DSTL.. Defence Science & Technology Laboratory
DTOEES ....Defence Technical Officer & Engineer Entry Scheme
ETPS ....Empire Test Pilots' School
EU OHQ...European Union Operational Headquarters
FCO .... Foreign & Commonwealth Office
FDS...Fleet Diving Squadron
FOSNI ....Flag Officer Scotland & Northern Ireland
FOST.. Flag Officer Sea Training
FPGRM .... Fleet Protection Group Royal Marines
FWO ....Fleet Waterfront Organisation
HMNB..Her Majesty's Naval Base
HQ 2 MED BDE..HQ 2 Medical Brigade
HQ EUFOR (SAR)..HQ European Force (Sarajevo)
HQ IADS ....HQ Integrated Area Defence System
HQ NI .... HQ Northern Ireland
HQLF .... HQ Land Forces
IBS .... Infantry Battle School

IMATT...International Military Advisory & Training Team
INM .... Institute of Naval Medicine
JCTTAT...Joint Counter Terrorism Training & Advisory Team
JEFTS ....Joint Elementary Flying Training School
JFC .... Joint Forces Command
JHC...Joint Helicopter Command
JSCSC ....Joint Services Command & Staff College
JSMTC .... Joint Services Mountain Training Centre
JSSU ....Joint Services Signals Unit
JSU .... Joint Support Unit
LATCC(MIL)..London Air Traffic Control Centre (Military)
LSP .... Loan Service Position
LWC .... Land Warfare Centre
MAA...Military Aviation Authority
MASF... Maritime Aviation Support Force
MCM1 ....Mine Countermeasures Squadron 1
MCM2 ....Mine Countermeasures Squadron 2
MCTC...Military Corrective Training Centre
MDHU .... Ministry of Defence Hospital Unit
MHRF(F).. Military High Readiness Force (France)
MOD .... Ministry of Defence
MSSG .... Military Stabilisation Support Group
MWC...Maritime Warfare Centre
MWS .... Maritime Warfare School
NAIC... Aeronautical Information Centre
NAS ....Naval Air Squadron
NATO... North Atlantic Treaty Organisation
NATO JFC ....NATO Joint Force Command
NATO JWC... NATO Joint Warfare Centre
NCHQ..Navy Command HQ
NCISS ....NATO Communication & Information Systems School
NDG ....Northern Diving Group
NETS..Naval Educational & Training Service
NOC .... Naval Outdoor Centre
NRC EE & CRF...... Naval Regional Commander Eastern England & Commander Regional Forces
NRC NE... Naval Regional Commander Northern England
NRC SNI..Naval Regional Commander Scotland & Northern Ireland
NRC WWE ....Naval Regional Commander Wales & Western England
OCLC... Officer Career Liaison & Recruiting Officer
OPTAG...Operational Training & Advisory Group
PJHQ.. Permanent Joint HQ
RBAF... Royal Brunei Armed Forces
RCDM..Royal Centre for Defence Medicine
RCDS ....Royal College of Defence Studies
RM BICKLEIGH..Royal Marines, Bickleigh, Plymouth
RM CHIVENOR.. Royal Marines, Chivenor, Barnstaple
RM CONDOR ....Royal Marines Condor, Arbroath

RM NORTON MANOR.. Royal Marines Norton Manor Camp, Taunton
RM POOLE ....Royal Marines Hamworthy, Poole
RM STONEHOUSE .... Royal Marines Stonehouse, Plymouth
RMSM .... Royal Marines School of Music
RMAS ....Royal Military Academy Sandhurst
RMBS...Royal Marine Band Service
RNAC .... Royal Naval Acquaint Centre
RNAESS ....Royal Naval Air Engineering & Survival School
RNAS .... Royal Naval Air Station
RNCR...Royal Naval Centre of Recruiting
RNEAWC .... Royal Naval Element Air Warfare Centre
RNIO... Royal Naval Infrastructure Organisation
RNLA ....Royal Naval Leadership Academy
RNLO..Royal Navy Liaison Officer
RNLT .... Royal Navy Liaison Team
RNPT...Royal Navy Presentation Team
RNSME .... Royal Naval School of Marine Engineering
RNSMS ....Royal Navy Submarine School
SACT .... Supreme Allied Commander, Transformation
SDG.. Southern Diving Unit Group
SETT .... Submarine Escape Training Tank
SGD...Surgeon General's Department
SHAPE ....Supreme Headquarters Allied Powers Europe
SHTC ....Salmond House Training Centre
SMC .... Sea Mounting Centre
SP WPNS SCH.. Support Weapons School
SPVA..Service Personnel & Veterans Agency
UKHO.. United Kingdom Hydrographic Office
UKJSU... United Kingdom Joint Support Unit
UK MCC ....United Kingdom Maritime Component Commander
UKTI-DSO ....United Kingdom Trade & Investment Defence & Security Organisation
UN... United Nations
US CENTCOM .... United States Central Command

Explanatory Notes

1. Any Officer who has the unit MCM1 or MCM2 will be assigned to one of the two Mine Countermeasure Squadrons and will be part of a rotating squad assigned to the Hunt & Sandown Class Mine Countermeasure vessels.

2. The location stated in the list of addresses may not necessarily be the Headquarters of that unit; it may simply be a location where an officer is serving.

3. Any Officer serving in a Defence Section, Exchange Post, Loan Service, Military Mission or Service Attache position, can be contacted by using the 'Yellow' book, as detailed on page 249.

ADDRESSES OF ORGANISATIONS WHERE OFFICERS SERVE WHEN NOT AT SEA

NAVAL STAFF & NAVY COMMAND HEADQUARTER FUNCTIONS

First Sea Lord & Chief of Naval Staff
1SL/CNS
Ministry of Defence
Main Building
LONDON
SW1A 2HB

Fleet Commander/Deputy Chief of Naval Staff
Leach Building
Whale Island
PORTSMOUTH
PO2 8BY

Second Sea Lord
Leach Building
Whale Island
PORTSMOUTH
PO2 8BY

Admiralty Interview Board
AIB
HMS Sultan
GOSPORT
PO12 3BY

Chief of Joint Operations
Building 410
C G 209
JHQ Northwood
HA6 3HP

Commander Fishery Protection Squad
CFPS
Lancelot Building
HMNB
PORTSMOUTH
PO1 3LS

Commander Operations
COM(Ops)
Maritime Operations Centre
Oswald Building
Northwood HQ
Sandy Lane
NORTHWOOD
HA6 3AP

Commander UK Amphibious Forces
COMUKAMPHIBFOR
Fieldhouse Building
Whale Island
PORTSMOUTH
PO2 8ER

Commander UK Maritime Forces
COMUKMARFOR
Fieldhouse Building
Whale Island
PORTSMOUTH
PO2 8ER

Commander Amphibious Task Group
COMATG
No.6 House
RMB Stonehouse
PLYMOUTH
PL1 3QS

Chaplain of the Fleet
Naval Chaplaincy Service
Navy Command HQ
Leach Building MP1.2
Whale Island
PORTSMOUTH
PO2 8BY

Flag Officer Scotland & Northern Ireland
Command Building
HMNB Clyde
HELENSBURGH
G84 8HL

Flag Officer Sea Training
FOST
Grenville Building
HMS Drake
HMNB Devonport
PLYMOUTH
PL2 2BG

Commander Core Naval Training
COMCORE
FOST
Raleigh Block
HHS Drake
HMNB Devonport
PLYMOUTH
PL2 2BG

Commander Operational Training
COMOT
FOST
Vernon Building
HMS COLLINGWOOD
Newgate Lane
Fareham
PO14 1AS

Flag Officer Sea Training (North)
FOST (North)
HMNB Clyde
HELENSBURGH
G84 8HL

Flag Officer Sea Training (South)
FOST (South)
Grenville Block
HMS Drake
HMNB Devonport
PLYMOUTH
PL2 2BG

Fleet Diving Squadron
FDS
Horsea Island
West Bund Road
COSHAM
PO6 4TT

**Headquarters Combined Cadet Force
(Royal Navy)**
HQ CCF (RN)
Room 21 South Terrace
PP 72
HMNB
PORTSMOUTH
PO1 3LS

Mine Warfare Centre
MWC
HMS Collingwood
Newgate Lane
FAREHAM
PO14 1AS

**Naval Personnel & Family Service
(Eastern)**
NPFS (EASTERN)
HMS Nelson
HMNB
PORTSMOUTH
PO1 3LS

**Naval Personnel & Family Service
(Western)**
NPFS (WESTERN)
HMS Drake
HMNB Devonport
PLYMOUTH
PL2 2BG

**Naval Personnel & Family Service
(Northern)**
NPFS (NORTHERN)
1-5 Churchill Square
HELENSBURGH
G84 9HL

Naval Regional Commander Eastern England and Commander Regional Forces
NRC EE & CRF
Naval Regional Headquarters Eastern England
HMS PRESIDENT
72 St Katherine's Way
LONDON
E1W 1UQ

Naval Regional Commander Northern England
NRC NE
Naval Regional Headquarters Northern
England and Isle of Man
80 Sefton Street
East Brunswick Dock
LIVERPOOL
L3 4DZ

Naval Regional Commander Scotland and Northern Ireland
NRC SNI
Naval Regional Headquarters Scotland and
Northern Ireland
MOD CALEDONIA
Hilton Road
Rosyth
KY11 2XH

Naval Regional Commander Wales and Western England
NRC WWE
Naval Regional Headquarters Wales and
Western England
HMS FLYING FOX
Winterstoke Road
BRISTOL
BS3 2NS

Officer Career Liaison & Recruiting Offices
OCLC
42 Tilton Road
BIRMINGHAM
B9 4PP

Officer Career Liaison & Recruiting Offices
OCLC
21 Hereward Centre
PETERBOROUGH
PE1 1TB

Officer Career Liaison & Recruiting Offices
OCLC
Pilgrim House
PLYMOUTH
PL1 2SW

Officer Career Liaison & Recruiting Offices
OCLC
Petersfield House
29 - 31 Peter Street
MANCHESTER
M2 5QJ

UK Hydrographic Office
UKHO
Admiralty Way
TAUNTON
TA1 2DN

SHORE BASES, ESTABLISHMENTS & OTHER NAVY ORGANISATIONS

Her Majesty's Naval Base Clyde
HMNB CLYDE
Faslane
HELENSBURGH
G84 8HL

Her Majesty's Naval Base Devonport
HMNB DEVONPORT
PLYMOUTH
PL2 2BG

Her Majesty's Naval Base Portsmouth
HMNB PORTSMOUTH
PORTSMOUTH
PO1 3LS

HMS Bristol
Whale Island
PORTSMOUTH
PO2 8ER

HMS Caledonia
ROSYTH
KY11 2XH

HMS Collingwood
Newgate Lane
FAREHAM
PO14 1AS

HMS Drake
HMNB DEVONPORT
PLYMOUTH
PL2 2BG

HMS Excellent
Whale Island
PORTSMOUTH
PO2 8ER

HMS Nelson
HMNB PORTSMOUTH
PORTSMOUTH
PO1 3LS

HMS Neptune
HMNB CLYDE
Faslane
HELENSBURGH
G84 8HL

HMS President
72 St Katharine's Way
LONDON
E1W 1UQ

HMS Sultan
Military Road
GOSPORT
PO12 3BY

HMS Temeraire
Burnaby Road
PORTSMOUTH
PO1 2HB

HMS Victory
HMNB PORTSMOUTH
PORTSMOUTH
PO1 3LS

Maritime Aviation Support Force
MASF
RNAS Culdrose
HELSTON
TR12 7RH

Naval Aeronautical Information Centre
NAIC
RAF Northolt
West End Road
RUISLIP
HA4 6NG

Royal Naval Air Station Culdrose
RNAS Culdrose
HMS Seahawk
HELSTON
TR12 7RH

Home to:
736, 750, 771, 814, 820, 824, 829, 849, 854
& 857 Naval Air Squadrons

Royal Naval Air Station Prestwick
RNAS Prestwick
HMS Gannet
PRESTWICK
KA9 2PL

Royal Naval Air Station Yeovilton
RNAS Yeovilton
HMS Heron
YEOVIL
BA22 8HT

Home to:
700W, 702, 727, 736, 815, 845, 846, 847,
848 Naval Air Squadrons & Commando
Helicopter Force HQ.

Royal Naval Presentation Team
RNPT
RAF Northolt
West End Road
RUISLIP
HA4 6NR

ROYAL MARINES ESTABLISHMENTS AND UNITS

3 Commando Brigade Royal Marines
3 CDO RM
Royal Marines Barracks
Stonehouse
PLYMOUTH
PL1 3QS

1 Assault Group Royal Marines
1 ASSLT GP RM
Triumph Building
HMNB Devonport
PLYMOUTH
PL2 2BG

10 Training Squadron 1 Assault Group
Royal Marines
10 Trg Sqn 1 Asslt Gp RM
RM Poole
Hamworthy
POOLE
BH15 4NQ

11 (Amphibious Trials & Training)
Squadron
11 (ATT) SQN
1 ASSLT GP RM
Instow
BIDEFORD
EX39 4JH

131 Independent Commando Squadron
Royal Engineers (Volunteers)
131 INDEP CDO SQN RE (V)
Training Centre

148 (Meiktila) Commando Forward
Observation Battery Royal Artillery
148 FO BTY RA
RM Poole
Hamworthy
POOLE
BH15 4NQ

1st Battalion the Rifles
1 RIFLES
Beachley Barracks
CHEPSTOW
NP16 7YG

24 Commando Regiment Royal Engineers
24 CDO REGT RE
RMB Chivenor
BARNSTAPLE
EX31 4AZ

29 Commando Regiment Royal Artillery
29 CDO REGT RA
Royal Citadel
PLYMOUTH
PL1 2PD

30 Commando Information & Exploitation
Group Royal Marines

30 CDO IX GP RM
RM Stonehouse
PLYMOUTH
PL1 3QS

40 Commando Royal Marines
40 CDO RM
Norton Manor Camp
TAUNTON
TA2 6PF

42 Commando Royal Marines
42 CDO RM
Bickleigh Barracks
PLYMOUTH
PL6 7AJ

43 Commando Fleet Protection Group
43 CDO FPG
Gibraltar Building
HM Naval Base Clyde
Faslane
HELENSBURGH
G84 8HL

45 Commando Royal Marines
45 CDO RM
RM Condor
ARBROATH
DD11 3SP

539 Assault Squadron Royal Marines
539 ASSLT SQN RM
RM Turnchapel
Barton Road
Turnchapel
PLYMOUTH
PL9 9XD

Armoured Support Group Royal Marines
AS GP RM
Yeovil Block,
RNAS Yeovilton
YEOVIL
BA22 8HT

Commando Helicopter Force HQ
CHF HQ
RNAS Yeovilton
YEOVIL
BA22 8HT

Commando Logistic Regiment Royal Marines
CDO LOG REGT RM
RM Chivenor
BARNSTAPLE
EX31 4AZ

Commando Training Centre Royal Marines
CTC RM
Lympstone
EXMOUTH
EX8 5AR

43 Commando Fleet Protection Group
43 CDO FPG
Gibraltar Building
HM Naval Base Clyde
Faslane
HELENSBURGH
G84 8HL

HASLER COMPANY
HMS Drake
PLYMOUTH
PL2 2BG

Royal Marine Band Service
RMBS
Walcheren Building
HMS Excellent
Whale Island
PORTSMOUTH
PO2 8ER

Royal Marine Band Collingwood
RM Band Collingwood
HMS NELSON
Queen Street
PORTSMOUTH
PO1 3HH

Royal Marine Band CTCRM
RM Band CTCRM
Lympstone
EXMOUTH
EX8 5AR

Royal Marine Band Plymouth
RM Band Plymouth
HMS RALEIGH
TORPOINT
PL11 2PD

Royal Marine Band Scotland
RM Band Scotland
HMS Caledonia
ROSYTH
KY11 2XH

Royal Marines Bickleigh
RM Bickleigh
Bickleigh Barracks
PLYMOUTH
PL6 7AJ

Royal Marines Chivenor
RM Chivenor
RM Chivenor
BARNSTAPLE
EX31 4AZ

Royal Marines Condor
RM Condor
RM Condor
ARBROATH
DD11 3SP

Royal Marines Norton Manor
RM Norton Manor
Norton Manor Camp
TAUNTON
TA2 6PF

Royal Marines Poole
RM Poole
Hamworthy
POOLE
BH15 4NQ

Royal Marines Stonehouse
RM Stonehouse
RM Stonehouse
PLYMOUTH
PL1 3QS

Royal Marines School of Music
RMSM
HMS NELSON
Queen Street
PORTSMOUTH
PO1 3HH

MEDICAL UNITS

Defence Dental Agency
DDA
Evelyn Woods Road
Aldershot
GU11 2LS

Defence Medical Rehabilitation Centre
DMRC
Headley Court
Headley
EPSOM
KT18 6PF

Defence Medical Services
DMS
DMS Whittington
Whittington Barracks
LICHFIELD
WS14 9PY

Defence Medical Services Training Group
DMSTG
Keogh Barracks
Ash Vale
ALDERSHOT
GU12 5RQ

Defence Medical Services Training Group
DMSTG
Selly Oak Hospital
Raddlebarn Road
Selly Oak
BIRMINGHAM
B29 6JD

Defence Post-Graduate Medical Deanery
DPMD
ICT Centre
Birmingham Research Park
Vincent Drive
Edgbaston
BIRMINGHAM
B15 2SQ

Department of Community Mental Health
DCMH
PP6, Sunny Walk
HMNB
PORTSMOUTH
PO1 3LT

HQ 2 Medical Brigade
HQ 2 MED BDE
Queen Elizabeth Barracks
Strensall
YORK
YO32 5SW

Institute of Naval Medicine
INM
Alverstoke
GOSPORT
PO12 2DL

MDHU Derriford
Derriford Hospital
Derriford Road
Crownhill
PLYMOUTH
PL6 5YE

MDHU Frimley
Frimley Park Hospital
Portsmouth Road
FRIMLEY
GU16 7UJ

MDHU Northallerton
Friarage Hospital
NORTHALLERTON
DL6 1JG

MDHU Peterborough
Peterborough District Hospital
Thorpe Road
PETERBOROUGH
PE3 6DA

MDHU Portsmouth
Queen Alexandra Hospital
Albert House
Southwick Hill Road
Cosham
PORTSMOUTH
PO6 3LY

Royal Centre for Defence Medicine
RCDM
Queen Elizabeth Hospital
Queen Elizabeth Medical Centre
Edgbaston
BIRMINGHAM
B15 2TH

Royal Centre for Defence Medicine
RCDM
Selly Oak Hospital
Raddlebarn Road
Selly Oak
BIRMINGHAM
B29 6JD

Surgeon General's Department
SGD
Coltman House
DMS Whittington
Lichfield Barracks
LICHFIELD
WS14 9PY

ROYAL NAVY & ROYAL MARINE RESERVE UNITS

ROYAL MARINE RESERVE UNITS

RMR Bristol
Dorset House
Litfield Place
Clifton
BRISTOL
BS8 3NA

RMR London
351 Merton Road
Southfields
LONDON
SW18 5JX

RMR Merseyside
East Brunswick Dock
80 Sefton Street
LIVERPOOL
L3 4DZ

RMR Scotland
37-51 Birkmyre Road
Govan
GLASGOW
G51 3JH

RMR Tyne
Anzio House
Quayside
NEWCASTLE-UPON-TYNE
NE6 1BU

ROYAL NAVY RESERVE UNITS

HMS Calliope
(Including Ceres Division)
South Shore Road
GATESHEAD
NE8 2BE

HMS Cambria
Hayes Point
Hayes Lane
Sully
PENARTH
CF64 5XU

HMS Dalriada
37-51 Birkmyre Rd
Govan
GLASGOW
G51 3JH

HMS Eaglet
Naval Regional Headquarters
Northern England & Isle of Man
East Brunswick Dock
LIVERPOOL
L3 4DZ

HMS Ferret
Building 600
DISC DHU
Chicksands
SHEFFORD
SG17 5PR

HMS Flying Fox
Winterstoke Road
BRISTOL
BS3 2NS

HMS Forward
42 Tilton Road
BIRMINGHAM
B9 4PP

HMS Hibernia
Thiepval Barracks
Magheralave Road
LISBURN
BT28 3NP

HMS King Alfred
Fraser Building
Whale Island
PORTSMOUTH
PO2 8ER

HMS President
72 St Katharine's Way
LONDON
E1W 1UQ

HMS Scotia
(Including Tay Division)
HMS Caledonia
Hilton Road
ROSYTH
KY11 2XH

HMS Sherwood
Chalfont Drive
NOTTINGHAM
NG8 3LT

HMS Vivid
Building SO40A
HM Naval Base Devonport
PLYMOUTH
PL2 2BG

HMS Wildfire
Building 99b
Northwood Headquarters
Sandy Lane
NORTHWOOD
HA6 3HP

ROYAL NAVAL RESERVE AIR BRANCH

RNAS Culdrose
Duke of Cornwall Building
RNAS Culdrose
HELSTON
TR12 7RH

RNAS Yeovilton
Cormorant House
Yeovilton
YEOVIL
BA22 8HL

UNIVERSITY ROYAL NAVAL UNITS

Birmingham University
Royal Naval Unit (HMS Exploit)
HMS FORWARD
42 Tilton Road
BIRMINGHAM
B9 4PP

Bristol University
Royal Naval Unit (HMS Dasher)
HMS Flying Fox
Winterstoke Road
BRISTOL
BS3 2NS

Cambridge University
Royal Naval Unit (HMS Trumpeter)
2 Chaucer Road
CAMBRIDGE
CB2 2EB

Edinburgh University
Royal Naval Unit (HMS Archer)
Hepburn House
89 East Claremount Street
EDINBURGH
EH7 4HU

Glasgow University
Royal Naval Unit (HMS Pursuer)
85 University Place
GLASGOW
G12 8SU

Liverpool University
Royal Naval Unit (HMS Charger)
RN Headquarters
80 Sefton Street
East Brunswick
LIVERPOOL
L3 4DZ

London University
Royal Naval Unit (HMS Puncher)
HMS President
72 St Katherine's Way
LONDON
EW1 1UQ

Manchester & Salford University
Royal Naval Unit (HMS Biter)
University Barracks
Boundary Lane
MANCHESTER
M15 6DH

Northumbrian University
Royal Naval Unit (HMS Example)
HMS Calliope
South Shore Road
GATESHEAD
NE8 2BE

Oxford University
Royal Naval Unit (HMS Smiter)
Falklands House
Oxpens Road
OXFORD
OX1 1RX

Southampton University
Royal Naval Unit (HMS Blazer)
Room 451/06
NOC
Waterfront Campus
European Way
SOUTHAMPTON
SO14 3ZH

Sussex University
Royal Naval Unit (HMS Ranger)
Army Reserves Barracks
198 Dyke Road
BRIGHTON
BN1 5AS

Wales Universities
Royal Naval Unit (HMS Express)
C/O HMS CAMBRIA
Hayes Point
Hayes Lane
Sully
PENARTH
CF64 5XU

Yorkshire & Humberside Universities
Royal Naval Unit (HMS Explorer)
Carr Lodge
Carlton Barracks
Carlton Gate
LEEDS
LS7 1HE

TRAINING ESTABLISHMENTS

Air Warfare Centre
AWC
RAF Waddington
LINCOLN
LN5 9NB

Armed Forces Chaplaincy Centre
AFCC
Amport House
Amport
ANDOVER
SP11 8BG

Army Aviation Centre
Aacen
Middle Wallop
STOCKBRIDGE
SO20 8DY

Britannia Royal Naval College
BRNC
DARTMOUTH
TQ6 0HJ

Central Air Traffic Control School
CATCS
RAF Shawbury
SHREWSBURY
SY4 4DZ

Commando Training Centre Royal Marines
CTCRM
Lympstone
EXMOUTH
EX8 5AR

Defence Academy of the United Kingdom
Greenhill House
SHRIVENHAM
SN6 8LA

Defence Chemical, Biological, Radiological & Nuclear Centre
DCBRNC
Winterbourne Gunner
SALISBURY
SP4 0ES

Defence College of Aeronautical Engineering
DCAE
RAF Cosford
Albrighton
WOLVERHAMPTON
WV7 3EX

Defence College of Communications & Information Systems
DCCIS
HMS Collingwood
Newgate Lane
FAREHAM
PO14 1AS

Defence College of Communications & Information Systems
DCCIS
Blandford Camp
BLANDFORD FORUM
DT11 8RH

Defence College of Electro-Mechanical Engineering
DCEME
HMS Sultan
Military Road
GOSPORT
PO12 3BY

Defence College of Logistics & Personnel Administration
DCLPA
Princess Royal Barracks
Deepcut
CAMBERLEY
GU16 6RN

Defence College of Logistics & Personnel Administration
DCLPA
Southwick Park
FAREHAM
PO17 6EJ

Defence College of Police & Guarding
DCPG
Southwick Park
FAREHAM
PO17 6EJ

Defence Cultural Specialist Unit
DCSU
RAF Henlow
HITCHIN
SG16 6DN

Defence Diving School
DDS
Horsea Island
West Bund Road
COSHAM
PO6 4TT

Defence Explosive Ordnance Disposal Munitions & Search School
DEMSS
Bldg 650
Marlborough Barracks
Southam
CV47 2UL

Defence Helicopter Flying School
DHFS
RAF Shawbury
SHREWSBURY
SY4 4DZ

Defence Intelligence & Security Centre
DISC
Chicksands
SHEFFORD
SG17 5PR

Defence Maritime Logistics School
DMLS
HMS Raleigh
TORPOINT
PL11 2PD

Defence Medical Services Training Group
DMSTG
Keogh Barracks
Ash Vale
ALDERSHOT
GU12 5RQ

Defence School of Languages
DSL
Wilton Park
BEACONSFIELD
HP9 2RP

Defence School of Marine Engineering
DSMarE
HMS Sultan
Military Road
GOSPORT
PO12 3BY

Defence School of Personnel Administration
DSPA
Worthy Down
WINCHESTER
SO21 2RG

Defence School of Transport
DST
Normandy Barracks
Leconfield
BEVERLEY
HU17 7LX

Defence Technical Officer & Engineer Entry Scheme
DTOEES
Defence Academy of the United Kingdom
SHRIVENHAM
SN6 8LA

Defence Technical Officer & Engineer Entry Scheme
DTOEES
Loughborough University
LOUGHBOROUGH
LE11 3TU

Defence Technical Officer & Engineer Entry Scheme
DTOEES
Southampton University
Capella House
Cook Street
SOUTHAMPTON
SO14 1NJ

Defence Technical Officer & Engineer Entry Scheme
DTOEES
South Shore Road
GATESHEAD
NE8 2BE

Empire Test Pilots' School
ETPS
RAF Boscombe Down
SALISBURY
SP4 0JE

HMS Raleigh
TORPOINT
PL11 2PD

Infantry Battle School
IBS
Dering Lines
BRECON
LD3 7RA

Institute of Naval Medicine
INM
Crescent Road
Alverstoke
GOSPORT
PO12 2DL

Joint Elementary Flying School
JEFTS
RAF Cranwell
SLEAFORD
NG34 8HB

Joint Services Command & Staff College
JSCSC
Faringdon Road
Watchfield
SWINDON
SN6 8TS

Joint Services Mountain Training Centre
JSMTC
Plas Llanfair
ANGLESEY
LL61 6NT

Land Warfare Centre
LWC
Imber Road
WARMINSTER
BA12 0DJ

Maritime Warfare Centre
MWC
HMS Collingwood
Newgate Lane
FAREHAM
PO14 1AS

Maritime Warfare School
MWS
HMS Collingwood
Newgate Lane
FAREHAM
PO14 1AS

Naval Outdoor Centre
NOC
PO Box 2021
SONTHOFEN
BFPO 105

Operational Training & Advisory Group
OPTAG
Risborough Barracks
FOLKSTONE
CT20 3EZ

Royal College of Defence Studies
RCDS
Seaford House
37 Belgrave Square
LONDON
SW1X 8NS

Royal Marines School of Music
RMSM
HMS Nelson
HMNB
PORTSMOUTH
PO1 3HH

Royal Military Academy Sandhurst
RMAS
CAMBERLEY
GU15 4PQ

Royal Naval Air Engineering & Survival School
RNAESS
HMS Sultan
Military Road
GOSPORT
PO12 3BY

Royal Naval Element Air Warfare Centre
RNEAWC
RAF Waddington
LINCOLN
LN5 9NB

Royal Naval Leadership Academy
RNLA
HMS Collingwood
Newgate Lane
FAREHAM
PO14 1AS

Royal Naval Leadership Academy
RNLA
Britannia Royal Naval College
DARTMOUTH
TQ6 0HJ

Royal Naval School of Physical Training
RNSPT
HMS Temeraire
Burnaby Road
PORTSMOUTH
PO1 2HB

Royal Navy Pre Deployment Training & Mounting Centre
RN PDTMC
HMS Nelson
HMNB
PORTSMOUTH
PO1 3HH

Royal Naval Centre of Recruiting
RNCR
Stanley Barracks
Bovington Camp
WAREHAM
BH20 6JB

Royal Navy Submarine School
RNSMS
HMS Raleigh
TORPOINT
PL11 2PD

Salmond House Training Centre
SHTC
Rheindhalen Military Complex
BFPO 40

Support Weapons School
SP WPNS SCH
Land Warfare Centre
Imber Avenue
WARMINSTER
BA12 0DJ

MINISTRY OF DEFENCE DEPARTMENTS & ORGANISATIONS

Ministry of Defence
MOD
Main Building
LONDON
SW1A 2HB

Defence Infrastructure Organisation Headquarters
DIO HQ
Kingston Road
SUTTON COLDFIELD
B75 7RL

Defence Infrastructure Organisation
DIO
RAF Wyton
Brampton and Wyton
HUNTINGDON
PE28 2EA

Defence Media Operations Centre
DMOC
RAF Halton
AYLESBURY
HP22 5PG

Defence Science & Technology Laboratory
DSTL
Ively Road
FARNBOROUGH
GU14 0LX

Defence Science & Technology Laboratory
DSTL
Porton Down
Salisbury
SP4 0JQ

Defence Science & Technology Laboratory
DSTL
P.O. Box 325
COSHAM
PO6 3SX

Defence Security & Assurance Services
DSAS
Minerva House
Welton Road
SWINDON
SN5 7XQ

DEFENCE EQUIPMENT & SUPPORT ORGANISATIONS AND LOCATIONS

Defence Equipment & Support
DE&S
Abbey Wood
BRISTOL
BS34 8JH

Defence Equipment & Support
DE&S
Basil Hill Site
CORSHAM
SN13 9NR

Defence Equipment & Support
DE&S
Gazelle House
YEOVILTON
BA22 8HJ

Defence Equipment & Support
DE&S
Dounreay Site
THURSO
KW14 7TZ

Defence Equipment & Support
DE&S
MOD Ensleigh
Granville Road
BATH
BA1 9BE

Defence Equipment & Support
DE&S
Castle Court
Coldharbour Business Park
SHERBORNE
DT9 4JW

Defence Equipment & Support
DE&S
Cormorant House
YEOVILTON
BA22 8HW

Defence Equipment & Support
DE&S
3100 Massachusetts Avenue
NW, 2008
WASHINGTON DC
USA

Defence Equipment & Support
DE&S
Unicorn House
Yeovilton
BA22 8HJ

Defence Equipment & Support
DE&S
Skimmingdish Lane
Caversfield
BICESTER
OX25 8TS

Defence Equipment & Support
DE&S
West Moors
WIMBORNE
BH21 6QS

Defence Equipment & Support
DE&S
Drummond Barracks
Ludgershall
ANDOVER
SP11 9RU

Augusta Westland
PO Box 188
Lysander Road
YEOVIL
BA20 2YB

BAE Systems Ltd
First Floor,
Main Shipyard Offices
BARROW-IN-FURNESS
LA14 1AF

British Forces Post Office
BFPO
RAF Northolt
West End Road
RUISLIP
HA4 6NG

UK Trade & Investment Defence &
Security Organisation
UKTI-DSO
Kingsgate House
66-74 Victoria Street
LONDON
SW1E 6SW

Vector Aerospace
Building 165
Fleetlands
Fareham Road
GOSPORT
PO13 0AA

TRI-SERVICE UNITS

Allied Rapid Reaction Corps
ARRC
Imjin Barracks
Innsworth
Gloucester
GL3 1HW

British Forces British Indian Ocean
Territory
BF BIOT
Diego Garcia
NP 1002
BFPO 485

British Forces Cyprus
BF C
BFPO 53

British Forces Germany
BF G
BFPO 40

British Forces Gibraltar
BF GIBRALTAR
BFPO 52

British Forces Post Office
BFPO
RAF Northolt
West End Road
RUISLIP
HA4 6NG

British Forces South Atlantic Islands
BFSAI
BFPO 655

Defence Intelligence & Security Centre
DISC
Chicksands
SHEFFORD
SG17 5PR

HQ EUFOR
Camp Butmir
SARAJEVO
Boznia Herzegovina

HQ Integrated Area Defence System
HQ IADS
185 Jalan Ampang
Kuala Lumpar

HQ Joint Forces Command Brunssum

Joint Counter Terrorism Training & Advisory Team
JCTTAT
Risborough Barracks
FOLKSTONE
CT20 3EZ

Joint Forces Command
JFC
Sandy Lane
NORTHWOOD
HA6 3AP

Joint Helicopter Command
JHC
HQ Land Forces
Marlborough Lines
Monxton Road
ANDOVER
SP11 8HJ

Joint Service Signal Unit
JSSU
Ayios Nikolaos
CYPRUS
BFPO 59

Joint Service Signal Unit
JSSU
Hubble Road
CHELTENHAM
GL51 0EX

Joint Support Unit
JSU
CASTEAU
Belgium
BFPO 26

Joint Support Unit
JSU
LISBON
BFPO 6

London Air Traffic Control Centre (Military)
LATCC(MIL)
Swanwick
SOUTHAMPTON
SO31 7AY

Military Aviation Authority
MAA
Abbey Wood
BRISTOL
BS34 8JH

Military Corrective Training Centre
MCTC
Berechurch Hall Camp
COLCHESTER
CO2 9NU

Military Higher Readiness Force (France)
MHRF(F)
238 Ave Auguste Batta
TOULON
France

Military Stabilisation Support Group
MSSG
Gibraltar Barracks
Blackwater
CAMBERLEY
GU17 9LP

NATO Supreme Allied Commander Transformation
NATO SACT
US Naval Base
NORFOLK
Virginia
NP 1964 via BFPO 63

NATO
MONS
Belgium
BFPO 26

NATO
BRUSSELS
BFPO 49

NATO Joint Forces Command Naples
NATO JFC
NAPLES
Italy
BFPO 8

NATO Joint Forces Command Brunssum
NATO JFC
BFPO 28

NATO Joint Forces Command Lisbon
NATO JFC
LISBON
BFPO 6

NATO Joint Warfare Centre
NATO JWC
4068 STAVANGER
Norway
BFPO 50

NATO School
OBERAMMERGAU
Box 2003
Germany
BFPO 105

Permanent Joint Headquarters
PJHQ
Sandy Lane
NORTHWOOD
HA6 3AP

Royal Brunei Armed Forces
RBAF
Bolkiah Camp
BRUNEI
BFPO 11

Sea Mounting Centre
SMC
Marchwood
SOUTHAMPTON
SO40 4ZG

Service Personnel & Veterans Agency
SPVA
Centurion Building
GOSPORT
PO13 9XA

Service Personnel & Veterans Agency
SPVA
Building 182
Imjin Barracks
Innsworth
GLOUCESTER
GL3 1HW

Service Personnel & Veterans Agency
SPVA
Kentigern House
65 Brown Street
GLASGOW
G2 8EX

Supreme HQ Allied Powers Europe
SHAPE
CASTEAU
Belgium
BFPO 26

UK Mission to the United Nations
UN
PO Box 5238
NEW YORK
NY 10150-5238 USA

ARMY UNITS

HQ Land Forces
HQLF
Marlborough Lines
Monxton Road
ANDOVER
SP11 8HJ

1st Battalion Irish Guards
1IG
Mons Barracks
Prince's Avenue
Aldershot
GU11 2LF

1 Regt Army Air Corps
1 REGT AAC
GUTERSLOH
BFPO 47

131 Independent Commando Squadron
Royal Engineers (Volunteers)
131 INDEP CDO SQN RE (V)
Training Centre
Honeypot Lane
Kingsbury
LONDON
NW9 9QY

148 (Meiktila) Commando Forward
Observation Battery Royal Artillery
148 FO BTY RA
RM Poole
Hamworthy
POOLE
BH15 4NQ

148 (Meiktila) Commando Forward
Observation Battery Royal Artillery
148 FO BTY RA
The Royal Citadel
PLYMOUTH
PL1 2PD

1st Battalion the Rifles
1 RIFLES
Beachley Barracks
CHEPSTOW
NP16 7YG

101 Logistics Brigade
101 LOG BDE
Buller Barracks
ALDERSHOT
GU11 2DE

102 Logistics Brigade
102 LOG BDE
GUTERSLOH
BFPO 47

24 Commando Regiment Royal Engineers
24 CDO REGT RE
RMB Chivenor
BARNSTAPLE
EX31 4AZ

26 Regiment Royal Artillery
26 REGT RA
GUTERSLOH
BFPO 47

29 Commando Regiment Royal Artillery
29 CDO REGT RA
Royal Citadel
PLYMOUTH
PL1 2PD

3 Regiment Army Air Corps
3 REGT AAC
Wattisham Airfield
IPSWICH
IP7 7RA

4 Regiment Army Air Corps
4 REGT AAC
Wattisham Airfield
IPSWICH
IP7 7RA

5 Regiment Army Air Corps
5 REGT AAC
JHCFS ALDERGROVE
BFPO 808

5th Battalion Royal Regiment of Scotland
5 SCOTS
Howe Barracks
CANTERBURY
CT1 1JU

7 Air Assault Battalion, REME
7 AA BN REME
Wattisham Airfield
IPSWICH
IP7 7RA

Army Aviation Centre
AAcen
Middle Wallop
STOCKBRIDGE
SO20 8DY

Army Recruiting & Training Division
ARTD
Trenchard Lines
Upavon
PEWSEY
SN9 6BE

Combined Arms Tactics Division
CATD
Land Warfare Centre
WARMINSTER
BA12 0DJ

Royal Military Academy Sandhurst
RMAS
CAMBERLEY
GU15 4PQ

ROYAL AIR FORCE UNITS

Air Command Headquarters
ACHQ
RAF High Wycombe
Walters Ash
HIGH WYCOMBE
HP14 4UE

Control & Reporting Centre
CRC
RAF Boulmer
ALNWICK
NE66 3JF

202 Squadron, E Flight
202 SQN E Flight
Leconfield
BEVERLEY
HU17 7LX

Joint Helicopter Command Flying Station
JHCFS
Aldergrove
BFPO 808

MOD Boscombe Down
SALISBURY
SP4 0JF

MOD St Athan
BARRY
CF62 4WA

RAF Barkston Heath
GRANTHAM
NG32 2DQ

RAF Benson
Benson
WALLINGFORD
OX10 6AA

RAF Boulmer
ALNWICK
NE66 3JF

RAF Brize Norton
CARTERTON
OX18 3LX

RAF Cranwell
SLEAFORD
NG34 8HA

RAF Digby
LINCOLN
LN4 3LH

RAF Halton
AYLESBURY
HP22 5PG

RAF Henlow
HITCHIN
SG16 6DN

RAF High Wycombe
Walters Ash
HIGH WYCOMBE
HP14 4UE

RAF Leeming
Gatenby
NORTHALLERTON
DL7 9NJ

RAF Linton-on-Ouse
YORK
YO30 2AJ

RAF Lossiemouth
LOSSIEMOUTH
IV31 6SD

RAF Northolt
West End Road
RUISLIP
HA4 6NG

RAF Odiham
Hook
BASINGSTOKE
RG29 1QT

RAF Shawbury
SHREWSBURY
SY4 4DZ

RAF St Mawgan
NEWQUAY
TR8 4HP

RAF Valley
HOLYHEAD
LL65 3NY

RAF Waddington
LINCOLN
LN5 9NB

RAF Wattisham
IPSWICH
IP7 7RA

RAF Wittering
PETERBOROUGH
PE8 6HB

RAF Wyton
Brampton and Wyton
HUNTINGDON
PE28 2EA

OTHER ADDRESSES

Ministry of Defence Police & Guarding Agency
MDPGA
Wethersfield
BRAINTREE
CM7 4AZ

Royal Navy & Royal Marines Charity
(Regn No. 1117794)
Registered Office:
Building 29
HMS Excellent
Whale Island
PORTSMOUTH
PO2 8ER

Sea Cadet Headquarters
202 Lambeth Road
LONDON
SE1 7JW

The Cabinet Office
70 Whitehall
LONDON
SW1A 2AS

The Foreign & Commonwealth Office
King Charles Street
LONDON
SW1A 2AH

ATTACHES AND ADVISERS

The Defence Engagement Strategy Overseas Directory, commonly known as The Yellow Book, lists the UK MOD Attaché corps based at Defence Sections in British Embassies and High Commissions, together with Loan Service Personnel and Special Advisors Overseas. The Directory is maintained by the Defence Engagement Strategy Overseas Support Division. It is an extensive and comprehensive publication that is updated throughout the year on the Web and bi-annually in a limited run of hard copy (DESTRAT Overseas Directory (The DESTRAT Yellow Book)).

For access to Attaches and Advisers you should refer to these sources for accuracy. A full and comprehensive listing of Attaches and Advisers can be accessed through the MoD intranet, the URL is:

http://defenceintranet.diif.r.mil.uk/Organisations/Orgs/HOCS/Organisations/Orgs/DSPO/DISP/Pages/YellowBook.aspx

Hardcopy: Authorised users without ready access to the DefenceNet can obtain copies of the concise Directory on application to the Editor:

        Peter McCarney
        Defence Engagement-Overseas Support-Admin
        Main Building
        Level 4, Zone B, Desk 36
        Whitehall
        LONDON, SW1A 2HB.

DIIF: DESTRAT-OS-Admin@mod.uk Role (UNCLAS)
            peter.mccarney781@mod.uk Personal (UNCLAS)

Phone: 020 7218 9176

OBITUARY

ROYAL NAVAL SERVICE

SURG LIEUTENANT COMMANDER

Surg Lt Cdr Alexander SHEARMAN RN   died 03 Feb 14

Surg Lt Cdr Vijay AHUJA RN   died 03 Dec 14

LIEUTENANT COMMANDER

Lt Cdr Leslie Hardy RN   died 01 May 14

AMENDMENTS TO NAVY LIST ENTRY

This edition of the Navy List has been produced largely from the information held within the Ministry of Defence's "Joint Personnel and Administration" system". The efficiencies and data handling of JPA affect the way in which individual entries are extracted and recorded in the Navy List.

Serving Officers who note errors or omissions in the Active or Seniority Lists should ensure that their data held within JPA is accurate and up to date. If you are unable to make these corrections within your JPA account you should seek assistance from either your JPA administrator or Career Manager.

Please note that all personnel data for the Navy List is derived through Career Managers/Data Owners and/or extracted direct from JPA; it is neither compiled nor maintained by the Editor. If you notice errors or omissions you should contact your Human Resources Manager.

All other errors or omissions should be brought to the attention of the Editor of the Navy List.

Readers who wish to comment on this edition of the Navy List are invited to write to:

Jacqui Farmer
The Editor of the Navy List
MP 2.2
West Battery
Whale Island
PORTSMOUTH
PO2 8DX

Service Number (mandatory)..

Surname..

Forenames..

Rank..

Comments:

Signed .... Date ....